DOCTOR, TEACHER, TERRORIST

DOCTOR, TEACHER, TERRORIST

THE LIFE AND LEGACY OF AL-QAEDA LEADER AYMAN AL-ZAWAHIRI

SAJJAN M. GOHEL

OXFORD
UNIVERSITY PRESS

OXFORD
UNIVERSITY PRESS

Oxford University Press is a department of the University of Oxford. It furthers
the University's objective of excellence in research, scholarship, and education
by publishing worldwide. Oxford is a registered trade mark of Oxford University
Press in the UK and certain other countries.

Published in the United States of America by Oxford University Press
198 Madison Avenue, New York, NY 10016, United States of America.

Library of Congress Cataloging-in-Publication Data
Names: Gohel, Sajjan M., author.
Title: Doctor, teacher, terrorist : the life and legacy of Al-Qaeda leader
Ayman Al-Zawahiri / Sajjan M. Gohel.
Description: New York, NY : Oxford University Press, [2024] |
Includes bibliographical references and index.
Identifiers: LCCN 2023019545 (print) | LCCN 2023019546 (ebook) |
ISBN 9780197665367 (hardback) | ISBN 9780197665381 (epub) |
ISBN 9780197665398
Subjects: LCSH: Ẓawāhirī, Ayman. | Terrorists—Egypt—Biography. |
Physicians—Egypt—Biography. | Qaida (Organization) | Tanẓīm
al-Jihād al-Islāmī (Organization) | War on Terrorism, 2001-2009.
Classification: LCC HV6430.Z38 G53 2024 (print) | LCC HV6430.Z38 (ebook) |
DDC 303.6/250962—dc23/eng/20230530
LC record available at https://lccn.loc.gov/2023019545
LC ebook record available at https://lccn.loc.gov/2023019546

ISBN 978–0–19–766536–7

DOI: 10.1093/oso/9780197665367.001.0001

Printed by Sheridan Books, Inc., United States of America

For those impacted by 9/11 and the women of Afghanistan.
Without history, we are lost.

Contents

Acknowledgements

This book has been a work in progress for more than 14 years, largely interrupted by life but also because Ayman al-Zawahiri himself would continue to confound his critics and indirectly force me to keep updating my draft manuscripts. Therefore, this book would simply not have been possible without the involvement of a large number of incredibly kind individuals.

I owe special thanks to several people who were extremely generous with their time, knowledge, ideas, and insights over the years. In particular, Alain Bauer, Kirsten Schulze, Amrullah Saleh, Hans Josef-Beth, Bruce Hoffman, Henry Crumpton, Douglas London, Mitchell Silber, Sebastian Rotella, Thomas Hegghammer, Sean M. Maloney, Ayesha Siddiqa, Peter Clarke, John Miller, Pieter Van Ostaeyen, Wuhong Shi, Chris Alexander, Joseph Votel, John Calvert, Bruce Rutherford, Sarah Adams, Lawrence Wright, Aaron Zelin, Edmund Fitton-Brown, Mary Fetchet, and Leon Panetta. Each deserves a personal testimony to express how indebted I am. The same applies to the countless number of colleagues and well-wishers at the London School of Economics and Political Science (LSE), NATO, and the Leadership in Counter Terrorism (LinCT).

I am sad that along the way, many people who spent time to add depth to my research are no longer with us. Their passing means that I can only attempt to repay their kind help in some small manner by recognising their support and encouragement. In particular, I would like to remember Sitara Achakzai, Anthony McDermott, Fred Halliday, Saleem Shahzad, D. A. Henderson, Mohamed Heikal, Reuven Paz, Martin Rudner, Christopher Dickey, Robert L. Tignor, and Jerrold Post. A special mention must be given to the late Lt. Col. Nick Pratt. Not only was he a mentor and inspiration, but also gave me the most important advice, to trust my instincts. It has been a lesson I've carried with me.

Two people have been a constant in my life from the time I was a teenager, and I am so fortunate to have had their guidance in my formative years right up till the present day with this book. They deserve special mention. Alex P. Schmid inspired me to study terrorism and has steered me in this discipline and helped me to grow as an academic. Bruce Riedel has taught me to think critically and ask clear questions. His sage guidance has been prophetic and his support, unwavering. They both have demonstrated to me that academic research can truly have real-world implications.

Understanding developments on the ground across the Middle East, North Africa, Afghanistan, and Pakistan can often prove extremely challenging, and I could not do so without the repeated assistance of my sources in these places and beyond. Although for obvious reasons I cannot name them here, I will forever remember their kindness. Equally, I'm grateful to many people who work in governmental organizations, law enforcement, and counter-terrorism. Understandably, most of them did not want to be identified because of the sensitive nature of their work, but I would like them to know that their willingness to talk to me was invaluable.

I am appreciative to my amazing students at the LSE whose research skills define why history is the greatest academic discipline. Their faith and dedication in my project was deeply valued, and I would like to acknowledge Marcus Andreopoulos, Alison Bailey, Cristina Cañiz Perez, Asta Chahal-Pierce, Kit Digby, Casey Hawkins, Sid Hirshberg, Victoria Jones, Sinéad Owen, Abby Perelman, Jackson Perry, Blanca Rivero-Anglada, and Leah Salley.

This project has been so long in the making and involved so many altruistic people that there are likely some I have forgotten to cite. I hope they will forgive me and trust they know the depth of my gratitude. This includes the constructive feedback from the anonymous peer-reviewers.

I must recognise my incredible cartographer, Ed Merritt, who designed and drew the maps in this book. What began as a simple idea at the start of our collaboration grew into a project itself which has provided another dynamic about al-Zawahiri and demonstrated the breadth of his role in terrorism.

I also want to thank my editor at Oxford University Press (OUP), David McBride, for not only instantly understanding the importance of such a project but also for his total and genuine commitment, drive, and support to see the manuscript published. I am very fortunate to have an editor who has had unyielding belief in this book from the moment we first spoke about it and then for shepherding it through during a global pandemic. Sarah Ebel, the project editor and Kavitha Yuvaraj, the project manager, provided constant kind support in seeing this through to publication. Also, my appreciation to the copy editor, Carrie Watterson, who meticulously went through the entire manuscript. I am most fortunate to have an incredible team of people that cared about this book as much as I do.

Finally, I owe an enormous amount of gratitude to my family who have all lived with this book, in one form or another, for as long as I have. Anupama, my sister and best friend, who during those long walks with our dog Hildy provided perspectives about my manuscript that would not have occurred to me otherwise. Also, to my father, M. J. Gohel. Everything I am is because of him, and without him nothing would be possible. Lastly, my late grandmother, Lady Sajjankunver Gohel, who taught me that women's rights is counter-terrorism. I miss you every day.

All these wonderful people in my acknowledgements have helped me through periods of doubt and struggle in completing this manuscript, whilst offering constant feedback. It has been a long journey, and I have learnt a lot. Thank you.

Note on Transliteration

The transliteration of Arabic words into English has been simplified. Arabic words are presented in the book in italics in their anglicised form and without diacritics. Arabic words that have come into common English usage, such as 'jihad', are not italicised.

Timelines

Historical Context

1798   The French general Napoleon Bonaparte invades and occupies Egypt

1801   British and Ottoman forces defeat the French, forcing their withdrawal and imposing their political and economic control

1805   Muhammad Ali, an ethnic Albanian officer, is imposed as governor of Egypt

1869   Construction of the Suez Canal is completed, with Britain and France retaining significant influence

1882   The 'Urabi Revolt' against colonial influence is defeated by the British, whose formal occupation of Egypt becomes known as the 'Veiled Protectorate'

1914   At the outbreak of World War I, Britain is pitted against the Ottoman Empire, part of the Central Powers alignment

1914   Britain officially declares its protectorate status over Egypt, deposing Khedive Abbas II and appointing his uncle, Hussein Kamel, as Egypt's first sultan

1916   Sykes-Picot Agreement confirms British and French spheres of influence following the expected collapse of the Ottoman Empire

1918   The Egyptian Expeditionary Force, led by Edmund Allenby, defeats Ottoman forces and occupies Palestine

1918   World War I ends with the defeat of the Central Powers and the gradual dismemberment of the Ottoman Empire

1919   British expulsion of Egyptian nationalist leader Saad Zaghlul leads to mass protests and the Egyptian Revolution

1922   Britain unilaterally declares Egyptian independence whilst retaining hegemony over Egypt's defence and foreign affairs

1923   The Ottoman Empire's collapse is completed and overseen by
       Britain and France

1928   The Egyptian ideologue Hasan al-Banna forms the Muslim
       Brotherhood, seeking the creation of an Islamic state

1929   Muhammad al-Ahmadi al-Zawahiri is appointed as grand imam of
       al-Azhar

1935   Facing widespread opposition, Muhammad al-Ahmadi al-Zawahiri
       is forced out of his position from al-Azhar

1942   The Muslim Brotherhood takes part in the Egyptian parliamentary
       elections, and once more in 1945, without attaining much success

1945   Following World War II, the Arab League is created, and Abdul
       Rahman Azzam becomes its first secretary general, tasked with
       promoting pan-Arab solidarity

1948   Egyptian ideologue Sayyid Qutb travels to the United States to
       research Western methods of teaching but uses the opportunity to
       lament Western culture and society

1949   The Palestine War concludes with Israeli victory over Palestinian
       and Egyptian forces

1952   Egyptian Revolution by the Free Officers movement led by Gamal
       Nasser, initially supported by the Muslim Brotherhood

1954   Sayyid Qutb arrested following a conspiracy by the Muslim
       Brotherhood to assassinate Nasser

1956   Nasser nationalises the Suez Canal, triggering the Suez Crisis

1964   Sayyid Qutb released from prison, and his seminal work, *Milestones*,
       is published

1965   Sayyid Qutb is rearrested because of Milestones' call for the
       overthrow of 'apostate rulers'

1966   Sayyid Qutb is executed in Egypt for sedition; Mahfouz Azzam acts
       as his lawyer

1970   Anwar Sadat succeeds Nasser as Egyptian president

1967   The June War, also known as the Six-Day War, results in Egypt's
       humiliating defeat

1973   The October War, also referred to as the Yom Kippur War, creates a
       stalemate between Egypt and Israel

1978   Camp David Accords signed by Egypt and Israel, with both sides
       establishing diplomatic ties

1979   Muhammad Abd al-Salam Faraj founds the clandestine al-Jihad
       terrorist group

1979   The Soviet Union invades and occupies Afghanistan

1981   Anwar Sadat assassinated by al-Jihad and succeeded by Hosni
       Mubarak

1987   Battle of Zazi between the Afghan-Arab *mujahideen* and the Soviets

1988   Founding of al-Qaeda

1989   Soviet withdrawal from Afghanistan

1989   Prime Minister Benazir Bhutto requests that all Arab *mujahideen*
       leave Pakistan

1989   Osama bin Laden funds a 'no confidence' bill to overthrow Bhutto's
       government

1995   During Bhutto's second term, Pakistan signs an extradition treaty
       with Egypt

2010   Beginning of Arab Spring in Tunisia

2011   Arab Spring uprisings in Egypt result in Mubarak falling
       from power

2011   Osama bin Laden is killed in a US Navy SEAL raid in Abbottabad,
       Pakistan

2012   Mohamed Morsi from the Muslim Brotherhood's affiliated
       Freedom and Justice Party is elected president of Egypt

2013   Morsi overthrown in a military coup led by General Abdel Fattah
       el-Sisi

2013   Iraqi ideologue Abu Bakr al-Baghdadi renames al-Qaeda affiliate in
       Iraq the Islamic State in Iraq and Greater Syria (ISIS)

2014   Abdel Fattah el-Sisi becomes president of Egypt

2014   Abu Bakr al-Baghdadi gives a sermon in Mosul, Iraq, proclaiming
       the ISIS caliphate and appointing himself its leader

2020   Doha Agreement signed by the United States and Taliban, leading
       to eventual departure of US and NATO troops from Afghanistan

2021   President Joseph R. Biden announces the complete withdrawal of
       US troops from Afghanistan by 11 September 2021 and cessation of
       combat operations in Iraq

2021   The Taliban, led by the Haqqani Network, retake complete control
       of Afghanistan and declare the Islamic Emirate of Afghanistan
       once again

2022 Sirajuddin Haqqani, the Taliban interior minister, and proscribed terrorist, consolidates his hold over Afghanistan

Al-Zawahiri's Origins and Education

1951 Born in Giza and raised in Cairo's Maadi neighbourhood
1966 Completes his studies at Maadi secondary school
1974 Graduates from Cairo University with a degree in medicine
1975 Joins the Egyptian army as a reservist working as a part-time surgeon
1978 Receives master's degree in surgery at the Faculty of Medicine Kasr Al-Ainy, Cairo University, but then opts to specialise as a paediatrician
1978 Marries his first wife, Izzat Ahmad Nuwair

Pivotal Moments

1966 Joins the Association of the Followers of Muhammad's Path
1967 Establishes the Organization, or Tanzeem, in his high school
1974 Abortive attempt to take over the Military Technical College near Cairo
1980 First experience with the Afghan jihad against the Soviets as part of a relief project in Pakistan
1981 Briefly visits Pakistan on behalf of the Kuwaiti Red Crescent Society
1981 Arrested for his peripheral role in the assassination of the Egyptian president Anwar Sadat in Cairo; sentenced to three years in prison
1983 Al-Jihad fractures in prison, with the formation of Egyptian Islamic Jihad (EIJ), which al-Zawahiri aligns with and al-Gama'a Islamiyya, led by Omar Abdel-Rahman
1984 Released from prison
1984 Former Egyptian army officer Ali Mohamed pledges an oath to al-Zawahiri and is sent to the United States to infiltrate the military and collect intelligence
1985 Visits Amman, Jordan, before moving to Jeddah, Saudi Arabia

1986   Travels to Afghanistan and meets Osama bin Laden in Peshawar,
        Pakistan
1989   The Palestinian-Jordanian ideologue Abdullah Azzam is killed in a
        car bomb in Peshawar
1990s* Publishes *Military Studies in the Jihad against the Tyrants*
1991   Publishes 'The Bitter Harvest'
1992   Joins Osama bin Laden in Sudan
1992   Bombings of the two hotels in Yemen
1993   Assumes official control of the EIJ
1993   Attack on US peacekeeping troops in Somalia, 19 killed
1993   Assassination attempt on Egyptian prime minister Atef Sedky
        in Cairo
1993   Travelled to Copenhagen for meetings with other jihadists
1993   Visited Bern and Zurich to plan impending trip to the
        United States
1993   Visits the United States to fundraise for the EIJ
1995   Publishes *The Compendium in the Pursuit of Divine Knowledge*
1995   Failed assassination attempt on President Hosni Mubarak in Addis
        Ababa, Ethiopia
1995   Bombing of the Egyptian Embassy in Islamabad, Pakistan
1995   Makes second and last trip to the United States
1996   Travels to the Caucasus and is detained by Russian authorities
1996   EIJ and al-Qaeda lose their safe haven in Sudan and relocate to
        Afghanistan
1998   Joint fatwa with Osama bin Laden, 'World Islamic Front against
        Jews and Crusaders', issued from territory in Afghanistan belonging
        to the Haqqani Network
1998   Al-Qaeda agrees to interviews with the international media to gain
        greater attention
1998   Foiled bombing of the US Embassy in Tirana, Albania
1998   Bombings of US Embassies in Kenya and Tanzania
1998   US Operation Infinite Reach results in airstrikes against al-Qaeda
        interests in Afghanistan and Sudan
1999   Plots with the Egyptian scientist Midhat Mursi to develop chemical,
        biological, radiological, nuclear, explosive (CBRNE) weapons

* Actual publication date is unclear, but the document is believed to have been created during
  the 1990s.

2000 Bombing of the naval destroyer USS *Cole* in port of Aden, Yemen

2000 Al-Qaeda launches its new media department, as-Sahab

2000 Met with Pakistani nuclear scientists to try to procure nuclear material

2001 The EIJ merges with al-Qaeda, splitting the organization

2001 Assassination of the Afghan Northern Alliance leader Ahmad Shah Massoud in Khodja Bahauddin, Afghanistan

2001 Attacks on the World Trade Center in New York and the Pentagon in Washington, DC

2001 United States issues $25 million reward leading to al-Zawahiri's capture or elimination; he seeks refuge in Pakistan

2001 Publishes *Knights under the Prophet's Banner*

2001 Escapes the US-led coalition bombing campaign of Tora Bora, Afghanistan

2002 Publishes 'Loyalty and Enmity: An Inherited Doctrine and Lost Reality'

2002 Al-Qaeda bombing of a synagogue in Djerba, Tunisia

2002 Publishes 'Allegiance and Disavowal'

2004 Begins creating al-Qaeda training camps in Malakand and Mansehra, Pakistan

2003 The Mubtakkar cyanide-dispersal plot on the New York subway is cancelled in preparation for a bigger plot

2004 Publishes 'The Defeat of America Is a Matter of Time'

2004 Evades a counter-terrorism operation on a hideout in Wana, Pakistan

2004 Ammonium nitrate plot in the United Kingdom disrupted by British authorities

2004 Dhiren Barot's terrorist cell attempt to assemble a radiological dispersal device (RDD) in the United Kingdom foiled

2005 Audiotape identifying the 'Three Foundations' of al-Qaeda's political ideology

2005 Criticises the Jordanian terrorist Abu Musab al-Zarqawi for killing Muslims in Iraq and urges him to stop

2005 Coordinated suicide bombings of the transit system in London, 52 dead

2005 Failed follow-up plot to target the London transit system, a second time in two weeks

2006	British authorities disrupt a large al-Qaeda cell planning to smuggle liquid explosives across several transatlantic flights with the intention to detonate them mid-air
2006	Authorities disrupt coordinated cells plotting attacks in Paris, Milan, Bologna, and Rabat
2006	Abu Musab al-Zarqawi killed in US airstrike
2006	Escapes the US airstrike in Damadola, Pakistan
2007	Open interview with al-Zawahiri organised by as-Sahab
2007	Assassination of former Pakistani prime minister Benazir Bhutto in Rawalpindi, Pakistan
2008	Attack on the Danish Embassy in Islamabad, Pakistan
2008	Publishes *The Exoneration: A Treatise Exonerating the Community of the Pen and the Sword from the Debilitating Accusation of Fatigue and Weakness*
2009	Plot to target the *Jyllands-Posten* newspaper offices in Denmark disrupted
2009	Recruits Jordanian triple agent Humam Khalil al-Balawi to eliminate a CIA team in Khost, Afghanistan
2011	Osama bin Laden killed in a US operation in Abbottabad, Pakistan
2011	Formally named al-Qaeda's new leader following bin Laden's death, and all the affiliates pledge their *ba'yah*
2012	Instigates coordinated attacks on US diplomatic missions in Cairo, Tunis, and Benghazi
2013	Publishes 'General Guidelines for Jihad'
2014	Reaffirms his *ba'yah* to Mullah Muhammad Omar
2014	Cuts ties with ISIS
2014	Creates the affiliate al-Qaeda in the Indian Subcontinent (AQIS) and attempts to hijack a Pakistani navy frigate to attack a US Navy vessel in the Arabian Sea
2015	Affirms his *ba'yah* to the new Taliban leader, Mullah Akhtar Mansour
2015	Presents Hamza bin Laden as 'Son of the Lion of Jihad'
2016	Releases Brief Messages to a Victorious Ummah series
2016	Gives *ba'yah* to the new head of the Taliban, Mawlawi Haibatullah
2016	The Haqqani Network's media wing releases a video celebrating the unbroken bond with al-Qaeda

2018   Recognises Sirajuddin Haqqani as the Taliban deputy leader
2017   Long-time nemesis Omar Abdel-Rahman dies in prison in the
        United States
2019   Abu Bakr al-Baghdadi killed in a US operation in Syria
2019   Hamza bin Laden killed in a US operation
2022   Releases a proof of life video demonstrating he is healthy
2022   Al-Zawahiri killed in a US drone operation in Kabul

Cast of Characters

Ayman al-Zawahiri's Family

PATERNAL SIDE

Ibrahim al-Zawahiri: Al-Zawahiri's paternal great-grandfather, who moved to Egypt from Saudi Arabia in the 1860s.

Rabīʿa ibn Ibrahim al-Zawahiri: Al-Zawahiri's paternal grandfather. He was an imam at al-Azhar Islamic seminary.

Shaykh Muhammad al-Ahmadi ibn Ibrahim al-Zawahiri: Al-Zawahiri's paternal granduncle. Grand imam at al-Azhar Islamic seminary during politically turbulent times in Egypt in the 1930s. Faced criticism that he had not done enough to defend Islam in the face of increasing Western Christian missionary activity.

Muhammad Rabīʿa al-Zawahiri: Al-Zawahiri's father. A respected doctor and academic in pharmaceutical sciences. He was deputy chair of the Department of Pharmacology at Cairo's Ain Shams University.

MATERNAL SIDE

Abdul Wahhab Azzam: Al-Zawahiri's maternal grandfather. The founder of King Saud University in Riyadh, Saudi Arabia, and the president of Cairo University, he was the Egyptian ambassador to Pakistan, Saudi Arabia, and Yemen. Respected for his high level of Islamic jurisprudence (*fiqh*).

Abdul Rahman Azzam: Al-Zawahiri's maternal granduncle. One of the founders of the Arab League and its first secretary general, 1945–1952. Strong proponent of pan-Arab nationalism. Advisor to the House of Saud. Friend and mentor of Malcolm X.

Umayma Azzam: Al-Zawahiri's mother. She hailed from a distinguished family from the Arabian Peninsula that settled in El-Shoubek Gharbi, Giza. Her family claimed lineage to the Prophet Muhammad.

Mahfouz Azzam: Al-Zawahiri's maternal uncle. Sayyid Qutb's lawyer and executor of his estate. Defended numerous Islamists in court, across generations.

SIBLINGS

Umnya al-Zawahiri: Al-Zawahiri's twin sister. She would go on to become a physician.

Heba al-Zawahiri: Al-Zawahiri's younger sister. She became a doctor specialising in oncology.

Muhammad al-Zawahiri: Al-Zawahiri's younger brother. An engineer and part of the EIJ before moving to Afghanistan. Involved in the Tirana, Albania, plot and the attacks on the US embassies in Nairobi and Dar-es-Salaam in 1998. Extradited to Egypt from the United Arab Emirates (UAE) and imprisoned. Released from prison following the fall of Hosni Mubarak during the Arab Spring. Incited protests at the US Embassy in Cairo.

Hussein al-Zawahiri: Al-Zawahiri's youngest brother. Worked as an engineer in Malaysia before being extradited to Egypt as part of a larger crackdown on anyone tied to al-Zawahiri and the EIJ.

WIVES

Izzat Ahmad Nuwair: Better known as Umm Fatima or Azza. Al-Zawahiri's first wife. Married in 1978. Hailed from a prominent and wealthy Egyptian family. Had five children with al-Zawahiri, four daughters and a son.

Umayma Hassan: Also known as Umm Khalid. She became al-Zawahiri's second wife in 2001. Survived Operation Enduring Freedom. They had a daughter together in 2005, called Nawwar. Occasional contributor to al-Qaeda propaganda.

Sayyida Halawa: Also known as Umm Tasneem. She became al-Zawahiri's third wife at some point post-9/11. Captured in a 2018 counter-terrorism operation in North Waziristan, Pakistan.

CHILDREN

Fatima al-Zawahiri: Al-Zawahiri's eldest child with Umm Fatima. She married the Jordanian jihadist Abu Turab al-Urduni.

Umayma al-Zawahiri: Al-Zawahiri's second child with Umm Fatima. She wedded the Egyptian jihadist Abu Dujana al-Masri.

Nabila al-Zawahiri: Al-Zawahiri's third child with Umm Fatima. She married the Moroccan terrorist Muhammad Abbatay.

Khadija al-Zawahiri: Al-Zawahiri's fourth child with Umm Fatima. She had a twin brother, Mohammed. She was married to Hamza bin Laden, son of Osama bin Laden.

Mohammed al-Zawahiri: Al-Zawahiri's fifth child with Umm Fatima. His twin sister is Khadija. He was killed in an airstrike in Afghanistan during Operation Enduring Freedom.

Aisha al-Zawahiri: Al-Zawahiri's sixth child with Umm Fatima. Diagnosed with Down syndrome, she was al-Zawahiri's favourite child. She was killed in an airstrike in Afghanistan during Operation Enduring Freedom.

Nawwar al-Zawahiri: Al-Zawahiri's seventh child and first with Umayma Hassan.

Politicians, Military, Ideologues, and Terrorists

Muhammad Abbatay: Alias: Abd al-Rahman al-Maghrebi. Moroccan. Al-Zawahiri's son-in-law, married to Nabila. Senior al-Qaeda operative. Spent extensive time in Iran. Served as director of as-Sahab, al-Qaeda's media arm.

Abdullah Ahmed Abdullah: Alias: Abu Muhammad al-Masri. Egyptian. Senior al-Qaeda operative. Al-Zawahiri's deputy and confidante. Oversaw the 1998 bombings on US embassies in Nairobi and Dar-es-Salaam. Spent extensive time in Iran. Killed in 2020 in Tehran in a mysterious drive-by shooting.

Saif al-Adel: Birth name: Mohammed Salah al-Din Zaidan. Egyptian. Former member of the Egyptian military specialising in tactics and strategy. Veteran of Afghan jihad. Al-Zawahiri loyalist and trusted aide. Al-Qaeda's chief of security. Al-Zawahiri tasked him with monitoring al-Zarqawi's activities. Married to Abu Walid al-Masri's daughter. Spent extensive time in Iran on behalf of al-Qaeda.

Abu Muhammad al-Adnani: Syrian. ISIS spokesperson. An outspoken critic of al-Zawahiri and al-Qaeda. Killed in a drone strike in Syria in 2016.

Mullah Mawlawi Haibatullah Akhundzada: Afghan. Successor to Mullah Mansour as leader of the Taliban. Al-Zawahiri pledged an oath of allegiance (*ba'yah*) to him in 2016, but Akhundzada did not publicly accept al-Zawahiri's pledge.

Mohammed Atef: Alias: Abu Hafs al-Masri. Egyptian. Bin Laden's brother-in-law and head of security prior to 9/11. Was al-Qaeda's military chief and wanted to prioritise the 'internal enemy'. With al-Zawahiri, involved in al-Qaeda's CBRNE programme. Killed in the Battle of Tora Bora, Afghanistan.

Yusuf bin Salih bin Fahd al-Ayeri: Alias: Abu Saleh. Saudi Arabian. Top al-Qaeda operative. Tasked with executing a terror attack in New York City in 2003 with the use of cyanide. The plot was later called off by al-Zawahiri. He was behind the 2003 suicide bombings in Riyadh coordinated with Saif al-Adel. Died in 2003 in a shoot-out with Saudi forces.

Maulana Masood Azhar: Pakistani. Leader of the Jaish-e-Mohammed (JeM), a Pakistani jihadist group with links to al-Qaeda and the Pakistani Inter-Services Intelligence (ISI). An ally of both bin Laden and al-Zawahiri, he helped al-Qaeda leaders escape Afghanistan to Pakistan using JeM's network of agents and safe houses.

Abdullah Azzam: Palestinian-Jordanian. Scholar and an Islamist ideologue. Helped craft the transnational brand of jihadism. Established the Services Office (Maktab al-Khadamat, MAK) to provide lodging, training, religious guidance, and logistical assistance for Arab *mujahideen* to fight the Afghan jihad. Bin Laden helped fund MAK. Azzam and al-Zawahiri differed over the strategy for the Arab fighters in Afghanistan after the Soviet withdrawal. Killed in a car bomb in 1989 in Peshawar, Pakistan.

Abu Bakr al-Baghdadi: Birth name: Ibrahim Awwad Ibrahim al-Badry. Iraqi. Founder of Jaysh Ahl al-Sunna wa-I-Jammah (Army of the People of the Sunna and Communal Solidarity), an Iraqi insurgent group that fought US troops in Iraq. Upon his release from Camp Bucca, he became part of al-Qaeda in Iraq. Established ISIS. Aimed to usurp and defy al-Qaeda and undermine al-Zawahiri.

Humam Khalil al-Balawi: Alias: Abu Dujanah al-Khorasani. Jordanian-Palestinian. Raised in Kuwait and Jordan. An online advocate for al-Qaeda. Recruited by the United States and Jordan to infiltrate al-Qaeda's upper echelons and locate al-Zawahiri. Detonated a suicide bomb at US base Camp Chapman in Khost, Afghanistan, killing his American and Jordanian handlers. Recruited by al-Zawahiri as a triple agent.

Hasan al-Banna: Egyptian. Founder of the Muslim Brotherhood. One of the key figures in the establishment of political Islam. Sought the total independence of Muslim lands from Western political, cultural, and economic domination and the re-establishment of Shariah law. Opposed to secular nationalism. Assassinated by Egyptian government forces in 1949.

Abu Ubaidah al-Banshiri: Egyptian. A founding and high-ranking member of al-Qaeda. Wanted to focus on the 'internal enemy'. Helped create military training bases in the border areas of Afghanistan-Pakistan (AfPak) to fight the Soviets and became al-Qaeda's head of operations in East Africa. Drowned in Lake Victoria in 1996.

Dhiren Barot: British. Muslim convert who led a terrorist cell plotting attacks in the UK, including using an RDD. Had the confidence of al-Qaeda's inner circle, especially al-Zawahiri. Arrested in 2004 and imprisoned in 2006 for his intention to commit mass murder on behalf of al-Qaeda.

Benazir Bhutto: Pakistani. Two-time prime minister of Pakistan, 1988–1990 and 1993–1996. Signed extradition treaty with Egypt. Opposed by al-Zawahiri and bin Laden over her efforts to rid Pakistan of foreign terrorists. Faced numerous plots before eventually being assassinated in 2007 in an al-Qaeda plot tied to al-Zawahiri.

Khalid Abu al-Dahab: Egyptian. Recruited to join the EIJ in 1984. Helped establish al-Kifah Refugee Center in Brooklyn, New York City, to raise funds for jihadist activities. His apartment in California served as an

EIJ communications hub, which also benefited al-Qaeda. Al-Zawahiri instructed him to recruit American citizens of Middle Eastern descent for the jihad. Became Ali Mohamed's second-in-command.

Muhammad Abd al-Salam Faraj: Egyptian. Leader of al-Jihad terrorist group. Author of *The Neglected Duty*, which provided the ideological underpinnings for Sadat's assassination and was viewed as al-Jihad's manifesto. Argued for the necessity of waging jihad against Muslim rulers who were deemed 'apostates' or 'pharaohs'. Sought to create an Islamic state. Executed in 1982 by the Mubarak regime for his role in the Sadat plot.

Adam Gadahn: Alias: 'Azzam the American'. American. Groomed by al-Zawahiri to be an al-Qaeda spokesperson. Killed in a drone strike in 2015.

Abu Mohammed al-Golani: Syrian. Leader of Jabhat al-Nusra, al-Qaeda affiliate in Syria. Refused to recognise Abu Bakr al-Baghdadi as his superior and instead pledged allegiance directly to al-Zawahiri. Opposed ISIS.

Jalaluddin Haqqani: Afghan. Founder of the criminal-terrorist militia, the Haqqani Network. Aligned with the Taliban and close ally of al-Qaeda. Died in 2019.

Khalil-ur-Rahman Haqqani: Afghan. Brother of Jalaluddin Haqqani and part of the Haqqani Network. Protected al-Zawahiri's family after 9/11. Became Taliban minister of refugees in Afghanistan. Smuggled al-Zawahiri and his family back into Afghanistan in 2022.

Sirajuddin Haqqani: Afghan. Half-Arab son of Jalaluddin Haqqani and nephew to Khalil-ur-Rahman Haqqani. Took over the Haqqani Network in 2019 and supported al-Qaeda tactically and strategically. Became Taliban interior minister in Afghanistan. Close ally of al-Zawahiri.

Seifallah Ben Hassine: Alias: Abu Ayyad al-Tunisi. Tunisian. Founder and leader of Ansar al-Sharia. Helped al-Zawahiri organise the assassination of Northern Alliance leader Ahmad Shah Massoud and sow insurrection in the aftermath of the Arab Spring. Procrastinated over the divisions between al-Qaeda and ISIS.

Safar al-Hawali: Egyptian. Al-Zawahiri's classmate at Maadi High School and member of al-Zawahiri's terrorist cell during the 1970s.

Rabiah Hutchinson: Australian. A convert to Islam who travelled to Afghanistan and into the inner circle of al-Qaeda's leadership. Invited by al-Zawahiri to run a women's hospital in Kabul. She was married to the journalist and jihadist Abu Walid al-Masri.

Khalid al-Islambouli: Egyptian. A captain in the Egyptian army and member of al-Jihad. Assassinated Sadat, along with three co-conspirators. Deeply influenced by the ideologue Muhammad Abd al-Salam Faraj.

Ilyas Kashmiri: Pakistani. Senior al-Qaeda operative. Organised 2008 al-Qaeda attack on Danish Embassy in Islamabad with al-Zawahiri's support. Al-Zawahiri appointed him to a special operations council after bin Laden's death. Killed in a drone strike in Pakistan in 2011.

Ahmed Khadr: Egyptian. In collaboration with al-Zawahiri, used several charities to fundraise in support of Egyptian jihadis travelling to Afghanistan and to pay their salaries.

Mohammad Sidique Khan: British-Pakistani. Ringleader of the London 7/7 attacks. Trained in al-Qaeda camps in Pakistan overseen by al-Zawahiri.

Momin Khawaja: Canadian-Pakistani. Worked within the Canadian Department of Foreign Affairs and passed information and money along to al-Qaeda. Plotted major attacks in the UK. Arrested in 2004 in Canada. Part of al-Zawahiri's strategy of recruiting Muslims born or brought up in the West to carry out attacks.

Hamza bin Laden: Saudi Arabian. Favourite son of Osama bin Laden. Spent time in Iran. Married to Khadija al-Zawahiri and the daughters of Mohamed Atta, the Egyptian lead hijacker in 9/11 attacks, and Abdullah Ahmed Abdullah. Al-Zawahiri groomed Hamza to be his successor since at least 2015. Encouraged lone-actor attacks in the West. Killed by a US airstrike in the AfPak region sometime between 2017 and 2019.

Osama bin Laden: Alias: Abu Abdallah. Saudi Arabian. Founder and leader of al-Qaeda (1988–2011). Al-Zawahiri's organization, the EIJ, became an official affiliate of bin Laden's al-Qaeda in 1998, and they merged in 2001. Al-Zawahiri is often referred to as bin Laden's 'lieutenant', and they issued a joint *fatwa* in 1998. Often perceived as the figurehead, charismatic communicator, and financier of al-Qaeda, compared to al-Zawahiri as the strategist, al-Qaeda ideologue, and operational planner. Killed in a US operation is Abbottabad, Pakistan.

Abu Faraj al-Libbi: Libyan. Senior al-Qaeda operative. Head of al-Qaeda's operational planning after Khalid Shaikh Mohammed's capture. Based in Abbottabad for a period. Apprehended in 2005 in Pakistan.

Abu Anas al-Libi: Birth name: Nazih al-Ruqail. Libyan. Member of the Libyan Islamic Fighting Group (LIFG). Fought in the Afghan jihad, where he first met al-Zawahiri. Became a top al-Qaeda operative. Granted political asylum in the UK during the early 1990s. Fled after being found in possession of al-Zawahiri's terror training manual. Spent time in Iran before joining the Libyan civil war. Died in 2015 from liver cancer whilst awaiting trial in the United States for his role in the East Africa embassy bombings.

Abu Yahya al-Libi: Birth name: Mohamed Hassan Qaid. Libyan. Senior al-Qaeda operative. Killed in a US drone strike in 2012 in Pakistan. Al-Zawahiri called for attacks on Americans in Libya to avenge al-Libi's death.

Ahmad Salama Mabruk: Alias: Abu Faraj al-Masri. Egyptian. Served in the Egyptian military briefly before joining al-Jihad. Mabruk was arrested in the sweep of jihadists following the assassination of Anwar Sadat and ended up in the same prison cell as al-Zawahiri, forming a lifelong friendship despite personal loss and setbacks. Accompanied al-Zawahiri on several trips and became his main interlocutor in Syria. Killed in a US drone strike in 2016.

Bashiruddin Mahmood: Pakistani. Nuclear scientist whom al-Zawahiri and bin Laden consulted about establishing an al-Qaeda nuclear weapons programme.

Abdul Majeed: Pakistani. Nuclear scientist who met al-Zawahiri and bin Laden on the prospects of providing nuclear material.

Mullah Akhtar Mansour: Afghan. Leader of the Taliban, 2015–2016. Successor to Mullah Omar. Killed in a US drone strike in 2016. Al-Zawahiri pledged *ba'yah* to him in 2014 after Mullah Omar's death was publicly announced.

Abu Ayyub al-Masri: Deputy to al-Zarqawi. Became leader of al-Qaeda in Iraq after al-Zarqawi's death in 2006. Died by suicide bomb to avoid capture by US forces in 2010.

Abu Ubaidah al-Masri: Birth name: Sheikh Abdul Hameed. Organised the bombing of the Egyptian embassy in Islamabad, Pakistan, in 1995. Spent time in the United Kingdom and Germany to develop an understanding of Western culture. Coordinated some of al-Qaeda's external operations in West, including the London transit bombings as well as the transatlantic airline liquid bomb plot. He was also implicated in the assassination of former Pakistani prime minister Benazir Bhutto. Died from hepatitis C.

Abu Walid al-Masri: Alias: Mustafa Hamid. Egyptian. Journalist and jihadist. Fought in the Afghan jihad. Associate of Jalaluddin Haqqani. Was married to the Australian convert Rabiah Hutchinson. Father-in-law to Saif al-Adel. Loyal to the Taliban and al-Zawahiri.

Essam Hafez Marzouk: Alias: Fawzi Harbi. Egyptian. Member of EIJ and sent by al-Zawahiri to be an operative in Canada. Involved in the preparation and planning of the attack on the US Embassy in Nairobi, Kenya, in 1998.

Abdul A'la Maududi: Pakistani. A theologian whose ideas about political Islam greatly influenced Sayyid Qutb. Founder and leader of the Islamist Jamaat-e-Islami movement. Died in 1979.

Ahmad Shah Massoud: Afghan. Legendary military commander and leader of the Northern Alliance. Ally of Abdullah Azzam. Fought against the Taliban in the 1990s before his assassination in 2001. Assassinated on 9 September 2001 (9/9) by al-Qaeda under direction of al-Zawahiri.

Ali Mohamed: Egyptian. Former member of Egyptian army. Member of al-Jihad and then the EIJ. Pledged *ba'yah* to al-Zawahiri and the EIJ after his discharge from the Egyptian army in 1984. Deeply trusted by al-Zawahiri. As an EIJ operative, he infiltrated the CIA, FBI, and US military. Considered the most lethal jihadist mole inside the US military and law enforcement. Worked closely with Khalid Abu al-Dahab in California. Al-Zawahiri instructed him to recruit US citizens of Middle Eastern descent for the jihad.

Khalid Shaikh Mohammed: Pakistani-Kuwait. Al-Qaeda operational planner. Mastermind behind 9/11. Behind the death of American journalist Daniel Pearl. Captured in Rawalpindi, Pakistan, in 2003.

Mohamed Morsi: Egyptian. President of Egypt, 2012–2013. Member of the Freedom and Justice Party, the Muslim Brotherhood's political wing.

Removed from power in a military coup in 2013 and imprisoned thereafter. Died in 2019.

Hosni Mubarak: Egyptian. Decorated air force officer. Made vice-president of Egypt under Sadat from 1975 to 1981. Succeeded Sadat as president of Egypt after his assassination from 1981 to 2011. Clamped down heavily on the jihadist terrorist groups, forcing many, including al-Zawahiri, into exile. Unseated from power following the Arab Spring in Egypt in 2011. Imprisoned in 2012 over corruption and misuse of power charges. Released in 2017. Died in 2020.

Pervez Musharraf: Pakistani. General and military ruler. Overthrew the Prime Minister Nawaz Sharif in a coup in 1999. President of Pakistan, 2001–2008. Following 9/11, was asked by the George W. Bush administration to track down the al-Qaeda leadership in Pakistan. Failed to deal with the rise of extremism in Pakistan.

Ahmed Ibrahim al-Sayyid al-Najjar: Egyptian. Member of the EIJ. Was active in Yemen and part of the cell in Albania. Extradited to Egypt, he became the state prosecution's primary witness against the EIJ networks that had been rounded up.

Gamal Nasser: Egyptian president, 1954–1970. Led the Free Officers movement that ushered in the Egyptian Revolution of 1952. Promoted pan-Arab unity. Nationalised the Suez Canal. Defeated by Israel in the June 1967 war. Imprisoned and executed Egyptian ideologue Sayyid Qutb.

Mullah Mohammed Omar: Afghan. Leader of the Taliban from 1994 to 2013. Educated and trained in Pakistan. Ally of al-Qaeda. Refused to hand over bin Laden and al-Zawahiri after 9/11. His death in 2013 was kept secret and only announced in 2015.

Isam al-Qamari: Egyptian. Former member of Egyptian military. Smuggled weapons to al-Jihad. Plotted to kill attendees at Sadat's funeral. Imprisoned in the same cell as al-Zawahiri after Sadat's assassination. Close ally and greatly admired by al-Zawahiri. Escaped from prison but was killed by Egyptian police.

Muhammad Qutb: Egyptian. Sayyid Qutb's brother and Egyptian Islamist intellectual. He edited and published Sayyid Qutb's works in Saudi Arabia and taught Islamic Studies at Umm al-Qura University. Al-Zawahiri met him several times.

Sayyid Qutb: Egyptian. An Islamist ideologue antagonistic towards Western culture. A prominent member of the Muslim Brotherhood, Qutb was greatly respected by jihadists as because of his time in the United Sates, where he wrote a critique of the corruption of Western society. Fell out with the Nasser government and imprisoned after being tied to a failed Islamist coup attempt. Wrote his seminal work, *Milestones*, which advocated the forced removal of 'apostate' governments who did not implement Shariah and were in a state of pre-Islamic ignorance. Executed by Nasser in 1966.

Atiyah Abd al-Rahman: Alias: Atiyah. Libyan. Senior al-Qaeda operative. First met bin Laden in 1988 in Afghanistan. Became al-Zawahiri's deputy. An al-Qaeda emissary in Iran and Algeria. Influential in helping the triple agent Humam Khalil al-Balawi infiltrate the US base Camp Chapman in Khost, Afghanistan.

Shaykh Omar Abdel Rahman: Alias: the Blind Shaykh. Egyptian. Spiritual leader of al-Gama'a al-Islamiyyah. Met al-Zawahiri when the two were imprisoned after Sadat's assassination. Rahman and al-Zawahiri became rivals because they disagreed about the best strategy to advance the jihad as well as who should be the *amir* of al-Jihad. Their disputes led to the split between al-Gama'a and the EIJ. Was also rivals with Mustafa Shalabi.

Rashid Rauf: British-Pakistani. A key al-Qaeda operational coordinator for plots in the UK. Married to a member of Maulana Masood Azhar family, providing a link between al-Zawahiri, JeM, and UK-based terrorist cells.

Anwar Sadat: Egyptian. Vice-president under Nasser, 1969–1970. President of Egypt, 1970–1981. Known as the Pious President, sought to transform Egypt strategically and economically by establishing closer ties with the United States and Israel, leading to a peace deal. Showed greater tolerance towards the Islamists. Unaware of their growing hostility towards him, culminating in his assassination in 1981 by al-Jihad terrorist group.

Hafiz Saeed: Pakistani. Co-founder and leader of Lashkar-e-Taiba (LeT), a Pakistani jihadist group with links to al-Qaeda and the Pakistani ISI.

Ijaz Shah: Served in the Pakistani military, ISI, and the Intelligence Bureau as well as being home minister for Punjab province. Established several clandestine relationships with terrorist groups including al-Qaeda and the JeM. Protected the terrorist Ahmed Omar Saeed Sheikh following his role in the abduction and murder of American journalist Daniel Pearl. Accused of having played a role in the death of former prime minister Benazir Bhutto.

Mustafa Shalabi: Egyptian. Helped establish al-Kifah Refugee Center in New York and fundraised for the *mujahideen* fighting against the Soviets. Per al-Zawahiri's instructions, he attempted to exclude Omar Abdel Rahman from the decision-making process within al-Kifah. His rivalry with Rahman led to his murder, which precipitated the disintegration of Azzam's US network.

Sayyid Imam al-Sharif: Alias: Dr Fadl. Egyptian. Met al-Zawahiri whilst both attended Cairo University as medical students. Established Tanzeem with al-Zawahiri in 1967. Made head of the EIJ and became its spiritual leader. Subsequently usurped from his role and became one of al-Zawahiri's biggest detractors. Differed with al-Zawahiri over the role of violence in jihadist strategy.

Tharwat Salah Shehata: Alias: Abu Samha al-Masri. Egyptian. A deputy of al-Zawahiri's in the EIJ. Involved in the disrupted Albania plot and failed attempt to assassinate former Egyptian prime minister Atef Sedky. Disagreed with the EIJ merger with al-Qaeda and continued to run a faction separately from al-Zawahiri. Detained in Iran after 9/11 and then travelled to Libya to fight in the civil war. Upon re-entering Egypt, he was arrested.

Ahmed Omar Saeed Sheikh: British-Pakistani. A member of the Pakistani terrorist group the JeM and close associate to Khalid Shaikh Mohammed. Responsible for abducting American journalist Daniel Pearl and took part in his brutal execution.

Aafia Siddiqui: Pakistani. A neuroscientist who was ideologically committed to al-Qaeda and offered to help develop its chemical and biological programme. Greatly admired by al-Zawahiri. Was arrested and prosecuted for attempting to murder members of the US military and law enforcement in Afghanistan. Al-Zawahiri long demanded Siddiqui's release.

Salih Abdullah Siriyya: Palestinian. *Amir* of Hizb ut-Tahrir al-Islami (Islamic Liberation Party), which condemned the existing political system in Egypt and believed in bringing about a Muslim social order through force. Siriyya conspired with al-Zawahiri for their attempt to take over Military Technical College building near Cairo on 17 April 1974.

Abdel Fattah el-Sisi: Egyptian. General and defence minister during Mohamed Morsi's brief tenure. Led the military coup that deposed Morsi. President of Egypt from 2014. Imprisoned Morsi and banned the Muslim Brotherhood, as well as other Islamist groups.

Qassem Soleimani: Iranian. Islamic Revolutionary Guard Corps (IRGC) general and commander who clandestinely enabled al-Qaeda to use Iran as a facilitation hub. Killed in 2020 by an American drone strike in Iraq.

Ismail Tantawi: Egyptian. Al-Zawahiri's classmate at Maadi High School. Co-founder of Tanzeem and member of al-Zawahiri's cell during the 1970s.

Hassan al-Turabi: Sudanese. Former secretary general of the Sudanese Muslim Brotherhood who institutionalised Shariah in northern Sudan. Invited bin Laden and al-Zawahiri to move to Sudan in the early 1990s. Al-Turabi and al-Zawahiri developed plans to confront the US military in the Horn of Africa.

Midhat Mursi al-Sayid Umar: Alias: Abu Khabab. Egyptian. Attained a biochemistry degree in 1975 and was a trainer at al-Qaeda's Darunta Complex. Gave courses on making and using toxins and poison gas. Head of al-Qaeda's biological, chemical, and nuclear weapons programme. Died in a 2006 US drone strike that was designed to also kill al-Zawahiri.

Ahmed 'Urabi: Egyptian. Military officer concerned about the economic, political, and military hegemony imposed on Egypt by Britain, France, and the Ottomans. Led an uprising named after him, the 'Urabi Revolt, which was eventually crushed by British forces. 'Urabi was sent into exile to Ceylon, later known as Sri Lanka.

Nasir al-Wuhayshi: Alias: Abu Basir, Abu Baseer. Yemeni. Leader of al-Qaeda in the Arabian Peninsula. Pledged *ba'yah* to al-Zawahiri and became his chosen successor. Killed in a US drone strike in Yemen in 2015.

Mustafa Abu al-Yazid: Alias: Sheikh Saeed al-Masri. Egyptian. Aide to al-Zawahiri. Claimed responsibility for the assassination of former Pakistani prime minister Benazir Bhutto. Contributed to the tactical planning of Humam Khalil al-Balawi's triple agent operation. Killed in a US drone strike in North Waziristan, Pakistan, in 2010.

Saad Zaghlul: Egyptian. Egyptian nationalist leader of the Wafd Party. Campaigned for independence for Egypt during and after World War I. Sent into exile on two occasions. Served briefly as Egypt's prime minister in 1924.

Muhammad Zia ul-Haq: Pakistani. Islamist military ruler who overthrew Prime Minister Zulfikar Ali Bhutto in a coup in 1977 and then had him executed. Initially ostracised, the West turned to Zia to help in creating the Afghan-Arab *mujahideen*. Died in 1988, in a mysterious plane crash in Pakistan.

Tariq al-Zumar: Egyptian. Imprisoned for his involvement in Sadat's assassination (1981–2011). Rivals with Shaykh Omar Abdel Rahman. The two disagreed over who was entitled to the role of *amir* of al-Jihad. Al-Zawahiri was loyal to al-Zumar. This disagreement and factionalisation led to the split between the EIJ and al-Gama'a. Subsequently became a leader within al-Gama'a.

Abbreviations

ANI-TV	Arabic News International
AQAP	al-Qaeda in the Arabian Penninsula
AQI	al-Qaeda in Iraq
AQIM	al-Qaeda in the Islamic Maghreb
AQIS	al-Qaeda in the Indian Subcontinent
AST	Ansar al-Sharia in Tunisia
CBRN	chemical, biological, radiological, and nuclear
CENTCOM	Central Command
CIA	Central Intelligence Agency
COAS	chief of army staff
DEVGRU	Naval Special Warfare Development Group
DNI	Director for National Intelligence
DSS	Diplomatic Security Service
EIJ	Egyptian Islamic Jihad
FATA	Federally Administered Tribal Areas
FBI	Federal Bureau of Investigation
FTF	foreign terrorist fighters
GIA	Islamic Fighting Group
GID	General Intelligence Department
GSPC	Salafist Group for Preaching and Combat
HCI	Human Concern International
HTI	Islamic Liberation Party (Hizb ut-Tahrir al-Islami)
HTS	Hay'at Tahrir al-Sham
HUJI	Harakat-ul-Jihad-Islami
HuM	Harkat-ul-Mujahidin
IB	Intelligence Bureau
ICRC	International Committee of the Red Cross
IED	improvised explosive device
IRGC	Islamic Revolutionary Guard Corps

ISI	Inter-Services Intelligence
ISIS	Islamic State in Iraq and Greater Syria
IS-KP	Islamic State Khorasan Province
JeM	Jaish-e-Mohammed
JI	Jemaah Islamiyah
LeT	Lashkar-e-Taiba
LIFG	Libyan Islamic Fighting Group
MAK	Maktab al-Khadamat
MJN	Muhammad Jamal Network
NGA	National Geospatial-Intelligence Agency
NIF	National Islamic Front
NDP	National Democratic Party
NDS	National Directorate of Security
PDPA	People's Democratic Party of Afghanistan
PLO	Palestinian Liberation Organization
PPP	Pakistan People's Party
RDD	radiological dispersal device
RFJ	Rewards for Justice
TCG	Tunisian Combat Group
TTP	Tehrik-e Taliban Pakistan
UAR	United Arab Republic
UTN	Reconstruction of the Muslim Ummah (Ummah Tameer-e-Nau)
WMD	weapons of mass destruction
WTC	World Trade Center

Illustrations

Photo acknowledgements are given in parentheses

Maps

Maps created by Ed Merritt

NORTH AFRICA / EUROPE

Tracking Ayman al-Zawahiri

① Ayman al-Zawahiri is born in Giza and raised in Maadi, Cairo, 1951.

② Abortive attempt to take over the Military Technical College in Cairo, 1974.

③ Arrested and imprisoned for the assassination of Egyptian President Anwar Sadat in Cairo, 1981.

④ Assassination attempt on Egyptian Prime Minister Atef Sedky in Cairo, 1993.

⑤ Visited Bern and Zurich to plan impending trip to the United States, 1993.

⑥ Foiled bombing of the U.S. Embassy in Tirana, 1998.

ATLANTIC OCEAN

DENMARK
⑪ Copenhagen

UNITED KINGDOM
⑧ London
⑨

GERMANY   EUROPE

⑩ Paris
SWITZERLAND
FRANCE   Zurich
Milan ⑤ ⑩
⑩ Bologna

ITALY   ALBANIA
Tirana
⑥

Black Sea

SPAIN

TURKEY

Mediterranean Sea

Rabat
⑩
MOROCCO

Tunis ⑫
TUNISIA Djerba
⑦

Benghazi   Cairo
⑫   ① 🏠 IIII
                ② ③
                ④
                ⑫

ALGERIA

LIBYA

EGYPT

AFRICA

SUDAN

⑦ Bombing of synagogue in Djerba, 2002.

⑧ Several mass-casualty al-Qaeda plots targeting transportation hubs and infrastructure are disrupted by British authorities, 2004 – 2006.

⑨ Coordinated suicide bombings of the transit system in London, 2005.

⑩ Authorities disrupt coordinated cells plotting attacks in Paris, Milan, Bologna and Rabat, 2006.

⑪ Plot to target the Danish Jyllands-Posten's newspaper offices disrupted, 2009.

⑫ Coordinated attacks on U.S. diplomatic missions in Cairo, Tunis and Benghazi, 2012.

0 km	500	1,000
0 miles		500

MAP KEY

☀ Terrorist Attack

▤ Terrorist Plot

IIII Imprisoned

🏠 Sanctuary / Abode

◉ Visited

Map 1

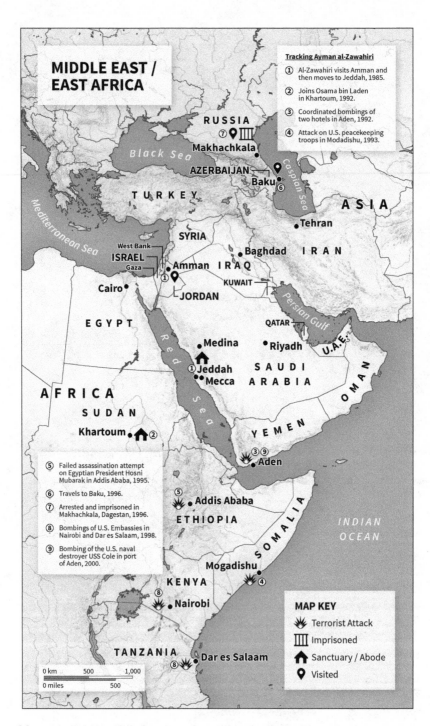

MIDDLE EAST /
EAST AFRICA

Tracking Ayman al-Zawahiri

① Al-Zawahiri visits Amman and then moves to Jeddah, 1985.

② Joins Osama bin Laden in Khartoum, 1992.

③ Coordinated bombings of two hotels in Aden, 1992.

④ Attack on U.S. peacekeeping troops in Modadishu, 1993.

RUSSIA
⑦
Makhachkala

Black Sea

AZERBAIJAN

Baku ⑥

Caspian Sea

ASIA

TURKEY

Tehran

Mediterranean Sea

SYRIA

West Bank
ISRAEL
Gaza

Baghdad

IRAQ

IRAN

Amman ①

KUWAIT

Cairo

JORDAN

Persian Gulf

EGYPT

QATAR

U.A.E.

Medina

Riyadh

Red Sea

① Jeddah
Mecca

SAUDI
ARABIA

OMAN

AFRICA

SUDAN

Khartoum ②

YEMEN

⑤ Failed assassination attempt on Egyptian President Hosni Mubarak in Addis Ababa, 1995.

⑥ Travels to Baku, 1996.

⑦ Arrested and imprisoned in Makhachkala, Dagestan, 1996.

⑧ Bombings of U.S. Embassies in Nairobi and Dar es Salaam, 1998.

⑨ Bombing of the U.S. naval destroyer USS Cole in port of Aden, 2000.

③⑨ Aden

⑤ Addis Ababa

ETHIOPIA

SOMALIA

INDIAN
OCEAN

Mogadishu

④

KENYA

⑧ Nairobi

MAP KEY

✹ Terrorist Attack

▥ Imprisoned

⌂ Sanctuary / Abode

⬤ Visited

TANZANIA

⑧ Dar es Salaam

0 km   500   1,000
0 miles   500

Map 2

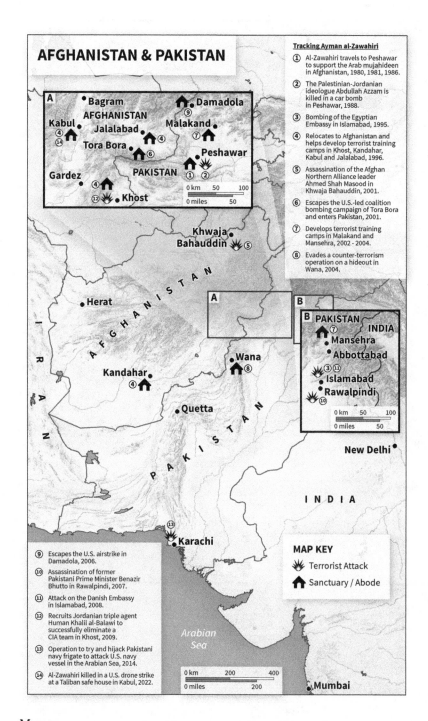

AFGHANISTAN & PAKISTAN

Tracking Ayman al-Zawahiri

① Al-Zawahiri travels to Peshawar to support the Arab mujahideen in Afghanistan, 1980, 1981, 1986.

② The Palestinian-Jordanian ideologue Abdullah Azzam is killed in a car bomb in Peshawar, 1988.

③ Bombing of the Egyptian Embassy in Islamabad, 1995.

④ Relocates to Afghanistan and helps develop terrorist training camps in Khost, Kandahar, Kabul and Jalalabad, 1996.

⑤ Assassination of the Afghan Northern Alliance leader Ahmed Shah Masood in Khwaja Bahauddin, 2001.

⑥ Escapes the U.S.-led coalition bombing campaign of Tora Bora and enters Pakistan, 2001.

⑦ Develops terrorist training camps in Malakand and Mansehra, 2002 - 2004.

⑧ Evades a counter-terrorism operation on a hideout in Wana, 2004.

⑨ Escapes the U.S. airstrike in Damadola, 2006.

⑩ Assassination of former Pakistani Prime Minister Benazir Bhutto in Rawalpindi, 2007.

⑪ Attack on the Danish Embassy in Islamabad, 2008.

⑫ Recruits Jordanian triple agent Human Khalil al-Balawi to successfully eliminate a CIA team in Khost, 2009.

⑬ Operation to try and hijack Pakistani navy frigate to attack U.S. navy vessel in the Arabian Sea, 2014.

⑭ Al-Zawahiri killed in a U.S. drone strike at a Taliban safe house in Kabul, 2022.

MAP KEY

🔥 Terrorist Attack

🏠 Sanctuary / Abode

Map 3

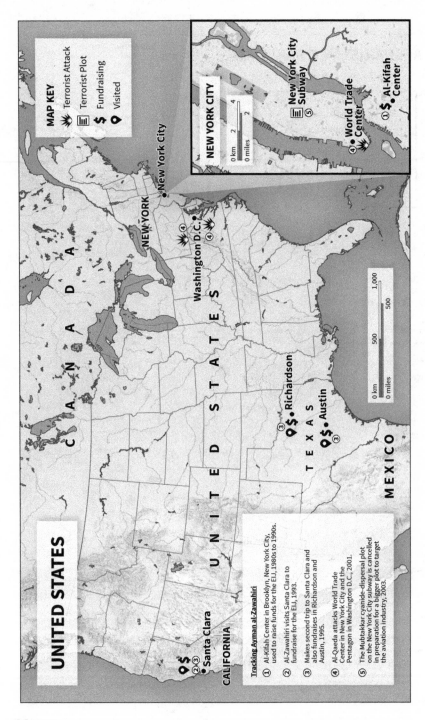

UNITED STATES

MAP KEY

☀ Terrorist Attack
▥ Terrorist Plot
$ Fundraising
◑ Visited

NEW YORK CITY

▥ New York City Subway ⑤
④ World Trade Center
① $ Al-Kifah Center

0 km   2   4
0 miles   2

CALIFORNIA
⑦ $ ② ③
● Santa Clara

TEXAS
③ ◑ $ ● Richardson
③ ◑ $ ● Austin

NEW YORK
● New York City

④ ● Washington D.C. ④

CANADA

UNITED STATES

MEXICO

0 km   500   1,000
0 miles   500

Tracking Ayman al-Zawahiri

① Al-Kifah Center in Brooklyn, New York City, used to raise funds for the EIJ, 1980s to 1990s.

② Al-Zawahiri visits Santa Clara to fundraise for the EIJ, 1993.

③ Makes second trip to Santa Clara and also fundraises in Richardson and Austin, 1995.

④ Al-Qaeda attacks World Trade Center in New York City and the Pentagon in Washington D.C., 2001.

⑤ The Mubtakkar cyanide-dispersal plot on the New York City subway is cancelled in preparation for a bigger plot to target the aviation industry, 2003.

Map 4

Introduction

On 31 July 2022, Ayman al-Zawahiri stepped out onto the balcony of his Kabul villa as the sun rose. Attired in his usual airy white robe, he felt the dawn's crisp breeze brush his skin in a rare moment before the summer heat came beating down midday. In what had become part of a recent routine, he was enjoying the precious fresh air. At the same time, an American weapons operator sat in an air-conditioned control room in the United States monitoring a live video stream of a drone's camera as it flew across Kabul. Al-Zawahiri had spent decades on the run, evading capture time and again but had finally been discovered, hiding in plain sight. Using the targeting brackets for the drone, the weapons operator calibrated the precision-guided laser at the leader of al-Qaeda.

Terrorists reflect their times and the events that define them, and if al-Zawahiri had time to process what was happening in the moments before the missile struck his villa, perhaps he thought of what led to that moment. It could be that al-Zawahiri remembered his own early years growing up in an illustrious Egyptian family of doctors, lawyers, clergy, and politicians or of leading his own terror cell as a teenager whilst studying medicine. Al-Zawahiri may have also reflected from the time he first gained international notoriety in a holding cage in a Cairo courtroom for the assassination of Egyptian president Anwar Sadat. Maybe he thought about his time in Afghanistan when he met and influenced Osama bin Laden, leading to al-Qaeda becoming the most powerful and deadly terrorist group in the world, capable of sophisticated attacks on a never-before-seen scale.

With the deft touch of a teacher, al-Zawahiri assigned his followers numerous murderous assignments that mandated their betrayal of the societies they lived in. The terrorist attacks he was responsible for were frightening and unpredictable, coming without warning. Whether it was office workers in downtown Cairo, commuters on a packed rush hour London train, Nairobi street vendors staking a prime spot near the US embassy, sailors aboard a naval vessel moored off the Yemeni port of Aden, an Afghan resistance fighter conducting a media interview, or American counter-terrorism agents being debriefed by an informant—Ayman al-Zawahiri's terrorism cut a swathe across continents both deep and wide.

Possibly, as the drone zeroed in on his Kabul villa, al-Zawahiri pondered how he lived on the razor's edge after 9/11, with the long years in hiding in Pakistan, surviving numerous US counter-terrorism operations. Yet al-Zawahiri repeatedly emerged from the shadows as a vengeful ideologue still hell-bent on changing history, as he pioneered the use of new media technology to convey al-Qaeda's zealotry. Al-Zawahiri may also have contemplated how he outlasted virtually all of his terrorist contemporaries and rivals. As al-Zawahiri was able to finally return to Afghanistan after his Taliban allies' helter-skelter victory over the West, he was likely pondering the next stage for the jihadist movement just as the glare of hindsight and the drone missile intersected. The Egyptian doctor did not think in terms of hours, days, or weeks, but in decades. He had been meticulously working for 55 years towards global insurrection. His death was not a comforting end to terrorism but instead raised important questions about the future of transnational terrorism and the legacy the al-Qaeda leader left behind.

Ayman al-Zawahiri led an incomparable life. By learning about his experiences and ideology devoted to violent rebellion and sedition, we can trace the growth and evolution of transnational jihadism from one of the longest-serving terrorists. Indeed, the Egyptian's role in insurrection commenced as far back as 1967 and spans several decades. Of all terrorists worldwide, al-Zawahiri had the highest reward on his head, $25 million, sanctioned by the George W. Bush administration after the September 11 attacks in the United States.

Al-Zawahiri's life mirrors the history of Islamism in the late twentieth century and well into the twenty-first. As has been touched upon, al-Zawahiri found himself in many of the places where history was being determined. Sometimes it was fortuitous, but it has also reflected his deliberate planning and calculating. He may not have started out playing the most essential role in unfolding global events, but he knew how to make his presence heard and felt. The journey of al-Zawahiri's life takes us across Egypt, Sudan, Afghanistan, and Pakistan, as well as more unexpected places such as the United States and Russia.

Al-Zawahiri succeeded his close ally and partner in terrorism, Osama bin Laden, as the head of al-Qaeda after the latter was killed by US forces in Pakistan in 2011. Although much has been published about al-Qaeda and bin Laden in academic and mainstream circles, the absence of a comprehensive account of al-Zawahiri remains an important gap in the literature. This book sets out to offer significant perspective and analysis about a man whose contribution to jihadism and global terrorism was of world-changing importance, but who received less serious and honest discussion.

A close examination of al-Zawahiri's life promises to yield important insights into how the Egyptian brand of militancy was mobilised globally and became an essential cog to al-Qaeda. For decades, al-Zawahiri had been sowing insurrection, fomenting terrorist attacks, and somehow always escaping the net to survive.

Not every terrorist is interesting enough to have their life story written about, but al-Zawahiri's provides a vivid account of transgression, trespass, and furious assault against the rule of law and international order. He engaged in the assassination of political leaders, sought to develop chemical and biological weapons, recruited double and triple agents as well as turned the tables on his enemies and rivals to isolate them. Al-Zawahiri had a knack for being in the right place at the right time.

There is a perception that al-Zawahiri was far less charismatic and infamous than bin Laden and that he lacked the tactical nous of Khalid Shaikh Mohammed, the ideological rigour of Abdullah Azzam, the gravitas of Abu Bakr al-Baghdadi, the menacing fear factor of Abu Musab al-Zarqawi, or the fluency to connect with zoomers in the West like Anwar al-Awlaki. Not only are these perceptions fundamentally flawed, but the point to remember is that these individuals were active for only a brief time before they were captured or killed, their fate decided. Al-Zawahiri outlived all of them. His propensity to endure for generations was one of his most important traits. In fact, al-Zawahiri was a strategic, pragmatic, and calculating individual who was forward-thinking and had a knack for networking. These characteristics made him a leader capable of strengthening and expanding the al-Qaeda organization across the globe as well as plotting and executing international attacks and operations.

Along with his aptitude for survival, al-Zawahiri had a shrewd understanding of what it would take to rebuild and reform his organization. There is an inaccurate perception of al-Zawahiri as a rigid micromanager with a preference for his own Egyptian cadres over those from other parts of the Arab world and that he was limited by his inability to inspire jihadists the way bin Laden would. In reality, al-Zawahiri focused on playing the long game and had the acumen to create a legacy for others to follow and develop by wanting to establish 'safe bases' within Afghanistan, Pakistan, the Middle East, North Africa, the Sahel, and the Horn of Africa.

Across this global network and the transnational jihadist movement at large, the Egyptian had an enduring impact. Indeed, he was a complex and multifaceted character whose victories and failures merit careful study on their own accord. Guiding readers through a fully integrated account, this book sheds light on al-Zawahiri by illustrating his determination and cunning in developing relationships and recruiting people to his cause. However, it also details the worst of him, including his treachery and betrayal of other jihadists, his tyrannical and vicious methods for running a terrorist organization, and the rivalries he formed.

Although Ayman al-Zawahiri warranted a reward of $25 million for his capture or elimination, there has been sparse scholarship that specifically focusses on his ideological context, personal history, or position in transnational terrorism, unless it's in conjunction with Osama bin Laden and al-Qaeda. Al-Zawahiri was engaged in political violence for more than a decade before bin Laden entered the scene in Afghanistan and more than a decade after bin Laden's demise in Pakistan.

The discourse produced on al-Zawahiri ranges from scholars to journalists and from lawyers to intelligence and law enforcement practitioners. Yet the literature specifically on al-Zawahiri is unusually concise. There is only one English-language book specifically about him. By comparison, there are a plethora of biographies of Osama bin Laden, and the Egyptian ideologue Sayyid Qutb, who inspired al-Zawahiri, is so widely studied that more than a dozen books analyse his life and works. The Arabic-language literature on al-Zawahiri is only marginally larger than the English-language contributions but is also mostly dated and focused on the dynamic of the Egyptian Islamic Jihad (EIJ).

Several larger works on al-Qaeda include chapters or sections on al-Zawahiri. One of the standouts is Lawrence Wright's seminal *The Looming Tower*; he was the first to discuss al-Zawahiri's background, his role and importance within the jihadist movement specifically al-Qaeda, and also the legacy he inherited by seeing himself as a continuation of Sayyid Qutb's doctrine.[1] This is supported by John Calvert, whose own extensive research into Qutb has demonstrated the pathway he left and the Egyptian ideological legacy al-Zawahiri saw himself carrying on.[2]

Ali Soufan has also provided an interesting overview on what transpired in parts of al-Zawahiri's life and role within al-Qaeda.[3] In addition, Cathy Scott-Clark and Adrian Levy address al-Zawahiri's significance in al-Qaeda's media strategy in shaping the narrative.[4] The prominent scholar Fawaz Gerges has looked at al-Zawahiri prioritising the jihadist campaign against the Hosni Mubarak regime of Egypt.[5] Other notable works include those by Seth G. Jones who considers some of the strategic aspects of al-Zawahiri's role in international terrorism.[6]

In the early 1990s, al-Zawahiri began working in conjunction with several other Egyptian and Libyan jihadists to produce the *Military Studies in the Jihad against the Tyrants.* The 180-page document contains 18 chapters, each of which is a blueprint for the tradecraft of terrorism. The noted psychiatrist and analyst on the psychology of terrorism Jerrold Post spent much time studying the terrorist training manual.[7]

Some have been cautious and sceptical about al-Zawahiri's importance within the jihadist movement. The lawyer Montasser al-Zayyat's *Road to al-Qaeda* provides the only English-language book on al-Zawahiri, and it is written through the prism of personal experiences within the Egyptian jihadist movements, including time in prison with al-Zawahiri. As it was published in 2004, it misses out on the key developments involving al-Zawahiri post-9/11.[8] Ironically, al-Zawahiri has heavily criticised al-Zayyat and suggested that he was a collaborator for the Mubarak regime.[9] Others have queried the impact of al-Zawahiri during specific moments in history. Abdullah Anas and Thomas Hegghammer were wary about al-Zawahiri's significance during the Arab *mujahideen* campaign against the Soviets.[10] Also, Peter Bergen has questioned al-Zawahiri's bearing and influence on bin Laden and al-Qaeda overall.[11]

Conversely, several practitioners have outlined the importance of al-Zawahiri as an ideologue, plotter, tactician, and strategist. This includes Mitchell Silber, who addressed al-Qaeda's global terrorism after 9/11.[12] John Miller, who interviewed bin Laden and also had a personal interaction with al-Zawahiri himself, has spoken about how much control al-Zawahiri was able to exert over bin Laden.[13] There have also been a number of contributions from the intelligence community seeking to outline the history of transnational terrorism covering the Egyptian and Pakistan dynamic. The most exemplary work is that of Bruce Riedel, whose rigorous research leaves an indelible imprint on what went wrong in the hunt for al-Qaeda, including al-Zawahiri, and the role of the Pakistani state.[14] Joby Warrick has evaluated some of the efforts by the counter-terrorism agencies to locate al-Zawahiri.[15]

Farhad Khosrokhavar described al-Zawahiri as a major jihadist intellectual and a key ideologue of al-Qaeda.[16] This has been supported by Bruce Hoffman, who has identified al-Zawahiri's importance to al-Qaeda as comparable to if not greater than that of bin Laden. Both scholars have also pointed out that al-Zawahiri was central to the key moments in transitional terrorism.[17]

Journal articles on al-Zawahiri are limited to a handful, one of which I wrote on the Egyptian's strategy to keep al-Qaeda functioning and re-building it within the Islamic world by creating 'safe bases' and looks at the disclosed Abbottabad documents that have provided a wealth of primary source material on the inner-workings of al-Qaeda.[18] Elsewhere, Nimrod Raphaeli was one of the first to provide a brief biographical account of al-Zawahiri back in 2002.[19] James Jacquier viewed al-Zawahiri's political psychology.[20] Similarly, Tim Huffman outlined al-Zawahiri's religious rhetoric.[21] Olivier Roy and Tore Hamming have evaluated the important relationship between al-Zawahiri and the Taliban.[22] Barak Mendelsohn has addressed the question of who may eventually succeed al-Zawahiri.[23]

It is important to acknowledge the essential and tireless work conducted by Rita Katz and Aaron Zelin, respectively. Their efforts in collecting, analysing, and translating speeches and statements by terrorists like al-Zawahiri have provided an essential clearinghouse of primary source material.[24]

A number of magazine articles, op-eds, and blog posts have been written on al-Zawahiri, but they are obviously confined to brief and cursory overviews. Overall, the substantive scholarship on al-Zawahiri has been sparse. The little that is out there is limited in scope, lacking important details, outdated, or fails to consider the entire wealth of primary sources which provide critical perspective on how al-Zawahiri sought to convert theory to practise, which he achieved with devastating effect on multiple occasions. Thus, there is a great need for an in-depth, thorough analysis of al-Zawahiri's ideological context, personal history, role in transnational terrorism, and ties with other terrorist entities spanning four continents, across several theatres, from Egypt to Pakistan and Sudan to Afghanistan as well as Europe and the United States.

The book fills these gaps by exploring two main lines of inquiry. The first is about al-Zawahiri's background. Where did he come from, and what historical events, ideologues, and family members shaped him as a thinker? What moments and experiences spurred the big decisions in his life? What were his opinions, and how did they evolve?

The second inquiry concerns the sources of al-Zawahiri's influence. Why did he become so influential? What did he do to recruit so many people to international jihadism? How did he shape the tactical and strategic ties with Osama bin Laden and al-Qaeda? How was he able to ensure his self-preservation longer than any other terrorist? What were the key relationships created with other jihadist and state elements that helped al-Zawahiri to plot and plan?

Answering these questions required working primarily as a historian to find, evaluate, and merge primary and secondary sources to identify key actors and events. This included conducting interviews with people who knew or met al-Zawahiri or observed his life up close and tried to capture him.

This book is not meant to be solely biographical but also to tell history through a series of episodes and vivid portraits of al-Zawahiri that have had a direct bearing on transnational terrorism from the 1970s to the 2020s (and potentially beyond). It is also a study of his ideas, the violent call to action, and their interwoven global impact. Instigating the assassination of politicians; fighting superpowers on the battlefield; plotting spectacular mass casualty attacks; recruiting sleeper agents, double agents, and triple agents; pioneering the use of modern technology; availing of sophisticated weaponry; expanding networks to other like-minded jihadists, creating a more widely aligned movement, and withstanding rivals and competitors—these are just some examples of what al-Zawahiri was involved in, not as a footnote but as an intrinsic, unparalleled, and irreplaceable actor.

There are three parts to al-Zawahiri's overarching life story: the Egyptian period, the time in Afghanistan, and then in hiding in Pakistan. The first part represents his grounding in doctrine and insurrection based on family heritage, ideological influences, and personal experiences. The second and third parts shift to building a base for transnational terrorism and moving back and forth between targeting internal and external enemies, a dynamic shaped and influenced by the alliances he created, especially with bin Laden. On occasion, the lines separating the three eras become blurred, illustrating the confluence of events and critical moments in al-Zawahiri's life.

At times, al-Zawahiri's story will be non-linear to incorporate different but interconnected periods, both historical and modern, and provide clearer context to important moments and the significance of certain characters and antagonists. This will also reveal greater insight into other aspects of al-Zawahiri, including unfolding subplots, gradually revealing details that will eventually become consequential to his life. This biography of al-Zawahiri is not meant to be for commemoration or reputation management. Nor will it handle his life with velvet gloves to demonstrate his global importance.

There is a need to understand al-Zawahiri's failures as much as his successes. As a writing task, this has been complicated by the fact that the outcome and legacy of al-Zawahiri had not been decided when I started researching and writing about him back in 2003. Subsequently, across two decades, this book seeks to provide a deep immersion from a lifetime of sources. The most interesting part was not entirely knowing from the outset what one would find on al-Zawahiri and have to report on.

This book also analyses al-Zawahiri's ideological treatises, statements, and military manuals which represent primary sources of al-Qaeda's ideology and political demands as well as their strategy and tactics. Included amongst them are the Abbottabad documents found in bin Laden's compound. A thorough understanding of al-Zawahiri's doctrine, views, and propaganda is essential to comprehending the seductive aspects of al-Qaeda's ideology as well as the terrorist attacks the group orchestrated. Although his fiery political commentary may be more relevant to the time it was released and the style and length easier to process, the longer written religious treatises are more instructive of al-Zawahiri's long-term goals. This book will use his terms, 'internal enemy' when assessing al-Zawahiri's commentary on governments and regimes in the Middle East and 'external enemy' when the Egyptian ideologue talks about the West and Israel.

Finally, this book seeks to show that al-Zawahiri has left a legacy and foundation for al-Qaeda's future on the world stage following the problems that emerged from the Arab Spring and the West's departure from Afghanistan. This is his story.

Chapter Outlines

Chapter 1, 'Reap What You Sow', starts with the Battle of Tora Bora during the opening stages of the US mission in Afghanistan in the aftermath of the September 11 terrorist attacks with the objective of capturing or eliminating the al-Qaeda leadership. Amidst the bombs dropping around him, al-Zawahiri penned his seminal treatise, *Knights under the Prophet's Banner*, which retraced his past experiences and influences. From the prism of his text, this chapter flashes back to Egypt's European colonial history, starting with Napoleon, and the key developments that al-Zawahiri deemed to have impeded Egypt and the Middle East, eventually expanding to the role of the United States. Al-Zawahiri's eminent family members contributed significantly to his thinking, and their legacies influence al-Zawahiri's formative years in Cairo, witnessing several events that shaped his thinking, from Nasser's nationalism to his regime's execution of the ideologue Sayyid Qutb, al-Zawahiri's primary influence.

Chapter 2, 'Insurrection and Transgression', looks at al-Zawahiri's entry into militancy when he concluded that global revolution and insurrection should start from home in his native Egypt. In 1974, al-Zawahiri was part of a clandestine group that attempted to overtake the Military Technical College near Cairo. The plot failed, and all the conspirators were arrested and executed except for al-Zawahiri, who managed to avoid any blame. He was later arrested in the massive round-up of Islamists following the 1981 assassination of then–Egyptian president Anwar Sadat. Although on the periphery of the plot, al-Zawahiri ended up becoming the face of the entire jihadist movement and developed an interest in utilising the media for propaganda. Both these incidents highlighted al-Zawahiri's knack for survival and evading punishment, a trait he would use to his advantage many more times.

Chapter 3, 'The Holy Warrior', continues from the trial of Sadat's assassins, with al-Zawahiri avoiding the death penalty but incarcerated, where he formalised his ties with some jihadists and rivalries with others. It then follows his journey as a member of the Arab *mujahedeen* in Afghanistan. It was there that al-Zawahiri met bin Laden and formed their pivotal terrorist partnership whilst also plotting against his adversary Abdullah Azzam. It was during this period that al-Zawahiri demonstrated long-term thinking, including recruiting Egyptians and sending them to the United States to infiltrate the military and spy for him, providing operational intelligence. Al-Zawahiri could also sense that bin Laden was on the rise in the world of jihadism, and he wanted to have his own stake in that growth whilst removing or ostracizing any detractors. This period was a moment of opportunity for al-Zawahiri.

Chapter 4, 'Building the Base', assesses al-Zawahiri's agenda in trying to defeat the Mubarak government in Egypt whilst facing setbacks and having to re-evaluate his approach by collaborating with bin Laden in Sudan and Afghanistan. This critical period reflected how al-Zawahiri saw the creation of al-Qaeda serving his strategic priorities including targeting US interests in the Middle East and Africa. It also evaluates his pivotal role in the assassination of Northern Alliance leader Ahmed Shah Masood as the precursor to the 9/11 attacks. During this period, al-Zawahiri developed a terrorist manual that became mandatory reading for all operatives and contributed to al-Qaeda's long-term strategy and tactics. Al-Zawahiri also aggressively pursued al-Qaeda's quest for biological, chemical, and nuclear weapons. It is during this period that al-Zawahiri pursues al-Qaeda's media propaganda development as part of an important outreach effort to control the narrative and optics.

Chapter 5, 'Live to Fight Another Day', picks up from the first discussion of the Tora Bora battle after 9/11 and explains how al-Zawahiri survived the bombing and sought to reconstitute al-Qaeda in Pakistan and evolve the group's ideology, tactics, and strategy against the West. This includes unleashing plots globally and inspiring affiliates. The convergence with Pakistani terrorist groups as well as the Haqqani Network coincided with al-Zawahiri taking control of al-Qaeda communiqués from bin Laden and directly engaging with the public. Other important dimensions include the opening of a new front in Iraq, which provided opportunities for al-Qaeda to expand but also coincided with the re-emergence of old rivalries. During this period, there were numerous efforts by the United States to apprehend or kill al-Zawahiri, who not only evaded capture each time but also turned the tables by recruiting triple agents.

Chapter 6, 'Changing of the Knights', looks at the setbacks al-Zawahiri and al-Qaeda encountered, from failing to capitalise on the vacuum created by the Arab Spring, to bin Laden being killed in a Navy Seals operation in Pakistan, and perhaps the biggest threat, the emergence of ISIS. ISIS challenged al-Qaeda's doctrine, recruiting fighters and expanding its territorial base. As al-Qaeda's leader, al-Zawahiri struggled to counter the perception that he had become marginalised amongst jihadists, fighting for significance as the head of a weakening terrorist franchise in fierce competition with ISIS. This chapter also delves into the Abbottabad documents from bin Laden's compound, providing greater insights into al-Qaeda's inner workings and al-Zawahiri's sometimes fractured relationships with other terrorists.

Chapter 7, 'The Elusive Terrorist', analyses how al-Zawahiri survived the challenges and sought to emerge from self-imposed hibernation whilst letting ISIS face the brunt of the international coalition operations in Iraq and Syria. At the same time, he sought to reconstitute al-Qaeda's infrastructure and networks across the Islamic world. Al-Zawahiri took the opportunity to create new affiliates and enhance the relationship with the Haqqani Network, enabling al-Zawahiri to quietly rebuild and fortify al-Qaeda's various branches. There is also an important dissection of al-Qaeda's opaque relationship with Iran as an alliance of convenience. The last part looks at the Taliban retuning to power to Afghanistan and with the Haqqani Network at the helm. This emboldened al-Qaeda and resulted in al-Zawahiri becoming more proactive in al-Qaeda's propaganda whilst pursuing the goal of creating 'safe bases' for operatives and fighters so that al-Qaeda can regrow. It also resulted in al-Zawahiri betraying his own instincts and choosing to return to Afghanistan, believing it would be safe. However, the United States was monitoring him and through a sophisticated intelligence gathering exercise, launched a drone strike at a villa in Kabul where al-Zawahiri was staying, killing the al-Qaeda leader.

The 'Conclusion: 55 Years of Terror' provides reflections on the implications of al-Zawahiri's influence, legacy, and long-term impact. Al-Zawahiri's priorities of survival and operational security remained paramount, and this longevity enabled him to outlast his rivals. It is vital to understand how far al-Zawahiri came, what ideology he imparted, why he was able to survive and withstand threats, and what legacy he left for other jihadists to follow in terms of propaganda, tactics, and strategy. All of this will provide an important reminder of why al-Zawahiri's legacy should not be underestimated, and why he has been one of the most effective terrorists whose own role spanned 55 years.

I

Reap What You Sow

The Battle for Tora Bora

On 7 October 2001, the George W. Bush administration authorised Operation Enduring Freedom with the intention to capture or kill the al-Qaeda leadership that had sent terrorists to launch the devastating attacks on the World Trade Center and the Pentagon on 11 September 2001. The mission was also to remove the Taliban militia, led by Mullah Omar, who provided al-Qaeda sanctuary and refused to cut ties with or hand over Osama bin Laden, his deputy Ayman al-Zawahiri, and the rest of the al-Qaeda command. With this, the US military commenced bombing al-Qaeda training bases and Taliban strongholds across Afghanistan, with two specific goals in mind: first, to operationally degrade the Taliban and second, to eliminate the al-Qaeda leadership. The immediate priorities were bin Laden, designated as 'High Value Target One' (HVT One) and al-Zawahiri as 'High Value Target Two' (HVT Two).[1]

An unprecedented combination of airpower and personnel orchestrated by US Central Command (CENTCOM), special operations commandos, and Central Intelligence Agency (CIA) personnel, along with Afghan Northern Alliance allies attempted to sweep the Taliban from power and either capture or kill al-Qaeda's leaders who were contemplating their next steps from Kabul.[2]

Kabul is situated high up in Afghanistan and nestled in a valley between distinct mountain ranges. During the winter when it snows, the capital turns white, creating a permeable boundary that temporarily separates itself from the rest of the country. As US forces and their Northern Alliance allies were closing in on Kabul, al-Zawahiri was preparing himself and his family to flee.[3] Ordering his wives and children to travel separately as they might be safer, al-Zawahiri provided an early indication of the calculated measures

Doctor, Teacher, Terrorist. Sajjan M. Gohel, Oxford University Press. © Oxford University Press 2024.
DOI: 10.1093/oso/9780197665367.003.0001

he was willing to take to evade capture. He sent his family to a safe house in Gardez in Paktia province, run by his allies the Haqqani Network, a faction of the Taliban who shared al-Qaeda's ideology but also dabbled in criminal enterprise. Such was the importance accorded to al-Zawahiri's family that the head of the Haqqani Network, Jalaluddin, instructed his brother Khalil-ur-Rahman to accompany them and ensure their safety in Gardez.[4]

The Taliban's occupation of Kabul ended on 12 November 2001 when the capital was liberated by Northern Alliance forces. By this point al-Zawahiri and the al-Qaeda leadership had fled to Jalalabad, in eastern Afghanistan.[5] However, they were not to stay there for long, as Jalalabad itself had descended into chaos.[6] The al-Qaeda leaders decided to head to Tora Bora, a string of mountain caves in Nangarhar near the Pakistani border.[7]

Towards the end of November 2001, a covert task force comprising officers from the CIA and US Special Forces had captured an al-Qaeda fighter who had with him a shortwave listening device. With it, they detected a voice which appeared to be that of al-Zawahiri himself, travelling with a large entourage. The US–Northern Alliance coalition tracked the Egyptian doctor from Jalalabad into the White Mountains and then Tora Bora, where al-Qaeda had been able to utilise a remote complex of high-altitude caves. The task force was hopeful that al-Zawahiri was trapped in the labyrinth mountains of Tora Bora, which means 'black dust' in Pashto. This moment had the prospect of being al-Zawahiri's last stand.[8]

Al-Zawahiri and bin Laden were effectively cornered. In seeking to initially enter the caves, the US task force encountered hundreds of al-Qaeda fighters providing ferocious resistance and ready to die to protect their leaders.[9] The battle for Tora Bora had begun. The US team called in a plethora of air strikes on the cave complex, up to one hundred a day, throwing every available weapon at the terrorists, who were determined to make a last stand at all costs. From 30 November to 17 December 2001, American airpower pounded the mountains with a sustained barrage of strikes in the hope that it would either flush out or crush al-Qaeda.[10]

In addition, the United States left no opportunity for bin Laden and al-Zawahiri to retreat elsewhere in Afghanistan. A rugged ridge that intersected the Tora Bora mountain cave complex and Milawa valleys marked the way to Pakistan and was seen as a potential escape path for al-Qaeda fighters. It too was hammered with an onslaught of bombs. The hills shook with 'daisy cutters', the world's largest conventional bombs at the time. The bombing created a mist of ammonium nitrate and aluminium that ignited and incinerated everything within a radius of 600 yards. The amount of munitions dropped would end up pulverising and changing the local landscape permanently.[11]

The bombing devastated al-Qaeda. Further conversations eavesdropped from captured al-Qaeda radios seemed to suggest that al-Zawahiri was seriously hurt. The tone of his intercepted communication conveyed a sense of desperation, and his demise seemed imminent.[12] On 15 December, bin Laden chose to make a statement on his shortwave radio which indicated a sense of resignation of his fate but also a degree of defiance by warning the battle against the 'crusaders' would continue multiple fronts.[13]

Meanwhile, to cover the backdoor and prevent any escape, the White House had received a guarantee from Pakistan's military ruler General Pervez Musharraf that his armed forces had posted hundreds of troops to cover the southern pass from the Tora Bora caves and prevent al-Qaeda from fleeing across the porous border. The Bush administration believed the Pakistani leader's assurances were sound despite classified CIA reports suggesting that 'the back door is open'.[14]

Northern Alliance fighters, supported by US Special Forces, were gradually advancing on al-Qaeda positions in Tora Bora, whose resolve was crumbling. This was precisely the moment that the United States had pressed inexorably towards. Three months after al-Qaeda had left New York and Washington, DC, in flames, a desperate al-Zawahiri was cornered. It was here that he chose to complete his monograph, *Knights under the Prophets Banner*, which was partly his memoir and his life experiences as well as his interpretation of historical injustices and an ideological reasoning for what he and al-Qaeda stands for and what they are fighting against. He hoped to present a vision and blueprint for al-Qaeda to grow and expand and for the mantle to be taken up by others should he be captured or killed.

Knights under the Prophet's Banner was being penned by al-Zawahiri even as the infrastructure he built in Afghanistan with bin Laden and the Taliban ruler Mullah Omar disintegrated. Initially it was serialised in the London-based *Asharq al-Awsat* broadsheet in twelve parts from December 2001. However, it is unclear whether al-Zawahiri began writing *Knights under the Prophet's Banner* before the events of 9/11. The word 'knights' in the title evokes the image of the defenders against the Christian Crusaders to refer to the members of the jihadist movement. The book's understated subtitle,

Meditations of the Jihadist Movement, is significant because it illustrates al-Zawahiri's introspection over past and future jihadist movements. The book begins:

> I have written this book for an additional reason, namely, to fulfil the duty entrusted to me towards our generation and future generations. Perhaps I will not be able to write afterwards in the midst of these worrying circumstances and changing conditions. I expect that no publisher will publish it and no distributor will distribute it.[15]

'Worrying circumstances' was a clear reference to the Tora Bora bombing campaign. The consequence was the loss of al-Qaeda's training camps, forcing them along with the Taliban to flee into neighbouring Pakistan, where they remain in hiding. Some of bin Laden and al-Zawahiri's closest supporters were killed in the US air strikes, including fellow Egyptian Muhammad Atef, who oversaw bin Laden's security.[16]

'I expect that no publisher will publish it and no distributor will distribute it' was probably a perception that he could either be captured or killed and therefore *Knights under the Prophet's Banner* would be his last will and testament. However, before any fate would befall him, al-Zawahiri wanted to articulate his experiences with terrorist groups and the events that made him infamous, including the September 11 attacks.[17] In its introduction al-Zawahiri explores 9/11 and the ensuing US air strikes:

> This book has been written as a warning to the forces of evil that lie in wait for this nation. We tell them: The nation is drawing closer every day to its victory over you and is about to inflict its rightful punishment on you step by step; your battle against this nation is destined to lead to inevitable defeat for yourselves, and all your efforts are no more than an attempt to delay this nation's victory, not to prevent it.[18]

Al-Zawahiri designated this period as 'the stage of the global battle now that the forces of the disbelievers have united against the *mujahideen* [warriors of Allah]'. He declared:

> In writing this book, I have sought to explain some of the features of the currently raging epic battle, and to alert the readers to the hidden and open enemies, their wolves, and their foxes, so that they can be on their guard against the brigands who wish to rob them.[19]

In an introduction to the first section of the book, titled 'A Look Back to the Past', al-Zawahiri opined, 'It is important to me at first to answer three questions about this book. Who wrote it? Why did he write it? For Whom did he write it?'[20] Describing himself, al-Zawahiri commented:

> It is a man who professes to have a connection with the *mujahideen* and to have forged a bond with them. He hopes to spend whatever is left of his life in serving the cause of Islam in its ferocious war against the tyrants of the new Crusade. He wrote it while being a wanted man, a fugitive.[21]

When explaining why the book was written and its relevance amidst 'large flood of daily books' by ideologues and jihadists, al-Zawahiri stated:

> This book was written in an attempt to revive the Muslim nation's awareness of its role and duty, its importance, and the duties that it needs to perform. The book also explains the extent of the new Crusaders' enmity to the Muslim nation and this nation's need to see the dividing line between its enemies and loyal subjects. ... We need to admit that successful attempts have been made to infiltrate our ranks, that these attempts have attracted some of our prominent names, and our enemies have added them to the crowds that serve their purposes, including the writers of falsehoods, those who exploit principles for personal gain, and those who sell their *fatwas* as commodities.[22]

Thinking about the target audience for the book, al-Zawahiri explained, 'I wrote this book so that it will be read by two kinds of people. The first is the intellectual group, the *mujahideen* group. For this reason, I have sought to write it in a clear, simple style and avoided the methods and inferences of specialists.'[23]

Al-Zawahiri wrote *Knights under the Prophets Banner* with the expectation that he would not survive Tora Bora. He therefore wanted to lay out historical motivations and legacy for others to follow.

> I am an emigrant fugitive, who gives his backing to other emigrants and *mujahideen*; he strengthens their resolve, and reminds them of Allah's bountiful mercy. ... These young men have revived a religious duty of which the nation [of Islam] had long been deprived, by fighting in Afghanistan, Kashmir, Bosnia-Herzegovina, and Chechnya. ... If I fall as a *shaheed* [martyr] in the defence of Islam, my son Muhammad will avenge me, but if I am finished politically and I spend my time arguing with governments about some partial solutions, what will motivate my son to take up my weapons after I have sold these weapons in the bargains' market? More important than all the foregoing is the fact that resistance is a duty imposed by Shariah [Islamic law].[24]

Who was this 'emigrant fugitive', and where did he come from? Understanding al-Zawahiri's interpretation of Egypt's past as well as his own his family legacy helps to elucidate the journey the Egyptian terrorist was to undertake. His path would take him from insurrections to assassinations to prisons to fighting superpowers in the battlefield to plotting mass casualty attacks, all whilst facing off against rivals and trying to stay alive. All of this would span more than five decades and contribute to a $25 million reward for his capture or elimination which came under the 2001 US Patriot Act, making al-Zawahiri the most wanted man on the planet alongside Osama bin Laden.[25]

The Boy from Maadi

Egyptians describe Cairo as the 'mother of the world', and the capital's rich history of religious and political changes has run parallel with the city's exponential population growth and expansion of its metropolitan boundaries. Emerging urban settlement areas within the fringe and northern edges was also absorbed. Greater Cairo, the largest city in Africa and the Middle East, served as the engine of the Egyptian economy.

Al-Zawahiri was born on 19 June 1951, in Giza with his twin sister Umnya to a very illustrious family. Initially raised in Heliopolis, on the outskirts of Cairo, the al-Zawahiri clan moved to the city's Maadi neighbourhood in 1960.[26] Maadi is a leafy and trendy suburb to the south of central Cairo situated at the southern end of the Hod al-Bassatine basin. When al-Zawahiri was growing up, Maadi was undergoing a vast expansion, fast becoming the home to embassies whilst developing a multicultural atmosphere. Many of its numbered streets are non-sequential and connected with multiple indistinguishable roundabouts.

During al-Zawahiri's childhood, Maadi was home to a plethora of international schools and the prestigious Maadi Sporting Club, which hosted the annual Egyptian Open tennis championship. Despite residing in a stronghold of Western culture, al-Zawahiri's parents lived modestly and were more pious and socially conservative than many members of their generation. Until the mid-1950s Maadi was dominated by the Mutamassirun, Egyptianized foreigners. Greeks dominated the shops and local businesses whilst the inhabitants were a mix of French, Italians, Germans, Britons, and Jews, along with some indigenous Egyptians. In Maadi's cultural melting pot, Christmas was celebrated as much as Eid. The number of churches was on par with the number of mosques. Parents competed in sending their children to the two most prestigious schools, the Cairo American College and the Lycée Français.[27]

However, al-Zawahiri did not go to either of Maadi's foreign-language schools. His family enrolled him in the local state-run school system, starting with the Qawmiyya Primary School and then the Maadi High School.[28] An al-Zawahiri family member revealed that 'Ayman came into contact with the dregs of Mutamassirun in his youth, but those interactions were limited and fleeting. Although his family was traditional, it was Ayman's choice to decide his future and he wanted to focus on his studies.'[29] According to his uncle Mahfouz Azzam, 'Ayman was a very bright boy and very well educated.'[30]

Even as a young boy in school, al-Zawahiri's intellect and reputation as an avid reader of Islamic philosophy and history was noted by his peers and teachers alike.[31] Though considered to be an especially astute student, according to a family member, 'He was intelligent but serious and guarded in expressing his views, especially depending on who he spoke to. He had a process in rationalising issues, but it was impossible to assume what he was ever thinking.'[32] Al-Zawahiri's siblings were all also very learned. His twin sister, Umnya, would graduate from medical school. Their younger sister, Heba, also became a doctor, specialising in oncology. The other two younger brothers, Muhammad and Hussein, became an architect and engineer, respectively. During their formative years, despite their religious upbringing, the al-Zawahiri siblings liked watching cartoons, especially ones by the three Frenkel brothers, Jewish Egyptians who pioneered animated films widely seen across the Middle East and North Africa and considered as comparable in quality to Disney animations.[33]

Al-Zawahiri's faith mattered a great deal to him too. He attended the Hussein Sedqi Mosque from an early age, which was close to where he lived, and participated in several of its classes in Qur'anic recitation, interpretation, and Islamic jurisprudence (*fiqh*). This would have a significant bearing on him. Al-Zawahiri developed a very strong interest in Egypt's colonial history, which he believed placed Egypt's religious orientation in precarious balance.[34]

Colonial History

Historic Cairo was synonymous with its narrow and winding streets and jumbled mix of monumental and decrepit buildings. At the centre of the

capital lay the iconic al-Azhar Mosque, established in 989, earning its his-
torical reputation as the greatest theological teaching institution in the
Islamic world for more than a thousand years. Scholars from all parts of the
Islamic world came to study the Qur'an and *fiqh*.[35]

The structure of al-Azhar is a microcosm of Cairo, as many additions
have been made by prominent leaders wishing to further embellish the
mosque. The main entrance is on Gamal Husayn, through the double arch
of the Ottoman Bab al-Muzainin (Gate of the Barbers). On either side are
two Mamluk religious schools (*madrasa*). On the left, the madrasa is topped
with a minaret and dating from 1340, and on the right, the Taybarsiya, dating from 1309, The latter contains some of the most precious manuscripts
of the library at al-Azhar.[36] In many ways al-Azhar served as the cradle
for Egypt's position as a major force and ballast in Islamic and Arab affairs.
When describing Egypt as a construct, the historian Afaf Lutfi al-Sayyid
Marsot observed:

> The native Egyptian, while coping with alien rulers, also clung to the fixed
> piece of territory that he identified and knew as Egypt. Even before the age
> of nationalism made people conscious of national affinities Egyptians were
> conscious of living in a land called Egypt.[37]

For al-Zawahiri, the puzzle behind what he saw as Egypt's un-Islamic mal-
aise was wrapped up in the country's colonial history stemming from the
eighteenth century. On 1 July 1798, the ambitious French general Napoleon
Bonaparte entered the northern port city of Alexandria and set a precedent for military interventions in Egypt. His vast armada included tens
of thousands of soldiers and more than 100 scientists and scholars. From
Alexandria, Napoleon strode to Cairo and designated himself as the saviour
of Egypt by defeating the Mamluks, who had been ruling the ancient land
that was under minimal control by the Ottoman Empire. Napoleon's initial
success marked the beginning of a three-year campaign.[38]

Because Napoleon required financial support to establish and pay for
his government in Egypt, he exacted several taxes that antagonised the
local population.[39] The primary rallying points for the Egyptian opposition
movement were centred around the mosques, where religious leaders called
for a jihad against their opponents.[40] For al-Zawahiri, the decline of Islam
coincided with the fall of the Mamluks and the Ottoman Caliphate, which
was part of a deliberate strategy by alien colonisers, begun under Napoleon:

Remember Bonaparte's call to the Jews, whom he referred to as the 'legitimate heirs to Palestine'; Bonaparte's message to the Muslims and his flirtation with Islam was a brazen act of deception while his call to the Jews was a different case.[41]

Al-Zawahiri believed Napoleon was aided by Zionists and fixated on his correspondence with Jewish leaders in the Levant when he occupied Palestine in 1799, which the Egyptian viewed as one of the earliest signs of Western imperialism. In al-Zawahiri's prism, the West has throughout history sought to control Palestine by exploiting Zionism for centuries.[42]

On 1 August 1798, British admiral Horatio Nelson thrust himself onto the Egyptian scene by destroying the French fleet and undermining Napoleon's attempts to push towards the Levantine coast. France's campaign eventually ended prematurely after its forced withdrawal from Egypt by British and Ottoman forces in September 1801.

The end of the French occupation of Egypt resulted in Muhammad Ali, a prominent ethnic Albanian army officer serving in the Ottoman Empire, filling the power void. Ali had credibility amongst Egyptians, as he had fought the French. However, Ali's role as Egypt's Ottoman governor (wali) commenced the start of a royal dynasty that would last till 1952 and result in endemic political and cultural changes to Egypt.[43] Ali ruled as autocratically as had his predecessors, the Mamluks and the Ottomans, except that he sought to come to terms with Western powers and brought the country into contact with Western culture. One of the unintended consequences of his opening to the West was the rise of a native-born, Western-educated Egyptian intelligentsia. This group would ultimately see Egypt as a prototypical nation-state, no different from France or Britain, and therefore deserving to be ruled by native-born Egyptians rather than by foreigners imposed on them, such as the dynasty of Muhammad Ali.[44]

According to al-Zawahiri, the debacle of French ambitions in Egypt was quickly replaced by those of the other leading European colonial power, Britain. He maintained a belief that since 1840, the British curtailed Ali's regime with impositions that 'prepared the grounds for a massive Jewish immigration to Palestine' which al-Zawahiri asserted was being plotted even prior to the twentieth century.[45]

Over time, the Ali dynasty adopted the grander title for its rulers as viceroy (khedive), which was accepted by the Ottoman Empire. By the 1870s, Egypt had become a strategically and financially important centre for the European powers. The Suez Canal Company, a French enterprise in which the *khedive* also had a commercial stake, had begun the process of constructing the canal in 1859. It took ten years to complete, consuming massive resources. However, it vastly reduced distances to parts of Africa and Asia and altered the course of global trade by markedly reducing freight costs. Yet the benefits were not being passed down to most Egyptians.[46]

Egypt had been poorly governed by Khedive Isma'il Pasha and was in a state of financial ruin partly created by his ill-fated war with Ethiopia between 1875 and 1876 as well as several infrastructure projects. Huge debts accrued by Isma'il could no longer be repaid, resulting in the country's finances being controlled by the treasuries of both France and Britain. Isma'il sold his shares in the Suez Canal Company but opposed the European hegemony over Egypt's affairs and was inevitably deposed, replaced by his more malleable son Tawfiq.[47] The consequences of using Egypt's revenue to repay these enormous debts resulted in economic hardship, particularly amongst the peasant farmers (*fellahin*). Elsewhere in Egypt, the senior levels of the civil service and commercial sector had become dominated by Europeans, who were more affluent than the native Egyptians. Furthermore, Turks, Circassians, and Albanians dominated the top tiers of the Egyptian military, which stymied the advancement of local Egyptians. Austerity measures in Egypt's military then resulted in the substantial downsizing of troops, many of whom were left financially destitute, fuelling simmering nationalist sentiments.[48]

In 1881, Egyptian army officers led by Ahmed 'Urabi, who had fought in the debacle with Ethiopia, drew up a petition listing their grievances, demanding a new constitution, an elected government, and greater transparency over senior government and military jobs. Under duress, Khedive Tawfiq agreed to the demands, and a new constitution was duly drawn up in which an indigenous parliament mandated control over Egypt's finances. 'Urabi had become the first political and military leader in Egypt to rise from the *fellahin*. In 1882 the French and British sent a joint communiqué that asserted the pre-eminence of the *khedive*'s authority.[49]

In June 1882 the ethnic tensions turned into violence on the streets of Alexandria, and European businesses were targeted, resulting in hundreds of deaths and widespread panic. The British believed their economic, political, and strategic interests in Egypt including the fate of the Suez Canal were in jeopardy, and Prime Minister William Gladstone dispatched a naval fleet that occupied Egypt and eventually crushed 'Urabi and his forces at the Battle of Tel el-Kebir. 'Urabi was subsequently tried and convicted for treason but, concerned that an execution would make him a martyr to the nationalist cause, the British instead exiled 'Urabi to Ceylon, later known as Sri Lanka.[50] Ostensibly short term, the British intervention persisted until 1952. For al-Zawahiri, the British occupation wasn't just meant to dampen Egypt nationalist aspirations but to undermine Islam:

> In 1882, Britain cited the existence of disturbances in Egypt and made a decision to occupy Egypt and quell the 'Urabi revolution. Britain's excuse was that 'Urabi was rebelling against the Sultan. Thus, the troops of infidelity marched into the homes of Islam under the protection of the Sultan![51]

Angry at the British being aided and abetted by royalty, what wasn't entirely clear was who al-Zawahiri was describing as the 'Sultan'. The Ottoman sultan at the time was Abdul Hamid II, but he chose to stay out of the conflict between the British and 'Urabi's forces. In Egypt, Tewfik was *khedive*, and the country did not have a sultanate till 19 December 1914, when Britain declared Egypt a protectorate and deposed the pro-Ottoman *khedive* Abbas Hilmi, claiming the Ottoman rights were 'forfeit', and replaced him with a relative, Hussein Kamel.[52]

For the World War I period and immediately thereafter, al-Zawahiri pinpointed his grievance once again to British and French machinations. In particular, he cited the Sykes-Picot Agreement, which had been formalised by the British diplomat Sir Mark Sykes and his French counterpart François George-Picot in 1916. It established a mutual understanding of how to fragment the Ottoman Empire between the allies should the war end favourably for them.[53] Al-Zawahiri saw the West wanting a Greater Israel to assert its dominance over the *ummah* in the Arab world and prop up the 'apostate' corrupt regimes created by the Sykes-Picot borders:

> In the spring of 1915 [1916], a few months after the start of the World War I, a person appeared in the scene of events who rendered invaluable services to the Jews. His name was Mark Sykes, who signed on behalf of Britain the famous Sykes-Picot Agreement, which blew the hopes of Britain's Arab allies up in the air along with the words of honour guaranteed by the British Crown.[54]

Despite getting the date wrong, al-Zawahiri saw the Sykes-Picot Agreement not only as a violation of the *ummah*'s right to decide its own future but also part of an overall Western strategy to permanently divide and rule the Muslim world via small and weak client states. Al-Zawahiri then went one step further and accused the leaders of the Arab revolt during World War I, namely the Hashemite Sharif Hussein of the Hijaz and the Saudi leader Abd al-Aziz al-Saud, of siding with the French and British, which was a 'stab in the back for the Ottomans'.[55] British officers, particularly the famed T. E. Lawrence of Arabia and W. H. I. Shakespeare, were cited by al-Zawahiri as colonial saboteurs, but his tirade was primarily directed at the Hashemite and Saudi rulers for enabling the demise of the Ottoman Caliphate and thus inaugurating Islam's downfall.[56]

Al-Zawahiri contended that the Ottomans had 'repelled the Crusaders from our countries for five centuries. It revived the Jihad. It defeated Constantinople. It defended Palestine.'[57] For him, the Saudi and Hashemite betrayal of the Ottomans set the stage for the establishment of Israel and the dissection of the *ummah* into the artificial states forged by the Sykes–Picot Agreement.[58] By connecting the Ottomans downfall to the Hashemite and Saudi royal dynasties, al-Zawahiri challenged the validity of the two most important kingdoms in the modern Arab world and therefore endorsed violence against their successors as their respective dynasties formed the start of the conspiracy against the *ummah* in 1915. According to al-Zawahiri, 'They are guilty of betraying the *ummah* at the moment of its greatest vulnerability. For this betrayal they were handsomely repaid over the next century as the local henchmen of the West. Moreover, they have given the West control of the energy resources of the *ummah* and its unique national wealth.'[59]

In Egypt, the British instituted martial law as the nation became a frontline state in the war when Ottoman troops entered the Sinai Peninsula in an abortive attempt to take the Suez Canal. Egypt served as a base of operations for Allied forces, producing mixed outcomes. It was the launch pad for the catastrophic Gallipoli campaign but also for the successful occupation of Palestine by the British Egyptian Expeditionary Force commanded by Edmund Allenby.[60] Keen to demonstrate his research skills as a historian, al-Zawahiri interpreted from the British archives that 'Jewish battalions within the General Allenby's army' were also utilised to enter 'Palestine and kicked the Turks out'.[61] Although there were Jewish battalions amongst Allenby's forces, they were not specifically assigned for service in Palestine and were essentially a modest labour corps. However, for al-Zawahiri this was enough to pinpoint the origin of the 'Zionist-Crusader' alliance and place Allenby at the forefront of it.[62] Al-Zawahiri would use future events to support his claims.

On 13 November 1918, the Egyptian nationalist leader Saad Zaghlul made an appeal to the British high commissioner Reginald Wingate for Egypt to provide a delegation to the planned Paris Peace Conference based on the aspirations of US president Woodrow Wilson for citizens of the world to benefit from 'self-determination'. The British rejected the request by Zaghlul and his cohort, who became known as the Delegation (Wafd), which evolved into a political party. On 8 March 1919, Zaghlul and several others were arrested by the British and exiled to Malta, triggering mass protests in Egypt and sparking the Egyptian Revolution. Egyptians from all segments of society demonstrated, which led to national general strikes that paralysed the country. There were also boycotts of British goods. Rioting broke out in Cairo and the countryside, but it was violently quelled by British forces.[63]

The British effectively lost control of most of Egypt during March 1919. Wingate was replaced by Allenby as high commissioner, and he pursued negotiations with Egyptian nationalist politicians including Zaghlul. However, British permission for them to travel to Paris for the peace conference coincided with the lobbying of President Wilson to state his support for the British protectorate to continue, which he agreed to.[64] The British faced a dilemma on how to deal with Egyptian demands for independence whilst faced with strikes and unrest. However, Allenby's anxieties over Zaghlul's growing status resulted in the Egyptian nationalist being exiled from the country whilst protests ensued. The British chose to pursue a path for Egypt's independence without consulting the Egyptians themselves, in large part to maintain their influence. On 28 February 1922, Britain unilaterally declared Egyptian independence, but real freedom was limited, as the British retained control over neighbouring Sudan and over Egypt's defence and foreign affairs.[65]

Egypt aside, al-Zawahiri saw the dismemberment of the Ottoman Empire in the aftermath of its defeat in the First World War as the fundamental moment of subjugation for Islam in modern history, and one he bemoaned. For him, the new Arab states that emerged from the demise of the Ottoman Empire were the immoral and contrived constructs of European colonialism that only undermined and diminished the standing of the *ummah*. For al-Zawahiri, this represented a 'global community of Muslims' of sorts, but as it was not unified it would spread what he saw as the start of un-Islamic doctrines like secularism and socialism.[66]

For al-Zawahiri, the fulfilment of the Sykes-Picot Agreement and the dismantling of the Ottoman Caliphate, as well as the creation of the British Mandate in Palestine, were the West's most invasive acts in destroying a pan-Islamic state because

> [the] Zionist entity is a foothold for the Crusader invasion of the Islamic world. The Zionist entity is the precursor of the American campaign to dominate the Islamic Levant. It is a part of an enormous campaign against the Islamic world in which the West, under the leadership of America, has allied with global Zionism.[67]

For al-Zawahiri, the fulfilment of the Zionist dream to create Israel had been 'a Western objective for over two centuries'.[68] Although far fetched, especially as the European powers were so preoccupied in fighting themselves for two centuries, for al-Zawahiri, no other calamity was so powerful as what he saw as the forfeiture of Palestine to the Zionists. Al-Zawahiri mourned the Balfour Declaration of 1917 which promised British support for Zionism as 'the crime of someone who didn't own the Holy Land of Palestine, giving it to someone who didn't deserve it'.[69] As al-Zawahiri argued, 'After the fall of the Ottoman Caliphate a wave of psychological defeatism and ideological collapse spread throughout the Islamic world.'[70] For al-Zawahiri, this despondency and spinelessness made it possible for Israel's victory in the 1948 war, regarded by Palestinians as a major catastrophe (*naqba*).

Perhaps the biggest weakness in al-Zawahiri's argument was that even before its collapse, the Ottoman Empire, although administered by a Muslim ruler, was a secular entity where minorities were increasingly given rights on par with the Muslim majority. The Ottoman Empire was home to many ethnic and religious minorities, including Jews who lived there through their protected status (*dhimmi*).[71] Nevertheless, despite the Ottoman Empire's religious opaqueness, in al-Zawahiri's doctrine, the agenda of the West mirrored past European colonial entities that had sought to subjugate Muslim empires and promote the Crusader narrative.

Muhammad al-Ahmadi al-Zawahiri

Al-Zawahiri hailed from a socially well-established family on both his father's and mother's sides. His paternal origins can be traced to the

Harbi tribe from Zawahir, a village in Medina province, Saudi Arabia. Al-Zawahiri's great-grandfather, Ibrahim al-Zawahiri, moved to Egypt in the 1860s and resided in Tanta on the Nile Delta. An existing mosque there was named after him. Al-Zawahiri's father, Muhammad Rabi'a al-Zawahiri, was a doctor and an academic in pharmaceutical sciences at Ain Shams University, where he attained the position of deputy chair.[72] His father was a beloved and somewhat comic figure in the Maadi neighbourhood as an inattentive eccentric. Nevertheless, Ayman al-Zawahiri admired his father and was dutiful to his mother.[73]

Many of al-Zawahiri's relatives practised medicine and were eminent in their respective fields, including dermatology, neurology, dentistry, and general practice. One uncle had served as dean of the Faculty Of Medicine Kasr Al-Ainy, Cairo University, and another was senior executive of the Egyptian branch of a pharmaceutical company. Some also practiced medicine at the renowned Islamic seminary al-Azhar in Cairo.[74] Family life encouraged his interest in medicine.

Ayman al-Zawahiri's paternal side also included religious scholars tied to al-Azhar. Whilst his paternal grandfather, Rabi'a al-Zawahiri, was also an imam at al-Azhar, it was in fact al-Zawahiri's granduncle, Muhammad al-Ahmadi al-Zawahiri, who was the better-respected and nationally recognised Imam, and he carried the honorific of *shaykh*. He was also part of the Supreme Council of Scholars which functions as the advisory body to the grand imam of al-Azhar as well as being a key decision-making institution.[75] The family name thus brought a degree of respect and prestige for their *fiqh*.[76] However, Shaykh al-Zawahiri soon became a highly unpopular figure following his elevation to the position of grand imam of al-Azhar in 1929.

The 1920s represented a period of great upheaval for Egypt, with the nation achieving independence in 1922 whilst the British retained significant political and economic influence. The role and importance of Islam within Egyptian society was also being closely observed, often with disdain. Viscount Alfred Milner had tasked the Foreign Office to monitor the impact of religion in Egypt and how it could shape politics. The diplomat Maurice Ingram, who served as assistant secretary to Milner's diplomatic mission to Egypt, commented on the role of Islam in Egyptian as a political tool:

> Islam perpetuates in the twentieth century the ideas and principles laid down more than one thousand yours ago for the guidance of a primitive society. Its

immutability clashes inevitably with the progress of modern civilization. . . .
In Egypt, therefore, the problem has been not solely one, as the Egyptians
would make it, to be, of oppressed versus oppressor, but of Moslem versus
Christian.[77]

Orientalist and derogatory sentiments like Ingram's were seized by upon by
Ayman al-Zawahiri, who revealed once again in *Knights under the Prophet's
Banner* that he too was a reader of the British archives. He argued that
the United Kingdom was focused on controlling Islam, and there was a
'dangerous idea that dominated the British policy during World War I and
continued to dominate it for a long time thereafter. The core of this idea is
that the holy sites of all religions in the Middle East must be placed under
British control.'[78] He strongly believed that Britain's ultimate desire was
that 'the holy sites of all religions in the Middle East must be placed under
British control'.[79] Indeed, the British were keen to take control of al-Azhar
with another of Milner's diplomats stating:

> It will doubtless be our duty to consider whether the best plan in the fu-
> ture would not be to take the Azhar and the religious establishments out
> of the control of the Sultan [Fuad] and his satellites and to place it under
> the control of the Prime Minister. . . . The moral influence of the Azhar is
> worth an Army Corps to whichever side succeeds in wooing it over. It is
> worth our while to try, and the sooner we begin the better for our policy
> in the East.[80]

In 1925, under British influence, a reform committee was created within
al-Azhar with the intention of placing the mosque under the control of
the Saad Zaghlul's Wafd government and, as a result, limit or control its
authority and religious influence in Egypt. Shaykh al-Zawahiri found himself on the reform committee, but he disagreed with such proposals and
disclosed the plans to the Egyptian king Fuad, who subsequently ensured
the committee was disbanded, earning Shaykh al-Zawahiri the ire of the
British.[81]

As a result, King Fuad desired to increase his own influence over al-
Azhar. By improving the financial position of the mosque, the king had
hoped to bring the *shaykhs* closer to him to exert further pressure upon
the Wafd government, which was under the influence of the British. For
this, the king had the constitution on his side, allowing him direct control
over both the Muslim scholars versed in theology (*ulama*) and the budget
of al-Azhar. The government, however, intent on preventing this alliance,

passed Law 15, making al-Azhar subservient to it, rather than the king, on such matters.[82]

The significance of this new law was first revealed following the death of al-Azhar's Grand Imam Shaykh Muhammad al-Jizawi in 1927. King Fuad wanted Shaykh al-Zawahiri to be appointed to the prestigious position.[83] However, it was to be his fierce rival, Mustafa al-Maraghi, who succeeded al-Jizawi, with the backing of both the Wafd government and the British. Shaykh al-Zawahiri's contempt for al-Maraghi due to different personalities and competing ambitions was well documented. Upon hearing the news of his nemesis' selection for the rectorship Shaykh al-Zawahiri fell seriously ill.[84]

Shaykh Al-Zawahiri and al-Maraghi were both al-Azhar graduates themselves, although since graduating al-Zawahiri had begun to believe strongly that his counterpart now took more interest in politics than in scholarship, taking particular issue with the fact that al-Maraghi had been so fervently endorsed by the British high commissioner at the time, Lord George Ambrose Lloyd.[85] In fact, for al-Azhar, the period between 1927 and 1945 came to be dominated by the public rivalry between the two *shaykhs*.

From 1927 until 1929, al-Maraghi served as al-Azhar's grand imam and attempted to push through sweeping reforms for the seminary. This included sending its students to Europe where they could study science and to East Asia as missionaries to proselytize Islam.[86] Furthermore, al-Maraghi was critical of the contemporary *ulama*, claiming that they had 'lost contact with society and had therefore become responsible for erecting false borders that has led to the widespread decline of Islam and morals', thus requiring immediate reform to the curriculum of young *ulama*.[87] Ultimately, al-Maraghi failed to achieve what he had intended and ended up making more enemies than friends and losing the support of the Wafd government.[88] Ultimately, this paved the way for King Fuad's preference, Shaykh al-Zawahiri, to finally attain the necessary government approval and succeed his rival as the new grand imam.

Under Shaykh al-Zawahiri the organization of higher education provided by al-Azhar was changed to resemble those of European universities, but admittance to the seminary was based on religious prerequisites including complete memorisation of the Qur'an and nine years of previous study in the al-Azhar system.[89] During his time as rector, al-Zawahiri also published a monthly al-Azhar journal, called *Light of Islam* (*Nur al-Islam*).

It focused on Islamic concepts such as *tafsir*, the exegesis of the writings of the Qur'an and the will of God (Allah). Another aspect was creating better understanding of *fiqh*, which is the understanding of Shariah through an interpretation of the Qur'an and the teachings of the Prophet Muhammad, provided by the *ulama*. Although this was at an advanced level of Islamic understanding, an al-Zawahiri family member pointed out that 'this would have a significant bearing on Ayman's [al-Zawahiri] thinking'.[90]

As Shaykh al-Zawahiri had been the initial choice of King Fuad, lectures in classrooms at al-Azhar were provided by the crown itself. In doing so, al-Zawahiri had aided King Fuad in overcoming Law 15, simultaneously increasing his sponsor's power.[91] As the Wafd government began to deny al-Azhar graduates access to jobs, al-Zawahiri retaliated by swiftly punishing both *shaykhs* and students who displayed any indications of support to a political party.

Despite weathering government excoriation, Shaykh al-Zawahiri faced a barrage of personal attacks from a range of critics, including some Islamic modernists, such as Rashid Rida. Rida, who hailed from Tripoli in the Levant, moved to Cairo in 1897 and would go on to have a monumental impact upon the nascent Islamic political movement within Egypt.[92] In his early life Rida experienced a Western model of education, spread by European missionaries, as well as later attending an Islamic school that attempted to synthesise Islamic ideals with Western modernity.

Heavily shaped by his own experiences and the collapse of the Ottoman Empire, Rida proclaimed a return to the first generations of Islam unadulterated, and not yet tainted by illegitimate Western innovations.[93] Rida's belief that the *ulama* were the biggest obstacle to the reform of Islam placed him on a collision course with the likes of Muhammad al-Zawahiri, with their public conflicts playing out through their respective periodicals during the 1930s.

As grand imam of al-Azhar, Shaykh al-Zawahiri faced accusations of not doing enough defend Islam in the face of attacks from Western Christian missionaries. Al-Zawahiri used *Nur al-Islam* to defend himself and resorted to unseemly criticisms of Rida's piety even though he descended from the Prophet Muhammad's Quraysh tribe.[94]

The issue of Christian missionaries spreading their religion and education throughout Egypt reignited the conflict between al-Zawahiri and al-Maraghi. In particular, European missionaries sought conversions to

Christianity, targeting Muslims directly, which included setting up schools. Despite opposition from Muslim communities, the missionaries were able to operate freely under the protection of the British occupation.[95] Much of the blame in failing to deal with the spread of Christianity was apportioned to Shaykh al-Zawahiri, whose apparent helplessness also impacted his health. In January 1935, a group of *ulama* presented a petition with 190 signatures attesting to the rector's incompetence. The final dagger to the heart of a now frail Shaykh al-Zawahiri came from the very man he had succeeded six years prior, Mustafa al-Maraghi, who would now resume his position. The downfall of al-Zawahiri and revival of al-Maraghi, who was preferred by the British, can be discerned from a Foreign Office memo:

> Shortly after accession of the new government there were partial strikes among students of Azhar and provincial religious institutions who demanded removal of present unpopular Rector and reappointment of Sheikh el-Marghi.... King is now inclined to get rid of Sheikh el-Zawahiri.[96]

Returning for a second term, al-Maraghi's agenda appeared to be centred on discrediting the changes made by his bitter enemy Shaykh al-Zawahiri. There was no room for reconciliation between al-Maraghi and al-Zawahiri. The committees established under al-Zawahiri were renamed, as was the journal *Nur al-Islam*. Eventually, all that was left of al-Zawahiri's legacy was the memory of a *shaykh* who ultimately lost in the power struggle over al-Azhar.[97] According to a relative of Ayman al-Zawahiri, 'The setback of being dismissed as grand imam and having his legacy tarnished was a grievance that had passed from generation to generation.'[98]

The Anglo-Egyptian Treaty, signed in London on 26 August 1936, officially ended the British occupation in Egypt. However, Egyptian independence remained inhibited by the terms of the treaty, which forced a 20-year military alliance on Egypt enabling Britain to enforce martial law. It also ensured the posting of British troops to the Suez and use of the naval base at Alexandria.

Abdul Rahman Azzam

Al-Zawahiri's mother, Umayma, also came from a very distinguished family. Their origins were from the Arabian Peninsula, and they settled in El-Shoubek Gharbi, Giza. Claiming lineage to the Prophet Muhammad, the

Azzams contributed several al-Azhar graduates too. Ayman al-Zawahiri's maternal grandfather, Dr Abdul Wahhab Azzam, grew up in the upper-class neighbourhood of Helwan in Greater Cairo. He was a very learned man and attained an academic scholarship to London. Because of his background in *fiqh*, he became the de facto preacher at the Egyptian Embassy. Attaining his degree in literature, he authored several books on Islam and became dean of the School of Literature at Cairo University, before becoming the president of the university.[99] He was nominated to the renowned Arabic Language Academy and served as Egypt's ambassador to Saudi Arabia, Yemen, and Pakistan. Highly respected for his piousness, he earned the epithet 'the devout ambassador'.[100] He was also accorded the Ottoman-era title of *bey*, traditionally given to rulers of small tribal groups and important officials. Upon retiring, Azzam helped create and establish the King Saud University in Riyadh, Saudi Arabia, where he became its first administrator. When he died in office on 18 January 1959, Azzam was eulogised by the elders of the House of Saud.[101]

Despite all Abdul Wahab's accolades, it was in fact al-Zawahiri's great-uncle, Abdul Rahman Azzam (1893–1976), who was the most renowned figure from the maternal branch of the family. He was one of the principal founders of the Arab League and served as its first secretary general, from 1945 to 1952. Azzam had a strong interest in Arab history and culture. However, he broke the mould with family tradition on several occasions, earning the reputation as a 'rebel'. He chose to study medicine in London instead of al-Azhar University. During his elective at London's St Thomas' Hospital, Azzam became a member of the student Sphinx Society, seeking an end to the British occupation of Egypt. He married the daughter of Khalid Abul Walid, a Libyan resistance leader.[102] Azzam fought for the Ottoman Empire during the First Balkan War between 1912 and 1913. The conflict provided Azzam with experience on the battlefield, fighting a losing battle against European powers and the Balkan League.[103]

Elsewhere, between 1915 to 1923, Azzam was an adviser and supporter for the anti-colonial resistance in Tripolitania against Italy, where he witnessed the weakness the continuing decline Ottoman Empire first-hand. These events led Azzam to express his ideas surrounding Arab history and nationalism in a newspaper that he founded called the *Banner of Tarabulsi* (*Al-Liwa al-Tarabulsi*). It was intended to act as the mouthpiece for the Tripolitanian Republic.[104] This was of great significance to Azzam as he believed in the importance controlling and shaping the narrative of the events that were unfolding in front of his eyes as a humiliation upon all Arabs.

Although the Azzam's family origins had links to both Egypt and the Arabian Peninsula, Azzam himself did not see himself as different from other Egyptians.[105] Azzam began to find sympathy in the Arab nationalist cause and returned to Egypt in 1923, but his profile was rising and was attracting the attention of the British authorities, who submitted an intelligence report on Azzam's early life and schooling:

> The Azzam family, though settled in Egypt for some generations, come of good old Arab stock, and have always clung tenaciously to Arab traditions and ideals of life. Abdul-Rahman was thus brought up in an atmosphere very different from that of the ordinary Egyptian or Turco-Egyptian family.... In estimating Abdul-Rahman's character, his early up-bringing and his Arab blood must never be forgotten.[106]

It was in this context that Azzam approached Saad Zaghlul, hoping that the prominent Egyptian nationalist leader and independence hero would welcome such ideas as Pan-Arabism. Zaghlul was, however, dismissive of Azzam's cause, stating, 'Our problem is an Egyptian problem and not an Arab problem.'[107] Zaghlul's response was to be expected of Egyptians during the 1920s and 1930s. Egyptian isolationism had been a result of their interactions with the British. Furthermore Pan-Arabism was not clearly defined at this time, and following the defeat of the Arab nations in the Arab Revolt of 1916, the movement appeared weaker than ever.[108]

However, Azzam would not be deterred. The tide appeared to turn in Egypt by the conclusion of the Second World War. In March 1945 Azzam helped develop and formalise the Arab League, which was intended to act as a voice and representative of the entire Arab world, promoting cultural bonds and sovereignty as well as cooperation amongst Arab nations in respect to economic and financial affairs. Within its first year it gradually came to be recognised by other powers as a most effective agency for peace and stability in the Middle East.[109] Azzam was made its first secretary general, and his vision for the group was to establish a unified Arab people who shared language, history, geography, and customs. Comparisons were drawn with the movements that led to the unification of Germany and Italy in the nineteenth century.[110]

Although Azzam was not calling for a caliphate outright, he did seek a union of Arab countries.[111] In essence, the Arab League wished to reunite the Arab peoples who had been divided by the colonial frontiers created by the West—partly emanating from the Sykes-Picot agreement—and which had brought with them differing systems of law and administration. In recognition of his efforts, King Farouk bestowed Azzam with the highest title of *pasha*, a step above *bey* and similar to a peerage or knighthood.[112]

Azzam saw pan-Arab nationalism playing a positive role as a community-mobilizing ideology to fight colonialism. However, he advocated that it was best achieved through the Egyptian ruling class, the vanguard. Azzam represented the social, intellectual, and political forces behind Egyptian Arab nationalism during the first half of the twentieth century.[113] However, during Azzam's tenure as secretary general of the Arab League, he was unable to overcome the difficulties of unifying multiple nations under one umbrella. Azzam, regularly found himself having to be 'in line with Egyptian and Saudi Arabian policy', rather than considering all Arab states.[114] Given the crucial role Azzam played in the league's early years, it is no surprise that he felt equally strongly about Palestine, as the Arab League resolutions made clear.

Following the partition resolution of November 1947, Azzam issued a sinister warning that the establishment of a Jewish state would result in 'a war of extermination and momentous massacre which will be spoken of like the Mongolian massacre and the Crusades'.[115] Azzam believed that Pan-Arabism could address the impact of the Palestine problem and the growth of Zionism. He also favoured Egyptian leadership of Pan-Arab policies.[116] Irrespective of his Pan-Arab ideology, Azzam, like al-Zawahiri would many years later, was a strong Egyptian nationalist, stating that he and his people were 'Egyptians first, Arabs second, and Muslims third'. He added:

> Egypt is the first nursery of mankind. Allah singled it out above all other nations. This is a characteristic of Egypt, and this is what always made of Egypt the shining place of the world. For here in Cairo, if we are angered, the whole world is angered. If we are contented, mankind from all shades of colour or ideology—whether they are the Negros of Africa or the white people of the North, whether they are Muslims or Christians, whether they respect our culture or are opposed to our ancient school, thousands of years old—is also contented.[117]

Azzam left his role as secretary general of the Arab League in 1953, having never truly been able to overcome his Egyptian and Saudi loyalties in the name of Pan-Arabism. Azzam's ties to Saudi Arabia were enhanced when his daughter Muna married Saudi crown prince Faisal's eldest son, Mohammed. It enabled Azzam to serve as Faisal's advisor. Azzam wrote several works on Islam whilst in Saudi Arabia, including 'The Eternal Message of Muhammed', which gained much attention after it was acclaimed by Malcolm X, the African American Muslim civil rights activist. Of their meeting in Jeddah, Malcolm X said, 'I never been so honoured in my life.'[118] Azzam then lent him his personal suite at the Jeddah Palace Hotel and agreed to help him resolve his visa issues so he could travel to Mecca for the hajj.

Malcolm X's undertaking of the *hajj* marked his formal entrance into the community of orthodox Islam, which would not have been possible without Azzam's intervention. Thanks to Azzam, Crown Prince Faisal also designated Malcolm X as an honoured state guest.[119] After completing the *hajj*, Azzam arranged for him to meet the crown prince. These experiences deeply impacted on the civil rights leader, and he recounted them on many occasions.[120]

Both Ayman al-Zawahiri's maternal and paternal branches had a set of beliefs and attitudes that were clearly passed down from generation to generation. The two branches had religious scholars and leading members of Egyptian society. One advocated Pan-Arabism and the other Shariah law, but both were hostile to Western cultural and religious influences. Elements of these ideas became part of al-Zawahiri's own world view. However, they were not instilled or indoctrinated into him. Al-Zawahiri felt a sense of burden and responsibility to challenge what he saw as non-Islamic beliefs, outside interference, and colonial hegemony being imposed on Egyptian society. This platform would go hand in hand with his promising career as a doctor. Ayman Al-Zawahiri had a reputation within his family for 'an inherited knowledge of medicine as well as zeal in his genes'.[121]

Knowing that his forebearers faced adversity meant that al-Zawahiri knew nothing would be achieved without sacrifices, which did not help him develop understanding, compassion, and empathy for others. For al-Zawahiri, 'weakness and lack of perseverance was their undoing'.[122] His family history convinced him to become more ideologically engaged and attempt to seek out ideas as well as think more deeply and critically about current events and world issues.

Interestingly, al-Zawahiri would not openly talk about his relatives. He strongly believed that there needed to be a separation between family and the larger mission. However, al-Zawahiri didn't hold back when it came to speaking about the Egyptian ideologues who came before him and from whom he would inherit the mantle of jihadism in pursuit of the restoration of caliphate. Yet, there was a degree of irony with his granduncle Shaykh al-Zawahiri being so close with King Fuad who had been appointed by the British as effectively a symbol of rejection of the Ottomans. It was an issue that Ayman al-Zawahiri would deliberately ignore.

The Brotherhood

Egyptian militancy has consistently exerted substantial regional influence across the Arab world. The question that gets raised often is, why Egypt? The reasons are varied. Egypt's stature as the largest Arab country with important religious institutions, such as al-Azhar, commands respect. Most people in the region are familiar with the Egyptian dialect, which makes it possible for recorded sermons and speeches by Egyptian thinkers to be understood throughout the region. Furthermore, the presence of large Egyptian expatriate communities in most Arab countries serves as a conduit for the export of ideas developed in Egypt.[123] These dynamics apply to Hasan al-Banna and Sayyid Qutb, who were foundational in Egyptian militancy and left a profound legacy.

Closely connected to Egypt's opening to the West is the politicization of Islam in Egypt, which can be traced back to the formation of the Muslim Brotherhood (al-Ikhwan al-Muslimun) by Hasan al-Banna in the late 1920s. Al-Banna rejected Western modernity and the imposition of non-Muslim, colonial rule. His lasting relevance is the articulation of a collective response to the perceived dire situation of Muslims by directly countering the apparent overbearing political, economic, and cultural Western influence that was pervading Egypt under British occupation, whilst also rejecting secular nationalism.[124]

The ineffectiveness of the different indigenous religious groups in practicing 'genuine Islam' and challenging the foreign presence compelled al-Banna to establish a movement with radical aims such as propagating Islam and its values, establishing a just Islamic society, and disseminating Islamic knowledge throughout society.[125] This movement was to become the Muslim Brotherhood, formalised in 1928, with al-Banna becoming its general guide (*al-murshid al-'amm*). All his followers gave him unquestioning obedience and allegiance.[126]

Al-Banna wanted the Muslim Brotherhood to accomplish two goals: first, the total independence of Muslim land from Western domination, and second, the re-establishment of Shariah law based on three pillars: the ruler's acceptance of God's sole sovereignty, the unity of the *ummah*, and the authority for the Muslim Brotherhood to remove rulers if they did not respect its will and opinions.[127] For al-Banna, 'The Arabs are the foremost *ummah* of Islam and its chosen army.'[128] As the spiritual vanguard of the *ummah*, only they have been entrusted with the mission of serving as the model for all the Muslims, leading them back to greatness and glory.

According to al-Banna, the most extreme expression of worship of a single territory and the unavoidable product of racial arrogance is pharaonism (*al-fir'awniyya*). The pharaoh was considered divine, a self-proclaimed God or the son of God, and religion was anchored in the state. The attempt to revive the national pharaonic pre-Islamic legacy was represented by al-Banna as 'the revival of pagan customs'.[129] Hence, pharaonism is clearly a 'nationalism of the pagans' (*qawmiyya al-jahiliyyah*).[130]

As a means of fighting the proselytizing and the attempts at conversion made by Western missionaries, various Islamic societies and organizations, including the Muslim Brotherhood, united under the new League for the Defence of Islam (Jama'at al-Difa' 'an al-Islam). Whilst al-Banna made Shaykh Muhammad al-Ahmadi al-Zawahiri aware of the Muslim Brotherhood's actions, it was to be his bitter rival Mustafa al-Maraghi who was nominated to serve as president of the league. Despite its best efforts to regain its status as the defender of Islam, for the most part al-Azhar was playing catch-up with the League for the Defence of Islam, because of its reputation as a 'royal stronghold' and ineffectiveness in religious guidance.[131] According to an al-Zawahiri family member, Shaykh al-Zawahiri being passed over in preference for al-Maraghi 'was viewed as a snub, and Ayman [al-Zawahiri] in particular felt the family name had been slighted by al-Banna'.[132]

Initially, al-Banna was willing to engage in the political process to gain power.[133] Al-Banna also decided to contest parliamentary elections twice, in 1942 and 1945. His second attempt was mired in alleged electoral corruption. Unsurprisingly, al-Banna concluded that political parties were immoral and hindering the development of Egyptian society. However, the mere fact that al-Banna was willing to engage in democracy undermined his status in the eyes of al-Zawahiri:

> All the religious transgressions committed by the Muslim Brotherhood were first committed by al-Banna whether by maintaining an armistice with the rulers of Egypt, by praising them or by accepting the legitimacy of the constitution, and by following the democratic rules and participating in the elections.[134]

Additionally, al-Banna stated that jihad was an obligation for all Muslims and being a martyr (*shaheed*) was a lofty act that would be rewarded in the hereafter. He claimed, 'Allah has imposed jihad as a religious duty on every Muslim, categorically and religiously, from which there is neither evasion nor escape.'[135] Al-Banna also pursued the creation of a paramilitary force which would carry out jihad against those who did not adhere to Islam. He believed Egyptians, as well as Arabs, required both internal regeneration and external defences against the Western occupation in the region. Al-Banna decided to create the Secret Apparatus (al-Jihaz al-Sirri) and the Special Organization (al-Nizam al-Khass), paramilitary organizations tied to the Muslim Brotherhood. Al-Banna painted a black-and-white picture in which he warned that the Muslim Brotherhood would not hesitate to declare war on anyone 'who d[id] not work for the victory of Islam'.[136]

Internally, the unit was structured around cells that operated almost independently, with militants not knowing about the activities of other clandestine cells. The vertical chain of command was short and had a tight hierarchical structure. Comparisons have been drawn with the organizational structure of al-Qaeda, but it is not something al-Zawahiri would endorse. Although he somewhat respected al-Banna, he did not follow his doctrine and viewed his beliefs as having inherent weaknesses:

> I did not consider him [al-Banna] deceptive and fallacious, as secularists and communists have done. I just studied and criticised his work according to my best ability, reporting him and the Ikhwan [Muslim Brotherhood] as best as I could. Regrettably, no Ikhwan leader has answered me, as far as I know.[137]

In the aftermath of World War II, the Muslim Brotherhood began to step up their political activity, organizing conferences against the pro-British Sa'diyyin government then headed by Mahmud Fahmi al-Nuqrashi. Many politicians began to accuse the Muslim Brotherhood of trying to grab power by violent means and terminate the constitution.[138]

In 1948, the Muslim Brotherhood had become very powerful and was a 'government within a government'.[139] Numerous acts of insurrection were attributed to them, including assassinations of politicians and judges as well as attacks on British soldiers.[140] Al-Nuqrashi's government dissolved the Muslim Brotherhood, confiscated its properties, and arrested all its senior members. Twenty days later, he was assassinated outside the Ministry of Interior by a member of the Muslim Brotherhood.[141] On 12 February 1949, the violent hostility between the government and the Muslim Brotherhood concluded in the assassination of al-Banna by the Royal Egyptian Intelligence Agency, which was also infamously known as the Iron Guard.[142]

During al-Banna's lifetime, Egypt experienced several competing ideologies and political movements. Ayman al-Zawahiri was not his greatest advocate, partly because he saw al-Banna compromise his principles by willingly conform to non-Islamic man-made laws that were created by Western-backed governments, as well as the perception of personal ill treatment by al-Banna to *Shaykh* al-Zawahiri. Nevertheless, al-Banna's most lasting and notable contributions were the creation of clandestine paramilitary movements and gathering ideas and concepts which had been scattered over the writings of the various pan-Islamic-oriented associations, movements, and individual intellectuals. Al-Banna weaved them into a single ideological system which could be formed into a well-defined doctrine for others to develop, expand, and evolve.

Beyond al-Banna, his contemporary, the ideologue Sayyid Qutb further solidified the foundations of political Islam in Egypt. Qutb's polemics have exerted a powerful hold on the imagination of many jihadists across generations, especially amongst Egyptians. Al-Zawahiri's respect and admiration for Qutb are palpable in *Knights under the Prophet's Banner*, where he dedicated an entire section to his ideological mentor. Al-Zawahiri described Qutb as 'the most prominent theoretician of the fundamentalist movements'.[143]

Qutb was born in 1906 in the relatively underdeveloped Upper Egyptian province of Asyut.[144] By age 10, he had memorised the entire Qur'an.[145] Like al-Banna, he later attended Dar al-'Ulum. Upon graduating in 1933, he was employed by the Ministry of Education as a teacher and then, after 1940, as an inspector of public schools.[146] In 1948, the ministry sent Qutb to the United States to learn about the benefits of the Western educational system.[147] The conventional account on Qutb is that his anti-Western ideas were shaped by his visit to the United States which he criticised for its capitalism, culture, music, decadence, and alleged liberalism, even during the McCarthy era.[148]

However, he was already castigating America for its support of Zionism in the late 1940s. His trip merely allowed him to justify his preconceived perceptions of Western materialism and decadence. For Qutb, Western influence was detrimental to the renewal of Islamic life, which necessitated 'the restoration of an Islamic life governed by the Islamic spirit and Islamic law in which the Islam we preach is combined with a genuine Islamic environment.'[149] Shariah for Qutb was paramount but because of the political and cultural hegemony of the West over Egypt, the creation of such a state was impossible.[150]

Ironically, in public, Qutb wore a European suit and tie, although in the comfort of his residence he would wear a *jallabiyya*. At one time, he had aspired to be part of the growing literate urban middle class Egyptians know as the *afandiyya*. In the 1920s and 1930s, their numbers had greatly increased owing to better educational facilities. However, British companies in Egypt dominated finance, commerce, and industry and preferred to employ their own countrymen, a factor which Qutb remained resentful of and blamed the government for, as well as the West.[151]

Much of Qutb's time in the United States was spent in Greeley, Colorado, home of the Colorado State College of Education as it was known at the time. By 1949, when Qutb was in Greeley, the town had a population of around 20,000, alcohol was banned, and there were more than 20 churches. According to the eminent writer and journalist Lawrence Wright, 'Greely is a town that reminds you of America as it used to be, lots of green lawns, enumerable churches. However, Qutb saw it as symbolic of the worst excesses of America.'[152] Qutb's American sojourn enabled him to write confirmatory letters to colleagues at home about the evils of the West, but without facing any real scrutiny about the veracity of his claims.[153] He viewed the nation not with fresh eyes but rather through the tinted spectacles of a man long captive to a particular view of the world.

Upon his return to Egypt in August 1950, Qutb spent several years aiding the Muslim Brotherhood through his writings before joining in an official capacity in 1953.[154] He admired the organization for its active involvement in the cause of Islam and Shariah law. Qutb's concept of God's sovereignty (*hakimiyyah*) mandates that people must live according to the Shariah, which he emphasises was ordained by God in the Qur'an and the Sunnah.[155] This means that all human activities, political, economic, and social, must fulfil the rules of the *hakimiyyah*. According to Qutb, Islam is 'a system in which all spheres aimed firstly and finally to fulfil the meaning of worship; in the system of government, economic, criminal law, civil law, personal status law and all laws and codes aimed to fulfil the meaning of worship'.[156] Qutb's pronouncement of *hakimiyyah* against man-made laws that totally contradict Shariah law, which according to al-Zawahiri, 'greatly helped the Islamic movement to know and define its enemies.

In turn, Abul A'la Maududi, the Pakistani theologian, was immensely influential in the development of Qutb's ideas and doctrines for an Islamic state, and Qutb was awed by Maududi's interpretations of the political aspects of Islam.[157] Maududi was the founder of the political party the Islamic Society (Jama'at-e-Islami) in Pakistan after Partition in 1947. He authored several books in Urdu on subjects ranging from Islamic law, political theory, and economics to philosophy and gender relations.[158] Maududi focused his criticism on Muslims he called 'neo-Westerners' whom he saw as Muslim only in name, more drawn to the ideas and customs of the West than to their Islamic traditions.[159]

Sayyid Qutb and the Free Officers

Despite the end of World War II, Britain continued to have an occupying presence in Egypt. However, things were about to take a major unprecedent turn. A group of young Egyptian military men, known as the Free Officers (al-Dubat al-Ahrar), plotted to seize the reins of authority with the promise of transforming Egyptian society. They included two future presidents, Gamal Nasser and Anwar Sadat. Their rancour intensified against King Farouk and the Wafd for continually submitting to British demands. Even as the war was coming to an end, the stage was being set for a pivotal moment in Egypt's future direction. Ironically, the military was transformed in the mid-1930s when it was opened to new working- and middle-class recruits and drew in Nasser and Sadat and other as well. Previously, it had been an organization tied directly to the landed aristocracy, but the new element created the Free Officers organization and concluded that it and it alone could better modernize Egypt.[160]

On 22 July 1952, the Executive Committee of the Society of Free Officers issued battle orders. Their slogan was 'Resolution and Boldness'. The password to mobilise and take over Egypt's political institutions and infrastructure was 'Nasr', which meant 'victory'. Zero hour was to be midnight. The revolution of 23 July 1952 led by Gamal Nasser and Mohamed Naguib went remarkably smoothly. Years of plotting paid off.[161] King Farouk's last words to those who overthrew him were, 'It isn't easy to govern Egypt.'[162]

On 18 June 1953, an Egyptian republic was formally declared by the Free Officers, with Naguib made president and Nasser the deputy prime minister of Egypt. The monarchy was entirely abolished, bringing an end to an institution that dated back to the time of Muhammad Ali. Any vestiges of the Ottoman legacy including the titles of *bey* and *pasha* were also outlawed. This deprived al-Zawahiri's relatives, Abdul Wahhab Mohammed Azzam and Abdul Rahman Azzam, of the honorifics that they had been afforded and which were seen as a source of prestige and respect.[163]

There were frictions between Nasser and Naguib over the direction Egypt was to take. For Nasser, Egypt's non-alignment in international affairs was of primary importance. He advocated for pan-Arab unity, self-reliance, and reduced dependence on the West. Egypt was simultaneously respected and feared because of its geography, history, politics, and culture, making it the centre of the Middle East and Arab conscience. It was admired for having deposed a corrupt monarchy. Nasser wanted to export his revolutionary nationalist experience to other Arab countries, whereas Naguib wanted a more cautious approach focused on Egypt itself. After a brief power struggle, Nasser succeeded Naguib as Egyptian president. With Nasser's ascension, according to the Egyptian author and political commentator Mohamed Heikal, 'For Egyptians, there was a belief that they were finally occupying their rightful position within the Middle East.'[164]

Paradoxically, Qutb was associated with the military coup d'état of the Free Officers and 'was warmly congratulated' by its leader, Nasser.[165] Nasser decided the Muslim Brotherhood under Qutb could be co-opted. Qutb in turn greeted the coup with guarded optimism and was accorded by Nasser an advisory role in the Revolutionary Command Council.[166] The

Free Officers abolished the establishment political parties, allowing only the Muslim Brotherhood to remain in existence.[167] The problem was that the Muslim Brotherhood did not want a secular government; they wanted an Islamic one.[168] Unsurprisingly, the relationship between Nasser and Qutb began to deteriorate when the latter was subsequently offered only a ministerial post for endowments (*waqf*) and an appointment to the Supreme Council of Scholars at al-Azhar.[169] It was therefore inevitable that this odd-couple relationship would disintegrate, and when the Muslim Brotherhood did not cooperate with the military, it too was outlawed.[170]

The significance of al-Azhar was also illustrated by the numerous visits by the leadership of the Free Officers, including Nasser, attending Friday prayers.[171] However, by putting al-Azhar under the control of the president's office, the institution became the main conduit and exponent of Nasser's revolution to the Egyptian people and the Arab world. The regime could rely on al-Azhar's leadership to intertwine the principles of Pan-Arabism and socialism with the goals of Nasserism.[172] This included the concept of social solidarity and mutual responsibility which al-Azhar said was at the crux of Nasser's Islamic socialism.[173] Qutb claimed that Nasser 'began to diverge on the programme' of liberating Egypt and as a result, the necessity for the Muslim Brotherhood as a bulwark against the socialist project 'was growing stronger'.[174]

Another important dynamic was how Qutb attempted to relate the biblical story of Moses and his opposition to the pharaoh to the present context. Qutb's treatment regarded Nasser as a repressive tyrant similar to the pharaoh. Qutb drew parallels to al-Banna's comparison of King Farouk to the pre-Islamic pharaonic legacy. According to Qutb, the pharaoh was a devious character who would alter his behaviour and attitude towards the people when the situation required it:

> Such is the habit of tyrants when they feel the very earth on which they stand shake. They soften their utterance after behaving as tyrants, and have recourse to help from the very people they had trampled underfoot. When in danger, they pretend to take advice, but when the danger is past, then, behold, they are tyrants and oppressors again, and rule despotically.[175]

Nasser was a charismatic, compelling, and inspirational soldier, highly respected within the Egyptian officer corps. Also, tough and uncompromising, he did not tolerate any dissent. Nasser had cast aside the trappings of power and lived a modest life with his wife and children, which further added to his appeal. He also preferred to be seen in civilian suits as opposed to military uniform. Perhaps most importantly, Nasser was a superb orator in the idiomatic Egyptian dialect which he preferred over classical Arabic. He fervently decried Egypt's suffering under colonialism as Western capitalism stripped the nation of its wealth and self-respect. Nasser believed that the only viable pathway for countering Western influences and the Arab-Israeli problem was through an Egyptian-led pan-Arab unity.

However, the Muslim Brotherhood saw Nasser capitulating to colonial dictates and viewed him as no different to previous Egyptian leaders. They believed that the British military observers would continue occupying military installations as well as the Suez Canal and something drastic needed to be done to prevent this from happening. In 1954, the Muslim Brotherhood attempted and failed to assassinate President Nasser as he was giving a speech in Alexandria's Manshiyya Square. Nasser seized the opportunity to galvanise his audience by saying that assassins might kill him, but 'other Nassers would arise to carry forward his mission'.[176]

In the wake of a failed attempt on Nasser's life, many members of the Muslim Brotherhood's Secret Apparatus were arrested along with Sayyid Qutb. The Muslim Brotherhood were accused of openly declaring war on the government with the aim of taking over by plotting attacks in Cairo, Alexandria, and along the Nile.[177] Nasser instructed al-Azhar to denounce the Muslim Brotherhood for 'deviating from the teachings of Islam' and declared that as they were plotting against the 'legitimate rulers of the Egyptian people', which meant the Free Officers, they were committing heresy.[178] Qutb and several other members of the Muslim Brotherhood were sentenced to 10 years in prison by a three-judge panel which included Anwar Sadat, Gamal Salem, and Hussein el-Shafei, a friend of the al-Zawahiri family.[179]

Nasser's next monumental achievement caught the West flabbergasted and unprepared when the Egyptian military moved into the Suez Canal zone in 1956 and took control, ousting the personnel employed by the Suez Canal Company.[180] Attempts by the British, French, and Israelis to regain control of the canal through a military operation proved futile and were criticised by the United States. Building on his momentum, Nasser saw the realisation of his much-heralded Pan-Arab dream when Syria and Egypt unified to create the United Arab Republic (UAR) in 1958. However, a plethora of divisions and disagreements contributed to the dissolution of

REAP WHAT YOU SOW

the UAR in 1961, with the Syrians claiming they were seen as second-class citizens by the Egyptians. Nasser also sought to codify a national ideology and political apparatus through the National Charter which was approved in 1962. This produced the Arab Socialist Union, governed by one political party, which Nasser would head, as well as a centralised economy.[181] For Qutb, the three vices that harm Islam were: secularism, nationalism, and socialism.

Whilst incarcerated, Qutb was tortured during long interrogation sessions. He experienced beatings and dogs were unleashed on him, all of which compromised his health.[182] It was also in prison that Qutb penned his final and most notorious book, *Milestones (Ma'alim fi'l-tariq)* which was written from a hospital prison and represented Qutb's vision for revolution, jihad, and fighting against 'apostates'. Qutb presented an emotive and provocative criticism, venting against what he described as *jahiliyyah* or *jahili*, that is, 'the condition of any place or society where oppression and transgression dominate over freedom, justice and equality'. This effectively meant a weakened mental and social condition akin to society living in darkness before Islam came about, which Qutb equated to the time of the pharaohs in Egypt.[183]

Qutb's approach in *Milestones* features three components: description, criticism, and alternative. Qutb criticises the non-Islamic affairs of society and offers an idealist alternative where the vanguard armed with *aqidah* (creed) alone could liberate the whole society from *jahiliyyah*.[184] Qutb intended to revive this extinct community through what he calls a 'Qur'anic message' which had created 'a generation of the companions of the Prophet without comparison in the history of Islam, even in the entire story of man'.[185] Qutb declared that the companions of the prophet did not see the Qur'an as an instrument of learning alone but also of direct action. Therefore, the pioneers of the modern Islamic revolution should take immediate action by cutting themselves off from the *jahili* society, the modern *jahiliyyah*.

Qutb's response to the global state of *jahiliyyah* was jihad. Jihad for Qutb was an all-encompassing affair that ranged from the personal study of the Qur'an to actual combat. Importantly, Qutb claimed that jihad is directed towards institutions and organizations which are the adversary, not the people who are forced to live under the *jahili* system. He criticised the perception that jihad should only be defensive against aggressive non-believers.

Qutb contended that not only could jihad be offensive, but it could also be waged against internal enemies including the state if it had lost its legitimacy. Jihad was vital and required to 'establish Allah's authority on earth ... to abolish all the Satanic forces and Satanic systems of life.'[186] These concepts would have a huge bearing on the thinking of al-Zawahiri, who regarded *jahiliyyah* not as a merely period in Islamic history but 'rather a condition that comes into existence every time its prerequisites are established or organised'.[187]

Qutb believed that jihad is a 'universal declaration of the freedom of man from slavery to other men and to his own desires'.[188] Qutb emphasised that jihad must be carried out universally because *hakimiyyah* did not confine itself to a country or ethnicity, and the whole *ummah* must reject *jahiliyyah* and accept Shariah law. The universality of Qutb's message is significant.[189] Additionally, he believed jihad was the obligation of every Muslim. These concepts had a deep influence on him. Al-Zawahiri would quote one of Qutb's key texts to illustrate the importance of Shariah, *hakimiyyah*, and *jahiliyyah*:

> Sayyid Qutb wrote in *In the Shade of the Qur'an*: '*Hakimiyyah* is the most exclusive prerogative of godhood. Therefore, whoever legislates to a people assumes a divine role among them and exercises its privileges. Men become his slaves, not the slaves of Allah; they accept his religion, not the religion of Allah.... This issue is extremely critical for the faith, for it is an issue concerning godhood and worship [i.e. the relationship between man and Allah], an issue concerning freedom and equality, an issue regarding the very liberation of man—nay, the very coming into being of man! And thus, due to all this, it is an issue of infidelity or faith, an issue of *jahiliyyah* or Islam. Instead, it becomes the duty of the Muslims to rise up against him, overthrow him, and place in his stead a just leader, if they are so able.... Even if this only occurs among a small group, still they are obligated to rise up and overthrow the infidel.'[190]

For Qutb, 'infidel' meant someone with without faith who rejects the central tenets of Islam. In Qutb's mind, although Nasser claimed to represent the interests of Egyptians and other Muslim peoples, his refusal to implement Shariah law qualified him as a usurper of *hakimiyyah*, an infidel, which it was incumbent for people to recognise and seek his removal, with violence if necessary. Although Qutb did not mention Nasser by name in *Milestones*, the inferences were explicit and could leave no doubt about who it was attacking. Interestingly, prior to publication, the text was smuggled out page by page by his sister, Hamidah, who was part of an elite underground Muslim Sisters and Muslim Brotherhood network.[191]

In terms of what Qutb was advocating to achieve his objectives, al-Zawahiri cites his mentor, 'Brother, push ahead, for your path is soaked in blood. Do not turn your head right or left but look only up to heaven.'[192] Al-Zawahiri was clearly inspired by Qutb's focus on the rulers of Muslim nations who administer without Shariah, which made them 'apostates'. It is an obligation to wage jihad against them and seek their removal from power, installing in their place legitimate Muslim rulers who adhere to *hakimiyyah*. Qutb wanted to take al-Banna's doctrine further through direct revolutionary means and challenge the existing system to its very foundation with jihad.

Qutb was released from jail in 1964, thanks to the intervention of the Iraqi president Abd al-Salam Arif. However, the effects of imprisonment had taken their toll on Qutb's health. To avoid the watchful eyes of the Egyptian intelligence, meetings of the Muslim Brotherhood were held in the houses of individual members such as Jabir Rizq, who exclaimed, 'Qutb explained to the youth whatever they had not understood.' A considerable organization of the Muslim Brotherhood thus re-emerged under Qutb's leadership.[193] For al-Zawahiri, it was this period when 'the jihad movement in Egypt began its current march against the government'.[194]

Crucially, Qutb 'helped [al-Zawahiri] to realise that the internal enemy was not less dangerous than the external enemy' since the internal enemy used the external enemy 'as a tool to launch its war on Islam'.[195] The dichotomy between local and distant enemies is critical in al-Zawahiri's ideology. It has also deeply influenced his militancy and shaped his terror strategy.

Qutb's *Milestones* was eventually presented to Nasser for approval before publication. Three editions had been approved by Nasser, who obviously had a personal interest in the subject.[196] When, however, it was presented to him the fourth time, he had concluded that there was a movement and organization behind it potentially conspiring against him.[197] On 3 April 1966, charges were laid against Qutb and 43 other Islamists for attempting to overthrow the Nasser government. On 9 April 1966, in a replay of the 1954 show trial, Qutb appeared in court facing charges of conspiracy and sedition. Qutb admitted that he believed the Nasser regime to be a *jahili* one.[198] He also admitted that he and the other members of the Muslim

Brotherhood desired change but insisted that this was to be accomplished gradually through the 'creation of a generation of young Muslims'.[199]

Anwar Sadat was sent to meet Qutb in prison and give him the opportunity to repent. If he did, the death sentence would be commuted, and he would be pardoned. However, Qutb told Sadat that he would rather die than renounce his stance.[200] By refusing to ask for pardon for his life, al-Zawahiri argues Qutb 'spoke justice in the face of the tyrant'.[201] Qutb was hanged on 29 August 1966. Al-Zawahiri's maternal uncle Mahfouz Azzam was the last person to see Qutb before his execution. Qutb had briefly taught Mahfouz Azzam in his youth which contributed to Azzam's lifelong deference to him, including serving as his lawyer.[202] Qutb also made Azzam an executor of his estate before he was sentenced to death and bestowed to him his own personal copy of the Qur'an.[203] Al-Zawahiri inherited his veneration for Qutb's doctrine from his uncle, who shared stories about his personal experiences with Qutb which impacted Ayman al-Zawahiri's 'self-perception and increased his resiliency'. In the need to oppose a state he believed was led by 'apostates',[204] Al-Zawahiri once exclaimed that Qutb was 'the most prominent theoretician of the jihadist movement'.[205]

For al-Zawahiri, Qutb's execution by the Nasser regime only made his words more omnipresent and 'became an example of sincerity and adherence to justice ... and [he] paid his life as a price for this'.[206] Qutb's revolutionary ideology and his execution by the Nasser regime had a weighty impact on al-Zawahiri. According to a former peer of al-Zawahiri's when they both studied medicine, 'Sayyid Qutb's words cut deep for al-Zawahiri because his words resulted in his execution.' Ultimately, Qutb's blueprint enabled al-Zawahiri to continue to develop his work.[207] Al-Zawahiri believed Nasser feared Qutb because of his potential impact, and that was why he was sent to the gallows:

> After the execution of Sayyid Qutb his words acquired dimensions not acquired by any other religious scholar. Those words, which Qutb wrote with his own blood, became the landmarks of a glorious and long road and the Muslim youth came to realise how much the Nasserite regime and its communist [allies] panicked from Qutb's call for unification.[208]

The effect of stories surrounding Qutb's experience in prison was undoubtedly of great significance to al-Zawahiri, and having that family connection to Qutb gave him a sense of direction and determination. This is particularly illustrated by one anecdote that occurred in the mid-1960s.

Al-Zawahiri and his younger brother Muhammad were returning home from Friday prayers. They came across Hussein al-Shafei, the vice-president of Egypt in his official government vehicle. He was known to the al-Zawahiri family: along with Anwar Sadat, he was part of a panel of judges in the 1954 roundup of Islamists that included Qutb. Al-Shafei asked the brothers whether they would like a lift home. They rejected his offer and apparently retorted, 'We don't want help from a creature who sentenced Muslims to the gallows.'[209] This incident became folklore amongst the jihadists in Egypt, and it was a narrative that al-Zawahiri promoted heavily.[210]

Al-Zawahiri would later say that it was at this period in life, during his final year of high school between 1965 and 1966, during the Nasser regime's mass incarceration of the Muslim Brotherhood, with many facing the death penalty (including Sayyid Qutb), that he was motivated to form a jihadist group of his own at the age of 15.[211] Al-Zawahiri describes his personal affinity for Qutb's thought and its influence on his journey to sow insurrection and terrorism:

> Although Qutb ... was oppressed and tortured by Nasser's regime, [his] influence on young Muslims was paramount. Qutb's message was and still is to believe in the oneness of Allah and the supremacy of the Divine path. This message fanned the fire of Islamic revolution against the enemies of Islam at home and abroad. The chapters of this revolution are renewing one day after another.[212]

According to al-Zawahiri, 'Sayyid Qutb's call for loyalty to Allah's oneness and to acknowledge Allah's sole authority and *hakimiyyah* was the spark that ignited the Islamic revolution against the enemies of Islam at home and abroad. The bloody chapters of this revolution continue to unfold day after day.'[213]

Qutb's writings detailed three responses to modernity: he first accepted it, then Islamised it, and finally rejected it. This trajectory has similarities his rejection of other key Western ideas. The books in which he set forth these views are still widely read and stand a witness to his profound repudiation of the existing system. Such was the level of respect and impact that Qutb had on al-Zawahiri that he would refer to him on occasion as 'Professor' and described him as one of the most important ideologues: 'Professor Sayyid Qutb played a key role in directing the Muslim youth to this road in the second half of the 20th century in Egypt in particular and the Arab region in general.'[214]

Al-Zawahiri also highlighted Qutb's endorsement of offensive jihad and the need to fight the 'internal enemy' in *Knights under the Prophet's Banner.* Al-Zawahiri said of Qutb, 'The Islamic movement had begun a war against the regime in its capacity as an enemy of Islam. Before that, the Islamic movement's ethics and principles—in which some believe until now— affirmed that the external enemy was the only enemy of Islam.'[215] In add- ition, al-Zawahiri specified Qutb and his followers 'decided to deal blows to the existent government in its capacity as a regime that was hostile to Islam ... and refused to apply the *Shariah.*'[216] Al-Zawahiri describes himself, with pride, as a disciple of Qutb, whose greatest contribution was to try to unite the *ummah* against the enemies of Islam:

> He affirmed that the issue of unification in Islam is important and that the battle between Islam and its enemies is primarily an ideological one over the issue of unification. It is also a battle over to whom authority and power should belong—to Allah's course and the Shariah, to man-made laws and material principles, or to those who claim to be intermediaries between the Creator and mankind. . . . This affirmation greatly helped the Islamic move- ment to know and define its enemies.[217]

For this reason, al-Zawahiri marked the beginning of Egypt's jihadist movement and 'its current march against the government' in the mid- 1960s when the Nasser government began its crackdown on the Muslim Brotherhood.[218] Thus, a jihadist nucleolus formed amidst the confrontation between the Nasser government and the Muslim Brotherhood, which al- Zawahiri joined. According to al-Zawahiri, Nasser's regime was mistaken in thinking that 'the Islamic movement received a deadly blow with the execution of Sayyid Qutb and his comrades and the arrest of thousands of Islamic movement members'. On the contrary, he argued 'Qutb's ideas and calls' were interacting, under the surface, with an emerging 'nucleolus of modern jihad'.[219] Hence, al-Zawahiri believed Qutb's death ultimately 'failed to stop his growing influence among the Muslim youth'.[220]

Al-Zawahiri's first foray into an Islamist organization came in 1966, with the Association of the Followers of Muhammad's Path (Jamiyyat Ansar al- Sunnah al-Muhammadiyya) under the tutelage of Shaykh Mustafa al-Fiqqi, but did not last for long when he attended Maadi High School.[221] It was here that al-Zawahiri started getting interested in religious books following the arrest, imprisonment, and eventual execution of Qutb. Al-Zawahiri's interest in religion was effectively an extension of what he had inherited from his family, which had so many distinguished religious scholars—although none promoted violence against the state. Part of this fascination was also because his uncle Mahfouz Azzam had a close relationship with Qutb.[222]

Despite being regarded as serious and focused on his studies, al-Zawahiri also enjoyed going to the cinema and listening to music. He was also known amongst his peers for his humour.[223] However, whilst at Maadi High School, al-Zawahiri came under the guidance of classmate Ismail Tantawi, who advocated the creation of clandestine cells that would infiltrate the Egyptian government.[224] Tantawi and al-Zawahiri were part of a clique in Maadi High School which also included Safar al-Hawali, a Saudi national who would go on to study at Umm al-Qura University in Mecca and write a master's dissertation on the weakness of secularism. His thesis supervisor was Sayyid Qutb's brother, Muhammad, who fled Egypt for Saudi Arabia following his release from prison in 1972 after having been accused of plotting against the Nasser regime.[225]

The three established a network within the school and called the Organization (Tanzeem) in 1967 whilst al-Zawahiri was still a teenager. The aim of the Tanzeem was the violent removal of the Egyptian government and the formation of an Islamic state practising Shariah Law.[226] Al-Zawahiri recalled about that moment in time, 'We were a group of students from Maadi High School amongst others.'[227] The inference was that al-Zawahiri believed he and his cohort were fulfilling the vanguard role that Qutb envisaged and that no others were suitable for it. With a reputation for secrecy, the Tanzeem mandated not growing beards to avoid displaying their religiosity and attracting attention from the authorities. As a result, they were aptly known as 'the shaved beards'.[228] The members of the cell tended to gather in one another's homes, at a mosque, or in a secluded area along the Nile. A friend of al-Zawahiri's, Kamal Habib, who joined the cell explained, 'We thought at the time that the goal to apply the laws of Islam can't be achieved with ways other than violence.'[229] Before long, al-Zawahiri became the leader (amir) of Tanzeem whilst admitting, 'Our means didn't match our aspirations.'[230]

Al-Zawahiri's younger brother Muhammad was also convinced of joining the group.[231] Muhammad al-Zawahiri was a dutiful brother and would often lead the prayers together with Ayman for their followers.[232] However, their cell was loosely organised and more a talking shop than an active militant organization. Over time, al-Zawahiri reached out to other like-minded jihadists to develop more serious capabilities. In addition to Qutb's execution, another important moment in al-Zawahiri's mind was when Nasser visited Moscow in 1967 and revealed his intention to crack down on the Muslim Brotherhood. Al-Zawahiri saw this as an ideological war against Islam which required the efforts of its youth to overthrow Nasser.[233]

The Arab-Israeli conflict in 1967 exposed Nasser's deeply flawed decision-making and brought about radical changes in the geopolitical environment of the Middle East. After the Suez invasion, Israel withdrew its troops to their original boundaries with Egypt, and Egypt permitted UN observers to station themselves along the border hotspots between Egypt and Israel, always, however, on the Egyptian side. In mid-May 1967, Nasser demanded that the United Nations withdraw its observers from Egyptian territory. Three weeks later, the Israelis, fearing that Egypt and Syria might launch an attack, took pre-emptive action and sent planes against the Egyptian air force and troops into Sinai. The airstrike was stunningly successful, destroying 300 of the 430 Egyptian combat airplanes and providing Israel with command of the airspace.[234]

Lacking air cover, the Egyptian forces stationed in Sinai were easy targets for advancing units of the Israeli army and air force. Egypt lost an estimated 20,000 soldiers, most of them in a desperate retreat across Sinai. When Syria and Jordan joined the battle to aid Egypt, the Israelis seized large chunks of their respective territories. By the time a ceasefire was imposed, six days after war had commenced, Israel had taken control of Jerusalem and the West Bank of the Jordan River from Jordan. It had also overrun the Golan Heights from Syria, and its forces had control over the Sinai.

For Nasser, the war was a disaster. Egypt could not hide or spin its military and political defeat. The defeat in the 1967 war with Israel was seen in some quarters as showing up the ineffectiveness of Pan-Arabism which al-Zawahiri's grandfather Abdul Rahman Azzam had long advocated, and it had severe consequences for Egypt and Nasser. Mass student protests vented on college campuses across Cairo and Alexandria with slogans shouted and graffitied on building walls: 'Stop the Rule of the Intelligence' and 'Down with the Police State'.[235]

The 1967 humiliation also had a profound impact on al-Zawahiri himself. After Nasser's push and sponsorship for Arab nationalism, the overwhelming defeat pushed many Egyptians like him to look for alternative responses. In *Knights under the Prophets Banner*, al-Zawahiri recalled this difficult episode of Egypt's history, arguing that after 1967 'the symbol Nasser, whose followers tried to depict to the people as the immortal and invincible leader, fell. The tyrant leader, who mistreated his foes and threatened them in his speeches, became a man panting after a face-saving peaceful solution.'[236] Unsurprisingly, Nasser's 1967 humiliation fuelled Egypt's incipient jihadist movement.

Nasser offered his resignation, accepting full responsibility for the failure, but the country was unwilling to see its fabled leader step down. Yet, by then, he was dispirited and disillusioned. Just over three years after the Six Day War, on 28 September 1970, Nasser died of heart failure.[237] For al-Zawahiri, Nasser's passing also represented the indictment of the statesman's legacy and belief in socialism and nationalism: 'The death of Nasser was not the death of one person but also the death of his principles, which proved their failure on the ground of reality, and the death of a popular myth that was broken on the sands of Sinai.'[238] Al-Zawahiri then cautioned, 'Soon they replaced him with another ruler, who took another turn and started to sell them a new illusion.'[239]

2

Insurrection and Transgression

The Pious Leader

In 1968, at a relatively young age, al-Zawahiri was admitted to the Faculty Of Medicine Kasr Al-Ainy at Cairo University, and he graduated in 1974.[1] Study was not his only priority, as the medical school at Cairo University was a hotbed for Islamist activism. Whilst there, al-Zawahiri spoke fervently of his religious convictions and had great influence amongst the students. Between 1969 to 1971, Lawrence Wright taught at the American University in Cairo, the same time al-Zawahiri was a medical student and leading a campaign to get women to cover their heads in public. Despite his reverent religious beliefs, the then-athletic-looking al-Zawahiri would often be seen wearing a Western suit and tie.[2] Yet al-Zawahiri never joined mainstream political activities during this period. He preferred to keep his own counsel and be a witness from the outside.[3]

It was here that al-Zawahiri would meet Sayyid Imam al-Sharif, also known as Dr Fadl. Al-Sharif would go on to play an important role in al-Zawahiri's ideological development, eventually becoming his biggest detractor within the ranks of the jihadists. Most of the people al-Zawahiri knew grew up in Cairo, but al-Sharif hailed from Beni Suef in northern Upper Egypt.[4] Islam had a profound impact on al-Sharif in his youth, which garnered instant respect from al-Zawahiri because of his deep understanding of *fiqh*. His ideological development would go hand in hand with his medical career as he earned a place at the surgery department at Qasr al-Ayni Hospital before obtaining his master's degree in surgery.[5]

In describing his time with al-Zawahiri, al-Sharif commented, 'We, together with other colleagues, used to discuss various Islamic issues. I knew from another colleague that Ayman was involved with an Islamic group.'[6] Al-Sharif joined al-Zawahiri's group when he was studying at the Qasr

Doctor, Teacher, Terrorist. Sajjan M. Gohel, Oxford University Press. © Oxford University Press 2024.
DOI: 10.1093/oso/9780197665367.003.0002

al-Ayni Hospital. Al-Zawahiri took pride in having recruited him.[7] This cemented their friendship and created a sense of kinship, which extended to their families becoming close as well.[8] This bond would run parallel with huge political changes taking place in Egypt.

Anwar Sadat was a founding member of the Free Officers movement. He had been imprisoned for four years by the British during just after World War II for collaborating with the notorious Nazi military officer Field Marshall Erwin Rommel. When Nasser launched his coup, Sadat was watching a movie in the theatre with his wife at the time and could not be contacted. For a while, this damaged his reputation and standing. He largely remained in subordinate roles thereafter.[9] This included being made editor-in-chief of a new newspaper, the *Republic (Al-Gumhouriya)* and then the secretary general of the Islamic Congress.[10] However, thereafter Sadat's role in Nasser's regime was largely nondescript. It was therefore a surprise when on 20 December 1969, he was appointed vice-president. Within a year, Nasser died, and Sadat succeeded him. Many Nasserists believed in an orderly changeover of the administration and that they could control Sadat, but that was not going to be the case.[11]

Nasser and Sadat were polar opposites in leadership style as well as on domestic and foreign policy issues. Sadat was known for being pious and made a point in highlighting the prayer mark high on his forehead to symbolise how often he would pray. Sadat would also absorb how the system worked both formally and informally. His experience as a newspaper editor gave him the understanding to control the narrative. However, the first challenge was to keep himself in power. There were many within Nasser's inner circle who viewed Sadat as an unworthy successor.[12] Al-Zawahiri could see Sadat's strategy in 'removing the proteges of the old regime. His strongest weapon in resisting those remaining proteges was his permission of some forms of freedom for the repressed people.'[13]

Soon after taking over from Nasser, Sadat chose to preserve Pan-Arabism in theory, as advocated by al-Zawahiri's maternal uncle Abdul Rahman Azzam, the former secretary general of the Arab League.[14] In reality, Sadat pursued a radically different approach for Egypt's foreign relations. In a startling move in 1972, Sadat expelled thousands of Soviet advisers along with their families, citing Moscow's lack of commitment to help Cairo counter Israel's well-established military arsenal. Concerning Sadat's political transformation of the country, al-Zawahiri argued, 'Anwar al-Mujahideen's

[Sadat's] assumption of power marked the beginning of a new political transformation in Egypt represented by the end of the Russian [Soviet] era and the start of the American era.'[15] Al-Zawahiri's reference to Sadat as 'Anwar al-Mujahideen' was deliberately sarcastic and disparaging, calling into question Sadat's religious credibility.

Another policy reorientation was the status of the Islamic establishment, which was enhanced considerably. Sadat needed Islamist allies beyond al-Azhar. He initially considered the Islamists in universities and the countryside. Sadat was cognisant of the political aspirations of the Muslim Brotherhood from the time he established dialogue with their founder, Hasan al-Banna, in the 1940s during World War II. He was open minded to a potential arrangement on the condition they did not challenge his authority or policies. Sadat referred to himself as the First Man of Islam, and his religiosity was a factor, but so was his need for the *ulama's* support in curbing the influence of Nasserist and leftist challengers and asserting his own authority.[16]

Part of Sadat's policy reorientation was engagement with the Islamists and releasing those who had been imprisoned by Nasser, including members of the Muslim Brotherhood.[17] Their denunciation of Nasser's Arabism for distorting Islam was a major reason for their initial support for Sadat, as he seemed willing to pursue a different path to his predecessor. Sadat amended the constitution of 1971 and declared Shariah law the principal source of all legislation.[18] Sadat, as the Pious President, was also developing his own style and slogans. He wanted to enhance his role as the head of the Egyptian family whilst exalting village ethics.[19]

Sadat had an even more audacious move to make. In October 1973, during the holy month of Ramadan, he launched a pre-emptive operation across the Suez Canal against Israeli forces. The strategy enabled the Egyptian army to make significant ground in the Sinai. The Israeli counter-attack was rapid and ferocious. With US support, the Israelis drove the Egyptians back across Sinai before the Americans prevailed on the Israelis to accept a truce. According to al-Zawahiri:

> During the 1973 October war between the Arabs and Israel, the United States began airlifting to Israel weapons, ammunition, equipment, and even tanks from the warehouses of the operating U.S. Army units directly into the battle-field. ... This tipped the balance of military power in favour of Israel. It also demonstrated the U.S. absolute support and backing for Israel in this war.[20]

Despite al-Zawahiri's assessment, Sadat had achieved one of his primary objectives in going to battle with Israel. He had forced the attention of the United States to the unresolved problems in the Middle East and kick-started diplomatic negotiations over the Sinai. Indeed, a succession of swift and defining events followed the ending of the 1973 war, with further courting of the United States. American advisers began to move into Egypt as quickly as their Soviet counterparts departed.[21]

During this period, al-Zawahiri encountered the Palestinian Salih Abdullah Siriyya, the *amir* of the Islamic Liberation Party (Hizb ut-Tahrir al-Islami, HTI), which was founded as a clandestine organization in Jordan.[22] The HTI affirmed that the legitimacy of the government should be gained from its ability to distribute wealth evenly. To this they added that the government should be based exclusively on the Shariah.[23] The HTI condemned the existing political system and believed it was their religious obligation to bring about a Muslim social order through force. Siriyya viewed Arab society as a victim of 'unscrupulous leaders' at the top of the 'apostate' political system that had no fear of God as in the Qur'an. He saw this 'victimised society' as eager but unable to get rid of its 'victimisers'—in this case the Sadat government, which represented the Party of Satan (Hizb al-Shaytan).[24]

Mirroring al-Zawahiri's beliefs, Siriyya developed a weighty conspiracy of the 'fall of the *umma*'. He argued that, on the one hand, nationalism was planted in the Arab world in the mid-nineteenth century by the British as a tool to subjugate Islam. On the other hand, the Ottoman Empire was dismantled by crusading missionaries as well as British and French colonial bureaucrats who endorsed the policy of secular Turkification by Kemal Ataturk.[25] Siriyya proposed the creation of an Islamic state, which to him necessitated the infiltration of the military and the police to speed up the destruction of the regime from within.[26] For al-Zawahiri, 'Sariyah was a mesmerizing speaker . . . his words carried weight and meaning on the need to support Islam.'[27]

On 17 April 1974, Siriyya and his militant group, Shabab Muhammad (Youth of Muhammad), along with al-Zawahiri and his cohort, gained notoriety for their abortive takeover the building of the Military Technical College in Heliopolis, near Cairo. Sadat was due to attend an event there marking six months since the 1973 October War. However, the presidential motorcade was late in arriving. According to al-Zawahiri:

A plan was prepared under which group members would silently overpower the policemen guarding the college gate, enter the college, and seize weapons and armoured vehicles with the help of students acting as night supervisors. They would then march toward the Arab Socialist Union headquarters to attack al-Mujahideen [Anwar Sadat] and his government officials who were meeting there.[28]

The plotters may have succeeded, at least to begin with, had not one member of the group panicked by the enormity of the task, and the potential fallout, and informed the authorities. Siriyya, assuming success was a forgone conclusion, had optimistically prepared a victory declaration to be aired on radio and television. However, Egyptian government forces, aware of the plot, were able to overwhelm Siriyya's group and made many arrests, although some escaped, including al-Zawahiri, who was not implicated in the plot at the time. The arrested jihadists, including Siriyya, were subsequently executed by the government.[29] After his escape, al-Zawahiri benefited from the political influence of his maternal Azzam family to shield him. Unlike his predominantly medical paternal family, the Azzams included politicians, governors, and several state counsellors and prosecutors, one of whom would later become a Supreme State Security Court chief justice.[30]

Al-Zawahiri claimed that 'the coup attempt failed because it did not take into consideration the objective conditions and the need to prepare well'. He also noted that he was 'mesmerised' by Siriyya. Siriyya believed a coup would be led by a vanguard similar to what Qutb had called for and what al-Zawahiri strongly believed in as well, but the overall plan was vague and undeveloped.[31]

Remarkably, following the Military Technical College revolt, al-Zawahiri worked for three years as a part-time surgeon in the Egyptian army. It was there that al-Zawahiri saw the legacy of Nasser's secularism within the army, which he loathed. He equally detested the peace overtures that were developing between Egypt and Israel. Subsequently, he followed in the footsteps of his friend al-Sharif and received a master's degree in surgery at Cairo University's Faculty Of Medicine Kasr Al-Ainy in 1978 and decided to specialise as a paediatrician.[32]

At the same time, Sadat's open-door (infitah) policy, took hold in Egypt and especially in Cairo, leading to the further development of the city.[33] This enabled capitalist entrepreneurs to re-emerge after being discouraged during the Nasser years, and Egyptian workers were able to work in Gulf Arab countries and send back remittances. Imported goods entered the Egyptian markets, as did foreign oil companies and banks. A property boom began to change formal Cairo's landscape, with residential tower blocks, new hotels, and office buildings transforming the city skyline. Infrastructure projects, mainly symbolised by the Sixth of October Bridge and flyovers, began to populate the horizon. During the 1976 parliamentary elections, Sadat maintained the backing of Islamic groups in his efforts to root out Nasser loyalists and socialists. This was the peak of his domestic standing.

In January 1977, the government significantly cut back on subsidies, causing a substantial rise in the cost of food staples such as sugar, flour, and oil.[34] This led to demonstrations which had widespread popular support. The chief *shaykh* of al-Azhar, Dr Abd al-Halim Mahmud, went on Radio Cairo to condemn the riots as 'the lowest that humanity could stoop to'. He declared that they were organised by 'the enemy lying in wait to destroy all our aspirations'.[35] However, not all religious groups would toe the government line. Some entities took advantage of the situation to criticise Sadat's policies. This was most reflected in the universities amongst the Islamic student groups that had been allowed to sprout up by the Egyptian president. Sadat's one-time allies turned into his most outspoken opponents. Their antagonism was not confined to domestic policies.[36] Al-Zawahiri viewed the situation as providing momentum for the jihadists:

> As soon as some pressure was lifted from the Islamic movement, the giant [the Islamic movement] emerged from the bottle and the extensive influence of the Islamists among the masses became clear. Muslim youth won the overwhelming majority of the seats in university and school student unions in a matter of few years. The Islamic movement began its march to control the trade unions.[37]

In continuation with his maverick tendencies, Sadat flew to Jerusalem on 19 November 1977. In a landmark speech in the Knesset, he offered a peace settlement between Egypt and Israel to resolve all outstanding issues between both countries.[38] In March 1978, at Mena House in Giza—the venue for peace talks—President Sadat met with President Jimmy Carter and Prime Minister Menachem Began to work out the terms of a peace accord. Some of the most complicated, contentious, and career-defining points between Egypt and Israel were being ironed out. Prior to that, Carter had addressed the Egyptian People's Assembly in Cairo, where he spoke about his hopes and expectations of peace between Israel and Egypt. Carter added, 'I know how deeply President Sadat is committed to that quest. And I believe its achievement will ultimately be his greatest legacy to the people he serves so well.'[39]

Following the speech, Carter and Sadat were interviewed by the American correspondent Peter Jennings of ABC News about their goals for the Mena House talks.[40] Mena House is one of the most unique hotels in Egypt, surrounded by 40 acres of verdant gardens in the shadows of the Great Pyramids of Giza. Originally a royal lodge, it was used as a rest house for the Khedive Ismail and would serve as host to other kings and emperors, heads of state and celebrities. The opulent setting for Sadat to play host to the leaders of the United States and Israel created the perception for the jihadists that Egypt's president was not pious but *jahili*.

The eyes of the world were also on Egypt, and for al-Zawahiri, this was a pivotal moment. One of his maternal cousins who was a freelance journalist got a job working as a stringer for ABC News assisting Peter Jennings.[41] Al-Zawahiri was fascinated by the editorial and production values of news media. He would discuss with his cousin the terminology and the differences between cutaways, B-rolls, overlays, montages, and sequences.[42] It was here that al-Zawahiri understood the importance of communications, engagement, and understanding the message being conveyed.

Through his cousin, al-Zawahiri also took interest in the ABC correspondents themselves. Peter Jennings had established the first US television news bureau in the Middle East. He also was widely known as Sadat's favourite journalist after completing a documentary on the Egyptian president in 1974, *Sadat: Action Biography*, which earned a Peabody Award.[43] Al-Zawahiri had seen the documentary, and it resonated not because he had any adulation for Sadat but rather because he had an appreciation for the medium of television. It provided an extra dimension to a person's character, making them interesting and understandable by blending history, commentary, and interviews.[44] For that era, Jennings was considered to have 'owned the Arab story', and this was not lost on al-Zawahiri.[45]

Al-Zawahiri's burgeoning interest in the media also extended to Sam Donaldson, the ABC News chief White House correspondent.[46] Donaldson was modish, wore English-cut suits, and had a distinctive accent. For al-Zawahiri, how one comes across on camera mattered a great deal as visually it conveys its own message. Donaldson, like Jennings, reported on Egypt. He once described Sadat as 'the Arab who dared to set aside hatred'.[47] Curiously, even before the age of the internet, according to a family member, 'al-Zawahiri was still able to follow developments within the US media'.[48] This is particularly remarkable when one considers that al-Zawahiri as a young man was living before the age of 24-hour satellite news, fibre-optic technology, and social media. It was even more unusual for Egyptians to be exposed to journalism from outside the Middle East, demonstrating al-Zawahiri's determination to understand how technology and communication from the West was utilised and what modalities could be borrowed to further his own agenda.

Meanwhile Sadat followed up the positive meetings at Mena House with another trip to Israel in May 1978, where he gave a talk at the Ben Gurion University in Beersheba. He emphasised the historic bonds between Islam and Judaism. He spoke about how the Prophet Muhammad had instructed the people of Yathrib (who were Jews) and Muslims to create one realm and to exercise and administer their respective faiths in harmony and mutual respect. Sadat went further and spoke about his desire to build a symbol for the Abrahamic faiths with a canal from the Nile to Jerusalem: 'In the name of Egypt and its great Al-Azhar and in the name of defending peace, the Nile water will become the new "Zamzam well" for believers in the three monotheistic religions. . . . The water will serve all pilgrims visiting the holy shrines in Jerusalem.'[49]

Subsequently, at Camp David, in the wooded mountains near Washington, DC, Sadat, Begin, and Carter signed the peace accord between Egypt and Israel on 17 September 1978. In return for formally recognising Israel, Egypt would receive back the whole of the Sinai Peninsula. Other terms of the agreement included promises on both sides to work to solve the underlying problems that separated Israel and the Palestinian peoples and to work to bring a Palestinian state into being. To the disappointment of some, Sadat did not make the Palestinian issue a deal-breaker.[50] Al-Zawahiri's interpretation of this illustrated that Sadat was substantially out of step with the Islamists:

> The United States handed a copy of this memorandum to al-Mujahideen [Anwar Sadat] a day before the peace treaty was signed, but this did not prevent al-Mujahideen from signing the treaty next day. He even signed a new document entitled 'A Complementary Agreement for Full Autonomy in the West Bank and Gaza'.[51]

To inflame the situation further, Sadat made decisive concessions. The final text of the peace accord with Israel removed all references to Jerusalem and referred only in general terms to UN Security Council Resolution 242 that spoke about the goal to create an enduring peaceful resolution in the Middle East, which had been signed after the 1967 Arab-Israeli War and the withdrawal of Israeli military from territories occupied in the conflict.[52] For Sadat, Egypt could not move forward domestically or internationally if its territorial integrity remained compromised. Therefore, ending hostilities with Israel resulted in all of the Sinai being returned to Egypt and Sadat aligning with the United States, who in turn would provide financial and technical assistance for his *infitah* policies. The agreement between Egypt and Israel ended thirty-one years of hostility between the two countries. However, for the Islamists, the only thing that mattered was that Egypt had become the first Arab state to reach an accommodation with Israel.

US economic assistance flowed after the peace treaty and totalled $1.8 billion in 1980 which made Egypt the largest recipient of American aid next to Israel.[53] The US Embassy expanded rapidly, from only six staff members when diplomatic relations were restored in 1974 to become the biggest US embassy in the world by 1980.[54] Although the Camp David Accords were heralded in the West and led to Sadat and Begin being awarded the 1978 Nobel Peace Prize, they triggered a storm of protests across the Arab world.

As expected, Arab nations ceased diplomatic relations with Egypt with some implementing economic sanctions. Egypt was expelled from the Organisation of the Islamic Conference and the Arab League, and the head-quarters was moved out of Cairo.[55] Egypt's newly acquired pariah status within the Arab world removed it as a cultural, intellectual, and political cen-tre. Sadat also faced opposition within Egypt. The noted academic on Egypt Robert Tignor commented, 'Sadat was right that Egypt and Egyptian families had suffered enough from the wars with Israel, but he failed to convince most of the professional classes and the rank and file of the population that a peace treaty with Israel was in the best interests of Egyptians going forward. He op-erated his own policy when it came to Israeli-Egyptian relations.'[56]

Sadat also faced opposition within his own government, as several minis-ters resigned. However, Egypt's political institutions felt compelled to support Sadat. The People's Assembly unsurprisingly rubber-stamped the treaty, and the referendum won 90% approval.[57] Al-Azhar repeated their endorsement of Sadat's policy, claiming, 'The peace treaty between Egypt and Israel is a blessed Islamic step, founded on the principles of religion.'[58] Furthermore, the chief *shaykh* of al-Azhar, Abd al-Halim Mahmud, presented a *fatwa* sanctioning the Camp David agreement. This was an embarrassing reversal of previous policy positions. In 1965, under Nasser's rule, al-Azhar had issued a *fatwa* prohibiting a Muslim ruler from concluding any peace agreement with Israel and condemning those who did so as unbelievers.[59] The revised position from al-Azhar was that if the Prophet Muhammad could parlay with the Jews of Medina, then the Arab states should be open to seeking dialogue with Israel. It was a sobering reminder of the constraints of al-Azhar's ability to take a position independent of the Egyptian state.[60]

Al-Zawahiri perceived the immorality of the West and Israel now influencing and controlling events within Egypt to the extent that even al-Azhar had abandoned its Islamic credentials: 'The Islamic movement began entering this phase of growth, spreading among its youth a deep awareness that that the internal enemy was not less dangerous than the external enemy. This awareness began to strongly grow on the basis of clear legitimacy and bitter historical and practical experience.'[61]

Despite the many denunciations within the Islamic world and Egypt itself of Sadat's peace with Israel as an act of treachery against the *ummah*, Sadat was unrelenting on the importance of the religious and cultural aspects of normalising ties with Israel, which he claimed went beyond strategic imperatives. In an interview with the *October Magazine* on 30 September 1979, Sadat stated, 'I regret to say that the Arabs have not changed but have instead regressed. Egypt alone has changed. We were and still are more civilised and advanced. The Arabs have become small in our eyes because we have grown bigger.'[62]

Although the Muslim Brotherhood could be viewed as a convenient bedfellow for Sadat against the Nasser loyalists and the leftist groups, this fragile arrangement deteriorated after the Camp David Accords in 1978. Sadat had a strong faith in Islam, but he used it opportunistically. At Camp David, the Americans provided a place for Sadat to pray, and the Egyptian president took advantage of that opportunity to demonstrate that his faith was still paramount and respected in the West.[63] However, the Islamists were unimpressed and began to pose a threat to the established order, denouncing Sadat's 'Egypt First' which to them meant a 'pagan pharaonic' approach.[64] The Islamists were no longer convinced by Sadat's religious credentials.

Away from the major foreign policy upheavals, al-Zawahiri married Izzat Ahmad Nuwair in 1978. She had also studied at his alma mater, Cairo University, earning a philosophy degree, and fulfilled his prerequisite of 'a devout wife'.[65] She was better known within her social circle as Umm Fatima and had a calm demeanour and a dry sense of humour. She was pe-tite, compared to al-Zawahiri's now rotund figure. She suffered from eczema that left her hands red.[66] Like al-Zawahiri, she came from a prominent and wealthy Egyptian family from Maadi, and they would eventually become dismayed by her association with al-Zawahiri. The Nowair family were not devout Muslims, but Umm Fatima was pious, and as a student she started wearing the hijab and eventually covered herself completely.[67] Al-Zawahiri was attracted to her piety, and she was dedicated to him. According to Lawrence Wright, 'She was a very strong uncompromising figure. This ap-pealed to al-Zawahiri as he wanted a partner who would go through the hardships, knowing they would come.'[68]

The couple got married in a traditional Islamic wedding in February 1978, at the Grand Continental Hotel in central Cairo. Overlooking Opera Square and the Azbakeya Botanical Gardens, the hotel was an iconic part of the capital. It was built in the 1860s as part of Egypt's modernisation projects that included the Suez Canal. It experienced a decline in fortunes after the al-Zawahiri wedding and became a dilapidated eyesore which eventually led to its demolition, leaving only memories. However, other than the recorded date, there was no trace of the wedding. Photographs were not allowed, and music was banned. The al-Zawahiris would have five children, including a girl with Down syndrome, who was al-Zawahiri's favourite. Once the couple was married, Umm Fatima drifted further from her family.[69]

By 1979, militant Islamist groups had mushroomed across Egypt, iron-ically emboldened by the freedom that Sadat had given them. People like 'Ayman [al-Zawahiri] viewed world Jewry as an agent whose services were used by both the United States and the Soviet Union against the Muslim world'.[70] In al-Zawahiri's mind, peace with Israel was equivalent to treason because every Muslim was conscientiously obligated to engage in the jihad against Israel.[71] In an effort to shift attention elsewhere, Sadat encouraged Egyptians to go to Afghanistan and Pakistan to engage in the emerging jihad against the Soviets.

Al-Zawahiri's medical background would enable him to travel to Afghanistan during the early stages of the Afghan-Arab *mujahideen* cam-paign. In his memoir, al-Zawahiri wrote, 'My connection with Afghanistan began in the summer of 1980 by a twist of fate.'[72] Whilst working part time at the Muslim Brotherhood clinic in al-Sayyida Zaynab, one of Cairo's most deprived districts, al-Zawahiri was queried whether he would be willing to travel to Afghanistan to 'work as a surgeon, to the medical relief effort among the Afghan refugees'. He looked at it as 'a golden opportunity to get to know closely the field of jihad, which could be a base for jihad in Egypt and the Arab world, the heart of the Islamic world where real battle for Islam exist'.[73] As al-Zawahiri expanded:

> The problem of finding a secure base for jihad activity in Egypt used to occupy me a lot, in view of the pursuits to which we were subjected by the security forces and because of Egypt's flat terrain which made government control easy, for the River Nile runs in its narrow valley between two deserts that have no vegetation or water. . . . When I came into contact with the arena of Afghan jihad in 1980, I became aware of its rich potential and realised how much benefit it would bring to the Muslim nation in general, and the jihadist movement in particular. I understood the importance of benefiting from this arena. Hence, after I stayed for four months there on my first visit, I returned in March 1981 and spent another two months there. I was then forced to return to Egypt because of pressing circumstances back home.[74]

According to his uncle Mahfouz Azzam, al-Zawahiri 'was willing to abandon his surgery here in Cairo—it was very successful, lots of clients. . . . The *mujahideen* needed his help when they were fighting the Russians [Soviets]. He treated all their top commanders and when he came back to Egypt he was a hero.'[75]

At the beginning of the war, there was no organised effort to transport Arab jihadists from their mosques in Cairo and Medina to the battlefields of Afghanistan. Arab volunteers were young, naive, and fanatically religious men drawn to the battlefields of Afghanistan by the promise of eternal life and fantasies of becoming *shaheeds*. Al-Zawahiri developed credibility amongst jihadist circles as one of the first Egyptians to engage in the jihad.

In 1980, he travelled to Peshawar, Pakistan, with some friends to do philanthropic work assisting the Afghan refugees escaping the nascent war against the communist regime propped up by the occupying Soviet forces. Al-Zawahiri stated, 'We were the first three Arabs to arrive there to participate in relief work.'[76] Assigned to the Kuwaiti Red Crescent Society, affiliated to the International Red Crescent Movement, al-Zawahiri spent several months in Peshawar providing medical care for the refugees based there.[77] Seeing the Afghan war close up enabled him to also meet members of the Afghan resistance, the *mujahideen*, who were fighting against the Soviets and their Afghan communist allies. On some occasions, al-Zawahiri would travel across the porous border to see the war with his own eyes. According to a family member, 'Tribesmen took Ayman over the border.'[78]

Upon his return to Cairo at the end of 1980, al-Zawahiri shared his experiences with other Egyptians and began recruiting to increase the ranks of the *mujahideen*. He spoke of 'miracles' that were occurring in the jihad against the Soviets. He wrote in *Knights under the Prophet's Banner* that he understood 'the importance of the benefit of this arena' and the 'rich potential' of the Afghan jihad.[79] The Pakistani military ruler General Zia ul-Haq was also keen to welcome Arab jihadists to Pakistan. He had overthrown the Prime Minister Zulfikar Ali Bhutto in a coup in 1977 and then had him executed. Zia had earned pariah status, but after the Soviet occupation in Afghanistan, the West turned to him for help in creating the Afghan-Arab *mujahideen*.

In early 1981, al-Zawahiri made a fleeting visit to Pakistan on behalf of the Kuwaiti Red Crescent Society once more. He returned to Cairo inspired by the battle-hardened *mujahideen*. These early exposures to the Afghan campaign would be very pivotal in enhancing al-Zawahiri's credibility and reputation as a proponent of the Jihad against the Soviet occupation of a Muslim country.[80]

Back in Egypt, another issue that caught the ire of the Islamists was Sadat's decision to give the shah of Iran and his family sanctuary in Egypt after they fled the country following the Islamic revolution. Kubba Palace, an extravagant presidential guest house in the Heliopolis suburb of northern Cairo, was provided to them. The shah had become vehemently unpopular amongst the Islamists for his close ties with the West and because he was seen as un-Islamic due to his secular regime. When the shah died on 27 July 1980 of ill health, his wife wanted a quiet burial, but Sadat decided that he should have a state funeral. Sadat was again heavily criticised by the Islamists for associating himself too closely with the 'un-Islamic Shah'.[81]

Sadat had begun to develop a sense of infallibility in his own judgement. It was perhaps not surprising that the accolades of the West accelerated the problem. Helmut Schmidt, the former West German chancellor, described Sadat as 'a deep-thinking peace-loving military man, very deeply rooted in religion and philosophy'.[82] Such was the adulation of Sadat that President Carter, in a toast at a White House dinner in April 1980, said he was glad he was not running against him for president of the United States.[83]

Like Nasser, Sadat had become isolated and arguably out of step with the sentiments within Egypt. More worryingly, he was quite naive of the growing strength of the Islamists, who had consolidated their infrastructure because of his lenient policies towards them when he took power.[84] Sadat was becoming the problem for the Islamists, who increasingly viewed him as an 'apostate' supported by the West and Israel.

Sadat announced through *Mayo*, the weekly organ of the National Democratic Party (NDP), that he was to devote all his time to countering the fundamentalist menace. He frequently appeared on television, speaking for hours at a stretch, often tongue-lashing 'his' Egyptians, which must have caused alienation. On 30 September 1981, he spoke to the nation with the chant 'with our lives and our blood we dedicate ourselves to you' ringing in the background.[85] On 5 September, when addressing a joint session of the People's Assembly and the Consultative Council (Majlis al-Shura), he spoke of Egypt being an 'island of democracy'.[86]

With tensions simmering to the boiling point between the Islamists and Sadat, the Egyptian leader authorised mass arrests of anyone being suspected as having anti-state views. One of the most volatile moments was on 2 September 1981, at the University of Assiut. Sadat sanctioned the arrests of more than 1,500 people for allegedly conspiring against the government. Amongst those arrested were Mohammed al-Islambouli, a prominent member of the campus community's Islamist society.[87] Little did Sadat know that a conspiracy against him was already brewing and that the arrest of al-Islambouli would contribute to the final part of a plot against him. The die had been cast.

Killing Pharaoh

On 6 October 1981, Egypt commemorated their battle with Israel in the 1973 October War, which is celebrated as an official holiday. Fighter planes flew in celebratory formation above the Grave of the Unknown Soldier in Heliopolis where a huge parade was taking place. Columns of soldiers marched past the reviewing stand, as President Sadat looked on. It was a proud day for him. He was in full uniform; epaulettes adorning his shoulders, dozens of medals clipped against his chest, and a blue sash displaying eleven gold stars celebrating his seniority. On his right, sitting next to him was Hosni Mubarak, his vice-president.

Mubarak was not one of the Free Officers, but he became a respected member of the military, a bomber pilot who over time established an exemplary record in the Egyptian air force. He rose quickly in the ranks, becoming commandant of the Air Academy in 1967 and air force chief of staff in 1969. Through distinguished action in the 1973 war, he was elevated to air marshal.[88] His highly impressive career in the air force was suddenly altered on 16 April 1975, when Sadat appointed Mubarak vice-president to quiet the fears of the powerful military establishment that Sadat's successor was not one of their own.

When the time came for the artillery unit to pass the reviewing stand, a military truck suddenly stopped, from which several uniformed men leapt and moved with precision and stealth towards the reviewing stand. Suddenly, one of the men, Captain Khalid al-Islambouli, brother of Mohammed al-Islambouli, threw a grenade followed by several more. His cohorts fired their weapons at the stand. Such was the audacity of the plotters that Sadat and many others thought it was part of the parade, especially as many of the grenades failed to detonate.[89] According to al-Zawahiri, the goal was to wipe out 'the upper echelons' of the Sadat administration.[90]

Pandemonium and panic ensued. People ran in multiple directions whilst Sadat was shot by one of the co-conspirators, Hussein Abbas, in the neck and chest.[91] Sadat fell to the floor, but another assassin, Abed al-Hamid, fired more shots from his rifle at Sadat.[92] Thirty seconds later, al-Islambouli reached the edge of the grandstand, where he continued to fire at the president. An additional twenty-seven were wounded, including Vice-President Hosni Mubarak. Al-Islambouli then shouted that he had 'killed Pharaoh'.[93] By calling Sadat 'Pharaoh' he was in effect declaring him as an apostate, following *jahili* beliefs, and therefore was condemned to death. Sadat was flown by helicopter to the Armed Forces Military Hospital in Maadi, coincidentally near al-Zawahiri's family home. However, Sadat had already passed away. The gunshots were fatal.

Al-Islambouli was part of the terrorist group al-Jihad, led by Muhammad Abd al-Salam Faraj. Al-Jihad sought to establish an Islamic state based on the Shariah by means of violent revolution. They pursued a policy to infiltrate the military to bring about a popular insurrection.[94] Faraj hailed from a lower-middle-class family in Beheira.[95] Unlike al-Banna and Qutb, Faraj did not have a religious education. He was an engineer but very interested in religion.[96]

Faraj advocated swift and forceful action to remove 'apostate regimes' through his political treatise, 'The Neglected Duty', which spoke of the necessity of waging jihad against Muslim rulers, who were deemed as the 'near enemy' or 'internal enemy', with the goal of establishing an Islamic state. For Faraj, jihad was not an end but an essential means to the end, the establishment of caliphate through violent revolution. Through this, he introduced the focus of first targeting the near enemy before looking at the 'far enemy' or 'external enemy'. The sole priority was first Egypt. He also justified targeting civilians, including children, to achieve the eventual goal of an Islamic state.[97]

Faraj raised fundamental issues regarding the legitimacy of a true Muslim ruler by delving into the past and citing the thirteenth-century jurist Ibn Taymiyyah as an authority and source to declare apostasy on Egypt's ruling establishment. Ibn Taymiyyah constructed a theory by which the invading Mongols hordes who destroyed the Abbasid Caliphate could still be portrayed as the enemy because even though they claimed to be Muslim, they followed their own customary laws and did not apply the Shariah. They were therefore 'apostates'. Applying history to the present reality, similar to Qutb, Faraj saw a link between the Mongols and the contemporary Arab rulers in their deviation from Islam.[98]

The use of the term 'pharaoh' by Faraj describes a ruler not as a Muslim but an 'apostate' who cannot be allowed to continue ruling over Muslims. With echoes of Qutb, 'The Neglected Duty' addresses the need and right to kill fellow Muslims in the name of jihad: 'First, to fight an enemy who is near is more important than to fight an enemy who is far. Second, Muslim blood will be shed in order to realise this victory.'[99] Faraj also claimed the existence of Western influences within the Islamic world is due to the very leaders he identified as needing to be removed.

In 1981, under the name of al-Jihad, a coalition of jihadist groups assembled several months before the assassination of Sadat. Faraj became the head of the clandestine partnership supported by a faction led by Kamal Habib, a graduate in economics. The other major component was the cadres from the Islamic Group (al-Gama'a al-Islamiyya) a radical Islamist alliance that emerged in the mid-1970s at university campuses. Its leader was Karam Muhammad Zuhdi, a student in the Institute of Cooperative Studies in Asyut. Most of al-Jihad's recruits were students from al-Gama'a.[100] The blind Shaykh Omar Abdel Rahman became the spiritual leader of the group. Rahman's significance was that he was an *'alim*, a professional man of religion, and therefore could issues *fatwas* with some authority.[101] Another key cog was Tariq al-Zumar, a colonel in Egypt's military intelligence, who eventually became his right-hand man. Al-Zumar came from a family of relatively high standing. His father was the village head (*'umda*) in Nahya, Giza. Al-Zumar also had an uncle who was a member of the upper house of the Egyptian parliament. In addition, four of his other relatives were senior officers in the Egyptian army.[102]

One of the group's first acts was to establish a its own Consultative Council to coordinate its activities. It drew parallels to al-Banna's structure of the Muslim Brotherhood. The Majlis al-Shura, with eleven members, was the supreme council of the movement.[103] The group also provided its members with social support, jobs and loans, which was designed to win hearts and minds and maintain loyalty. The group also focused its anger towards al-Azhar for being ideologically ineffective, failing to implement the Shariah and having no independence from the government.[104]

Al-Jihad had two main branches, with the one in Cairo under the leadership of Faraj, and the one in Upper Egypt, covering Minya and Asyut, under the control of Zuhdi.[105] Through its networks, al-Jihad was able to recruit more university students and graduates from all walks of life. Some were from underprivileged rural backgrounds, and others represented the upper echelons of society like al-Zawahiri, who was initially tasked with working with the Asyut branch.[106]

The defining and transformative moment in al-Zawahiri's life was the assassination of Sadat. He would often speak about it in later years. In his book *Allegiance and Disavowal*, al-Zawahiri stated that Sadat was killed for signing the peace treaty with Israel which recognised 'the state of Israel, acknowledged its capture of Palestine, prevented Egypt from assisting any country being subjected to Israeli aggression and disarmed Sinai to guarantee Israel's security'.[107] Al-Zawahiri would later emphasise the importance of killing Sadat: 'The Islamic movement began entering this phase of growth, spreading among its youth a deep awareness that the internal enemy was not less dangerous than the external enemy. This awareness began to strongly grow on the basis of clear legitimacy and bitter historical and practical experience.'[108] Al-Zawahiri recognised the need to 'capitalise' on young students' interest in attacking local secular government.

There were several reasons why the Sadat assassination succeeded. Tariq al-Zumar's military intelligence background provided a strong operational and organizational base. Another factor was that the civil and military intelligence services had been victims of rivalry between the Interior and Defence Ministries for years. As a result, the religious zealotry of soldiers who were to take part in the parade were inadequately checked.[109]

Major security failures also lay behind Sadat's assassination. He refused to wear body armour for reasons of personal appearance. He asked security forces and bodyguards to stay out of sight, and snipers who were positioned on nearby tall structures to protect the president, were instructed not to be visible lest the optics betray the president's unpopularity and the instability of his regime. Flaws of overconfidence and hubris, which had manifested themselves repeatedly during Sadat's career, finally proved his undoing. Lastly, luck played an important role. On the day of the parade, these three elements intersected.

In *Knights under the Prophet's Banner*, al-Zawahiri also underscored the success of the Islamic movement in killing Sadat, calling it a 'fundamental gain'.[110] He praised the 'courage of the fundamentalists' who attacked the regime and showed 'the offensive nature of the fundamentalist movement' along with the 'utter failure of the security services'.[111] However, the subsequent Islamist rebellion to seize power was crushed by the government's special forces. Thus, al-Zawahiri regarded Sadat's assassination as only a partial success for the Islamist movement, given that the Islamist uprising failed came up short because of 'poor planning and insufficient preparation.'[112] Nevertheless, it demonstrated the extensive growth of Islamist militancy under Sadat's rule and the serious consequences of leaving the movement unchecked.

Al-Zawahiri was made aware of the Sadat plot from around 9 a.m. on 6 October 1981, a few hours before it occurred.[113] Although he may not have been directly involved, his life would now take an irreversible turn, and the events on that fateful day would contribute to al-Zawahiri's infamy.[114] Following the death of Sadat, the second part of al-Jihad's actions focused on Asyut, where its faction, including al-Zawahiri, was tasked to immobilise the police and political leadership and take control of the radio building.[115] Al-Zawahiri was responsible for stockpiling weapons, explosives, and ammunition.[116]

The Asyut cell launched their attack on 8 October, the first day of the
Feast of the Sacrifice ('Id al-Adha), two days after Sadat's assassination. A
group of al-Jihad members attacked the police headquarters, where only
a few officers were on duty because of the holiday. They were all killed.
Al-Jihad occupied the headquarters and were not overpowered until the
next day when paratroopers were flown in from Cairo and crushed the rebellion.[117] Al-Jihad's staggered insurrection enabled the Egyptian military
to regroup and aggressively reassert themselves. Because of the delay in the
Asyut al-Jihad operation, al-Zawahiri said, 'the army succeeded in controlling the country and securing the regime'.[118]

Sadat's funeral was attended by dignitaries from all over the Western
world, including three American presidents—Jimmy Carter, Gerald Ford,
and Richard Nixon. However, it was boycotted by the entire Arab world
except for President Gaafar Nimeiry of Sudan. The funeral procession
passed through the same military review ground on which Sadat had been
shot. In fact, al-Zawahiri's cell briefly considered the viability of attacking
the funeral procession and killing his successor, Hosni Mubarak, and 'the
[former] Presidents of the United States and the leaders of Israel.'[119] Another
plot entailed trying to assassinate Mubarak whilst he was enroute to conduct Eid prayers in a mosque. The bombs and guns were ready and stored in
al-Zawahiri's medical clinic.[120] However, both plots did not develop beyond
the drawing board, as the Egyptian government arrested every Islamist and
jihadist in sight.

Defendant Number 113

Upon becoming Egypt's president, Hosni Mubarak, a military man, was
deeply perturbed that the jihadists version of Islam had replaced Arab nationalism as the ideology of mass mobilisation.[121] Anyone deemed to have
been an enemy of the Sadat regime or harbouring religious views that
could present a threat to the Egyptian state was rounded up. The prison
vans filled to the brim, and the Mubarak regime was going to make examples of all of them, without exception.

At the end of October 1981, perhaps anticipating that Mubarak's dragnet
on al-Jihad would catch him, Ayman al-Zawahiri planned another trip to
Pakistan to join his brother, Muhammad, who was also part of al-Jihad but

had moved to Pakistan before Sadat was assassinated. Ayman al-Zawahiri's other brother, Hussein, was accompanying him to the airport when the police, armed with additional powers following Sadat's death, halted their vehicle and took Ayman to the Maadi police station. In an incident that would define al-Zawahiri amongst young Egyptian jihadists for generations, the chief of the police station smacked him on the face, and al-Zawahiri whacked him back.[122] This time, al-Zawahiri's well-connected relatives were not going to be able to protect him. Following his arrest and incarceration at Mazra'at Tora prison, al-Zawahiri became known as 'the man who struck back'.[123]

The maximum-security Mazra'at Tora prison located in Cairo's Maadi suburb, where al-Zawahiri hailed from, became infamous for housing high-profile inmates tied to the Sadat assassination as well as for the inhumane conditions the prisoners were subjected to. It began with 'welcome parades' during which inmates are made upon arrival to walk through a gauntlet of prison guards where they are subjected to physical assault and electric shocks. Sounds of men screaming in distress could be heard every two to three minutes. They would then often face indefinite solitary confinement.[124]

Prison cells measuring 10 by 3 metres were filled with dozens of jihadists. The bedlam of being in a shoebox with so many people during the day was matched with sleeping on the concrete floor at night, competing for space not just with each other but also with the cockroaches and ants.[125] Sanitary conditions were traumatising. The toilet was a tiny, carved-out area demarcated by a dirty sheet with a lone squat-style toilet and a cracked tap with water constantly cascading down the wall. Garbage was piled next to the toilet and when pieces of rubbish would block the drain, raw sewage would often seep into the cell.

People would yell at each other, and on occasions it devolved into physical violence. However, what the Egyptian authorities didn't anticipate, or perhaps even care about, is that the conditions in the prison cells served as fertile ground for radicalising the detainees, including al-Zawahiri, and fuelling the rise of violent ideological extremism. Hundreds were standing trial, so the proceedings were held at one of the main halls of the Nasr City Exhibition Centre in north-east Cairo. The accused were spread across twelve cages. At a preliminary hearing each person was summoned to give his name, age, and profession. There was open defiance, many objecting to being tried before a civil court, which in their minds was un-Islamic and not under Shariah law.[126]

The first session of the Higher State Security Court that looked into the Sadat assassination, which became known as the 'Great Jihad' case, was held on 4 December 1982. More than 300 people stood accused of playing a role in the murder of Sadat and causing sedition. Many were shown on display behind bars. The accused were divided by the Egyptian authorities into two categories. The primary grouping of detainees included those accused of specifically plotting and planning the Sadat assassination, including Khalid al-Islambouli, Abdel al-Hamid, and Hussein Abbas as well as Muhammad Abd al-Salam Faraj and Omar Abdel Rahman. They were all tried for assassination, accessory to assassination, and incitement, with 'The Neglected Duty' produced in court as al-Jihad's manifesto and primary source evidence of intention to murder Sadat and sow insurrection.[127]

Before being sent to the gallows after conviction, al-Islambouli made his infamous confession: 'I killed him but I am not guilty. I did what I did for the sake of religion and of my country. I killed Pharaoh.'[128] For al-Zawahiri, 'Khalid al-Islambouli and his righteous comrades killed Sadat amid his soldiers in the most courageous operation in contemporary history and thus set a pattern for future operations that strike at the enemies of Islam and its corrupt apostates.'[129]

Faraj and the other primary plotters were also sentenced to death. As for Rahman, he faced trial twice for his role in Sadat's assassination. However, on both occasions, in 1982 and 1984, he was acquitted. Rahman, defending himself, denouncing secularism and asserted that the *ummah* had a duty to wage jihad. He condemned the impact Western materialism and sinful immorality had on Egyptian culture. Yet Rahman was very careful as to not state clearly that he supported the specific assassination of Sadat, although it was implied. On both occasions he faced trial, Rahman mesmerised the court. One person who was somewhat awestruck was al-Zawahiri, who recounted:

Shaykh Omar Abdel Rahman was roaring in the courtroom and speaking these words to the judge: 'I am a Muslim who lives only for his religion and is prepared to die for it. I can never remain silent while Islam is being fought on all fronts.' The trial was unique and full of surprises. But the most important events in the trial were the delivery by Dr. Omar Abdel Rahman of his famous testimony for three days. . . . [H]e put the judge in the dock, holding him responsible for the injustice which he might mete out on Muslims, warning him of Allah's wrath and punishment, and urging him to judge in accordance with the *Shariah*. Indeed, the judge did not issue any death sentence in that case. He cited extenuating circumstances, such as the defendant's just cause and noble intention.[130]

The second cluster of detainees were tired for being on the periphery of the plot without knowing the full details of how the assassination would unfold. As a result, almost every Islamist in the country was implicated in the plot. This included al-Zawahiri, who as defendant number 113 stood accused of plotting with the Asyut al-Jihad cell and handling weapons, including possession of a firearm which belonged to Tariq al-Zumar.[131]

The scenes at the trials were chaotic. The large number of jihadis were packed tightly into holding cells with a total absence of fear as they gawked defiantly from behind the confines of the steel bars, smirking grins plastered across insolent faces. They were loud and boisterous. It was as if they were celebrating an event and not about to face a possible death penalty. In front of them, their lawyers and government officials congregated the gallery.[132]

Al-Zawahiri was placed in the same prison cell as a former tank commander named Isam al-Qamari, whom he knew from before during the Military Technical College plot. Ironically, al-Qamari had become a respected officer in the Egyptian army and attained the rank of major. He smuggled weapons and ammunition from the armoury of Egyptian army bases for al-Jihad. Al-Zawahiri reminisced, 'He used to tell us that this Corps must be the Corps of Muslims since it teaches people how to win battles and deter the enemy.... Al-Qamari's outstanding performance in the Armoured Corps was noticeable. Isam [al-Qamari] gave all his time to studying and understanding military affairs and acquiring field experience in practice.'[133]

In his memoir, al-Zawahiri described al-Qamari as 'a noble person in the true sense of the word.... Most of the sufferings and sacrifices that he endured willingly and calmly were the result of his honourable character.'[134] Al-Qamari was oblivious that al-Zawahiri was already in custody when they arranged a meeting at the Zawya Mosque in Embaba, a district in Giza. Al-Zawahiri, arguably under duress, had betrayed al-Qamari, who was then apprehended when he reached the mosque. In *Knights under the Prophet's Banner*, al-Zawahiri makes a vague but important reference to the 'humiliation' of having to confess: 'The toughest thing about captivity is forcing the *mujahid*, under the force of torture, to confess about his colleagues, to destroy his movement with his own hands, and offer his and his colleagues' secrets to the enemy.'[135] Al-Zawahiri informing on al-Qamari was a traumatic event that propelled much of his career, which he spent trying to reclaim his dignity amongst the jihadists. The concepts of humiliation and shame are rooted in the doctrine of al-Qaeda shaped by al-Zawahiri.[136]

Whilst in jail, al-Zawahiri was electrocuted, stripped naked, beaten, and humiliated in every way possible. As Lawrence Wright added, 'The Egyptian authorities would bleed al-Zawahiri to extract information. Either you end up broken or full of rage. Some were not affected and became more focused and single-minded on rampage when the opportunity presented itself.'[137] The experience had a searing impact on al-Zawahiri's psyche—so much so that he published a short book on the subject, *The Black Book: Torturing Muslims under President Hosni Mubarak*. Much of it was a refutation of the interrogation report the Egyptian government produced which al-Zawahiri alleges was through torture.[138] The only aspect of al-Zawahiri's interpretation of his interrogation that matched the official Egyptian government account was when al-Zawahiri was asked what the goals of al-Jihad were. He answered, 'Jihad means removing the current government through resistance and changing the current regime to establish an Islamic government because it does not rule according to the Shariah of Allah, glorified be His name.'[139]

The international media closely covered the unfolding trial, and al-Zawahiri, who had the best level of English as well as a background as a physician, became the de facto spokesperson for all those incarcerated.[140] He understood early on the media's potential as a propaganda tool to spread information across a large audience. It was here that al-Zawahiri began his iconic hand gesture of using a single, raised index finger as the symbol of al-Jihad's cause. At the time, some interpreted it as either a sign of power and victory following Sadat's assassination or a disrespectful gesture to single out the Mubarak regime as the 'apostate enemy'. In fact, the index finger signified the defining doctrine of Islam known as *tawhid*, which professes the complete monotheism, unity, and uniqueness of God as creator and preserver of life upon which a Muslim's entire religious adherence resides. The *tawhid* forms part of the shahada, which is an affirmation of faith, one of the five pillars of Islam, and an intrinsic element of daily prayers: 'There is no God but Allah, Mohammad is the messenger of Allah.'

More specifically, al-Zawahiri's interpretation of the *tawhid* rejected any other view, including other Islamic interpretations, as idolatry. Al-Zawahiri's finger gesture was affirming a powerful ideology that demands the defeat of any form of pluralism whilst commanding obedience from other jihadists and symbolising himself as the supreme leader of this movement. Al-Zawahiri would use his index finger on countless subsequent occasions across the decades, and it would always be reflected in propaganda videos.

Al-Zawahiri's experience in prison produced the first stirrings of his drive for leadership and power. Whilst there he spoke openly on behalf of other prisoners.[141] Because of the prominence of his family, they were allowed to bring food via a servant to al-Zawahiri, who in turn would distribute it amongst his cellmates. This wasn't just about being generous, it was primarily about winning adherents to his cause.[142] Thanks to his language skills, al-Zawahiri was able to speak to foreign journalists from his cramped jail cell, and he chastised the Egyptian government for torturing prisoners and declared his fidelity to Islam. Clothed in a white robe with a grey scarf over his shoulder, al-Zawahiri shouted:

> Now we want to speak to the whole world! Who are we? Who are we? Why they bring us here, and what we want to say? About the first question, we are Muslims! We are Muslims who believe in their religion! We are Muslims who believe in their religion, both in ideology and practice, and hence we tried our best to establish an Islamic state and an Islamic society![143]

Between his pronouncements, the other prisoners chanted in Arabic, 'There is no God but Allah!' At one point they cried out, 'We will not sacrifice the blood of the Muslims for the Americans and the Jews.'[144]

Al-Zawahiri declared, 'We are not sorry, we are not sorry for what we have done for our religion, and we have sacrificed, and we stand ready to make more sacrifices!' The others would again shout, 'There is no God, but Allah!' He continued, 'We are here the real Islamic front and the real Islamic opposition against Zionism, Communism, and imperialism!' He paused, then stated, 'And now, as an answer to the second question, Why did they bring us here? They bring us here for two reasons! First, they are trying to abolish the outstanding Islamic movement . . . and, secondly, to complete the conspiracy of evacuating the area in preparation for the Zionist infiltration.'[145]

The prisoners removed their shoes and raised their clothes to exhibit the results of torture. Al-Zawahiri stated the torture occurred in:

dirty Egyptian jails ... where we suffered the severest inhuman treatment. There they kicked us, they beat us, they whipped us with electric cables, they shocked us with electricity! They shocked us with electricity! And they used the wild dogs! And they used the wild dogs! And they hung us over the edges of the doors ... with our hands tied at the back! They arrested the wives, the mothers, the fathers, the sisters, and the sons![146]

Al-Zawahiri identified several prisoners he claimed had died because of torture. 'So where is democracy?' he shouted. 'Where is freedom? Where is human rights? Where is justice? Where is justice? We will never forget! We will never forget!'[147]

Thus, al-Zawahiri loudly but articulately proclaimed in both Arabic and English to the world's media that he and his co-conspirators had undergone countless hours of torture from the Egyptian military in the Mazra'at Tora prison.[148] The mention of wild dogs referred to the alleged use of dogs to attack the prisoners' genitals. He claimed this was punishment because he and his co-conspirators were advocating an Islamic state to replace the corrupt Sadat regime. According to the journalist Anthony McDermott, who attended the trials, 'Occasionally, someone would climb up the side of the cage and call to his fellow prisoners to order and comply with the court procedures, which they did. This discipline was also a sign of what might have been possible for the jihadists if they had an actual plan following Sadat's assassination. Al-Zawahiri saw this as a powerful learning opportunity.'[149]

Al-Zawahiri displayed no signs of being subdued by the prison system. To the contrary, he stood proud, confident, and unashamedly defiant as he gave audience to waiting journalists, brandishing sheets of white paper containing a list of complaints that detailed the abhorrent and unacceptable way he was being treated by prison guards. He wore black-rimmed spectacles and had a brown moustache and beard. This image and vocal recording taken before the age of social media was to become iconic and would lionise him in the eyes of the jihadists.[150] Al-Zawahiri may not have been directly involved in the assassination of Sadat, but events in prison galvanised his status amongst the jihadists and was further amplified by the international media. He was the face of Egypt's jihadists.

Though al-Zawahiri was the most senior participant of the so-called Maadi gang, named after those who hailed from the Cairo suburb, out of respect he deferred to al-Qamari. Yassir al-Sirri, a member of the Maadi gang, commented, 'Al-Qamari saw that something was missing in Ayman but knew he had much potential.'[151] Al-Qamari saw that al-Zawahiri had zeal and drive but needed to assume a leadership role to fulfil his potential, which would directly challenge the Egyptian state.

The Mazra'at Tora prison ended up serving as an incubator for extremism. The dark gloominess of the prison walls combined with the awful sanitary conditions made the situation stark for all those who were incarcerated there. Despite spending time in prison, al-Zawahiri had filled out and was a slightly heavyset five feet, seven inches tall. His religious devotion was evident in his face. He sported a *zebiba*, which translates literally as 'raisin' and refers to the patch of hardened skin on a devout Muslim's forehead where it touches the mat during prayers. It gave al-Zawahiri an air of religious piety.[152]

During the trial, the state prosecutor asked al-Zawahiri what 'jihad' meant. Al-Zawahiri responded that it involved 'removing the current government through resisting it and changing the current regime to establish an Islamic government instead [Shariah law]'.[153] When asked how he would usurp the government with a Shariah one, al-Zawahiri retorted, 'Through a military coup. We were convinced that civilians and the military should cooperate to achieve this end.'[154] Al-Zawahiri explained that al-Jihad was endeavouring towards incremental stages of the revolution by recruiting educated individuals who could form part of a vanguard, whilst also continuing to pursue individuals within the military and security community. In this way, al-Zawahiri can be said to have aligned more with Qutb, who also wanted to wait until the right moment for revolution.

Al-Zawahiri went on to articulate that revolution required exhaustive planning and therefore requiring someone with a military background.[155] In court transcripts, al-Zawahiri highlighted how his beliefs diverged from those of the Muslim Brotherhood. He stood for the revolution and toppling of the Egyptian government with no dialogue or conciliation. Although the Muslim Brotherhood were blatantly opposed to Egyptian government policies, al-Zawahiri accused them of too often cooperating with the government, which only weakened the organization and failed to create an Islamic state. He condemned those who would drift from this mission and be co-opted by the state to receive privileges and rewards from the government.[156] Looking back years later, al-Zawahiri would argue that al-Jihad's hurriedly devised plan to assassinate Sadat and ignite a mass uprising was 'doomed to fail' because it was an emotional uprising that was poorly planned. The rebellion occurred two days after the assassination of al-Sadat and was based on an unrealistic plan to seize Asyut and then advance northward toward Cairo, disregarding any figures about the enemy's strength and materiel. . . . Thus the 1401 [1981] Hijra uprising ended with a fundamental gain—the killing of al-Sadat. The attempts that followed it were not successful because of poor planning and insufficient preparation.[157]

Al-Zawahiri was critical of the implementation of the doctrine behind Sadat's assassination as advocated by the ideologue Faraj. Faraj believed that the Egyptian *ummah* would overwhelmingly and spontaneously endorse the formulation of an Islamic state after the elimination of an 'apostate ruler', in this scenario, Anwar Sadat. However, this never transpired. For al-Zawahiri that was proof of why there needed to be greater dependence on a vanguard.[158]

The prosecution could not directly prove that al-Zawahiri was involved in the plot to assassinate Sadat. However, he was convicted for being a member of al-Jihad and for weapons possession and sentenced to three years in prison.[159]

Al-Zawahiri met many other leaders of the Egyptian underground Jihadist movement in jail, including the blind Shayk Omar Abdel Rahman, who was short and stocky, his eyes blank and milky, with an unkempt beard. Whilst al-Zawahiri and Rahman shared time in jail, they and their respective followers argued forcefully about the best strategy to advance the jihad. Although impressed by his defence at court, al-Zawahiri disputed with Rahman about who should take up the role of *amir* for al-Jihad. There was no doubt that egos and power also played a role in the disagreements. Al-Zawahiri questioned the legitimacy of Rahman's claim to the leadership mantle because he was blind.[160] There was also some scepticism about the level of Rahman's *fiqh*, with accusations amongst other jihadists that his 1972 graduate dissertation from al-Azhar entitled 'Repentance' was an unfocused study of a Qur'anic chapter.[161]

These differences eventually caused a permanent and consequential fracture, leading to al-Jihad splitting into two. Al-Zawahiri created the Egyptian Islamic Jihad (Tanzim al-Jihad) and had the backing of people like al-Qamari.[162] Also supporting al-Zawahiri was Ahmad Salama Mabruk. Like al-Zawahiri, Mabruk was born in Giza but raised in Cairo and was active in student politics. He would often visit Faraj at home for ideological guidance. Whilst he was studying at Cairo University, he befriended al-Zawahiri, and like many in al-Jihad who encouraged infiltration of state apparatuses, Mabruk joined the Egyptian army and briefly served in their intelligence division. However, his radical beliefs and open hatred of Sadat led to Mabruk's transfer to another unit before being discharged from the army entirely in 1981. Soon after, he conspired with al-Jihad in their goal to take over the country by assassinating Sadat. He had been tasked with trying to seize control of the Egyptian state-run national broadcaster's headquarters. However, he was unsuccessful and was arrested by the Egyptian authorities as part of their pursuit of all Egyptian jihadists. He was sentenced to seven years in prison.[163]

Meanwhile, Rahman took control of the faction that originally belonged to al-Gama'a, where he became its spiritual leader and was supported by Karam Zuhdi.[164] The EIJ adopted an elitist posture and rejected the notion of a mass movement, favouring the use of a vanguard to launch attacks against the Mubarak regime, leading to its eventual collapse. On the contrary, al-Gama'a advocated a more active community presence to organise violence whilst engaging in proselytizing.[165] Al-Zawahiri saw himself as the Egyptian exemplar to continue Qutb's legacy. The eminent scholar John Calvert points out that the 'similarities between Qutb's and al-Zawahiri's ideas reflected in al-Zawahiri's Tanzim al-Jihad were elitist and clandestine and was similar to Qutb's notion of the vanguard'.[166]

Meanwhile, politically, President Hosni Mubarak continued Sadat's policies, including the peace agreement with Israel, the free market orientation of the economy, and the reliance on the United States in economic and foreign policy matters. Mubarak demonstrated that he was a resourceful political leader, able to outsmart rivals and retain a stranglehold on power.[167] He earned the nickname of the 'bulldozer man' because of his somewhat sturdy and unforgiving appearance.[168] To show his religious credentials, Mubarak claimed he was avowedly Muslim. In a media interview he stated, 'I am a religious man but not an extremist. I am a very moderate religious man.'[169] Upon assuming power, Mubarak proclaimed a state of emergency, which would remain in place till 2012, some 31 years later.[170] Eventually, the Muslim Brotherhood accepted Mubarak's legitimacy and sought to take part in elections although their candidates could not openly declare themselves to be members of a banned organization, which Mubarak did not remove sanctions on.

3

The Holy Warrior

The Afghan–Arab Jihad

After serving three years in prison for handling weapons in the Sadat assassination, al-Zawahiri was eventually released in 1984 by the Mubarak regime. The Egyptian courts could not link al-Zawahiri directly to Sadat's assassination. When al-Zawahiri emerged from prison, he was a changed man, more intensely focused on fighting the Mubarak regime.

In 1985, he travelled to Amman, Jordan, before moving to Jeddah, Saudi Arabia, to work as a doctor at the Ibn al-Nafees clinic. Jeddah is also a commercial hub in the holy Hijaz region and a primary path for pilgrims travelling to Mecca. Al-Zawahiri used the opportunity to take the hajj, perhaps not realising this would be his last opportunity. He reunited with his brother Muhammad who was employed as an architect in nearby Medina. Al-Zawahiri also managed to see Sayyid Qutb's brother, Muhammad, who taught at the King Abdul Aziz University in Jeddah. Muhammad Qutb advocated and advanced Sayyid Qutb's anti-Western ideas on crusaderism. Albeit brief, al-Zawahiri's time in Saudi Arabia would help amplify what would be his priority, finding allies to help him defeat the Mubarak regime and imposing an Islamic state in Egypt. After that, he would leave Saudi Arabia for Pakistan for the third and most important time to join the tens of thousands of Arabs in their battle against the Soviet occupation of Afghanistan.[1]

Al-Zawahiri arrived in Peshawar in 1986 at a time when the anti-Soviet jihad was in full momentum. He drew a symbolic comparison between the Mubarak regime and a Communist superpower that also shunned religion as well as invaded a Muslim country. 'In Afghanistan the picture was completely clear,' al-Zawahiri wrote: 'a Muslim nation carrying out jihad under the banner of Islam, versus a foreign enemy that was an infidel aggressor

Doctor, Teacher, Terrorist. Sajjan M. Gohel, Oxford University Press. © Oxford University Press 2024.
DOI: 10.1093/oso/9780197665367.003.0003

backed by a corrupt, apostate regime [Egypt] at home.'[2] Although Egypt was not an ally of the Soviets anymore, for al-Zawahiri, there was no clear or substantive difference been the 'apostate' Egyptian government and the 'infidel' Soviet state.

Peshawar is a sprawling, boisterous city with a population of millions. It had been the winter capital of Afghanistan during the nineteenth century, and its residents were predominantly Pashtuns who had ended up on the wrong side of the border when Sir Mortimer Durand, a British civil servant, put pen to paper and drew up the artificial boundary separating the Pashtuns based on topography rather than ethnic fault lines. In the 1980s, Peshawar was home not just to many Afghan refugees but also to the headquarters of the Arab *mujahideen* groups fighting the Soviets.

Peshawar had altered considerably in the five years since al-Zawahiri's last visit. Some 2 million Afghan refugees had poured into what was then Pakistan's North-West Frontier Province. Some of the Arabs had financial resources by virtue of either coming from well-to-do families or benefiting from generous private donors from Arab Gulf oil states. The resources that flowed in also enabled Islamic charities and NGOs to operate in Peshawar.[3]

Even as refugees continued to stream eastwards into Pakistan, armed Afghan men returned westwards to join and supply the *mujahideen*. For the Arab fighters, there were three ways to get to Peshawar—roads, trains, and planes. The security on the roads between Pakistan's Punjab province and Peshawar was non-existent. There were no checkpoints or roadblocks, but this was intentional.

The other way was through the Peshawar railway station, which was a run-down, ramshackle affair. It had neither the junction status of Lahore nor the military garrison importance of Rawalpindi. There was a perceptible chill in the air from the proximity to the Himalayas. The Peshawar airport at the northwest border of Pakistan also evinced a unique atmosphere, with armed soldiers everywhere. The purpose was not to hinder would-be Arab *mujahideen* travelling to Peshawar but to ease their passage. One of the beneficiaries was al-Zawahiri, but he had issues with the distinctions being made between the Afghans and Arabs seeking to fight the Soviets.

> The name Arab Afghans is a tendentious description because these *mujahideen* have never been solely Arab, but *mujahideen* from all parts of the Islamic world, though the Arabs have been a distinctive element in this group. In this way the *mujahideen* young men and the jihadist movements came to know each

other closely, exchanged expertise, and learned to understand their brethren's problems.[4]

Peshawar's ancient market was like a conventional souk. It shimmered with sienna and coral colours, spicy odours, rhythmic sounds, and the agitated goings-on of a crowd that call all the senses into action. Languages from all over the Islamic world were spoken as volunteers to fight the Soviets were seeking justice and glory. Large signs dotted around the bazaar screamed in Pashto: 'U.S.S.R. OUT OF AFGHANISTAN'.[5] The go-to place in Peshawar to for the jihadists to congregate was centred on the Jami Asirya Madrasa.[6]

Al-Zawahiri returned to Pakistan during a time when the Red Army was mounting large sweep operations in the Afghan countryside, but Soviet military activity still consisted primarily of air strikes. Whole sectors of Afghanistan had become virtually 'free-fire' zones. In areas where the *mujahideen* attacked convoys, Soviet ground and air forces took particularly brutal acts of reprisal, raiding villages, destroying crops, and bayonetting women and children.[7] Al-Zawahiri and his wife Umm Fatima made their home in Hayatabad, an outlying western suburb of Peshawar where many other Arabs also settled, using the place as a launchpad to fight the Soviets in Afghanistan.[8]

The Peshawar *mujahideen* groups were backed by Pakistan's shadowy military intelligence agency, the Inter-Services Intelligence (ISI), who played a crucial role as conduits for supplying fighters in Afghanistan.[9] For al-Zawahiri, 'in the training camps and on the battlefronts against the Russians [Soviets], the Muslim youths developed a broad awareness and a fuller realization of the conspiracy that was being weaved. They developed an understanding based on Shariah of the enemies of Islam, the renegades, and their collaborators.'[10]

However, as the war was progressing, several Afghan commanders fighting on the front line began to attract followings of their own and constitute a political leadership in the resistance that the Pakistani military could not control or influence. Most prominent amongst them was Ahmad Shah Massoud, a young ethnic Tajik. Outwardly, Massoud may have appeared gentle and even tempered, but there was no mistaking the decades of experience in warfare. His imposing height and broad shoulders served to further enhance his legendary reputation as a skilled warrior.

Operating up and down the long Panjshir Valley in the Hindu Kush mountain range north of Kabul, Massoud and his forces repeatedly repelled the Soviet and Afghan army attempts to assert control over that strategic area. During 1983, having established a position of strength, Massoud entered a temporary ceasefire with Soviet forces, an act that provoked accusations and the ire of Arab *mujahideen* groups but enabled Massoud to begin coordinating strategy with non-Arab commanders operating outside of the Panjshir Valley. Massoud's efforts underscored that the allegiances and rivalries of *mujahideen* factions in Peshawar often had little to do with actual arrangements on the ground inside Afghanistan. Massoud's actions during this period planted the seeds of hatred that Arab *mujahideen* fighters would develop for him, especially al-Zawahiri.[11]

What Peshawar lacked in ethnic violence it made up for with almost daily car bombs planted by Soviet agents trying to destabilise Pakistan for sheltering and supporting the *mujahideen*. Dead bodies, victims of political vendettas, started turning up in Peshawar's sewage-filled canals. Wounded fighters would cross back into Pakistan, joining the growing number of amputees limping around the city. Crudely made posters of fallen commanders appeared on walls and electricity poles in increasing numbers. *Mujahideen* magazines would feature black-and-white photos of 'martyrs' to serve as inspiration. Khalid al-Islambouli, who had assassinated Egyptian president Anwar Sadat, was included in a 'caravan of martyrs' collage that showed images of long-dead Afghan activists, some of whom had cut their ideological teeth while studying and mingling with the Muslim Brotherhood in Egypt during the 1960s.[12]

By the time al-Zawahiri arrived in Peshawar, the United States and Saudi Arabia were bankrolling the war, and Egypt was supplying weapons. Hostels in Peshawar and recruitment centres around the world, often in the guise of refugee charities, attracted thousands to Pakistan.[13] Saudi Arabia's ardent support of the jihad, along with the Egyptian government's aid with arms, was common knowledge. What was less known was that many Egyptian 'volunteers' were political prisoners the government wanted to dispose of. Al-Zawahiri was one of them, and most of the Egyptians who came to fight in the Afghan jihad coalesced around him. They ruminated on current affairs and focused on the need to promote and spread an ideological revolution throughout the Muslim world.[14]

The Mubarak regime saw the transfer of jihadists to Afghanistan as a win-win situation for Egypt. They conveniently rid themselves of troublemakers whilst currying favour with the religious establishment and a sympathetic public. It was an equally ideal arrangement for the jihadis, as Afghanistan provided a safe and remote haven for their leaders to gain military experience that would prove useful when they would try to topple the Egyptian government. As al-Zawahiri put it in *Knights under the Prophet's Banner*, 'The opportunity to go to Afghanistan was a gift handed on a gold platter. I was always searching for a secure base for jihadist activity in Egypt because the members of the fundamentalist movement were the target of repeated security crackdowns.'[15]

The Egyptian jihadists were not entirely central to the overall Afghan-Arab community, and al-Zawahiri did not take it upon himself to be front-line commander. He had yet to establish the same status amongst the jihadists outside Egypt as he had attained inside his country.[16] In many ways, this played to al-Zawahiri's advantage. He did not seek the limelight and preferred to work behind the scenes, building up his list of contacts and allies quietly and steadily. The jihad against the Soviets may not have been the most intrinsic part of al-Zawahiri's life, but by being in Pakistan, his goal was to spread the jihad to Egypt, and the battle for Afghanistan was a means to that end by finding the right allies.

Al-Zawahiri worked as a surgeon in the Kuwaiti Red Crescent Society hospital.[17] It was here that he was reunited with Sayyid Imam al-Sharif, working alongside him as a surgeon. Al-Sharif, who was exonerated of the Sadat assassination, managed to slip out of Egypt in 1982. He moved to the United Arab Emirates, then to Saudi Arabia, and finally landed in Pakistan in 1983.[18] Al-Zawahiri then asked al-Sharif whether he would be willing to join the Egyptian Islamic Jihad (EIJ) to overthrow the Mubarak government and supplant it with an Islamic state. 'The matter calls for exhaustive canon law study and is not as simple as you imagine,' al-Sharif bureaucratically mused, noting that it was critical to ground the group in a proper understanding of Islam. Yet al-Zawahiri insisted that Sharif join, pointing out 'the importance of exploiting the Afghan jihad and the importance of bringing young men from Egypt to participate in it'.[19] For al-Zawahiri, the Afghan war offered an extraordinary opportunity to train members of Egyptian Islamic Jihad, who could eventually use their skills to overthrow the Egyptian government.

Despite some misgivings, al-Sharif became the EIJ's ideological leader and headed the group's Shariah committee. Al-Zawahiri was left to handle the strategy and tactical operations, as he deferred to al-Sharif's knowledge in *fiqh* to provide religious justification for EIJ's armed operations.[20] Al-Zawahiri wielded significant power within Egyptian jihadist circles, and some who joined the EIJ pledged allegiance directly to him.[21]

One of al-Sharif's most important contributions was the 1988 publication of a 500-page book, Treatise on the Pillar of Preparing Oneself for Jihad in the Way of Allah the Almighty. Originally written in Arabic whilst he was in Peshawar, it was translated into nine languages and read by jihadists from Algeria to Indonesia. The book's five chapters outline the EIJ's objectives, highlight its ideological underpinnings, and offer strategic and operational tenets. Sharif asserted that members of the *ummah* who did not commit to the jihad against 'apostate' rulers were 'impious' and equally part of the problem. Controversially, the book was also used as religious justification for jihadists to commit atrocities against civilians, including women and children.[22]

On the Front Lines

Al-Zawahiri would travel with the *mujahideen* and perform surgery on wounded fighters. He also opened the Islamic Jihad Office (Maktab Jihad al-Islamee) in Peshawar to serve both as a connecting hub for new *mujahideen* and a recruitment centre for Egyptian radicals. Peshawar was strategically important as it served as a gateway for the *mujahideen* into Afghanistan.[23] Al-Zawahiri stated:

> The Muslim youths in Afghanistan waged the war to liberate Muslim land under purely Islamic slogans, a very vital matter, for many of the liberation battles in our Muslim world had used composite slogans, that mixed nationalism with Islam and, indeed, sometimes caused Islam to intermingle with leftist, communist slogans.[24]

In Afghanistan, the scenario was blatant for al-Zawahiri, 'a Muslim people fighting [a jihad] under the banner of Islam against an infidel external enemy supported by corrupt internal system'. He added that the jihadist victory over the Soviets, a superpower, was viable:

> The most important thing about the battle in Afghanistan was that it destroyed the illusion of the superpower in the minds of the young Muslim *mujahideen*. The Soviet Union, the power with the largest land forces in the world, was destroyed and scattered, running away from Afghanistan before the

eyes of the Muslim youth. This *Jihad* was a training course for Muslim youth for the future battle anticipated with the superpower which is the sole leader in the world now, America.[25]

A seismic figure in the Arab-Afghan jihad was Abdullah Azzam, a Palestinian-Jordanian professor and a respected Islamist ideologue.[26] Azzam was a barrel-chested man whose enormous beard was dark in the centre with vertical grey streaks on either side. It blended in with his black-and-white checked Palestinian kaffiyeh that marked him as a combatant and ideologue. His fiery rhetoric and ability to articulate doctrine for jihad made him a commanding presence. His well-established formula for victory was 'Jihad and the rifle alone: no negotiations, no conferences, and no dialogues'.[27]

Azzam's relevance in developing the jihad against the Soviets would have a profound impact on Islamists around the world and long-term consequences for the West. Azzam would also become the centre of attention for al-Zawahiri. Azzam came from a village in Jenin when it was part of the British Mandate for Palestine.[28] His life was disrupted by the 1967 June War, when Israel occupied the West Bank, forcing Azzam and his family to flee to a refugee camp in the town of Zarqa in Jordan before relocating to the capital, Amman. Distressed by the circumstances of the Israeli occupation, he joined the local branch of the Muslim Brotherhood.[29]

Azzam shared the Muslim Brotherhood's cynicism of secular Arab nationalism largely promoted by Egyptians, including al-Zawahiri's uncle Abdul Rahman Azzam. He saw the left-leaning secular philosophy of the Palestinian Liberation Organization (PLO) as weak, enabling Israel to take advantage of a partitioned and lifeless *ummah*. In Azzam's view, the battle to 'liberate Jerusalem' was inherently part of the emancipation of the entire *ummah* from 'infidel' occupation.[30]

In the 1970s Azzam studied at al-Azhar in Cairo, and he graduated with a master's degree in Shariah and a PhD in the principles of jurisprudence (*usul al-fiqh*). Whilst in Egypt, Azzam familiarised himself with the ideological thought of Sayyid Qutb. However, he did not agree with Qutb's doctrine that Muslim regimes were in a total state of *jahiliyyah* and therefore ought to be deposed through jihad. Instead, Azzam recognised Qutb's belief that Western ideas and beliefs should be directly opposed and confronted, violently if needed.[31]

Azzam also came into contact with Sayyid Qutb's brother, Muhammad, in Saudi Arabia.[32] However, it was another influential member of Qutb's extended family who shaped Azzam. Kamal al-Sananiri, a prominent Saudi-based Egyptian ideologue, handled the political affairs of the Muslim Brotherhood as well as the Saudi kingdom's support of the Arab *mujahideen* factions. Kamal al-Sananiri was married to Sayyid Qutb's sister Aminah. Like Qutb, al-Sananiri was incarcerated during Nasser's clampdown on the Muslim Brotherhood in 1954 and subsequently spent twenty years in prison. As a brother-in-law of Sayyid Qutb—which gave him legitimacy in the eyes of the jihadists—al-Sananiri rallied the Arab *mujahideen* groups, making trips to Pakistan to evaluate the situation of the Afghan jihad.[33]

Tellingly, al-Sananiri's early role in liaising with the Afghan *mujahideen* was acknowledged by al-Zawahiri: 'Although I never knew al-Sananiri personally, the evidence of his presence in Peshawar and Afghanistan used to precede us wherever we went. He had played a pioneer role in establishing the hospital where we worked and whenever we met with *mujahideen* leaders, they would speak of his assistance to them and his efforts to unite them.'[34]

Around September 1981, al-Sananiri went to Mecca, Saudi Arabia, for the hajj. Whilst there, he happened across Abdullah Azzam, who at that point was a lecturer at the King Abdul Aziz University in Jeddah and former leader of the Jordanian Muslim Brotherhood.[35] Al-Sananiri shared with Azzam his experiences in Afghanistan and encouraged him to come with him to Islamabad, Pakistan, once he had returned to Egypt to bring his family to join him there. However, soon after the meeting with Azzam, al-Sananiri was arrested in the massive October 1981 crackdown following the assassination of Sadat. He died in detention, and according to al-Zawahiri, 'Al-Sananiri was killed by acts of torture personally carried out by Hasan Abu-Basha, director of the State Security Investigation Department and later interior minister.' Al-Zawahiri then lamented the Muslim Brotherhood's choice not to 'avenge his blood, although they knew all the details about the way he was killed'.[36]

Although he was pious and intellectual rather than a combatant, Azzam withdrew from his successful academic career to support the Afghans in their battle against the Soviet occupation. He was granted a leave of absence from the King Abdul Aziz University and travelled to Afghanistan alone and gradually took over as the liaison between the Arab militants and the Afghan *mujahideen*. Azzam's first prospect to partake in the Arab-Afghan jihad came when he took up a teaching role at the International

Islamic University in Islamabad in November 1981. From Islamabad, Azzam frequently visited Peshawar to be in close proximity to the *mujahideen*. He met several *mujahideen*, wrote articles, and gave speeches that publicised their mission.

Azzam developed a particularly close relationship with the Afghan Tajik leader Ahmad Shah Massoud, whom he described as 'the most brilliant commander in Afghanistan'.[37] Massoud was a lanky, charismatic commander of the Panjshir Valley, recognised by his trademark *pakol* hat. Azzam's friendship with Massoud would carry enormous symbolic relevance 20 years later. In 1984, Azzam established the Services Office (Maktab al-Khadamat, MAK) to provide lodging, training, religious guidance, and logistical assistance for the Arab volunteers flocking to Pakistan from around the Islamic world to aid the *mujahideen* in their jihad.[38]

Aiding him in this endeavour was Osama bin Laden, the son of a wealthy Yemeni-Saudi construction magnate. Bin Laden was motivated by the Soviet occupation of Afghanistan. They first met when Azzam lectured at King Abdul Aziz University in Jeddah. Azzam handed the administrative duties to bin Laden.[39] Working with Azzam, bin Laden offered housing and monthly remuneration for every individual who joined their jihad in Afghanistan. Prior to this, bin Laden had arranged the journey of Saudi fighters from Jeddah through his House of Helpers (Bait ul-Ansar), which served a similar function to Azzam's MAK.[40]

Bin Laden had gone through a metamorphosis from a spoilt rich young man into the front-line *mujahideen* leader that he believed was his destiny. Gone were the Western clothes he wore in Beirut nightclubs. He now preferred traditional Arab robes. Whilst in Pakistan, bin Laden transferred a portion of his personal fortune to the MAK. Some of the funds went into the publication of *Al-Jihad Magazine*, which was circulated throughout the Arab world and beyond to increase awareness and understanding of the jihad against the ungodly Soviets.[41]

For Azzam the MAK's purpose was to 'gather the Arabs and send them inside Afghanistan . . . to save them from the political games of the Afghans'.[42] Azzam inspired in bin Laden the belief that only jihad could unite Muslims and, through that help, reverse the tide of Muslim humiliation around the world. Bin Laden pledged loyalty to Azzam in April 1986 as they fought side by side against the Soviets. Through Azzam's ideological zeal and bin Laden's funding, MAK assumed a commanding role within the community of *mujahideen* volunteers fighting in Afghanistan, proliferating globally, with bureaus dispersed across Europe and North America.[43] Azzam's greatest feat was disseminating the jihad amongst the Arabs during the war against the Soviets, bringing in some 35,000 from the Middle East and North America.[44] What allowed for Azzam's success in recruiting jihadists from around the world was the political crackdowns on Islamists in their respective countries. Azzam was able to utilise this to influence the transnational brand of jihadism we know today.[45]

Azzam articulated his vision of jihad in two discourses, which he declared as *fatwas*: *Defence of the Muslim Lands* and *Join the Caravan*. Azzam's period at al-Azhar in Egypt educated him to an appropriate level to issue a *fatwa*. The central ethos of these texts provided religious sanction that the Afghan jihad represented the concern of Muslims everywhere.[46] Azzam organised and galvanised a plethora of volunteers from all over the Islamic world. He wasn't a tactician or a strategist on the battlefield, but his warrior-scholar reputation resonated with many of the Arab *mujahideen*, who would read his treatises and listen to his sermons disseminated via audio cassettes.

Azzam pointed out that it was an individual religious duty (*fard'ayn*) for Muslims, as well as a collective community responsibility (*fard'kifaya*), to support the jihad against the Soviets because the Afghans were powerless against the onslaught of ungodly invading forces. Azzam would frame this as defensive jihad.[47] According to Azzam, 'If they fail to repel the infidels due to a lack of resources or due to indolence then the duty spreads to those behind, and if they fail, to those beyond them until the enemy is finally repelled.'[48] For Azzam, jihad could take precedence over other pillars of Islam, such as the hajj, especially when Muslim land is occupied and is in need of 'liberation' by people who share the same faith.[49]

Al-Zawahiri had a very tense relationship with Azzam, based more on personality than ideology. In fact, from the instant al-Zawahiri arrived in Afghanistan, he deliberately avoided him and refused to show him any respect, despite Azzam's burgeoning reputation amongst the Arab *mujahideen*.[50] Instead, al-Zawahiri focused on getting close to bin Laden. Bin Laden sometimes gave speeches at the Red Crescent where al-Zawahiri worked, but at that point, the two were more acquaintances than friends. Bin Laden had a stronger alliance with Azzam. Al-Zawahiri recalled one of his earliest encounters with bin Laden:

> I remember that he [bin Laden] visited us in those days at the Kuwaiti-funded Al-Hilal Hospital in Peshawar and talked to us about those lectures of his. I remember that I told him: 'As of now, you should change the way in which you

are guarded. You should alter your entire security system because your head is now wanted by the Americans and the Jews, not only by the communists and the Russians [Soviets], because you are hitting the snake on its head.[51]

The MAK guest houses were now facing competition with the rising numbers from the EIJ led by Sayyid Imam al-Sharif and al-Zawahiri.[52] Al-Zawahiri refused to even pray behind Azzam, he had to be in front and told others not to pray with Azzam at all. At the same time al-Zawahiri would accuse Azzam and the MAK of being corrupt or working for foreign powers.[53] However, al-Zawahiri's reputation amongst the *mujahideen* was also questioned. Those loyal to Azzam have claimed al-Zawahiri was not regarded as a *mujahid* but instead someone who remained focused on Egypt.[54] Al-Zawahiri wasn't ashamed of his focus on Egypt. He believed that the Afghan jihad had served its purpose as an external incubator for the political, religious, and military mobilisation of the Arab *mujahideen*, who now had a historic opportunity to take this fight back home to Egypt and Syria.

Azzam was more focused on building an Islamic army in Afghanistan. Both al-Zawahiri and Azzam saw bin Laden as crucial to their plans—the question was whose agenda bin Laden would choose to support. Although relations between bin Laden and Azzam were cordial, there were areas of dispute. Bin Laden became exasperated by the bickering and corruption that was engulfing the MAK.[55] A particular point of contention was Azzam's nepotism in the MAK bureaucracy.

In was perhaps inevitable that bin Laden and al-Zawahiri would form a bond because of their similar family backgrounds. Bin Laden came from a wealthy industrialist family, and al-Zawahiri, who was several years his senior, hailed from a prominent family in Egypt. Both were educated, pious, and claimed to be politically disenfranchised, despite their elitist backgrounds. Whilst in Afghanistan, issues such as fighting apostasy and ushering in Shariah resonated between these two men. They tried to develop and synchronise their respective ideas and goals.[56] One complemented the other. Bin Laden had the resources but sought direction, and al-Zawahiri had the long-term strategic plan and ideological tract to support it.

At the time, al-Zawahiri and the EIJ were fighting a losing battle with their Egyptian rivals al-Gama'a for reputation, resources, and recruits. However, in the affluent Saudi, al-Zawahiri saw a chance to reignite his own battle against the Mubarak regime. For al-Zawahiri, bin Laden was a saviour with nearly limitless financial support and open to new ideas. Bin

Laden had a general knowledge of Islam, but he didn't understand the issues of apostasy that had grown within the jihadist movement.[57] According to Lawrence Wright, 'Bin Laden was acting as a *mujahideen* aimlessly to no real effect. Al-Zawahiri already had a terrorist organization, which may not have been well led, but it existed in exile and surrounded bin Laden. The EIJ and al-Zawahiri became the nucleus for bin Laden as they provided a plan, direction, and experienced operatives.'[58]

Al-Zawahiri would find other allies in his agenda. Ahmed Khadr had grown up in Egypt but migrated to Canada in his 20s to study computer programming at the University of Ottawa, where he obtained a master's degree.[59] After the Soviet invasion of Afghanistan Khadr travelled to Pakistan to work as a volunteer in the Afghan refugee camps, joining a Canadian-based charity in Peshawar, Human Concern International. In the mid-1980s Khadr and his wife Maha Elsamneh moved their family to Peshawar but returned regularly to Canada to raise funds at mosques for their projects.[60] Khadr would claim that the money raised through his charity in Canada would be used to purchase livestock to sustain families and purchase artificial limbs for children disabled by landmines.[61]

Khadr also worked for a Kuwaiti organization called Islamic Call Committee (Lajnat al-Dawa), one of the largest charities responsible for major reconstruction projects in Pakistan and Afghanistan.[62] In Peshawar, Khadr worked with Abdullah Azzam, bin Laden, and al-Zawahiri; the latter was working at the Red Crescent hospital treating the wounded *mujahideen* where Khadr's wife worked as a volunteer. Khadr was impressed by al-Zawahiri and sympathetic to his fight against the Mubarak government. The two men became close friends and would spend long evenings talking about the plight of the Afghans and their aspirations for an Islamic government in Egypt.[63]

In late 1986, during a trip to the front lines against the Soviets near Khost, bin Laden concluded that he needed to begin the process of creating a new Arab movement.[64] Subsequently, bin Laden instituted a training camp in Zazi, Paktika province, in eastern Afghanistan, about ten miles from the Pakistani border. The base was known as al-Masada (Lion's Den).[65] He prioritised enlisting support from the Egyptian contingent of the *mujahideen*, who were fighting alongside the Paktika-based Afghan warlord Jalaluddin Haqqani.[66] They had not been engaged with MAK's activities.[67]

Bin Laden was accompanied by several Egyptians, including his military chief and confidante Mohammed Atef, Abu Ubaidah al-Banshiri, and al-Zawahiri. Al-Banshiri was essential in helping to set up the infrastructure for what would eventually be known as al-Qaeda.[68] Atef and al-Banshiri were also the key cords tying al-Zawahiri and bin Laden. During the spring of 1987, it was from the Lion's Den that bin Laden was involved in the Battle of Zazi against the Soviets. Although the outcome was a stalemate, bin Laden arose from it as a *mujahideen* hero due to his leadership skills in uniting a diverse group of Arabs.[69] It was at this moment that he believed an Arab vanguard was best positioned to withstand and repel the Soviets because they were zealous and pious compared to their Afghan counterparts, who seemed less focused.[70]

Al-Zawahiri was able to build a relationship with bin Laden by acting as his personal doctor. In this role, al-Zawahiri had ongoing intimate access to build a relationship with bin Laden. Because of his chronic health problems, bin Laden became dependent on al-Zawahiri for medical care, even on the battlefield.[71] Al-Zawahiri was trying to revitalise his EIJ against the Egyptian regime and was drawn to bin Laden's financial resources and his burgeoning reputation amongst the jihadists.[72] As Lawrence Wright points out, 'Al-Zawahiri wasn't interested in being the leader but wanted someone to fund him. At the same time, Azzam was bleeding bin Laden financially. Al-Zawahiri wanted bin Laden but did not need Azzam hanging around.'[73]

Bin Laden respected al-Zawahiri for his experience and track record in the Islamist movement. At the same time, al-Zawahiri was fixated on uncoupling bin Laden from Azzam's MAK, which he believed was haemorrhaging bin Laden's resources on ventures inconsequential to fighting the jihad against the Soviets. Problems also began to emerge with bin Laden and Abdullah Azzam. The MAK's failure of bureaucratic oversight left projects incomplete amidst corruption allegations that were becoming louder. Despite frustrations with Azzam and facing pressure from the Egyptian contingent, bin Laden did not seek to openly fall out with Azzam. He did, however, keep his own counsel whilst accepting that Azzam's influence was waning.[74]

Al-Zawahiri sought to add to these tensions.[75] Atef, al-Banshiri, al-Zawahiri, and al-Sharif lobbied bin Laden of the need to focus the future battles against Arab regimes.[76] Al-Zawahiri also advised bin Laden to bulk up his own security because of his increasing notoriety and began surrounding bin Laden with lieutenants from the EIJ.[77] The Egyptians who were loyal to al-Zawahiri included his deputy Mohammed Atef and the group's trainer, Saif al-Adel, whose real name is Mohammed Salah al-Din Zaidan. Atef would become bin Laden's brother-in-law.[78]

This collection of Egyptian al-Qaeda members with long-held ties to him would prove seminal to al-Zawahiri's strategy during the 'exile years', particularly when it came to moving the jihadist battle back to the Middle East and to 'internal enemy' targets. Those individuals tried to redirect bin Laden's capital to their agenda.[79] The Saudi faced criticism from the Egyptians cadres for being considered soft and indifferent about removing 'apostate rulers' by force.[80]

Along with Azzam, al-Zawahiri still faced a parallel challenge with the leaders of al-Gama'a, who sent a delegation to Peshawar in 1987. They were led by Mohammed al-Islambouli, brother of one of Sadat's assassins, Khaled al-Islambouli. The faction of al-Gama'a was tasked to confront and challenge al-Zawahiri directly. At the same time, news reached al-Zawahiri that his close ally Isam al-Qamari, who had escaped from prison, had been killed in an encounter with the Egyptian police. Clearly troubled in retelling the story, al-Zawahiri revealed, 'He [al-Qamari] was hit in the stomach, and he fell. His companions returned to carry him, but he declined and gave them the pistol he had. He ordered them to continue to run away. He died on the spot.'[81]

Al-Zawahiri was frustrated by bin Laden's lack of support for his bid to be seen as the head of the Egyptian jihadists. 'The young men are willing to give up their souls, while the wealthy remain with money,' he wrote in *The Word of Truth* (*Kalimat Haq*), an Islamist magazine.[82] Meanwhile, bin Laden himself was frequently infuriated by the tensions between the EIJ and al-Gama'a.[83] The situation flared up between the two Egyptian terrorist groups, which was reflected in the publication of their respective magazines, *The Holy Fighters* (*Al-Murabitoon*), by al-Gama'a, and *The Opening* (*Al-Fath*), by al-Zawahiri. Both publications traded insults and accusations of corruption. Tension intensified with mutual accusations of apostasy to tit-for-tat assassinations.[84] Paradoxically, whilst the EIJ and al-Gama'a were often at odds, many of their members had familial ties to both groups and even co-operated temporarily for convenience and operational necessity.[85]

Amidst these very public tensions between the different Egyptian jihadist groups, a narrative began to emerge of the 'evil Egyptians', implying these radicals had a negative, overbearing, and damaging influence on other Islamist groups, through their ideology and doctrine, which intensified political and social instability and drew the wrath of various Arab governments whom the Egyptians were seeking to overthrow. There were rivalries with all these different factions, and other Arab Islamists resented the Egyptians for their overbearing attempt to dominate the jihadist agenda. According to the scholar Fred Halliday, 'The evil Egyptian narrative is really big. Why is there radicalism in Saudi Arabia? It's because of Egyptian teachers who were here. And the Egyptians brought all these evil ideas into our [Saudi] pure society. And you see that throughout the Middle East. It's a fascinating macro-narrative of the different factions.'[86]

Amongst the plethora of characters swarming across Afghanistan and Pakistan, one would have a deep and indelible relationship with al-Zawahiri. Jalaluddin Haqqani was born in Karezgay, located in the Zadran District of Paktia province, Afghanistan, in 1939. In 1964, he began his education at the Darul Uloom Haqqania in Akora Khattak, Pakistan, and earned the religious honorific title of *mawlawi* (master) after receiving a doctorate in 1970. The Haqqani part of his name is directly associated to the seminary, which also became the finishing school for tens of thousands of jihadists from Afghanistan and Pakistan.[87]

After the overthrow of Afghan king Mohammad Zahir Shah in 1973 and the subsequent rise of his cousin, Mohammed Daoud Khan, Haqqani emerged as a vocal critic of the new regime. He moved to Pakistan. After the fall of President Mohammed Daoud Khan in the April 1978 Saur Revolution and the installation of the pro-Soviet People's Democratic Party of Afghanistan (PDPA), Haqqani joined the ranks of the Afghan *mujahideen* group Islamic Party of Khalis (Hezb-e Islami Hezb-e Islami Khalis), led by its commander Mohammad Yunus Khalis.[88]

The Hezb-e Islami Khalis factions were highly autonomous, and this decentralized structure allowed Haqqani to take command of a force of *mujahideen* fighters who adopted the name of the Haqqani Network. Throughout the 1980s, the Haqqani Network fostered relationships with Pakistan's intelligence agency, the ISI, a close affiliation that has been maintained ever since. The Haqqani Network received extensive resources, arms, and training from the ISI. The ISI's supply chain to the *mujahideen* was primarily routed through Khost and Paktia, where Haqqani maintained significant influence.[89] He established a series of training and support bases in North

Waziristan, Pakistan, with the help of the ISI and later created his own institution there, the Fountainhead of Knowledge (Manba'-al-Uloom).[90]

Haqqani also forged ties with multiple private Arab donors in the Persian Gulf and the Egyptian faction of the Arab *mujahideen*. According to Nick Pratt, who served as an officer in the US Marine Corps and commanded a Central Intelligence Agency (CIA) Special Operations Group during the Soviet occupation of Afghanistan, 'the Haqqani Network was the first *mujahideen* group to incorporate Arab volunteers. It was here that Haqqani became friends with bin Laden, al-Zawahiri and Atef.'[91] Through these ties, Haqqani met one of his wives, who was from Kuwait and of Yemeni origin.[92] The Canadian diplomat Chris Alexander, who served as the Ambassador to Afghanistan, pointed out, 'Jalaluddin Haqqani and his sons were regarded as the most ruthless, most kinetic, and therefore most effective of the ISI military proxies operating in Afghanistan.'[93]

Embarrassingly, Haqqani was once lauded by the US Embassy in Islamabad as the finest Afghan *mujahideen*.[94] Furthermore, former Texas congressman Charlie Wilson, who played a critical role in ensuring that the *mujahideen* and ISI received significant US funding to defeat the Soviets was also full of praise for Haqqani. Recalling his 1987 visit to Afghanistan, Wilson commented, 'I adored Haqqani. When I was in Afghanistan, Haqqani was the guy who made sure I would get out. He was a marvellous leader.'[95]

Wilson was escorted to the Haqqani base in Paktia province, across the border from Pakistan, by the ISI's Afghan bureau chief Brigadier Mohammad Yousaf.[96] Yousaf oversaw the ISI's Afghanistan operations from 1983 to 1987. His role illustrated the nexus between Haqqani and the Pakistani army. This relationship would stand the test of time.[97]

The Mole

Upon his release from an Egyptian prison, al-Zawahiri understood that the United States intended to firmly support the Mubarak regime. To undermine and otherwise damage the Egyptian government whilst he was in Afghanistan, al-Zawahiri needed to recruit people who could embed themselves within the US security apparatus instead of Egypt's. It was at this moment that al-Zawahiri's path would cross with Ali Mohamed, who hailed from a devout farming family in Kafr el-Sheikh, Lower Egypt.[98]

Just like his father, Mohamed joined the Egyptian Army in 1971 after his enrolment in the Egyptian Military Academy.[99] He eventually joined the military's special forces.

In 1981, Mohamed clandestinely joined al-Jihad, the very same year it assassinated President Anwar Sadat in Cairo, which seems unsurprising considering the extent to which Mohamed's military career had been permeated by his religious fervour. It made Mohamed a target of the Mubarak regime, which was eager to purge the military of potential jihadists. Mohamed's association with the EIJ raised suspicions. Consequently, he was discharged in 1984 with the rank of major. He was 'bitter' but, soon after, he would attract the attention of al-Zawahiri. Ali Mohamed's military training would become a strong determinant of his value to al-Zawahiri and eventually al-Qaeda.[100]

Soon after his discharge from the army, Mohamed pledged a *ba'yah*, an Islamic oath of allegiance, to both al-Zawahiri and the EIJ.[101] The practice of *ba'yah* is one of the traditional methods for sanctifying relations between individuals and entities in the Muslim world, and it was profoundly important for al-Zawahiri to maintain loyalty. With the words, 'You're my *shaykh*. You're my *Emir*. . . . I pledge my *ba'yah* to you,' Mohamed began his career as a de facto spy. He quickly proved his worth by obtaining a job at EgyptAir, the Egyptian state airline.[102] The scholar John Calvert pointed out that 'Qutb's distinction between "authentic/inauthentic" Muslims finds resonance in al-Zawahiri's refashioned concept of "loyalty and enmity". Both men preached the offensive jihad and were unapologetic about it: the vanguard of true believers must strike the powers that be. Both foregrounded the idea of martyrdom.'[103]

For the next year and a half, Mohamed's role as a counter-terrorism security adviser enabled him to obtain sensitive information about airline security and the existing gaps for the EIJ, who wanted to explore the potential of hijacking a plane.[104] Under al-Zawahiri's orders, Mohamed gained abilities with which he would eventually excel in training terrorists to hijack planes.

So impressed was al-Zawahiri that he trusted Mohamed with a more challenging task: infiltrate the US intelligence services.[105] In 1984, Mohamed presented his services to the CIA Cairo station and was quickly assigned to Hamburg, Germany. However, his success was short lived. Having been sent to infiltrate a Hezbollah-linked mosque, Mohamed announced himself as a CIA recruit. Seeing him as a liability, the agency dropped him.[106] Despite the setback with the CIA, the Federal Bureau of Investigation (FBI) had no knowledge of Ali Mohamed's activities, as everything was compartmentalised. This enabled Mohamed to enter the United States in 1985.[107]

Prior to arriving via a flight from Athens to New York, Mohamed met his future wife, Linda Lee Sanchez. The Egyptian jihadist and the medical technician from Santa Clara, California, would wed six weeks later in Reno, Nevada.[108] In August 1986, almost a year after his arrival to the United States, Mohamed enlisted in the US Army. Under the name of Ali Aboualacoud Mohamed, the former Egyptian special forces major thrived and rose quickly through the ranks.[109] Such was his exemplary performance that he received both an Army Commendation Medal and an Army Achievement Medal.[110]

He was then sent to the Special Operations Command at Fort Bragg, North Carolina, where he had coincidentally trained once whilst he was serving in Egyptian army years ago. At Fort Bragg, Mohamed was elevated to supply sergeant for the Fifth Special Forces Group and subsequently seconded as an instructor at the John F. Kennedy Special Warfare Center as a teacher on Islamic culture and Middle East politics.[111] In addition to Arabic, Mohamed was fluent in English, French, and Hebrew. Al-Zawahiri's mole had earned the trust of the people around him and was able to not only provide intelligence to the EIJ but also cause significant harm to human life if he was ordered to do so.[112]

Mohamed's accelerated rise paralleled his ascent within EIJ. Indeed, it was not only his skills as an exemplary soldier that he brought from his time in the Egyptian army, but also his visible devotion of praying five times a day and undertaking to memorise the Qur'an.[113] What's more, his unabashed piety was evident when speaking his mind, most notably on his support for the assassination of Sadat.[114] Occasionally, he would give away such radical views to his American colleagues as his opinion that Sadat was a traitor and deserved to die.[115] With a reputation as an 'exemplary soldier', however, Mohamed took advantage of his skills to advance al-Zawahiri's agenda.

In 1987, soon after Mohamed enlisted in the US Army, al-Zawahiri requested that he travel to Pakistan to train Arab fighters.[116] Dutifully, Mohamed complied. Without revealing his destination, he obtained authorisation to travel overseas to Paris during his upcoming 30-day leave.

After a month of honing the skills of Arab recruits in navigation, survival techniques, and weapons identification in Pakistan, Mohamed returned to Fort Bragg.[117]

Beginning in the spring of 1989, Mohamed would meet with EIJ members in New Jersey and New York to provide military training intel.[118] The group would meet in the Masjid al-Salaam in New Jersey and drive to several shooting ranges they frequented across upstate New York, Connecticut, New Jersey, and Pennsylvania. The cell would train using AK-47s and other weapons[119] Mohamed would also use these trips as an opportunity to give his EIJ contacts documents he had stolen from the JFK Special Warfare Center,[120] including assault rifle and antitank weapon operation manuals as well as Special Forces training manuals.[121] Many of these documents would be used as a template for training manuals in the various Afghan camps in the 1990s, like the manual *Military Studies in the Jihad against the Tyrants* al-Zawahiri was developing.[122]

Mohamed's activities with the EIJ go beyond simply passing sensitive information along. He was al-Zawahiri's most lethal asset inside the US military. On 9 November 1989, Mohamed was 'honourably discharged from active duty'.[123] Praise for his 'patriotism, valour, fidelity, and professional excellence' were amongst the commendations in his file,[124] and Mohamed returned to live with his wife in Santa Clara, as a member of the US Army Reserves.[125] From this point onward, Mohamed's involvement with al-Zawahiri and bin Laden would intensify especially as the Saudi increasingly depended on the Egyptian doctor and his EIJ assets.

Soviet Withdrawal

After nine years of occupation, Soviet troops pulled out of Afghanistan in mid–February 1989, leaving behind the embattled Najibullah regime. The George H.W. Bush administration initially pushed to bring more moderate forces to power, but the half-hearted effort was quickly abandoned. Many Arab fighters, including al-Zawahiri, saw the victory in Afghanistan as the first step in a larger jihad:

> A further significant point was that the jihad battles in Afghanistan destroyed the myth of a [superpower] in the minds of the Muslim *mujahideen* young men. The USSR, a superpower with the largest land army in the world, was

destroyed and the remnants of its troops fled Afghanistan before the eyes of the Muslim youths and as a result of their actions.[126]

After the Soviets announced their intention to withdraw from Afghanistan, the Arab *mujahideen* led by bin Laden needed to decide their ideological focus. An important new strategy had emerged during the Afghan jihad that defied Azzam and sought to alter the jihad towards *jahili* regimes in the Muslim world. This dimension came from the Egyptian groups.

The Afghan *mujahideen* debated about what to do with foreign Arab fighters who remained in the country. Sibghatullah Mojaddedi, the interim Afghan president, requested that all Arabs leave. Burhanuddin Rabbani, Mojaddedi's successor, wanted some to remain as an auxiliary force to aid his militia against rival Afghan warlords.[127]

Al-Zawahiri was concerned that if Arab fighters lingered in Afghanistan, they would be caught in the middle of tribal conflicts and therefore side-tracked from his priority of the violent overthrow of the Mubarak government. Al-Zawahiri's family hoped he would return to Egypt and assume a respectable career as a general practitioner, despite spending time in prison for the Sadat assassination. They had written to him complaining that they had been paying rent for his clinic in Maadi for years. However, al-Zawahiri knew he could never return, and wanted to move to a more proximate country to conduct a new guerrilla campaign inside Egypt, based on the lessons from the Afghan model.[128]

The environment in Peshawar had come to be dominated by those who sought to use the trained and mobilised Arab contingent for overseas action.[129] Much of the leadership present in Peshawar and the region in the early 1990s were still committed to revolutionary jihad but the question of where the next battle was remained. Al-Zawahiri summed it up:

> Another important issue is the fact that these battles that were waged under non-Muslim banners or under mixed banners caused the dividing lines between friends and enemies to become blurred. The Muslim youths began to have doubts about who was the enemy. Was it the foreign enemy that occupied Muslim territory, or was it the domestic enemy that prohibited government by Islamic *Shariah*, repressed the Muslims, and disseminated immorality under the slogan's progressiveness, liberty, nationalism, of liberation. This situation led the homeland to the brink of the abyss of domestic ruin and surrender to the foreign enemy, exactly like the current situation of the majority of our [Arab] countries under the aegis of the new world order.[130]

As the internal debates continued amongst the Arab *mujahideen*, the Soviet withdrawal was formalised as part of the 1988 UN Geneva Accords between Afghanistan and Pakistan, undersigned by the United States and the USSR.[131] Although Afghanistan and Pakistan agreed to non-interference in each other's sovereignty, the USSR had difficulty enforcing Pakistan's cooperation. In 1989, Soviet leaders discussed Pakistan's problematic role: 'Pakistani border troops are actively participating in military operations on Afghan territory. . . . [Pakistan] is the source of a continuous flow of weaponry, and armed bands also cross over unimpeded from there.'[132]

Soviet leaders were aware that the period following their withdrawal would determine Afghanistan's fate and reveal the consequences of their occupation. Declassified Politburo meetings reveal that 'everybody understands that the main fight is still ahead'. There was also a prophetic warning: 'In case of [our] Afghan friends' misfortune, Islamic fundamentalists are most likely to come to power.'[133]

Between 11 and 13 August 1988, several meetings took place in Peshawar with Arab jihadists from the campaign against the Soviets attending. The Egyptians such as al-Zawahiri and al-Sharif took part as observers but were not involved in the minutiae. That meeting has now been viewed as the date when al-Qaeda, the organization, came into being. Attendees agreed in principle to a set of bylaws for the new organization, including its top-down hierarchy. The focus would be a new military entity with three principle parts:

1. General Camp
2. Special Camp
3. Al-Qaeda (base)

Bin Laden's then-aide, a US national of Syrian heritage, Mohammed Loay Bayazid, was tasked with taking the minutes of the meeting. Notes from the gathering outlined, 'This future project is in the interest of the Egyptian brothers.'[134] This was likely done to appease the EIJ, especially al-Zawahiri, who wanted to use their cadres to overthrow the Mubarak government.

Strategically, Azzam was not convinced that the existing conditions were conducive to depose existing 'apostate' Muslim rulers and scorned those advocating revolutionary violence against the 'internal enemy'.[135] For Azzam, it was of paramount importance to regain control of once-Muslim lands, like Palestine. Liberating Palestine should be the 'primary issue on the mind of every Muslim'.[136] Yet Azzam argued that the strategy dictated 'jihad should begin with Afghanistan before Palestine'.[137] For Azzam, a successful jihad in Afghanistan would also create a jihadist cadre able to challenge Israel and reclaim lost Muslim lands. When the Soviet Union began the process of withdrawing from Afghanistan in April 1988, Azzam's *Al-Jihad* magazine made the case for the jihad to spread to Palestine.[138]

Sayyid Imam al-Sharif's conception of jihad differed from Azzam's in several important respects, which would impact on al-Zawahiri. The EIJ's goal was to remove the Egyptian regime of Hosni Mubarak and establish an Islamic state in its place. Consequently, when evaluating the long-term goals of jihad, al-Sharif pinpointed the 'apostates' and not the 'infidels'. He was indifferent to Azzam putting prominence on the 'external enemy'. For al-Sharif, jihad against apostates was the *ummah*'s most important religious duty.[139]

In addition, al-Sharif's framework for the 'preparation for jihad' had a different outlook from Azzam's. Whilst Azzam viewed jihad as an incremental progression commencing with the obligation to 'emigrate' and then engage in jihad, al-Sharif believed the initial step was creating a committed cadre: 'Preparation for *jihad* begins with the formation of a Muslim group ... and the path to *jihad* begins with the formation of a group of believers who believe in the duty of *jihad*, call upon others to undertake this duty.'[140]

Neither al-Zawahiri nor Azzam had the financial resources to pursue their goals without support. In contrast, bin Laden had his own vision of creating an all-Arab jihadist movement that could fight the Marxist regime in southern Yemen. Al-Sharif and al-Zawahiri proposed supporting bin Laden with members of the EIJ, but they faced stiff opposition from Azzam, which in turn created a rift with bin Laden.[141] Yet, instead of al-Qaeda's foundational meeting focussing on Azzam's aspirations, the participants wanted to focus on 'mismanagement and bad treatment in Maktab al-Khadamat', the organization created by Azzam and bin Laden to fundraise and recruit *mujahideen* for the war against the Soviets in Afghanistan.[142]

Accusations about MAK's malfeasance had been mounting for a while. Back in 1987, Azzam had approached Ahmed Khadr about creating a new grassroots organization in Peshawar called al-Tahaddi (the Challenge). However, Khadr and Azzam soon fell out over how the money raised in the West was to be used. Azzam accused Khadr of being both a 'spy' and a 'Westerner' as well as being manipulated by al-Zawahiri and al-Sharif.[143] For al-Zawahiri, this was an opportunity to tarnish Azzam's credibility amongst the jihadists. In an early example of his propensity for propaganda, al-Zawahiri orchestrated a coordinated plan to circulate flyers and posters in mosques and guest homes in Peshawar demanding that Azzam be brought to trial for spreading lies against Khadr.[144] Feeling overwhelming pressure to act, bin Laden held an informal Shariah court trial, which Azzam chose not to attend and sent his son instead.[145] Al-Zawahiri's plan to create a wedge between bin Laden and his mentor Azzam had begun. Azzam was found guilty of spreading false claims but did not face any consequence other than damage to his reputation.[146]

Even if al-Zawahiri could not entirely convince bin Laden about prioritising Egypt, the 'near enemy', at that exact moment, his other objective in isolating Azzam was bearing fruit. Azzam soon felt his influence over bin Laden fading whilst al-Zawahiri's effect over the Saudi was increasing. Azzam complained to his son-in-law Abdullah Anas about the proliferation of Egyptians causing *fitna* (discord) within the Arab *mujahideen*.[147] He specifically identified al-Zawahiri as one of the agitators.[148] Al-Zawahiri continued to undermine Azzam's status by disseminating rumours that he was an infiltrator, working for the Americans. The criticisms stuck and tainted Azzam in some circles.[149]

The dilemma over the purpose and direction of thousands of resilient and battle-hardened Arabs in Afghanistan came to a forceful climax in 1989 when, conveniently for al-Zawahiri, Azzam and his two sons were killed. A sophisticated device was used to blow up the car they were driving to a mosque in Peshawar. The result was bin Laden taking full control of the MAK. Since 1989, no clear evidence has linked Azzam's assassination to any individual or intelligence organization despite suspicion pointing to the KGB, CIA, or ISI, and even Mossad. However, there was another suspect, al-Zawahiri.

The ISI nurtured jihadists and saw strategic convergence with them especially in their emerging strategy of creating an insurgency in Indian-administered Jammu and Kashmir. If the KGB were going to target jihadists, several others were more directly involved in bleeding Soviet troops on the battleground than Azzam. For the CIA, the mission of defeating the Soviets in Afghanistan was achieved, and Azzam had been well received in the United States for his fundraising tours. He was not deemed a threat.

The person who benefited the most in Azzam's death was al-Zawahiri. With Azzam out of the way, al-Zawahiri became the primary indispensable advisor and ally to bin Laden and was able to exert his sole influence without any competing narratives.[150] As the passage of time would demonstrate, al-Zawahiri would specialise in assassinations. Furthermore, throughout his life, al-Zawahiri would face accusations from competing jihadist factions about his role in Azzam's death, something the Egyptian would continuously deny.

One month after Azzam's mysterious death, one of his remaining sons, Huthaifa Azzam, went to Peshawar airport to receive a group of young men from Jordan. Recently released from prison, they had come to fight in the emerging civil war in Afghanistan between the various militias that had defeated the Soviets.[151]

Amongst them, a single person would stand out, Ahmad Fadhil Nazzal al-Khalaylah. He was a reformed individual. In his youth he had been involved in heavy drinking and narcotics, and tattoos were scrawled across his arms. He enjoyed fighting and spent time in prison for sexual assault. However, whilst incarcerated he became more religiously zealous. Eager to engage in the battlefields of Afghanistan, this individual would end up being one of the world's most notorious terrorists, adopting the name Abu Musab al-Zarqawi.[152] The name was taken from the town he grew up in, Zarqa, a shambolic industrial city rife with militancy, inevitably contributing the most Jordanian volunteers to fight in theatres abroad, first in Afghanistan and then in Iraq.

Al-Zarqawi had read the books Azzam had written, including *Join the Caravan* and *The Lofty Mountain*. He took inspiration from Abullah Azzam and was clearly crestfallen that a man he wanted to be his mentor was no longer alive.[153] Azzam had fought against the Soviets, and al-Zarqawi was determined that he would fight in the war's second phase, to ensure the Najibullah government would fall. However, his first stay did not last long. Al-Zarqawi was not utilised the way he wished to be. Although he did engage in some battles in Afghanistan, he was largely side-lined to work more on propaganda for the jihadists, a skill that would enhance his reputation in later years.[154] Whilst in Afghanistan, al-Zarqawi became aware of the rumour that al-Zawahiri may have played a role in Azzam's death, an issue that would lead to permanently fraught relations between them.[155]

Elsewhere, in December 1989, the EIJ, now unencumbered by Azzam's competing agenda, aggressively conspired against the Mubarak regime. It ambushed Interior Minister Zaki Badr's convoy using a hidden explosive placed under the car by the driver who had been recruited by the EIJ. However, it malfunctioned, and the driver was arrested.[156] At the same time, the Bush administration renewed its support to Mubarak against the jihadists and continuation of substantial US military aid.

Meanwhile, the crumbling Soviet Union provided financial and military assistance to Afghan president Mohammed Najibullah for three years. It was only after the USSR dissolved in 1991 that support evaporated, which had a knock-on effect for Najibullah's government. In 1992, the Afghan *mujahideen* captured Kabul. In Washington, this was viewed as a success of US strategy, especially as Najibullah was deemed to be on the wrong side of the Cold War. According to al-Zawahiri, 'In the wake of the USSR's collapse, the United States monopolised its military superiority to dictate its wishes to numerous governments and, as a result, has succeeded in imposing security agreements on many countries.'[157] One superpower may have been defeated, but another was now standing in the way of al-Zawahiri's agenda, and an inevitable confrontation was gathering momentum.

4

Building the Base

Bitter Harvest

Whilst in Pakistan, al-Zawahiri produced his first treatise in 1991, 'The Bitter Harvest: The [Muslim] Brotherhood in Sixty Years' ('Al-Al-Hisad al-Murr: al-Ikhwan al-Muslimin Fi Sitin Aman). The book is a history dedicated to how and why Egypt's Muslim Brotherhood lost its way by choosing to participate in politics and elections instead of waging jihad against the 'apostate' Mubarak government of Egypt:

> Not only have the Brothers been idle from fulfilling their duty of jihad, but they have gone as far as to describe the infidel governments as legitimate and have joined ranks with them in the *jahiliyyah* governing, that is, democracies, elections, and parliaments. Moreover, they take advantage of the Muslim youths' fervour by bringing them into their fold only to store them in a refrigerator. Then, they steer their onetime passionate Islamic zeal for jihad against tyranny toward conferences and elections.[1]

To justify his scathing condemnation of the Muslim Brotherhood's interactions with the Egyptian government and willingness to participate in elections, al-Zawahiri defined two theological concepts to validate his accusations:

1. The Islamic obligation to fight and overthrow any leader who does not govern according to the Shariah of Allah
2. The belief that democracy and Islam are paradoxical and can never coexist[2]

The fundamental question that al-Zawahiri dwelt upon is, how can Muslims establish Shariah law which has been created by God except by violent offensive jihad? He criticises the Muslim Brotherhood for sacrificing

Doctor, Teacher, Terrorist. Sajjan M. Gohel, Oxford University Press. © Oxford University Press 2024.
DOI: 10.1093/oso/9780197665367.003.0004

hakimiyyah for *jahiliyyah*, which Sayyid Qutb had suggested regarding the Nasser regime, by participating in the political process and therefore accepting that the people are the primary source of sovereignty:

> Though they have concluded that it is dangerous to openly confront Islam as enemies, these current organizations [Muslim Brotherhood] lording over our Islamic *ummah* continue betraying Islam and cheating its people by, above all, scattering and dividing them—all which lead to two situations: 1) They as Muslims abandon the *Shariah* and guidance of Allah in [exchange for the opportunity to] participate in *jahiliyyah* democracies—thus ultimately yielding Allah's absolute truths for human truths, meaning submission to the right of humanity to choose what it wants from laws and ideologies. 2) They attack and belittle those who call for that [jihad], slander them, and call on the [apostate] governments to destroy them. They disavow themselves from [those who call for jihad] in front of those idolaters, contrary to Allah's Word: 'Fight against them [infidels] until idolatry is no more and Allah's religion reigns supreme' [2:191].[3]

In this text al-Zawahiri also warned that the Muslim Brotherhood's path was especially dangerous given the status of Muslims around the world. He claimed that the 'false' governments in Arab states in the present are reminiscent of the medieval governments established by Mongol invaders in the time of Ibn Taymiyyah, the medieval Islamist jurist:

> For the majority of Islamic nations today are on the verge of adopting these laws that are at variance with the *Shariah* and that resemble the yasiq [Mongol oral law code], which itself was formulated by an infidel [Genghis Khan]—a man who publicly revelled in his infidelity. Such also are the laws being promulgated by people associated with Islam today. The sons of the Muslims go on to learn them, and both fathers and sons take pride in them, letting their rebellious wills embrace it—the modern-day yasiq.[4]

'Bitter Harvest' also emphasised al-Zawahiri's priorities arguing that 'fighting against apostates that govern Muslim lands takes primacy over fighting others'. 'The Bitter Harvest' highlighted the requirement to create an Islamist core within the Islamic world to restore the caliphate and former glory:

> The Islamic movements must answer the questions: are the governments in the Muslim countries true Muslims or are they infidels? These rulers are obviously infidels and apostates because they rule with a law other than that of Allah. Therefore, it is the individual duty to wage Jihad against them and remove them from their positions.[5]

Al-Zawahiri contended that it was an individual obligation for Muslims not only to fight against the 'occupation' of Muslim lands but also to overthrow *jahili* Arab regimes. Al-Zawahiri had learnt from bitter experience over Sadat's assassination and the failure of al-Jihad that an actual strategy was needed to achieve a Shariah state. It would be simplistic to attribute al-Zawahiri's overwhelming anger against Arab governments to his prison experience. Al-Zawahiri's argument was primarily about Western cultures that had imposed a new religion on the *ummah* and had helped apostasy grow and ascend to power—in essence, the Mubarak regime. Regarding this, Qutb's friend and collaborator Abdul A'la Maududi purportedly said, 'democracy is the deification of man . . . and rule of the masses' which resonated with al-Zawahiri.[6] For al-Zawahiri, this meant that:

> democracy is a man-made infidel religion, devised to give the right to legislate to the masses—as opposed to Islam, where all legislative rights belong to Allah Most High: He has no partners. In democracies, however, those legislators [elected] from the masses become partners worshipped in place of Allah. Whoever obeys their laws [ultimately] worships them.[7]

In effect, the Muslim Brotherhood's willingness to engage in participatory politics and elections meant placing man-made laws above Shariah law. Therefore, for al-Zawahiri, these people invalidate themselves as Muslims: 'For he who legislates anything for human beings would establish himself as their Allah.'[8]

In *Knights under the Prophet's Banner*, al-Zawahiri would double down on the failings and hypocrisy of the Muslim Brotherhood and use his memoirs to justify the acerbic criticism he unleashed on them in 'Bitter Harvest'. Despite the pretence of having no regrets, Al-Zawahiri also showed a sign of defensiveness, feeling compelled to defend his previous comments point by point:

> The Muslim Brotherhood is growing organizationally but is committing suicide ideologically and politically. The history of the Muslim Brotherhood is full of mistakes and failures and adds that the mistakes committed by the biggest Islamic movement in the world prompted me to write The Muslim Brotherhood's Bitter Harvest in 60 Years.
>
> Some of my brothers have blamed me because of the book's contents. Some of them are proud of their relationship both with me and with the Muslim Brotherhood. Their criticism was that this book is unfair because it pinpoints the mistakes of the Muslim Brotherhood and does not mention any of their good deeds although their history is full of good deeds.[9]

Al-Zawahiri uses his treatise to draw a strict distinction between his Egyptian Islamic Jihad (EIJ) and other Islamist movements like the Muslim Brotherhood, which he characterises as 'apostates'. He writes in *Knights under the Prophet's Banner* that:

> the Muslim Brotherhood has reneged on its history of struggle and what this history contains in terms of the blood of the *shaheed* [martyrs], the wounds of the detainees, and the agony of the fugitives. Not only that, the Muslim Brotherhood has also reneged on its principles and creed. The Muslim Brotherhood is drifting away from its history, creating a new generation who only cares about worldly things now and in the future.[10]

In a small sign of contrition, al-Zawahiri acknowledged he could have perhaps phrased things differently with the benefit of hindsight and that he would think about devising some comments in an updated volume of 'Bitter Harvest' should he manage to survive the Battle of Tora Bora: 'I do not deny that there are some unnecessary phrases in the book; however, their removal will not affect the topic of the book. I have revised the book twice and have thought of publishing a second edition. I do not know whether Allah will help me to do this or not.'[11]

Egyptians in America

Ali Mohamed's immediate post-1989 mission for al-Zawahiri can be charac-terised by his partnership with fellow Egyptian Khalid Abu al-Dahab, who travelled to California in 1987 at Mohamed's request. Al-Dahab was born to a wealthy family in Alexandria, Egypt. He was deeply influenced by both his parents. His mother was a physician, which led al-Dahab to pursue a career in medicine. However, his father's career as an airplane pilot shaped al-Dahab's path as an EIJ operative. The 1974 downing of a Cairo-bound Libyan Arab Airlines Flight 114 by Israel's air force, after it entered Israeli-controlled air-space over the Sinai Peninsula, killed 108 people, including al-Dahab's father. Sadat had managed to convince the Libyan government to refrain from any direct military retaliation. However, Egypt's failure to 'avenge' his father's death turned al-Dahab against Egypt, Israel, and the United States too. Al-Dahab abandoned his medical studies in Alexandria and enlisted with the EIJ.[12] Mohamed would become al-Dahab's companion in terrorism, specif-ically in the San Francisco Bay Area, for many years.[13]

In 1987, a year after his arrival in America, al-Dahab had helped Abdullah Azzam found al-Kifah Center, a non-governmental organization that would become the American branch of the MAK.[14] It was surreptitiously referred to as the al-Kifah Refugee Center, with the word 'refugee' designed to give it the veneer of humanitarian outreach. Situated out of al-Farooq Mosque in Brooklyn, it was run by another Egyptian and al-Zawahiri confidante, Mustafa Shalabi. Al-Kifah would serve to recruit members for the EIJ and help finance it, with Shalabi becoming the most influential Egyptian jihadist in New York.[15] Ironically, it was al-Zawahiri's nemesis Abdullah Azzam who had initially sent Shalabi to New York in 1986 to set up al-Kifah Center and fundraise for the *mujahideen* against the Soviets.[16] Shalabi found donors for his Afghan operation.[17] Al-Zawahiri's mole Ali Mohamed would often visit the place on weekends.[18]

However, the mosque's board brought in another al-Zawahiri rival, Omar Abdel Rahman, who had arrived in the United States seeking asylum from Egypt.[19] Initially, Shalabi helped Rahman settle in an apartment. He also paid for his food and telephone bills.[20] However, the relationship soon turned sour. Under instructions from al-Zawahiri, Shalabi soon excluded Rahman from any decision making regarding the earnings from fundraisers and tours for al-Kifah.[21] In turn, Rahman denounced Shalabi as a 'bad Muslim' and subsequently tried to excommunicate him through the concept of *takfir*, which involved the killing of Muslims accused of having abandoned Islam.[22]

Rahman was also accused of stealing donations to serve his own purposes and promote al-Gama'a. The EIJ/al-Gama'a rivalry was now playing out in the streets of New York City. As a result, two months after being named temporary imam, Rahman was dismissed. Undeterred, he chose to continue his campaign against Shalabi, including distributing flyers discouraging people from giving money to him.[23] Things were coming to a head.

On 1 March 1991, Shalabi was found dead at his home near Coney Island. He had been shot in the head and stabbed in the back and neck. The assassination-style murder had a purpose.[24] Whilst the crime remains unsolved, important information came to light two weeks after the 1993 bombing of the World Trade Center (WTC), which killed six and injured more than 1,000. Rahman's former driver, Mahmud Abouhalima, was also behind the WTC plot and fled to Egypt, where he was arrested.[25] After being turned over to US authorities, he implicated himself and Rahman in

Shalabi's murder. Still, neither individual was ever charged, as the priority was to prosecute them for the 1993 WTC bombing.[26] Abouhalima had also been in regular touch with Ali Mohamed, and for a while the two were exploring ways of working together until al-Zawahiri ordered Mohamed to cut ties.[27] Ultimately, Shalabi's death precipitated the disintegration of al-Kifah Refugee Center in Brooklyn, which closed down in 1993.[28]

Unhindered by the turf war at al-Kifah, al-Dahab established an EIJ communications and money laundering hub in his Santa Clara apartment in California using satellite communications equipment given to him by al-Zawahiri. He would act like a phone operator, patching through EIJ calls and messages to operatives around the world.[29] The hub, which would eventually serve al-Qaeda, carried out tasks including sending money through the underground banking hawala networks and front companies, as well as manufacturing forged passports and stealing IDs. The beneficiaries were al-Zawahiri and his cohorts.[30] Mohamed's return to California led to a significant increase in these activities. Al-Dahab would become Mohamed's second in command.[31]

In 1990, Mohamed directed al-Dahab towards the camps in lawless Afghanistan after the Soviets left. Al-Dahab attended one near Jalalabad, where he received military-style training, including flying hang gliders, in preparation for future EIJ plots to free imprisoned jihadists.[32] Upon his return, the 'Santa Clara duo' were assigned a new task by al-Zawahiri to recruit people of Middle Eastern descent.[33] Al-Zawahiri understood early on that passports and ID theft could be useful to identify target locations.[34]

Around this time, Mohamed began his ploy to infiltrate the Federal Bureau of Investigation (FBI). Applying for a job as a translator at their offices in San Francisco, Mohamed was interviewed for the role. To attain trust, he told the FBI about a criminal network involved in fraudulent ID documents tied to the Palestinian militant group Hamas. The information was inconsequential for the EIJ, as they had no affiliation with Hamas. This event marked Mohamed's 'career' as a criminal informant for the FBI. He had, once again, managed to infiltrate a US intelligence service, as per al-Zawahiri's request.

Interestingly, in the following years, Mohamed would play host to al-Zawahiri during two separate US fundraising tours, first in the spring of 1993 and then in 1995. In 1993, al-Zawahiri was able to enter the US through the forged papers Mohamed provided him with.[35] Under the pseudonym Dr Abdel Muez, al-Zawahiri impersonated an official from the humanitarian

Red Crescent based in Pakistan.[36] Acting as his hosts, Mohamed and al-Dahab brought 'the doctor' to solicit resources at Californian mosques in Santa Clara, Stockton, and Sacramento.[37] Al-Zawahiri would inform people of his experiences providing medical care in Afghanistan as well as fighting the Soviets. Overall, the 1993 tour raised a substantial amount of cash for the EIJ.[38] Such was the success that al-Zawahiri chose to return to the United States in 1995 for another fundraising tour, where he returned to Santa Clara and travelled to Austin and Richardson in Texas.[39] This time, however, the trip resulted in only $2,500. Al-Zawahiri berated al-Dahab for the paltry amount collected. Still, this capital and the money raised previously was to contribute to the costs of future EIJ plots.[40]

Some of the money raised would also facilitate wider jihadist travel to North America. In 1993 al-Dahab received a wire transfer from bin Laden and al-Zawahiri to go to Vancouver, Canada, and help post bail for an Egyptian, Essam Hafez Marzouk.[41] Marzouk had arrived at Vancouver airport from Frankfurt. He produced a Saudi passport in the name of Fawzi Harbi and applied for a visitor's visa. However, Canadian customs agents searching his luggage discovered a doctored Egyptian passport with his photo with another name. Unsurprisingly, Marzouk was arrested but not before he claimed he had fled Egypt because of religious persecution. Helping al-Dahab secure Marzouk's release was his old friend Ali Mohamed, who was supposed to collect him from the Vancouver airport. Mohamed vouched for Marzouk by citing his own trusted relationship with the FBI and US military. Ali Mohamed even provided the name of the FBI agent who could verify his credibility. Marzouk was subsequently released and obtained refugee status and lived in the Vancouver area for several years.[42] What neither Canadian or American authorities knew was that Marzouk had briefly served in the Egyptian military and Ali Mohamed had trained him in manufacturing improvised explosive devices (IEDs) in Afghanistan during the battle against the Soviets. The two would go on to help al-Zawahiri and bin Laden move to Sudan.[43]

Exodus to Sudan

The battlefields of the Afghan jihad were key to the early operational development of Pakistani Islamist militancy. Whilst the jihadists were working out what their next mission would be following the withdrawal of Soviet forces from Afghanistan, the Pakistani military under General Zia ul-Haq had already started planning for the next stage of jihad. The Inter-Services Intelligence (ISI) devised two intersecting Islamist projects: first, to formulate the ascent to power in Afghanistan of a pro-Pakistani Pashtun Islamist movement, and second, an attempt to wrestle control of the territory of Jammu and Kashmir from India by inciting an insurgency.[44] Under the command of General Akhtar Abdur Rehman, the ISI planned to use the extensive jihadist networks that were created during the Afghan jihad.[45] Rehman was consequently elevated to the position of chairman of the Pakistani military's Joint Chiefs of Staff Committee.

However, on 17 August 1988, Zia died along with several top military brass, including Rehman, and two American diplomats in a mysterious plane explosion near Bahawalpur, Pakistan.[46] Zia's death dramatically ended his dictatorship and enabled Benazir Bhutto to return to Pakistan after years in exile, following Zia executing her father, former prime minister Zulfikar Ali Bhutto. The aftermath resulted in democratic elections in Pakistan with Bhutto chosen as the first female prime minister of Pakistan. Unbeknown to Bhutto, Rehman's successor as head of the ISI, Hamid Gul, assertively continued to implement the dual projects covertly.[47] Along with the military, the ISI ensured it remained the real controlling force in Pakistan.[48]

Bhutto was not prepared to tolerate the visible presence of Arab jihadists who had made Pakistan their home, and she sought their removal. To destabilise her government, bin Laden, in collaboration with the ISI, attempted to bribe Pakistani parliamentarians to support a 'no confidence' bill in 1989 to overthrow her government. Bin Laden committed $10 million for this purpose but ultimately failed.[49] However, he had made himself persona non grata and eventually had to leave Pakistan. The only country openly willing to take the Arab *mujahideen* was Sudan.

Sudan was seen as an ideal base for Arab jihadists to establish their networks. Back in 1989, Lt. Gen. Omar Hasan Ahmad al-Bashir deposed the democratic civilian government of Sadiq al-Mahdi.[50] The ideologue Hassan al-Turabi, a former secretary general of the Sudanese Muslim Brotherhood, was given a prominent role in Sudanese politics through his National Islamic Front (NIF), an Islamist political organization.[51] Al-Turabi was instrumental in institutionalizing Shariah in Sudan.[52]

Sudan offered an amenable government for Arab jihadists. Bin Laden had accepted al-Turabi's open invitation to move there in 1991.[53] Bin Laden invested in Sudan, and his wealth provided refuge for Arab fighters.[54] Ali Mohamed, al-Zawahiri's American mole, was assigned with the task of helping relocate bin Laden to Sudan. Having provided the logistics and security, he went on to stay in Sudan to help establish camps to provide training in weapons, explosives, counter-intelligence, and creating cells.[55]

Bin Laden lived in Sudan for five years. During this time, he fell out with the House of Saud in his native Saudi Arabia over the US-led campaign against Saddam Hussein's occupation of Kuwait. Al-Zawahiri mirrored bin Laden's criticisms of the Saudi Arabian government for requesting assistance from the United States to base its troops in the Saudi kingdom as part of Operation Desert Shield. This was the first phase of a military response to Iraq's invasion of Kuwait designed to repel Saddam Hussein's forces from attacking Saudi Arabia. For al-Zawahiri, the House of Saud allowing non-Muslims to 'occupy' a nation which is home to the two holiest cities for all Muslims, Mecca and Medina, was sacrilegious; Saudi Arabia was emulating Egypt by surrendering its sovereignty to the West.[56]

In Sudan, bin Laden was based in the coincidentally named al-Riyadh quarter of Khartoum, a neighbourhood where wealthier Sudanese who had made their money in the Middle East lived.[57] It was a settlement of winding roads and rundown buildings that straddles the confluence of the Blue and White Nile Rivers. His secluded art deco several-story pinkish house lay behind a high white wall topped with razor wire along an unpaved road. Flanking his house was a series of walled-in compounds. Bin Laden owned guest houses on both sides of the street. They were the homes of his top officers. Travelling terrorists, such as al-Zawahiri, would receive accommodation at the guest houses beside his Saudi friend. Bin Laden maintained an office on the second floor.[58] But he often preferred to sit on plastic chairs in the front garden and talk jihad with the men.[59]

Al-Zawahiri confidant Abu Ubaidah al-Banshiri became al-Qaeda's head of operations for East Africa and the Horn of Africa. He communicated with bin Laden regularly.[60] In the 1990s Khalid al-Fawwaz, who would later become a cog in al-Qaeda's emerging media set-up, started a company in Nairobi, Kenya, called Asma Limited, which was later reassigned to Abu Ubaidah al-Banshiri.[61] Al-Banshiri also created a gem mining enterprise and a transportation hauler company in Tanzania. They would serve as front companies to demonstrate legitimate business but beneath the surface would help to raise funds for al-Qaeda and provide logistical support when

required. Despite al-Banshiri drowning in Lake Victoria in 1996, his infrastructure was utilised to plan the 1998 US Embassy bombings in Kenya and
Tanzania.[62]

In neighbouring Egypt, the economic boom continued into the 1980s,
with the introduction of the first metro line and new highways. Numerous
subdivisions were added onto the existing urban layouts. Thanks largely to
US assistance, long-neglected infrastructure began to receive attention. A
completely revamped sewerage system was installed on both sides of the
Nile. Huge power plants were installed to deal with the growing public
demand for electricity. For al-Zawahiri, Egypt's progress was being shaped
by the West which he predicted would result in the country falling further
into a state of *jahiliyyah*.

Al-Zawahiri and al-Sharif eventually followed bin Laden to settle in
Sudan in 1992.[63] Bin Laden gave al-Zawahiri $100,000 to aid the EIJ's
battle against the Mubarak government and prevent it from losing ground
to al-Gama'a. Bin Laden continued to fund al-Zawahiri's group during
the Sudan years.[64] Khartoum was supposed to provide a refuge from international intelligence pressure, but cracks quickly emerged between al-
Zawahiri and al-Sharif about the legitimacy of violence, especially in Egypt.

The EIJ attempted several daring plots against the Egyptian government,
but they either failed or didn't achieve the necessary jolt to trigger a popular
uprising. Frustrated that the United States was supporting Mubarak, al-
Zawahiri felt even more determined that the Mubarak government was
illegitimate and that this was a 'battle of ideologies' as much as it was a
military contest. As he expressed in the *Knights Under the Prophet's Banner*:

> An analysis of the political situation in Egypt would reveal that Egypt is strug-
> gling between two powers.... An official power and a popular power that
> has its roots deeply established in the ground, which is the Islamic movement
> in general and the solid jihad nucleus in particular. This meant an all-out, vio-
> lent war. It is a battle of ideologies, a struggle for survival, and a war with no
> truce.[65]

On 29 December 1992, al-Qaeda launched its first ever attack against US
interests. The plot was designed to kill members of the US military in
Yemen transferring to Somalia to stabilise the country and provide humanitarian support as part of Operation Restore Hope. Two Yemenis who
had fought alongside bin Laden and al-Zawahiri in Afghanistan, Tariq
Nasr al-Fadhli and Jamal al-Nahdi were assigned the role.[66] Al-Fadhli and

al-Nahdi planted bombs at both the Gold Mohur Hotel and Mövenpick Hotel in Aden. However, the bombing did not achieve its objectives, as no American soldiers died, but two Austrian tourists were killed in the attack.[67] Years later, bin Laden identified the attack as the beginning of al-Qaeda's war against the United States:

> The Arab *mujahideen* related to the Afghan jihad carried out two bomb explo- sions in Yemen to warn the United States, causing damage to some Americans staying in those hotels. The United States received our warning and gave up the idea of setting up its military bases in Yemen. This was the first al-Qaeda victory scored against the Crusaders.[68]

Aiding al-Fadhli and al-Nahdi in the Aden attacks was al-Zawahiri's former EIJ cellmate Ahmad Mabruk. Released in 1988, Mabruk moved to Afghanistan the following year just as the Soviet occupation was coming to an end. He had developed a close bond with al-Zawahiri in prison and sought to renew ties in Afghanistan and Sudan.[69]

The Yemen attack was often overlooked despite its importance as the first collaboration between bin Laden and al-Zawahiri against the United States. Greater emphasis was placed on events in Somalia the following year. Between 3 and 4 October 1993, US Army Rangers and commandos from Delta Force conducted a successful operation to capture deputies of Somali warlord Mohamed Farah Aideed. However, subsequently, they were forced into street battles with hundreds of Somali gunmen which resulted in 18 US soldiers killed, dozens wounded, and two Army Black Hawk choppers shot down. The Clinton administration ordered a hasty exit from Operation Restore Hope.[70]

What was not apparent at the time was that bin Laden and al-Zawahiri had a direct role in training and equipping the Somali militias, which at the time inflicted the largest ever number of casualties for US Special Operations Forces.[71] Al-Qaeda military chief Mohammed Atef was directed by bin Laden to Mogadishu in 1992, where he supported Aideed's fight against US and UN forces. Accompanying Atef was Mohammad Sadiq Odeh and al-Zawahiri loyalist Saif al-Adel. All veterans of the Afghan jihad, they were tasked to train some of the Somali militias fighting. This included utilising the rocket-propelled grenades to target the tail rotors of US Black Hawks.[72] Al-Zawahiri also advised on low-tech steganography to direct the Somalis in protecting themselves. This included Aideed telling his fighters to bang out messages on drums instead of using telephones to thwart the efforts of US forces to intercept his communications.[73]

Whilst in Sudan, al-Zawahiri's EIJ also fought an intense clandestine battle to overthrow the Mubarak regime. However, al-Gama'a's higher pro- file and larger resources forced al-Zawahiri to modify his strategy, which he termed 'the flea and the dog'. His EIJ would hover around the Mubarak regime like a flea to a dog and, through a succession of attacks, wear down its morale and public trust and bring about its collapse.[74] November 1993 saw the initiation of al-Zawahiri's 'flea and the dog' strategy with one of his protégés, Tharwat Salah Shehata, tasked with implementing it. Also known by his alias Abu Samha al-Masri, Shehata was a lawyer by training, and had spent time in prison with al-Zawahiri over the Sadat assassination. Shehata led an EIJ cell which attempted to assassinate former prime minister Atef Sedky by targeting his motorcade with a hidden explosive. However, the prime minister missed the explosion by a split second, and the EIJ cell inadvertently killed a 12-year-old schoolgirl, Shayma Muhammad Abdel Halim. This was a significant setback to any support for al-Zawahiri's aims.[75] The incident clearly tainted al-Zawahiri as it was something he highlighted in his memories: 'I deeply regret her death and am willing to pay blood money. This girl was as old as my own daughter.'[76]

As al-Zawahiri explained, 'The government used the death of Shayma, may Allah bless her soul, and portrayed the incident as an attack by the al-Jihad group [EIJ] against Shayma, not against Prime Minister Sedky.'[77] Al-Zawahiri's EIJ continued to attack Egyptian government targets and in- frastructure, but the Mubarak regime was ever more invulnerable to assault. Thus, their attacks were on softer targets aimed at weakening the Egyptian economy, especially at Western and Israeli tourists frequenting Egypt's an- tiquities and artifacts.[78]

Although successful in intimidating the United States and shaping US decision making in Somalia, al-Zawahiri's EIJ suffered a major blow in 1993 when Egyptian authorities uncovered the names of more than 800 members of the group known as Vanguards of Conquest (Talaa' al-Fateh). Most were subsequently arrested. Al-Zawahiri would reflect on this later by claiming the United States was aiding Mubarak in undermining the jihadists: 'This arbitrary separation between the external enemies and their internal agents led to many disasters and setbacks because the movement's members faced their enemy with their chests but left their backs exposed to his ally. Thus, they were stabbed in the back on the orders of those whom they faced with their chests.'[79]

After years of advocating unrestrained violence, al-Sharif began encouraging abstention from 'excesses of Islamic action'.[80] Al-Sharif believed the war against Mubarak was futile and that the EIJ should focus on recruiting cadres, including within the Egyptian military, and bide their time for the right moment when internal opposition against Mubarak grew naturally. Many within the EIJ began opposing al-Sharif and pushed for his removal from the EIJ, and al-Zawahiri sensed an opportunity.[81] Al-Sharif castigated al-Zawahiri: 'Who is further astray than the one who follows his own whims with no guidance from Allah? Truly Allah does not guide those who do wrong.'[82]

In the ensuing fallout members of the movement who had taken refuge in Sudan demanded a new leader. As a result, al-Sharif was forced to relinquish control and was immediately replaced by al-Zawahiri, who showed no reluctance to take over. Inevitably, al-Sharif's departure was acrimonious. He decided to move to Yemen in 1994 to start a medical practice in Sana'a,[83] but not before leaving behind an unpublished draft of the major treatise he had finished whilst in Sudan entitled *The Compendium of the Pursuit of Divine Knowledge*. The book painstakingly defined and categorised apostasy, which included the rulers of Egypt and other Arab nations. Yet al-Zawahiri rewrote sections and removed al-Sharif's caveats such as the fanatical reliance on violence. As a result, the text defined Islam so rigidly that virtually everyone was a heretic who merits extermination.[84]

After *Al-Mujahideen*, an organ of the EIJ, published excerpts from the text in 1995, al-Sharif issued a seething statement: 'I do not know anyone in the history of Islam prior to Ayman al-Zawahiri ... who engaged in such lying, cheating, forgery, and betrayal of trust by transgressing against someone else's book and distorting it.'[85] He was particularly incensed that al-Zawahiri had altered a profoundly religious document. However, al-Zawahiri's loyal base within the EIJ saw his actions as a refinement of Sharif's flawed draft.[86]

Upon becoming the EIJ *amir*, al-Zawahiri revamped its executive committee, known as the Shura Council, and made Tharwat Salah Shehata his deputy, tasking him with developing both the EIJ's financial network and taking charge of the organization's intelligence unit to plot activities and prevent infiltrations from Mubarak's security forces. Shehata began a

forensic process of documenting all EIJ members, noting down their physical attributes, level of education, religious knowledge, and social skills.[87]

In the mid-1990s, the EIJ and al-Gama'a began negotiations to see
whether a merger between the two terrorist organizations was possible.
Inevitably, there were several sticking points, including the allocation of
seats each faction would have in an amalgamated Shura Council. There
was also a major ideological fault line.[88] Both groups adhered to Sayyid
Qutb's doctrines including punishing Muslims who were voluntarily living
in *jahili* society and adopting the policy of *takfir* against 'apostates'. A large
part of this was fuelled by the grievance jihadists had towards Muslims
they deemed apostate who also tolerated Christians and Jews. However,
al-Gama'a had its own internal divisions on this issue, as some in its leadership believed there was a need to excuse Muslims for failing to observe
Qutb's articles of faith. They wanted to adopt the principle of 'excusing on
the basis of ignorance' (*al-'udhr bi'l-jahl*), which effectively meant forgiving
Muslims who are unintentionally ignorant that they are committing unbelief or tolerating polytheism.[89] For al-Zawahiri's EIJ, this was a red line.
Inevitably, the fissures between the EIJ and al-Gama'a were intractable, and
as both sides were unwilling to comprise, the negotiations petered out and
hostilities continued.

During this time, a very difficult scenario arose for the EIJ. Ahmad
Mabruk's teenage son, Musab, and another boy, Ahmad, the son of one of
the EIJ's administrators, Mohammed Sharaf, were detained by Egyptian security. Allegations within the EIJ were that the two boys were coerced into
becoming informants for the state. They were serious enough that when al-
Zawahiri discovered what happened, he had them both executed in Sudan.
Despite al-Zawahiri ordering the death of his son, Mabruk stayed loyal to
the EIJ leader and blamed the Mubarak regime.[90]

On 27 June 1995, President Hosni Mubarak was supposed attend the
opening session of a conference of the Organization of African Unity in
Ethiopia. As his motorcade was travelling from the Addis Ababa airport, EIJ
assassins used automatic weapons in an ambush, killing two of Mubarak's
bodyguards. The situation could have been more catastrophic had the
grenade launcher not malfunctioned. A second cell was lined up further
down the road, but sensing the strategy Mubarak had the presence of mind
to order his security detail to return to the airport. Al-Zawahiri later admitted in *Knights under the Prophet's Banner* that there were 'shortcomings'

and 'weaknesses' inherent to this plot that rendered it unsuccessful, including that 'one of the two cars that participated in the attack broke down.'[91] Al-Zawahiri also resented the financial, intelligence, and military support Egypt was receiving from the United States which aided their efforts against the EIJ.[92] The result was that al-Zawahiri was failing to destabilise the Mubarak regime at home but making himself an even bigger pariah. Worse, his Sudanese hosts were deemed complicit in the attack by the United States, resulting in the imposition of UN sanctions.[93] Al-Zawahiri's ire towards the United States was growing.

According to his uncle Mahfouz Azzam, 'The [Mubarak] regime bows to the Americans and doesn't allow Ayman to return. He has not been back since the mid-80s, but the family kept his paediatrician surgery open, we paid the rent for 20 years, thinking he would come back. . . . [W]e know he'll never be able to return.'[94] Not all of al-Zawahiri's relatives were sympathetic to his exile status, including his father, Dr Muhammad Rabi'a al-Zawahiri, who passed away on 9 August 1995 in Cairo knowing that his son had become Egypt's most wanted terrorist and had badly tarnished the family name.[95]

Despite failing to undermine the Mubarak regime, the EIJ clearly concerned the government, which began to try to apprehend those who remained in Pakistan following the Soviet withdrawal from Afghanistan. In April 1993, Egypt's cooperation with Pakistan became particularly irksome for al-Zawahiri when the names of 600 Egyptians living in Pakistan and identified as terrorists were passed to Pakistani prime minister Nawaz Sharif.[96] The subsequent Benazir Bhutto government continued the assistance by expelling several Egyptians. In 1994, Bhutto's justice minister Syed Haidar visited Egypt to sign an extradition agreement ensuring that Egyptians detained in Pakistan would be swiftly returned to Egypt.[97] A concerned al-Zawahiri stated, 'The Egyptian Government began to pursue the Arabs, but particularly Egyptian nationals, who had stayed on in Pakistan.'[98]

In 1995, al-Zawahiri declared an expansion of his campaign against Mubarak outside Egypt. Shortly thereafter, on 19 November 1995, two men approached the Egyptian Embassy in Islamabad. One, armed with a machine gun, shot the security guards dead. The other drove a truck loaded with 250 pounds of explosives and detonated it, blowing open the barriers. Then came a 4x4, packed with explosives. It entered the embassy compound before exploding, destroying a side of the embassy. Fourteen people died, and 60 were wounded.[99] One of al-Zawahiri's EIJ deputies, Sheikh Abdul Hameed, better known by his alias Abu Ubaidah al-Masri, helped coordinate the attack.[100] This was the EIJ's first overseas success under al-Zawahiri's own direction. The bomb 'left the embassy's ruined building as an eloquent and clear message', al-Zawahiri wrote in his memoir.[101] He was a pioneer of the use of suicide bomb attacks for the EIJ. To get around the religious prohibitions surrounding suicide and murder, al-Zawahiri would term them 'martyrdom operations' against the 'apostate regime' and their compliant citizens. Al-Zawahiri would also record the would-be bomber's vows of martyrdom on the eve of the attack.[102]

Al-Zawahiri himself had helped financially support the attack during his visits to the United States as part of a fundraising agenda.[103] Al-Zawahiri had also considered targeting American interests in Islamabad. However, according to the Egyptian teacher, 'after extensive surveillance, it was decided that hitting the U.S. Embassy was beyond the team's capability. Surveillance was conducted on another U.S. target in Islamabad, but it was discovered that it had a very small number of U.S. personnel and that most of the casualties would be among Pakistani nationals.'[104] After the attack, to avoid being caught and extradited to Egypt from Pakistan, al-Zawahiri sent Abu Ubaidah al-Masri to live in Germany and the United Kingdom from 1995 to 1999.[105]

In his book *Knights under the Prophet's Banner*, al-Zawahiri took full responsibility for the Islamabad embassy attack: 'We decided our response should be an attack on a target that would harm this vile alliance of Egyptians, the U.S. and India.'[106] It was a bizarre comment, particularly as it was unclear what the Indian government had to do with the Egyptian Embassy in Islamabad. However, the attack served only to put the spotlight further on al-Zawahiri and the Sudanese who were harbouring him. Al-Zawahiri and bin Laden might have stayed in Sudan had the Egyptian and Saudi governments not pressured Khartoum to hand them over.[107] A return to Pakistan was inevitable. In collaboration with Pakistan's intelligence agency, the ISI, al-Zawahiri was also looking at the potential of assassinating Benazir Bhutto, who was now serving her second term as prime minister.[108] Although the plot was never developed beyond a concept, al-Zawahiri considered Bhutto a constant thorn in the interests of the EIJ, and he knew eventually there would be a reckoning.

The attack on the Egyptian Embassy can also be seen as a critical juncture in al-Zawahiri's career. It was at this moment, when he sensed the upswing in the EIJ's momentum, that al-Bashir demanded al-Zawahiri and bin Laden leave Sudan along with their cadres. Undermining and unseating Mubarak remained a key goal and desire for al-Zawahiri, but that objective was now being undermined. The trust deficit amongst his Sudanese hosts had also been growing over the years. Back in 1994, the Sudanese ideologue and ally of bin Laden and al-Zawahiri Hassan al-Turabi was approached by the French authorities concerning Ilich Ramirez Sanchez, more infamously known as Carlos the Jackal, a far-left terrorist and at the time, the best-known terrorist globally. The Sudanese authorities negotiated a deal where Sanchez would be extradited to France against his will.[109] It would not have gone unnoticed by bin Laden and al-Zawahiri that if Sanchez was expendable to the Sudanese establishment, then they could potentially be next, especially as the United States had more international clout and economic muscle. However, America was not the only threat. In February 1994, al-Zawahiri asked Ali Mohamed to train a new security detail after an attempt was made on bin Laden's life at Khartoum.[110]

Many years later, al-Bashir faced an international arrest warrant for war crimes and crimes against humanity in the Darfur genocide. Al-Zawahiri was quick to issue a fiery audio statement, saying al-Bashir was paying the price for succumbing to Western pressure and selling his soul for money: 'The Bashir regime is reaping what it sowed. . . . For many long years, it continued to back down and backtrack in front of American Crusader pressure.' Al-Zawahiri also railed against what he saw as 'an audacious lie that they [bin Laden and al-Zawahiri] had left Sudan voluntarily' whilst al-Bashir was allegedly financially rewarded by 'the Saudi regime and the Americans'.[111]

The AfPak Base

Bin Laden coaxed and convinced al-Zawahiri that focussing on the United States, and ending its influence within the Arab world, was essential to creating the pan-Islamic state in the Middle East and North Africa.[112] The 'external enemy' narrative would be propagated through both ideology and planned attacks.[113] Al-Zawahiri's statements continued to emphasis his ire at the 'internal enemy', although the United States was by no means excluded from his vitriol.[114]

The United States had begun to rethink its foreign policy priorities, and under President George H. W. Bush it shifted its attention away from Afghanistan after the Soviet defeat.[115] As a consequence, opposing agendas amongst the Pashtuns, Tajiks, and Uzbeks soon emerged, and they began to seize Afghan territory whilst simultaneously trying to usurp each other. Major cities including the capital Kabul were reduced to rubble.[116] Amidst the anarchy, Pashtun cleric Mullah Mohammed Omar emerged on the scene as the leader of the Taliban, a cohort of Deobandi militants trained in Pakistani *madrasas*. The Deobandis are a Muslim revivalist movement that arose in British colonial India in reaction to the threat to Islam from both Western and Hindu influences. In Pakistan, Deobandism emphasises a puritanical understanding of Islam that discards the Sufi influences prevalent in Central and South Asia's Islam. During the military rule of Zia ul-Haq, the Deobandi movement in Pakistan was radicalised by his Islamisation policies, exemplified by the movement pushing to institute the doctrine of Sawad-e-Azam Ahl-e-Sunnat (Greater unity of the Sunnis), which categorised Shiites as apostates.[117]

At the same time, the Deobandi movement was also cultivated by the Pakistani military establishment during the Soviet invasion of Afghanistan. The subsequent Afghan jihad transformed the Deobandi movement in Pakistan, with its *madrasas* becoming centres for jihad.[118] The Pakistani Deobandi *madrasas* contributed strong links to the insecurity in Afghanistan by providing Taliban fighters who were ideologically radicalised, shaped by a narrow, dogmatic, and misogynistic doctrine.[119] However, before their agenda became apparent to Afghan society and the world, the Taliban began their conquest to take control of Afghanistan by demonstrating piety and seeking to end the nation's lawlessness and warlordism by offering security and stability. The fine print in the Taliban's true agenda was overlooked by war-weary Afghans. Within just two years, the Taliban captured major towns and cities.[120] Seeing this as an opportunity, bin Laden and al-Zawahiri left Khartoum on 18 May 1996, fearing that Sudan would betray them if they stayed there much longer. They arrived in Afghanistan as the Taliban was ascendant.[121]

According to the *9/11 Commission Report*, the ISI facilitated bin Laden and al-Zawahiri's arrival in Afghanistan and their meetings with Taliban leader Mullah Omar.[122] The ISI held significant power by controlling funds and providing recruits as well as logistical support to the Taliban, who in turn delivered Pakistan's agenda of strategic depth in Afghanistan with the aim of deflecting unfriendly states by operating within its borders.[123] Immediate, short-term support such as the provision of safe havens, training, and assets was the most significant factor in cementing the Taliban's dependence upon the Pakistani military.[124]

The ISI has primacy in determining Pakistan's national security agenda and has become a state within a state.[125] Indeed, no other force has so strongly and consistently driven Pakistan's agenda. The ISI has used its authoritative position to influence Pakistani politics and maintain Pakistani influence in Afghanistan and suppress Pashtun secular nationalist calls for Greater Pashtunistan. It hoped to forge a wider Islamic block of Pakistan, Jammu and Kashmir, Afghanistan, and Central Asia to balance India by installing an Islamist regime in Kabul and to secure Pakistan's position in the wider Muslim world.[126]

Although the Afghan Taliban was not yet in operation in the 1980s, significant groundwork was laid for their emergence during this period. One of the most significant factors leading to the relationship between the Taliban and the Pakistani military was the rapid expansion of the network of *madrasas* in Pakistan, which catered largely to Afghan refugees and *mujahideen*. In 1971, there were only 900 *madrasas* in Pakistan, which increased to 8,000 official *madrasas* and more than 25,000 unregistered religious schools by 1988.[127] Some of these schools taught an extreme and warped interpretation of the Deobandi subsect of Sunni Islam to 3 million Afghan refugees between 1979 and 1989, which became the ideological bedrock of the Taliban world view.[128]

The ISI served as gatekeeper to favour and manipulate certain Afghan *mujahideen* groups to achieve its own regional policy aims.[129] It was against this background that the Taliban emerged in Kandahar in the south of Afghanistan under the leadership of Mullah Mohammed Omar, a teacher in an ISI-funded *madrasa* and a former *mujahideen* fighter.[130] Pakistan's support for the Taliban was therefore a 'tactical adjustment', rather than a 'strategic policy shift'.[131] The rise of the Taliban was the result of a collaboration between the ISI manipulating Afghan affairs during the war and Afghan Pashtun religious insurgents.[132] This collaboration characterised their continued relationship, and the biggest beneficiaries would be bin Laden and al-Zawahiri. According to Ambassador Henry Crumpton, who served in both the FBI and CIA and was President George W. Bush's coordinator for counterterrorism:

> There's a convergence of some political interests between al-Qaeda and the Taliban. Clearly there is a degree of shared ideology, but al-Qaeda has been managing and manipulating the relationship. They're far more sophisticated

than the Taliban, even to the extent of encouraging marriage. So increasingly over the years, it's not just political and ideological, but it is social, clan family related, and that's not a small thing.[133]

For al-Qaeda to exist in Afghanistan meant depending on terrorist allies in Pakistan with ties to the ISI. One such ally was Ilyas Kashmiri, who would become one of the few non-Egyptian confidantes of al-Zawahiri. Ilyas Kashmiri began jihadi life as one of the anonymous and nondescript *mujahideen* foot soldiers from Pakistan-administered Kashmir during the era of the Afghan-Arab *mujahideen* war against the Soviets in 1980s.[134] Kashmiri specialised in guerrilla warfare and explosives. Subsequently, he became part of the Pakistani terrorist group Harakat-ul-Jihad-Islami (HuJI), which focused on the insurgency against India in Jammu and Kashmir.[135] Kashmiri later formed and led the 313 Brigade, an offshoot of HuJI, following operational differences with its leadership.[136] Kashmiri established his training base in Razmak in North Waziristan, Pakistan, and recruited Pakistani militants who had earlier fought in Kashmir. At his Razmak camp, Kashmiri was in regular contact with one of al-Zawahiri's lieutenants, Mustafa Abu al-Yazid, also known as Sheikh Saeed al-Masri.[137]

In September 1996, the Taliban advanced on Kabul, where they publicly castrated and hanged former president Najibullah after dragging him out of a United Nations building.[138] It was at this stage that the Taliban declared the Islamic Emirate of Afghanistan over which they were to be its rulers. Meanwhile, also in 1996, bin Laden issued his personal *fatwa* 'Declaration of War against the Americans Occupying the Land of the Two Holy Places'. His focus was the 'occupation' of Muslim lands by the United States and parts of the world where Muslims had allegedly been subjugated.[139] In the 1996 *fatwa*, bin Laden taunted the United States over the events in Somalia which al-Zawahiri was involved in: 'You left [Somalia] carrying disappointment, humiliation, defeat and your dead with you.' For bin Laden, the US withdrawal and inability to absorb loses was painting an image of his mind that bigger attacks would have greater impact on the American psyche.

Meanwhile, a bin Laden and al-Zawahiri ally from the Afghan Arab *mujahideen* days, Jalaluddin Haqqani, was seeking to assert his own authority in Afghanistan. He had been named minister of justice in the coalition government of Burhanuddin Rabbani in 1992 when Najibullah's administration collapsed. Haqqani became increasingly disenchanted with the government and in 1995 joined the Taliban. When the Taliban overthrew the

Rabbani government in 1996, Haqqani was appointed minister of borders and tribal affairs, a portfolio that was regarded as nondescript but which over time would transform his influence and power.[140]

Haqqani tapped into the growing trade in heroin which he would arrange to be smuggled into Pakistan, using mountain trails previously used by the *mujahideen*. Many of the traffickers were from Haqqani's own Zadran tribe, and they moved the narcotics across the porous border into the Waziristan agencies in Pakistan. This illicit lucrative trade made Haqqani very wealthy and enabled him to create numerous front companies to funnel his ill-gotten proceeds which included car dealerships and construction and pharmaceutical companies. He had mastered money laundering, which also benefited al-Qaeda.[141] At the same time, the Pakistani military, particularly the ISI, was also active in ensuring corruption flourished across the Afghan state and Afghan society, often using recruits from the 1980s and 1990s, including major figures in the drug trade, as vectors of transmission for corrupt practices.[142]

In essence, four separate but overlapping systems were created through al-Qaeda's alliance with the Taliban and Haqqani Network with the ISI's shadow in the background.[143] First, there was a training plan that ushered in local Afghan Pashtun recruits from the Pakistani *madrasas* and foreign jihadists to support the Taliban in its battles against the Northern Alliance. Second, a variety of Pakistani terrorist groups, mostly involved in attacks against India in Jammu and Kashmir, established training facilities in Afghanistan and acted as a funnel for bin Laden's agenda. Third, this provided foreign terrorists an outlet to fight but also a level of deniability concerning their Pakistani military sponsors. Lastly, there was bin Laden and his band of affiliates and foreign terrorist fighters who arrived from Sudan in 1996. According to Nick Pratt, 'All four groupings operated in tandem in Afghanistan but also in Pakistani jihadist hostels known as "guest houses" in order to enable recruits to move freely inside and outside of Afghanistan.'[144]

Kandahar possessed numerous facilities for potential jihadists. One of the most important for al-Zawahiri was the 'Airport Camp', also known as Tarnak Farms, where recruits were trained in surveillance, counter-surveillance, and intelligence by his trusted fellow Egyptian Saif al-Adel.[145] The Pakistani military facilitated fighter movement from the Waziristans to southern Afghanistan.[146] The other major camp in Kandahar was the al-Farooq one. It was here that al-Zawahiri would meet his future son-in-law and trusted deputy, Muhammad Abbatay, a Moroccan who also went by the alias Abd al-Rahman al-Maghrebi.[147] Abbatay had taken a software engineering course in Germany before moving to Afghanistan in 1999 to join al-Qaeda.[148] He married al-Zawahiri's daughter Nabila.[149] The al-Zawahiri household became a central point for the wives and families of al-Qaeda terrorists whilst the men plotted and planned.[150]

Though Kandahar received the most attention because of the presence of the al-Qaeda hierarchy, the main part of the jihadist training was centred in and around Kabul, where it was able to utilise the airport and existing Soviet-era military facilities.[151] In addition, the Kabul guesthouses acted as a precursor to the training camps. The most prominent one al-Zawahiri used for Arabs was the Khana Ghulam Bacha Guesthouse, which served to partly support the Taliban frontlines against the Northern Alliance.[152] Bin Laden was able to finance the camps, but Pakistan's ISI also helped to subsidize the cost as their intention was to fuel the terrorism in Jammu and Kashmir.[153]

The Egyptians were part of the 'faculty' at several of these camps.[154] By far the most important terrorist training facility in the Kabul area for al-Zawahiri was the Khalden Camp, which was ironically originally established by Abdullah Azzam's MAK. Al-Zawahiri would situate himself there when visiting Kabul. Al-Zawahiri had an office there with a sign outside the door, reading 'This is a workplace! For those who do not work here, please do not enter at all. Dr. Ayman.'[155] Khalden was utilised as a funnel for al-Qaeda to select the best recruits for the future operations.[156]

Another vital al-Qaeda camp for al-Zawahiri was the Darunta Complex, situated near the eastern city of Jalalabad in Nangarhar province. Documents discovered there revealed plans for a biological-processing facility. Manuals illustrated the handling and storage of a variety of chemical and biological agents as well as explosives. However, al-Qaeda also had a special interest in anthrax.[157] Al-Zawahiri was heading up the programme himself, joined by Mohammed Atef.

Whilst developing al-Qaeda's infrastructure in Afghanistan and Pakistan, al-Zawahiri was also very keen on creating an effective security apparatus to evade detection and penetration by foreign intelligence agencies. Personal safety and avoiding notice were synonymous with the Egyptian teacher. Al-Zawahiri kept a tight leash on terrorists abroad to adhere to security protocols and warned against lax security. In one communique, he ordered recruits to stop 'writing my name on messages ... start using two envelopes ... place my name on the inner envelope'.[158]

Returning to Afghanistan around the same time as al-Zawahiri, the Khadr family were initially living in Hayatabad, a suburb on the western outskirts of Peshawar, in 1994, and their children were all attending Abdullah Azzam's school.[159] Ahmed Khadr stood out from the other Arabs in Peshawar, preferring to wear Western pants and dress shirts.[160] Eventually, Khadr and his family moved into the bin Laden compound in Kabul. When bin Laden moved to Kandahar, the Khadr family shifted to Karte Parwan, a neighbourhood in north-western Kabul, from which Khadr ran his supposed new charity, Health and Education Projects International.[161]

In late 2000 Khadr's baby granddaughter Sofia had a serious medical problem. The circumference of her head had an abnormal growth causing fluid on the brain. Khadr spoke with al-Zawahiri, whom he viewed as a 'medical genius'.[162] According to John Miller, who met al-Zawahiri when he was working for ABC News, 'as a paediatrician, al-Zawahiri had an ability to connect both with people and children'.[163] Al-Zawahiri visited the Khadr family home in Karte Parwan, to make a physical assessment. As part of his ideological beliefs, the women of the house stayed behind a curtain whilst some of the men sat with al-Zawahiri.[164] Al-Zawahiri spoke in clear English throughout and recommended the baby should be taken to Canada for treatment and the Khadr family made the arrangements.[165]

Rabiah Hutchinson, an Australian convert who had found her way into radical Islamist circles prior to 9/11, was a mutual friend of the Khadr and al-Zawahiri families. In this period, Hutchinson became close friends with al-Zawahiri's favourite wife, Umm Fatima. It was Rabia who first said Sofia Khadr had fluid on the brain, which impressed al-Zawahiri, who asked her to run a women's hospital in Kabul he wanted to create.[166] Curiously, the second in command of al-Qaeda chose a foreign woman with no formal medical training for this position, but it demonstrated al-Zawahiri's pragmatism and interest in women demonstrating their knowledge and confidence.

The Caucasus Interlude

Throughout the early 1990s, al-Zawahiri had travelled far and wide, setting up training camps and cells. He was especially drawn to the Balkans and particularly the civil war in Bosnia-Herzegovina, as one of Europe's largest Muslim communities was located there.[167] Another region that mattered a great deal to him was the Caucasus. Around December 1996, al-Zawahiri sought to travel to Chechnya to create a new base for EIJ cadres.[168] Along with Afghanistan, Chechnya for al-Zawahiri 'became the safe haven and destination of emigrants and *mujahideen* from various parts of the world'.[169] Al-Zawahiri added, 'Conditions there [in the North Caucasus] were excellent.'[170] The Russians had started withdrawing from Chechnya in 1996 after agreeing to a humiliating ceasefire with the rebellious region during the First Chechen War. Chechnya presented a chance to create an Islamic state in the Caucasus and a base theatre from which the Islamists could wage jihad throughout the Central Asian region.[171] Al-Zawahiri wrote in *Knights under the Prophet's Banner*:

> The liberation of the Caucasus would constitute a hotbed of jihad ... and that region would become the shelter of thousands of Muslim *mujahideen* from various parts of the Islamic world, particularly Arab parts. This poses a direct threat to the United States represented by the growing support for the jihadist movement everywhere in the Islamic world. ... This will form a *mujahid* Islamic belt to the south of Russia that will be connected in the east to Pakistan, which is brimming with *mujahideen* movements in Kashmir. The belt will be linked to the south with Iran and Turkey that are sympathetic to the Muslims of Central Asia.[172]

Al-Zawahiri saw much of the potential of the Caucasus as a way to undermine not just Russia but the United States too. The neighbouring Russian province of Dagestan also held promise for al-Zawahiri. Situated in Russia's North Caucasus, it has a Muslim population and was the birthplace of Imam Shamil, the legendary nineteenth-century fighter who led tribesmen to resist the growing Russian Empire. Dagestan served as a strategic doorway between the Middle East and the Eurasian steppes. The rugged topography and rebellious and truculent inhabitants has proven to be a forbidding experience for every regional power that attempted to subdue the North Caucasus.

After the fall of the Soviet Union, Dagestan remained part of Russia, but the region also suffered from neglect, anarchy, and corruption. Organised crime flourished, with kidnappings and violence being routine. Firearms were omnipresent, and assassinations became regular occurrences. The head of Dagestan's government since 1987 was Magomedali Magomedov, a shrewd politician who had the ear of the Kremlin by controlling local discontent through clan-corporate associations. Under Magomedov's rule, Dagestan became part of his family fiefdom.[173] The 1990s also witnessed the Islamist insurgency in Chechnya spill over on occasions into

Dagestan.[174] Bomb blasts would kill police officers, separatist assailants assassinated local politicians, and rebel leaders were shot in skirmishes with Russian security forces.[175] For al-Zawahiri, the conditions were ripe to spread the jihad from Chechnya whilst using the opportunity to recruit for the EIJ. He saw the strategic benefits of aiding Dagestani Islamists to gain access to and control more than two-thirds of Russia's Caspian Sea shelf, making the EIJ a regional force to be reckoned with whilst serving another blow to Russia. Of all Chechnya's neighbours,[176] as al-Zawahiri explains,

> the liberation of the Muslim Caucasus will lead to the fragmentation of the Russian Federation and will help escalate the jihad movements that already exist in the republics of Uzbekistan and Tajikistan, whose governments get Russian backing against those jihadist movements.[177]

Thus, in an effort to connect with Chechen and Dagestani fighters, al-Zawahiri took a small cohort into Russian territory via Azerbaijan. They included EIJ stalwarts Mahmud Hisham al-Hennawi and Ahmed Salama Mabruk, who lived in Azerbaijan and ran a front company raising funds for the EIJ. On 1 December 1996, upon crossing the border into Russia's Dagestan province they were arrested for illegal entry.[178] Al-Zawahiri was carrying thousands of dollars in cash, a satellite phone, and forged identity documents, including a Sudanese passport, which helped him move back and forth from Khartoum.[179]

Under interrogation, al-Zawahiri claimed he was a merchant interested in the price of leather and purchasing medicines for sick relatives. He feigned ignorance that he was crossing the border illegally and avoided speaking clear English. Not knowing who al-Zawahiri was, the Russians treated him and the others as illegal immigrants, and he was imprisoned in Makhachkala for six months.[180]

Makhachkala is a city by the sea where portraits of Imam Shamil often appear in front of public buildings. Al-Zawahiri was hoping to emulate him but instead was confronted with a major setback to his grand ambitions in the Caucasus. Evading the attention of Russian intelligence, the EIJ's deputy Tharwat Salah Shehata arrived in Makhachkala on the premise that he was al-Zawahiri's legal representative and bribed the local authorities to release him and the others in May 1997.[181] In an often understated but important moment in the history of the global jihadist movement, the senior leadership of the EIJ were all together in the North Caucasus but left without incident or notice. Years later al-Zawahiri commented, 'Allah blinded them [the Russians] to our identities.'[182]

Al-Zawahiri went back to Kandahar accompanied by Shehata.[183] However, other EIJ members were not pleased with al-Zawahiri's Dagestan sojourn. An email from associates in Yemen described al-Zawahiri's escapade as 'a disaster that almost destroyed the group'.[184] Frustration with al-Zawahiri sometimes bubbled over into potential mutiny. Records from an al-Qaeda computer outlined a memorandum of gripes presented to 'the doctor'. They suggested the EIJ was swamped by feuds. 'What was the point of a visit to Chechnya?' the memorandum questioned, 'management methods that have led to the departure of some brothers from the company and nearly led to the temptation of others.'[185]

The World Islamic Front

In 1998, al-Zawahiri wrote in the EIJ journal *Al-Mujahideen* on Jewish influence in the United States. His anti-Semitic tropes included, 'America is now controlled by the Jews, completely, as are its news, its elections, its economy, and its politics.'[186] This was building up to a much wider indictment of Jews and the West that al-Zawahiri believed sponsored them. On 23 February 1998, al-Zawahiri issued a joint *fatwa* with bin Laden under the title 'Declaration of the World Islamic Front for Jihad against the Jews and the Crusaders'.[187] The language had been in negotiation for some time, as part of the consolidation of ties between bin Laden's organization and al-Zawahiri's EIJ. Although the *fatwa* signified the EIJ becoming an official affiliate of al-Qaeda, it did not signify a full-scale merger of the two terrorist groups yet.[188] However, al-Zawahiri contributed to the drafting of the *fatwa*, which meant the EIJ was slowly becoming absorbed into al-Qaeda.[189]

Bin Laden and al-Zawahiri were joined by three other leaders of prominent terrorist groups. Abu Yasir Rifai Ahmad Taha, who led a splinter faction of al-Gama'a that had merged with the EIJ; Mir Hamza, secretary general of the Assembly of the Pakistani Clergy (Jamiat Ulema-e-Pakistan), a Pakistani militant group; and Maulana Fazlur Rahman, the leader of a Bangladeshi militant group, Movement of Islamic Holy War (Harkat-ul-Jihad-al-Islami). These entities signed a declaration, defined by al-Qaeda as a *fatwa*, declaring the establishment of the World Islamic Front to unite the global jihadist movement.

Other members of the alliance were jihadist groups in Afghanistan, Sudan, Saudi Arabia, Somalia, Yemen, Bosnia-Herzegovina, Algeria, Tunisia, Lebanon, the Philippines, Tajikistan, Pakistan, and the Caucasus. The document delineated the transnational threat that was starting to take shape. 'In compliance with Allah's order,' the text read, 'we issue the following *fatwa* to all Muslims: the ruling to kill the Americans and their allies' civilian and military is an individual duty for every Muslim who can do it in any country in which it is possible to do it.'[190] The *fatwa* outlined its grievances against what would be al-Qaeda's biggest Western enemy:

> The United States has been occupying the lands of Islam in the holiest of places, the Arabian Peninsula, plundering its riches, dictating to its rulers, humiliating its people, terrorising its neighbours, and turning its bases in the Peninsula into a spearhead through which to fight the neighbouring Muslim people.[191]

A *fatwa* is an edict based on the interpretation of Islamic law by a respected Islamic authority or scholar of *fiqh*, but neither bin Laden nor al-Zawahiri were authorities or scholars on Shariah, a criticism other ideologues who preceded them did not have to face. Both bin Laden and al-Zawahiri lacked formal religious training, and their pronouncements should not have been religiously qualified *fatwas*. However, very little was done to invalidate the 1998 declaration or even try to expose the ideological limitations of both men. Instead, there was greater focus on the threat they presented, which only heightened their own importance within the global jihadist movement. Unlike bin Laden's 1996 *fatwa*, the 1998 *fatwa* had a degree of religious authority due to Mir Hamzah's inclusion, as he was a qualified cleric.

The 1998 *fatwa* signalled an unparalleled moment in which jihadist terrorist groups united openly to assert their intentions. The 1998 *fatwa* cited three reasons for its creation. First, the 'American occupation' of the 'holy' Arabian Peninsula; second, the 'massacre' of Iraqis by the United Nations sanctions enforced in 1991; and third, the existence of Israel and the occupation of Jerusalem. For al-Qaeda, these crimes were orchestrated by the United States to further their strategic interests. According to the *fatwa*, all the attacks on Muslim countries were to 'serve the interests of the petty Jewish state, diverting attention from its occupation of Jerusalem ... and to fragment all the states in the region, like Iraq, Saudi Arabia, Egypt, and Sudan, into paper mini-states whose weakness and disunity will guarantee

Israel's attacks'[192] The *fatwa* effectively formally established al-Qaeda's doctrine, whose purpose was to

> kill Americans and their allies . . . in order to liberate the al-Aqsa Mosque [in Jerusalem] and the Holy Mosque [in Mecca] from their grip so that their armies leave all the territory of Islam, defeated, broken and unable to threaten any Muslim. This is in accordance with the words of almighty Allah, 'and fight the pagans all together as they fight you all together' and 'fight them until there is no more tumult or oppression, and there prevail justice and faith in Allah'.[193]

The call to alter the priorities by reducing the level of importance in the battle against the 'internal enemy' and target the West was an extraordinary strategic move amongst jihadist groups and signalled al-Zawahiri's move away from the tenets of Sayyid Qutb and Muhammad Abd al-Salam Faraj on removing 'apostate' rulers. However, the decision to target the West was not a spontaneous reaction. It came after three decades of unsuccessful and futile attempts against the 'internal enemy'. The conflict with the Mubarak regime was too costly for al-Zawahiri. He targeted the 'external enemy,' principally the United States, through a series of attacks resulting in casualties, to hurt their morale and economy, which in turn would force them to withdraw their support for the '*jahili*' rulers. Al-Zawahiri had long blamed the United States for preserving Mubarak. An EIJ lieutenant testified in a 1999 court trial that

> Usamah bin Laden said that the organization's [al-Jihad] activities were too costly because militants had to change hideouts continuously. He also argued that attacks being carried out in Egypt were costing too much money and too many militant lives and called on both the country's main Islamic groups to 'turn their guns' on the U.S. and Israel.[194]

The *fatwa* also demonstrated a reversal in who shaped the jihadist direction. It was now bin Laden enlisting al-Zawahiri to be part of his jihad against the United States, unlike during the aftermath of the Soviet defeat in Afghanistan, when al-Zawahiri held sway over bin Laden. However, even within al-Qaeda's leadership, there were divisions over the benefits of broadening the jihad to include the West because it could inadvertently unify public support and further the agendas of Western governments who planned to isolate and undermine al-Qaeda.[195]

Significantly, the *fatwa* was issued from Khost, in territory controlled by Afghan warlord Jalaluddin Haqqani, and not Kandahar where the Taliban and Mullah Omar focused their power and influence.[196] There was a degree of reluctance for Mullah Omar to publicly endorse al-Qaeda's activities because of the international scrutiny it would attract. Although the Haqqani Network was not a signatory of the *fatwa*, by hosting al-Qaeda for its announcement they were by extension supporting it. At the time, the United States described the Haqqanis as being 'ideologically close to bin Laden's internationalist Islamist positions, [and] these men have successfully argued with other Taliban in recent months to reduce controls on bin Laden'.[197] As the Pakistani scholar Ayesha Siddiqa pointed out, 'The Haqqanis maintained a close relationship with al-Qaeda because it's ideological. That's what is different with Mullah Omar's Taliban who were not expansionist. Jalaluddin Haqqani was more of an Islamic globalist.'[198]

Haqqani was essential to providing support and sanctuary to various Pakistani, Kashmiri, and Arab jihadists like al-Qaeda 'in exchange for weapons and money ... in areas of Paktia province'.[199] Paktia, Paktika, and Khost provinces are dominated by the Haqqani Zadran tribe. This area is known as Greater Paktia (Loya Paktia) as well as the 'Zadran Arch', because of the common culture across the provinces. The Canadian diplomat Chris Alexander pointed out, 'The tribal standing of the Haqqani family in certain areas of Loya Paktia is indisputable. Relatives of those Haqqanis active as Pakistani proxies have been living in the Zadran district for generations.'[200] The Haqqani Paktia sanctuary for al-Qaeda would eventually pay a heavy toll for hosting al-Zawahiri.

Aside from using Khost as a location to broadcast their propaganda, bin Laden and al-Zawahiri also produced multiple videos and conducted several media interviews from Jalalabad in Nangarhar province.[201] The Airport House, also called the Najim al-Jihad Guesthouse, was used by al-Zawahiri when he visited Jalalabad.[202] On 26 May 1998, bin Laden, al-Zawahiri, and Mohammed Atef continued to show their independence from the Taliban and held a press conference in one of the training camps in Khost province. The press conference was attended by the two Pakistani journalists Rahimullah Yusufzai and Jamal Isma'il.[203] At the same time, bin Laden paid several journalists in Pakistan to ramp up their coverage of his statements and al-Qaeda's agendas.[204]

However, for al-Zawahiri, recruiting local journalists wasn't sufficient for al-Qaeda to get maximum coverage, especially if the group was going to escalate its war against the West. It needed attention that could be controlled, meaning that al-Zawahiri wanted to shape the narrative. He later reflected that during this period the 'tools' that the 'Western powers' used to fight and subjugate Islam included the 'international news agencies and satellite television'.[205] Al-Zawahiri sensed an opportunity. From his experiences in Egypt learning how journalists reported on political events, as well as his time in prison, al-Zawahiri understood that the media in its various formats can spur political violence through manipulation. Under his influence, al-Qaeda began to devote time and resources to its media propaganda to adapt to the growing dominance of satellite and cable television as well as the emergence of the internet.

To achieve this, al-Qaeda needed to court the attention of the international media to enhance their status and notoriety, but also it presented an opportunity to see close up how the editorial process works. Almost simultaneously with the *fatwa*'s announcement, a fax arrived at the London office of *Al-Quds al-Arabi* newspaper on 23 February 1998. It was verbatim the 1,053-word declaration of war from bin Laden and al-Zawahiri.[206] At the time, fax machines provided a level of near real-time interaction previously unimagined. Al-Qaeda were no longer encumbered by time delays for their content to get the oxygen of publicity. All they needed was a phone line, and the indoctrination began.

Terrorist propaganda was not new, but the way it was transmitted illustrated how evolving technology could be used for terrorism. Al-Zawahiri understood that faxing provided an inexpensive and faster way of transmitting words and images and data. Faxing an ideological message was akin to publishing a manifesto.

'There Will Be No B-roll'

Under al-Zawahiri's guidance, Osama bin Laden wanted to 'introduce himself' to the United States and agreed to take part in an ABC News television interview in May 1998. It was the same network al-Zawahiri's cousin had once worked for as a stringer back in the 1970s. Then–ABC correspondent John Miller had the task of quizzing bin Laden. However, he and his production team first had to take a very circuitous journey to secure the interview. This included multiple plane flights within Pakistan, a night-time border crossing into Afghanistan, numerous al-Qaeda protocols and checkpoints, and being escorted through several camps in Kandahar before finally being able to meet bin Laden, al-Zawahiri, and Atef. For Miller, the immediate priority was to try to figure out their roles and seniority.

> When we got there, we meet al-Zawahiri, who is all about being the political director of the event. He said, 'I'm sure you had a long journey, it must have been very difficult, we're just going to check out some things here, and then we'll get you to where you're going to sleep. It's probably not the accommodation you're used to, but around here, it's the Ritz!'[207]

Al-Zawahiri spoke in perfect English, with confidence, and he was keen to show Miller that he was in control of matters. Conversely, Mohammed Atef only spoke in single-syllable words, focusing on bin Laden's security by confiscating the camera equipment, searching it, and returning some but holding onto the rest. For Miller, Atef was the military leader, playing the role of bodyguard. During their stay at the al-Qaeda camp, al-Zawahiri would visit Miller and his team every day.[208] Ahead of the interview with bin Laden, al-Zawahiri wanted to know in advance what the questions were going to be. Miller explained, 'We don't really give out the questions, it's not the way we work.' Al-Zawahiri retorted:

> We have a translator here. You're going to ask the questions in English, he's going to translate them into Arabic. And he's not a translator from the United Nations. He'll do the best he can, but if you write the questions out, then he can copy them into Arabic, and when you ask question number one and he reads it, it's going to be exactly the question you're looking for the answer to, not an approximation.[209]

For Miller, this showed 'a practical ability for al-Zawahiri to deal with problems, to deal with people, to navigate cultural and business issues. I ended up writing out 16 questions.'[210] Miller then explained to al-Zawahiri that his news network did not just want bin Laden to be a talking head for an hour, speaking about whatever he deemed was pertinent. The ABC team planned to build a story around why should people listen to bin Laden and get to understand who he is. For Miller,

> that meant we've got to show bin Laden moving around the camp, watching the soldiers train, riding in a jeep, whatever it is that he normally does. We

need to have some B-roll, which is when the narrator is talking, there's some footage that goes over that, of him doing what he does here, in his element.[211]

At which point al-Zawahiri laughed and said, 'There will be no B-roll. . . . This is not like your Sam Donaldson walking through the Rose Garden with the President of the United States.'[212] Al-Zawahiri's reference to Sam Donaldson was very intriguing, as Miller explains:

> Donaldson was the dean of White House reporters for ABC news. And he covered every president back to Lyndon Johnson, and he always got that ex- clusive interview with the president where they walked around through the Rose Garden of the White House and then sat down on the veranda and spoke frankly. I don't remember what he said after that because the whole time I was thinking 'Wow, Ayman al-Zawahiri knows who Sam Donaldson is.' It was a very Western-media-savvy reference.[213]

Al-Zawahiri's knowledge of Sam Donaldson harks back to the time prior to the Sadat assassination when Donaldson was the White House corres- pondent for ABC and al-Zawahiri's cousin worked as a stringer for the network in Egypt. Since then, al-Zawahiri had showed a huge interest in Donaldson. By the time Miller interviewed bin Laden, Donaldson was once again the White House correspondent. Al-Zawahiri clearly wanted to demonstrate his knowledge of the American media, but it also revealed how closely he was following it. For Miller, the trip to Afghanistan helped clarify the leadership roles of al-Qaeda and the relationship with the EIJ as well al-Zawahiri's influence with bin Laden:

> Al-Zawahiri did the mechanics of getting the interview done and getting us in there. He was in the formulation of the message part of the business. Essentially, bin Laden was the leadership and the inspiration and the money. Al-Zawahiri was there for what is the doctrine, the method, the cause, the compelling storyline that needs to go with that. And Atef was all about oper- ations. That was the troika at the time.[214]

During his interview with Miller, bin Laden made his notorious remark about the US withdrawal from Somalia in 1993: 'The American soldier was just a paper tige . . . unable to endure the strikes that were dealt to his army, so he fled,' which to al-Qaeda meant there would be future opportun- ities to challenge America's global standing and the 'paper tiger' theory.[215] Al-Zawahiri's departing words to Miller predicted what al-Qaeda's future activities entailed: it was 'every Muslims duty to kill the Americans and their allies, civilians and military'. It was a clear statement of intent that for al-Qaeda the lines between civilians and the military were not just blurred; they were effectively one in the same for al-Zawahiri.[216]

Interestingly, al-Qaeda's media engagement created a rare moment of tension between Mullah Omar and bin Laden and al-Zawahiri. Omar did not like bin Laden meeting foreign journalists without informing the Taliban in advance. In fact, in July 1998 a secret memo highlighted the near fissure in ties between the two groups.[217] Addressed to al-Zawahiri, the note describes a tense meeting between the Taliban leader and 'Abu Abdullah', a bin Laden alias.[218] The memo blames the spat on a 'bankrupt failure to achieve any real external victory'.[219] It cautions that Arabs based in Afghanistan are in danger of losing access to training camps in Taliban-held territory. This was something al-Qaeda could ill afford, having already been forced to leave Sudan.

Amidst all of this, al-Zawahiri had begun to see a merger with bin Laden as a logical next step, which would also ensure a more consistent revenue stream thanks to bin Laden's largesse.[220] However, al-Zawahiri's cadres did not acquiesce to his desire, and the potential strategic change produced extensive friction in the EIJ. Al-Zawahiri hurriedly convened an EIJ gathering in Afghanistan to discuss the legacy of the 1998 *fatwa* for the EIJ, which some were opposed to.[221] Yet al-Zawahiri had already made up his mind before the EIJ's Majlis al-Shura could form a consensus. For al-Zawahiri, signing the *fatwa* was of paramount importance. Humiliatingly, most of the EIJ learnt about the union with bin Laden only from newspapers, television, and radio.[222] The foot soldiers and mid-level operators were outraged that their leader signed it without consulting them. Many of the Egyptians were equally disillusioned that al-Zawahiri had abruptly altered the EIJ's long-standing 'internal enemy' strategy. According to an EIJ member:

> The [1998] *Fatwa* to kill the Americans contravenes the principles of Islamic *Shariah*. It also contravenes the strategy and principles of the Jihad Organization [EIJ], which believes that . . . it is more appropriate to fight the ruler than to fight a faraway enemy, like Zionism and imperialism.[223]

The EIJ had significant financial problems, and al-Zawahiri realised the group had sustainability issues. Its failure to achieve its primary goal of unseating the Mubarak regime, as well as the mass incarceration of their members resulted in demoralization. The EIJ's attacks impacted negatively on Egypt's economy and resulted in a backlash from the urban poor who struggled to eke out a living. Having generated widespread opposition, the Egyptian cadres in disarray, and the rival al-Gama'a imprisoned leaders negotiating a ceasefire with Mubarak, al-Zawahiri concluded that his options were limited.[224]

Indeed, al-Zawahiri saw the partnership with bin Laden as a marriage of convenience to keep the EIJ alive. At the same time, al-Zawahiri silenced the dissenters within the EIJ by accusing them of being seduced by Western culture and materialism.[225] The EIJ would not merge with al-Qaeda for the time being but instead would function in tandem as a transnational organization with a Shura Council hierarchy at the helm overseen by bin Laden, with al-Zawahiri as his deputy and a network of recruits across the world.[226] In the meantime, the EIJ would have autonomy to carry out terrorist operations of its own.

One of the EIJ's major international plots was well underway when the 1998 *fatwa* was signed. However, in July 1998, Ahmed Mabruk was detained in Baku, Azerbaijan, in a joint operation between the Azeris and the Americans. Mabruk's heavy-duty Toshiba laptop was also seized, which contained information about EIJ members in Egypt and in the Balkans. Consequently, the Mubarak regime was able to round up a large portion of the EIJ in Egypt.[227] This was devastating for al-Zawahiri and led to the discovery of seven cells including one in Tirana, Albania, which was subsequently dismantled by the Albanian authorities in cooperation with US counter-terrorism agencies.[228] Mabruk was returned to Egypt and offered a deal to provide more details on the EIJ's networks including al-Zawahiri's location. However, Mabruk refused and was imprisoned for 15 years in 1999.[229]

On 6 August 1998, al-Zawahiri sent a fax to the office of the Egyptian newspaper *al-Hayat* in Cairo admitting that an EIJ cell had been unearthed by the Central Intelligence Agency (CIA) in Tirana, Albania. *Al-Hayat* published an article on it the next day.[230] The EIJ had planned to target the US Embassy in Tirana with a truck bomb, but the plot was foiled in one of the largest counter-terrorism operations on record.[231] The EIJ cell in Tirana was assembled by Ayman al-Zawahiri's younger brother, Muhammad, in the early 1990s soon after the Albanian communist regime collapsed in 1991. The EIJ members in Albania were extradited to Egypt.[232] What became known as the 'Trial of the Returnees from Albania' turned out to be second-biggest terrorist trial in Egypt, after the case of al-Jihad and the assassination of Anwar Sadat in 1981. Ayman al-Zawahiri was involved in both.

The prosecution of the EIJ plotters commenced in 1999 with 43 people on trial in person at the Higher Military Court at Haekstep, north of Cairo.[233] This included Muhammad al-Zawahiri, who had fled to the United Arab Emirates but was arrested and extradited to Egypt.[234] Sixty-four were being tried in absentia with Ayman al-Zawahiri. More than 20,000 pages of investigation report contained the defendants' detailed confessions to their 'anti-regime' activities, violent acts inside and outside Egypt, and future plans to destabilise the Mubarak regime. Many of the accused had been members of the EIJ for the nearly 20 years since its inception. They had served time in Egyptian prisons after the killing of Sadat.[235]

During the trial, several EIJ members revealed that al-Zawahiri arranged for forged passports to enable their travels between Yemen, Afghanistan, and Sudan. The EIJ also had safe houses in Sudan, Yemen, Austria, Germany, the United Kingdom, Azerbaijan, Afghanistan, Saudi Arabia, and Southeast Asia. The EIJ maintained bank accounts in many European countries and sent small amounts, less than $2,000 at a time, to support other members including for the US Embassy Tirana plot. To finance the plot, they also siphoned proceeds meant for an Albanian orphanage and raided an Italian diplomat's home in Amman, Jordan. The cell also acquired doctored university certificates.[236]

One of the EIJ operatives extradited from Albania was Ahmed Ibrahim al-Sayyid al-Najjar, who became the Egyptian state prosecution's primary witness. Following the failed assassination attempt of Egyptian prime minister Atef Sedky, al-Najjar was put in charge of the EIJ's Yemen cell and tasked with building up supporters and recruits under the guise of an 'urban planning committee'. Al-Najjar revealed that financial support for the EIJ would be based on every recruit providing between 10% and 26% of any income they made, which would then be supplemented by Osama bin Laden. Importantly, bin Laden would not interfere with organizational matters. They would be left to al-Zawahiri, as both men had a good understanding and mutual respect.[237]

During the court hearings, some of the EIJ members revealed that they had been in touch with al-Zawahiri's deputy Tharwat Salah Shehata, who was guiding them on the Tirana plot, with al-Najjar serving as his deputy. They both received instructions from al-Zawahiri via fax. Al-Najjar also revealed that al-Zawahiri kept strict control over the various cells and pursued a policy of compartmentalisation: 'Al-Zawahiri prohibited any of the cell officials from conducting direct coordination . . . [so] there was no confusion between the cells and his experience proved that when there was an overlap.'[238]

Al-Najjar revealed it was permissible for EIJ operatives to use telephones to communicate, but al-Zawahiri preferred faxes and increasingly the internet, which was a relatively new phenomenon at the time. It was clear how important clandestine communications were to al-Zawahiri. Safety and concealment from being uncovered by the Egyptian authorities were paramount. Individuals attached to specific cells also had to go through a protracted process anytime they wanted to travel outside the country. They needed consent from the Special Action Committee, of which Muhammad al-Zawahiri was a member.[239]

Al-Najjar revealed that the EIJ in Albania learnt of the 1998 *fatwa* only when it was revealed to the world. Although there were massive internal disagreements within the EIJ over the merits of this pact, al-Najjar said, 'there is a direct benefit from the merging of the groups under bin Laden, financial strength being the most important'.[240] The most controversial revelation that came out of the trial was that al-Qaeda and the EIJ were collaborating on creating biological and chemical weapons. This was a project al-Zawahiri was particularly keen on, and over time his agenda would become more apparent.

To try to get to al-Zawahiri, the dragnet was closing in on some of his family and closest allies. Khalid Abu al-Dahab, who had represented the EIJ in California and New York and was a loyal al-Zawahiri confidante, was spending an increasing amount of time in Egypt. Despite the coordinated dismantlement of several EIJ cells, al-Dahab bizarrely chose to remain in Egypt, in the hope that being close to home would attract the least suspicion. However, on 28 October 1998, al-Dahab was aboard a flight to the United States nearing take-off when the Egyptian security police arrested him on board. Al-Dahab was sentenced to 15 years in prison.[241]

Al-Dahab confessed to the Egyptian authorities his role in the EIJ, including the Albania plot. During the trial he revealed that he had been tasked by al-Zawahiri with planning a near-impossible raid on the Mazra'at Tora prison to facilitate the escape of EIJ terrorists. The plot involved dropping explosives from a hang glider onto the prison from overhead. The intended result was to create panic, enabling the EIJ members to flee. Al-Dahab even learnt how to use a glider at a civil flying school in San Francisco and went to Afghanistan to train three EIJ operatives how to use it. However, the plot never went further.[242] Behind the walls and watchtowers of Mazra'at Tora prison, in 1993, many years after the EIJ old guard had left, a new 320-cell annex was created to house all the EIJ terrorists and other high-level extremists. It was known as el-Aqrab, or the Scorpion. No visitors are ever allowed within its walls.[243]

Eventually, the court convicted 87 EIJ members and sentenced 10 of them to death, including al-Zawahiri, who was tried in absentia. His brother Muhammad was given a life sentence.[244] According to a former EIJ jihadist, 'At the time, we were under severe scrutiny and real pressure from both the Egyptian and American governments, and it was a tough, tough situation to find ourselves in.'[245] Al-Zawahiri's association and ties with bin Laden had caught the attention of the US intelligence community. According to Ambassador Henry Crumpton, al-Zawahiri's name would come up often within the US intelligence community:

> From 1998, it was pretty constant. Coming from the Egyptian Islamic Jihad and their collaboration with al-Qaeda, we followed all that closely, almost daily in terms of his name coming up in the work we were doing. We understood how serious the issue was and even in the sort of broader operational discussions we would have of the al-Qaeda leadership, and al-Zawahiri in particular.[246]

In his fax to *al-Hayat*, al-Zawahiri warned that the United States would soon be punished for the disruption of the EIJ Tirana cell: 'We should like to inform the Americans that, in short, their message has been received and that they should read carefully the reply that will, with Allah's help, be written in the language that they understand.'[247]

Raising the Stakes

As al-Zawahiri was alluding to, the Tirana plot was not the only operation being planned. Al-Qaeda and the EIJ had concluded that their objectives in targeting US interests may be more successful in Africa. Al-Zawahiri had sent his double agent Ali Mohamed to Nairobi, Kenya, to look for viable targets. Mohamed, who had successfully embedded himself both in the FBI and US Army, scouted the US Embassy, USAID headquarters, and the US Agricultural Office. In July 1998, al-Zawahiri summoned Essam Marzouk to Afghanistan to help with the final preparations of the US Embassy attack.[248] Without any hesitation, Marzouk sold off his company assets and left Canada permanently. Marzouk was assigned to train two men, a Saudi, Mohamed al-Owhali, and an Egyptian, Jihad Mohammed Ali, for a suicide bombing mission.[249]

The 7 August 1998 marked exactly eight years to the day that US troops arrived in Saudi Arabia to take part in Operation Desert Shield, to counter Iraq's invasion of Kuwait. At the time, hardly anyone in East Africa, or even the United States, was wary or concerned about the anniversary. Iraq had been expelled from Kuwait, and the House of Saud continued to rule Saudi Arabia. The world had moved on, except for al-Qaeda, and in particular, bin Laden and al-Zawahiri. On 7 August, 1998, the day after al-Zawahiri's fax to *al-Hayat*, two US Embassies were attacked concurrently by suicide truck bombers in Nairobi, Kenya, and Dar es Salaam, Tanzania.[250] A thousand pounds of explosives were assembled into the explosives.[251] In Nairobi, a truck slowed in front of the US Embassy, and Mohamed al-Owhali jumped out and tossed a stun grenade at the security guard. Behind the steering wheel, Jihad Mohammed Ali opened fire with a handgun whilst manoeuvring the bomb-laden truck before it detonated. Seven hundred miles away, a similar scene was unfolding outside the US Embassy in Dar es Salam. The bombers executed their mission with deadly effect. They had been well trained in part by the EIJ.

Another Egyptian al-Zawahiri confidante, Abdullah Ahmed Abdullah—also known as Abu Muhammad al-Masri—oversaw the two terrorist attacks. The ensuing blast in Nairobi killed 247 people and wounded another 5,000.[252] Amongst the dead were 12 Americans.[253] The bomb in Tanzania exploded outside the embassy gate, killing 11 Tanzanians and injuring 72.[254] Al-Qaeda soon advertised their now global notoriety in the *al-Hayat* newspaper: 'America will face a black fate. . . . [S]trikes will continue from everywhere, and Islamic groups will appear one after another to fight American interests.'[255] For al-Zawahiri, the East Africa embassy attacks also importantly dispelled several notions which had clearly weighed on his mind and may have been shaped by his experiences with the American media:

The Arab and Western media are responsible for distorting the image of the Arab Afghans by portraying them as obsessed half-mad people who have re-belled against the United States that once trained and financed them. This lie was repeated more frequently after the Arab Afghans returned to Afghanistan for the second time in the mid-1990s in the wake of the bombing of the U.S. embassies in Nairobi and Dar es-Salam.[256]

Al-Qaeda's approach was intended to create maximum carnage by coordin-ating attacks on American interests in different locations whilst at the same time assessing how the United States might react.[257] The group's global jihad against the 'external enemy' had officially begun. Al-Zawahiri ration-alised that the arrangement with bin Laden and the shift to the 'external enemy' would bring together the different strands of the jihad movement against the United States and Israel. As he explained in *Knights under the Prophet's Banner*:

> The one slogan that has been well understood by the nation and to which it has been responding for the past 50 years is the call for the Jihad against Israel. In addition to this slogan, the nation in this decade is geared against the U.S. presence. It has responded favourably to the call for the Jihad against the Americans.[258]

Al-Zawahiri viewed the East Africa embassy bombings as a measure of revenge for his brother's detention in the UAE and extradition to Egypt. Al-Zawahiri was pained by that and had a sense of guilt that he was not able to protect his younger brother, which possibly contributed to his fur-ther intrinsic support of bin Laden.[259] Ayman al-Zawahiri later commented on his brother's extradition which he argued was on 'America's orders to Egypt, thus taking part with America in its war on Islam after the events of Nairobi and Dar al-Salaam'.[260]

Files uncovered in al-Qaeda's compound years later showed a congratu-latory message to al-Zawahiri by an unidentified author for the embassy bombings praising him for 'what you did and all the works and the labours that you did to plague the enemy of Allah'. The author added, 'We should not look for the easier targets, but we should look for the more strategic places, the targets which will harm the enemy and exact revenge upon them.'[261]

Following the US Embassy bombings, Ali Mohamed, who was in California, intended to travel to Afghanistan via Egypt. Before doing so, however, he was subpoenaed to appear before a grand jury in the Southern

District of New York.[262] On 10 September 1998, before the grand jury, Mohamed perjured himself.[263] This led to his secret arrest.[264] It was only on 19 May 1999 that he pled guilty to conspiracy.[265] He had been indicted 'on federal charges that he provided training to members of [al-Qaeda]'. Around a year after his arrest, on 20 October 2000, he also pled guilty to his involvement in the US Embassy bombings of 1998.[266] Subsequently, he cooperated with the US government, providing information about al-Qaeda.[267] Since then, Mohamed has not been sentenced and remains in US custody at an unknown location.

In large part because of al-Zawahiri's judgement of Mohamed's potential, he remains arguably the only jihadist to have successfully infiltrated both the US military and federal law enforcement. His record as a terrorist was more astounding when considering all the occasions when US intelligence and law enforcement failed to put an end to his illicit activities in collaboration with al-Zawahiri. Al-Zawahiri's name had been on US intelligence radar since the mid-1990s. He became a person of interest after the EIJ bombing of the Egyptian Embassy in Islamabad. Although he was still viewed as primarily an Egyptian problem, when al-Zawahiri signed the 1998 *fatwa* with bin Laden, the FBI opened a file on him. Following the East Africa embassy bombings, US intelligence had their worst suspicions confirmed, that bin Laden was no longer the only transnational terrorist they had to be worried about. Al-Zawahiri had become a full-time director with bin Laden in global terror.[268]

Thirteen days after the embassy bombings, on 20 August, President Bill Clinton gave the order to launch Operation Infinite Reach, which identified two al-Qaeda targets for air strikes. One was the Khost terrorist training camp in Afghanistan where some 500 al-Qaeda fighters were based, including on occasions bin Laden and al-Zawahiri. The other target was the El-Shifa pharmaceutical factory in Khartoum, Sudan, that was suspected of producing materials for chemical weapons.[269]

Even though most of the missiles struck their planned locations, neither bin Laden nor al-Zawahiri was killed or even injured. It was likely that they managed to escape hours before the missiles hit the camp. For the Khost operation, the cruise missiles that headed for Afghanistan had to cross Pakistan. The US vice chairman of the Joint Chiefs, General Joseph Ralston, spoke with the Pakistani chief of army staff (COAS) General Jehangir Karamat to point out that the missiles were from the United States and not from their arch-rival, India.[270] In May 1998, both India and Pakistan had conducted nuclear bomb tests which had created tensions in the region. In hindsight, US officials concluded by alerting the Pakistani military of the airstrike, the military in turn likely tipped off al-Qaeda either directly or through the Taliban.[271] Ambassador Henry Crumpton commented, 'It would be surprising to me if some elements of the Pakistani leadership, particularly the military, were not aware and perhaps even aiding and abetting al-Qaeda.'[272]

The day after American missile strikes in Afghanistan and Sudan, US president Bill Clinton called the Pakistani prime minister Nawaz Sharif, who was forced by his military 'to take a hard line against the strikes'. A State Department memo, revealed that the Sharif government 'operates in an environment dominated by conspiracy theories and paranoia'.[273] The Sharif government could not denounce bin Laden without disaffecting key elements in Pakistan, especially the local jihadists who retained close ties to al-Qaeda and who also received backing from the Pakistani military. Another State Department memo revealed, 'The U.S. Embassy in Islamabad disclosed that Pakistan is not disposed to be especially helpful on the matter of terrorist Usama bin Laden.'[274] Directly following the air strikes, Taliban commander Mullah Omar defiantly stated the Taliban 'will never hand over bin Laden to anyone and [will] protect him with our blood at all costs'.[275] For bin Laden, the US response encouraged his belief that America was very much a 'paper tiger'.

Mischievously, al-Zawahiri also posited a 'wag the dog' story to his followers to explain Clinton's decision for the airstrikes as an attempt to distract the world's attention from his relationship with White House intern Monica Lewinsky.[276] The reference was to the 1997 film *Wag the Dog*, based on a 1993 novel by Larry Beinhart. The plot was based on a presidential scandal which needed to be forgotten, and the best way to achieve that was to fabricate a war. It again demonstrated al-Zawahiri's knowledge of pop culture and Western media. The fiction intruded into real politics. Three days after admitting he had inappropriate relations with White House intern Monica Lewinsky and two weeks after the East Africa embassy bombings, Clinton ordered missile strikes in Sudan and Afghanistan.

Following the East Africa embassy bombings, John Miller tried to arrange a second interview with bin Laden for ABC News and contacted the network's freelance stringer in Pakistan to help arrange a meeting. Eventually, after the airstrikes in Afghanistan and Sudan, the stringer got back to Miller saying he had spoken to al-Zawahiri, who had refused another interview, but had a message from bin Laden: 'Tell the Americans that we aren't afraid of bombardment, threats, and acts of aggression. We are ready for more sacrifices. The war has only just begun, [and] the Americans should now await the answer.'[277]

In October 1999, al-Zawahiri's youngest brother, Hussein, was arrested in Malaysia, where he was working as an engineer. Initially accused of being involved in the Albania plot, he was then extradited to Egypt. Like his notorious brothers, Hussein had been arrested a few times in Egypt on suspicion of being part of the EIJ but was never indicted. In this instance he was eventually released after no evidence to link him to the EIJ's plotting was found.[278] The experience of the EIJ cell being exposed was particularly traumatic for al-Zawahiri, especially as it permanently impacted the ability of the EIJ to operate at the same level. Thereafter, al-Zawahiri made it an absolute priority to ensure his own personal safety and not ever end up in prison again or meet the fate of his colleagues and brothers. In particular, al-Zawahiri understood the value of the Haqqani Network in Afghanistan and realised that the group's infrastructure could serve him well and provide guaranteed protection.

Also in 1999, US officials covertly met directly with Jalaluddin Haqqani to discuss cooperation on isolating al-Qaeda. At that point, Haqqani was the Taliban's minister of borders, which was a very lucrative portfolio, as it gave him access to the traffic between Pakistan and Afghanistan and enabled him to increase his burgeoning shadow businesses. Tensions were palpable since the US missile strike destroyed the Haqqani-linked terrorist camp in Khost in August 1998. Inevitably, talks reached an impasse.[279] At the same time, the Clinton administration had identified the Haqqani Paktia safehouses as al-Qaeda sanctuaries for potential future airstrikes if required.[280]

In the meantime, al-Qaeda kept trying to escalate the conflict with the US. On 14 December 2000, Ahmed Ressam, an Algerian al-Qaeda member, was arrested crossing the border from Canada to the United States with components used to manufacture IEDs. It transpired that he was planning to bomb the Los Angeles International Airport on New Year's Eve 1999.[281] Notably, Ressam trained at Darunta for several weeks to use explosives and poisons. He was a graduate of al-Zawahiri's terrorist ambitions for al-Qaeda.[282]

US frustrations with the Taliban were growing substantially over the impasse on the question of al-Qaeda. Yet a few weeks after Ressam was

arrested, Amir Khan Muttaqi, the Taliban minister of education and minister of information warned of serious consequences if any action was taken
to kill bin Laden. In a meeting with US officials in Islamabad, Pakistan,
Muttaqi claimed bin Laden posed no threat whilst he was in Afghanistan:
'We would like to assure you [the United States] that he will not operate
against you as long as he is in our hands. . . . If he is captured or killed, there
will be big reactions. Therefore, his stay in Afghanistan is in your interest. . . .
His supporters are not acting against the U.S. now due to the fear that it will
bring harm to bin Laden.'[283] Yet bin Laden's biggest supporter, al-Zawahiri,
continued his evolving strategic orientation and support for further attacks
on US interests. This was demonstrated on 12 October 2000, when al-
Qaeda carried out a maritime suicide bomb attack against the US naval
destroyer the USS *Cole*, whilst it was harboured in the Yemeni port of Aden.
The attack was carried out by local Yemenis under the order and guidance
of al-Qaeda.[284] Seventeen American sailors were killed. However, worse was
yet to come.

During this time, Pakistan was under the military regime of General
Pervez Musharraf, who refused to assist the Clinton administration in apprehending al-Qaeda leadership.[285] Musharraf had overthrown the democratically elected Prime Minister Nawaz Sharif in a coup, which resulted in
the general becoming a global pariah. However, he was a wily chameleon
of sorts. He had a penchant for changing effortlessly from Western suits to
full military uniform when it was politically convenient, depending on who
and which country he wished to dupe or manipulate.

After the al-Qaeda bombing of the American warship USS *Cole* in
Yemen in October 2000, bin Laden separated his key leaders so that in the
event of an American attack they could not all be eliminated at once. Al-
Zawahiri was headquartered in Kabul and lived in an expansive but run-
down colonial-era mansion in the embassy quarter of Wazir Akbar Khan,
northern Kabul. The house had double-glass doors that opened onto an
unkempt English garden.[286] Inside, it was quite spartan, with very few home
furnishings, as al-Zawahiri believed it was important to convey the right
message to other jihadists to live humbly. Security guards protected the
front entrance.[287]

Amidst the terrorist plotting against a superpower, al-Zawahiri also
had to juggle family life too, with six children and eventually three wives.
Because of his jihadist activities, his children were growing up in Sudan,

Afghanistan, and Pakistan. They did not know Egypt very well, but they were brought up in a conservative lifestyle. Al-Zawahiri had five daughters with his first wife Umm Fatima—Fatima, Umayma, Nabila, Khadija, and his favourite, Aisha, who was born in 1997 and diagnosed with Down syndrome. All wore black abayas and were not allowed to mix with men outside the family. Al-Zawahiri also had a son, Mohammed, who was a twin to Khadija.[288]

Al-Zawahiri would also go on to have a second wife, Umayma Hassan, known as Umm Khalid, in 2001, with whom al-Zawahiri would have a daughter called Nawwar. His third wife was Sayyida Halawa, more commonly known as Umm Tasneem. Both his second and third wives were widows of fallen jihadists. Al-Zawahiri's daughters were betrothed to jihadists. Fatima married a Jordanian called Abu Turab al-Urduni. Umayma wedded an Egyptian named Abu Dujana al-Misri al-Sharqawi. Nabila's spouse was the Moroccan, Muhammad Abbatay.[289] Khadija would go on to marry Hamza bin Laden, son of Osama bin Laden.[290]

In an email dated 3 May 2001, al-Zawahiri resurrected the issue of merging the EIJ with al-Qaeda. He discussed the need for international collaboration to 'increase profits'.[291] However, this idea was still met with dissatisfaction by some of al-Zawahiri's colleagues in the EIJ, one of whom wrote that proceeding with such a plan was like 'throwing good seeds onto barren land.'[292]

Al-Zawahiri did not want the EIJ to fall to the wayside like other Egyptian terrorist groups. His rivals in al-Gama'a decided that they had failed to win popular support for their mission and a military victory was now impossible. Their strategy had failed following the death of many innocents. In 1998, al-Gama'a proposed to end their attacks and declare a ceasefire. The Mubarak government responded positively. Al-Gama'a had the support of their imprisoned leadership.[293] Al-Zawahiri responded with a combination of disbelief and anger. In an October 1998 letter to the al-Gama'a leadership, al-Zawahiri castigated them: 'This initiative has undoubtedly shaken the image of the captive leaders in the eyes of the youth and shocked them hard. It represents a severe loss for the jihad movement as a whole.'[294]

Even from an American prison, Omar Abdel Rahman continued to issue *fatwas* and give instructions to al-Gama'a members in Egypt. Al-Zawahiri was particularly scornful that Rahman was willing to enter into a negotiations: 'Rahman made a statement after the initiative was made under the slogan—Halt [the operations] for the sake of Allah's pleasure.'[295]

Yet, on 14 June 2000, Rahman's lawyer, Lynne Stewart, announced on Rahman's behalf that a ceasefire was to be lifted in Egypt, meaning that al-Gama'a members could once again engage in terrorism. This revealed Rahman's enduring relevance in Egyptian affairs. Stewart, who often arrived at court with a New York Mets baseball cap and floral-print dresses seemed like an odd person for Rahman to retain. Stewart was charged and convicted for issuing prohibited information in a press release. After a protracted process, she received 10 years in prison in the United States. Al-Zawahiri deemed it important enough to highlight Rahman's contradictions as well as his use of Americans to disseminate his messages. The aim was to undermine Rahman whilst also making it clear their mutual animosity could not be mended:

> Early in June 2000 Dr. Omar Abdel Rahman issued a statement from his jail that was relayed by his lawyer Lynn Stewart in which she said that *Shaykh* Omar was withdrawing his support for the no-violence initiative because it had not brought any positive results for the Islamists. Stewart cited Abdel Rahman as saying: 'There has been no progress. Thousands of detainees are still in jail, the military tribunals are still prosecuting people, and the death penalty continues to be carried out.'[296]

Destructive Weapons

In the midst of the EIJ Tirana cell being dismantled and the planning that went into the East Africa embassy bombings, al-Qaeda and the EIJ also began discussing their most disturbing project: creating a chemical, biological, radiological, and nuclear (CBRN) weapons programme. Bin Laden had some concerns on the practicalities of these destructive tools and whether their use would draw comparisons with Iraqi dictator Saddam Hussein's deploying chemical weapons against the Kurds in the 1988 Halabja massacre.[297] It seemed bizarre that bin Laden was concerned about the propriety of weapons and tactics, based on what else al-Qaeda had done and was planning. However, to avoid creating a rift in his terrorist coalition, particularly al-Zawahiri and Atef, he decided to support the investigation and development of CBRNs.[298]

In February 1999, al-Zawahiri and Atef began discussing the modalities of the programme. Al-Zawahiri wrote a memo to Atef citing peer-reviewed journal papers as well as books, which although were old and outdated in terms of their utility, nevertheless demonstrated his pursuit of chemical and biological weapons.[299] In prioritising chemical and biological weapons, al-Zawahiri told Atef that 'the destructive power of these weapons is no less than that of nuclear weapons'.[300] Al-Zawahiri also cited several other benefits of such weapons. They could inflict a significant number of casualties and were nearly impossible to defend against. Finally, they offered the fastest and most practical way to proceed. The programme was code-named 'al-Zabadi', which is Arabic for 'curdled milk'.[301]

Al-Zawahiri was also encouraged about the potential utility of a nerve gas produced from insecticides and other chemicals to accelerate penetration of the skin. As part of the plan to manufacture a nerve gas, al-Qaeda recruits were provided with extensive reading material that included a study entitled 'Current Concepts: Napalm'. Al-Zawahiri lamented al-Qaeda's slow realisation of the destructive properties of these weapons, noting that 'despite their extreme danger, we only became aware of them when the enemy drew our attention to them by repeatedly expressing concern that they can be produced simply'.[302]

In another document from May 1999, after vising the Darunta Complex, al-Zawahiri talked about some 'very useful ideas' that arose during a visit to the Egyptian scientist Midhat Mursi al-Sayid Umar, who also went by the alias Abu Khabab. Al-Zawahiri added, 'It just needs some experiments to develop its practical use.' During this period al-Zawahiri used the aliases Abdel Moez, Nur al-Din, or Salah al-Din. The latter two were warrior rulers during the Second Crusade who conquered Syria and Egypt, respectively. Al-Zawahiri drew inspiration from both because they fought against 'hypocrites' and ensured 'Egypt and Syria were unified'.[303]

Mursi obtained a biochemistry degree from Alexandria University in 1975. He spent time in prison after being rounded up following the assassination of Egyptian president Anwar Sadat in 1981. Whilst in jail, he encountered al-Zawahiri, who appreciated Mursi's intelligence and potential.[304] At the Darunta Complex, Mursi oversaw Project al-Zabadi and produced training manuals and gave courses to al-Qaeda recruits on how to make toxins and conduct unethical experiments, including subjecting dogs and rabbits to cyanide. Mursi was also developing a project involving poison gas, called al-Mubtakkar al-Farid (the Unique Invention). Copies of his training manuals were discovered by the US military after Operation Enduring Freedom.[305]

In collaboration with al-Zawahiri, Ahmed Khadr's Human Concern International (HCI) supported the project.[306] Khadr's charity paid salaries to Egyptian terrorists, amongst them Mursi. Khadr also used his charity office, and the money raised, to provide logistical support for Egyptian jihadis travelling to Afghanistan, and it serve as the front for the chemical and biological weapons programme that al-Zawahiri was planning.[307]

Despite the infrastructure and the finance to sustain the programme provided by bin Laden, al-Zawahiri's desire to create destructive weapons was being frustrated. Mursi lacked the support of recruits with the scientific and engineering know-how required to put together a viable biological or chemical device. Al-Zawahiri advocated using al-Qaeda operatives to infiltrate scientific educational institutions to learn the necessary expertise. Al-Zawahiri also spoke to Pakistani interlocutors in the business community with ties to the criminal underworld to identify Pakistani scientists for recruitment.[308]

Enter Abdur Rauf, a Pakistani microbiologist with ideological sympathies towards al-Qaeda. Rauf reported directly to al-Zawahiri and was given a stipend to fund his travel to the UK so that al-Zawahiri could understand the layout of a laboratory for bacterial cultures, the equipment required to outfit it, and other requirements. According to D. A. Henderson, an expert on biological weapons who had served as an advisor to the US Health and Human Services Department, 'Rauf communicated with al-Zawahiri and in one dialogue, Rauf spoke about visiting a facility in the United Kingdom where he allegedly was shown a pathogen collection. It was clear he wanted to export the pathogens but also procure vaccines to protect the people working on al-Qaeda's programme.'[309] Rauf was also told by al-Zawahiri to travel across Europe to attend scientific conferences and learn more about the application of anthrax. Rauf had some understanding of the requirements to make a biological weapon, but he was not willing to take the lead in any of the laboratory work himself. This led to a disagreement between him and al-Zawahiri, and as a result, none of the bacterial cultures were obtained and the relationship with al-Qaeda ended.[310]

With Rauf no longer part of the project, al-Zawahiri turned to Riduan Isamuddin, who was better known by his alias, Hambali, the military leader of the Indonesian terrorist organization Jemaah Islamiyah (JI). He would develop an infamy of his own by orchestrating some of the biggest terrorist attacks in South-East Asia, including the 2002 Bali bombings that killed 202 people, including 88 Australians. Hambali met al-Zawahiri in Kandahar and introduced him to his deputy Yazid Sufaat, from Malaysia, who had a degree in biological sciences from California State University, Sacramento, where he had obtained clinical laboratory knowledge. Sufaat had even developed his own pathology laboratory which tested blood and urine samples. On Christmas Eve 2000, JI and al-Qaeda coordinated a series of explosions across Indonesia, killing 18 people and injuring more than 100. Hambali oversaw the plot, and Sufaat led the operation that targeted several churches in Medan, North Sumatra.[311] Sufaat and Hambali made several trips between Kandahar and Karachi to purchase biological and chemical materials, but based on unspecified logistical issues they proved unsuccessful. Frustrated, al-Zawahiri viewed these efforts as a waste of money.[312]

However, al-Zawahiri then received help from a surprising figure who would end up developing a relationship of mutual respect with him. Pakistani neuroscientist Aafia Siddiqui offered her scientific services to aid al-Qaeda's programme. She had been awarded an undergraduate degree in biology from the Massachusetts Institute of Technology before studying neuroscience at Brandeis University. Likely, it was because she was a woman that al-Qaeda rejected Siddiqui's offer. However, al-Zawahiri appeared to genuinely appreciate Siddiqui's willingness to help al-Qaeda develop one of their most important and deadly programmes.[313] It was something he would never forget.

Al-Zawahiri had known about Siddiqui for a while. Throughout her undergraduate career in the early 1990s, she became heavily involved with MIT's association for Muslim students and preoccupied with the war in Bosnia. Siddiqui started working with the Brooklyn-based al-Kifah Refugee Center, helping to fundraise and distributing pamphlets, and she encouraged fellow students to do the same.[314] At one time, Siddiqui was part of the Banaat-e-Ayesha, the women's wing of al-Qaeda's affiliate in Pakistan, the Jaish-e-Mohammed (JeM), and moved to Balakot where JeM had a training camp. Siddiqui also represented the first female jihadist who attained respect and influence within both the JeM and al-Qaeda.[315]

Unsurprisingly, the Taliban would aid al-Qaeda's agenda. In August 2001, bin Laden and al-Zawahiri met in Kabul with Dr Bashiruddin Mahmood and Dr Abdul Majeed, two Pakistani nuclear scientists.[316] Their discussions focused on the development and employment of chemical and biological weapons.[317] However, the four men also spent days conferring on al-Qaeda's desire to attain nuclear material. This was one month before 9/

11.[318] In June 2000, Mahmood and Majeed had founded Reconstruction of the Muslim Ummah (Ummah Tameer-e-Nau, UTN), which claimed to help in educational reform. UTN were also openly providing training to the Taliban in 'science-related matters' and had the rare distinction of being praised by Mullah Omar, the head of the Taliban. When UTN officials visited Afghanistan from Pakistan, their visas were sanctioned by the Taliban's Minister for Mines and Industry Ahmad Jan.[319] Jan was also a close friend of bin Laden and al-Zawahiri.[320]

Majeed retired as a scientist in 2000 from the Nuclear Materials Division of the Pakistan Institute of Nuclear Science and Technology in Rawalpindi. Mahmood was a former chairman of Pakistan's Atomic Energy Commission and had been associated with Pakistan's nuclear programme, overseeing the Kahuta uranium enrichment plant in the early 1990s.[321]

Mahmood resigned from Pakistan's Atomic Energy Commission in 1999 to protest the willingness of Nawaz Sharif's civilian government to sign the Comprehensive Test Ban Treaty. However, Sharif never signed the treaty, as he was removed from office in a coup orchestrated by General Pervez Musharraf. Curiously, Mahmood's stance was supported by al-Zawahiri that he respected Pakistan's refusal to sign the Nuclear Non-Proliferation Treaty of 2000:

> It is both astonishing and disturbing at the same time to see that a country such as Pakistan, which has strong ties with the United States, has refused to sign the [Non-Proliferation] treaty so long as its enemy India has not signed it. Unlike Egypt, Pakistan has not stepped down into the level to which the Egyptian regime reached in giving up everything to obey the United States.[322]

This indicates al-Qaeda's awareness of nuclear weapons and their potential usefulness in fighting the West. Al-Zawahiri sought to justify al-Qaeda's goals for seeking WMDs:

> It is worth noting here that Britain, one of the superpowers, has given itself the right to determine the legitimate defence needs of weaker governments. Whatever exceeds these needs is considered illegitimate. This is the same law that is being applied by the United States and major states against other countries. The United States and the major powers have the right to possess weapons of mass destruction while the weaker nations are denied this right.[323]

After the fall of the Taliban, coalition forces searched UTN offices in Kabul. Some of the documents they found revealed that the UTN was very interested in radiological and biological weapons such as anthrax. Other

documents found showed linked the UTN to the JeM. The Bush administration added the UTN to the list of entities supporting terrorism and had
its assets be frozen under Executive Order 13224. Mahmood and Majeed
were also sanctioned.[324] Neither Mahmood nor Majeed faced any sanction
from the Musharraf regime.

Despite the inherent weakness within Pakistan's own security apparatus,
it was deeply disconcerting that some Pakistani nuclear scientists were so
willing to aid al-Qaeda in its efforts to develop a CBRN programme. This
thinking would consume US foreign policy for years to come. As former
Central Command (CENTCOM) commander, General Joseph Votel, aptly
pointed out, 'The concern with Pakistan was their nuclear weapons. It was
the fear that they were not well-controlled, they could fall into the hands
of al Qaeda and then be used for nefarious purposes. That was prioritized
over their support to the Taliban.'[325]

Military Studies

In the 1990s, several members of the Libyan Islamic Fighting Group (LIFG)
moved to Britain, mostly living in London and Manchester. Some were
given sanctuary after claiming asylum due to their calls for the overthrow of
the Muammar Qadhafi regime in Libya.[326] This included Nazih al-Ruqail,
also known as Abu Anas al-Libi, who had been granted political asylum and
chose to reside in Manchester. Al-Libi was part of the Arab *mujahideen* during the Soviet occupation of Afghanistan, where he first met al-Zawahiri.[327]

In 1992, he relocated with bin Laden to Sudan.[328] He was known to
have participated in one of al-Zawahiri's failed plots to assassinate Egyptian
president Hosni Mubarak. Under pressure from Qaddafi, al-Libi was expelled in 1995.[329] Al-Libi was also implicated in the US Embassy bombings in Kenya and Tanzania, after travelling to Nairobi to train al-Qaeda
cadres in surveillance methods.[330] As a senior member of the LIFG, al-Libi
oversaw running the Afghanistan section of the Sanabel Relief Agency
in Manchester. Although it was a British registered charity, allegations
emerged of it siphoning funds to the LIFG. In 1999, al-Libi was arrested
but released because of a lack of formal evidence.[331] Sensing the net closing
on him, al-Libi fled the United Kingdom and relocated to the al-Qaeda
camps in Afghanistan.

A subsequent raid on al-Libi's Manchester apartment by Britain's counter-terrorism agencies in 2000 led to the discovery of one of the most important jihadist terrorist training manuals: *Military Studies in the Jihad against the Tyrants*. This handbook of terrorism was also used by Ali Mohamed. It was deemed so secret that on the front page was emblazoned 'It Is Forbidden to Remove This from the House'[332] According to the scholar Martin Rudner, 'Those words reflected the position of Ayman al-Zawahiri. He was at the forefront of it and did not want anyone knowing about his manual and exposing the strategy of the jihadists.'[333]

In the early 1990s, al-Zawahiri began working in conjunction with several other Egyptian and Libyan jihadists to produce the *Military Studies in the Jihad against the Tyrants*. The 180-page document contained 18 chapters, each of which was a blueprint for the tradecraft of terrorism. The noted psychiatrist and analyst of the psychology of terrorism, Jerrold Post, spent much time studying the terrorist training manual. According to him, 'Its origins are not entirely clear. It was likely started in the aftermath of the Soviet occupation of Afghanistan and added to as events unfolded. It has the hallmark of the Egyptian jihadist contingent, especially Ayman al-Zawahiri, who was pivotal to the manual's formulation. One could call him the Editor of it, with assistance from Tharwat Salah Shehata.'[334] Al-Zawahiri was seeking to formulate strategies and tactics for the jihadist movements and codifying them in training manuals. Many of the 'lessons', each with its own subheading, was based on al-Zawahiri's own experiences and activities of the EIJ.

This preliminary lesson, 'General Introduction', delineated a mission statement that highlighted the importance of uniting all Muslims to 'resist this state of ignorance'. The chapter then outlined a basic vision for a military organization whose goal is to overthrow 'apostate' regimes and replace them with an Islamic one. The medieval Islamic jurist Ibn Taymiyyah was cited to justify the claim that jihad is an Islamic obligation.

'Necessary Qualifications and Character for Organization's Members' provided the traits and skills that individuals must possess to be members of a jihadist organization. First and foremost, they must be Muslim and committed ideologically. Some other attributes are related to one's personality traits or disposition, including the ability to keep a secret, to observe and analyse, to act, and to conceal oneself. The goal is to be an effective spy. Al-Zawahiri became extremely close with some recruits who possessed these characteristics, such as Ali Mohamed and Khalid Abu al-Dahab.

'Counterfeit Currency and Forged Documents' listed precautions, such as dispersing and hiding funds, that should be taken to ensure the network's financial health. It also describes the precautions one should take when going undercover and using doctored identity documents. Al-Zawahiri himself entered the United States using forged documents under a pseudonym impersonating an official from the humanitarian Red Crescent of Pakistan. Separately, using fake documents, al-Zawahiri illegally entered Russia in 1996 disguised as a merchant to connect with Chechen and Dagestani jihadis. 'Organization Military Bases' described how to select and set up safe houses in cities whilst avoiding detection. These safe houses were to be used as hiding places and command centres for organizing and executing attacks.

'Means of Communication and Transportation' illustrated in detail the security protocols that should be adhered to for five types of covert communication: telephone calls, in-person meetings, messengers, letters, and faxes and wireless. It also highlighted security protocols for using both public and private transportation. Al-Zawahiri was very concerned with developing an effective security apparatus that avoids detection by state intelligence agencies. [335]

'Training' identified the security precautions that should be taken whilst training recruits. The location should be remote and secret, with many entrances and exits. Trainees should be carefully selected, and they should not know one another in advance. The size of the trainee group should be small, only 7–10 individuals. 'Weapons: Measures Related to Buying and Transporting Them' explained how to purchase, store, and transport weapons and appropriate cover for the purchase. Trainees should make sure that the weapon is functional and stored safely, free from excessive heat and humidity.

'Member Safety' outlined security measures specific to each type of member: the overt member, the covert member, and the commander, who together constitute a network. The commander may be involved in overt or covert work but is also distinguished by his leadership role and the instructions he receives. Unlike the overt members, the covert contingent should adopt a persona that conceals their religious or ideological orientation. A covert member should maintain his normal daily routines when working on an operation. Contact between overt and covert members should be on a 'need to know basis'. Married members should not tell their wives about their work, as women did not engage in jihadist activities.

'Security Plan' was meant to minimise losses in the event of detection by the 'enemy' security apparatus. Precautions and plans should be established to enact upon detection. This includes training members on how to answer questions under interrogation if they are caught whilst travelling to or from Afghanistan, including the camp they were trained at as well as the operations they were tasked with. Security plans also outline the procedures for a 'group mission' to assassinate an important individual.

'Special Tactical Operations' included 'assassinations, bombing and demolition, assault, kidnapping hostages and confiscating documents, freeing prisoners'. The bulk of the lesson focused on how to stage a tactical operation, including detailed advice for the research, planning, and execution stages. Al-Zawahiri was involved in the planning of numerous 'special tactical operations' that were meant to inflict psychological pain on Egypt and the United States whilst boosting the EIJ's and al-Qaeda's morale.

'Espionage: Information-Gathering Using Open Methods' sought to use religious texts to justify espionage and hiding one's religious identity whilst spying. It also offered a distorted religious justification for hostage taking as well as interrogating and killing hostages. The lesson further highlighted the importance of acquiring up-to-date information about the enemy's capabilities and plans, so the organization can counter them. Information can be gathered from public and secret sources. Public sources, such as the newspapers, magazines, public documents, radio, and television, could fulfil approximately 80% of the terrorist organization's information-gathering needs, but 20% of the necessary information was secret, and clandestine methods are necessary to acquire it. 'Espionage: Information-Gathering Using Covert Methods' summarised security measures to be taken when gathering information about 'governing personalities or establishments' through covert means. Much attention was given to recruiting smugglers, political asylum seekers, employees at transportation hubs, and workers at restaurants and hotels.

'Secret Writing and Ciphers and Codes' explained how to create and decipher invisible ink. It also outlined the history of ciphers and codes, and how to create, encode, and decode them. 'Kidnapping and Assassinations Using Rifles and Pistols' explained how each of type of weapons works, its advantages and disadvantages, and how to handle it. Guidance about where to aim on a human target to inflict maximum damage was included in this lesson as well as the best locations to use them against a designated target.

For each assassination type, sample operations from the past in Egypt were included with an analysis of the operation's successes and shortcomings.

'Assassination Using Explosives' provided very detailed, technical explanations of how to create and detonate explosives. There was also guidance about how to create and place booby traps. Examples of past assassination operations using explosives were included. 'Assassination Using Poisons and Cold Steel' discussed instructions about how to acquire and use poisons and toxins and how to use knives, blunt objects, and rope to assassinate a target.

'Interrogation and Investigation' addressed psychological warfare and 'intellectual combat' by distinguishing interrogation and questioning as well as ensuring the legal rights of jihadists were preserved under the rule of law. Lastly, 'Prisons and Detention Centres' provided instructions for a member to follow when sentenced to prison, including what activity one can engage in without drawing scrutiny of the prison authorities.

Two common themes in each chapter were lessons learnt from past mistakes, as well as best practises for success in terrorism or dealing with scenarios for a jihadist if detained by the authorities. Reflecting another al-Zawahiri hallmark, many of the guidelines contained detailed justifications, citing suras, Hadiths, and verses from the Qur'an. Curiously, the suras were not numbered.

Some of it was based on strategies al-Zawahiri had already utilised with the EIJ. Often overlooked and regularly understated, the *Military Studies* was groundbreaking, as it drew on some conceptual approaches by state intelligence agencies as well as law enforcement and military. Although it may have not been entirely original, al-Zawahiri reworked it to serve as a disturbingly pioneering guide to political violence, with each task flowing from the primary goal to overthrow 'apostate' regimes. Importantly, there was no mention of the United States or countries in Europe, reflecting al-Zawahiri's and the EIJ's 'internal enemy' focus.

Virtually all al-Qaeda plots that had emerged at this point and in the subsequent decades can trace their tactics and strategies to the *Military Studies*. Based on its significance, in some circles it was known as the 'Al-Qaeda Handbook' or the 'Manchester Manual', from where it was first discovered. With the advent of new media technology and enhanced communications, the plots would evolve, but they too owe their origins to the *Military Studies*, courtesy of al-Zawahiri. According to Jerrold Post, 'Al-Zawahiri was tasked with most day-to-day decisions for al-Qaeda including plotting the large-scale attacks.' Many of the concepts in the *Military Studies* would be used in subsequent al–Qaeda manuals and magazines such as *Inspire*. Even ISIS's online magazines *Dabiq* and *Rumiyah* can be said to have taken ideas from the *Military Studies*. The manual also has several sections on lessons earned, which reviews past plots against state elements that ultimately failed and ways to improve future operations. Curiously, the case studies centered on Egypt and dealt with groups that al–Zawahiri had been critical of, such as the Muslim Brotherhood. Equally significant, he deliberately avoided specifying EIJ operations, either successful or not, very likely to avoid exposing ongoing plots and clandestine cells. Much of the manual concentrated on avoiding detection by the military and law enforcement.

Military Studies was very detailed, logical, and systematic in its approach. It was also very pragmatic, as terrorist plots don't always go to plan, and therefore improvisation was important. It was groundbreaking in terms of its 'open-source jihad' guidance on how to handle weapons and create bombs, and it would serve as a template for future terrorist guides as technology evolved. Unlike *Milestones* and 'The Neglected Duty', which spoke about revolution, *Military Studies* focused on how to plan and execute insurrection.

Some sections required an advanced level of guidance and knowledge that resembled the training of state intelligence agencies. The manual was also very detailed and even gave guidance and permission for operatives to not follow Islamic traditions in order to blend into the civilian fabric of society. The *Military Studies* also revealed that whilst economic, military, and political targets featured prominently in manual, it also sought to target civilians: 'In every country we should hit their organizations, institutions, clubs and hospitals. . . . [T]he targets must be identified, carefully chosen and include their largest gatherings so that any strike should cause thousands of deaths.' The significance of this was that al–Zawahiri was willing to escalate a war with the West. Although he wanted to prioritise the 'internal enemy', it was the 'external enemy' that was sustaining regimes like Mubarak, and therefore everyone in the West was a legitimate target.[336]

Al-Zarqawi's Shadow

Although al–Zawahiri and bin Laden were forging a formidable partnership and had free reign to conduct their activities in Afghanistan, there remained a thorn in their side, by the name of Abu Musab al–Zarqawi. After returning to Jordan from Afghanistan, al-Zarqawi was incarcerated in 1992 for possession of weapons and explosives. In 1999, al-Zarqawi was released from prison as part of a national pardon by Jordan's King Abdullah II upon his coronation to the throne of the Hashemite kingdom.[337] Upon release, Zarqawi didn't waste time. He had unfinished business in Afghanistan.

In December 1999, 10 years after his first visit, al-Zarqawi returned to Afghanistan, where the Taliban were now the presiding power. Later that month he met al-Zawahiri and bin Laden at an al-Qaeda guest house in Kandahar. There was seething hatred from both sides. Al-Zawahiri distrusted and disliked al-Zarqawi because the upstart saw Azzam as his ideological mentor. He also believed that the Jordanian prisoners who had been granted amnesty, along with al-Zarqawi, had been penetrated by Jordanian intelligence. Al-Zawahiri was all too aware that something similar had occurred not long ago in Egypt. Al-Zawahiri also disliked 'al-Zarqawi's abrasive, and overbearing manner and apparent lack of respect'.[338]

In early 2000, al-Zarqawi created his own training camp in Herat, away from al-Qaeda's. In homage to the origins of his mentor Azzam, al-Zarqawi's goal was to build an army known as Jund al-Sham, or Soldiers of the Levant, that he could export globally.[339] Al-Zarqawi had developed an obsession to overthrow the Jordanian monarchy and establish a caliphate in the Levant. According to the investigative journalist Sebastian Rotella, 'People talk about al-Zawahiri as an old sage, respected figure, whereas al-Zarqawi was a gangster jihadi and seen as a hands-on killer.'[340] To keep an eye on al-Zarqawi, al-Zawahiri requested one of his trusted aides, Saif al-Adel, watch him and act as the designated middleman. Al-Adel served as the EIJ's chief of security and had previously been in the Egyptian army, having attained the rank of colonel at an early age with training in special operations. Al-Zawahiri depended on al-Adel a great deal. Al-Adel made regular visits to al-Zarqawi's Herat training camp, reporting back to the al-Qaeda leadership.[341]

On several occasions between 2000 and 2001, bin Laden summoned al-Zarqawi to personally visit him in Kandahar and pledge a *ba'yah* to him as the leader of the global jihadist movement. Using a *ba'yah*, bin Laden and al-Zawahiri wanted to achieve a global expansion by establishing allegiance relationships. It was also an effective process of demonstrating their power, to both its adherents and enemies. However, on every occasion, al-Zarqawi refused.[342] It was clear he did not believe that either bin Laden or al-Zawahiri shared his vision for jihad and to preserve the doctrine and legacy of Abdullah Azzam.

When the United States launched Operation Enduring Freedom in Afghanistan on 7 October 2001, al-Zarqawi was wounded in an air strike on his Herat camp. He managed to escape Afghanistan, without the help of al-Qaeda. During the next year, al-Zarqawi based himself primarily in northern Iraq. He first rebuilt his network and then created camps whilst recruiting fighters locally and from abroad.

Preparing for Battle

Al-Zawahiri viewed the United States as eradicating Islam from power through rigged elections in 'apostate nations' like Egypt. Al-Zawahiri also claimed that there were two competing authorities in Egypt, an official one, supported by the West, Israel, and many Arab rulers; and the second, which he argued was led by people like him and depended on God alone. For al-Zawahiri, the first power sought 'to drive Islam out of all spheres of life by force, tyranny and forged elections'.[343] Al-Zawahiri drew parallels to Faraj's 'The Neglected Duty' when he cited al-Qaeda's policy of fighting apostate rulers which he affirmed was the duty of every Muslim to

> Expose the rulers who are fighting Islam; Highlighting the importance of loyalty to the faithful and relinquishment of the infidels in the Muslim creed; Holding every Muslim responsible for defending Islam, its sanctities, nation and homeland; Cautioning against the *ulama* of the sultan [apostate ruler Mubarak] of the virtues of the *ulama* of Jihad and the *imams* of sacrifice and the need for the nation to defend, protect, honour and follow them and exposing the extent of aggression against our creed and sanctities and the plundering of our wealth.[344]

Al-Zawahiri had advocated a similar agenda to Faraj. He identified 'apostate' Muslim rulers who need to be fought. In addition, he talked about the weakness of the *ulama* and that any individual can have as much religious experience as a cleric, who may have compromised his religious beliefs by obedience to the state and as a result harm the interests of the *ummah*. He also stated that every Muslim has a personal obligation to defend Islam and that sitting on the sidelines was not an answer. However, unlike Faraj, al-Zawahiri's primary focus was shifting to targeting the 'external enemy', which would in turn weaken the 'internal enemy'.

Al-Zawahiri warned that 'the victory of the struggle of the Islamic movement against the international alliance will not be accomplished without acquiring an Islamist base in the heart of the Islamic world'.[345] He recognised that it would not be an easy or quick goal to achieve, but it was the only way forward to 'restore its fallen caliphate and regain its lost glory'. Al-Zawahiri added, 'Do not precipitate collision and to be patient about victory.'[346]

Most importantly, as a hallmark of al-Zawahiri, self-preservation surpassed jihad, although he would frame it as being smart to live to fight for another day, as opposed to being crushed. Reflected in his *Military Studies*, al-Zawahiri asked the rhetorical question of what happens if al-Qaeda's membership or its plans were discovered, its resources confiscated and its existence in danger? 'The answer in my view, is for the movement to withdraw as much as it can to a safe place and carry the war against the Americans and the Jews in their homes and against their bodies.'[347]

Al-Zawahiri's direct purpose and intention was to incite a conflict between the *ummah* and the West, designed to unite the Muslim world, similar to the Afghan-Arab jihad against the Soviets, something which Arab rulers appeared incapable of achieving. He concluded with a call to arms:

> The Crusader-Jewish alliance under the leadership of America will not permit any Muslim power to govern in any of the Islamic countries. It will mobilise all its resources to strike at the (Islamic power) in order to remove it from governing. . . . The alliance will wage a war worldwide. . . . We have to prepare ourselves for a battle not only in one region but a battle that will include both the internal enemy [ruling government] and the external Crusader-Jewish enemy.[348]

Knights under the Prophet's Banner presented a blueprint for future jihadists that al-Zawahiri began developing during his time in Afghanistan battling the Soviets. He wrote, 'A Jihadist movement needs an arena that would act like an incubator, where its seeds would grow and where it can acquire practical experience in combat, politics and organizational matter.'[349] Al-Zawahiri implored his adherents to inflict the highest number of fatalities on the West by whatever means necessary. Again, borrowing from *Military Studies*, al-Zawahiri also incited followers to attack Americans individually:

Killing the Americans with a single bullet, a stab, or device made up of a popular mix of explosives or hitting them with an iron rod is not impossible. Likewise, burning their property with Molotov cocktails is not difficult. Suicide operations are the most successful in inflicting damage on the opponent and the least costly in terms of casualties among the fundamentalists. . . . Cause the greatest damage and inflict the maximum casualties on the opponent, no matter how much time and effort these operations take, because this is the language understood by the West.[350]

Al-Zawahiri saw the conspiracy continuing indefinitely against the *ummah* on every front. The *ummah* has remained under attack not just from the West, the United States, Europe, and Israel but also from the East, from India. In his eyes:

India has never accepted the partition of the subcontinent in 1948 at the end of the British Raj. India's Hindu governments want to dominate South Asia and restore the borders of the Raj, meaning to recover Pakistan and under their control. To do so they actively plot with America and Israel against Pakistan to subvert it and ultimately subjugate it.[351]

Although he got the date of Partition wrong, which was actually 1947, by mentioning India, al-Zawahiri was looking to gain favour with the Pakistani terrorist groups that al-Qaeda depended upon and would rely on in the coming years, should they make it out of Afghanistan alive. The picture al-Zawahiri conveyed was one of an unparalleled subjugation of the Islamic world by its enemies; namely, Crusaders and Zionists. However, al-Zawahiri also advocated not standing still but resisting the suppression, defending the *ummah*, and restoring the caliphate. For al-Zawahiri it was the obligation of every Muslim to fight the 'infidels' and the corrupt 'apostates' who align themselves with the infidels. Al-Zawahiri warned that it would be a long-term challenge:

If our goal is comprehensive change and if our path, as the *Qur'an* and our history have shown us, is a long road of *Jihad* and sacrifices, we must not despair of repeated strikes and recurring calamities. We must never lay down our arms, regardless of the casualties or sacrifices.[352]

Al-Zawahiri accepted that al-Qaeda had not yet attracted the full support of the *ummah*. Indeed, he viewed the masses as still being under the thumb of their 'corrupt apostate leaders'. Thus, for al-Zawahiri the path to victory must be forged by a small cadre of brave Islamic warriors, whom he described as 'Knights' who are courageous, have valour, inspire the *ummah* in to following their lead in jihad, and if required, make the ultimate sacrifice of their lives for the cause. The first of the group were the assassins of Sadat in 1981 whom al-Zawahiri described as 'giving inspiration to the *ummah*'.[353] In al-Zawahiri's mind, the attacks on the World Trade Center and the Pentagon were the latest example of his knights acting bravely.

Significantly, *Knights under the Prophet's Banner* justified attacking the 'external enemy' first. By making this official, al-Zawahiri was superseding the previous accepted 'internal enemy' strategy of al-Banna, Qutb, Azzam, and Faraj. Al-Zawahiri sought to justify this departure by stating it was the result of a prudent strategic decision by him and bin Laden following the failures of the Muslim Brotherhood, al-Gama'a, and even the EIJ to topple the 'internal enemy'. Based on the successes of the Afghan-Arab *mujahideen* over the Soviets, the calculation was that the 'external enemy' strategy, especially against the United States, was the sager course of action, because it would unify and rally and motivate the *ummah*. According to al-Zawahiri, 'That jihad [against the Soviets] was a training course of the utmost importance to prepare Muslim *mujahideen* to wage their awaited battle against the superpower that now has sole dominance over the globe, namely, the United States.'[354]

For these reasons, al-Zawahiri claimed al-Qaeda shifted its focus to the 'external enemy' and the United States in particular. However, these views contradicted the stance al-Zawahiri initially held soon after the Soviet defeat, when he believed the focus of the Afghan experience needed to be converted to fight the 'internal enemy'; namely, the Egyptian regime of Mubarak. For al-Zawahiri, the intent of large mass casualty attacks against the United States was to force the West out of the Middle East and other Islamic nations, which would weaken pro-Western secular 'apostate' regimes and increase al-Qaeda's status amongst the jihadists. The theory was that attacks on the West would provoke a foreseeable reprisal that would rally the *ummah* to global jihad and defence of Islam. Consequently, the 'apostate' regimes would be the first casualties of this war and collapse. They would be replaced by Shariah law, setting the platform for further conquests by the vanguard created by bin Laden and al-Zawahiri.

One obvious flaw in *Knights under the Prophet's Banner* was the absence of a specific template on ruling and administration, what an Islamic state would entail, and how it would deal with matters like socio-economic difficulties. In al-Zawahiri's doctrine, God's will simply provides all. He uses religious history, imagery, and zeal to directly influence young, impressionable people by seeking acceptance and vindication for his actions on behalf of Islam. Whilst al-Zawahiri long derided democracy as an enemy of Islam, writing in his earlier text, 'The Bitter Harvest', that democracy would put 'no limit on apostasy' and 'everyone agreeing to [democracy as authority] is an infidel', he offered no alternative solution in his follow-up memoir.[355] Al-Zawahiri never clarified what the mechanisms of a 'proper' Islamic government would be.

Interestingly, al-Zawahiri sought to address the notion that the Afghan-Arab *mujahideen* were created and funded by the United States and other Western nations. It seemed more important for the al-Qaeda deputy to make clear that the United States had never enjoyed any control over al-Qaeda and that what al-Zawahiri and bin Laden were seeking to achieve was entirely through their own initiative. It was a reflection that al-Zawahiri did not want al-Qaeda's brand to be tainted with unfounded conspiracy theories:

> This lie is self-contradictory. If the Arab Afghans are a U.S. creation, why did the United States seek to expel them over a period of two years? The truth that everyone should learn is that the United States did not give one penny in aid to the *mujahideen*. If the Arab Afghans are the mercenaries of the United States who have now rebelled against it, why is the United States unable to buy them back now? Would not buying them be more economical and less costly than the security and prevention budget that it is paying to defend itself now?[356]

Al-Zawahiri was perhaps keen to illustrate that Muslims can achieve revolution on their own without assistance from the West, and it would undermine his own efforts to state that the United States was trying to subjugate Muslims. He resented that the United States took credit for defeating the Soviets in Afghanistan and did not acknowledge the Arab Muslims for their contribution in the war. However, al-Zawahiri ignored the fact that the West and in particular the United States provided not just financial support but also arms and weapons via the Pakistani military.

Priorities

A leader needs a right-hand person to complement his abilities. Bin Laden understood the vital importance of choosing the appropriate second in command and avoided the temptation to have someone who was too similar to him but at the same time, shared the common ideological agenda of a pan-Islamic state and matching ideas for instigating insurrection. Although al-Zawahiri's EIJ collaborated with al-Qaeda and they planned joint operations, the consolidation was not complete as yet. However, in June 2001 the EIJ and al-Qaeda formally merged into one entity that would be officially known as al-Qaeda al-Jihad.[357] As John Miller reflected about the merger:

> Al-Zawahiri had been tortured, tried, and deported from the world of Egypt, where he could not return, and was trying to. He found his way to bin Laden, who in terms of being on message, wasn't exactly the same, but was close enough, and al-Zawahiri could influence the Saudi. He merged EIJ with al-Qaeda because his attempts against Mubarak failed, and he needed someone [who] had a structure, sanctuary, and resources. And bin Laden had all three of those.[358]

An element of personal cost with questionable judgement whilst wanting to be a supportive ally and concluding there was no alternative led al-Zawahiri to demonstrate a commitment to al-Qaeda's cause that impacted on the EIJ. Although the EIJ number of shock troops was no longer as significant as it used to be after the global disruption of plots, following the full-scale merger with al-Qaeda, bin Laden gave the Egyptians in al-Qaeda six out of nine of the Shura Council seats. This was done partly because of the fighting prowess of the existing EIJ fighters but also in the hopes that the Egyptian contingent would support the September 11 plot, which was still being developed. However, almost all voted against it, much to bin Laden's displeasure.[359]

One of the dissidents was al-Zawahiri's deputy Tharwat Salah Shehata. The 1998 *fatwa* was something that al-Zawahiri managed to square with the EIJ despite considerable internal opposition. However, the formal merger with al-Qaeda was a step too far for some. Understanding the reasons for the opposition and realising that he could no longer keep the EIJ united, al-Zawahiri permitted the creation of an independent offshoot of the EIJ, with Shehata at the helm. Several other senior members joined him, including Mahmud al-Hennawi, who had been detained in Russia with al-Zawahiri. Al-Zawahiri had to make a significant sacrifice to align with bin Laden.[360]

Unlike bin Laden, who remained firm in his belief that the United States was a 'paper tiger' that could be easily humbled, al-Zawahiri was reluctant to attack the American homeland. Instead, he argued it would be more judicious for al-Qaeda to focus its efforts on US targets within the Islamic world, which would be more manageable and unlikely to force Americans into an all-out war with them.[361] This was more in sync with al-Qaeda's current position, as seen in its bombings of the US embassies in Kenya and Tanzania in 1998 and the 2000 maritime attack on the USS *Cole*. However, despite failing to sway the al-Qaeda leadership, al-Zawahiri committed himself to al-Qaeda's future plots as envisaged by bin Laden, and he would be at the forefront of those operations, earning him the long-standing trust of al-Qaeda's *amir*. This meant al-Zawahiri was diverging from the doctrine of Sayyid Qutb, whom he had long sought to emulate. The scholar John Calvert pointed out that whilst 'Qutb was attuned to the internationalist dimension of the jihad, his practical focus was Egypt. He had no interest in luring the Western powers into existential conflict or conceived of attacking non-combatants. Whereas al-Zawahiri matured into a terrorist.'[362]

However, there was more vocal opposition from other Egyptian Jihadists including Abu Walid al-Masri, also known as Mustafa Hamid. Abu Walid was married to Rabiah Hutchinson, whom al-Zawahiri took a shine to. Abu Walid was an unusual combination of journalist and jihadist.[363] Born in Egypt, he graduated with an engineering degree in 1969 from Alexandria University. Eventually, he chose to work as a journalist but moonlighted as a jihadist for various campaigns. This included in Lebanon, where he fought against occupying Israeli forces. When he joined the Afghan jihad in 1979 against the Soviets, he wrote about the conflict for several publications.[364] Whilst there, he came across Jalaluddin Haqqani in 1979, and he later worked with him from 1982 until 1990.[365]

In 1986, Abu Walid first met al-Zawahiri in Peshawar. He was also in Sudan for few a months but left the same time as bin Laden and al-Zawahiri.[366] When the Taliban seized control of Kabul, Abu Walid returned to journalism as the Kandahar correspondent for al-Jazeera between 1998 and 2001.[367] However, he also retained a loyalty to his hosts, the Taliban, and pledged allegiance to Mullah Omar as commander of the faithful (*amir al-muminin*) in 1997.[368] On occasion, Abu Walid represented the Taliban in dialogue with Iran, including seeking to unlock the Iranian embargo put in place by Tehran after several Iranian diplomats were murdered in 1998 by Taliban forces in Mazar-i-Sharif.[369]

Abu Walid's personal ties of loyalty were less to bin Laden than to fellow Egyptians al-Zawahiri and Saif al-Adel, who was married to Abu Walid's eldest daughter.[370] Abu Walid and al-Adel opposed any plot to target the United States directly on both strategic and ideological grounds, as the 'internal enemy' should remain the priority.[371] Abu Walid was unimpressed by bin Laden.[372] This spoke to the factionalism within the jihadist movement, particularly the internal rivalry between the Saudis and the Egyptians. Al-Zawahiri fitted more in the middle of this debate. He was still not motivated in targeting the US mainland as much as bin Laden was but realised the importance of bin Laden for the wider agenda of defeating the Arab regimes.[373] The differences between bin Laden and al-Zawahiri were also what made their partnership successful. As al-Qaeda began to grow, so did al-Zawahiri's influence as both a leader and ally of bin Laden, and he would seek to check the Saudi's impulses so that the terrorist group continued along the path where it would be able to shape events within the Islamic world.[374]

9/9 and 9/11

In August 2001, US agents came close to apprehending al-Zawahiri as news surfaced that he was planning to travel to Yemen for medical treatment for his daughter Aisha. Egyptian intelligence got wind of the information about the hospital in Sana'a. However, as would become apparent about al-Zawahiri's own obsession with security, EIJ operatives were sent to case the hospital and they came across a joint American-Egyptian surveillance operation. Al-Zawahiri avoided the trip and stayed in Afghanistan especially as he was needed by bin Laden for al-Qaeda's biggest plots to date.[375]

Bin Laden made only a handful of his aides aware of 9/11 terrorist attacks because he desired to minimise knowledge of and, hence, opposition to it. There have been suggestions that al-Zawahiri was not consulted in the planning the coordinated attacks on the United States and that he was aware of the specifics of the operation only twenty-four hours in advance.[376] Moreover, in late-August 2001, bin Laden informed his Shura Council of an impending attack on US soil without disclosing the full details, and although the majority of council members opposed it, especially the Egyptian faction, bin Laden was adamant that it should go ahead as planned.[377]

However, other evidence points to the fact that al-Zawahiri was not only aware of the plans to target the US mainland but was also involved in the preparation and planning of 9/11. Bin Laden had taken steps to establish an optimal relationship with al-Zawahiri so that he would be a co-creator, collaborator, confidant, and in-house critic. Al-Zawahiri had bin Laden's trust and a defined role to play so that both individual responsibilities and where control lay were clear to the rest of al-Qaeda. By the same token, al-Zawahiri may have been reluctant to support the September 11 attacks because of the consequences it would create for a-Qaeda as well as his own obsession in removing the Mubarak regime in Egypt, but he felt enormous loyalty to bin Laden, who had supported him over Azzam and al-Gama'a. Al-Zawahiri needed bin Laden.[378]

Al-Zawahiri may not have directed the 9/11 plots or decided the specific targets, but the plans were presented to him, especially as bin Laden had a specific and highly challenging task he needed al-Zawahiri to take on that needed to be synchronized with 9/11 for the attacks to be successful. The mission was to assassinate the Northern Alliance leader Ahmad Shah Massoud. Massoud had become the West's ally in Afghanistan and was in dialogue with the CIA to explore pathways to capture or kill bin Laden. Under Massoud, the Northern Alliance had managed to stop the Taliban from taking full control of Afghanistan, much to the frustration of Taliban leader Mullah Omar and, by extension, bin Laden too. Massoud was blocking the way towards achieving their respective agendas.[379]

To ensure the success of 9/11, al-Zawahiri had to oversee the assassination of Massoud, which was planned some 18 months in advance.[380] This was not going to be an easy assignment. Massoud was secure in the north of Afghanistan and had multiple security layers protecting him. Bin Laden wanted to help the Taliban in advance of the 9/11 operation to neuter any US response against al-Qaeda by removing their Northern Alliance ally on the ground, especially if its leader Massoud was eliminated.[381]

A strategy needed to be formed which would not arouse the suspicion of the very astute Massoud, who had survived numerous attempts on his life by foes ranging from the Soviets to the Taliban. Aiding al-Zawahiri were Tunisian jihadists who provided their own unique skill sets. In 2000, Seifallah Ben Hassine, also known by his alias Abu Ayyad al-Tunisi relocated to Afghanistan from London and created the Tunisian Combat Group (TCG) with another Tunisian, Tarek Maroufi, who was based in Brussels.

The TCG aligned itself to al-Qaeda and Abu Ayyad became a close confidant of bin Laden's. With bin Laden's resources, al-Zawahiri overseeing the Massoud plot, and the Tunisians providing the manpower, a plan was hatched. The TCG had an extensive network of recruits across France, Belgium, Italy, and the United Kingdom. They were known for their criminal activity, especially document forgery.[382]

In May 2000, pretending to be journalists from a London-based Islamic information agency, Arabic News International, al-Qaeda operatives contacted Massoud requesting an interview to be conducted by 'one of our best journalists, Mr. Karim Touzani'. The message added, 'We ... are at your service in the hope that our collaboration will be long and fruitful.' Massoud, who had been the bane in the Taliban's conquest of Afghanistan, willingly agreed.[383] What didn't appear in the message to Massoud but which was later found on an al-Qaeda laptop, which also contained the all the communications about this plot, was that the message was penned by a 'Mohammed al-Zawahiri'.[384] It was ambiguous whether this referred to Ayman al-Zawahiri, who sometimes used the alias Abu Mohammed or possibly to his brother, Muhammad al-Zawahiri. However, he was serving a sentence for his role in setting up the terror cell in Albania and the East Africa embassy bombings. Al-Zawahiri was very close to him and may have chosen to use his name as an alias for symbolic solidarity.[385]

On 9 September 2001, two Tunisian men, Dahmane Abd al-Sattar and Bouraoui al-Ouaer, both French-speaking Arabs carrying stolen Belgian passports, posed as television journalists to meet Massoud in Khwaja Bahauddin, in northern Afghanistan near the border with Tajikistan. They behaved and dressed like Westerners, but they were carrying a bomb hidden inside the camera which they had stolen from a French news network.[386] Dahmane Abd al-Sattar pretended he was 'Karim Souzani', who had been in official dialogue with Massoud, and Bouraoui al-Ouaer assumed the role of the cameraman, 'Kassim Bocouli'.[387] Continuing the pretence of holding an interview with Massoud, they posed a question to him, 'Commander, what will you do with Osama bin Laden when you have reconquered all of Afghanistan?'[388]

Before Massoud could answer, the bomb was detonated. One of the terrorists died instantly from the concealed explosive. The other, injured by the shrapnel, was shot dead by Northern Alliance guards. Massoud, the legendary Afghan commander who had out-thought and outfought the

Soviets, was mortally wounded. The next day, Muhammad Yunes Kanuni, the spokesman for Northern Alliance, released a statement stating, 'Ahmad Shah Mas'ud [Massoud] was the target of an assassination attempt organised by the Pakistani ISI and Usamah bin Laden.'[389] However, before anyone could fully establish what had just transpired and why the Northern Alliance were accusing the Pakistani spy agency of playing a role, far worse was to come.

Al-Qaeda's longstanding threat to strike the heart of the United States became a stark reality on 11 September 2001. Four commercial passenger planes were hijacked leaving Boston's Logan Airport and smashed into both the north and south towers of the World Trade Center in New York, the Pentagon in Washington, DC, and into a field in rural Pennsylvania. In total 2,998 people were killed as a direct consequence of the attacks itself. Al-Qaeda had recruited 19 terrorists to carry out the attack which would leave deep, indelible scars on the American psyche across generations. It would also have long-term consequences for global security by redefining international threats and altering the nature of warfare as well as ushering in the 'war on terrorism' and the recalibration of law enforcement and intelligence communities.[390] Immediately after the collapse of the Twin Towers, layers of thick dust and ash combined with destroyed building materials, industrial chemicals, and jet fuel residue to engulf the surrounding area. More than 400,000 survivors, first responders, and Lower Manhattan residents were exposed to the toxic atmosphere on 9/11 itself and during the nine-month rescue and recovery operations at Ground Zero. Tens of thousands endured chronic illnesses, including respiratory diseases, cancer, and mental health issues. More than 2,000 of those exposed have died.[391] The actual death toll from the 9/11 fallout continues to grow every year.

Although 9/11 has been well documented by commissions, practitioners, journalists, and academics, an important comment that Faraj had made in 'The Neglected Duty' more than two decades prior was overlooked, which some jihadists believed was prophetically fulfilled following 9/11:

> Only when all important centres [positions] are filled with Muslim doctors and Muslim engineers, will the existing pagan order perish automatically and the Muslim ruler will establish himself.[392]

For many jihadists, it was notable that al-Zawahiri, as a trained doctor, was connected to the planning behind 9/11. For al-Zawahiri himself, his role

was a continuation in the Egyptian jihadist struggle following in the footsteps of both Qutb and Faraj. The Egyptian Mohamed Atta, the hijacker-
pilot of American Airlines Flight 11 which crashed into the North Tower of
the World Trade Center whom al-Zawahiri mentored, was a qualified engineer.[393] Months later, an al-Qaeda operative apprehended in Afghanistan
claimed the 9/11 hijackers were following through on 'the doctor's programme', which was a refence to al-Zawahiri.[394]

The day after the 9/11 attacks, Deputy Secretary of State Richard Armitage
met with the director general of Pakistan's ISI Lieutenant General Mahmud
Ahmed. Armitage warned Ahmed that 'Pakistan must either stand with the
United States in its fight against terrorism or stand against us. There was no
manoeuvring room.' Ahmed, who had very close ties to the jihadist network in Pakistan and Afghanistan, assured Armitage that the United States
'could count on Pakistan's "unqualified support", that Islamabad would do
whatever was required of it by the U.S.'[395] On 13 September 2001, Armitage
met again with Ahmed and presented him with specific requests including to 'stop al-Qaeda operatives at your border, intercept arms shipments
through Pakistan and end all logistical support for bin Laden'.[396]

General Pervez Musharraf had been a pariah after overthrowing the
democratically elected prime minister Nawaz Sharif. In a twist of fate, because of 9/11, he was in the right place and at the right time. Based on
the flawed recommendations by the US secretary of state Colin Powell,
the Bush administration chose to depend on Musharraf and the Pakistani
military.[397] That support would derail counter-terrorism efforts for the
next 20 years across several American administrations and contribute to al-
Zawahiri's endurance. Under Musharraf, the Pakistani state and intelligence
services strategically intensified their relationship with the terrorist groups
and did not degrade the nexus, which was what the Bush administration
was expecting and hoping for.[398] However, officially, the Musharraf regime
accepted the actions the Bush administration requested 'without conditions'.[399] Yet, as the Pakistani scholar Ayesha Siddiqa reveals, 'When the U.S.
said, "Are you with us or against us?" that didn't leave a lot of options for
the leadership. But there was a lot of sympathy among certain elements of
the military with al-Qaeda.'[400]

With some concern that the Pakistanis might play a double game, a senior CIA officer stationed at the US Embassy in Islamabad, Bob Grenier,
established a separate dialogue with a Taliban interlocutor, Mullah Akhtar

Mohammad Osmani, one of Mullah Omar's closest advisors. Grenier presented Osmani with three choices—hand over the al-Qaeda leadership; allow US special forces into Afghanistan to eliminate them; or lastly, bring bin Laden, al-Zawahiri, and the others to justice themselves by executing them. Unsurprisingly, the Taliban rejected all three proposals.[401] Around the same time, on 17 September 2001, ISI director Mahmud Ahmed arrived in Afghanistan to meet Taliban leader Mullah Omar and ostensibly convey the same US orders.[402]

Whether these demands were genuinely conveyed to the Taliban has never been fully established. Without doubt, Ahmed was always playing a double game.[403] On 7 October 2001, the same day Operation Enduring Freedom was launched, Ahmed was forced to resign as the head of the ISI under considerable US pressure after allegations of his close connections to both the Taliban and al-Qaeda became apparent. FBI investigators uncovered evidence that in early September 2001 Ahmed directed the British-Pakistani terrorist Ahmed Omar Saeed Sheikh to transfer $100,000 to Mohamed Atta, ringleader of the 9/11 hijackers.[404] However, more revelations would eventually emerge about the ISI's nefarious ties with terrorist groups as well as Sheikh's own activities with them.[405] According to Ayesha Siddiqa, 'For those in the ISI who were engaged with the Taliban and al-Qaeda, there was a lot of sympathy. Another concerning example was General Mahmud Ahmed advising Mullah Omar on how to make an escape from Afghanistan during American bombings.'[406]

The response to al-Qaeda was failing before any operation had begun. Washington was divided over how to handle the duplicity of the Pakistani military, which through their statecraft had invested substantially in creating 'strategic depth' inside Afghanistan and were not simply going to abandon it. As a senior US intelligence official pointed out, 'The Pakistanis can put on the charm with people that visit. Arrange trips to wherever one wants to go, provide vehicles, helicopters. They really do have this ability to orchestrate the information campaign in support of what they wanted. And it's very very effective in terms of that.'[407]

In the meantime, al-Qaeda was preparing for the US invasion. The reasoning for al-Zawahiri's elaborate plot to kill Ahmad Shah Massoud had become abundantly clear. Bin Laden had predicted correctly the United States would retaliate massively after 9/11, invading Afghanistan to eliminate al-Qaeda and their hosts, the Taliban. The most strategically valuable asset for an invading army was reliable on-the-ground logistical support, which the Northern Alliance was well placed to provide. Therefore, by eliminating Massoud beforehand, the Northern Alliance would be much weaker, divided, and unable to assist the United States. Furthermore, the US would be embroiled in a long-drawn-out conflict of attrition, just as the Soviets had been.[408] According to Lawrence Wright, 'The assassination of Ahmed Shah Masood was in the service of 9/11. This was a big assignment to get rid of Masood. And demonstrated al-Zawahiri was not a peripheral figure within al-Qaeda. He did a very effective job in taking down Masood and demonstrated the level of trust bin Laden had in him.'[409] There was also a touch of symbolism for al-Zawahiri in removing Massoud. He was an ally of Abdullah Azzam during the jihad against the Soviets.

Another intention was that the invasion of Afghanistan would instigate a mass revolution whereby the *jahili* rulers would be toppled. This was similar to Faraj's intention when Sadat was assassinated. Al-Zawahiri hoped that a highly visible attack against the 'external enemy' followed by the inevitable retaliation would unite the *ummah* to 'strengthening the main struggle, the one against the current regimes of the Muslim world'. According to him, 'The Jihad movement must . . . make room for the Muslim nation to participate with it in the Jihad for the sake of empowerment. The Muslim nation will not participate with [the Jihad movement] unless the slogans of the *mujahideen* are understood by the masses.'[410]

However, this was a gross miscalculation by al-Qaeda, as the Northern Alliance was able to rally around the murder of Massoud and, with American air support, unseat and eject the Taliban from Afghanistan. As the United States commenced Operation Enduring Freedom in Afghanistan, bin Laden had seriously overestimated the fundamentalist motivation in the Muslim world. However, al-Zawahiri knew that defeating the United States wasn't going to be imminent. It could take years, possibly decades, and didn't necessarily involve a victory on the battlefield but withstanding the inevitable onslaught. For that reason, this phase of al-Qaeda's jihad and the ideological component to justify the struggle was especially important for their long-term goals.

1 Ayman al-Zawahiri through the ages. As a toddler, to school-boy, to university student, to international terrorist. (*ABACA PRESS/PA Images*).

2   Maadi, the treelined suburb in Cairo where al-Zawahiri grew up. (*Wael Aboulsaadat*).

3 Al-Zawahiri's paternal granduncle, Shaykh Muhammad al-Ahmadi ibn Ibrahim al-Zawahiri, was grand imam at the prestigious al-Azhar seminary in the 1930s. He was allegedly ousted by British interference. (*Author's own collection*).

4 Abdul Rahman Azzam, al-Zawahiri's maternal granduncle, served as the Arab League secretary-general between 1945 to 1952. He was a proponent of Arab nationalism. (*Keystone-France*).

5 Egyptian president Gamal Abdel Nasser in Mansoura, Egypt, 1960. Al-Zawahiri despised Nasser's Arab socialism. (*Bibliotheca Alexandrina*).

6 Sayyid Qutb on trial in 1966 for his seminal book, *Milestones*, which spoke about overthrowing 'apostate' regimes. Qutb was subsequently executed by the Nasser regime, which had a huge impact on al–Zawahiri. (*Wikimedia Commons*).

7 Mahfouz Azzam, al–Zawahiri's maternal uncle, was Sayyid Qutb's lawyer. Azzam's stories of Qutb had a profound impact on al–Zawahiri's worldview. (*Hossam el-Hamalawy*).

8 The Military Technical College in Egypt. Al–Zawahiri along with his cohorts tried but failed to take it over in 1974. This was his first act of insurrection. (*Author's own collection*).

9 Egyptian vice-president Hosni Mubarak (*left*) and president Anwar Sadat (*right*), pray over the tomb of Gamal Abdel Nasser. Hours later, Sadat would be killed by the al-Jihad terrorist group. 6 October 1981. (*AFP*).

10 World leaders follow the flag-draped coffin of Anwar Sadat. Al-Zawahiri plotted to attack the funeral procession but was unsuccessful. 11 October 1981. (*Bryn Colton*).

11 Al-Zawahiri, incarcerated following the assassination of Anwar Sadat. He forged ties and established his status amongst other jailed Egyptian jihadists who were galvanised by his fiery rhetoric. 1982. (*Getty Images*).

12 The prestigious al-Azhar seminary in Cairo which was always at the centre of Egypt's major political upheavals. (*US National Archives*).

13 The Jordanian-Palestinian ideologue Abdullah Azzam (right) with Afghan *mujahideen* commander Ahmad Shah Massoud (left) in Afghanistan during the battle against the Soviets in the 1980s. Over time, al-Zawahiri would play a hand in both of their deaths. (*Al-Bunyan al-Marsus magazine, no. 30 p. 17*).

14 Front page of the *Ethiopian Herald*, with pictures of a failed assassination attempt against Egyptian president Hosni Mubarak as his motorcade drove from Addis Ababa airport. Al-Zawahiri orchestrated this plot with his EIJ fighters. 27 June 1995. (*Alexander Joe/AFP/GettyImages*).

15 The ruins of the Egyptian Embassy in Islamabad, Pakistan, following an EIJ suicide car bomb attack. Fifteen people were killed and scores injured. The attack was part of al-Zawahiri's expanding terrorist campaign against the Mubarak regime outside Egypt. 19 November 1995. (*Tanveer Mughal/AFP via Getty Images*).

16 Omar Abdel Rahman, the blind spiritual leader of the Egyptian terrorist group al-Gama'a Islamiyya. He and al-Zawahiri had a consequential falling out over the future direction of al-Jihad resulting in a split between the EIJ and al-Gama'a. (*Mike Nelson/AFP/GettyImages*).

17 Muhammad al-Zawahiri, younger brother to Ayman al-Zawahiri. He was involved in EIJ activities, including a terror cell in Albania. Released from prison during the fall of the Mubarak regime, he engaged in the protests outside the US Embassy in Cairo. (*Bisson / Jdd / Sipa / Shutterstock*).

18 Ayman al-Zawahiri, Osama bin Laden, and Mohammed Atef hold an al-Qaeda press conference at a terrorist training camp in Khost, Afghanistan. 26 May 1998. (*Getty Images / Staff*).

5

Live to Fight Another Day

The Great Escape

President George W. Bush was sitting in the Oval Office receiving near-simultaneous updates on the progress of the Battle of Tora Bora. He had a chart in his office with photos of the al-Qaeda hierarchy. During a presidential daily briefing in early December 2001, information had come through that al-Zawahiri may have been killed in the bombing of Tora Bora. Al-Qaeda's deputy could be dead, so soon. Bush prepared to mark an X across the bespectacled face of the Egyptian doctor. There was quiet satisfaction that a big figure within al-Qaeda would soon fall. However, the White House was incredibly naïve as to the type of person al-Zawahiri was and his propensity to defy the odds for self-preservation.[1]

Before the war against the Soviets, Tora Bora was a network of tall, intertwined, rugged, and sparsely forested mountains with numerous caves where goats and sheep and occasionally nomads took shelter in chilly weather. During the Soviet occupation, the caves served as refuge for the *mujahideen*. At Tora Bora, caves honeycombed the valley, some primitive and untouched, others fortified and expanded.

In the years leading up to 9/11, bin Laden maintained a mountain hideaway near Tora Bora called Milawa. It was situated across narrow snow-covered valleys.[2] Using his vast resources, bin Laden began the complicated work of turning the site into a forbidding sanctuary should the need ever arise. He constructed a road linking it to Jalalabad and fortified the natural caves and engineered new ones so he and his al-Qaeda fighters could move undetected between locations.[3] Near the bottom of the valley, two long, triangle-shaped caves had been enlarged to hold hundreds of rifles, machine guns, rocket launchers, and boxes of ammunition.[4] In the years that followed, bin Laden and al-Zawahiri developed an understanding of

Doctor, Teacher, Terrorist. Sajjan M. Gohel, Oxford University Press. © Oxford University Press 2024.
DOI: 10.1093/oso/9780197665367.003.0005

the surrounding geography and the routes used by traders and smugglers to navigate into Pakistan. For al-Qaeda, Tora Bora was known as a bastion. It wasn't a place of last resort, but it would serve to protect them when, or if, the time was needed.

Bin Laden described his experiences at Tora Bora in an audio message in 2003. He remembered that, on the morning of 3 December 2001, intense and incessant US bombing was taking place. According to bin Laden, 'American forces were bombing us by smart bombs that weigh thousands of pounds and bombs that penetrate caves.'[5] Bin Laden and al-Zawahiri were being hemmed in and their operational space confined. Senior figures within al-Qaeda—Mohammed Atef and Juma Namangani—were killed during this bombing of Tora Bora.[6]

For al-Zawahiri, news arrived from Gardez to inform him that his wife Umm Fatima, his son Mohammed, and favourite daughter Aisha had all been killed in a US air strike. Bin Laden comforted a distraught al-Zawahiri, who had thought his family would be safe if he kept them apart from him.[7] The bombing campaign was furious and focused on the Haqqani Network assets including safe houses. Several of al-Zawahiri's family members were trapped under the rubble. Al-Zawahiri's second wife Umayma Hassan wrote about her experiences: 'Khalil-ur-Rahman Haqqani said to me, "give me your hand my sister." I hesitated and the [bombing] plane came again and I thought I would die, so I was prepared, to be happy with them [the family members already dead]. Haqqani shouted to me "please sister quickly come," so I gave him my hand and he pulled me out of the rubble. He said "Do not be afraid, I will take you to a safe place."'[8]

This was the steep cost al-Zawahiri and his family had to endure as part of his alliance with bin Laden. He chose to alter his goal from unseating Mubarak in Egypt to declaring war against the United States which had exacted an unbearable toll. Al-Zawahiri's protégé Saif al-Adel, who had opposed the 9/11 attacks and foresaw the likely US response, did not follow al-Zawahiri to Tora Bora and instead headed to Iran, as did many other Egyptian members of al-Qaeda.[9]

Usually by November in Afghanistan, snow blankets much of the country. Temperatures dropped well below freezing. Anyone at Tora Bora would have endured a harsh winter of snow and isolation in dark caves and bunkers. There was concern within US intelligence circles that bin Laden and al-Zawahiri might try to escape Tora Bora and sneak into Pakistan. Despite assurances from Pakistan's General Musharraf, his military took no meaningful concrete measures to cover their side of the border.

The only way to mitigate that was to have more US elite soldiers strike the complex of caves where bin Laden and al-Zawahiri were hiding and to block their escape routes. General Tommy Franks, as Central Command (CENTCOM) commander, rejected positioning more US troops on the ground to close off the mountain paths that lead to Pakistan.[10] On 14 December 2001, bin Laden's voice was identified by US special forces. It sounded more like a pre-recorded speech than a live broadcast. Bin Laden spoke to his fighters with the expectation he would die. His comments reflected this fatalism:

> Allah commended to us that when death approaches any of us that we make a bequest to parents and next of kin and to Muslims as a whole.... Allah bears witness that the love of jihad and death in the cause of Allah has dominated my life and the verses of the sword permeated every cell in my heart ... and fight the pagans all together as they fight you all together.... If I live or die the war will continue.[11]

The reality was that this was a ruse, and bin Laden and al-Zawahiri were preparing to leave the battlefield area. Abdullah Tabarak, bin Laden's Moroccan bodyguard, used bin Laden's satellite handset as the others escaped, knowing that it was being tracked by US intelligence, to give the impression the al-Qaeda leadership was still in Tora Bora.[12]

Another development would aid the escape. On 19 December 2001, six individuals from the Pakistani terrorist group Jaish-e-Mohammed (JeM) attacked the Indian parliament in New Delhi after penetrating the first security cordon layer. A gun battle ensued between the terrorists and the parliament's security forces. In the end, all six JeM attackers and eight members of the security forces died.[13] The brazen attack of India's seat of democracy was designed to create repercussions.

Indian authorities accused the JeM attackers of being under the directive of the Pakistani military.[14] The Atal Bihari Vajpayee government gave several ultimatums, which included Pakistan banning the JeM and Lashkar-e-Taiba (LeT), two groups established by the ISI that were implicated in several attacks in India. This was followed by the mobilisation of hundreds of thousands of troops, heavy tanks, artillery, and fighter bombers deployed on each side of the border, with Pakistan repositioning troops from the Afghan border to the Indian border.[15]

The resulting India–Pakistan military stand-off was no coincidence. Indeed, it had been engineered by JeM to create a diversion to allow the al-Qaeda leadership trapped in the Tora Bora mountains to escape.[16] Their leader, Maulana Masood Azhar, helped bin Laden and several other al-Qaeda leaders to cross over to Pakistan using JeM's network of safe houses and agents across Pakistan's Parachinar tribal regions. For Azhar, this was an opportunity to help the al-Qaeda leadership who had supported him in the past.[17] The Pakistani scholar Ayesha Siddiqa provided more detail on the ties bonding al-Qaeda with the terrorist outfits in Pakistan:

> Groups like the Lashkar-e-Taiba, and Jaish-e-Mohammed looked up to al-Qaeda. Jaish-e-Mohammed people would say "Brother Osama" and "Brother Ayman." Some of Jaish-e-Mohammed's initial financing came from al-Qaeda. It was not so much how much the Pakistani-based terrorist groups helped al-Qaeda but more how al-Qaeda helps these groups.[18]

Under the cover of a cold December night, bin Laden and al-Zawahiri descended from the caves of Tora Bora to the valley floor to commence what would have been a three-day journey to Parachinar. No clearly marked border indicated where Pakistan ended and Afghanistan began. Forested mountains with snow-covered peaks soaring more than 14,000 feet cut between both countries. They then travelled in disguise and were sent first to Dera Ismail Khan, a city on the edge of the tribal areas. From there, journeys were coordinated by senior al-Qaeda planner Abu Zubaydah's allies in the JeM.[19] Once in Pakistan, the al-Qaeda leadership separated and dispersed to multiple locations to avoid detection and plan their next moves.

By 20 December 2001, the Battle of Tora Bora was over. As the US forces gauged the devastation of the bombing campaign, some 220 dead al-Qaeda fighters and 52 captured were accounted for.[20] Most were Arabs, Afghans, and Pakistanis. Yet the senior leadership of al-Qaeda were safely in Pakistan. Questions were raised about the role of the Pakistani military. Although the Taliban collapsed as a regime and lost territory, they were not defeated. They went into Pakistan together with al-Qaeda and the Pakistani military advisors based in Afghanistan helping the Taliban, also had to evacuate.[21] Ambassador Henry Crumpton provided a devastating assessment of Pakistan's lack of cooperation:

> I had some doubts about the Pakistani military before 9/11, and I remember thinking it must be isolated incidents or individuals within the Pakistani military, the government, or local leaders. Now I think it was worse than I

thought. I really realised that about October 2001 when the Pakistanis were allowing us access and helping to a degree, but when we really needed some hard intelligence, we really needed some support, I saw that not happening. For me that was a benchmark, a particularly important moment, and I remember later on in December at Tora Bora, having zero confidence that if bin Laden and al-Zawahiri got away and went into Pakistan that we would have no help from the Pakistanis. I knew that with great confidence, and sadly it was true.[22]

President Bush had to remove the *X* he had prematurely put on al-Zawahiri's picture when it was assumed he had died in Tora Bora. This would not be the last time al-Zawahiri would foil the US efforts in capturing or killing him. Nor would it be the last time that the Pakistani military would mislead the White House about its intensions. In *Knights under the Prophet's Banner*, al-Zawahiri praised the Taliban for refusing to hand over the al-Qaeda leadership to the United States:

> The defiance shown by the Islamic principality of Afghanistan, under the leadership of 'Prince of the Faithful, the *mujahid* Mullah Mohammad Omar' when it refused to comply with the U.S. request to hand over Osama Bin Laden and his companions and its firm steadfastness in continuing to reject this request even in the wake of the U.S. missile strikes against Afghan territory, represented a challenge that the United States could neither absorb or adapt to.[23]

Al-Zawahiri was promoting the idea that the Taliban was indispensable to the jihadist cause. However, not all were optimistic. Abu Walid al-Masri's ire was reserved for Osama bin Laden, whom he blamed for the Taliban's fall. He described the al-Qaeda leader as a traitor (*kha'in*) for betraying Mullah Omar's offer of refuge and hospitality.[24] Abu Walid typified the rift within al-Qaeda, which would leave the organization weakened in the aftermath of September 11.

Reflecting this split, as the US bombardment continued, bin Laden and his colleagues fled in two separate directions. Bin Laden and loyalists including al-Zawahiri headed towards Pakistan.[25] Given their opposition to bin Laden, Abu Walid and his son-in-law Saif al-Adel fled in the opposite direction to Iran.[26] Their destination was a smugglers' post beyond Herat, a few kilometres from the Iranian border.[27] Al-Qaeda's members now had to live in the shadows, both in Pakistan and Iran, and depended on allies for sanctuary. The Taliban too had been driven from power and needed to regroup in Pakistan. Post-9/11, whilst in hiding, al-Zawahiri would manage to find the time to have his seventh and last child, a daughter, Nawwar, the first with his second wife, Umayma Hassan.[28]

Meanwhile, the Afghan American diplomat Zalmay Khalilzad had begun serving as the special assistant to President George W. Bush, making him the most influential person in Afghanistan. As part of a roadmap for a post-Taliban Afghanistan, Khalilzad oversaw the 2001 Bonn Conference in Germany, which led Afghanistan to the crisis it would face for decades to come.[29] It also outlined the problematic aspects of Khalilzad's role in Afghan ethno-politics. Khalilzad's own ethnic group, the Pashtuns, accused him of blocking former king Mohammad Zahir Shah from a position in the new government.[30] The Tajik-dominated Northern Alliance who ousted the Taliban were frustrated with Khalilzad for over-centralizing the political system to benefit Pashtuns. Subsequently, Khalilzad became US ambassador to Afghanistan. He successfully alienated parts of the Afghan population and earned the unfortunate sobriquet as the "viceroy" because of his micro-managing of Afghanistan's internal affairs.[31]

Vex and Exhaust

On 11 April 2002, Djerba, Tunisia—a place frequented by Western tourists—was changed forever when Tunisian al-Qaeda operative Niser bin Muhammad Nawar drove a truck at full speed past a security cordon and smashed the vehicle filled with liquid propane into the side of the historic el-Ghriba Synagogue, one of North Africa's oldest Jewish places of worship. Like 9/11, the attack was conceived by Khalid Sheikh Mohammed and in consultation with al-Zawahiri was given the go-ahead.[32] The suicide bombing killed 14 Germans, three Tunisians, and two French whilst leaving dozens injured. It was al-Qaeda's first external operation following the 9/11 attacks and demonstrated a commitment by al-Zawahiri to continue attacking soft targets especially those that would attract people from the West.

Statements ascribed to al-Zawahiri after 2001 sought to validate al-Qaeda's targeting of civilians by claiming that Western societies were morally corrupt and should be held answerable for the policies of their governments in the Islamic world. Al-Zawahiri's statements had variations in tone and content, but all were designed to appeal to specific audiences. More than a year after 9/11, al-Zawahiri issued a lengthy treatise, 'Loyalty and Enmity', which portrayed a world divided into two warring camps: Muslims and the rest. For al-Zawahiri, Muslims were duty bound to protect, without question, the jihadists who were waging war on behalf of Islam.

> Waging Offensive Jihad against the infidels becomes even more logical and palatable, since Muslims can never love or befriend infidels anyway until the latter submit to Islam. All Muslims would be obliged to help, fund, and shelter the *mujahidin*, since they must at all times be loyal to fellow Muslims. And so forth. In short: the Muslim must 'know that he is obligated to befriend a believer—even if he is oppressive and violent toward you, while he must be hostile to the infidel even if he is liberal and kind to you'.[33]

This treatise was further revealing in that it acknowledges another little-known doctrine, *taqiyya*, which for al-Qaeda meant 'deception'. According to al-Zawahiri's definition, *taqiyya* meant that Muslims can under certain situations deceive 'infidels' by feigning amity or kindness, even apostasy, provided they remain true to al-Zawahiri's vision of how Islam should be practiced. The purpose had a simple goal, to enable al-Qaeda recruits living in the West and parts of the Islamic world to operate without divulging their true intentions. This tactic was a continuation and development from the methods al-Zawahiri envisaged in the *Military Studies* manual he developed in the 1990s:

> Taqiyya [self-preservation through dissembling] was a novelty of Islam before the Muslims grew strong. . . . However, taqiyya is permitted only should one fear being killed, scarred, or severely harmed. But whoever is forced into apostasy, it is his right to resist and refuse to respond to any utterance of infidelity, if he can.[34]

By speaking to Western audiences as well as Muslims, al-Zawahiri could both scorn Western governments' anti-terror tactics and shame Muslims who accept Western ideals and pull away from the *ummah*. Furthermore, although there was often a perception that al-Zawahiri and bin Laden had a consensus-driven approach, internal communications provided glimpses of the al-Qaeda leaders differing over the group's direction in the post-9/11 environment. On one such occasion in August 2003, al-Zawahiri wrote to bin Laden about a speech being developed on the ideological justification for jihad, which would then be made available to their supporters as well as to the wider world, 'The author does not greedily intend to add to his predecessor's works, but rather seeks to clarify several points.'[35] Al-Zawahiri, using carefully thought-out language, was clearly uncomfortable with bin Laden's version of the speech and wanted to rephrase parts which to him would better reflect al-Qaeda's narrative.

Al-Zawahiri's editing of bin Laden's original text included extensive verses from the Qur'an. He goes on to say, 'This meaning is very important to highlight to the righteous people of this time, for their hearts to be reassured that they are engaging in the same battles that were conducted by Allah's messengers and their followers of the faithful people for all time. . . . We hope that this message would enlighten the connection between the internal and external enemies in their goals and in their soldiers.'[36] For al-Zawahiri, it was important to ensure that there was a religious justification and rationale for potential future actions.

With his hair still messed up from sleep and wearing only his undergarments, Khalid Shaikh Mohammed was captured in Rawalpindi, Pakistan, on 1 March 2003. He was apprehended near the ISI headquarters. According to a senior US intelligence official, 'KSM was photographed by the CIA looking doped-up, hirsute, and bedraggled looking like an obese manager of a seedy nightclub.'[37] The mastermind of the 9/11 attacks was paraded for the world to see. No doubt al-Zawahiri was watching this and thinking about his own safety and security. Worse news was to follow. Al-Zawahiri was distraught when his long-time friend and ally Ahmed Khadr was killed on 2 October 2003 in South Waziristan, Pakistan, in a military operation. His death was a personal blow for al-Zawahiri, as the two had established a close relationship that was sustained even though they were in hiding.[38]

However, al-Zawahiri would continue to taunt the West with his ability to evade detection. In March 2004, the American intelligence community informed Pakistan's ISI that they thought al-Zawahiri was in Wana, a town in South Waziristan.[39] The development coincided, perhaps blatantly, with US secretary of state Colin Powell's visit to Pakistan. Pakistani forces were supposed to be preparing for a dawn raid on a mountain stronghold identified as al-Zawahiri's hideout. President Pervez Musharraf had appeared on the Western media boasting that al-Zawahiri was cornered and described him as 'a high-value target'.[40]

US forces were not directly involved in the operation, as it was in Pakistani territory, but were positioned across the border in Afghanistan, should al-Zawahiri try to move westwards. Oddly, despite the momentum, the Pakistani military then chose to suspend operations against the fortified compound that the US had identified and launch a dawn raid instead. By the time Pakistani units made it to this destination, al-Zawahiri was not there. According to Sebastian Rotella, 'al-Zawahiri has had very good connections in Pakistan which is why he was able to stay a step ahead of any hunt against him.'[41]

The suspicion was that al-Zawahiri had been tipped off by the ISI. Yet again, American faith in the Pakistani military establishment had been betrayed, and once more it was put down to 'rogue elements'.[42] When officers of the ISI are caught aiding terrorists, they are immediately termed rogues or isolated elements to shield the real culprits from justice and accountability and enable people like al-Zawahiri to continue to live to fight another day.[43]

It was at this time that North and South Waziristan witnessed local agitation against the Pakistani military's 'three Ds' security policy, which represented death, destruction and dislocation. For Pakistan's military establishment, the Taliban's insurgency in Afghanistan was essential to regain their 'strategic depth'. However, to achieve this, their military operations also resulted in some 3 million civilians becoming internally displaced persons. This created a security vacuum where the Taliban were able to operate freely which benefited al-Qaeda too. It also created tensions with the United States. As the former Commander of CENTCOM, General Joseph Votel commented:

> The Taliban reconstituted their support from Pakistan in quite a significant way. We were unable to really impact that sanctuary, and that allowed them to grow. And they were moving leaders, fighters, and supplies back and forth. As we tried to address that, this is when the friction began to go up with Pakistan. We kept trying to push, to put more and more pressure on Pakistan. And as we pushed, the pushing came back from Pakistan.[44]

Iraq

Another seismic foreign policy dynamic would inadvertently aid bin Laden and al-Zawahiri. When it looked like al-Qaeda may well be in sharp decline, US president George W. Bush and British prime minister Tony Blair led a new campaign to remove Iraqi dictator Saddam Hussein from power in 2003, ostensibly over allegations that Saddam Hussein possessed weapons of mass destruction (WMD). The Iraq war would drain coalition resources and focus from Afghanistan, providing al-Qaeda and the Taliban much needed breathing space.

Several members of the Bush administration saw Iraq as a crucial issue. In 1998, 18 Republicans wrote a letter to President Clinton urging him to 'aim at the removal of Saddam Hussein's regime from power'.[45] This document played a significant role in shaping the George W. Bush administration's decision to launch the 2003 war in Iraq, which would have lasting consequences for regional insecurity in the Middle East. Most of its authors became officials in the George W. Bush administration, including John Bolton, Donald Rumsfeld, Paul Wolfowitz, and Zalmay Khalilzad. Two years after the invasion, Khalilzad was made US ambassador to Iraq.

However, as the build-up to a war in Iraq gathered momentum, al-Qaeda planned to attack the New York City subway system using cyanide gas. The gas was to be dispersed simultaneously at several stations by devices placed in train carriages.[46] The primary objective for al-Qaeda was to create panic, fear, and disruption which would impact on safety and confidence in the subway system. That in turn would hurt an economy still recovering from 9/11. There would also be fatalities, but the numbers would be less than if an explosive device was used.

Al-Qaeda had revived a project it first conceived in Afghanistan pre-9/11 with the intention of unleashing a chemical and cyanide dispersal system, called the 'Unique Invention' (al-Mubtakkar al-Farid). Originally conceived by the Egyptian Midhat Mursi, the belief was that the project had stalled after al-Qaeda was forced to vacate its bases in Afghanistan and go into hiding in Pakistan. However, it was still being clandestinely developed. The Mubtakkar was a portable contraption composed of a widely available combination of chemicals and sodium cyanide that creates hydrogen cyanide, a highly volatile liquid that when turned into gas is fatal in minutes if inhaled within a closed environment.[47]

The person tasked with executing the plot in New York was a Saudi, Yusuf bin Salih bin Fahd al-Ayeri, al-Qaeda's top operative in the Arabian Peninsula.[48] Born into an upper-middle-class family in Dammam, Saudi Arabia, al-Ayeri was reckless in his youth, keen on joyriding fast cars on the streets of Dammam, which he saw as a way of confronting the security forces. He was known as Abu Saleh.[49] Al-Ayeri was shaped by the jihadist youth culture that proliferated in the 1990s following the Gulf War and was under the influence of the Awakening (Sahwa), a Saudi Salafi apolitical reform movement.[50] As a teenager he travelled to Afghanistan and trained at al-Faruq camp in Kandahar. He briefly served as a minder for Osama bin Laden, with whom he relocated with to Sudan in 1994, and was involved in the conflict with US peacekeepers in Somalia 1993. He returned to Afghanistan under the Taliban before being asked by Osama bin Laden to create, recruit, and organise the al-Qaeda branch in Saudi Arabia.[51]

Al-Ayeri visited al-Zawahiri in Pakistan in January 2003 to inform him of progress on the plan, which would soon be operational. A large quantity of cyanide salts and potassium permanganate had been procured near Riyadh to test the Mubtakkar. However, to al-Ayeri's surprise, al-Zawahiri called off the attack.[52] There has been much speculation as to what the reasons were. Al-Zawahiri reluctantly supported the 9/11 attacks, an operation that divided al-Qaeda, but this time al-Zawahiri was concerned that another attack in New York, albeit on a lesser scale, would prompt the Bush administration to directly escalate its counter-terrorism operations in Pakistan, rather than rely on the murky ISI, whose loyalties at best remained divided.[53] Another concern al-Zawahiri had was the attack would be used to justify connecting al-Qaeda to Saddam Hussein in Iraq.[54]

However, reflecting on what al-Zawahiri said in *Knights under the Prophet's Banner*, the al-Qaeda deputy believed that a terrorist attack should 'cause the greatest damage and inflict the maximum casualties on the opponent, no matter how much time and effort these operations take, because this is the language understood by the West'.[55] Al-Zawahiri had a much bigger and more devastating plot in mind which was being developed over years, and the Mubtakkar plot was not the priority. Mitchell Silber, who had served as director of intelligence for the New York Police Department commented that 'al-Zawahiri felt compelled to intervene and call off the 2003 poison gas Mubtakkar plot against the New York City subway due to larger dynamics'.[56]

On the Mubtakkar plot, al-Zawahiri played an important centralised operational role and was involved in its conception. The plot initiation and cancellation illustrated that al-Zawahiri wielded direct power and was very hands-on.[57] If the New York subway plot had been executed, a number of people would have died, but it would not have inflicted massive casualties as it involved a cyanide-based, chemical dispersal device. It would frighten people from venturing into the mass transit system and being in confined spaces with limited open air circulation. Although it was going to have a massive impact, both psychological as well as economic, al-Zawahiri had something even more devastating up his sleeve which was why Mubtakkar was shelved.[58]

Al-Ayeri was behind the 12 May 2003 suicide bombings of the Muhaya residential compounds in Riyadh, killing 39 and injuring 160.[59] The plot was coordinated with al-Zawahiri's trusted deputy Saif al-Adel from Iran. Soon after, on 31 May, al-Ayeri was located in Turbah, in the Saudi province of Najd, and killed in a shoot-out with Saudi security forces.[60]

Visualising Terror

Iraq also served as an opportunity for several jihadists, especially Abu Musab al-Zarqawi's faction, known as Jama'at al-Tawhid wal-Jihad (Group of Monotheism and Jihad), to extend their operations against the West inside an Islamic country. In fact, aside from the claim of Saddam Hussein being in possession of WMDs, al-Zarqawi also played a crucial role in the George W. Bush administration's decision to invade Iraq. On 5 February 2003, Secretary of State Colin Powell addressed the UN Security Council and cited al-Zarqawi's presence in Iraq as evidence of ties between Saddam Hussein and al-Qaeda.[61] Ironically, Powell failed to understand the enmity between al-Qaeda and al-Zarqawi. These alleged ties, which were never proved, were partly used to 'justify' US-led military intervention in Iraq, but al-Zarqawi's reputation amongst the jihadists grew in stature.

Al-Zarqawi was behind a deluge of atrocities in Iraq including against Iraqis themselves. On 19 August 2003, Baghdad's UN headquarters was bombed, killing 22 people including the UN special envoy Sergio Vieira de Mello. Soon afterwards a huge explosion killed the Shiite cleric Ayatollah Mohammad Baqer al-Hakim and 83 worshippers outside the Imam Ali Mosque in Najaf. A letter seized by US forces in January 2004, from al-Zarqawi to Osama bin Laden, called for instigating civil war between Iraq's Sunni minority and Shiite majority. He called Shiites 'a sect of treachery and betrayal . . . the lurking snake, the crafty and malicious scorpion'.[62] His requests were rejected but this didn't stop him. Explosions on 1 February 2004, during the Ashura festival, killed 185 Shiite pilgrims in Karbala and Baghdad.[63] All of this added to al-Zarqawi's notoriety, and he continued fomenting sectarian conflict against Shiite Muslims.

Al-Zarqawi also escalated visually disturbing and graphic terrorism content by filming live beheadings on camera. The Jordanian did not just want to have terrorism reported by others; he wanted it to be seen by everyone. Al-Zarqawi was also a pioneer in utilising the evolving new media for terrorism. Al-Zarqawi would often dress in black clothes with ammunition pouches strapped across his chest. He was well built, with short black hair and a cropped beard. The key feature of his often-expressionless face was the glare in his eyes that served to intimidate his enemies. When appearing in videos he would often have either an assault rifle or a sword in the background, the latter of which would be used to execute his hostages.

Behind the scenes al-Qaeda's leadership had been debating what to do with al-Zarqawi. He was too unhinged and pathologically violent for some in al-Qaeda like al-Zawahiri, but at the same time, al-Zarqawi's insurgency against the United States was galvanising a segment of the jihadist movement. If al-Qaeda didn't capitalise on it, they could lose global relevancy. In a statement in September 2004 entitled 'The Defeat of America Is a Matter of Time', al-Zawahiri claimed that 'the *mujahideen* fighters in Iraq turned America's plan upside down' and that 'Americans in both countries [Iraq and Afghanistan] are between two fires. If they carry on, they will bleed to death, and if they pull out, they lose everything.'[64] Al-Zawahiri was encouraging Americans to have doubts about their government and its military capabilities. By addressing Americans directly, al-Zawahiri tried to undermine American solidarity and urge US citizens to pressure their government to pull out of the Iraqi and Afghan theatres. However, all was not well within the ranks of al-Qaeda and their Iraqi franchise.

On 17 October 2004, al-Zarqawi finally pledged a *ba'yah* (oath of allegiance) 'to the *mujahid Shaykh* Osama bin Laden, to listen and obey in times of difficulty and prosperity'.[65] Al-Zawahiri also revealed that several months of communications with al-Qaeda had led to this moment. Despite the optics, al-Zawahiri and al-Qaeda did not immediately accept al-Zarqawi's pledge. The leadership wanted more reassurances from the Jordanian about his overall plans. As a result, Abu Faraj al-Libbi, the head of al-Qaeda's external operations, was tasked in finalising the arrangement with al-Zarqawi and his deputy Abu Ja'far al-Iraqi.[66]

For al-Libbi, Iraq was 'ablaze' courtesy of al-Zarqawi, which offered so much promise for al-Qaeda that he proposed to the organization's leadership that its external operations section move to Iraq, where the conditions were more conducive to launch attacks against the West and recruit new adherents. It was also safer from US counter-terrorism operations. The one problem was that although al-Zarqawi was in alignment over killing Americans and targeting the 'apostate' governments of the Middle East, al-Zarqawi also had a strong hatred for Iraq's Shiite Muslims and was unwilling to lower the intensity of his sectarian attacks against them. Al-Libbi sent a memo back to bin Laden and al-Zawahiri outlining his discussions with al-Zarqawi. Significantly, al-Zawahiri stated his opposition to 'opening a front' against the Shiites in Iraq. Not wanting this to be an issue of contention, al-Libbi conferred separately with bin Laden and concluded not to pass on al-Zawahiri's concerns to al-Zarqawi, as it was more important to consolidate the relationship. Once al-Qaeda accepted al-Zarqawi's *ba'yah*, then reining him in would be more straightforward, according to al-Libbi.[67]

Subsequently, al-Zarqawi wrote to al-Libbi, explaining the urgency of al-Qaeda's pending recognition of his *ba'yah* and for its leadership to understand and support the violence he was unleashing in Iraq: 'There were some opinions that oppose the nature of our work here. . . . There is no doubt that there will be disturbances and differences and we are well aware of this during these difficult times. We would not accept this matter if it weren't for the good of victory of this religion and the rise of our two head Brothers [bin Laden and al-Zawahiri].'[68] Significantly, al-Zarqawi attached greater importance to getting al-Zawahiri's support, likely because he knew that this was where he faced the most opposition, even though his reservations had been withheld by al-Libbi. Nevertheless, al-Zarqawi showed significant reverence to al-Zawahiri by stating, 'As long as the Doctor [al-Zawahiri] is in the picture . . . I wanted him to know about the issue, so that the matter would be completely clear.'[69]

Continuing to filter messages to al-Zawahiri, al-Libbi managed to attain the endorsement for al-Zarqawi and sent a message to his group informing them that 'the companion of the father [al-Zawahiri] tells Ahmad [al-Zarqawi] to put his trust in Allah and announce what has taken place. And he suggests that the announcement be made in the name of your group'. In addition to giving the blessings for al-Zarqawi's *ba'yah*, al-Libbi stated the al-Qaeda leadership did require a 'more detailed report concerning your conditions in order to put our brothers here in the picture. More so that they can consult with you on some issues, and you can choose the appropriate means [attacks on Shiites]', implying the persistent concerns over the sectarian violence.[70] However, although al-Zarqawi received what he wanted with the creation of al-Qaeda in the Lands of the Two Rivers, better known as al-Qaeda in Iraq (AQI), he not only continued his attacks against Iraqi Shiites but extended the violence to Sunni Muslims too. Al-Libbi would not be able to compartmentalise matters for much longer.

In October 2005, the Bush administration revealed that US forces in Iraq had intercepted a 17-page, 6,000-word letter from al-Zawahiri to al-Zarqawi criticising his tactics and methods. He wrote that the beheadings of hostages and bombings of mosques may push away the 'Muslim masses'. Al-Zawahiri had a reputation for long, nuanced messages, but instead he chose to be clear and direct with al-Zarqawi on several important themes that the Egyptian doctor believed would define al-Qaeda in the years to come (which may also have been fuelled by al-Libbi misleading him). On the one hand al-Zawahiri was trying to appease al-Zarqawi and be respectful as he realised he was a potent force for al-Qaeda's brand. But he also concerned that al-Zarqawi was out of control and felt the need to scold him. One aspect was that al-Zawahiri's violent tactics in Iraq were undermining the al-Qaeda brand:

> The *mujahid* movement must avoid any action that the masses do not understand or approve, if there is no contravention of *Shariah* in such avoidance, and as long as there are other options to resort to, meaning we must not throw the masses, scant in knowledge, into the sea before we teach them to swim.[71]

Although al-Qaeda has often spoken of its disdain for the Shiites, al-Zawahiri doubled down on giving them the benefit of the doubt even if they were in contravention of the Shariah. He spoke about the need to educate them first before resorting to killing them. He was concerned that attacking Shiite tombs, which carry a great deal of symbolic significance, would be counterproductive and damaging:

> We must repeat what we mentioned previously, that the majority of Muslims don't comprehend this and possibly could not even imagine it. For that reason, many of your Muslim admirers amongst the common folk are wondering about your attacks on the Shiite. The sharpness of this questioning increases when the attacks are on one of their mosques and it increases more when the attacks are on the mausoleum of Imam Ali Ibn Abi Talib, may Allah honour him. My opinion is that this matter won't be acceptable to the Muslim populace however much you have tried to explain it, and aversion to this will continue.[72]

Al-Zawahiri also questioned the timing of al-Zarqawi's tactics and suggested he could postpone his operations until al-Qaeda in Iraq were a much
stronger entity and had the ability to control swathes of territory through
a series of questions: 'Is it something that is unavoidable? Or, is it something can be put off until the force of the *mujahid* movement in Iraq gets
stronger? And if some of the operations were necessary for self-defence,
were all of the operations necessary? Or, were there some operations that
weren't called for?'[73] What was particularly troubling al-Zawahiri was that
al-Zarqawi's tactics and notoriety would create an opportunity for the
United States to exploit to win over those who felt completely alienated by
al-Zarqawi's violence. In addition, al-Zarqawi's actions would create a permanent divide in al-Qaeda's attempts to win the masses over in the future:

> And is the opening of another front now in addition to the front against the
> Americans and the government a wise decision? Or, does this conflict with
> the Shiite lift the burden from the Americans by diverting the *mujahideen* to
> the Shiite, while the Americans continue to control matters from afar?[74]

Perhaps the most telling aspect of al-Zawahiri's concerns was an important
but opaque and often understated aspect of al-Qaeda's existence post-9/
11, which entailed the relationship with the Iranian Shiite theocratic state.
Al-Zawahiri avoided any vagueness when he explained that members of al-
Qaeda and their family were being held by the Iranians and continued sectarian attacks against Shiites could put their people in jeopardy inside Iran:

> And do the brothers forget that we have more than one hundred prisoners—
> many of whom are from the leadership who are wanted in their countries—in
> the custody of the Iranians? And even if we attack the Shiite out of necessity,
> then why do you announce this matter and make it public, which compels
> the Iranians to take counter measures? And do the brothers forget that both
> we and the Iranians need to refrain from harming each other at this time in
> which the Americans are targeting us?[75]

Al-Zawahiri also commented on the tactics al-Zarqawi employed by be-
heading hostages on video. Al-Zawahiri tried to caution al-Zarqawi that
the impressionable youth he associated with were effectively feeding his
ego but were not reflective of Iraqi society:

> Among the things which the feelings of the Muslim populace who love and
> support you will never find palatable—also—are the scenes of slaughtering
> the hostages. You shouldn't be deceived by the praise of some of the zealous

young men and their description of you as the *shaykh* of the slaughterers, etc. They do not express the general view of the admirer and the supporter of the resistance in Iraq, and of you in particular by the favour and blessing of Allah.[76]

Al-Zawahiri had also long spoken about controlling the media narrative and not depending on others to distinguish what al-Qaeda stood for. Al-Zawahiri wanted to make clear to al-Zarqawi that winning hearts and minds went hand in hand with the media strategy; if al-Zarqawi's only purpose for the media was to murder people, it would indelibly hurt al-Qaeda.

> However, despite all of this, I say to you: that we are in a battle, and that more than half of this battle is taking place in the battlefield of the media. And that we are in a media battle in a race for the hearts and minds of our *ummah*. And that however far our capabilities reach, they will never be equal to one thousandth of the capabilities of the kingdom of Satan that is waging war on us. And we can kill the captives by bullet. That would achieve that which is sought after without exposing ourselves to the questions and answering to doubts. We don't need this.[77]

Al-Zawahiri then chose to talk about a clearly personal and painful moment in his life, which was the loss of his wife and and children in Afghanistan. The Egyptian only heard the details himself after he survived the Battle of Tora Bora. Al-Zawahiri had ordered some of his family members to an al-Qaeda safe house in Gardez, the capital of the Paktia near the Pakistan border, and to take shelter. It belonged to the infamous Taliban leader and crime lord Jalaluddin Haqqani of the Haqqani Network. For that reason, it was a target for the US bombing mission, and the safe house was struck with a missile.[78] Umm Fatima was pinned under the collapsed cement roof and died. Four-year-old Aisha, who had Down syndrome, had a severe open head wound and froze to death. Al-Zawahiri's son, Mohammed, was crushed to death, covered in a mixture of sand and dirt. Al-Zawahiri was not with them. According to al-Zawahiri:

> And I say to you with sure feeling and I say that the author of these lines has tasted the bitterness of American brutality, and that my favourite wife's chest was crushed by a concrete ceiling and she went on calling for aid to lift the stone block off her chest until she breathed her last.... As for my young daughter, she was afflicted by a cerebral haemorrhage, and she continued for a whole day suffering in pain until she expired. And to this day I do not know the location of the graves of my wife, my son, my daughter, and the rest of the three other families who were martyred in the incident and who were

pulverised by the concrete ceiling. . . . [W]ere they brought out of the rubble, or are they still buried beneath it to this day?[79]

Al-Zawahiri also never enjoyed the same deep bond with the Taliban leader Mullah Omar that bin Laden did. At times the relationship was terse, although it never fractured entirely. The al-Qaeda leader was probably not expecting that the contents of his letter to al-Zarqawi would end up in the public sphere, especially when he urged al-Zarqawi not to follow in the footsteps of the Taliban, who discriminated against other Muslims:

> We don't want to repeat the mistake of the Taliban, who restricted participation in governance to the students and the people of Kandahar alone. They did not have any representation for the Afghan people in their ruling regime, so the result was that the Afghan people disengaged themselves from them. Even devout ones took the stance of the spectator and, when the invasion came, the emirate collapsed in days, because the people were either passive or hostile. Even the students themselves had a stronger affiliation to their tribes and their villages than their affiliation to the Islamic emirate or the Taliban movement or the responsible party in charge of each one of them in his place.[80]

Al-Zawahiri agreed tangentially with al-Zarqawi over what they both saw as fraudulent governments in the Arab world sponsored by the West, but he insisted that the violence against civilians within these countries had to be balanced to avoid alienating themselves from potential supporters. Aside from dressing down al-Zarqawi, al-Zawahiri also curiously seemed to demonstrate the franchise model by asking for money, noting that 'many of the lines [of financing] had been cut off. Because of this we need a payment'.[81] However, despite all the important themes al-Zawahiri addressed as well as his recounting of personal experiences and losses, al-Zarqawi would not heed the call to show restraint. He intensified the violence inside Iraq, including against Muslims. Al-Zarqawi understood that everyone considered him the most dangerous man in Iraq, and it was a source of vanity for him. He believed that if other jihadists like al-Zawahiri tried to dissuade him from violence so insistently, it was above all to try to weaken him.

On 7 June 2006, al-Zarqawi was killed in a targeted US air strike whilst attending a meeting in at a safe house north of Baqubah in Diyala Governorate. The safe house itself was monitored for weeks, and Jordanian intelligence helped to identify his location. A couple of weeks later, al-Jazeera aired a video in which al-Zawahiri memorialised al-Zarqawi as 'a soldier, a hero, an imam and the prince of martyrs, [and his death] has defined the struggle between the crusaders and Islam in Iraq'. Based on the enmity between the two, it was highly unlikely that al-Zawahiri shed any tears for al-Zarqawi's demise. On the contrary, he was probably satisfied that someone he saw as an unruly upstart and rival for global jihadism had been eliminated.

Al-Zawahiri's relationship with al-Zarqawi intersected through three major moments in history. The first was al-Zarqawi's first trip to Afghanistan after the Soviet occupation had ended and Abdullah Azzam was killed, allegedly by al-Zawahiri. A civil war was emerging between rival *mujahideen* factions at that point. The second was al-Zarqawi's return to Afghanistan, where he created a jihadist movement separate from al-Qaeda, much to al-Zawahiri's chagrin. Finally, al-Zarqawi's time in Iraq became pivotal, as the insurgency ensured that al-Qaeda was revitalised through the graphic violence it inflicted and was able to recruit new adherents to their cause.

However, al-Zawahiri's words of concern to al-Zarqawi that his propensity for violence would harm al-Qaeda's cause proved to be prophetic. In February 2007 General David Petraeus was appointed by President George W. Bush as the new US commander in Iraq. Petraeus wanted to move away from unsuccessful counter-insurgency practices and focus on securing the environment for Iraqi civilians. Part of this involved the deployment of more than 20,000 soldiers in Iraq in what would be known as the 'surge'. Fearing what this would mean for AQI, al-Zawahiri attempted to influence events through intimidation:

> I ask him [George W. Bush], why send 20,000 [troops] only, why not send 50,000 100,000? Aren't you aware that the dogs of Iraq are pining for your troops' dead bodies? ... So send your entire army to be annihilated at the hands of the *mujahideen* to free the world from your evil ... because Iraq, land of the Caliphate and Jihad, is able to bury 10 armies like yours, with Allah's help and power.[82]

This bluster was meant to make Americans question their political and military leaders' strategy and play on the political divisions within the United States over the extension of the parameters of the Iraq War. In a subsequent message, al-Zawahiri spoke specifically to the Democratic Party: 'As for the Democrats in America, I tell them, the people chose you due to your opposition to Bush's policy in Iraq, but it appears that you are marching with him to the same abyss.'[83]

However, following Petraeus's plan, there was a substantial decline in attacks by terrorists and insurgents. The Sunni tribal uprising against al-Qaeda in Iraq also worked to Petraeus's advantage. The Sunni Awakening, designed to win over disenfranchised Sunni Iraqis, some of whom had fought the United States, began in 2006 before Petraeus arrived in Iraq, but it aligned with the surge strategy. The Arab fighters of the Awakening formed part of the 'Sons of Iraq' programme, which by the spring of 2009 had expanded to around 100,000 men. As al-Zawahiri feared, AQI was being isolated and its operational space confined.

Revisiting Knights

Following the Djerba attack, between 2002 until 2006, the Taliban chose to reconstitute in Pakistan. As the attention of the United States was diverted to Iraq, Afghanistan paid the price. General Joseph Votel, pointed out, 'The Taliban and affiliates were badly beaten in 2001. There was an opportunity at that point to settle out, but it was missed. We failed to capitalize on it strategically and took our eye of the ball. Space was given for the Taliban to reconstitute itself, and they did. They came back stronger.'[84]

At the same time, al-Zawahiri also sought to consolidate the relation-ship with the Haqqani Network which would provide him with the most effective protection. When the US-led coalition overthrew the Taliban in 2001, Jalaluddin Haqqani fled to Pakistan and relaunched the Haqqani Network with support from Pakistani jihadists and the ISI. His son, Sirajuddin Haqqani, had a growing role in the network and acted as the group's main military commander, whilst Jalaluddin remained the spiritual leader.[85] The Haqqani Network was able to maintain its autonomy and at the same time ensconce itself under the Taliban umbrella.

Sirajuddin Haqqani, the half-Arab son of Jalaluddin Haqqani's Kuwaiti-Yemeni wife, worked closely with al-Qaeda and served as a key conduit for the escape of its operatives into Pakistan after the US-led invasion and pro-vided sanctuary in the tribal areas.[86] Sirajuddin Haqqani's dual ethnicity and fluency in Arabic helped to further solidify the Haqqani Network's lethal alliance with al-Zawahiri. Sirajuddin Haqqani was keen to include foreign Egyptian fighters in his operations because of the training and knowledge they could provide.[87] In January 2003, the Haqqani Network commenced operations in the areas of Loya Paktia. It provided an access corridor from the Haqqani Network's bases in Pakistan into Afghanistan.[88] In collaboration with the Taliban, attacks soon spread rapidly across the country, including against foreigners.

On 27 March 2003, the Taliban killed water engineer Ricardo Munguia, an El Salvadoran employee of the International Committee of the Red Cross (ICRC). Often forgotten in the annals of time, the incident marked the start of the Taliban's resurgence and its agenda to rid Afghanistan of all foreigners. Munguia was traveling in the province of Oruzgan towards Kandahar for a humanitarian mission when the convoy was stopped by a group of about 25 heavily armed Taliban fighters. Munguia was dragged from his car and shot in the head point blank.[89] They deliberately targeted a foreigner. Munguia's death shattered the time-honoured assumption that the ICRC's reputation for neutrality in Afghanistan would protect its staff from attacks. Munguia was portrayed by the Taliban and al-Qaeda as a symbol of the 'imperialist West'. For the Taliban, his assassination blurred the lines between military and civilian targets and demonstrated their ruthlessness about who was expendable in regaining a foothold in Afghanistan through a climate of fear and intimidation.[90]

A second turning point was the renewed use of conventional tactics, starting in 2005, by the Taliban and the Haqqani Network, particularly in southern Afghanistan. A third inflection point was the expanded use of suicide attacks as a tactic in 2005–2007. At each juncture, there were targeted assassinations of humanitarian workers, increased conventional attacks in Afghanistan's four southern provinces, and suicide attacks as an irregular and psychological warfare tactic.[91] Reflecting on that period, Sirajuddin Haqqani commented, 'At the beginning of this war, the coordination between our fighters was useless. . . . But there are so many attacks now, we can't count them ourselves. But it's still not enough. The future will show what I mean.'[92] During this time, Chris Alexander was the deputy special representative of the secretary general of the United Nations, and he concluded that 'the military doctrine, training, weapons, intelligence, and logistics were provided by ISI. The Haqqanis and ISI are seen as virtually synonymous.'[93] The biggest beneficiaries of this relationship was al-Qaeda, who were given safe sanctuary in Pakistan following their dramatic departure from Afghanistan and would use this opportunity to recalibrate and reconstitute. Concerns within Afghanistan's security apparatus about this murky nexus were being ignored by the West. According to Amrullah Saleh, who at the time was the director of the Afghan National Directorate of Security:

> We paid the price because we would say Pakistan is not cooperating, the Taliban and al-Qaeda leadership is hibernating in Pakistan, it is a matter of time that they will come back. But all of our claims would be refused or would find very little attention or audience in the Western capitals. Then a lot of times we would be accused of not detaching ourselves from the past.[94]

Reflecting on the past, al-Zawahiri had expressed some closing thoughts in *Knights under the Prophet's Banner* about what plans the al-Qaeda leadership had should they escape unscathed from Tora Bora:

> The mujahid Islamic movement must escalate its methods of strikes and tools of resisting the enemies to keep up with the tremendous increase in the number of its enemies, the quality of their weapons, their destructive powers, their disregard for all taboos, and disrespect for the customs of wars and conflicts. In this regard, we concentrate on the following:
> 1. The need to inflict the maximum casualties against the opponent, for this is the language understood by the West, no matter how much time and effort such operations take.
> 2. The need to concentrate on the method of martyrdom operations as the most successful way of inflicting damage against the opponent and the least costly to the mujahideen in terms of casualties.
> 3. The targets as well as the type and method of weapons used must be chosen to have an impact on the structure of the enemy and deter it enough to stop its brutality, arrogance, and disregard for all taboos and customs. It must restore the struggle to its real size.
> 4. To reemphasise what we have already explained, we reiterate that focusing on the domestic enemy alone will not be feasible at this stage.[95]

It was here that al-Zawahiri made the important conclusion that al-Qaeda would need to focus and prioritise future operations against the West if the jihadist movement was ever to achieve its objectives in the Islamic world:

> Liberating the Muslim nation, confronting the enemies of Islam, and launching jihad against them require a Muslim authority, established on a Muslim land, that raises the banner of jihad and rallies the Muslims around it. Without achieving this goal our actions will mean nothing more than mere and

repeated disturbances that will not lead to the aspired goal, which is the restoration of the caliphate and the dismissal of the invaders from the land of
Islam.[96]

As part of this, the new media and controlling the narrative became even
more central to al-Qaeda's strategy and identity after the loss of its Afghan
base. For al-Zawahiri in particular, the absence of a physical safe space,
and an environment constricted by global counter-terrorism operations
made the media the primary source for al-Qaeda's oxygen of publicity.
Al-Zawahiri sought to fundamentally restructure the ideological discourse
within the Islamic world.

Al-Qaeda initially placed enormous value on the benefits generated
by featuring in the evening news. Although brief, the mere appearance
in news bulletins enabled al-Qaeda to strengthen the psychological effects of their actions, to call society's attention to their agenda and power.
Al-Zawahiri sought to abandon the preconceived notion that the media
were an enemy and were, in fact, a valuable resource to further al-Qaeda's
objectives. Al-Zawahiri could see across the 1970s, 1980s, and 1990s that
the TV news bulletins focused mainly on what is known as 'visual culture',
which meant that the attention an event receives is entirely dependent
on the amount of audio-visual material available for it. Furthermore, time
on TV has limitations, preventing deep analysis and historical context.
Al-Zawahiri wanted to ensure the sanctity and ownership of al-Qaeda's
messages and visuals whilst having global connectivity which resonated
with its target audience.

The internet was rapidly becoming the new medium for al-Zawahiri.
Beyond greater access to information, it offered several dynamics that the
fax machine lacked, including dedicated hyperlinks and search engines. Al-
Zawahiri never viewed the fax in isolation but always in comparison with
other ways of communicating that would give al-Qaeda an edge. To aid
him in this endeavour, a dedicated production vehicle called The Cloud
(as-Sahab) was created by al-Zawahiri. It was established back in September
2000, and in one of its first videos, bin Laden called for more attacks on
the United States three weeks before the bombing of the USS *Cole*. Yet
the media platform had not been properly or consistently utilised pre-9/
11. With the recruitment of people with technical capacity and the advent
of as-Sahab's more sophisticated production as well as web-based technological innovations, al-Qaeda was able post its own audio-visual content to

the internet, making the turnaround from production to broadcast shorter and more responsive to geopolitical events.

Instead of being dependent on the mainstream media, the news networks would be competing with al-Qaeda's coverage of global issues. Because as-Sahab can serve as an official source, it would help verify the legitimacy of al-Qaeda's propaganda. By 2005, as-Sahab was producing its videos in formats that could be watched on any media platform, broadening its reach and influence. The video and audio recordings would also galvanize recruits and fighters by providing claims of responsibility for successful attacks, issuing threats, and offering guidance to aspiring recruits. Through this process of direct communications, al-Qaeda would be able to reach wider audiences, attract a new generation of adherents, and bypass government censorship. For al-Zawahiri, there were 10 principal themes that featured in as-Sahab which were also tied into past and unfolding global events:

1. The importance of jihad and a religiously sanctioned 'call to arms'
2. Claims of responsibility for an act of terrorism
3. General tactical and strategic guidance
4. 'Clash of civilizations' narrative
5. Apostate leaders betraying Islam
6. The United States–Zionist connection
7. The West subjugating Muslims globally
8. Uniting the *ummah*
9. The United States is weakening
10. Other nations in Europe, Africa, and Asia undermining Islam

The media communiqués, whether video, audio, or text, were focused on identifying the audiences that bin Laden and al-Zawahiri were attempting to connect with. Al-Zawahiri adroitly played on local grievances of different Muslim communities globally to demonstrate empathy for local interests. Interestingly, a substantial number of as-Sahab videos were filmed in territory belonging to the Haqqani Network.[97]

Like they did previously, bin Laden and al-Zawahiri also selected verses from the Qur'an to use in every media release to demonstrate that their movement represented the true tenets of Islam and was the most pious. And they could ensure those Qur'anic quotations would be aired via as-Sahab. There was also a purpose to show that Islam was at a critical period in history, and the future caliphate hung in the balance. Although al-Qaeda's media releases imparted their interpretation of current events, their primary goal was also the intentional repetition of these themes, enhancing the chances that these messages would proliferate. This was the crux of the entire strategy.

Al-Qaeda's video releases also provided visual proof that bin Laden and al-Zawahiri were still alive. However, sometimes to try to avoid providing clues of their whereabouts, bin Laden and Zawahiri also produced audio messages that were either broadcast over a still photo of them or old video material. For al-Zawahiri, al-Qaeda's messages needed the technical capacity to reach a global audience as well as the substance required to reverberate. One of al-Zawahiri's strengths was his intuition in identifying what potential adherents wanted to hear and when they wanted to hear it.

Post-9/11, capitalising on their heightened international infamy, bin Laden and al-Zawahiri released anniversary messages for 9/11 to spread their message whilst captivating a global audience, knowing the mainstream media would compete to give them airtime. The additional capabilities of al-Qaeda's media wing, as-Sahab, who started the novel idea of posting videos directly to the internet, made a significant difference by dictating control over their content and having the ability to have real-time impact.

On a 30 January 2005 audiotape, al-Zawahiri identified the 'three foundations' of al-Qaeda's political doctrine. Some elements could be found in various messages by al-Qaeda over the years, but al-Zawahiri sought to formalise them under one specific directive. The first foundation supported the formation of an Islamic state governed solely by Shariah. Secular governments or those that practise 'man-made law' were considered unacceptable, *jahili*, and in contravention of Islam.[98]

The second foundation demanded the 'liberation of the homelands'. Al-Zawahiri argued that elections cannot take precedence over establishing 'the freedom of the Muslim lands and their liberation from every aggressor'. He also emphasised the importance of having ownership over the Middle East's natural energy resources and spoke of the *ummah* as 'impotent and exposed to the Israeli nuclear arsenal'.[99]

The third foundation advocated the' liberation of the human being.' Al-Zawahiri proposed a contractual arrangement permitting the *ummah* to choose their leaders but also resist and overthrow those who fail to adhere to the Shariah. He criticised hereditary regimes and identified a 'need to specify the power of the Shariah based judiciary and ensure that no one can dispose of the people's rights, except in accordance with this judiciary'.[100]

Al-Zawahiri oversaw the development and reshaping of al-Qaeda's strategy to recruit foreign terrorist fighters who were Muslims but brought up in the West. Much of this was based on what he had envisaged in *Knights under the Prophet's Banner*. He developed a point-by-point approach encompassing two phases, planning and preparation. In a statement released 21 February 2005, al-Zawahiri told citizens of Western countries that they cannot trust their 'false governments': 'If you, the people of the West, think that these cardboard governments can protect you, you are wrong. Real security is based on mutual cooperation with the Islamic nation on the basis of mutual respect and the stopping of aggression.' By claiming this, al-Zawahiri displaced blame onto Western countries. In another video, released 30 January 2006, al-Zawahiri criticised Americans for 'drowning in illusions' and failing to pressure their American government to accept bin Laden's offer of a 'truce'.

The Next Stage

In the United Kingdom, the discovery of terrorist plots after 9/11 directed by senior al-Qaeda figures in Pakistan including al-Zawahiri raised serious security concerns. The training provided by al-Qaeda members was a key component along with Pakistan-based facilities for support. This entailed having 'planning' and 'preparation' phases for each terrorist cell which al-Zawahiri helped to devise based on his *Military Studies* manual. The planning phase entailed coordinated communication between cell members and centralised tasking by al-Qaeda's leadership. As part of this, recruits were instructed to research and download jihadist propaganda material, conduct preliminary reconnaissance of potential targets, and prepare for international travel. The preparation phase focused on securing a property that could be used to prepare for the unfolding plot which also necessitated weapons material procurement and manufacture. Target locations would be finalised following additional reconnaissance, and financial activity would be required to fund all of this.[101]

During this period, al-Zawahiri detailed 'a near-term plan and a long-term plan' for attaining al-Qaeda aims that renewed its commitment to several theatres of conflict:

The near-term plan consists of targeting Crusader-Jewish interests, as everyone who attacks the Muslim *ummah* must pay the price, in our country and theirs, in Iraq, Afghanistan, Palestine and Somalia, and everywhere we are able to strike their interests. ... And the long-term plan is divided into two halves: The first half consists of earnest, diligent work, to change these corrupt and corruptive regimes. ... As for the second half of the long-term plan, it consists of hurrying to the fields of Jihad like Afghanistan, Iraq, and Somalia, for *Jihad* preparation and training. Thus, it is a must to hurry to the fields of Jihad for two reasons: The first is to defeat the enemies of the *ummah* and repel the Zionist Crusade, and the second is for Jihadi preparation and training to prepare for the next stage of the Jihad.[102]

The 'next stage' was to build on the carefully constructed strategy by al-Qaeda, led by al-Zawahiri, to conduct a series of plots in the West by recruiting Muslims born or brought up in the West. The goal was to inflict economic, political, and social consequences. Contrary to claims that al-Zawahiri was a micromanager, he tended to have a light managerial touch, allowing the al-Qaeda head of external operations, the number 3, the full ability to command and control those operations.[103]

This light touch was utilised in the case of Momin Khawaja, a Canadian national of Pakistani origin. In June 2002 Khawaja obtained employment with the Canadian Department of Foreign Affairs and International Trade (DFAIT) as a software developer, and his responsibilities included assisting DFAIT employees posted overseas. This provided Khawaja access to the list of Canadian diplomatic residences overseas, putting each employee at risk.[104] Khawaja planned to transfer money from Canada to the United Kingdom and Pakistan to fund al-Qaeda plots. Khawaja represented another jihadist recruit following the advice in al-Zawahiri's *Military Studies* manual on governmental infiltration.[105]

In the summer of 2003, Khawaja travelled to Pakistan and was trained in bomb making along with two Britons of Pakistani origin, Omar Khyam and Mohammad Sidique Khan.[106] All of this was building up to a series of al-Qaeda plots to target the United Kingdom over several years. The first major plot uncovered was in the spring of 2003 with the investigation of an al-Qaeda cell based in Greater London. The plotters sought to create a series of mass casualty attacks at nightclubs, stadiums, pubs, and shopping malls with 1,300 pounds (600 kg) of ammonium nitrate fertilizer. They were arrested at the end of March 2004 before they were able to commence their bombing campaign.[107] In 2004, Momin Khawaja was arrested and became the first Canadian charged under Canada's anti-terrorism act. He was convicted and handed a life sentence.[108] Khawaja and Khyam were the two leading figures in the UK plot.

Between 2002 to 2008, Peter Clarke served as the deputy assistant commissioner of the Metropolitan Police and was the head of Britain's Counter Terrorism Command that oversaw all counter-terrorism investigations and developed a deep understanding of the ties the terrorist cells had to al-Qaeda core. According to Clarke, 'Omar Khyam and others in the group had been to Pakistan and attended training camps there. There was contact between the British network and Pakistan seeking advice on details of how to manufacture a large IED. There was full knowledge and approval for the attack plans from al-Qaeda in Pakistan.'[109]

On Friday 15 September 2006, during his trial, Khyam recounted how he had initially been recruited by the ISI to fight with the JeM in the insurgency in Jammu and Kashmir. He stated that he had attended a training camp in Malakand, Pakistan, where he learnt to use AK-47s and RPGs and in the evenings would read JeM leader Maulana Masood Azhar's book *The Virtues of Jihad*. He was later co-opted by al-Qaeda. Khyam had not finished testifying on Friday and would continue on Monday. However, on 18 September, when the trial resumed, Khyam shocked the court by refusing to provide any more testimony. Khyam revealed that over the weekend the ISI had threatened his family in Pakistan over his disclosures in court. The intimidation of individuals by an overseas intelligence agency in a terrorism trial in the United Kingdom set an often overlooked and disturbing precedent.[110] It resembled scenes from gangster movies, but in Khyam's case, life was imitating art in the most dramatic sense.

In 2004, Briton Dhiren Barot led a terrorist cell plotting various attacks in the United Kingdom. The most developed plan was the 'gas limos project' designed to blow up three limousines, with gas cylinders and explosives attached, in an underground carpark near commercial buildings. There were also plans to explode a radiological dispersal device (RDD), also known as a 'dirty bomb', which was akin to the New York subway plot and an idea al-Zawahiri had long been interested in prior to 9/11.[111] Barot was trained in the use of weapons and explosives in Pakistan under the tuition of al-Qaeda. He was significant for representing the cohort that connected the founders of al-Qaeda with the new generation that had been born or brought up in the West.[112] Barot was regarded as one of the most senior al-Qaeda figures British counter-terrorism agencies had ever dealt with. He had the confidence of its inner circle, especially al-Zawahiri.[113]

Like Khawaja, Barot was a student of al-Zawahiri's *Military Studies* manual and its 'lessons'. This included assuming several identities to cover his tracks. He managed to maintain numerous bank accounts, credit cards, and a number of fraudulent passports.[114] Barot also adopted counter-surveillance techniques which included creating temporary email accounts to send coded messages. He would also travel from London to Swansea in Wales just to use a cybercafe. He wouldn't stay in one location for more than one night and used several different vehicles and mostly avoided using mobile phones.[115] As part of al-Zawahiri's desire to enhance 'cipher and code' encryption methods to protect data, Barot utilised new techniques to protect research material hidden within computer files. So well protected were they that police have still not been able to crack all the encrypted files to date.[116] Barot was the definition of a 'full-time terrorist' with long-term ties to al-Qaeda and wide linkages, committed to mass murder on both sides of the Atlantic.[117] On 3 August 2004, police arrested Barot and dismantled his cell.[118] Although these plots had al-Zawahiri's imprint, they were all disrupted by the British authorities, and the culprits were given lengthy prison sentences. Al-Qaeda chose not to publicly associate themselves with failed operations, as a disrupted plot in their mind damaged their reputation.

However, al-Zawahiri took responsibility for one of its most important attacks post-9/11, which was the 7 July 2005 (7/7) attack on the London transportation system in which 52 people were killed by four suicide bombers on three London Underground trains and one bus. Al-Zawahiri described it as 'the blessed raid on London which came as a blow to the insolent British Crusader pride and made it take a sip from the same glass from which it had long made the Muslims drink. The blessed raid which, like its illustrious predecessors in New York, Washington and Madrid took the battle to the enemy's own soul.'[119]

Al-Qaeda deemed 7/7 a massive success in terms of its political, economic, and social consequences. As a result, al-Zawahiri addressed the British public several more times. In his video 'A Message to the British' on 4 August 2005, he tied the 7/7 bombings to Britain's foreign policy and the war in Iraq:

> The lies and the actions of [British prime minister Tony] Blair are responsible for bringing destruction to you, to the centre of London and he will

bring you more of the same inshallah [Allah willing]. The lion of Islam, the
mujahid Shaykh Osama bin Laden, may Allah protect him, before offered you a
truce, if you would leave the lands of Islam. Our message to you is clear, non-
negotiable, and you must do it immediately.[120]

In another video, al-Zawahiri called the London bombings 'a slap in the
face of the arrogant British Crusader hegemony [and] a raid that moved the
battle to the land of the enemy after it kept moving the battle for many ages
to our land'.[121] The video also spliced in the last will and testament of 7/7
ringleader Mohammad Sidique Khan, a British-Pakistani who provided a
chilling statement:

> Until we feel security, you will be our targets. And until you stop the bombing,
> gassing, imprisonment, and torture of my people we will not stop this fight.
> We are at war and I am a soldier. Now you too will taste the reality of this
> situation. . . . I myself, I make *dua* [pray] to Allah . . . to raise me amongst
> those whom I love like the prophets, the messengers, the martyrs [*shaheed*]
> and today's heroes like our beloved Shakyh Usamah bin Laden, Dr Ayman
> al-Zawahiri and Abu Musab al-Zarqawi and all the other brothers and sisters
> that are fighting in . . . this cause.[122]

Khan spoke in a West Yorkshire accent, but his allegiance was not to the
country he was born in but to the Islamist ideology and doctrine purported
by al-Qaeda. Critically, this illustrated the fusion of his identity with his religion. Khan did not associate himself as a British national but part of the
worldwide *ummah* as articulated by al-Banna, Qutb, Faraj, and al-Zawahiri.
Al-Qaeda may have lost its safe bases inside Afghanistan, but al-Zawahiri
could recruit from within Western societies and use those individuals to
serve in the name of al-Qaeda. Several weeks later, al-Zawahiri provided
further justification for the attack in London. He lauded the 'knights of
monotheism who carried out the London raid' and recognised that they
were 'sons of Pakistani immigrants' to the United Kingdom.[123]

As-Sahab produced an interview with al-Zawahiri celebrating the fourth
anniversary of 9/11. The al-Qaeda deputy sought to mock Tony Blair and
the failure to find weapons of mass destruction in Iraq, the pretence for
occupying Iraq: 'Britain's "open-mindedness" could not tolerate the suspicion that the fictional weapons of mass destruction existed in Iraq, and so it
destroyed Iraq under the false pretext of searching for them. Blair considers
his people to be fools, and they, for their part, act like fools for his sake.'[124]

For all these plots to be viable, al-Zawahiri wanted to recreate places
in Pakistan for al-Qaeda recruits to be trained to carry out mass casualty

attacks. This included the Mansehra training camp. It was surrounded by the wooded hills and was primarily used to train Pakistanis and foreigners to fight in the insurgency in Jammu and Kashmir and elsewhere in India.[125] However, many foreigners would then be side tracked into joining al-Qaeda. The strategy was decided by a senior ISI officer of the rank of colonel or brigadier general.[126] British individuals who were either born or lived in the West, mostly of Pakistani heritage, contributed significantly to what is known as the 'Kashmir Escalator'.[127] This refers to members of the diaspora initially radicalised in the West travelling to Pakistan, utilising familial ties to connect with terrorist groups like JeM, LeT, and the Harkat-ul-Mujahidin (HuM). However, many would also be rerouted towards becoming part of al-Qaeda and engaging in transnational attacks in the West.

Omar Khyam was a case in point. After wanting to join a Pakistan terrorist group, his relatives in the Pakistani military redirected him to al-Qaeda.[128] Mohammad Sidique Khan's involvement in the 'Kashmir Escalator' began in July 2001 when he joined a training camp at Mansehra in Pakistan's Khyber Pakhtunkhwa run by the HuM, a Pakistani al-Qaeda affiliate with close ties to al-Zawahiri.[129] In December 2004, Khan, along with Shehzad Tanweer, returned to Pakistan. The two men stayed in the country for several weeks. On this trip, they were based in Mansehra and Balakot and met with al-Zawahiri. The Egyptian teacher led al-Qaeda's efforts to formalise control over the Mansehra camp, which also conveniently happened to be near the JeM's training camp in Balakot, known as Madrasa Syed Ahmad Shaheed Balakot.[130] Both Khan and Tanweer received bomb-making training in Mansehra, and they also recorded martyrdom videos overseen by al-Zawahiri.[131]

Two weeks after the 7/7 attacks, London was still reeling from its first-ever suicide bombings, when an identical plot known as 21/7, was launched on matching targets, three London Underground trains and a bus. However, when the four plotters tried to trigger the devices, they failed to detonate, as the explosive material had degraded.[132] All these British cells received guidance from British-Pakistani Rashid Rauf, who was al-Qaeda's operational coordinator and in close contact with al-Zawahiri.[133]

Rashid Rauf was married to a member of JeM leader Maulana Masood Azhar's family, which provided the link between al-Zawahiri, JeM, and the 'British' terrorist recruits.[134] Rauf also played a role in recruitment of British nationals who travelled to Pakistan, maintaining communications with them and issuing directives as they prepared their plots.[135]

Rauf met the 7/7 ringleaders, Mohammed Siddique Khan and Shezad Tanweer, shortly after they arrived in Pakistan in late 2004 and sent them to al-Qaeda camps in Pakistan's tribal areas as well as one in Mansehra, Pakistan.[136]

Al-Zawahiri had demonstrated his ability to put together multiple cells for transnational attacks. If he had been underestimated pre-9/11, Western counter-terrorism agencies were taking him far more seriously now. As an American intelligence official stated, 'Bin Laden and al-Zawahiri were the two that mattered most, and the agency's [Central Intelligence Agency (CIA)] efforts and resources were directed towards the objective of finding them'.[137] On 13 January 2006, the United States carried out a drone strike in the Pakistani village of Damadola in the Bajaur District of Federally Administered Tribal Areas (FATA). The strike was meant to target al-Zawahiri, who was thought to be attending a meeting in the village at a mud-walled compound. Bajaur was a safe haven for the Taliban. One of these individuals was Maulvi Faqir Muhammad, who had invited al-Zawahiri to meet him in Bajaur in January 2006.[138]

Intelligence was provided to the United States that al-Zawahiri was attending a dinner to mark the Islamic holiday of Eid al-Adha at the compound.[139] However, once the CIA had gotten word of this scheduled meeting, al-Zawahiri was subsequently tipped off and thus decided at the last minute not to attend.[140] Al-Zawahiri decided to move further into the mountains of South Waziristan to avoid drone operations and evade capture. US frustration was growing. As General Joseph Votel commented, 'We had so many reports, so-called sightings of al-Zawahiri in Afghanistan and efforts to try to stand up and target him that it almost became a little bit of a running joke.'[141]

Although al-Zawahiri was elusive, he lost some of his key allies in the Damadola drone strike. Midhat Mursi, al-Qaeda's head of biological and chemical weapons programme, was killed.[142] Others also thought to have died included al-Zawahiri's son-in-law, Muhammad Abbatay, who at the time was put in charge of al-Qaeda's Afghanistan's eastern Kunar province.[143] Not surprisingly, it was not long before an irate and unscathed al-Zawahiri commented on the drone strike and condemned the operation. The video release put to bed rumours of al-Zawahiri's death. Many refer to this video as his 'I'm Alive' video.

The American airplanes, in collaboration with their agent of the Jews and the Crusaders, Musharraf, launched an airstrike on Damadola near Peshawar around the Eid al-Adha holiday, during which 18 Muslims—men, women and children—died in their fight against Islam, which they call terrorism. Their claim was to target this poor man and four of my brothers. The whole world discovered the lies as the Americans fight Islam and the Muslims.[144]

The fact al-Zawahiri felt compelled to comment on the airstrike meant he was fully aware it was designed to target him. As was becoming a common theme, the al-Qaeda deputy may have once again received intelligence of the impending airstrike by allies in Pakistan. It was also possible that al-Zawahiri wanted to use as propaganda the significant loss of civilians killed in the drone operation. He singled out President Bush in particular, taunting him: 'Bush, do you know where I am? I am among the Muslim masses enjoying their care.' He then castigated Bush as a 'failed crusader'.[145] The second half of his message was directed to the American people, whom al-Zawahiri reproached for continuing to 'drown in illusions' and allowing their leaders to reject bin Laden's truce offer which entailed the West staying away from 'Muslim lands'.[146] This message carried the repeated threat that soon Americans would be seeing terrorist operations in their very own homes.

In a March 2006 videotape broadcast by al-Jazeera, al-Zawahiri repeated his calls on Muslims to 'inflict losses on the crusader West, especially to its economic infrastructure, with strikes that would make it bleed for years'.[147] An al-Qaeda plot was afoot which if successful would have matched 9/11 in scale and casualties. In the summer of 2006, British and American law enforcement jointly disrupted al-Qaeda's plan to place suicide bombers, with concealed liquid explosives, on board seven flights leaving London's Heathrow airport for cities across the United States and Canada and detonate their devices during a three-hour period, which would have killed thousands. The plotters were later convicted of terrorism and other offences.[148] Significantly, the airline liquid bomb plot was the primary reason al-Zawahiri stopped the Mubtakkar plan of unleashing a chemical and cyanide dispersal system in the New York subway. At the time of the plot, John Miller had become assistant director of the Federal Bureau of Investigation (FBI), and to him the reasons were now clear:

> If one measures impact based on al-Zawahiri's mindset, would you rather have a frightening cyanide dispersal device that would kill 20 people and cause a

lockdown of regional public transportation? Or would you rather have the second version of 9/11, where half a dozen planes would explode over the ocean and kill over 2,000 people, causing chaos across the Atlantic? The latter meant for al-Qaeda that they're back in 9/11-style casualties in the triple dig-its but on a shoestring budget. No flight training was required or spending a quarter of a million dollars on travel and logistics and tuition in the planning arc.[149]

Furthermore, al-Zawahiri rationalised that the Mubtakkar would increase security in ways that had not been seen yet at train stations, possibly airports too, and that could impact negatively on the airline liquid bomb plot. He therefore opted for the airline liquid bomb plot because it would have far greater fatalities and greater economic, political, and social impact. It also meant the Mubtakkar could be planned at a later time but not in tandem with the airline liquid bomb plot.[150] Although the airline liquid plot was disrupted, al-Zawahiri's secondary objective was achieved: extraordinary se-curity measures were put in place at airports globally, including prohibiting passengers carrying liquid containers larger than 100 millilitres onto commer-cial aircrafts. These restrictions would remain in place for many years to come.

Assisting in organising the airline plot was Muhammad Abbatay, who it now transpired did not die in Damadola, Pakistan.[151] Rashid Rauf's role was to help coordinate with Assad Ali, the leader of the airline liquid bomb plot, as well as Assad Sarwar, the bomb-maker.[152] They both had been to train-ing camps in Pakistan, where they were taught how to construct IEDs that could bypass airport security. The batteries that were recovered from the bomb factory in London had been manufactured as part of a batch that was sold only in Pakistan. The operation was brought to a slightly premature conclusion when Rashid Rauf was arrested in Pakistan at the instigation of the United States. According to Peter Clarke, 'It is very clear that the whole attack plan was designed and implemented under the control of al-Qaeda in Pakistan.'[153]

However, soon after appearing in an Islamabad court to face extradition to the United Kingdom, Rauf escaped. Rauf asked the police tasked with guarding him to let him pray at a roadside mosque. Rauf took the oppor-tunity to escape through the back door.[154] The questionable circumstances of Rauf's escape shone a further spotlight on the relationship militants have with the Pakistani security establishment. It was not until 2012 that US au-thorities were able to track down Rauf and eliminate him in a drone strike operation in Pakistan.[155]

The United Kingdom was not the only country in al-Zawahiri's sights. In 2006, al-Qaeda in collaboration with its Algerian ally, the Salafist Group for Preaching and Combat (GSPC) were looking to carry out a series of daring coordinated attacks across Morocco, Italy, and France. Similar to the 7/7 attacks and the 2004 Madrid train bombings (11M), the plans were to target transportation hubs such as the Milan Metro as well as the Paris Metro and Orly airport.[156]

Other GSPC targets included the Basilica of San Petronio in Bologna, with the aim of carrying out attacks to be timed before the Italian general elections. The effect of an attack on the eve of Italians going to the polls would have mirrored that of the Madrid train bombings, which contributed to the defeat of the Spanish government of Jose Marie Aznar, who had supported the Iraq War. Equally, al-Zawahiri and the GSPC pondered that an attack in Italy would undermine Prime Minister Silvio Berlusconi's re-election bid and force Italy to withdraw its troops from Iraq.[157] Other locations being discussed for an attack included the US Embassy in Rabat, Morocco, the Paris headquarters of the French intelligence agency the Directorate-General for External Security (DGSE), and the Milan police's command centre. However, because of the number of people involved in this ambitious scheme, the plot was uncovered by authorities in Morocco, who in collaboration with their European counterparts were able to make multiple arrests.[158] The al-Qaeda strategy of large-scale coordinated attacks was becoming harder to pull off. Global counter-terrorism efforts were becoming more effective in sharing information, foiling plots, and gathering intelligence. Al-Qaeda needed to recalibrate its approach. Despite the plots failing, al-Zawahiri remained unrepentant about targeting the West outside the United States. In 2007, al-Zawahiri said, 'Whatever its form, method, and means, force remains a necessary element for bringing about change.'[159]

Q&A

On 5 August 2006, al-Zawahiri announced that al-Gama'a had aligned with al-Qaeda, with one of its leaders, Muhammad Hakaima, standing beside him. Al-Zawahiri commented that the two groups would form 'one line, facing its enemies'.[160] However, not all from al-Gama'a agreed with Hakaima. Several members had been set free from Egyptian prisons, including veteran Karam Zuhdi, who expressed regret for conspiring in the assassination of Egyptian president Anwar Sadat and condemned al-Zawahiri for continuing with terrorism.[161] As time would attest, al-Gama'a was irretrievably divided, much to the satisfaction of al-Zawahiri, who finally triumphed in ensuring the primacy of the Egyptian jihadist narrative, as his rivals were either dead, incarcerated, or tainted by associating with the Mubarak regime. For al-Zawahiri, there was an opportunity to expand the Egyptian jihadist narrative, but it needed the right opportunity and moment.

In December 2007, al-Qaeda's media arm, as-Sahab, requested individuals, organizations, and journalists to propose questions for an 'open interview' with al-Zawahiri. Bulletins posted on jihadist online forums said questions sent to them would be passed to al-Zawahiri 'without alteration, whether it comes from someone who agrees or disagrees'.[162] This was an interesting and unusual moment for al-Zawahiri, who was seeking to keep the international spotlight on al-Qaeda's global relevance, especially in the international media. Despite having a reputation for being rigid and inflexible, al-Zawahiri was ahead of the curve in utilising communications and technology in order to have a direct and personal impact. The number of questions submitted for the Q&A was in the hundreds and would have been higher if more people knew how to access the jihadist forums.

Although al-Zawahiri answered a number of questions from people all around the world, he appeared to only respond to those from the Islamic world. Perhaps unsurprisingly, al-Zawahiri was asked a question about allegedly calling Abdullah Azzam an unbeliever and seeing himself as superior to the Palestinian-Jordanian ideologue. The al-Qaeda deputy denied having a troubled relationship with Azzam: 'As for the third question about my declaring *Shaykh* Abdullah Azzam an unbeliever and that I wouldn't pray behind him, it is a statement which is the complete opposite of the truth.'[163] Al-Zawahiri's response was short and did not provide any real insight, but he chose to answer this question to suggest that he had nothing but respect for Azzam, who still carried a significant standing amongst many jihadists.

Al-Zawahiri was then asked why al-Qaeda has not carried out any attacks in Israel, to which he angrily responded:

> I challenge you and your organization to do that in Tel Aviv, I don't know—
> hasn't the questioner heard that Qa'ida al-Jihad struck the Jews in Djerba,

Tunisia, and struck the Israeli tourists in Mombasa, Kenya, in their hotel, then fired two missiles at the El-Al airliner carrying a number of them?[164]

The Djerba attack on 11 April 2002 and the 28 November 2003 Mombasa strike were indeed both carried out by al-Qaeda, although the attack in Kenya was by an affiliate.[165] It seemed important for al-Zawahiri to burnish al-Qaeda's credentials for targeting Jewish interests particularly as they have always posited an intimate relationship between the 'Zionists and Crusaders'. It was also noteworthy that al-Zawahiri referred to al-Qaeda as 'Qa'ida al-Jihad', which implied the Egyptian EIJ angle of the al-Jihad group that assassinated Sadat. It was also a reference to its supporters and critics that al-Zawahiri, as an Egyptian, remained a very important part of al-Qaeda. When whether the 'internal enemy', and mainly Egypt, was no longer his primary focus, al-Zawahiri responded:

> In regard to Egypt, our independent judgement to which we invite the *ummah* in Egypt and elsewhere is: the striking of the Jewish Crusader interests wherever they are found to force the invaders to depart the lands of the Muslims and stop backing the corrupt regimes in their countries, and to mobilise the *ummah* to confront them, and to lay bare the treasonous governments which defend them, in addition to exhorting the Muslims to diligently strive to rid themselves of the corrupt, corruptive governments which are sitting on their chests. Egypt and the rest of the lands of the Muslims are not out of our sight, but victory comes through patience.[166]

Although al-Zawahiri did not dismiss the importance of removing *jahili* rulers in the Arab world and in particular Egypt, he renewed his commitment for Muslims to make it their priority to strike at Western interests throughout the world, wherever they may be. Al-Zawahiri saw the benefit in using the principle of recruiting supporters who live in the land of the 'external enemy' who could localise the conflict. Al-Zawahiri did face several questions about Egypt, including his opinions of the intelligence and security forces which played a pivotal role in dismantling his EIJ's infrastructure:

> I believe that the officers of the State Security–Anti-Religious Activities Branch and who investigate Islamic causes and torture the Muslims are infidels, each and every one of them. They know more about the Islamic movements than many of those movement's members know about them. And it is permissible to kill the officers of State Security and the rest of the personnel of the police.[167]

Al-Zawahiri calling for the killing and direct targeting of Egypt's state intelligence was perhaps shaped by his own treatment by them after he was
arrested following the Sadat assassination. His deep resentment was also
shaped by how they dismantled numerous EIJ cells and imprisoned his
brother Muhammad. Interestingly, al-Zawahiri offered a caveat, as he recalled that there are some people within the military who were loyal to
the cause including Khalid al-Islambouli, who assassinated Sadat, and Isam
al-Qamari, whom al-Zawahiri betrayed under torture from his Egyptian
interrogators. Clearly, that incident still affected him:

> The Egyptian army which produced Khalid al-Islambouli and 'Isam al-
> Qamari (may Allah have mercy on him) continues to be full of those whose
> hearts boil with jealousy for Islam and Muslims and who long for the oppor-
> tunity to remove the corrupt gang which rules Egypt.[168]

Echoing Qutb's call for an Islamic vanguard, al-Zawahiri also cited the
gradual decline of the United States; although it would still take generations, the process had begun, and for the Egyptian doctor, it was inevitable that the US military would leave Iraq and Afghanistan. According to
al-Zawahiri:

> there is no doubt that the American collapse has begun, and the myth of
> uni-polarity has ended. And the raids on New York and Washington were
> identifying marks of this collapse, but I point out that the collapse of empires
> doesn't come in a single moment, but rather, may take decades, and the col-
> lapse of the Soviet Union is the nearest example of that. And the withdrawal
> of America from Afghanistan and Iraq will be in the interest of the Muslims
> with Allah's permission, and the Jihadi vanguard has announced that its ob-
> jective on which it will not compromise.[169]

Helping al-Zawahiri to field questions was 'Azzam the American', also
known as Adam Gadahn, who became spokesperson for al-Qaeda. Gadahn
was chosen for the role to signal a true about-face for the organization. By
putting a fresh-faced American who knew the ins and outs of American
culture and history online, al-Zawahiri hoped to stimulate donations and
support throughout the Islamic: even a home-grown American could become an al-Qaeda operative. Although Gadahn was a somewhat comic
figure because of his Californian hipster background, together with al-
Zawahiri he began digitising all al-Qaeda content, and a new distribution
network was established called al-Fajr Media Centre.

Another aspect of the propaganda was whether al-Qaeda needed an emblem or flag to better identify themselves as an entity. In January 2007, al-Fajr Media Centre released a picture of what it conceived to be the global jihadist movement's flag for its caliphate. There was no clear explanation behind its methodology but its style sent a clear message. It was a black banner that recalled the one the Prophet Muhammad had spoken of a black flag as the Messenger of God. The standard had white writing across the top, 'No God but Allah', and 'Mohammed is the Messenger' was featured in black writing inside an uneven white circle. It appeared to be hand drawn, which was deliberately meant to hark back to a bygone era, even if ironically the flag was likely designed on a computer. Al-Qaeda's goal was to convey that it had inherited the prophet's seal, just as the early caliphs had. Al-Qaeda wanted a single banner to unify its supporters as its franchises grew, and this this flag was a sign of the coming together of their doctrines and goals.

Al-Qaeda had never institutionalised an emblem, which resulted in variations of the Islamic black banner being used by supporters and affiliates and were meant to represent the battle standards carried by various armies throughout Islamic history. This was supposed to reflect the Prophet Muhammad's goal to spread Islam. However, without a clear notion of the Prophet's true designated flag, jihadist groups were left to interpret history for themselves as the flags they adopted were manifestations of historical warfare, but there was never any consistency. Al-Qaeda's affiliates were wanting clear direction from the leadership, which was lacking. Al-Qaeda was reluctant to use this new banner as often or as frequently as some of its adherents wanted such as al-Qaeda in Iraq who were the most frequent proponents of the black flag. Al-Qaeda felt the virtual world was the best way to visually convey its agenda, even if a banner was not the priority for the optics the group was trying to create.

Indeed, al-Qaeda used the internet for more than simply distributing information and communicating. It manufactures new forms of action and interaction, shaping the control over content and social life. Freed of dependence on mainstream media for publicity, al-Qaeda would use the internet as a recruiting tool and a rallying call. Images and video clips served as tools of empowerment for al-Qaeda and increased their levels of support and general appeal. Not all who read and saw al-Qaeda's commentary on the internet would instantly be inspired to act. Not all would remember the content of al-Zawahiri's proclamations or quotations of the Qur'an.

However, the key point was to get their attention even if it was for the briefest of moments. For the Egyptian doctor, it was about starting the process and attacking from all fronts, from the ideological, to the social, to the economic, to the political.

Al-Sharif's Revenge

Up until 2007, al-Zawahiri and bin Laden did not face any serious challenge to their agenda from other jihadists. However, a face from the past would come back to haunt al-Zawahiri and present the first real attempt to undermine and discredit al-Qaeda. Sayyid Imam al-Sharif had helped al-Zawahiri create the EIJ and discredit Abdullah Azzam. He disappeared into obscurity after leaving Sudan for Yemen following his falling out with al-Zawahiri, who had usurped the EIJ leadership. However, in 1999 his name cropped up again when he was tried in absentia by an Egyptian military court and given a life sentence in the EIJ Albania plot. Although al-Sharif had never set foot in Albania many of those arrested in Tirana identified him as the former spiritual leader of the group.[170]

In October 2001, under pressure from the Egyptian government, al-Sharif was arrested by Yemeni authorities at Dar al-Shifa Hospital in the city of Ibb. After several years in detention, he was transferred to Cairo in February 2004.[171] He was sent to the notorious Mazra'at Tora Prison where Qutb, Faraj, al-Zawahiri, and al-Rahman had done time. Under prison life, al-Sharif began reviewing his ideas about the jihadist doctrine in which he had previously based his ideology. Under the close review of al-Azhar seminary, al-Sharif formulated new ideas for stopping the violence against the West and Arab regimes. In 2007, he issued his initiative 'The Document for Rationalization of Jihad in Egypt and the World' which was serialised between 19 November and 3 December 2007 in the Kuwaiti newspaper *Al-Jarida* and the Egyptian broadsheet *Al-Masri al-Yawm*.[172] The central premise of al-Sharif's argument was that the jihadist movement strayed from the true tenants of jihad as stipulated by the Shariah.

Al-Sharif added that jihadist groups are weak and do not have the sustained means to wage successful jihad, and therefore terrorism was futile. Al-Sharif also said it was not permitted to kill Western tourists and civilians in Western countries. Al-Sharif did not mention al-Qaeda or al-Zawahiri

by name, but they were heavily implied. Al-Sharif opined, 'We are prohibited from committing aggression, even if the enemies of Islam do that.'[173]
Al-Sharif's treatise was meant to serve as a cessation of violence and was
supported by some imprisoned members of the EIJ in Egypt.

What was significant was what al-Sharif did not say, such as whether
the current rulers of Muslim countries were 'apostates'. He also did
not renounce his previous ideological tract. Interestingly, he did not
condemn all militant activity. On Afghanistan, al-Sharif supported the
Taliban efforts to retake the country: 'Jihad in Afghanistan will lead to
the creation of an Islamic state with the triumph of the Taliban, Allah
willing.'[174]

In conjunction with 'The Document for Rationalization of Jihad in
Egypt and the World', al-Sharif also gave an interview to the al-Hayat
newspaper, during which he aggressively and openly attacked al-Qaeda
and especially bin Laden and al-Zawahiri.[175] However, despite making several startling assertions, al-Sharif's assertions need to be tempered within
the context of his history with al-Zawahiri and his emerging ties with the
Egyptian state. Al-Sharif initially claimed in al-Hayat that his disagreements
with al-Zawahiri were unbiased and factual and not personal, but he later
contradicted himself, stating sharply:

> He [al-Zawahiri] was a burden to me on the educational, professional, juris-
> prudential, and sometimes personal levels. . . . He was ungrateful for the kind-
> ness I had shown him and bit the hand that I had extended to him. What I got
> for my efforts was deception, betrayal, lies.[176]

Al-Sharif clearly resented the attention that al-Zawahiri received, saying he
was 'enamoured of the media and a show off', which enabled al-Zawahiri
to take the limelight and assume control over EIJ's ideas and doctrines, and
thereafter al-Qaeda.[177] Mocking the al-Qaeda leaders, al-Sharif stated:

> Usamah bin Laden, Al-Zawahiri, and others fled at the beginning of the
> American bombing [in Afghanistan], to the point of abandoning their wives
> and families to be killed along with other innocent people. . . . I think that
> a Shariah court should be established, composed of reliable scholars, to hold
> these people accountable for their crimes, even if in absentia, so that those
> who are ignorant in their religion do not repeat this futility. . . . Ramming
> America has become the shortest road to fame and leadership among the
> Arabs and Muslims. But what good is it if you destroy one of your enemy's
> buildings, and he destroys one of your countries? What good is it if you kill

one of his people, and he kills a thousand of your people? . . . That, in short, is my evaluation of 9/11.[178]

Al-Zawahiri faced criticism from al-Sharif for his perceived lack of credibility as a religious jurist and *fiqh*. Al-Sharif boasted to *al-Hayat* that 'al-Qaeda has no one who is qualified from a *Shariah* perspective to make a response. All of them, bin Laden, al-Zawahiri, and others, are not religious scholars on whose opinion you can count. They are ordinary persons.' Of course, al-Sharif ignored the fact that he himself had no formal religious training, either.

Al-Sharif's comments were damaging to al-Qaeda. They also got the attention of al-Zawahiri, who issued a video message, entitled 'The Power of Truth':

> Do the prison cells of Egypt now have fax machines? And I wonder, are these fax machines connected to the same line as the electric shock machines, or do they have a separate line? . . . Thus, I caution my Muslim brothers everywhere against the statements and retractions of the graduates and guests of the prisons on the peninsula and in Egypt, Yemen, Algeria, Indonesia, and all lands of Islam. They are either those who have been coerced and before whose eyes the memories of the torture, lashing, suspension and shocks play like a film, or are those who are disheartened and fallen and looking for a way out of prison and a little comfort. Neither type is to be listened to or relied upon in his statements and opinions.[179]

The sarcastic reference to the fax machine was not a reference to al-Zawahiri's penchant for that technology but a more provocative insinuation that al-Sharif had reached some form of compromise with the Egyptian authorities. There was no way to be sure whether he had a genuine ideological revision. Also, al-Sharif did not renounce all forms of violence, just those that threaten the Egyptian state and its Western allies. That was very telling and why al-Zawahiri's retort demanded that people do not listen to these statements. Al-Zawahiri was seething and felt it necessary to respond. Al-Zawahiri argued that the revisions, which he termed as 'retractions' 'were simply the result of torture in the Egyptian prisons'. He provocatively added that the Mubarak regime seemed very keen to promote al-Sharif's book. He compared the Egyptian government to 'gravediggers' who wait for someone to die so they can earn money from burying him, reputationally. Al-Zawahiri then issued a challenge to al-Sharif:

Thus, I tell these enemies: This is not a noble fight, to be alone with an isolated prisoner and squeeze him physically and psychologically until he agrees
with you, for you then to applaud that. If you are real men, then compete with
us by yourselves, in the arenas of ideology, invitation and information, which
are the arenas in which you yourselves have admitted your defeat.[180]

The personal animosity between al-Sharif and al-Zawahiri was palpable.
Indeed, al-Sharif's biggest motivation was his hatred of al-Zawahiri and a
desire to settle scores with him. Al-Sharif may have held a severe grudge
towards the al-Qaeda deputy for forcing him out of the EIJ, allegedly misin-
terpreting his *Compendium of the Pursuit of Divine Knowledge,* and for having
him convicted in the Returnees from Albania case. Al-Sharif may also have
envied al-Zawahiri's global notoriety. Many of the assertions against al-
Qaeda were highly personal. It was also difficult to comprehend how a
hardened ideologue could suddenly experience a transformation and doc-
trinal reinterpretation.

On 2 March 2008, al-Zawahiri published an entire book online, titled
*The Exoneration: A Treatise Exonerating the Community of the Pen and the Sword
from the Debilitating Accusation of Fatigue and Weakness.*[181] In it, he responded
to al-Sharif's November 2007 criticisms. *The Exoneration* was also an official
declaration of al-Qaeda's ideological platform and of its religious justifications for its terrorism. Al-Zawahiri referred to 'the author of the Document'
rather than specifying al-Sharif by name. Al-Zawahiri claimed, 'This message I present to the reader today is among the most difficult I have ever
written in my life.'[182] Building upon his video message, al-Zawahiri claimed
that al-Sharif wrote his book 'in the spirit of the Minister of the Interior'.[183]
He inflammatorily comments were an indictment of al-Sharif's about-face
as a hopeless attempt by the West, Zionists, and the 'apostate' rulers of the
Muslim world to 'stand in the way of the fierce wave of Jihadi revivalism
that is shaking the Islamic world'.[184]

Al-Zawahiri admitted some mistakes: 'I neither condone the killing of
innocent people nor claim that Jihad is free of error.'[185] He then qualified
his remarks: 'Muslim leaders during the time of the Prophet Muhammad
made mistakes, but the Jihad did not stop. ... I'm warning those Islamist
groups who welcome the document ["The Document for Rationalization
of Jihad in Egypt and the World"] that they are giving the government
the knife with which it can slaughter them.'[186] Many of the themes and
arguments in the book illustrate al-Qaeda's strategic orientation including

shifting the violence in Iraq away from Shiite civilians. Al-Zawahiri also wanted like-minded jihadists in Egypt to prepare to seize the opportunity when the Mubarak regime falls. At the time it may have been overly optimistic to assume that its demise was imminent, but al-Zawahiri was picking on issues that he believed could resonate with targeted audiences, especially in Egypt:

> If Muslims wait until they have full parity with their enemies then how will they ever be able to defeat an oppressive ruler or powerful foreign nation who has invaded their lands? . . . If a Muslim's family is threatened by an oppressive regime or foreign power, why would he adopt non-violence to protect them? . . . If a Muslim never attacks the enemy for fear of killing fellow believers or innocent people, how can he put pressure on a much more powerful enemy?[187]

Al-Zawahiri added that because civilians in the West voluntarily choose their elected officials through the act of voting, they are legitimate targets.[188] He elaborated about the September 11 attack:

> Concerning the operations of the blessed Tuesday [9/11] . . . they are legally legitimate because they are committed against a country at war with us, and the people in that country are combatants. Someone might say that it is the innocent, the elderly, the women, and the children who are victims, so how can these operations be legitimate according to *Shariah*? And we say that the sanctity of women, children, and the elderly is not absolute. There are special cases Muslims may respond in kind if infidels have targeted women and children and elderly Muslims, [or if] they are being invaded, [or if] the non-combatants are helping with the fight, whether in action, word, or any other type of assistance, [or if they] need to attack with heavy weapons, which do not differentiate between combatants and non-combatants.[189]

Al-Zawahiri adhered to a mentality that was black and white: either you are on the side of God, or on the side of Satan. Following in the footsteps of Qutb, al-Zawahiri echoed the call for a revolutionary vanguard to mobilise and inspire the masses against apostate governments that suppress the people: '[This method] was our means of raising the awareness of the *ummah* and awakening it.'[190]

Cartoons and Sieges

In 2005, *Jyllands-Posten*, a Danish newspaper, published several controversial cartoons depicting the Prophet Muhammad that ignited demonstrations across the Muslim world. In early 2008, *Jyllands-Posten* and other Danish newspapers republished the cartoons. On 2 June 2008, al-Qaeda attacked the Danish Embassy in Islamabad, Pakistan, organized in part by Ilyas Kashmiri with al-Zawahiri's blessings.[191] In August 2008, al-Qaeda released a video calling for follow-up attacks as a reprisal for the republication of the Prophet Muhammad cartoons by several European newspapers. Al-Zawahiri aide Mustafa Abu al-Yazid appeared in a video demonstrating this had backing from the al-Qaeda deputy.[192]

Making the situation murkier, Ilyas Kashmiri also received support from Pakistan's ISI.[193] One of the most notorious connections was with Abdur Rehman Hashim Syed, a retired major in the Pakistani military. Abdur Rehman also has used the names 'Major' and Pasha. Back in 2001, when the al-Qaeda leadership, including al-Zawahiri, fled Afghanistan to Pakistan during the Tora Bora campaign, Abdur Rehman oversaw a military unit given orders by the United States to intercept the Taliban and al-Qaeda, but he refused to do so.[194]

In collaboration with the LeT, Abdur Rehman and Kashmiri played a central role in one of the most audacious terrorist attacks ever. Starting on 26 November 2008, and continuing for two days, 10 terrorists trained by the LeT carried out multiple synchronised assaults against targets in Mumbai, including the Taj Mahal and Oberoi Hotels, the Leopold Café, the Jewish cultural centre Chabad House, and the Chhatrapati Shivaji train station. Each of the locations had been scouted in advance by the American-Pakistani David Headley. By the end of the carnage, 164 people had died, including six Americans.[195] Prior to the attack, Tahawwur Rana, a Canadian, and Headley were involved in the logistics and surveillance of targets for the plot and were supported by Ilyas Kashmiri and Abdur Rehman, who was in regular contact with the leaders of al-Qaeda.[196]

Mumbai was a state-sponsored terrorist attack overseen, funded, and directed by the ISI in conjunction with the LeT. That was why it was so successful—and so outrageous.[197] As the investigative reporter Sebastian Rotella, who researched the LeT in detail, pointed out, 'The ISI and LeT were intertwined, working together, and had a symbiotic relationship. Every single LeT figure had a handler in the ISI—it's hard to imagine the LeT interacting with the fugitive al-Qaeda and the ISI didn't know about it.'[198]

What remained unclear was the role of the civilian government in Pakistan at the time, which was led by the widower of Benazir Bhutto, Asif Ali Zardari of the Pakistan People's Party (PPP). The PPP was either complicit in or ignorant of what the ISI and the LeT hatched in Mumbai, especially as it initially denied that the attackers hailed from Pakistan. It was later embarrassingly forced to accept responsibility when one of the gunmen, Ajmal Kasab, was captured alive by the Mumbai police. The siege in Mumbai explained once more how powerful the military is in Pakistan and that ultimately, it is the institution that oversees the security, and insecurity, that emanates from the country.[199]

In a separate plot, Headley and Rana conspired with Kashmiri and Abdur Rehman to murder journalists at *Jyllands-Posten*. Headley communicated with Abdur Rehman to coordinate a trip to Copenhagen, Denmark, to carry out reconnaissance. Headley travelled in January 2009 from Chicago to Copenhagen to observe the newspaper headquarters in Copenhagen and Aarhus and to videotape the surrounding areas. The Copenhagen plot involved Headley taking hostages to initially get attention and then decapitate the journalists in front of the gaze of the media.[200] In February 2009, Abdur Rehman took Headley to meet Kashmiri in Razmak in North Waziristan, Pakistan. Kashmiri renewed his support for the operation with al-Zawahiri's backing but cautioned that the LeT's participation could no longer continue owing to the pressure on Pakistan from the US following the Mumbai attacks.[201]

However, the plot failed to come to pass, as both Headley and Rana were arrested in the United States. Rana was found guilty of providing material support for terrorist activity and playing a supporting role in the Denmark plot and handed a 13-year prison sentence.[202] Headley was found guilty for his role in both the Denmark and Mumbai plots and sentenced to 35 years in prison.[203] The Denmark and India plots demonstrated an unprecedented level of cooperation amongst state actors from Pakistan, the LeT, and al-Qaeda through Ilyas Kashmiri, who was given considerable autonomy by al-Zawahiri to plot and wreak devastation.[204]

Malcolm X

On 5 May 2007, al-Qaeda released a video featuring al-Zawahiri taking part in an 'interview' appealing to the African American community as a source of recruitment by capitalising on domestic social tensions.[205] Interestingly, al-Zawahiri discussed, quoted, and displayed video clips of the civil right activist Malcolm X, whom al-Zawahiri's granduncle Abdul Rahman Azzam helped get a visa to visit Mecca for the *hajj* in 1964. Al-Zawahiri appealed to African Americans by opportunistically citing the ability of black leaders to mobilise for social justice matters. Al-Zawahiri cited Malcolm X's activism:

> Would that those who insist on peaceful resistance had heard what was said by the struggler and martyr [*shaheed*] al-Hajj Malik al-Shabaaz [Malcolm X], may Allah have mercy on him: 'Anytime you beg another man to set you free, you will never be free. Freedom is something you have to do for yourself. . . . The price of freedom is death.'[206]

Although Malcolm X did not support random violence as a means of achieving one's objectives, al-Zawahiri interpreted him as a case study of radical activism of which al-Qaeda could benefit by highlighting histor- ical grievances of institutionalised discrimination and subsequent disen- franchisement within the African American community. To demonstrate his point further, al-Zawahiri showed another excerpt of Malcolm X, stating, 'No, I'm not American. I'm one of the 22 million black people who are the victims of Americanism, one of the 22 million black people who are the victims of democracy. . . . I see America through the eyes of a victim.'[207] Al- Zawahiri then comments that the United States 'will throw you [African Americans] into the street without mercy like an old shoe'.[208]

Provocatively, al-Zawahiri then described former secretaries of state Colin Powell and Condoleezza Rice as 'house slaves' who help keep 'field slaves' down. Al-Zawahiri was seeking to interlace al-Qaeda's global jihad with domestic racial tensions in the United States, and those that wil- fully pledged their adherence to the establishment, to conflate issues. Al- Zawahiri told African Americans that they can defeat the 'most powerful tyrannical force in the history of mankind'.[209] Significantly, al-Zawahiri was knowledgeable of the divide in US racial politics between mainstream African American leaders and revolutionaries like Malcolm X.

Al-Zawahiri saw much potential in tapping into resentment and vulner-ability within communities and using the Malcolm X card. On 19 November 2008, soon after Barack Obama was elected as the first-ever Black president of the United States, al-Qaeda released a video with al-Zawahiri describing the president-elect as a 'race traitor' and 'hypocrite'. Al-Zawahiri claimed Obama did not represent a genuine change for America, and said he was the 'direct opposite of honourable Black Americans' such as Malcolm X.[210]

Al-Zawahiri went into a vicious diatribe: 'America has put on a new face, but its heart full of hate, mind drowning in greed, and spirit which spreads evil, murder, repression and despotism continue to be the same as always.'[211] He then returned to racial slurs, calling Obama a 'house slave' who served at the behest of his white masters. Even though the Egyptian could speak English, he always chose to talk in Arabic but allowed his messages to have subtitles. As-Sahab translated al-Zawahiri's reference of Obama as a 'house slave' as 'house negro'.

The al-Qaeda video then showed a clip of Malcolm X using the term 'house Negroes' to describe several people who were submissive to white people. To further demonstrate al-Zawahiri's point, footage of Malcolm X praying at a mosque was set against pictures of Obama with a *kippah* at the Western Wall in Jerusalem. Al-Zawahiri concluded by accusing Obama of betraying his father to enhance his political goals: 'You were born to a Muslim father, but you chose to stand in the ranks of the enemies of the Muslims, and pray the prayer of the Jews, although you claim to be Christian, in order to climb the rungs of leadership in America.'

Recalling stories about Malcolm X from his granduncle Abdul Rahman Azzam, al-Zawahiri sought to identify himself and al-Qaeda as allies of African Americans by utilising the same tone as Malcolm X as well as calling out problems of discrimination that the African Americans have historically faced.[212] Al-Zawahiri was continually seeking to fuel the fires of extremism, laying the groundwork for the next incident of terrorism, whilst undermining the middle ground. The success of his strategy cannot be judged entirely on direct linkage to cause and effect but more the pro-motion of a narrative that African Americans could be preyed upon and re-cruited by exploiting social tensions. It was this narrative that other jihadist groups and lone actors would be motivated to pursue.

However, one topic that al-Zawahiri was keen to avoid addressing was the racism of his ideological mentor Sayyid Qutb towards African Americans.

Qutb was once asked to define jazz. He wrote that it was 'the music that the savage bushmen created to satisfy their primitive desires, and the desire for noise on the one hand, and the abundance of animal noises on the other'.[213]

The Bhutto Assassination

After fleeing Pakistan for a second time over corruption allegations and having to spend eight years in exile, Benazir Bhutto returned to Pakistan for the final time in October 2007 after a US-brokered deal with General Pervez Musharraf gave her immunity from charges of corruption during her two terms as prime minister. Under pressure from the George W. Bush administration, Musharraf also announced that general elections would be held on 8 January 2008 which Bhutto fully intended to take part in despite facing death threats from jihadists. However, on 18 October 2007, within hours of landing in Karachi, she narrowly escaped with her life when two bombs were detonated near her motorcade, killing 130 people. Bhutto claimed the ISI was involved in the attack and condemned the presence of foreign jihadists in Pakistan and vowed to expel them. However, worse was to come.[214]

On 27 December 2007, Bhutto was actively campaigning in Rawalpindi, buoyed by the prospect of an unprecedented third term. Whilst travelling in a bullet-proof vehicle, waiving to huge throngs of people from the open roof of the car, a face in the crowd wearing dark glasses pulled out a pistol and fired three shots at Bhutto. The assassin then detonated a powerful explosive device attached to his body. In the wake of the explosion, the scene was one of panic and confusion filled with blood and smoke. Dozens had been killed, and Bhutto was pronounced dead shortly after.[215]

While much debate and speculation surrounded the circumstances of Bhutto's death, the consequences were clear. It damaged a fragile political process in a country already enduring tremendous instability and a rising terrorist threat. Making matters worse, the crime scene was hosed down two hours after the killing, washing away any potential forensic evidence. The failure to conduct an autopsy aggravated the situation and heightened suspicions.[216] A subsequent United Nations investigation determined that the failure of the Musharraf regime to investigate the Bhutto killing was 'deliberate' and 'severely hampered' by the ISI.[217] Asif Ali Zardari, Bhutto's widower, suggested Musharraf himself played a role in the assassination, referring to the military establishment as the 'Killer League'.[218] The PPP's 2007 manifesto promised to curtail the powers of the military and intelligence agencies with civilian, democratic oversight as well as greater transparency over the military's secretly guarded budget.

Shortly after, al-Qaeda claimed responsibility for Bhutto's murder. Mustafa Abu al-Yazid contacted the Italian news agency Adnkronos International, stating that al-Zawahiri had planned the assassination back in October when Bhutto returned to Pakistan and claimed, 'We terminated the most precious American asset which vowed to defeat [the] *mujahideen*.'[219] Al-Yazid then repeated the claim of responsibility to the *Asia Times* whilst commenting on Bhutto's speeches against al-Qaeda, adding, 'This is our first major victory against those who have been siding with infidels in a fight against al-Qaeda.'[220] Taking the lead for al-Qaeda in the Bhutto plot was Abu Ubaidah al-Masri, the man tied to the EIJ attack on the Egyptian Embassy in Islamabad in 1995 and al-Qaeda's plots in the United Kingdom. Following the Bhutto assassination, Abu Ubaidah relayed a message to the al-Qaeda leadership about the successful 'operation in [Rawal]Pindi'.[221] In April 2008 Abu Ubaidah died of hepatitis C.[222]

The PPP also accused the then head of the Intelligence Bureau (IB), Brigadier Ijaz Shah, of having impeded the Bhutto investigation. Prior to her death, Bhutto had written to Musharraf naming several likely culprits if there were an attempt on her life. It included Ijaz Shah, a man with close ties with terrorist groups, who was made the IB head in 2004 by Musharraf and was regarded a long-term close ally and confidant.[223] The military was concerned about Bhutto's return, as she wanted to limit its overbearing influence over Pakistani society. This meant taking away the military's monopoly on counter-terrorism and allowing a degree of civilian control where there would be no question of divided loyalties regarding al-Qaeda. Therefore al-Zawahiri personally ordered Benazir Bhutto's murder.[224]

Much of the focus had fallen on Ijaz Shah as the cog connecting the military, local jihadists, and foreign terrorists. Back in 2002, Shah had already incensed the United States for housing the British-Pakistani Ahmed Omar Saeed Sheikh, who was responsible for the abduction and murder of the American journalist Daniel Pearl. Pearl was investigating the military-backed Ummah Tameer-e-Nau (UTN), which had been in discussions with al-Zawahiri and bin Laden over selling nuclear material prior to 9/

11.[225] Sheikh was trained at al-Qaeda's camps in Khost.[226] Given his English education, Western social skills, and London upbringing, Sheikh was a valuable resource for al-Qaeda. He was also close to the Pakistani military.[227]

Bhutto was al-Qaeda's nemesis because she was a liberal and also a woman. They had tried to undermine her twice before and failed. The idea of a liberal woman politician returning to govern Pakistan was an abomination to the terrorists now ensconced there. They were determined to prevent Bhutto's election. Prior to her assassination, al-Qaeda's most infamous targeted political killing was of Ahmad Shah Massoud, the head of the Northern Alliance, two days before 9/11, which al-Zawahiri also played a direct role in organising. Al-Qaeda's killing of Bhutto was designed to plunge the country into chaos and divert it from the democratic path. However, elections were still conducted on schedule, and Bhutto's PPP won enough seats to form the next government.

The Mujahidat

As willing as al-Zawahiri was to sanction the targeted killing of women, there remained the sensitive issue of what role female jihadists, *mujahidat*, could serve within al-Qaeda. In 2008, al-Zawahiri held another public session entitled 'Open Discussion', where he was asked by a woman, 'Does al-Qaeda accept women in its ranks?' Zawahiri bluntly replied, 'No.'[228]

Another person asked, 'Who is the highest-ranking woman in al-Qaeda? Don't mention names if you do not want to do so, but what is their duty in the organization?' Al-Zawahiri responded, 'Al-Qaeda has no women, but the women of the *mujahideen* do their heroic part in taking care of their homes and sons in the roughness of the immigration, movement, unity, and expecting the Crusader strikes.'[229] His comments were criticised by some jihadists across the world, including women who wanted to become an active part of al-Qaeda.

To deal with this potential fissure within the jihadist movement, al-Zawahiri would turn to an unlikely source. In December, 2009, as-Sahab produced a message by al-Zawahiri's second wife, Umayma Hassan, 'A Message to the Muslim Sisters', where she encouraged her 'Muslim sisters' to bring up their children on the love of jihad in God's path, 'to incite their

brothers, husbands, and sons to defend Muslims' territories and properties
... to assist [the male] jihadist with prayers and money.'[230]

If women are not satisfied with this childcare mission, Umayma Hassan
claimed al-Qaeda may allow women to raise money for jihadists, to establish a network amongst mosques, and to print publications for the organization: 'I call upon them also to help the *mujahideen* with prayer and money,
and help the families of the wounded and imprisoned with money and
donations to their children and women.'[231]

Umayma Hassan referred to the importance of the *mujahidat* accompanying their husbands, and although there are some cases when a Muslim
woman may fight, the paramount priority must be in the service of the
man: 'The Muslim woman must work beside the man to defend her religion and land. ... Jihad is an individual obligation on every Muslim man
and woman, but the path of combat is not easy for a woman. It requires a
Mahram [a male Muslim relative], because the woman must have a Mahram
in her comings and goings.'[232] Umayma Hassan's role for women participating in jihad was ambiguous. On the one hand, she said jihad was an individual obligation but then contradicted herself by saying a woman needs a
male companion. Much of Umayma Hassan's commentary was designed to
deal with the problems al-Zawahiri created during his 'Open Discussion'.

Umayma Hassan's comments were therefore twofold. First, to repeat her
husband's advice to women but also to try to acknowledge that women
do desire to fight in the battlefield alongside men. Whilst supporting those
women who have waged jihad, she insists it is 'difficult for women to travel
to a land of jihad.'[233]

A few years later, in 2012, in an effort to bolster al-Qaeda's standing in
the Arab world and widen its appeal from its previous male focus, Umayma
Hassan praised the contribution of Muslim women in the Arab Spring to the
overthrow of four Arab rulers whom she described as 'tyrant criminals':[234]

> I congratulate all females of the world for these blessed revolutions, and I
> salute every mother who sacrificed her loved ones in the revolutions. It is
> really an Arab Spring and will soon become an Islamic Spring.[235]

Hassan also urged Muslim women to raise their children for jihad:

> I advise you to raise your children in the cult of jihad and martyrdom and to
> instil in them a love for religion and death. ... [E]ach woman would raise her
> child to be a new Saladin [a 12th century Kurdish general who defeated the

Crusaders in battle] by telling him it is you who will restore the grandeur of
the Islamic nation and you will liberate Jerusalem.[236]

Umayma Hassan's statement would have been authorised by al-Zawahiri,
but the al-Qaeda leader also believed it was necessary to get his wife to
issue this unusual statement. Up till now, al-Zawahiri had adopted a very
rigid view of the role women could play in conflict, to the extent that he
did not want them even talking about it. This was a major departure for al-
Zawahiri. However, although the narrative that women should not be on
the front line of conflict remained, the scope had changed, as women were
being encouraged to indoctrinate their children into fighting against the
so-called 'apostate' regimes as part of a modern crusade and to be willing to
lose their children in battle as a result.

Many of the discussions about the role of women in al-Qaeda and
al-Zawahiri's views coincided with the fate of a female jihadist whom
al-Zawahiri had held in high esteem for her loyalty to al-Qaeda's agenda.
Pakistani neuroscientist Aafia Siddiqui was at the centre of an al-Qaeda
cell based in Karachi between 2002 and 2003 led by 9/11 mastermind
Khalid Sheikh Mohammed. Siddiqui's role was to obtain safe houses provided by the JeM terrorist group and give organizational support to the
operation. Around February 2003, Siddiqui married Pakistani national
and Khalid Sheikh Mohammed's nephew, Ammar al-Baluchi, who was
ultimately apprehended by American counter-terrorism officers in the
Pakistani city of Rawalpindi close to a military headquarters. At the time,
Siddiqui was conducting research on biological weapons for Pakistan's
defence capabilities.[237]

In July 2008, Siddiqui was detained by the US military in Ghazni,
Afghanistan. She had in her possession two pounds of sodium cyanide, a
poisonous substance that can be lethal in small quantities. She also had
papers that included handwritten notes referencing attacks on American
landmarks, as well as printed material. According to court records, more
specifically, they consisted of several handwritten notes. Excerpts included:

Do the unthinkable: Attack enemies on gliders. . . . Attack using laser beams.
   Dirty Bomb: Need few oz. radioactive material (e.g. cobalt 60 from food
irradiation facility) . . . wrap cobalt 60 around a [u/i] bomb, detonate it &
shower a city w deadly fall out. . . . To detect dirty bombs, gamma, and other
radiation sensors @ airports [or] seaports [or] police depts (but still not all
covered in America). . . . Practical dirty bomb would work by causing FEAR,
not much deaths.

It is better to die while fighting infidels than to die or become handicapped by one's own negligence and carelessness when making weapons.[238]

These notes were significant for demonstrating several terrorist-related activities that al-Zawahiri was not only involved in, but directing: he had been seeking to use chemical, biological, radiological, and nuclear (CBRN) weapons, including a dirty bomb with the Briton Dhiren Barot, and he had tasked the Egyptian Khalid Abu al-Dahab with using a hang glider to storm Mazra'at Tora prison. Siddiqui was subsequently taken to an Afghan National Police facility for questioning following her arrest. A team of American personnel was sent in, and as the US chief warrant officer set down his M4-A1 rifle next to him, Siddiqui grabbed it, shouting exclamations like, 'I want to kill Americans' and 'Death to America', according to some witnesses, before an interpreter tackled her and an American officer shot her in the stomach.[239]

On 23 September 2010, a US court sentenced Siddiqui to jail for 86 years for attempting to kill US federal agents in Afghanistan.[240] Soon after, al-Zawahiri issued a message titled 'Who Will Support Scientist Aafia Siddiqui?' Al-Zawahiri also threatened the United States with reprisals: 'We will fight you until the hour of judgment, or until you stop your crimes. . . . So whoever wants to free Aafia Siddiqui and take revenge on those who violated her and all Muslim women should join the *mujahideen* because there's no dearness [to be had] except by Jihad and no pride but by it.'[241]

A seething al-Zawahiri doubled down on his threats to the United States, warning that the 'Islamic Ummah (community) [would] respond strike for strike and kill for kill, and destruction for destruction, and attack for attack', a message that has resonated with jihadist groups since its proclamation. Al-Zawahiri would go on to repeat his demands for Siddiqui's release in years to come. Al-Zawahiri's full ties with Siddiqui were yet to be unravelled. Likely, they were platonic, and he respected her zeal. Yet his level of empathy for her was unmatched with anyone else, other than the family he lost during the bombing of Tora Bora.[242]

Siddiqui also became a cause célèbre within Pakistan, earning the moniker of 'ransom girl' by both jihadist groups and politicians and senior members of the military due to her close proximity with them. This raised further concerning questions over the murky nexus between Pakistan's establishment and terrorists. Upon Siddiqui's sentencing in the United States Pakistani prime minister Yousaf Raza Gilani, called her the 'daughter of the nation'.[243] Gilani hailed from the same political party, the PPP, as the slain Benazir Bhutto. Disturbingly, during Imran Khan's stint as prime minister, he proposed exchanging Siddiqui for Shakil Afridi, a doctor who was imprisoned in Pakistan for helping the United States track down Osama bin Laden in Pakistan.[244]

Triple Agents and Middlemen

Whilst al-Zawahiri was willing to plot against an 'internal enemy' like Benazir Bhutto, bin Laden was getting frustrated that al-Qaeda was not extending its operations once more to the West. A Mauritanian operative, Younis al-Mauritani, had proposed plans to carry out attacks across continental Europe which bin Laden was receptive too. However, for al-Zawahiri, there was a far greater opportunity emerging to kill important people from the West, without having to travel to Europe or North America.[245]

Humam Khalil al-Balawi was a Palestinian whose family left Beersheba following the 1948 Arab-Israeli war. They settled in Kuwait, where al-Balawi was raised.[246] In 1991, following the removal of Saddam Hussein's Iraqi forces from Kuwait, the Kuwaiti government ejected the Palestinian community because Palestinian leader Yasser Arafat had endorsed Hussein's occupation of the emirate. Al-Balawi's family became exiles. Al-Balawi then lived in Jordan before receiving a medical degree in Istanbul, Turkey.[247]

Al-Balawi had another role, as an online promoter for al-Qaeda. Through his blogs, he demonstrated interest in al-Qaeda's ideas and terrorist tactics, using the alias Abu Dujanah al-Khorasani.[248] In particular, al-Balawi assessed and supported as-Sahab messages by al-Zawahiri and posted his musings on them. In this way, al-Balawi became a sort of unofficial mouthpiece for al-Qaeda.[249]

In January 2009, the Jordanian General Intelligence Department (GID) arrested al-Balawi. His interrogator, Captain Sharif Ali bin Zeid al-Oun, was a cousin of King Abdullah II of Jordan. Zeid was educated and trained in the United States and had established close ties with the American intelligence community. The GID sought to cultivate al-Balawi as a double agent by seeing whether he could penetrate al-Qaeda, and Zeid would act as his handler. The hope and intention was for al-Balawi to embed himself within the leadership of al-Qaeda hiding in Pakistan. The trail of the senior leadership—primarily al-Zawahiri and Osama bin Laden—had gone cold, and there were no concrete leads, with little help forthcoming from the ISI.

Al-Balawi convinced Zeid that he was the asset that the Jordanians and Americans were looking for. For the US counter-terrorism community, any intelligence related to the senior leadership of al-Qaeda, especially bin Laden and al-Zawahiri, was of the highest priority.[250] Over the many years they were at large, they had become difficult to locate. Specific intelligence was very hard to come by, especially as it was clear that the Pakistani military could not be trusted.[251]

For the CIA, al-Zawahiri was considered not only the intellectual ideo-logue behind al-Qaeda but also the overall operational commander as well. He was believed as important to capture or eliminate as bin Laden in order to degrade al-Qaeda.[252] On the basis of Zeid's endorsement, al-Balawi was dispatched to Pakistan. He was seen as the best chance to locate al-Zawahiri and maybe bin Laden.

In the spring of 2009, al-Balawi travelled to South Waziristan under the invitation from the Taliban. He subsequently dropped off the radar for sev-eral months. Eventually, he resurfaced, and increasingly al-Balawi began to report to his handler that he was infiltrating the Taliban leadership and al-Qaeda in Pakistan using his online reputation as Khorasani.[253] The Jordanians and Americans had significant hope and expectation that they had a dependable and consistent source in him.

Al-Qaeda reached out to al-Balawi and introduced him to the Libyan Atiyah Abd al-Rahman and the Egyptian Mustafa Abu al-Yazid. Atiyah had known bin Laden and al-Zawahiri since he was a teenager in Afghanistan, after leaving Libya in 1988 to fight towards the end of the Soviet occupa-tion. Atiyah's intelligence saw him rise within al-Qaeda's hierarchy and bin Laden sent Atiyah to Algeria in 1993 to act as an emissary for him and the jihadists fighting in the civil war. Atiyah was eventually betrayed by a member of the Islamic Fighting Group (GIA) who was working for the Algerian military as a double agent and was imprisoned. Infiltration by a governmental entity would serve as a life lesson that Atiyah would learn from and use with deadly effect against al-Qaeda's enemies. Eventually, he managed to escape and traveled to Pakistan after 9/11 to take up a senior role within al-Qaeda.[254]

Through Atiyah, al-Zawahiri used al-Balawi as a triple agent. Though al-Zawahiri guided overall strategy, tactical planning for this operation was led by Atiyah and Mustafa Abu al-Yazid, Atiyah cunningly used extracts of information, supported by video clips, to show that al-Balawi was inside an al-Qaeda terror camp. Then, news came in the autumn of 2009 that the CIA and Zeid was hoping for. Al-Balawi reported back to Zeid that he had met al-Zawahiri, who required medical attention. He provided details of al-Zawahiri's health, which cross-checked with the information the Americans had gathered over many years. The trap was being set.

Al-Balawi used a video of senior terrorists including Atiyah to further convince the CIA of his credentials. The footage was staged as part of a plan concocted by Atiyah to bait the Jordanian and American intelligence communities.[255] Al-Balawi also claimed to have access to al-Zawahiri by acting as his doctor. Al-Qaeda's leadership directed al-Balawi to send detailed medical descriptions and evaluations to the Jordanians and Americans to prove that he was in fact seeing al-Zawahiri as a patient. Despite being one of the world's most wanted terrorists, al-Zawahiri's health was fragile. He had multiple medical conditions, including coronary artery disease as well as diabetes. Al-Balawi provided the CIA with news that al-Zawahiri was running out of the multiple prescription medicines that he needed and was struggling to get more whilst living in the shadows.[256]

The CIA were able to tally the medical conditions and medicines that al-Balawi said al-Zawahiri needed with their own information. They then decided that to help build al-Balawi's credentials with al-Zawahiri, they would obtain the medicines and hand them over to the Jordanian the next time they met him.[257] Having close contact with such a high-ranking al-Qaeda official was a significant development, and Jordanian as well as American intelligence officials were eager to use al-Balawi to gain as much information about al-Qaeda's second in command as possible.[258] Al-Balawi's status dramatically altered from the periphery of the CIA's radar to suddenly becoming one of their most important potential assets. Al-Balawi was the closest the United States had come to al-Zawahiri since the 2006 Damadola drone strike which al-Zawahiri narrowly managed to escape after being tipped off. However, it was now essential for a personal meeting with the CIA operations team to get a real assessment of what they were dealing with.

Unbeknown to them, al-Zawahiri wanted to use al-Balawi to kill Zeid, al-Balawi's Jordanian contact, as well as the CIA officers.[259] Both the CIA and GID wanted to interview al-Balawi in a secure location. Al-Balawi had tried to lure his handlers to a meeting in Pakistan, but it was deemed too risky. After much back and forth, Forward Operating Base Chapman in Khost was designated as the venue. It was just over the border from South Waziristan in Pakistan. Al-Zawahiri also had enormous experience in grooming people to act as double agents, working in sensitive positions and earning the trust of the intelligence community, as we saw with Ali Mohamed. However, al-Balawi was a step up for the Egyptian, and the risks were far greater. According to Bruce Riedel, who served on the US National Security Council and advised four American presidents on the Middle East and South Asia, 'Al-Zawahiri is a big thinker and a dangerous thinker. Just look at the sheer audacity of his plans for terrorism. He was the architect behind the Khost attack.'[260]

Several senior CIA officers who had spent years analysing intricate details on al-Qaeda would accompany Zeid, who would lead the debriefing with the aim of using the information al-Balawi was going to provide to target al-Zawahiri. They also had with them al-Zawahiri's medicines. On 30 December 2009, al-Balawi arrived in a car with a driver, slumped in the back seat. Critically, he was not searched upon entering the base. Several senior and experienced CIA officers were waiting for him. The CIA security team asked for al-Balawi to step out of the car, as they were going to search him as a standard security requirement. Before they could get close enough to realise there was a problem, al-Balawi detonated his hidden suicide vest killing himself, seven CIA officers, and two others, one of whom was Zeid.[261]

Back in Langley, Virginia, the CIA were monitoring the meeting in real time. Suddenly, their communications went silent, dark. A deep sense of foreboding ensued. Eventually, a secure call from a senior operational officer confirmed that the entire US team had been killed by al-Balawi.[262] Al-Zawahiri had once again evaded the intelligence net and this time helped orchestrate a devasting reversal, with the death of several experienced counterterrorism agents. He had also scored a symbolic victory against Jordan, as al-Zawahiri had often blamed the Hashemite Kingdom for the destruction of the Ottoman Caliphate.[263] Just inside the main entrance of CIA Headquarters in Langley Virginia is a white marble wall with a collection of stars etched into the stone. Each star memorialises a life of a CIA agent lost in the line of duty. Al-Zawahiri was responsible for seven of those engraved stars.

In May 2010, the CIA got a measure of retribution against al-Qaeda through a drone strike that killed Abu al-Yazid in North Waziristan, but al-Zawahiri remained elusive.[264] Al-Qaeda was developing close ties with the Pakistan Taliban, also known as the Tehrik-e Taliban Pakistan (TTP), who had developed a strong presence in the tribal areas of Pakistan. The TTP had emerged on the scene in 2007 as an alliance of Pakistani Pashtun tribes opposed to the flawed military strategy in Pakistan's tribal areas that resulted in significant socio-economic upheaval and the displacement of the local population. Ironically, the TTP began to emulate the Afghan Taliban, who were backed by the Pakistani military. However, the TTP's goals were the expulsion of the Pakistani military in the Pashtun areas and the implementation of a strict interpretation of Shariah law. Pakistan's military has no qualms enabling the Afghan Taliban to further their objectives in Afghanistan but were opposed to the TTP doing the same in Pakistan. This paradox would blight Pakistan's strategic statecraft and undermine counter-terrorism efforts in the region.

Just like with the Bhutto assassination, the location, sophistication, and planning of the Khost attack, required the collaboration of several other entities with al-Qaeda. Following the attack, al-Qaeda released a statement claiming that the 'the appropriate media entity will publish his [al-Balawi's] story . . . in a proper production'.[265] Curiously, not long after, the TTP claimed responsibility with a video that featured al-Balawi and TTP leader Hakimullah Mehsud.[266] There was notable silence from the Haqqani Network. However, it was not practical for the operation to have taken place in Khost without the full knowledge and direct participation of the Haqqani Network in territory where they exert significant influence and control the flow of clandestine traffic to and from Pakistan.[267] Jalaluddin Haqqani once noted the value of Khost's mobilisation networks: 'Khost is one of four strategic places in Afghanistan. It is very important because Khost has more than tens of routes to Pakistan.'[268]

Several months after the attack, as-Sahab posthumously released a pre-recorded video of al-Balawi in which he spoke in English of how he lured American and Jordanian intelligence officers into a trap by sending them misleading information about al-Zawahiri. The Jordanian revealed,

'Death will come to you in unexpected ways.... [W]e will get you CIA Team ... inshallah, we will get you down.' Al-Balawi then pointed to the suicide bomb's detonator discretely strapped to his watch and boasted, 'Look, this is for you, it's not a watch, it's a detonator to kill as much as I can. This is my goal, to kill you, to kill your partner, Jordanian partner.'[269]

One of the most troubling aspects of the attack was that Pakistan's ISI may have supported it financially, according to declassified US State Department cables obtained by the George Washington University's National Security Archive. Two weeks after the suicide bombing, the State Department reported on a meeting between Haqqani Network operatives and unidentified officers with the ISI in Islamabad around the time of the Khost attack in which they 'discussed funding for operations' including to 'enable the attack on Chapman'. According to the cable, the ISI gave the Haqqani Network $200,000 for the attack in Khost. The documents also revealed that the ISI provided 'direction to the Haqqanis to expedite attack preparations and lethality in Afghanistan'. The nexus amongst al-Qaeda, the Haqqanis, and the ISI demonstrated the challenges in capturing the al-Qaeda leadership, especially if they are protected by state elements who in turn harbour murky strategic ties with proscribed terrorist groups.[270]

The ties between the Haqqani Network and the ISI caused deep consternation amongst the US military and intelligence communities. In 2011, Admiral Mike Mullen, the then chairman of the US Joint Chiefs of Staff, said that the Haqqani Network acted 'as a veritable arm of Pakistan's intelligence'.[271] The additional problem was that this 'veritable arm' would also then extend to providing sanctuary for al-Qaeda and cooperation in 'special operations'.[272]

The senior leader of the Taliban-affiliated Haqqani Network, Sirajuddin Haqqani, never hid his relationship with al-Qaeda. In 2011, he published a Pashto-language manual, *Military Lessons: For the Legions of Jihadists*, proclaiming that followers who volunteered to become suicide bombers demonstrated 'good character', and anyone who did so 'is favoured by Almighty Allah'. The text also lauds al-Qaeda as an entity that 'terrifies' its adversaries and urges all jihadists to emulate the group's ability to 'stay and live among people who are against our faith and ideology, like those militants operating in Europe and the U.S.'. Much of the manual was devoted to the best methods and weapons for killing and destroying targets as well as guidance on how to set up a cell, attain financing, recruit, and train. This manual was

used to recruit and train the cadres of Haqqani Network fighters responsible for killing Afghans as well as coalition soldiers in Afghanistan.[273]

Inevitably, in 2012, the United Nations and the United States proscribed
the Haqqani Network as a terrorist group. At the same time, Sirajuddin
Haqqani was designated as an international terrorist, in large part because
of his relationship with al-Qaeda as well as his responsibility for the death
of countless American and Afghan soldiers as well as thousands of Afghan
civilians. The State Department's Rewards for Justice Program offered a reward of up to $10 million for information leading to Sirajuddin Haqqani's
capture.[274] However, he continued to operate freely in Pakistan and embraced his notoriety. The Haqqani Network retained a unique role as an
intermediate between the Afghan Taliban and al-Qaeda, protecting al-
Zawahiri. Even as the Taliban wavered in their support to the Egyptian
doctor, the Haqqani loyalty remained steadfast.

6

Changing of the Knights

The Arab Spring

Rumours had long persisted that Hosni Mubarak had orchestrated a plan to transfer power to his son Gamal in Egypt when he was appointed as general secretary of the Policy Committee of the ruling National Democratic Party (NDP), the third-highest-ranking position. Resentment intensified towards Mubarak, who had not nominated a vice-president since he replaced Sadat in 1981.[1] Between 2004 and 2007, Egypt witnessed an unprecedented rise in civil resistance. The main movement was named Kefaya, meaning 'Enough'. Founded in 2004, Kefaya was a loose-knit grouping of distinct factions across Egypt's political and ideological spectrum, many of whom were part of the student movements in the 1970s during the regime of Anwar Sadat.[2] They represented a broad political range, from Nasserists and Marxists to liberals to Islamists, including the Muslim Brotherhood, who agreed to refrain from pushing religious ideology in the Kefaya movement's activities.[3]

Together, street demonstrations and other acts of civil disobedience underscored a demand for multiparty elections, judicial independence, and an end to hereditary succession. Still, Mubarak was able to withstand the opposition, and Egypt's authoritarian power structure remained intact.[4] Curiously, al-Zawahiri was closely monitoring events and condemned Kefaya's peaceful non-religious approach, asserting that 'the only way to confront tyrannical rulers and the crusader forces is through jihad'.[5] The Kefaya movement may have not achieved its aims, but it laid the groundwork for more monumental events to come with the Arab Spring.

Zine El Abidine Ben Ali had been Tunisia's president since 1987. His rule was controversial, and he faced continual accusations of brutal repression complemented by corruption and nepotism especially through his wife, Leila Ben Ali. Yet in one of the most spontaneous and astonishing chapters

Doctor, Teacher, Terrorist. Sajjan M. Gohel, Oxford University Press. © Oxford University Press 2024.
DOI: 10.1093/oso/9780197665367.003.0006

in modern Middle Eastern history, he was toppled by a popular uprising, sparking the Arab Spring which had been ignited by the despairing act of one man. Mohammed Bouazizi, from the town of Sidi Bouzid, decided he could no longer accept the unfair and corrupt practices of the Ben Ali regime.[6] On 17 December 2010, he went to a petrol station, filled up a container, positioned himself in the middle of the road and stopped oncoming vehicles, poured gasoline over himself, and shouted, 'How do you expect me to make a living?' Then he lit a match setting himself alight. He barely survived, with burns over 90% of his body.[7]

News soon spread about Bouazizi's act of self-immolation. Hundreds of people came from all over Sidi Bouzid to protest even though demonstrating in Tunisia was illegal. The anger spread to other towns in the country. The police started shooting at protestors, killing hundreds, but protestors uploaded images that went viral nationally, regionally, and globally.[8] On 4 January 2011, Bouazizi died from his severe burns. Within days tens of thousands thronged the nation's capital, Tunis. Realising the inevitable was nigh, Ben Ali fled into exile in Saudi Arabia. In an unprecedented event in Middle East and North Africa, an Arab ruler was deposed by a popular, non-violent uprising. However, Tunisia was not a one-off stand-alone event. The seeds for change had already been planted in Egypt.[9]

Following the scenes in Tunisia, social media activists urged Egyptians to participate in nationwide anti-government demonstrations on 25 January 2011, which coincided with National Police Day. Young Egyptian protestors came out in large numbers chanting, 'The People Want to Bring Down a Regime.'[10] On 28 January 2011, aided by social media, hundreds of thousands of protestors turned up in Cairo. Many were students and other youths exasperated by government corruption and the lack of economic prospects. For the first few days, Tahrir Square in Cairo was filled by thousands of demonstrators. It was orderly and non-violent and captured the attention of the Egyptian people and the entire world. The water cannons, rubber bullets, and tear gas so often used with great effect by the security police under Hosni Mubarak did not deter the crowds or dampen their sense of making history.[11]

Despite the army's deployment to end the protests, soldiers were unwilling to fire on crowds, and many protestors embraced them as potential allies. These were unparalleled moments in modern Egypt.[12] The word *irhal*, meaning 'leave' appeared on countless posters. Protesters also used the colloquial Egyptian word *imshi* which can mean 'scram' or 'beat it' and is usually reserved for annoying children. On 29 January 2011, Mubarak addressed the nation and in a feeble attempt to placate the protesters, announced he was appointing national intelligence chief Omar Suleiman as his vice-president. This was the first time anyone had held that position under Mubarak. However, the move failed to calm public fury.[13] Protests continued and the army said that they would not intervene or use force against the Egyptian people, stating they understood 'the legitimacy of your demands'.[14] On 1 February 2011, with protests increasing, Mubarak announced that he would not run for re-election in the autumn of 2011 and wanted to oversee a 'peaceful transfer of power' once his term ended. He added, 'History shall judge me and others in terms of what we owe and what we are owed.'[15]

Mubarak believed he could outlast the protestors by separating and isolating them through some proposed concessions and political reform whilst preserving his dominance. However, widespread labour strikes soon spread across Egypt and generated renewed momentum for the Arab Spring.[16] Al-Azhar in Cairo adopted a cautious position on the Arab Spring protests. Initially, it requested that people vacate the streets and return home for the sake of peace and stability. However, some younger members of al-Azhar did participate in the demonstrations. Protests eventually spread to al-Azhar's campuses, involving university faculty and students.[17]

Up till now, the voice of the jihadists had been noticeably absent from events in Egypt. However, in early February 2011, al-Zawahiri's former EIJ deputy Tharwat Salah Shehata resurfaced, issuing a statement emulating the words of Anwar Sadat's assassin, Khalid al-Islambouli: 'The Pharaoh and his rotten party must depart.' The message raised two important developments. The first indicated that Shehata had engaged in a rapprochement with al-Zawahiri after disagreeing pre-9/11 over the direction of the EIJ including the merger with al-Qaeda and the September 11 attacks. Shehata's message would not have appeared on the specific forums without al-Zawahiri's consent. The other important aspect was that his statement was issued whilst he was based in Tehran. Yet another example of a jihadist located in Iran but operating with impunity. Iran was no friend of Egypt after all.[18]

On 11 February 2011, after 18 days of relatively peaceful protest, Mubarak finally resigned, with massive ramifications for Egypt and beyond. The announcement was made by Vice-President Suleiman, who also revealed that the Supreme Council of the Egyptian Armed Forces had taken control of the country. Unlike Ben Ali, Mubarak choose not to flee and seek sanctuary in another country.[19]

Undermining al-Qaeda, nationalist and democratic values drove the popular uprisings.[20] According to Mohamed Heikal, 'Events in Egypt showed that power of the masses, opposition to an authoritarian regime and religion alone could not address economic and social concerns.'[21] Mubarak may have successfully moved aggressively against the jihadists, isolating them with widespread arrests, detention, torture, and collective punishment, but this created a culture within the security services of tolerating and encouraging brutality against anyone suspected of threatening the state. According to the noted historian Bruce Rutherford, 'This culture contributed to the increasingly haphazard violence against civilians that contributed to the 2011 uprising and eventually eroded public confidence in Mubarak's leadership and contributed to his removal from office.'[22]

Seeking to exploit the situation, al-Zawahiri released a series of statements. All of them shared the same title: 'Missive of Hope and Joy to Our People in Egypt'.[23] For al-Zawahiri, the frustrations on the Arab streets stemmed from the oppressive secular rulers in Egypt, past and present. He connected them to historical events that saw Western intrusions of Egypt. In these statements, Al-Zawahiri returned to an important aspect he raised in *Knights under the Prophet's Banner*: that Egyptian frustrations stemmed not from just the Mubarak regime but from the eighteenth century with Napoleon's conquest and subjugation of Egypt, followed by the British occupation which lasted for nearly two more centuries via economic, political, and military hegemony. The historical background of these problems was compounded by American influence over Sadat and Mubarak, whom al-Zawahiri described as 'pharaohs who have oppressed the Egyptians to advance their interests and those of the United States'.[24]

In an obvious reaction to the events in Egypt in the aftermath of the Arab Spring, al-Zawahiri acknowledged the 'free and the noble people' who made their presence felt. However, he was keen to claim that they were all fighting the same foe: 'Your jihadi brethren are confronting alongside you the same enemy, America and its Western allies, those who set up [tyrants] like Hosni Mubarak.'[25] Focussing on the United States, al-Zawahiri claimed that nothing would change regarding Western interference:

America that is weeping over the victims of torture in Egypt is [the same America] that resorts to torture in the prisons of Guantanamo, Bagram, and Abu Ghurayb and in its secret prisons in Egypt, Jordan, Morocco, Poland. . . . America is the last [entity] that is allowed to speak of [the virtues of] democracy and human rights.[26]

Beyond highlighting his usual narrative of American and Western hypocrisy, al-Zawahiri cautioned the Egyptian people that the successes of the revolution would be wasted if they did not create an Islamic government once and for all based on 'principles of consultation' (nizam islami shuri).[27] Al-Zawahiri reminded fellow Egyptians not to forget the other Arab Spring revolutionaries, including the Libyans who were fighting against the Muammar Qadhafi regime. He lamented the Arab regimes, asking whether 'their role is limited to oppressing the people'. Al-Zawahiri called on Libya's Muslims and those in neighbouring countries to rise and fight against 'Qadhafi mercenaries and those of the Crusader-NATO'.[28] Indeed, al-Qaeda also saw opportunities in Libya, having called for fighters from neighbouring countries to assist the revolution.[29] Al-Zawahiri's deputy Atiyah Abd al-Rahman claimed, 'Libya is now ready for the jihad. . . . Because of its important location, it will be a jihadist battlefield opening on Algeria and the Sahara, Sudan, Darfur, Chad, and the depth of Africa.'[30]

On 13 April 2011, Egypt's prosecutor general, General Abdel Meguid Mahmoud, ordered Mubarak and his two sons be detained over accusations of corruption and abuse of authority.[31] Several months later, after falling ill, Mubarak arrived in a Cairo court on a stretcher, charged with the unlawful killing of protesters in the uprising and profiteering by abusing his position of power.[32] Mubarak's appearance in court was a defining event. For the first time in the Middle East, an Arab ruler was being held to account because of popular will. An Egyptian court found Mubarak guilty of complicity in the deaths 800 demonstrators during protests against his rule and sentenced him to life in prison.

In March 2012, Muhammad al-Zawahiri, Ayman's younger brother who was involved in al-Qaeda's Albania plot, was released from prison as part of an amnesty for many jihadists. This was a similar strategy that Sadat had employed in the 1970s, one that would eventually contribute to his assassination.[33] Personality-wise, Muhammad is very different to his elder brother. He has intense eyes and his face is encompassed by a long greyish beard, but unlike Ayman, Muhammad has a humorous side, often dark. He would often be seen smiling and laughing even during tense situations.[34]

Muhammad al-Zawahiri quickly became a prolific advocate for his brother and at the same time publicly condemned Western democracies and advocated al-Qaeda's doctrine. He would be surrounded by a large gathering of followers in Tahrir Square issuing fiery messages through a megaphone. He also was a regular fixture on Egyptian television and radio programmes and was willing to be interviewed by Western journalists.[35]

In May 2012, Egyptians went to the polls to take part in the nation's first free and transparent elections. By mid-June it was announced that Mohamed Morsi of the Freedom and Justice Party, the Muslim Brotherhood's political wing, attained a marginal win. Once thought unimaginable, Morsi, who opposed Mubarak and had been a political prisoner, became the democratically elected president. Morsi's election, preceded by the Freedom and Justice Party's victory in the January 2012 parliamentary elections, led to the writing of a new constitution based on Islamic tenets.[36] Despite the jubilation within Egypt, problems would quickly emerge with Morsi's governance. In November 2012, fearing that the constitutional court was going to reject an Islamist-slanted constitution that the Egyptian assembly had drafted, Morsi sent his spokesman to read a proclamation on television preventing any court from countering his decisions.[37] It effectively framed him as another Egyptian autocrat.

On 10 September 2012, in a video arranged for the eleventh anniversary of 9/11, al-Zawahiri called for attacks on Americans in Libya to avenge the death of senior al-Qaeda operative Abu Yahya al-Libi, who had been killed in a drone strike in Mir Ali, Pakistan, several months prior. An angry al-Zawahiri stated, 'His blood urges you and incites you to fight and kill the crusaders.'[38] The reality is that this video was likely a coded message for al-Qaeda and its allies and affiliates to launch audacious attacks on US interests in North Africa.

Upon hearing his brother's call to avenge the death of Abu Yahya al-Libi, Muhammad al-Zawahiri helped instigate a large-scale protest of around 2,000 people outside the US Embassy in Cairo the following day. The gathering included both EIJ veterans and the new generation of Egyptian jihadists. The most prominent was Rifai Ahmed Taha Musa, who was named as a signatory to al-Qaeda's 1998 *fatwa* announcing an Islamic Front for

Jihad against Jews and Crusaders. The mob, led by Muhammad al-Zawahiri, helped inflame the situation which led to the US Embassy's walls being breached. The American flag was ripped off the flagpole, set alight, and replaced with the 2007 flag that al-Fajr Media Centre produced for al-Qaeda, as protesters chanted, 'Obama, Obama, we're all Osama [bin Laden]!'[39]

The black banner was experiencing a revival as a symbol of Islamist resistance and dissent during the Arab Spring in Tunisia, Libya, and Egypt, where it was flown at political demonstrations during anti-Mubarak protests in Cairo. Crucially, this flag was a central symbol in the attempted takeover of the US Embassy in Cairo. As a result, the flag became a symbol of revolutionary jihadist protests in the Middle East and North Africa.[40]

The situation across North Africa was already tense following the release of an obscure but provocative short film titled *Innocence of Muslims* released on YouTube to maximise publicity. The low-budget and poorly acted portrayal of the Prophet Muhammad was bigoted propaganda designed to inflame. Although the video may have been a contributing factor to the US Embassy protests, Muhammad al-Zawahiri's actions were in fact premeditated and coordinated with Ayman al-Zawahiri.[41]

The role of al-Qaeda in the US Cairo embassy protests was later documented in a video released by al-Faroq Media. Although not an official media arm of al-Qaeda, al-Faroq embraced Ayman al-Zawahiri's doctrine. Al-Qaeda would even use clips from al-Faroq's productions in its own as-Sahab videos. Muhammad al-Zawahiri can be seen at the embassy rally in al-Faroq's video.[42] In fact, he admittedly helped stage the Cairo protest.[43] Despite not having physically seen each other since 1996, technology brought the al-Zawahiri brothers together for one of the most turbulent periods in Egypt.

Later, on the same day as the Cairo embassy attack, dozens of jihadists tied to al-Qaeda raided the US Consulate and the Central Intelligence Agency (CIA) annex in Benghazi, Libya. The guards at the consulate were five unarmed men facing 50-plus heavily armed fighters equipped with AK-47s, light and heavy machine guns, and RPGs. The attackers ordered them to open the pedestrian gate or be shot dead. In a series of attacks involving arson, small arms fire, machine-gun fire, and rocket-propelled grenades, US ambassador to Libya J. Christopher Stevens was killed, along with Foreign Service information management officer Sean Smith and former Navy SEALs Glen Doherty and Tyrone Woods.[44]

The Benghazi attack was not a random, spontaneous event. It was well planned, and much thought went into coordinating it. The plotters behind the Benghazi attack were not acting independently of al-Qaeda. Al-Zawahiri, without knowing the nuts and bolts of the operation, had been consulted head of time about organising an attack on US interests in Benghazi, for which he gave his consent.[45]

Fighters tied to Muhammad Jamal Abu Ahmad, an EIJ member who was an ally of both Ayman and Muhammad al-Zawahiri, played a key role in the Benghazi attack. Muhammad Jamal sought permission from al-Qaeda's leaders for permission for his Muhammad Jamal Network (MJN) to launch an attack on the US Consulate in conjunction with al-Qaeda in the Islamic Maghreb (AQIM). Liaising with the MJN was Muhammad al-Kashef, an EIJ military commander during the 1990s who remained loyal to Ayman al-Zawahiri whilst in prison. After al-Kashef's release he reached out to al-Zawahiri to establish new al-Qaeda affiliates in North Africa whilst solidifying efforts to cooperate with AQIM and al-Qaeda in the Arabian Peninsula (AQAP). Al-Zawahiri assigned him to lead the organization in Egypt and Libya, and Kashef established training camps in the latter. Some of his trainees took part in the Benghazi attack.[46]

As much as al-Zawahiri was fixated in seizing the advantage in Egypt and Libya by sowing disorder, he was equally interested in Tunisia, especially following the rise of the Ennahda movement, which in 2011 had won the first free election held in Tunisia since the country's independence in 1956. In a June 2012 video message, al-Zawahiri stated, 'They [Ennahda] are inventing an "Islam" that pleases the American Department of State, the European Union and the Gulf. . . . [T]he masks have fallen and the faces have been unveiled, so rise up to support your sharia. Incite your people on a popular uprising to support the *Shariah* and affirm Islam and rule with the *Qur'an*.'[47] Within days of the shocking events in Cairo and Benghazi, on 14 September, the US Embassy in Tunis also came under attack. It was led by Abu Ayyad al-Tunisi, who had conspired with al-Zawahiri 11 years previously to assassinate the Northern Alliance leader Ahmad Shah Massoud. The staff were able to seek refuge within the building, but the attackers raised the same black flag used by protesters at the US Embassy in Cairo.[48]

In the aftermath of 9/11, al-Tunisi had been found and arrested in Turkey before being extradited to Tunisia and imprisoned for terrorism-related activities. In February 2011, after the overthrow of Ben Ali, al-Tunisi was

freed under a general amnesty along with hundreds of other jihadist prisoners. Following his release, he created Ansar al-Sharia in Tunisia (AST).
The group retained allegiance to al-Qaeda and cooperated with its leadership.[49] The Libyan branch of AST was involved in the Benghazi operation,
aided by fighters from Egypt and Tunisia. Following the events at the US
Embassy in Tunis, al-Tunisi managed to evade capture.[50]

Al-Qaeda's direct involvement in the three plots demonstrated that its
command-and-control features were still strong.[51] The coordinated attacks
on the US missions were the biggest threats to the American diplomatic
presence since the simultaneous truck bomb attacks at the US Embassies in
Dar es Salaam and Nairobi in 1998, which al-Zawahiri was also involved in.

Aiding al-Qaeda and AQIM in Libya was al-Zawahiri ally Abu Anas al-
Libi, who had fled Manchester back in 2000 and travelled to al-Qaeda's
camps in Afghanistan. After Operation Enduring Freedom, al-Libi slipped
into Iran, where he remained for nearly nine years under the purview of
the Iranian authorities before being allowed to leave and seek sanctuary in
Pakistan. In 2010, under al-Zawahiri's guidance, al-Libi was appointed to al-
Qaeda's security committee. In March 2011, he requested permission to return to fight in the Libyan civil war against Qaddafi.[52] Another jihadist freed
from Iran was former al-Zawahiri protégé Thirwat Salah Shehata, who had
refused to align with al-Qaeda. Shehata and al-Libi both were involved in
training Libyan jihadists and working with al-Zawahiri.[53]

Al-Libi was captured by US commandos in Tripoli on 5 October 2013
in a raid and transferred to the United States to face trial for the embassy
bombings in Kenya and Tanzania in 1998. On 2 January 2015, al-Libi died
from liver cancer before his trial could commence.[54] In 2014, Shehata was
arrested in a Cairo suburb after smuggling himself into Egypt. He had previously been sentenced to death in absentia in the 1990s for an attempted
assassination of the former Egyptian prime minister Atef Sedky.[55]

Al-Qaeda were initially caught off guard by the Arab Spring and were
forced to develop a clear and consistent narrative to address the new realities. Ironically, their narrative carried more credibility under the Mubarak
regime, as there was a clear enemy they could identify. Al-Zawahiri was
unsure what would transpire in a post-Mubarak Egypt, but he cautioned
that real change would not take place unless Shariah law was properly institutionalised. In al-Zawahiri's seventh statement of 2011, he celebrated the
fall of Arab 'despots', as well as what he called 'the defeats of their master

America', such as 9/11 and the withdrawals of US troops from Iraq and the reduction of American forces in Afghanistan. He added that the Libyans should move quickly to establish Shariah law:

> Be careful of the plots of the West and its agents as you are building your new state and do not allow them to trick you and steal your sacrifices and suffering.... [B]e sure to take the first, most important step for reform and apply *Shariah*.... If the West talks about extremists and militants, they are talking about the honest and the free who defend their religion, sanctities, families, and countries.[56]

Al-Zawahiri was clearly determined to contest the charge that al-Qaeda had lost influence during the Arab Spring. Effectively, he was claiming that his work over the previous two decades had set the conditions for Mubarak's removal. Al-Zawahiri also sought to craft a narrative of the Arab Spring as only the first revolution in a greater struggle that would eventually usher Islam to its rightful paramount place in society.

In 2013, protests soon erupted over Morsi's rule, with some turning violent between the president's opponents and supporters. At the same time, food prices and unemployment began to rise. General Abdel Fattah el-Sisi, who had been appointed by Morsi as Egyptian defence minister and head of the armed forces, made a disconcerting address, warning that the military would intervene if the demonstrations continued to paralyse Egypt.[57] Days later, el-Sisi, supported by the military, deposed Morsi.[58] Within a year, he became the next Egyptian president, winning 96% of the vote. Morsi was imprisoned, the Muslim Brotherhood were banned along with several other Islamist groups, and protests were crushed.[59] There was a strong sense of déjà vu with what unfolded following the assassination of Anwar Sadat.[60]

Al-Zawahiri often reflected upon the downfall of Mohamed Morsi and considered his demise a mistake of the Muslim Brotherhood's ongoing attempt to find a compromise with non-Islamist sections of the Egyptian state, such as the military. This approach failed Morsi and resulted in the old politics being reinstated without much protestation from Western countries. Al-Zawahiri elaborated on Morsi's downfall in 'Glad Tidings of Victory to Our People in Egypt', which he saw as an opportunity to promote 'new beginnings'. He also pointed out that Morsi could never be 'the hope of the Islamic Community' because he was willing to take part in man-made politics which undermined the goal creating a caliphate and imposition of Shariah.[61]

Al-Qaeda saw the Arab Spring as a 'historical opportunity'.[62] Al-Zawahiri cunningly anticipated that the political and social turmoil of the post-revolutionary environment could be further exploited by introducing al-Qaeda's ideology to new generations disillusioned with the lack of change under el-Sisi and the return to the status quo. Even after Morsi was overthrown, al-Qaeda sought to promote the narrative that the Egyptian military regime of el-Sisi continued the 'apostate' status quo of the Mubarak regime.[63]

What was quite unique about al-Zawahiri was his ability to take lessons from Islamic history to teach his followers and learn from the mistakes of the past against perceived enemies. The Arab Spring was a period which al-Zawahiri tended to highlight as an 'abject failure in Islamic history'.[64] In various speeches he argued that the Arab Spring uprisings failed because they tried to make meaningful incremental changes within the framework of the nation-state and bring religion to the fore. Instead, they should have enforced a wholesale radical 'purification' by launching coordinated jihadist revolutions that respected no frontier, violently uprooted the old order, and implemented the Shariah. Al-Zawahiri urged his followers to 'reflect thoroughly on these bitter experiences, let us learn from where the enemy was able to rally against these mighty revolutions'.[65] The lesson for al-Qaeda here was that, without violent revolution, Islamist politics would not have any opportunity for success. But equally, if one refuses to learn from these experiences, progress will be stunted.

In April 2015, Morsi was convicted for inciting violence outside the presidential palace and sentenced to 20 years in prison.[66] A year later, he was handed a life sentence for allegedly passing state secrets to Qatar.[67] Appeals and counter-appeals were filed, but then on 17 April 2019, Egyptian state television announced that Morsi had collapsed during a court inquiry on espionage charges at Cairo's infamous Mazra'at Tora Prison. He was pronounced dead of a heart attack.[68] Suspicions and accusations abound over the prison conditions Morsi had to endure. They provided ample reason for the Islamists to describe Morsi as a *shaheed*.

Separately, in 2015, Mubarak was sentenced to three years in prison and fined after a court found him guilty of corruption.[69] However, on 2 March 2017, Egypt's appeals court acquitted Mubarak of conspiring to kill protesters during the 2011 revolution. He was released from prison in 2017. Mubarak returned to his residence in the prosperous northern suburb of

Heliopolis.[70] Three years later, Mubarak died and was accorded a military burial. Al-Zawahiri had outlasted and survived his nemesis, a fact that would not have been lost on the Egyptian ideologue and teacher.

However, events in Egypt curtailed hopes that political and military leaders would answer for corruption and suppression of civil liberties. They would also be used as propaganda by terrorist groups to illustrate the corruption within the Egyptian establishment and the incompatibility of democracy and transparency with man-made laws. In April 2019, Egypt held a referendum on constitutional amendments allowing el-Sisi to remain in power until 2030, as well as broadening the power of the military in civilian affairs and undermining judicial independence. El-Sisi also reimposed the state of emergency that had been removed following the Arab Spring.[71] At the time, faculty members favoured greater independence such as electing the grand imam of al-Azhar instead of being appointed government.[72] The seminary issued the *Al-Azhar Document*, an 11-point programme recommending institutional changes and greater transparency.[73] However, the recommendations were not taken onboard, and al-Azhar remained under strict government oversight by the el-Sisi regime.

Geronimo EKIA

Following the September 11 attacks, there were $25 million rewards for information that led to the whereabouts of both bin Laden and al-Zawahiri through the Rewards for Justice (RFJ) programme which was created through the 1984 Act to Combat International Terrorism. The programme is administered by the US Department of State's Diplomatic Security Service (DSS).[74]

The RFJ programme was partly intended to recompense people who provided actionable information leading to the capture of terrorists who have planned or committed attacks against US targets. It sanctioned a 'favourable resolution', which meant a military operation resulting in the death of the terrorist. Equally important, it was also designed to obtain information that prevents future plots from occurring. The law enables those willing to provide tangible information to become part of the US Department of Justice witness protection programme to ensure their safety.[75] Originally, the rewards were up to $500,000. That amount was increased to $1 million in

1990. The RFJ programme gained the ability to offer large payments such as $25 million for al-Zawahiri under the 2001 Patriot Act, which was passed after the 9/11 attacks on 26 October 2001.[76]

The RFJ programme was utilised in the February 1995 capture of Ramzi Yousef in Pakistan. He was the bombmaker in the 1993 World Trade Center bombing and the nephew of 9/11 planner Khalid Shaikh Mohammed.[77] In June 1997, the RFJ was successfully used to encourage Pakistani tribesmen to turn in Mir Amal Kansi, who shot two people dead and injured several outside the CIA headquarters in Langley, Virginia, in 1993.[78] Much of the RFJ reward money was paid out in Iraq, such as the information that led to the discovery of Saddam Hussein's sons, Uday and Qusay, who were valued at $15 million each. Although a $25 million reward was offered for Saddam Hussein, it was not authorised when he was apprehended because the information that led to his capture came under duress and from several people.[79] Al-Zawahiri remained the last individual who had the $25 million dollar bounty and although that amount may not seem as significant now as it was back in 2001, partly because of inflation, there is no other individual that had a bounty anywhere near as close.

For the largest reward to be sanctioned such as that offered for al-Zawahiri or bin Laden, a case must be made to an interagency rewards programme committee chaired by the director of the DSS. The committee includes members of the Department of Justice, the Federal Bureau of Investigation (FBI), the National Security Council, the CIA, the Department of Defense, the Department of the Treasury, and the Department of Homeland Security. The secretary of state must personally authorise any reward offer exceeding $5 million. Separately, the CIA also has specially designated funds that can be used as payments for intelligence leading to a prominent terrorist.[80] Despite widespread interagency support. both bin Laden and al-Zawahiri managed to elude the spotlight. However, things were about to change.

On the night of 1 May 2011, two stealth Black Hawks and two Chinooks left Jalalabad Airfield in eastern Afghanistan and entered Pakistani airspace flying low and fast to evade the low-altitude radar system. They were carrying Navy SEALs from Team Six, also known as also known as the Naval Special Warfare Development Group (DEVGRU). They were tasked with a high-risk career-defining covert mission, code-named Operation Neptune Spear, to kill a terrorist in Pakistan who for the mission was named 'Geronimo'.[81] The person in question was Osama bin Laden. To do get to him, they would have to target the al-Qaeda leader in his safe haven located in an urban centre in Pakistan.

The specific destination for DEVGRU was a compound in the small town of Abbottabad, about 60 miles north of Islamabad, Pakistan's capital. Abbottabad, part of the Hazara region, is also the home of the prestigious Pakistan Military Academy, Pakistan's version of West Point or Sandhurst. It is a town bristling with security facilities, including an ISI intelligence cen-tre.[82] Bin Laden's compound was only 92 metres from the military academy and 3 miles from a Pakistani infantry battalion. It was little wonder that of-ficials in the Obama administration had grave concerns that senior elements within the country's military and intelligence echelons could be protecting bin Laden. Therefore, every safeguard had to be factored in to ensure the Pakistanis did not learn what the United States was planning.

Under Leon Panetta, who had been made the director of the CIA in 2009, all efforts were made to intensify intelligence-collection to track bin Laden and al-Zawahiri, especially after the attack on the CIA personal at Forward Base Chapman in Khost. As Secretary Panetta stated, 'What hap-pened at Khost was tragic but it became a tremendous inspiration to the CIA and to the military, to not stop the mission of going after bin Laden, al-Qaeda, and those involved in 9/11.'[83] Almost 10 years after September 11, every previous lead had come to a dead end for both High Value Target (HVT) One, bin Laden, and HVT Two, al-Zawahiri, who had been able to turn the tables on the CIA.[84]

Under Panetta, a task force was created to find the al-Qaeda leaders, and in August 2010, CIA analysts identified two of bin Laden's couriers and tracked them to the Pakistani town of Abbottabad visiting what they initially described as a 'fortress' with very few windows. The large con-crete compound in Abbottabad lacked a phone or internet connection. Twelve-foot-high walls at the front were shadowed by 18-foot-high walls in the rear, and the compound was entirely encircled in barbed wire. There was also a 7-foot wall on the third floor where a 'mysterious family' was living. Bin Laden's compound was set on a hilltop at the end of a narrow dirt road, and it was three times bigger than any other building in the area.[85] Bin Laden had lived there since 2005, when it was built. The only access was through two security gates. There was clear emphasis on privacy.[86]

Panetta ordered around-the-clock surveillance of the compound for any comings and goings, especially after the couriers were found travelling 90 miles away to make phone calls.[87] To ascertain further that it was bin Laden at the compound, a Pakistani doctor, Shakil Afridi, was recruited to assist. Afridi had been involved in various US funded vaccination programmes, and under the guise of conducting a hepatitis B vaccination drive Afridi managed to obtain the blood of one of bin Laden's children. He was able to confirm to the Americans that bin Laden was staying there as well as sections of the internal layout.[88] From that moment, Operation Neptune Spear was given the green light.[89] The highly tactical plan used red-teaming, where a group assembling the strategy adopts the role of an enemy engaging in full-scope, multi-layered attack simulation, which in Abbottabad could end up being those protecting bin Laden or even the Pakistani military.[90] Within the Obama administration opinions were divided on whether the operation would work, including opposition from Vice President Joe Biden. Ultimately, the sage advice of Secretary Panetta prevailed:

> When the president asked me what I thought, I said, 'Mr. President, I have an old formula I used when I was in Congress, which was when I was facing a tough decision, pretend I was talking to an average citizen in my district and saying, if you knew what I knew about this issue, what would you do? And that helped me make decisions. In this instance, if I told the average citizen that we had the best evidence on the location of bin Laden since Tora Bora, I think they would say we have to go. And that's what I'm recommending to you, Mr. President.'[91]

As the Black Hawk helicopters entered Pakistan's airspace, they managed to evade detection by the Pakistani military. The engine on one of the Blackhawks stalled in close proximity to the compound and its tail hit one of the walls.[92] Upon entering the Abbottabad compound, the SEALs moved with stealth and began checking every inch of the ground floor of the main house. They then proceeded up the stairs and chanced upon bin Laden's son, Khalid, carrying an AK-47. The SEALs shot and killed him.[93] After climbing another set of stairs, the SEALs confronted a tall man peering out from behind a door. It was Osama bin Laden, HVT One. The SEAL pinpointed the laser of his M4 on bin Laden's chest and shot him dead.[94] The outcome was relayed to the US officials who had been monitoring events unfold, 'For God and country, Geronimo, Geronimo, Geronimo EKIA [enemy killed in action].'[95]

Two other SEALs unfurled a nylon body bag and placed the body of bin Laden inside the bag. Stage 1 of Operation Neptune Spear was complete. Stage 2 of the mission focused on intelligence gathering from the

Abbottabad compound. With plastic bags, the SEALS scoured the compound for 45 minutes, collecting documents, CDs, DVDs, computers, hard drives, and more than 150 storage devices that held some 15,000 documents and close to 25,000 videos.[96] The helicopters landed back in Jalalabad around 3 a.m. the following day. Bin Laden's corpse was sent to Bagram and then flown to the aircraft carrier the USS *Carl Vinson* in the Arabian Sea, off the Pakistani coast. His body was then buried at sea to avoid a shrine being made for him by his followers.[97] Just like that, the world's most wanted terrorist became a footnote. Bin Laden's death provided an important moment for counter-terrorism as the head of al-Qaeda and author of numerous terrorist attacks, including 9/11, had been eliminated. Killing bin Laden was an important milestone, but it was more symbolic than impactful, more tactical than strategic, and it did not mean an end to al-Qaeda or global terrorism.

Nine years, seven months, and twenty days after 9/11, the United States finally were able to locate and eliminate bin Laden. The operation was the result of enormous interagency cooperation, including the CIA and the Department of Defense as well as the often unheralded National Geospatial-Intelligence Agency (NGA). The NGA combines several fundamental intelligence roles, including rendering imagery from satellites and drones.[98] Through this, the NGA can ascertain from great distances what an object or a building is made from. It also conducts complex assessment of human characteristics: gender, body size and shape, as well as pioneering facial recognition. This enabled the planners of the Abbottabad raid to make very accurate assessments of the number of people who lived inside the compound.[99]

Such was the level of technology and sophistication at the disposal of the United States that it makes it even more remarkable that with all these tools, al-Zawahiri was able to remain elusive. HVT Two, al-Zawahiri, was still at large. Al-Zawahiri clearly took fewer risks than bin Laden—a hallmark of his obsession with self-preservation. According to Douglas London, who was a CIA chief of station handling the threat of al-Qaeda, 'Al-Zawahiri has been a priority and it's hard to determine with absolute confidence how he has evaded capture all these years. But his long-standing focus on security and tradecraft in communications and limits on those with whom he surrounds himself are significant factors.'[100]

In 2005, this author had publicly stated, 'We have to look at the fact that since September 11, the leading members or figures of al-Qaeda have all been caught inside Pakistan.'[101] This concern was expressed countless times prior and thereafter; it was believed that al-Zawahiri too was hiding within Pakistan. The success of the bin Laden operation raised a debate within the military and intelligence communities whether other terrorists worth daring another commando raid were in a Pakistani city, such as Ayman al-Zawahiri.

However, according to Ambassador Henry Crumpton, 'After Osama bin Laden was killed, that took some of the political pressure off. And al-Zawahiri had less communications links, which means less exposure, and you become a less viable intelligence target or intelligence opportunity. If he is entirely isolated, there's very little signature, and therefore it's just much more difficult from an intelligence perspective.'[102] Furthermore, individuals who might be induced by the cash rewards, such as from the RFJ programme, require protection against reprisal not only from the terrorist groups but also from the governments they live under. The medical doctor, Shakil Afridi, who helped locate Osama bin Laden in Abbottabad, was accused of high treason by the Pakistani establishment and has remained incarcerated.[103]

The initial shock and humiliation caused by the Abbottabad operation soon turned into anger and humiliation within Pakistan's military ranks as well as global suspicion that they had never been a genuine ally against al-Qaeda. This should never have been very surprising. Even before bin Laden's death, the town of Abbottabad carried enormous significance in terms of the murky relationship between the Pakistan military and the terrorists that inhabit the country.

Bin Laden had been living in his Abbottabad abode near the Pakistan Military Academy since around 2005–2006. Interestingly, the time overlaps with the appointment of General Nadeem Taj as commandant of the academy. Taj was a close confidant of the then–military ruler of Pakistan General Pervez Musharraf and was with Musharraf on the airplane that was refused entry into Pakistani airspace in 1999 by then–prime minister Nawaz Sharif. This sparked the military coup which facilitated Musharraf's seizure of power.[104]

Taj knew the town of Abbottabad very well, including who travelled through it, and he even permitted a number of jihadists to situate themselves in Abbottabad as a transit hub which links Pakistan, Kashmir, Khyber Pakhtunkhwa, and Punjab. This included al-Zawahiri and bin Laden allies like Hafiz Saeed, the leader of the Lashkar-e-Taiba (LeT), and Maulana Masood Azhar, the leader of the Jaish-e-Mohammed (JeM). Aside from

Abbottabad, the Hazara region includes the town of Mansehra, where many of the British-Pakistanis behind al-Qaeda's plots in the United Kingdom were trained.[105] Cell phones retrieved from bin Laden's compound had the contact details for senior terrorists belonging to Harkat-ul-Mujahidin (HuM), JeM, and LeT, all of them being Pakistani jihadi group affiliated with al-Qaeda which also had close ties to the ISI.[106] After serving as commandant of the Pakistan Military Academy, Taj was appointed as the director general of the ISI by Musharraf, but he was forced to step down in 2008 under pressure from the United States because of his ties with terrorist groups.[107]

Since the discovery of bin Laden in Abbottabad, the spotlight also fell on former Pakistani military ruler Pervez Musharraf and how much both he and Taj knew about al-Qaeda's whereabouts in the urban centres of Pakistan. Musharraf had been provided with information in 2007 by the Afghan government about al-Qaeda's activities in Pakistan but rejected it. According to Amrullah Saleh, who at the time was the director of the Afghan National Directorate of Security (NDS):

> I provided evidence directly to President Musharraf in 2007. I said, 'Mr. President, we are seeing a lot of al-Qaeda in the Hazara region of Pakistan.' He banged the table and stood up physically to start a fistfight with me, and President Karzai told him, 'I am your counterpart, Mr. President, calm down.' Now you see they found bin Laden in Abbottabad eventually.[108]

Musharraf's own memoir, *In the Line of Fire*, written whilst he was still both the head of the military and president of Pakistan, is also a key source of inadvertent information. He acknowledged Abbottabad was an al-Qaeda hub and described how the Pakistani army was tracking but failed to apprehend al-Qaeda operational planner Abu Faraj al-Libbi in the Hazara region in April 2004:

> The second miss was again in Abbotabad [sic]. We were tipped off that someone important in al-Qaeda was living in a house there, and that someone else, also very important, someone we were looking for, was supposed to come and meet him. We did not know that the second someone was Abu Faraj al-Libbi.[109]

Al-Libbi was eventually apprehended in Mardan in May 2005, at a mosque in Khyber Pakhtunkhwa province, Pakistan, which got al-Zawahiri's attention. He considered it important enough to comment to al-Zarqawi in an intercepted message of October 2005. Al-Zawahiri wrote with some concern:

> The enemy struck a blow against us with the arrest of Abu al-Faraj, may Allah break his bonds. However, no Arab brother was arrested because of him. The brothers tried, and were successful to a great degree, to contain the fall of Abu al-Faraj as much as they could. . . . [Abu al-Faraj] was lured by one of his brothers, who had been taken into custody, to meet him at a public location where a trap had been set.[110]

What al-Zawahiri did not know at the time was that the actual hunt for bin Laden started in 2005 when Abu Faraj al-Libbi, whilst being held at Guantanamo Bay, provided the nickname for bin Laden's most trusted courier, Maulawi Abd al-Khaliq Jan. It took another 12 months to unearth the man's identity, and it was not until 2009 that it could be established that he was situated near Islamabad and Rawalpindi. The fact that the courier was performing his tasks with relative freedom near the Pakistani capital and the military headquarters convinced US intelligence officials that al-Libbi may have been protected by the ISI. Leon Panetta, who was made US Defense Secretary after the Abbottabad raid, pointed out, 'When we were doing surveillance, a Pakistani military helicopter actually went right over the compound. So, I have to believe that they were aware that something was happening at that compound.'[111] This underlined the US conclusion not to share information with the Pakistanis.

The killing of bin Laden served as a kind of breaking point for the trust between the United States and Pakistan. Pakistan had repeatedly insisted that bin Laden was not in their territory, but he was in fact hiding there comfortably.[112] After the raid, the ISI adopted a campaign of intimidation against the US diplomatic presence in Pakistan. They aggressively stopped consular motorcades and confiscated weapons used for the protection of American diplomats. They also intimidated Pakistanis who worked for the US Embassy and consulates in Pakistan. Perhaps most egregiously, they would have Pakistani newspapers publish the names of American diplomats travelling to Pakistan and label them as CIA agents or part of private military organizations.[113]

It was becoming very hard for the US intelligence and law enforcement community to operate on the ground in Pakistan. Ironically, the biggest beneficiary of the Abbottabad operation was al-Zawahiri. Not because he was the most likely successor of al-Qaeda but more because the United States had used its one-time covert operations card in Pakistan to kill bin

Laden and would now end up with even less cooperation from the Pakistani military than before.

From Deputy to Leader

In the coming weeks, a US task force scrutinised the files which illustrated that despite being logistically separated from the other al-Qaeda commanders, bin Laden had remained intrinsically involved in the group's operational activities. The information obtained from bin Laden's Abbottabad compound helped the United States identify, evaluate, and monitor senior members of al-Qaeda including Abu Yahya al-Libi, Ilyas Kashmiri, Anwar al-Awlaki, Saeed al-Shehri, Abu Yahya al-Libi, Atiyah Abd al-Rahman, and Abu Zaid al-Kuwaiti.[114]

Yet al-Zawahiri remained at large, partly because he remained physically separate from bin Laden's communication apparatus. Inadvertently, the elimination of al-Qaeda figures close to bin Laden would only serve to strengthen al-Zawahiri's hand within al-Qaeda. In the aftermath of bin Laden's death, Ilyas Kashmiri was appointed by al-Zawahiri to be part of a 'special operations council' alongside Saif al-Adel.[115] However, on 3 June 2011, Kashmiri was killed in a US drone attack at a village near Wana, South Waziristan, Pakistan.[116]

Despite much chatter on the web forums, al-Qaeda's leadership did not comment on bin Laden's death, nor did they announce who was taking over despite the general belief that al-Zawahiri would assume the mantle. On 8 June 2011, al-Zawahiri finally ended a month's silence by releasing a video message in which he swore vengeance for bin Laden's death-'blood for blood'. Seething, al-Zawahiri used a chopping gesture with his hands and asked his followers to remember the 9/11 attacks against the United States, saying the attack 'destroyed the symbol of American economy in New York and the symbol of American military might in the Pentagon'.[117]

Al-Zawahiri also highlighted one of bin Laden's apparent achievements and objectives, above all others, which was motivating the *ummah*. He argued, '[Bin Laden's] message reached from East to West and all over the world ... al-Qaeda is a mission before it is an organization or a group.'[118] Speaking in a measured tone, al-Zawahiri denounced the Americans for the 'un-Islamic' burial of his former leader at sea. Controversially, his invective that Obama was a traitor to Islam was laced with antisemitic tropes: 'the compromised Islam of America, the Islam of Obama who sold his father's religion, became a Christian and prayed like the Jews to gain favour with the rich and powerful'.[119] He added, 'The *Shaykh* [bin Laden] has departed, may Allah have mercy on him, to his Allah as a *shaheed* [martyr] and we must continue on his path of jihad to expel the invaders from the land of Muslims and to purify it from injustice.'[120]

Al-Zawahiri did not proclaim himself as the new leader of al-Qaeda, but his attitude and words suggested he had assumed the terrorist mantle to succeed bin Laden. He urged al-Qaeda's followers to emulate those in Egypt, Tunisia, Libya, and Syria seeking to overthrow their governments.[121] During this period, al-Zawahiri was thinking ahead about finding ways to prioritise against the 'internal enemy'. As result, he sent veteran al-Qaeda fighters to eastern Syria to set up a jihadist movement with like-minded Syrians against the Bashar al-Assad regime in the nascent Syrian civil war.[122]

Soon after, al-Qaeda issued a formal statement announcing al-Zawahiri's appointment as their new *amir*. Posted on a jihadist blog and attributed to al-Qaeda's General Command, it stated, '*Shaykh* Dr Ayman al-Zawahiri, may Allah guide him, assumed responsibility as the group's Amir [leader].'[123] The time lag may have been an indicator that there were some disputes within al-Qaeda over al-Zawahiri's claim to the leadership, but more likely it reflected the challenges in logistics in getting his endorsement from the leadership dregs hidden across Pakistan and the rest of the Islamic world. Al-Zawahiri had been seen in some militant quarters as a micromanager unwilling to delegate responsibilities. He also did not carry the same level of respect and influence that bin Laden had.

Clearly, to try to halt the speculation of any perceived opposition to al-Zawahiri's appointment as the head of al-Qaeda, several jihadist factions offered their loyalty to him, albeit somewhat late. However, the number of responses was rather small, and the level of discourse was superficial. On 7 July 2011, al-Qaeda in the Islamic Maghreb (AQIM) released the audio of an interview with Shaykh Abu 'Ubayda Yousef al-'Annabi, part of the AQIM's Shariah Council. In the interview, Abu 'Ubayda pledged allegiance on behalf of AQIM to al-Zawahiri. However, one should note that the AQIM oath taking was not made by the organization's *emir*, Abdelmalek Droukdel.[124]

On 26 July 2011, Nasir al-Wuhayshi, the leader of al-Qaeda in the Arabian Peninsula (AQAP), pledged his *ba'yah* to al-Zawahiri in an audio message released on jihadist forums: 'I give you allegiance of obedience in good and hard times, in ease and difficulty and in fighting the enemies of Allah as much as I can—myself and your loyal soldiers who are with me [on] the Arabian Peninsula.'[125] In the sixth issue of al-Qaeda's English-language online publication, *Inspire*, the magazine's editor, Yahya Ibrahim, also referenced to al-Zawahiri's appointment: 'Now *Shaykh* Ayman carries the banner. He had been at the forefront of Islamic work and now would lead the organization he helped found. We ask Allah to assist *Shaykh* Ayman in this great task.'[126] Bin Laden's death left al-Zawahiri burdened with a greater sense of responsibility for the future of the global jihadist movement. Even prior to his death, bin Laden's own actions were negatively impacting upon al-Qaeda and left no resources behind for al-Zawahiri and his contemporaries.

The Abbottabad Documents

Over the years, the Office of the Director for National Intelligence (DNI) gradually began a declassification process by releasing a trove of information concerning Osama bin Laden and other senior members of al-Qaeda seized amidst the raid that killed bin Laden in Abbottabad in 2011. Files included tens of thousands of image and text files as well as audio and video files. These files date between 2003 to 2011, but the precise time frame is unknown, as most items are missing their dates. Some of the letters are incomplete, and not all letters explicitly identify their correspondents. Some were also handwritten letters.

The Abbottabad documents revealed in laborious detail the tensions within al-Qaeda's external networks, including finding capable operatives and searching for resources to plot and plan. Many of the letters were pertinent to al-Zawahiri, which showed both his frustration with regional jihadi groups and the inability to exercise control or communicate effectively among all sides. When al-Zawahiri was discussed by other members of al-Qaeda, there appeared to be a direct split in opinion. Some praised him for his knowledge and influence as a scholar, whereas others tended to chide him for his various faults.

The Abbottabad documents presented a complicated story of a terrorist organization struggling with living in the shadows with its leadership scattered across Pakistan. We also learn from the letters that bin Laden was effectively off the radar after 9/11 to even his al-Qaeda colleagues, and he did not regain command until 2004. Till that point, al-Zawahiri was directing the terror networks operations and propaganda which we now know involved the plots to target European countries including 7/7. When bin Laden resumed contact with al-Qaeda, he was eager to renew the terrorist plots against the West, but he faced recriminations from his associates who felt abandoned mostly by bin Laden and to a lesser extent al-Zawahiri.[127]

Al-Zawahiri had also written some letters to bin Laden advising him on changes to be made within al-Qaeda, complicated by the irregular correspondence. He discussed the terrorist group's day-to-day strategies, tactics, targets, and funding. Despite this, al-Zawahiri was highly valued by bin Laden. When bin Laden resurfaced in 2004, he made it clear that al-Zawahiri must be protected at all costs. Overall, these documents demonstrated that al-Zawahiri was a key player in working behind the scenes of al-Qaeda and effective in presenting his group as the only effective jihadist movement. In fact, in terms of shaping al-Qaeda strategy, the documents reveal that whilst bin Laden was still very much in contact with al-Qaeda operatives around the world, even before his death in 2011, it was al-Zawahiri who was chiefly responsible for making major decisions.

As the Abbottabad documents strenuously demonstrated, al-Zawahiri's ability to play the long game preserved the option of al-Qaeda becoming a serious threat in the future.[128] The papers also reveal that al-Zawahiri was leveraging his control of al-Qaeda's organization long before bin Laden's death. In one letter thought to be written by al-Zawahiri to bin Laden using aliases, the author claimed it was 'very essential for al-Qaeda to confirm and declare its linkage with its branches'[129] and urged bin Laden to announce al-Qaeda's formal relationship with the Somalian al-Shabaab. Bin Laden never formally solidified them as an affiliate of al-Qaeda, despite a myriad of requests from al-Shabaab's leadership. Bin Laden wanted to maintain the association underground to thwart further American mobilisation against al-Shabaab, whilst enabling the free flow of donations to support the group.[130] Bin Laden also did not see the group as having the same standing as the other al-Qaeda affiliates. However, after bin Laden's death, al-Zawahiri formally recognised al-Shabaab in Somalia as an al-Qaeda affiliate in February 2012.[131] The decision directly countermanded bin Laden's position.

Under bin Laden, al-Qaeda had traditionally set more specific and nuanced caveats before creating a formal alliance with any group and its leaders. There was a rigid hierarchical approach. Bin Laden was concerned about lending al-Qaeda's name to other groups over which al-Qaeda's

Shura Council could not maintain control, especially after the debacle with al-Zarqawi.[132] Ironically, al-Zawahiri, who once had a reputation of being bureaucratic and traditional on issues like a ba'yah, had evolved his approach, adjusting with the challenges and threats al-Qaeda was facing. Effectively, al-Zawahiri advocated a template that began with a citation from the Qur'an or Hadith. It would then go on to a statement of unconditional loyalty by the jihadist on behalf of the group he represented.[133] A common template would resemble the following:

> To our Shaykh and our Emir, Abu Muhammad Ayman al-Zawahiri, I pledge my allegiance to you, will obey you at all times, and will not dispute your orders. And I pledge you to jihad for the sake of Allah, to establish the law of Allah on the earth, and this allegiance from me and all my brothers in Al-Qaeda . . .[134]

Al-Zawahiri wanted to shore up al-Qaeda's allies amidst mounting fears that al-Qaeda in Iraq (AQI) would damage al-Qaeda's movement through its campaign to eliminate non-Sunni Muslims. According to the Abbottabad documents, bin Laden was cautious in bringing affiliates under the umbrella of al-Qaeda whilst his second in command saw an opportunity to 'protect' the al-Qaeda movement.

It was also probable that al-Zawahiri saw a chance to shift al-Qaeda's focus to 'internal enemy' battles through its links with affiliates. It was apparent that these tensions were felt throughout the organization and that al-Qaeda operatives as far away as Saudi Arabia were aware that al-Zawahiri was asserting his authority. In many ways this displays al-Zawahiri's prescience. He knew that to maintain its relevance, al-Qaeda would need to mould its strategy and rhetoric to focus on local battles in the Muslim world whilst refraining from damaging its public image through identifying with groups that killed Muslims.

A good example of this was al-Zawahiri's 'change of heart' in regard to the Taliban. Previously, al-Zawahiri was hesitant to cultivate close ties with the organization and even lobbied against bin Laden's pledge of ba'yah to Mullah Omar. However, as al-Qaeda amir, al-Zawahiri realised that al-Qaeda could not survive in Afghanistan without the Taliban's continued protection. As a result, al-Zawahiri's rhetoric continually mentioned and praised the Taliban, and he never missed an opportunity to show al-Qaeda's support of its goal of establishing itself throughout Central Asia.

Some of the Abbottabad documents show that al-Qaeda's relationship
with its affiliates had problems over leadership and direction. Some senior
al-Qaeda leaders wanted to keep their distance from their jihadist allies.
Others believed that including regional groups would help al-Qaeda's expansion within the *ummah*. Bin Laden was open to having channels of
communication with these groups, to advise and provide guidance, but
at the same time he was hesitant to deepen relationships with affiliates
and urged constraint in that regard. Al-Zawahiri was somewhere in the
middle. During the mid-2000s, al-Zawahiri was pivotal in establishing franchise status with al-Qaeda for AQIM and AQAP without bin Laden's un-
equivocal support.[135]

In a letter to bin Laden, al-Zawahiri advised that al-Qaeda should take
on more branches and affirm their affiliates: 'Al Qaeda needs to confirm
and declare its linkages with its branches, in order to become a reported
fact.'[136] He believed this was necessary in case they were later pressured to
announce their disassociation. An example was a dispute over the connection with the Somali jihadi group, al-Shabaab.

However, in an August 2010 letter to al-Shabab leader Mukhtar al-
Zubayr, bin Laden declined his proposal to combine with al-Qaeda, preferring to 'say that there is a relationship with al-Qaeda which is simply
a brotherly Islamic connection and nothing more'.[137] Four months after
this, al-Zawahiri sent this letter pressuring bin Laden to reconsider: 'Please
reconsider your opinion not to declare the accession of the brothers of
Somalia.'[138] The rationale behind al-Zawahiri's critique was that if the leadership did not declare which groups are affiliates, then anybody can claim
to be al-Qaeda.

However, having such affiliates did not come without obstacles. One
al-Shabab member undermined al-Zawahiri's leadership in 2007, stating,
'We're not [al Qaeda]. . . . And if al-Zawahiri says [our] people should do
this or that, it could be wrong. He is not from here.'[139] Furthermore, in
2011, one of al-Shabab's leaders, Harun Fazul, did not view al-Zawahiri as
bin Laden's legitimate successor and considered EIJ and al Qaeda to be two
separate entities. In early June 2011, around one month after bin Laden was
killed, Fazul was murdered in Somalia. Some believe that this was a hit orchestrated by al-Zawahiri himself, as al-Shabab conveniently proceeded to
pledge *ba'yah* to the new al-Qaeda leader shortly thereafter.[140] This sheds
light on the February 2012 merger of al-Qaeda and al-Shabab, eight months

after bin Laden's death and al-Zawahiri ascent to power, illustrating a shift at al-Zawahiri's behest.[141]

Al-Zawahiri was not entirely satisfied. In one letter, the tone with which al-Zawahiri addressed bin Laden was far more direct and instructive than expected. The letter was composed of a list of issues which al-Zawahiri wanted bin Laden 'to look into carefully'. At the end of the letter he instructed bin Laden to 'please destroy the letter after reading it', an instruction which was obviously ignored.[142] Al-Zawahiri's concern was that 'al-Qaeda has become a broad field; each can enter to declare his allegiance, does not wait to see whether he has been accepted or not'.[143] He feared that the organization had become vague in its membership requirements which threatened their control. He thus urged his resolution to bin Laden, 'Therefore, starting from now, please think about controlling the matter with a system that deals with people, each according to his religion, piety and contribution.'[144]

The words deferred to bin Laden's role as the movement's 'thinker' whilst at the same time the tone was directive, the phrase 'starting from now', indicates not only a sense of urgency in the command but also a sense of hierarchy, as al-Zawahiri gave bin Laden a time frame to begin working from. This tells us that within al-Qaeda, al-Zawahiri was a key advocate for maintaining a close working relationship with affiliate groups and was crucial to the change in the organization's strategy. For him, if they were to win battles, al-Qaeda and its affiliates must secure sanctuaries across the Islamic world.

This strategy towards al-Qaeda's affiliates was supported by the document 'Addendum to the Report of the Islamic Maghreb', which described the battle between al-Qaeda and supporters in Algeria and the unnamed 'foe'.[145] Here, the writer, Salih al-Mauritani of the AQIM, strongly promoted al-Zawahiri's 'unity project'. Al-Mauritani described the situation before al-Zawahiri's intervention as one 'of desolation and weakness affecting their souls' with the brothers in Algeria fighting a losing battle.[146] But after al-Zawahiri introduced this 'unity project', al-Mauritani described how the brothers regained their strength and were waging a more advantageous battle:

> The morale of the foe dropped as they suffered throughout all these years from the brothers. When they believed they could eradicate them in the

reconciliation project, the brothers came with the most dangerous unity being with *Shaykh* Usamah Bin Laden, Dr. Ayman Al-Zawahiri.[147]

One can see al-Zawahiri's intervention in the Maghreb as being responsible for preserving the North African jihadist movement. Al-Mauritani was demonstrating respect for al-Zawahiri as a wise scholar and praised his efforts in unifying this affiliate group and his ability to expand al-Qaeda's territory across Algeria and other territories. Al-Mauritani noted that by unifying with al-Qaeda, the jihadists 'received an external support that America was unable to thwart'.[148] This allowed them to expand under the name of al-Qaeda. This document demonstrated al-Zawahiri enforcing his strategy on an affiliate group by 'extending a hand to the brothers in the Islamic Maghreb,' he was ensuring communication between groups to expand their influence.

A persistent theme which continued to crop up throughout these letters was defined leadership roles. Bin Laden's authority was in relative decline, and his perpetual state of anxiety over the safety of his family and the scarcity of his public appearances led to speculation that he might be dead. In a letter from an unnamed individual tied to AQAP and the Libyan terrorist Atiyah Abd al-Rahman in January 2007, the unidentified person bemoaned al-Zawahiri's overbearing influence on al-Qaeda's hierarchy and questioned the benefits if the Egyptian doctor was to eventually replace bin Laden:

> How true is what I hear from people aligned with religious students, who may be biased, that *Shaykh* Ayman al-[Zawahiri] is the most influential man in the organization, and that Abu 'Abdallah [Osama bin Laden] is like a puppet on his hand, and that Abu 'Abdallah has given authority to al-Zawahiri to run everything, though the former disagrees with some of the *Shaykh* Ayman's behaviour?[149]

It was statements such as these that reveal the deep fissures within the al-Qaeda leadership. Bin Laden and al-Zawahiri had different visions of al-Qaeda's future, and these disagreements signalled that al-Zawahiri was willing and able to challenge the man who deputised him. Since bin Laden often went by the pseudonym Abu 'Abdallah, this suggests that bin Laden was already beginning to step away from his role as leader of al-Qaeda and was allowing al-Zawahiri to 'run everything'. The fact that he was described as a 'puppet' and that he granted al-Zawahiri authority despite 'disagreeing with some of *Shaykh* Ayman's behaviour' also suggests that al-Zawahiri had convinced bin Laden of his 'internal enemy' ideology and had thus granted authority within al-Qaeda to ensure its adoption. Being described as 'the most influential leader in the organization' meant that even four years before the death of bin Laden, al-Zawahiri was already vying for the leadership position. What was interesting here was that the speaker, a middleman for Mahmud, was explicitly unhappy about this prospect:

> This really has me agitated and I don't accept it. But I wanted to verify with you the role of *Shaykh* Ayman. Has al-Qaeda been tinged with his ideology and opinions, and is Abu 'Abdallah not the most influential man in the organization?[150]

The tone of this piece was remarkably negative. The prospect of al-Zawahiri taking over from bin Laden left the speaker 'agitated', using words such as 'tinged' to imply that al-Zawahiri's ideas and ideologies were acting as a disease that was contaminating the organization. Again, this shows that al-Zawahiri was influential from early on in pushing for ideological change within al-Qaeda and changing their terrorist strategy. Despite this, al-Zawahiri remained conspicuously distant from bin Laden's immediate circle even though he was the deputy leader. He was rarely spoken about nor did he address many letters here. On occasion, bin Laden referred to al-Zawahiri as 'Abu Muhammad' as a sign of respect, but despite the honorific, bin Laden was seeking his advice in the same way he did with Atiyah.

Perhaps seeking to curry favour with al-Zawahiri, Atiyah described the Egyptian's son-in-law, Muhammad Abbatay, as a 'rising star' in al-Qaeda and wanted al-Zawahiri to mentor him. According to Atiyah, Abbatay 'has a fine intellect, and as far as I can judge, his faith is strong.... He has high morals, he can keep a secret, and he is patient. His ideology is prudent, and he has excellent awareness.'[151] This provided an interesting dynamic in which senior members of al-Qaeda sought al-Zawahiri's guidance and experience to shape the next generation of jihadists.

Despite bin Laden's reliance on Atiyah over al-Zawahiri, the Egyptian doctor showed no ill will or jealousy towards him. In fact, he appointed Atiyah for a very special and secretive role of travelling into and out of Iran and linking up with other al-Qaeda fighters.[152] Atiyah was also a key cog for al-Qaeda to communicate with the notorious Abu Musab al-Zarqawi, whom Atiyah tried and failed to rein in on major strategic issues.[153] Atiyah was concerned about espionage and surveillance on him and other al-Qaeda members. In secret communiqués, Atiyah grumbled that most of al-Qaeda's problems were due to infiltrators and moles creating 'grave shortages in personnel. . . . [It] has really taken its toll on us.'[154]

Atiyah also spoke about their reliance on the Taliban to keep them safe. He told bin Laden, 'Our bothers and other Pashtun security units [the Taliban] are constantly uncovering and destroying spies' networks.' But, he added, 'that has not kept airstrikes from hitting us repeatedly because we continue to make mistakes'.[155] Atiyah was appointed deputy leader of al-Qaeda under al-Zawahiri but he was unable to consolidate his position. On 22 August 2011, a missile struck a house in Norak, North Waziristan, killing him.[156]

The Abbottabad documents also revealed al-Qaeda's laboured editing process for their official statements. There are editors, unidentified, who went through al-Zawahiri's drafts, often with a more modest writing style. Al-Zawahiri was known for his prolific statements on behalf of al-Qaeda, offering opinions on a multitude of topics. Adam Gadahn was tasked with fact-checking some of al-Zawahiri's unpublished speeches, including one about US politics in 2011, warning that:

> Benjamin Franklin was not a president, but a 'statesman' and one of the founders of the United States and its Constitution. . . . [S]uch a mistake may be used to slander the *shaykh* and accuse him of talking about something which he does not master [politics]. . . . [T]his mistake is not usually committed by those talking in politics, analysing, and discussing.[157]

Gadahn's tone was relatively respectful, but in a rare lapse by the American, he used certain words and phrases which indicate an underlying patronising voice, such as suggesting that this mistake may be used to expose al-Zawahiri of 'talking about something which he does not master (politics)'. Here, Gadahn was hinting at al-Zawahiri's liability as a leader due to his failure to master basic political terminology and the potential for the media to expose his lack of understanding. Gadahn then hints again that 'this mistake is not usually committed by those talking in politics', suggesting again that al-Zawahiri lacked the credentials to be in such as position of authority in al-Qaeda. The way Gadahn explains things may also be that he was not a natural Arab speaker and was more direct in his approach. It remains unclear whether al-Zawahiri rebuked him.

In general, al-Zawahiri disregarded most of the edits tempering, preferring to stick to what he had drafted.[158] Of course, as with any leader, al-Zawahiri clearly maintained a base of support amongst other al-Qaeda members. Amongst other things, he was praised mainly for his knowledge as 'the sage of the Islamic groups' and, in direct contrast with the previous source, al-Zawahiri was in fact celebrated as the pinnacle of knowledge on *jihad*.[159] In 'Letter Providing Direction', the unknown author instructs the unknown addressee to examine al-Zawahiri's works and use them to teach young insurgents:

> I have read 98 articles written by him; the articles are useful in their totality emphasizing the approach of Jihad, the understanding of faith by the Sunnis, and their role in the change. I ask that you review the articles, select the most important and suitable ones for the youths to read, and praise the articles in some of your writings, especially, the ones dealing with contemporary problems, citing the Book, and religious practice; rebutting all sorts of the opponents' approaches that may have taken on unlawful legitimacy causing disagreements and arguments.[160]

This shows the influence al-Zawahiri retained within al-Qaeda as a learned scholar, as he was not only being read by *shaykhs* within the organization, but he was also being celebrated as a model of understanding and a specialist in his field for educating the younger generation. This demonstrated his ability to recruit and radicalise youths to their cause, much like his predecessor, bin Laden. The fact that the speaker was also asking for al-Zawahiri to be 'praised in your writing' suggests that his influence was also expanding amongst scholarly debate and his work was being instructed to be both read and applauded unconditionally.

Despite his obsession with security, al-Zawahiri was also praised for his ability to maintain good contact with others and ensure the smooth running of operations. In a letter by an unknown author, the issue of weak communication lines within al-Qaeda is raised, but despite this, al-Zawahiri was reliable and easy to confer with:

> There are some obstacles in the correspondence of letters between the brothers and me, so when any message is sent to me, please send a copy to Abu-Muhammad *Shaykh* Ayman al-Zawahiri; he is in constant contact with the brothers and is in charge of following up the affairs in the Islamic Maghreb.[161]

Al-Zawahiri had become the undisputed authority in al-Qaeda, and thus all correspondence and communication lines needed to be directed through him. The fact that he was in 'constant contact with the brothers' indicates his key position as a conduit for communication and his reputation for having his finger on the pulse.[162] The Abbottabad documents demonstrate al-Zawahiri's general success. Initially, bin Laden and al-Zawahiri shared a common strategic outlook, with documents such as 'Terror Franchise' providing a united strategy between the two leaders, 'the leaders of jihad, commencing with al-Qaeda's leaders *Shaykh* Osama and Doctor Ayman al-Zawahiri to the efficient idea of shutting down the source of energy from which the Zio-Crusade invaders keep on refuelling with money, soldiers and support'.[163]

Here, both leaders promoted the strategy of going to the root of the problem and cutting off the supply at the source. However, other correspondence demonstrated that bin Laden and al-Zawahiri had divergent ideologies. In a letter from 2003, al-Zawahiri sought to 'clarify' the narrative of his leader's speech by asserting his 'internal enemy' ideology:

> The author does not greedily intend to add to his predecessor's works, but rather seeks to clarify several points. . . . For this we hope that this message would enlighten the connection between the internal and external enemies in their goals and in their soldiers . . . to expose the veil and take off the mask of the enemies of Islam that were hiding behind it and diluting the issue of governing, to serve the interest of the enemies of Islam.[164]

Al-Zawahiri's tone was cautious but firm in his bid to clarify bin Laden's jihadist ideology. When mentioning 'the internal and external enemies', al-Zawahiri was pushing for bin Laden to adopt the 'internal/external enemy' policy in his narrative. This illustrates how early on al-Zawahiri was promoting this strategy and attempting to embed it within the rhetoric of al-Qaeda. It had also become apparent that al-Zawahiri was overseeing many aspects of bin Laden's leadership, providing an alternative perspective without appearing to be blatantly patronising. However, the subtle tension in the words was noticeable.

When writing to bin Laden, al-Zawahiri often showed a tendency to lace his arguments or corrections with excessive references to Qur'anic anecdotes or quotes, perhaps to assert his scholarly authority over bin Laden and justify his critiques. In 'Why This Letter?' after seeking to merely 'clarify a few points', al-Zawahiri loads his argument with lengthy quotes from the Qur'an: 'Allah said, praise be to him . . . The curse of Allah be on them! How are they deluded (away from the truth!) *Surah* 64 verse 4.'[165] Again, this can be seen in other correspondence with bin Laden, when al-Zawahiri lists a series of organizational and communication matters he wanted bin Laden to 'look into' concerning al-Qaeda's affiliates, and he ends his letter with a rambling anecdote concerning the Prophet Muhammad's son-in-law 'master Uthman' and the spread of sedition.[166] Al-Zawahiri was likely doing this as precautionary measure given that he was critiquing bin Laden's ideas and promoting his own views. Perhaps, he felt it necessary to reaffirm his scholarly credentials.

In another letter, al-Zawahiri again talked of fighting the 'internal' and 'external' enemies. Although we cannot be sure, as the letter cites no recipient, date, or speaker, we can deduce from the content that it was most likely written by al-Zawahiri. Here he revealed that they learnt from the 'hasty, poor decisions' made in Iraq, where they 'did not think about the consequences beforehand'.[167] Because of this, the tribes retracted their support for the *mujahideen* and stirred up bad feelings and 'vengeful wars'.[168] He thus stressed the need to 'gain support of tribes who enjoy strength and influence before building a Muslim state'.[169]

Al-Zawahiri acknowledged that the United States was too powerful at the moment to attack, so in the meantime he advocated that al-Qaeda 'concentrate our jihad efforts in areas where the conditions are ideal for us to fight. Iraq and Afghanistan are two good examples. . . . [W]e do not have to rush to other areas of conflict.'[170] This goes back to the idea of self-preservation. Al-Zawahiri was prioritising courses of action that were local to the Arab world to gain safe bases to regenerate, reconsolidate, and eventually redirect towards the West.

Despite previous assumptions that al-Zawahiri was often portrayed as awkward and ineffectual by the media, he was in fact far more effective in promoting his ideology through various media portals than some might have expected. Other al-Qaeda members who were likewise very assertive about increasing the media coverage of al-Zawahiri's doctrines and statements on strategy. Gadahn mentions this change in stance:

> We should not forget that there are millions of admirer's of the *shaykh* in the Islamic world, who are eager for his appearance to ensure his health and that he is well. Those should be targeted in our speeches and messages, before the Americans and Europeans, who do not listen or evaluate what is being said.[171]

This indicates a clear turn away from the 'external enemy' by al-Qaeda, and instead of directing their messages to the West, they decided to focus instead on supporters of the West in the Islamic world. The Abbottabad documents made for heavy reading, but brought to light very important information concerning the web of alliances and source of internal tensions within al-Qaeda. Based on these documents, it was apparent that bin Laden was not the puppet master pulling the strings. It was more his trusted deputy Ayman al-Zawahiri who, through the promotion of his 'internal enemy' ideology, worked his way to the top. From early on, al-Zawahiri played a critical role in pushing al-Qaeda to adopt different policies and tactics, ultimately changing their strategy for terrorism.

The Usurper

Ibrahim Awwad Ibrahim al-Badry was born in 1971 in Samarra, an Iraqi city north of Baghdad. He claimed his ancestors were descendants of the Prophet Muhammad, but this may well have been part of the myth he wanted to create for himself, assuming the sobriquet as the 'Believer'.[172] Yet in his formative years, al-Badry was withdrawn, reticent, and, when he spoke, it was barely noticeable. In 2003, al-Badry helped found the Army of the People of the Sunna and Communal Solidarity (Jaysh Ahl al-Sunna wa-l-Jamaah), a jihadist insurgent faction that clashed with US troops in Iraq. In February 2004, al-Badry was arrested in Fallujah and detained at Camp Bucca in southern Iraq for 10 months.[173] Al-Badry made connections with many inmates who had served in Saddam Hussein's regime, as well as some of Abu Musab al-Zarqawi's inner circle.[174] Much like al-Zawahiri's time in prison and mujahideen campaign in Afghanistan and Pakistan, al-Badry was in the right place at the right time.

Upon leaving Camp Bucca, al-Badry travelled to Damascus to perform tasks for al-Qaeda and to enhance his religious credentials by becoming an academically trained religious scholar.[175] In 2006, al-Badry's terrorist faction aligned itself with al-Zarqawi. When al-Zarqawi was killed in a US airstrike in 2006, his deputy, Abu Ayyub al-Masri, took over. Abu Ayyub was impressed with al-Badry and nominated him to the 11-member AQI Consultative Council tasked with religious and propaganda matters. In April 2010 Abu Ayyub detonated a suicide vest, killing himself before US forces could apprehend him. The head of the military council, Hajji Bakr, a former colonel in Saddam Hussein's army who became part of the insurgency after losing his privileged status, manipulated the succession in favour of al-Badry, based on favourable statements by those who were imprisoned with him in Camp Bucca.[176]

Al-Badry then took his now-infamous nom de guerre, Abu Bakr al-Baghdadi, a double homage to religion and the goal of conquest and expansion. Abu Bakr was Prophet Muhammad's father-in-law and the first caliph. Baghdad was the capital of the Abbasid Caliphate that came to power in the eighth century over the Umayyad Caliphate. The name combined power and religious authenticity.[177] Al-Baghdadi also adopted the title Commander of the Faithful (Amir al-Muminin).[178] This was a title usually reserved for caliphs, although the Taliban's Mullah Omar had also assumed this designation.

In April 2013, Abu Bakr al-Baghdadi made a dramatic move in the jihadist landscape and insisted that al-Qaeda's ally in Syria the Support Front for the People (Jabhat al-Nusra) was answerable to him. However, its leader, Abu Mohammed al-Golani refused to acknowledge al-Baghdadi as his superior and instead pledged a ba'yah directly to al-Zawahiri, with the intention of making Jabhat al-Nusra an al-Qaeda affiliate. Undeterred, al-Baghdadi took unilateral control over all al-Qaeda operations in both Syria and Iraq and renamed AQI as the 'Islamic State in Iraq and Syria (ISIS)'.[179] By the summer of 2013, ISIS had ejected Jabhat al-Nusra and proclaimed its authority over parts of northern and eastern Syria. It then set up a front in the Syrian city of Raqqa, making it the de facto capital whilst seizing oil-fields and moving with stealth towards Fallujah and Ramadi in Iraq's Anbar province.

In trying to deal with this deeply concerning dispute, al-Zawahiri sent an edict, stating that al-Baghdadi was wrong not to consult with al-Golani, who equally should not have pledged a ba'yah to al-Zawahiri without first obtaining permission from al-Qaeda.[180] Al-Zawahiri's approach in admonishing both al-Golani and al-Baghdadi backfired. Al-Baghdadi rejected the al-Qaeda leader's directive, as he believed al-Zawahiri was dividing the jihadists according to the borders created by the imperialist Sykes-Picot agreement, which ironically al-Zawahiri had himself been deeply opposed to.[181] Over time, through an incremental process, al-Baghdadi would systematically separate ISIS from the purview of al-Zawahiri's al-Qaeda.

In September 2013, al-Zawahiri issued his 'General Guidelines for Jihad' where he again stressed self-discipline and restraint, commenting that al-Qaeda's strategy 'is a long one, and jihad is in need of safe bases'.[182] Through maintaining 'safe bases', al-Zawahiri wanted to pursue a multipurpose

agenda through a multi-pronged strategy which focused on the recruitment, organization, and eventual deployment of cadres. In other places he
was more interested in intelligence gathering and identification of hostile
elements whilst embedding with local allies and affiliates to avoid as much
local friction as possible.

However, al-Zawahiri added, 'if we are forced to fight [local regimes],
then we must make it clear that our struggle against them is a part of our
resistance against the Crusader onslaught'.[183] The 'General Guidelines for
Jihad' in 2013 represented the culmination of several years of internal debates amongst al-Qaeda's hierarchy about institutionalised reforms and
a strategic blueprint and for al-Qaeda's strategy in Syria. It was meant
to avoid the problem that al-Zarqawi had created in Iraq. Since 9/11,
much had changed geopolitically around the world when al-Zawahiri
published his 'General Guidelines for Jihad', which stipulated not only
rules of behaviour in jihad but also on how to deal with it via media
publications.[184]

The document was an important indicator of al-Qaeda's move to a more
cautious approach in winning the hearts and minds of the *ummah*. In it, al-
Zawahiri ordered his cadres to avoid violence against religious minorities
and 'deviant sects' such as Shiite Muslims unless provoked, as it could result
in a 'revolt of the masses'. He cautioned against killing women and children as well planning attacks in markets and mosques. Al-Zawahiri added
that should they still occur, those responsible should show contrition and
compensate the family members of those who were harmed. Interestingly,
al-Zawahiri also suggested potentially working with other jihadist groups,
even those with clear ideological differences. This was a huge departure
from al-Zawahiri's previous rigidity, a reflection of the practical necessities
for al-Qaeda's continued existence.[185] It reveals a more population-centric
strategy. The mission of keeping the people content and supportive in local
populations was in stark contrast to the approach ISIS would take in its
theatres of operations.

Although al-Zawahiri defined targeting the 'external enemy' as the primary aim, he also believed that until it was realistic and sustainable, realising
a more local strategy against the 'internal enemy' would ultimately benefit
al-Qaeda's long-term approach against the West. Al-Zawahiri emphasised
the need for operational space to function and then expand, without being
under coercion or pressure.[186] Syria was becoming increasingly important

for al-Zawahiri as part of this strategy, and the al-Qaeda leader decided to send around a dozen of his acolytes and members of affiliates to Syria from Pakistan, Iran, Yemen, and Lebanon. Several fighters were part of al-Qaeda's Shura Council and senior military commanders. Al-Zawahiri hoped this would engender more collaboration and loyalty from the jihadists fighting the Bashar Assad regime.[187]

Aiding al-Zawahiri in this mission was another Egyptian jihadist who had been released from Egypt's prisons after Mubarak was overthrown. Ahmad Salama Mabruk, the veteran EIJ operative who worked for al-Zawahiri for decades, was initially often seen in the company of the younger Muhammad al-Zawahiri, proselytizing on behalf of al-Qaeda. However, Ayman al-Zawahiri and Mabruk had other plans. Towards the end of 2013, al-Zawahiri sent Mabruk to try to reconcile differences that were emerging between ISIS and Jabhat al-Nusra.[188] Mabruk brought with him funds to help support al-Golani and curry favour with him. As a result, Mabruk became a senior figure within Jabhat al-Nusra and sat on its Shura Council. The hope was that this would keep the *ummah* united.[189]

In an interview with al-Qaeda's media wing, al-Sahab, in April 2014, al-Zawahiri was even more plain in his reflections, speaking that al-Qaeda's priority was to unite the *ummah* and work 'to restore the rightly guided caliphate that is based on a consultation and accepted by Muslims'.[190] He also commented that it would be impossible to united the *ummah*, 'if our image is that of a dominator, someone who usurps the rights of others, and an attacker'. This was an obvious criticism of ISIS, which had attained growing notoriety in Syria and Iraq. Yet ISIS would not heed al-Zawahiri's call.

In June 2014, ISIS made a seismic statement and launched an assault on Mosul, Iraq's second-largest city, followed by occupying Saddam Hussein's hometown of Tikrit. Cities were taken with little effort. ISIS had put paid to al-Zawahiri's demand for the jihadists to adopt a cautious strategy. Al-Zawahiri's goal was one of de-escalation and containment. However, the situation was now spiralling out of his control. For a micromanager like al-Zawahiri, who couldn't just take a flight to Syria to resolve matters, the inability to direct events was excruciating and the biggest challenge he faced as al-Qaeda leader.[191] An Iraqi intelligence official revealed that that 'al-Baghdadi desired to usurp and defy al-Zawahiri. There were private communications between them for months. The last one was days before ISIS occupied Mosul and Tikrit. These intercepted letters showed al-Zawahiri complaining about al-Baghdadi's approach, adding that he did not have the authority to conduct these operations.'[192]

ISIS's rapid accession threatened to disrupt al-Qaeda's position of supremacy that al-Zawahiri had worked so hard to craft. ISIS's strategy was diametrically opposed to al-Qaeda. Whilst al-Qaeda tended to grow covertly, ISIS stole the spotlight at every opportunity. Although al-Qaeda utilised new media to act as their oxygen of publicity, it was ISIS that built a sophisticated propaganda machinery churning out a stream of videos, images, and statements demonstrating its victories that were then instantly circulated by its proliferating social media groups.

Al-Zawahiri was never fully in sync with Islamists in Iraq and even less so in Syria, given his rudimentary understanding of the dynamics on the ground. Abu Khaled al-Suri, al-Zawahiri's handpicked representative in Syria, was appointed to mediate the divisions that were emerging between al-Baghdadi and al-Golani.[193] Al-Zawahiri and al-Suri had been colleagues since the days of the jihad in Afghanistan.[194] Al-Suri, whose real name is Mohamed Bahaia, was an al-Qaeda veteran and at one time served as bin Laden's messenger between Afghanistan and western Europe.[195] He was also a co-founder of Ahrar al-Sham, a Syrian-based jihadist group seeking the overthrow of President Bashar Assad. The group were part of the Islamic Front, a loose coalition of jihadist militant groups been embroiled in infighting against ISIS.[196]

Al-Suri ultimately came down on al-Golani's side, condemning al-Baghdadi's cause for harming Muslims and having ties to foreign intelligence entities.[197] However, al-Suri failed to find a resolution and in February 2014 was killed by ISIS in a suicide attack inside his compound in the northern Syrian city of Aleppo.[198] The attack specifically targeted him. Following al-Suri's death, al-Zawahiri released a video memorialising his fallen comrade, which highlighted al-Suri's relationship with bin Laden and called out ISIS in all but name.[199]

During this same period, al-Zawahiri also instructed Nasir al-Wuhayshi, the leader of AQAP who was also effectively acting as al-Qaeda's deputy with al-Zawahiri's blessings, to help facilitate discussion between al-Golani and al-Baghdadi.[200] Previously, al-Zawahiri had tasked al-Wuhayshi with plotting attacks against the West, including targeting Yemeni infrastructure as well as American foreign outposts around the Middle East. However, these attacks were ultimately foiled.[201] Al-Wuhayshi was not successful in negotiating with al-Baghdadi either, as the latter simply refused to respond to al-Wuyayshi's requests.[202] Thus, this stalemate, together with al-Suri's death, signalled that ISIS had no desire to find an amicable solution with other jihadist groups short of total submission, something al-Zawahiri was unwilling to do.

Clearly, the emergence of ISIS had shaken the foundations of al-Qaeda and highlighted the vulnerability of al-Zawahiri's position. In February 2014, al-Zawahiri disavowed any association with ISIS. This was significant, as it marked the first occasion al-Qaeda disowned an affiliate and meant the organization could lose its grip on Iraq and Syria.[203] However, the back-biting and trading of barbs continued publicly for the world to see. In a video released in May 2014, al-Zawahiri responded to a statement made by a spokesman of ISIS denying that al-Qaeda had ever been under the command of AQI, and thus al-Zawahiri's expulsion of ISIS from al-Qaeda in February 2014 was a meaningless gesture. The speech, entitled 'Testimonial to Preserve the Blood of the *Mujahideen* in Syria' shows al-Zawahiri arguing to the contrary by drawing on documents sent by ISIS leaders to al-Qaeda, some of which are in the Abbottabad document archives. One of the examples was from a Shura member of ISIS:

> We are letting you know, O our *shaykhs* and *Wulaat al-Amr* that your State in Iraq is fine and firm. . . . [T]he brothers here and Abu Bakr and the *Majlis Shura* have no problem [with the idea] that this leadership is temporary, and if anyone is sent from you, and you find that it will ensure the *Maslaha* for him to take over the leadership.[204]

With al-Zawahiri powerless to stem the rise of al-Baghdadi, ISIS fighters continued to seize cities, towns, and villages across Iraq and Syria. Following ISIS's capture of Mosul, some jihadists concluded that there was an opportunity to mend the rift between al-Qaeda and ISIS. Al-Zawahiri ally Abu Ayyad al-Tunisi released a statement saying, 'I recommend that the two *shaykhs*, Ayman al-Zawahiri and Abu Mohammad al-Golani, rush to congratulate [ISIS on] these victories. This may lead the leaders of the organizations that are fighting each other to put an end to the battle and the struggle between them. Likewise, I call upon Abu Bakr al-Baghdadi to hurry and respond to the calls [for reconciliation issued] by the honourable commanders and clerics.'[205]

On 4 July 2014, al-Baghdadi rose to the stage in Mosul to deliver the Friday sermon, his first official appearance since taking the helm of ISIS.

The aesthetics and visuals were important to convey a message. He wore black robes to symbolise the memory of the Abbasid caliphs. Al-Baghdadi then made a pivotal speech, one that would shake the foundations of the jihadist movement and challenge al-Zawahiri directly:

> I was appointed to rule you, but I am not the best among you. . . . If you see me acting truly, then follow me. If you see me acting falsely, then advise and guide me. . . . If I disobey Allah, then do not obey me.[206]

This was a rewording of what the first caliph, Abu Bakr, is believed to have said when he was chosen by the Prophet Muhammad's companions. Al-Baghdadi emphatically laid down a challenge not only to the Iraqi government and the West but also to al-Qaeda and al-Zawahiri. Al-Zawahiri was ill prepared to handle the spiralling events in Syria and Iraq, especially as ISIS, without consulting al-Qaeda, formalised a global caliphate with Abu Bakr al-Baghdadi as its caliph. Thus, after a year of turmoil and ISIS's refusal to follow al-Zawahiri's orders, al-Zawahiri was compelled to release a new statement disowning ISIS on the basis that

> we were not informed about its creation, nor counselled. Nor were we satisfied with it: rather, we ordered it to stop. ISIS is not a branch of al-Qaeda and we have no organizational relationship with it, nor is al-Qaeda responsible for its actions and behaviours.[207]

To add further salt to al-Qaeda's wounds, ISIS took sole ownership of the black banner that al-Zawahiri's brother, Muhammad, had raised aloft in 2012 at the US embassy in Egypt, to highlight their control over the towns and cities of Iraq and Syria. Following ISIS's acrimonious split with Jabhat al-Nusra in Syria, the flag became inseparable from its own project and signified its demarcation or any affiliation with al-Qaeda. Their now official flag was flown atop buildings, hillsides, vehicles, and other landmarks as a way of marking their possession of territory which they claimed evoked the eighth-century Abbasid Revolution that had overthrown the corrupt rule of the Umayyad dynasty and replaced it with a new caliphate based in Iraq. The blackness of the flag reflected ISIS's apocalyptic connotations and was to become one of their most infamous and widespread symbols. The irony was that it was al-Qaeda's flag to adopt but they did not seize the opportunity. The momentum was now with ISIS, and al-Zawahiri faced an enormous challenge to not only compete with al-Baghdadi but keep al-Qaeda relevant within the jihadist spectrum.

With the rise of ISIS and the creation of its caliphate in 2014, the jihadist landscape changed greatly. ISIS also sought to appropriate al-Zawahiri's *tawhid* single raised index finger as a sign of their violent and uncompromising agenda towards their opponents, both in the Middle East and in the West. Although the al-Qaeda affiliates stayed loyal to al-Zawahiri, several groups, like Boko Haram in Nigeria, who had previously shown a close ideological affinity with al-Qaeda, chose to alter their allegiances to ISIS by reciting the *ba'yah* to al-Baghdadi.[208]

In the aftermath of the caliphate announcement, al-Tunisi haphazardly wrote to al-Zawahiri bizarrely suggesting the al-Qaeda leader could pledge a *ba'yah* to al-Baghdadi. Al-Tunisi naively thought al-Zawahiri might be able help temper ISIS and 'weaken the extremists of the [Islamic] State who have no project besides murder and *takfir* (excommunication of Muslims)'.[209] However, in a subsequent letter, al-Tunisi told al-Zawahiri to ignore his previous message, as he had concluded that there were no good people left amongst ISIS. However, the damage was done. By not taking a firm position on where he stood on the divide and in fact, leaning towards al-Baghdadi, al-Tunisi inadvertently made it permissible for many Tunisian jihadists to join ISIS if they chose to. Around 2,500 of the eventual 2,900 Tunisian foreign terrorist fighters that had arrived in Iraq and Syria chose to align themselves with ISIS.[210] Despite al-Tunisi's paradoxical communications and the consequences they created for al-Qaeda and its allies in Syria and Iraq, al-Zawahiri didn't appear to hold a grudge and the two stayed on good terms. The Egyptian teacher could not afford to lose any more allies.[211]

As Syria and Iraq's plight continued, al-Zawahiri sought to re-establish a strong foothold for al-Qaeda in the Middle East, which meant jostling with ISIS. As a result, their battle of ideas was no longer confined to Syria and Iraq but became an open conflict with each side vying for global legitimacy. To compete with ISIS, al-Zawahiri adopted a series of tactics: first, to undermine ISIS's legitimacy using Qur'anic evidence; second, to counter the litany of allegations from ISIS; and third, to present al-Qaeda as the more moderate of the two organizations by berating the brutal methods of ISIS.

The combination of a new rival on the scene and deep-seated divisions from within the organization meant that al-Zawahiri constantly had to re-state al-Qaeda's goals and aims to conceal his vulnerable position as leader. To undermine their authority, al-Zawahiri began by publicly denouncing ISIS's formation as illegitimate because it did not align with the Qur'anic rubric: a caliphate must have 'the essential foundations to function and defend itself. If our state is not supported by the proper foundations, the enemy will easily destroy it.'[212]

This asserted an organizational hierarchy placing al-Qaeda above ISIS. Al-Zawahiri concluded by calling for ISIS to return to the fold and accept his orders to leave Syria and return to Iraq for the sake of jihadi unity and to avoid the shedding of Muslim blood. Yet ISIS would not stop their provocations in Syria and Iraq. On 5 November 2014, al-Baghdadi sent a message to al-Zawahiri ordering him to cease his allegiance to Taliban leader Mullah Mohammed Omar, whom he labelled as 'an ignorant, illiterate warlord, unworthy of spiritual or political respect'.[213] Instead, al-Baghdadi demanded al-Zawahiri swear allegiance to him as caliph. Al-Zawahiri did not reply, assuming it would give more credibility to al-Baghdadi to even acknowledge his message. However, his silence only created more confusion and enabled ISIS to seize control of the jihadist narrative once again.

Ahead of the fourteenth anniversary of 9/11 in 2015, al-Zawahiri launched his Islamic Spring series of messages. It represented his first rebuke to al-Baghdadi's declaration of the caliphate, reflecting ISIS's indiscretions, flawed doctrines, and the illegitimate overpowering (taghallub) of the jihadist order. Al-Zawahiri warned that al-Baghdadi's actions would 'irreconcilably' divide the jihadist movement. Al-Zawahiri accused al-Baghdadi of 'sedition' and insisted that he was not the leader of all Muslims. The Egyptian al-Qaeda leader stated that 'everyone was surprised' by al-Baghdadi's declaration anointing himself the caliph 'without consulting the Muslims'. Al-Zawahiri was also hoping to set the record straight and once again control the jihadist narrative that ISIS was aggressively seizing. In the Islamic Spring series, al-Zawahiri provided his interpretation of how the fallout with ISIS began and the negative impact of intra-jihadi conflict.[214]

Initially reluctant to openly condemn al-Baghdadi and ISIS for fear that it would give them undue publicity, al-Zawahiri was now openly revealing how deep and irreconcilable the divisions had become between al-Qaeda and ISIS. Referring to him by his real name, in a derogatory way, al-Zawahiri also complained that al-Baghdadi had ignored Muslims suffering elsewhere:

> We preferred to respond with as little as possible, out of our concern to extinguish the fire of sedition, but al-Badry [Abu Bakr al-Baghdadi] and his

brothers did not leave us a choice, for they have demanded that all the *muja-hideen* reject their confirmed pledges of allegiance, and to pledge allegiance to them for what they claim of a caliphate.[215]

Whilst castigating ISIS, al-Zawahiri also offered an olive branch, reflecting a pragmatism that he wasn't renowned for. Although al-Zawahiri saw a potential rapprochement as a 'strategic necessity', he laid out several conditions to ISIS, including to stop the unmitigated violence against other Muslims and jihadists who disagreed with them and assent to the creation of a Shariah court to administer justice in Syria and Iraq. In return, al-Zawahiri offered an amnesty for all of the violence unleashed by ISIS. However, as al-Baghdadi and ISIS were in ascendency at the time, they inevitably rejected al-Zawahiri's proposal and chose to graphically intensify the violence. The jihadist civil war would continue unabated.[216]

ISIS's emergence and expansion presented al-Zawahiri and al-Qaeda with a direct challenge unlike anything else they had experienced. Up till that point, al-Qaeda had managed to preserve an unrivalled supremacy within the global jihadist movement. With its unabashed approach, ISIS openly courted al-Qaeda's affiliates, attempting to integrate its rival's allies. In return, rather than trying to compete or replicate ISIS's model, al-Zawahiri reduced al-Qaeda's public profile and embedded it further within the civilian fabric of Pakistani society. According to the noted academic Bruce Hoffman:

> The situation in Syria has had its ups and downs for al-Zawahiri. Initially, al-Qaeda benefited from the Arab Spring, by taking advantage of the problems in Syria. The mistake was relying on al-Baghdadi. There was always going to be a personality clash between al-Baghdadi and al-Zawahiri. Al-Zawahiri couldn't exercise the type of control al-Baghdadi was able to, as he was in hiding.[217]

ISIS was always more direct and open to publicising whatever they did, but al-Qaeda did not always do so and had to play catch-up. Al-Qaeda also did not post the garish violence which ISIS specialized in. The editorial quality of ISIS output generally was significantly higher than that of al-Qaeda.[218] However, al-Zawahiri's decision to cut ties with ISIS and let the phenomenon 'flame out' on its own allowed him to earn back the trust of many who were sickened by ISIS's treatment of Muslims. The international community's overt focus on ISIS in turn allowed al-Qaeda to reform itself inconspicuously. Thus, in many ways, ISIS's brutal march into the Levant worked to the benefit of al-Qaeda, as the world obsessed about ISIS and ignored al-Qaeda as it rebuilt itself in its repudiated child's shadow. Al-Zawahiri took full advantage of this, adopting a pragmatic strategy, strengthening ties with the franchises, creating new ones, and seeking to enhance the sanctuary inside Iran.[219]

19 A Northern Alliance soldier returns from the Tora Bora front line, showing a leaflet bearing the photograph of al-Zawahiri (*left*) and bin Laden (*right*). The leaflets, written in Farsi and Pashto, tell of a $25 million reward for each. The leaflets were dropped by US warplanes over the Tora Bora mountain area. 17 December 2001. (*Romeo Gacad/AFP via Getty Images*).

MOST WANTED TERRORIST

AYMAN AL-ZAWAHIRI

Murder of U.S. Nationals Outside the United States; Conspiracy to Murder U.S. Nationals Outside the United States; Attack on a Federal Facility Resulting in Death

DESCRIPTION

Aliases: Abu Muhammad, Abu Fatima, Muhammad Ibrahim, Abu Abdallah, Abu al-Mu'iz, The Doctor, The Teacher, Nur, Ustaz, Abu Mohammed, Abu Mohammed Nur al-Deen, Abdel Muaz, Dr. Ayman al Zawahiri

Date(s) of Birth Used: June 19, 1951	**Place of Birth:** Egypt
Hair: Brown/Black	**Eyes:** Dark
Height: Unknown	**Weight:** Unknown
Build: Unknown	**Complexion:** Olive
Sex: Male	**Citizenship:** Egyptian
Languages: Arabic, French	**Scars and Marks:** None known

REWARD

The Rewards For Justice Program, United States Department of State, is offering a reward of up to $25 million for information leading directly to the apprehension or conviction of Ayman Al-Zawahiri.

REMARKS

Al-Zawahiri is a physician and the founder of the Egyptian Islamic Jihad (EIJ). This organization opposes the secular Egyptian Government and seeks its overthrow through violent means. In approximately 1998, the EIJ led by Al-Zawahiri merged with Al Qaeda.

CAUTION

Ayman Al-Zawahiri has been indicted for his alleged role in the August 7, 1998, bombings of the United States Embassies in Dar es Salaam, Tanzania, and Nairobi, Kenya.

SHOULD BE CONSIDERED ARMED AND DANGEROUS

If you have any information concerning this person, please contact your local FBI office or the nearest American Embassy or Consulate.

Field Office: New York

20 FBI poster for al-Zawahiri, who is listed as one of the world's most wanted terrorists, including the $25 million reward and details about his background and aliases. (*FBI*).

21 Pakistani terrorists Maulana Masood Azhar (right) of the Jaish-e-Mohammed (JeM) and Hafiz Saeed (left) of the Lashkar-e-Taiba (LeT). Both helped al-Qaeda's leaders escape from Afghanistan into Pakistan and provided sanctuary and support. (*Author's own collection*).

22 General Pervez Musharraf (*left*) and General Ashfaq Kayani (*right*) separately served as Pakistan's chief of army staff during the US hunt for al-Qaeda. Both turned out to be unreliable, as they maintained ties to Pakistani terrorist groups and the Haqqani Network, who in turn protected al-Qaeda. (*Aamir Qureshi/AFP via Getty Images*).

23 A view of the bus destroyed by an al-Qaeda suicide bomber. Three other
suicide bombers detonated their devices on London Underground trains. Fifty-
two people were killed and more than 700 others injured. Al-Zawahiri oversaw
the 7/7 plot. 7 July 2005. (*Peter Macdiarmid/Getty Images*).

24 A video statement by one of the 7/7 London bombers, Shehzad Tanweer,
who had been trained by al-Qaeda at a terror camp in Pakistan. His remarks were
spliced in with al-Zawahiri's comments. 6 July 2006. (*jihadist website*).

25 An image grab from al-Qaeda's as-Sahab Media shows footage of al-Zawahiri vowing to avenge the death of al-Qaeda in Iraq's leader, Abu Musab al-Zarqawi, who was killed in a US operation on 7 June 2006. The two, however, had a very poor and tense relationship and they frequently clashed. The video is dated 23 June 2006. (*AFP via Getty Images*).

26 The debris of a home in Damadola, Pakistan, following a US air strike seeking to eliminate al-Zawahiri, who narrowly escaped death. 13 January 2006. (*Tariq Mahmood / AFP via Getty Images*).

27 Former prime minister Benazir Bhutto addresses thousands of supporters at an election campaign rally minutes before being assassinated in a suicide bombing in Rawalpindi, Pakistan. Al–Zawahiri gave his sanction for the attack. 27 December, 2007. (*John Moore / Getty Images*).

28 Destroyed cars and the damaged building of the United Nations Development Programme, following a suicide attack in Islamabad, Pakistan. It was adjacent to the Danish Embassy. The attack, ordered by al–Zawahiri, left several dead. 2 June 2008. (*Aamir Qureshi / AFP via Getty Images*).

29 An image grab of triple agent Humam Khalil al-Balawi preparing his suicide bomb attack in Khost, Afghanistan, on a CIA team and his Jordanian intelligence handler after convincing them he would lead them to the whereabouts of al-Zawahiri. 30 December 2009. (*jihadist website*).

30 The former US Forward Operating Base Chapman in Khost, Afghanistan, where al-Balawi murdered the CIA team and Jordanian handler. He was aided by the Haqqani Network, who now occupy the base. (*Andalou Images*).

31 ISIS leader Abu Bakr al-Baghdadi speaking in Mosul, Iraq, declaring himself the leader of the Islamic State. This resulted in a permanent fracture with al-Zawahiri and al-Qaeda. 4 July 2014. (*jihadist website*).

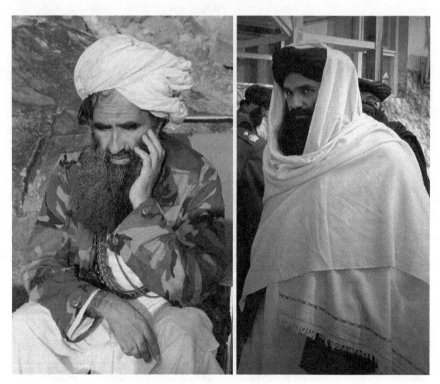

32 Jalaluddin Haqqani (*left*) and his son and successor as the head of the Haqqani Network, Sirajuddin (*right*). Both protected al-Zawahiri pre- and post-9/11. The Haqqani Network became an internationally proscribed terrorist group in 2012. (*Author's own collection*).

33 Somalis hold placards including a portrait of al-Zawahiri as they demonstrate against the al-Shabaab terrorist group following the announcement that they will officially join al-Qaeda. Al-Zawahiri announced the union. Unlike bin Laden, al-Zawahiri was keen to expand the number of al-Qaeda affiliates. 15 February 2012. (*Mohamed Abdiwahab/AFP via Getty Images*).

34 Al-Zawahiri's arch-nemesis, former Egyptian president Hosni Mubarak, sits inside a cage in a courtroom similar to the one he put al-Zawahiri in back in 1981. Mubarak faced allegations of corruption and extrajudicial killings during his rule. 2 June 2012. (*STR/AFP via Getty Images*).

35 Egyptian protesters, led by Muhammad al-Zawahiri, tear down the American
flag and wave various black jihadist flags at the US Embassy in Cairo during
a demonstration against a film deemed offensive to Islam. The protests were
instigated by Ayman al-Zawahiri on the eleventh anniversary of 9/11. Over time
one of those black flags would be appropriated by ISIS. 11 September 2012.
(*AFP/GettyImages*).

36 Flyers offering a reward for information leading to the capture of al-Zawahiri in Arabic, Pashto, and Farsi. Part of the US State Department's Rewards for Justice Program. (*US Rewards for Justice, US State Department*).

37 Al-Zawahiri's Sherpur residence in Kabul, Afghanistan. Provided to the Egyptian by the Haqqani Network, it was here that the United States finally tracked him down and killed him in a drone operation. 31 July 2022. (*Author's own collection*).

7

The Elusive Terrorist

Isolation and Hibernation

Since the mid-1990s al-Zawahiri repeatedly swore *ba'yah* to Mullah Omar to strengthen and protect al-Qaeda residing under the protection of the Taliban. Yet prior to 9/11, al-Zawahiri had some reluctance in showing Mullah Omar the same level of reverence as bin Laden accorded to the Taliban leader.[1] Al-Zawahiri did not want to remain in Afghanistan indefinitely, as he always harboured a desire to return to Egypt.[2] However, al-Zawahiri's oath to the Taliban would now carry more significance after the emergence of ISIS. Al-Zawahiri, being challenged and undermined by al-Baghdadi, began to vocally promote Mullah Omar as the 'Commander of the Faithful'. On 20 July 2014, al-Qaeda circulated an online newsletter *Call to Arms* (*An-Nafir*), and the organization used its inaugural issue to publicly renew its *ba'yah* to Mullah Omar:

> Al-Qaeda with its branches all over, are his [Mullah Omar's] soldiers working under his victorious banner with help and support from Allah, to make the word of Allah the highest, for Islamic *Shariah* to prevail in ruling and not be ruled, commanding, and not commanded, for every area of Islamic land to be free.[3]

Al-Zawahiri wanted to prepare in advance a terrorist movement that he envisaged would continue long after him. As part of that strategy, on 3 September 2014, al-Zawahiri, released a video announcing the creation of a new affiliate called al-Qaeda in the Indian Subcontinent (AQIS) to 'help raise the flag of jihad and return Islamic rule to the subcontinent, which used to be part of the land of the Muslims until the infidel enemy occupied it and fragmented it and split it'.[4] It was also announced at the same time that the leader of AQIS would be Shaykh Asim Umar, a Pakistani Islamic

Doctor, Teacher, Terrorist. Sajjan M. Gohel, Oxford University Press. © Oxford University Press 2024.
DOI: 10.1093/oso/9780197665367.003.0007

scholar with long-standing ties to al-Qaeda. Umar was also a close ally of Ilyas Kashmiri. Soon after Kashmiri was chosen by al-Zawahiri to be part of al-Qaeda's 'special operations council', he introduced the Egyptian to Umar, and they subsequently established a strong relationship.[5]

In his statement, al-Zawahiri declared that the formation of AQIS was the 'blessed result' of a two-year effort to 'gather the *mujahideen* in the Indian Subcontinent into a single entity'.[6] This included uniting jihadist factions across Pakistan, India, and Afghanistan with the goal of establishing a caliphate. Citing examples of discrimination and marginalisation facing South Asian Muslims, al-Zawahiri anticipated that AQIS would be welcomed by South Asian Muslims 'who sought liberation from oppression and injustice'.[7]

AQIS's official name, Organization of the Base of Jihad in the Indian Subcontinent denotes both its geographic focus and, in keeping with al-Qaeda core's other regional proxies, signifies its explicit dedication to jihad against both the 'near' enemy of India, Myanmar and Bangladesh, and the 'far' enemy of American targets in the Indian subcontinent. The end goal was the 'liberation' of the Indian subcontinent from 'infidel occupation' and the re-establishment of a caliphate evoking the Mughal Empire. Al-Zawahiri aimed at distinguishing AQIS from competing jihadist groups by reminding South Asian Muslims of the 'long-lost glorious past' of Muslim governance under the Mughals, thus constructing an alternative political order to the competing order offered by ISIS.[8] Al-Zawahiri would speak about the 'Ghazwa al-Hind', or the 'Battle to Reunite India'.[9] Al-Zawahiri sought to capitalise on pre-existing tensions, particularly between Hindus and Muslims, to give AQIS momentum.

The timing of AQIS also coincided with al-Zawahiri's attempt to counter the competition al-Qaeda faced from ISIS for fighters, impact, and attention on the international stage as well as seeking to capitalise on the extensive Islamic history in South Asia to justify the pursuit of a caliphate in the subcontinent as a viable and legitimate alternative to travelling to Iraq and Syria to achieve an Islamic state there. Importantly, AQIS was also established to bolster the Taliban's position and status, resulting in the inclusion of Taliban fighters who considered themselves loyal to al-Zawahiri's leadership.[10] The Taliban was crucial to al-Qaeda's broader strategy. Being located in Pakistan was also important as there was a support base of other like-minded jihadist groups, tribal areas to operate in, urban centres in which to find safe havens, and sections of the Pakistani military sympathetic to Islamist ideals.[11] Indeed, the creation of AQIS essentially formalised the historic operational relationships between al-Qaeda and various jihadist groups based in Afghanistan, Pakistan, and India.[12] In some measure, AQIS was an attempt to revitalise al-Qaeda and act as a buffer and additional layer of security for al-Qaeda core, as they would be locally based.

In terms of operations, AQIS engaged in assassinations and suicide attacks but were also focussing on something far bigger and more chilling. On 6 September 2014, AQIS operatives tried to hijack the Pakistani navy frigates PNS *Zulfiqar* and PNS *Aslat* at the Karachi port.[13] This was the same place where the Lashkar-e-Taiba (LeT) cell behind the Mumbai siege attack departed from. The AQIS goal was to destroy the American navy oil tanker, the USS *Supply*, as well as an additional frigate, whilst a separate cell on the PNS *Aslat* were plotting to sail towards India and attack Indian warships. The plots would resemble the 2000 USS *Cole* attack but on a much larger scale. Although some AQIS operatives were able to get onboard the frigates, they failed to launch the ships and were killed in the ensuing shootout.[14]

The most striking aspect of AQIS's maritime hijacking was its boldness, especially for a relatively new terrorist group. More significantly, the plot was ordered by al-Zawahiri himself.[15] The US counter-terrorism community took notice. In September 2019, AQIS leader Asim Umar was killed in a joint US-Afghan military operation at a Taliban compound in Helmand, Afghanistan.[16] Umar's death in a Taliban stronghold demonstrated the strategic relationship AQIS had with the Taliban, which was what al-Zawahiri had hoped would grow, despite setbacks.

On 12 July 2015, ISIS simultaneously released an audio message and an article in its *Dabiq* magazine, shockingly revealing that Taliban Supreme Leader Mullah Omar was dead and had been for a while. This exposé by ISIS compelled the Taliban to admit that Mullah Omar had died.[17] The revelation came to al-Zawahiri's detriment, as it looked like he had been advertising loyalty to a dead man and that ISIS were able to dictate the Taliban's narrative. Three of al-Qaeda's franchises, Jabhat al-Nusra, al-Qaeda in the Arabian Peninsula (AQAP), and al-Qaeda in the Islamic Maghreb (AQIM), issued a shared eulogy lauding the late Mullah Omar and his contribution to the global jihad movement.[18] Yet al-Zawahiri maintained a noticeable silence which was exploited by ISIS. Mohamed Mahmoud, an ISIS commander who defected from al-Qaeda because of his resentment over al-Zawahiri promoting his Egyptian cadre, published a series of tweets on 30 July 2015, claiming that al-Zawahiri himself had been long dead and al-Qaeda was concealing it.[19]

In fact, soon after formalising the creation of AQIS, between October 2014 and August 2015, al-Zawahiri avoided making any public statements, audio, video, or print. This created enormous uncertainty as to the direction al-Qaeda was heading. His silence was deafening, especially as many senior leaders within al-Qaeda and the affiliates were killed in US operations. This included al-Zawahiri's designated successor Nasir al-Wuhayshi, who led AQAP, and the US-born as-Sahab spokesman Adam Gadahn.[20] Ahmad Farouq, deputy leader of AQIS, and Muhsin al-Fadhli, leader of the Khorasan group in Syria, who was involved in plotting the 9/11 attacks, also died. There was no reaction or obituary from al-Zawahiri for any of them.

Eventually, after eleven months of silence, in August 2015, al-Zawahiri re-emerged and instantly declared his *ba'yah* to the new head of the Taliban, Mullah Mansour, designating him as the Amir al-Muminin in direct challenge to Abu Bakr al-Baghdadi's claim of *caliph*.[21] Mansour recognised al-Zawahiri's *bayat* and responded by identifying him as 'the leader of international Jihadi organization'.[22]

Al-Zawahiri's message was on 1 August 2015 and had been produced just two days after the Taliban conceded that Mullah Omar had in fact died on 23 April 2013. Remarkably, that was over two years before the Taliban were forced to publicly acknowledge Mullah Omar's death.[23] The Taliban contended it was kept a secret for strategic reasons, but the revelation that its founder's death had been concealed for years was detrimental for them and resulted in numerous splits and fractures within the different elements of the Taliban.

Curiously, al-Zawahiri avoided commenting on whether he had known. He was in a difficult position. Awareness of Mullah Omar's death could have been construed as evidence that he had been misleading his followers for years, whilst pledging *ba'yah* to a dead person. However, not being amongst the few insiders with this knowledge would confirm suspicions that al-Zawahiri was not as close to the Taliban leadership as bin Laden had been, which would have been equally damaging. Therefore, keeping silent on the issue was al-Zawahiri's best option. The problem for both al-Qaeda and the Taliban was that ISIS knew about Omar's demise sitting several thousand miles away in Syria. The fact that they outed Omar's passing caused huge internal fractures within the Taliban militias.

However, when al-Zawahiri pledged allegiance to Mullah Mansour, he received some derision by subordinating himself to a man whose succession to Mullah Omar was opposed by factions of the Taliban militia. Arguably, he had little choice, having found himself in a dependent position due to the rise of ISIS and his continued residence in the Taliban's strongholds in Pakistan.[24] Following Mansour's elimination in a US drone strike on 21 May 2016, al-Zawahiri pledged another *ba'yah* to his successor, Mawlawi Haibatullah Akhundzada, in the hope of strengthening the relationship with al-Qaeda.[25] Interestingly, Akhundzada never publicly accepted al-Zawahiri's pledge.

Al-Zawahiri presented the relationship between the Taliban and al-Qaeda as a model for jihadists around the globe. To show how far back the relationship went, al-Zawahiri lauded Mullah Omar for rejecting America's demand to turn over the al-Qaeda leadership after the September 11 attacks.[26] Al-Zawahiri would consistently express his endorsement for the Taliban and called on all jihadists globally to 'rally around the emirate', referring to the Taliban's pre-9/11 Islamic Emirate of Afghanistan.[27] Al-Zawahiri's open backing for the Taliban was not surprising, as al-Qaeda remained dependent on them for protection and sanctuary in both Afghanistan and Pakistan. Although al-Zawahiri's ties with the Taliban had been strained on occasions, he maintained them out of necessity. Allies can have areas of divergence. Yet they both shared a desire to force Western troops out of Afghanistan and reinstate Taliban rule. Furthermore, al-Zawahiri benefited from better ties with the Haqqani Network.

After the deaths of Mullah Omar and Mullah Mansour, and as Mawlawi Haibatullah struggled to secure his leadership, Sirajuddin Haqqani, the leader of the Haqqani Network, assumed the position of deputy *amir* of the Taliban's Islamic Emirate of Afghanistan. Haqqani wasted no time in taking control of many of the Taliban's day-to-day military operations, including renewing its support of al-Qaeda.[28] In December 2016, the Haqqani's media wing, Fountainhead of Jihad (Manba' al-Jihad) released a video celebrating the unbroken bond between the Taliban and al-Qaeda. Much of the production emphasized the close relationship between the two. An archival audio clip of Sirajuddin was included in that same video. The development of Manba' al-Jihad demonstrated Sirajuddin Haqqani's focus on propaganda and shaping the narrative. He was not just aiming at an Afghan audience. He once took part in an online question-and-answer session in an Arabic-language jihadist forum, making him the only known Taliban leader to engage in this format. It was reminiscent of the one al-Zawahiri took part in back in December 2007. It was clear the al-Qaeda leader was having an significant influence on Haqqani.[29]

An Assortment of Enemies

On 29 August 2016, al-Zawahiri released his fourth message in the series 'Brief Messages to a Victorious Ummah', entitled 'The Solid Structure'.[30] Symbolically, it was released on the 50th anniversary of the execution of his ideological mentor Sayyid Qutb. In 'The Solid Structure', al-Zawahiri borrowed from Qutb's formative book *Milestones*, about the need for the 'revival' of Shariah to adjudicate differences and disputes, and a Shura Council that would 'harness the power of the *ummah* against the tyrants and invaders'.[31] Al-Zawahiri was seeking to redress a criticism he had long faced, which was the importance of consistency behind the jihadist message.

Al-Zawahiri also castigated ISIS and al-Baghdadi for creating schisms and fragmentation amongst the jihadists with their 'innovated *caliphate*'.[32] Al-Zawahiri described them as 'neo-*Kharijites*' based on the term *khawarij* which effectively means 'outsiders', a historical and pejorative allusion to a sect, active during the first century of Islam, which rebelled against the fourth *caliph*, Ali, whom they later assassinated.[33] In classifying ISIS as *khawarij*, al-Zawahiri was calling for their total extermination (*qatl ad*).[34] The original *khawarij* pursued *takfir*, the excommunication and killing of Muslims accused of having abandoned Islam. Abu Musab al-Zarqawi was notorious for declaring Muslims as *takfir* to justify his violence against the Iraqi population. Years later, it was the same doctrine that ISIS used against Iraqi and Syrian Muslims.[35]

In retaliation for the plethora of verbal attacks by ISIS against al-Qaeda, al-Zawahiri sought to counter several of the damaging claims including that he had become soft and weak towards the enemies of the global jihadist movement. Some of the most egregious inferences by ISIS were that al-Zawahiri had endorsed Mohamed Morsi of the Muslim Brotherhood, opted against targeting Shiite Muslims, and abandoned the goal of targeting the United States. Regarding Shiites, al-Zawahiri blasted ISIS for trying to cast aspersions on his character: 'The liars [ISIS] insist upon their falsehood, to the extent that they claimed we do not denounce Shiites.'[36] He clarified that there should be no violence towards Shiite civilians, but plots should be redirected on Shiite-led Iraqi forces. Al-Zawahiri labelled them with the derogatory and sectarian word *rafidah*, which meant effectively calling the Shiite militias 'rejectionists' of the first three caliphs of Islam. Al-Zawahiri also repeated that al-Qaeda remained focused on attacking the West, regardless of their current focus on the 'internal enemy':

> We must not be prisoners to the terrorism of Western propaganda and politics, nor to the deceit of their hustling agents and those liars with [hidden] objectives, who accuse al-Qaeda of all types of betrayal, including being agents of America, created in Afghanistan during the Russian invasion.[37]

Al-Zawahiri was keen to illustrate his criticism of the West and conflating it with the 'hustling agents and liars' of ISIS as being the same enemy. Al-Zawahiri also once again specifically referred to the ISIS leader, Abu Bakr al-Baghdadi by his real name, Ibrahim al-Badry.[38] The Egyptian teacher preferred to do it behind closed doors, but he had learnt that the only way to defeat the ISIS narrative was to publicly challenge them.

After the strongholds of ISIS began to disintegrate because of international coalition efforts, al-Zawahiri's criticisms against them become more audible and fervent. In January 2017, he said that ISIS was 'exceeding the limit of extremism' and called on its fighters to defect from the 'madness'. He also asked those who 'seek truth' to follow al-Qaeda. He criticised ISIS for 'slandering' its own jihadists and branded ISIS members as 'cowards' with a 'thirsty desire for authority'.[39] Al-Zawahiri was finally feeling more confident that the global jihadist narrative could swing back to al-Qaeda. He had always had an extended time frame for his vision of jihad and viewed ISIS as a fad that would fail over time. To appear as the more 'moderate' terrorist group of the two, al-Zawahiri attempted to separate the tactics and methods of al-Qaeda from those of ISIS. Al-Zawahiri advocated kidnapping Western civilians and soldiers in Iraq and Afghanistan and exchanging them for imprisoned jihadists in the West, in evident contrast with the ISIS tactic of executing hostages and videotaping their decapitations.[40]

When al-Zawahiri gave a speech marking the 15th anniversary of 9/11, entitled 'The Defiers of Injustice', he commented on the racial discord in the United States and provocatively urged African Americans to join al-Qaeda:

> America is the source of calamity and the head of evil in this world, and it is the thief of [all] nations and their aliment, and it is the one who humiliate the Africans [i.e., African Americans] until this day, and no matter how much

they try to reform and obtain their rights according to the law and the [US] constitution, they will not attain it, for the law is in the hands of the white majority, [who] control it as they wish. And they [i.e., African Americans] will not be saved but by Islam.[41]

This opportunistic approach to expansion was pragmatic, adaptive, and less ideologically bound. It harked back to al-Zawahiri's May 2007 video in which he displayed video clips of Malcolm X and praised him as an example of long-term activism and radicalisation.[42] It was also a reminder of how much influence al-Zawahiri's granduncle Abdul Rahman Azzam had on him, as he was also an inspiration for Malcom X. Ironically, both Azzam and Malcolm X would likely not have appreciated al-Zawahiri's usage of the civil rights activist.

Al-Zawahiri's directives to affiliates provided a more nuanced strategic approach. In a May 2015 interview with al-Jazeera, Abu Mohammed al-Golani, the leader of Jabhat al-Nusra in Syria revealed that al-Zawahiri had directed him away from planning attacks against the West and to focus on Assad instead: 'We received clear orders not to use Syria as a launching pad to attack the U.S. or Europe in order to not sabotage the true mission against the [Bashar al-Assad] regime.'[43] Al-Golani's disclosure illustrated that al-Zawahiri was navigating al-Qaeda away from Osama bin Laden's directive to target the 'eternal enemy'. Al-Zawahiri's 'internal enemy' ideology became defined by playing the long game by first buying al-Qaeda time to rebuild whilst concurrently focussing on the 'internal enemy' within Muslim lands. Only when the organization was strong enough would they then revert to attacking the 'external enemy'. Al-Zawahiri learnt from 9/11 about prioritising which enemy could be the centre of their attention during certain phases and not to open new fronts which al-Qaeda is then unable to defend.

In July 2016, Abu Mohammad al-Golani announced that Jabhat al-Nusra was uncoupling from al-Qaeda and changing its name to Jabhat Fateh al-Sham (Front for the Conquest of Syria). Al-Zawahiri's trusted Egyptian deputies Abu al-Khayr al-Masri and Saif al-Adel helped formalise the delinking. Saif al-Adel's voice carried weight amongst many jihadists, as he was one of the few al-Qaeda leaders who openly opposed the September 11 attacks because it would put al-Qaeda under the direct spotlight of the United States. Al-Qaeda had approved the uncoupling so that its forces could concentrate on their fight against the Assad regime and form closer bonds with other Islamist groups fighting in Syria.[44]

The decision by al-Golani to cease fighting under al-Qaeda's banner was months in the making and overseen by al-Zawahiri himself. In May 2016, he released an audio recording saying Jabhat al-Nusra leaving al-Qaeda would not be an obstacle to 'the great hopes of the Islamic nation'.[45] Al-Zawahiri's message was an explicit clearance that enabled Jabhat Fateh al-Sham to uncouple from al-Qaeda without breaking the *ba'yah* to al-Zawahiri. He had hoped the group's break was more about organizational practicalities than any ideological conflict. Al-Zawahiri felt reassured because his close ally Ahmad Salama Mabruk had become a part of al-Golani's inner circle, and with the robust resistance to the Assad regime, it could provide al-Qaeda a more resilient base from which to operate in for future plotting.[46] However, on 3 October, 2016, this plan unravelled dramatically when it was revealed that Mabruk was killed in an airstrike by an American drone near Jisr al-Shughour in northern Syria.[47]

Without Mabruk, al-Zawahiri lost his key cog within Jabhat Fateh al-Sham. In less than a year, the group distanced itself further from al-Qaeda and rebranded itself as Hay'at Tahrir al-Sham (HTS) whilst at the same time absorbing other jihadist groups that had been reluctant to join previously because of the al-Qaeda connection.[48] With the emergence of HTS, the differences between them and al-Qaeda became more pronounced but not anywhere near the scale of animosity al-Qaeda had towards ISIS. With HTS, the differences were more strategic and reflective of current ground realities in Syria.[49] Therefore, the prospect of a future rapprochement cannot be ruled out.

The False Dawn

Al-Zawahiri adopted a three-pronged strategy to revive al-Qaeda just as ISIS was heading towards its decline. This began with bolstering the affiliates, which bin Laden had previously been against. Al-Zawahiri determined that it was the support of affiliates, including those in Pakistan, which had enabled al-Qaeda to survive. In turn, al-Qaeda was able to incorporate local agendas into a global narrative as part of an all-encompassing grand strategy. Second, in 2013, al-Zawahiri requested restraint in mass casualty attacks, especially those that could lead to Muslim casualties. Al-Zawahiri intended for al-Qaeda to present itself as a more 'moderate' terrorist group compared to ISIS.[50] The third part of this revival process was grooming his successor, Hamza bin Laden.[51] Al-Zawahiri was shrewd enough to see the enduring benefits of the bin Laden brand name to reconstitute al-Qaeda's appeal. Hamza bin Laden was another al-Qaeda figure who spent time in Iran, where his activities remain a mystery.[52]

Hamza bin Laden was the favourite son of Osama bin Laden. Hamza's mother, Khairiah Sabar, was living with her husband, Osama bin Laden, in the Abbottabad compound when he was killed.[53] Following his father's death, Hamza began to assume an increasingly prominent role in al-Qaeda's propaganda. Despite his youthful appearance, Hamza sought to symbolically emulate his father both in the tone and doctrine. When appearing in al-Qaeda propaganda videos, he would wear robes and don a *ghutrah*, a piece of white cotton cloth. This was meant to symbolise and convey that despite growing up in Pakistan, Afghanistan, and Iran, Hamza bin Laden retained his Arab heritage.

Together, al-Zawahiri and Hamza bin Laden synchronised the release of al-Qaeda's online missives that spoke of retribution against the United States for the death of Osama bin Laden.[54] Al-Zawahiri had also hoped to cultivate Hamza bin Laden's potential, as he was married to al-Zawahiri's daughter, Khadija, and had two children from her, Khairiah and Saad.[55] Through the strategic marriage alliance, al-Zawahiri could keep the bin Laden legacy firmly ensconced in his own doctrine. Hamza bin Laden also married the daughter of Mohamed Atta, another Egyptian protégé of al-Zawahiri and the lead hijacker in the 9/11 terror attacks.[56]

In a 2015 speech, Ayman al-Zawahiri presented Hamza bin Laden as 'son of the lion of jihad' a play on the honourific of his father Osama. Hamza summoned al-Qaeda's followers to battle against the 'Americans, Jews, and the rest of the West'.[57] Hamza bin Laden's speeches revitalised the image and words of his father: 'We [al-Qaeda] will continue striking you and targeting you in your country and abroad.'[58] He was unnervingly direct when he threatened America and the West. Because of that, Hamza bin Laden was listed as a 'global terrorist' by the United States.[59]

Al-Zawahiri was working on Hamza's coronation as a terrorist figurehead, and in an August 2015 audio message, al-Zawahiri introduced 'a lion from the den of al-Qaeda' and Hamza bin Laden acclaimed the 'martyrdom' of his father and his brother Khalid at Abbottabad. He also commended al-Qaeda's leaders in Syria, Yemen, and the Maghreb; glorified the attacks on

Fort Hood and the Boston Marathon; and called for al-Qaeda's followers to 'take the battlefield from Kabul, Baghdad and Gaza to Washington, London, Paris and Tel Aviv'.[60]

This promotion of Hamza was a clear, calculated move by al-Zawahiri to appeal to young militants who still admired bin Laden. However, Hamza was not necessarily following his father's exact approach to terrorism. Osama bin Laden looked at specific large-scale mass casualty attacks, whereas Hamza was more interested in urging lone actors to seize any opportunity that became available against soft targets. In a recording on 13 May 2017, Hamza bin Laden stated, 'It is not necessary that it should be a military tool. . . . [I]f you are able to pick a firearm, well and good; if not, the options are many.'[61]

During a spring 2019 meeting in Afghanistan's Helmand province, the Taliban 'met with Hamza Usama [Osama] Muhammad bin Laden to reassure him personally' that the Taliban 'would not break its historical ties with al-Qaeda for any price'.[62] The fact that US intelligence was fully aware of this meeting meant the young bin Laden was less guarded about his personal security than al-Zawahiri.[63] Hamza bin Laden provided the link between the old al-Qaeda leadership and the next generation, and just as it looked like al-Qaeda was facing a new dawn in its re-emergence and growth, rumours began to surface of Hamza bin Laden's death. They were confirmed days after the eighteenth anniversary of 9/11 by the Trump administration: 'Hamza bin Laden was killed in a United States counter-terrorism operation in the Afghanistan/Pakistan region.'[64] The demise of Hamza bin Laden ended al-Zawahiri's efforts to carefully nurture his protégé and the symbolic connection to Osama bin Laden. As with Operation Neptune Spear, the United States did not consult Pakistan in their plans. The trust deficit remained.[65]

ISIS sought to capitalise on this and spread rumours that al-Zawahiri was either dead or had suffered a stroke on hearing the news about Hamza bin Laden, and that al-Qaeda was covering up the news to avoid a potential setback or disunity. To dispel recuring rumours of al-Zawahiri's health, on 11 September 2019, to commemorate the eighteenth anniversary of the 9/11 attacks, al-Qaeda released a special edition in English of their magazine *One Ummah*. The propaganda was originally launched in Arabic as *Majallah Ummah Wahida* in April 2019, but this was their first English-language version. *One Ummah* sought to be an alternative to the theological, doc-trinal messages from as-Sahab and focused on current events, history, eco-nomics, and personal stories from jihadists. The 9/11 issue had an extensive feature on al-Zawahiri, who described *One Ummah* as seeking to spread 'jihadi maturity and political understanding'. Al-Zawahiri added, 'Jihad is one of several methods to call people to Allah and spread the message of His Oneness so that there is no persecution in the world.'[66]

After dispelling rumours of his death once more, al-Zawahiri received some good news about ISIS. On 26 October 2019, helicopters carrying members of the elite US Army Delta Force landed on a compound near the town of Barisha, in the Idlib Governate, in northwest Syria, triggering a firefight with ISIS fighters. Abu Bakr al-Baghdadi escaped through a tunnel with two of his children. With Delta Force commandos in hot pursuit, al-Baghdadi, the world's *other* most wanted terrorist, detonated his suicide vest, killing himself and his offspring. The man who built a terrorist nation across the lands of Syria and Iraq and galvanised thousands of jihadists globally spent his last minutes crawling in a tunnel.[67] One can imagine al-Zawahiri's wry smile seeing yet another nemesis depart before him. Al-Baghdadi tried to usurp al-Zawahiri as the leader of the global jihad movement and ques-tioned the al-Qaeda leader on everything including the merits of creating an openly declared pseudo-state. According to Bruce Riedel, 'Al-Zawahiri was proven right in his dispute with Abu Bakr al Baghdadi about the via-bility of the Islamic caliphate, and he outlasted al-Baghdadi.'[68]

The operation to eliminate al-Baghdadi drew parallels with the bin Laden raid. Again, the United States capitalized on human intelligence, covert cooperation, and operational capability. Factoring in the huge, so-phisticated efforts to locate al-Baghdadi and bin Laden, the fact that al-Zawahiri had not been found at this point was even more remarkable. The al-Qaeda leader had sought to avoid the same pitfalls that brought about al-Baghdadi and bin Laden's demise. Luck may have also played a role. However, the Egyptian ideologue had repeatedly shown a desire and pro-pensity to survive despite the sophistication in technology and intelligence employed by counter-terrorism agencies, whilst also letting the burden fall on ISIS. Bruce Hoffman commented that 'al-Zawahiri was smart enough to let ISIS take all the heat. Al-Qaeda's slow, deliberate strategy is down to al-Zawahiri and his ability to implement it.'[69]

Kingdom of Heaven

In 2018, during the Trump administration, al-Zawahiri spoke about Saudi crown prince Mohammed bin Salman vowing to clamp down on Islamists and jihadists. Al-Zawahiri claimed that the United States was 'working with Saudi Arabia to train imams and rewrite religious textbooks'. Al-Zawahiri then called on Muslims 'to unite around confronting America'.[70] This demonstrated the terrorist group's gradualist approach of 'remaining loyal and steadfast on the path of jihad', a veiled poke at the ideological and strategic recklessness of ISIS, which had accused al-Zawahiri of being a weak leader, out of touch with the *ummah*.

Subsequent messages issued by al-Zawahiri continued the theme of making the United States the primary focus of al-Qaeda's ire. Following critiques of the Bush and Obama administrations, al-Zawahiri described President Donald Trump a 'blatant crusader' who has 'revealed the true face of America, and the true psychology of a majority of the American people toward Muslims'.[71] Al-Zawahiri's statement on the 17th anniversary of the September 11 attacks entitled 'How to Confront America?' stressed jihad against the United States anywhere in the Islamic world, conducted as a single campaign, as a unified force on many fronts.[72]

Al-Zawahiri wanted to identify the United States as the primary enemy to unite the *ummah*, but at the same time he wasn't planning any plots that would then undermine al-Qaeda's recovery. In the meantime, the United States would remain a reliable target for criticism and a method for recruitment. Instead, al-Zawahiri retained more willingness to focus on American interests in the Islamic world as opposed to the US North America and Europe, in regions where al-Qaeda and its affiliates had a functioning network.

Another example of this tactic by al-Zawahiri was demonstrated in a speech released on 18 September 2018 in reaction to the Trump administration's transfer of its embassy in Israel from Tel Aviv to Jerusalem: 'America [is] the number one enemy of Muslims ... despite of its professed secularism.'[73] Al-Zawahiri regularly cited US support for Israel as an example of subjugating Muslims, and he was increasingly using the US Embassy move to Jerusalem to drive his point home. Al-Zawahiri also made explicit reference to Trump's declaration that the Golan Heights belongs to Israel to encourage Palestinians to carry out suicide attacks on Israelis. His opinion hadn't changed since his debates with Abdullah Azzam over the flaws of targeting Israel; decades later, al-Zawahiri knew it was not a winnable issue, even though it was emotive.

On 11 September 2020 the al-Qaeda media organ as-Sahab released a video message from al-Zawahiri. It was the first instalment in a series entitled 'The Deal of the Century or the Crusade of the Century'. It coincided with the anniversary of 9/11, although curiously it did not deal with the attacks directly. The message did not comment on the emergence and impact of the global COVID-19 pandemic either.[74]

Al-Zawahiri instead commented on US president Donald Trump's 'peace plan' for the Middle East and then refuted claims from a 2019 al-Jazeera documentary regarding alleged cooperation between al-Qaeda and governmental elements in Gulf Arab countries. He angrily called these 'illusions' and part of a disinformation campaign 'falsely linked to Al-Qaeda'.[75] Clearly, al-Zawahiri's prickly nature came out, similar to when al-Sharif's refutation had rankled him.

Al-Zawahiri then sought to highlight some 'historical facts about the struggle between the Muslims and the Crusaders', stressing that the battle is a zero-sum religious conflict, based on the Zionist-Crusader alliance against Muslims.[76] In an important moment of reflection, al-Zawahiri emphasised that the 'jihad of da'wah and raising awareness . . . is more important than the military jihad itself'.[77] The context can be lost, but it was a continuous trait of al-Zawahiri to speak about biding one's time and not fighting the enemy too early when one is not ready. He identified the enemies of the *ummah*, aside from Israel, as 'America and its hirelings among the local rulers, Russia, China, India, and Iran.'[78]

Clearly fearing that Gulf Arab nations would normalise relations with Israel and seek diplomatic ties under Trump's plan, al-Zawahiri condemned the rulers of those countries as being 'among the dangerous type of enemies. . . . [They] claim to defend the *ummah* while in reality they are effective tools in the inimical plot against Islam and Muslims . . . while in reality they are fully submerged in the swamp of their security agreements with Israel, and their lands are occupied by American bases.' Al-Zawahiri's perceptions of Arab nations normalising ties with Israel turned out to be well-founded.[79]

Despite COVID-19, the Abraham Accords resulted in four Arab countries—the United Arab Emirates, Sudan, Morocco, and Bahrain—forging diplomatic ties with Israel in 2020 which became one of the most significant outcomes in the Arab-Israeli conflict since the 1990s.[80] In various peace talks over decades, Arab normalisation with Israel was contingent on Israel creating conditions for a viable independent Palestinian state comprising the West Bank and Gaza Strip. The fact that Israel achieved diplomatic relations with four Arab states in quick succession without any changes for the Palestinians, signalled that the issue was no longer considered important enough by some Arab regimes. Saudi crown prince Mohammed bin Salman, the architect of this enhancement of Arab ties with Israel, held a private meeting with Benjamin Netanyahu in the presence of US secretary of state Mike Pompeo, demonstrating unprecedented Saudi-Israeli coordination aimed at Iran, which both consider the bigger and primary threat to their respective security. Iran mattered to al-Zawahiri too.[81]

Iran and AQ: Best of Frenemies

In August 2020, Abu Muhammad al-Masri, one of al-Zawahiri's deputies, was mysteriously killed in a drive-by shooting in Tehran, allegedly an Israeli operation. Abu Muhammad was killed along with his daughter, one of the three widows of Hamza bin Laden. Abu Muhammad had originally been in Iran's 'custody' for more than a decade but overtime was allowed to live more freely in Tehran.[82] His death raised an often underreported but critically important tangential dynamic—namely, al-Qaeda's ties in Iran.

The relationship between al-Qaeda and Iran is contentious. On the one hand, there are obvious ideological barriers and profound suspicion affecting the relationship. On the other hand, there are temporary, tactical, and strategic imperatives for both sides. We can see the connection between al-Qaeda and Iran slowly unravelling through a combination of declassified documents by al-Qaeda's own leadership, such as the Abbottabad files, and intercepts by counter-terrorism agencies, as well as publicly disclosed US governmental assessments.

Following the 9/11 attacks, numerous EIJ and al-Qaeda fighters sought refuge in Iran but were largely kept in detention centres or under house arrest. Iran initially provided passage and sanctuary for al-Qaeda during Operation Enduring Freedom and continued to do so when US counterterrorism operations intensified in Pakistan, but with caveats attached.[83] The presence of al-Qaeda leaders and their family members in Iran has been a type of insurance that this understanding stays intact. However, it did not necessarily mean that Tehran was providing material or tactical assistance to al-Qaeda.[84]

For its part, al-Qaeda would instruct its followers that aside from the usual anti-Iranian sectarian rhetoric, they must avoid any action that could be detrimental to the al-Qaeda members based in Iran and put them at the receiving end of punitive action by the paramilitary Islamic Revolutionary Guard Corps (IRGC). As bin Laden stated in a 2007 letter, 'Iran is our main artery for funds, personnel, and communication.'[85] In turn, Iran wanted assurances that al-Qaeda would not conduct terrorist attacks against them.

Qassem Soleimani, the head of the IRGC, had approved sanctuary for al-Qaeda members without consulting then Iranian president Mohammad Khatami first. It is unclear if Ayatollah Ali Khamenei was involved in the policy, but the IRGC has always operated in lockstep with the Iranian Supreme Leader.[86] The IRGC itself was created in the aftermath of Iran's 1979 revolution to protect the Islamic theocratic regime whilst furthering its strategic interests. The IRGC has sought to provide assistance to militant groups in Afghanistan, Iraq, Lebanon, the Palestinian territories, Syria, and Yemen. Sometimes, the policy is based on supporting groups that are opposed to Israel, Saudi Arabia, or the United States. On other occasions, it is about having certain organizations placated so that they do not threaten Tehran whilst also using them to gain intelligence on their inner-workings. Iran has been a geostrategic location for al-Qaeda and a key pathway between the AfPak region and the Middle East.[87] The Saudi Arabian government alleged that Saif Al-Adel masterminded the 12 May 2003 suicide bombings of the Muhaya residential compounds in Riyadh whilst based in Iran.[88] Despite being involved in sectarian rivalry, al-Zawahiri appeared to have been in clandestine dialogue with Hezbollah. In an Abbottabad document, 'Letter regarding Working in Islamic Countries', an al-Qaeda operative questions bin Laden on Iraq and Hezbollah:

> Some of which is your silence regarding the Iranian strategy in the region, and the nature of the relationship to it, especially after the repeated calls to Muslims by Dr. Ayman to support Hizballah, knowing that Hizballah is a part of the Iranian rejectionist agenda.[89]

Soleimani took personal responsibility for Osama bin Laden's family when they sought sanctuary in Iran in 2002 and justified them as 'non-combatants'. However, in 2008, bin Laden learnt about the poor conditions to which his family and other detainees were subjected to in Iran, when his son, Saad, managed to escape. Upon his arrival in North Waziristan, Saad wrote a long letter to his father detailing the conditions that members of al-Qaeda and their families were subjected to by the IRGC while in detention.[90] The al-Qaeda leadership needed to steer a cautious path with Iran, but they also were willing to up the ante if required. In 2010, Iran and al-Qaeda engaged in a prisoner exchange where several al-Qaeda members, including Abu Walid al-Masri and bin Laden's son Hamza were freed and allowed into Pakistan in exchange for Heshmatollah Attarzadeh-Nyaki, an Iranian diplomat abducted in Pakistan in 2008.[91]

Events like this resulted in a very surreal situation in Pakistan's tribal areas such as Kurram, where the Pakistani Frontier Corps would encounter on occasion IRGC intelligence operatives trying to leverage influence amongst the disproportionately large Shiite population in the area. The Iranians wanted to know what was happening in Afghanistan and Pakistan, and the Pakistanis tolerated it as long as it did not impact on their own security. This dynamic became more complicated as al-Qaeda fighters would often be caught moving from Pakistan to Afghanistan and Iran and vice-versa.[92]

Post-Abbottabad, al-Zawahiri's most persistent problem was his inability to communicate regularly with senior aides and affiliates. However, countering this isolation, he cultivated a hub of loyal cadres in Iran, known as the Hittin Committee, who liaised with jihadists in Syria, the Sinai, Maghreb, and sub-Saharan Africa.[93] The name was derived from the Battle of Hittin in 1187 between the founder of the Ayyubid dynasty, Saladin, and the Latin Crusader states. The Christians were defeated, bringing about an effective end to the Christian occupation of the Holy Land, including Jerusalem. The losses prompted the Third Crusade in 1189.

Over time, al-Qaeda's resilience and ambivalence towards Iran served the IRGC's ability to focus on ISIS, which had no qualms in killing Iranians and Shiite affiliates in Iraq. This also prevented al-Qaeda from being paired with ISIS by Tehran. In 2014, Abu Muhammad al-Adnani, the head of external operations for ISIS, issued a message entitled *Iran's Heavy Debt to al-Qaeda*, attacking al-Zawahiri for inhibiting jihadists from launching attacks in Iran 'pursuant to al-Qaeda's order to maintain its interests and lines of supply in Iran'.[94] Ironically, before al-Zawahiri succeeded bin Laden, al-Adnani viewed the Egyptian teacher as the 'wise man of the *ummah*'.[95]

In 2015 there was a prisoner exchange between Iran and al-Qaeda which involved the release from Iranian confinement of five senior of al-Qaeda operatives, including three close allies of al-Zawahiri, the Egyptians Saif al-Adel, Abu Muhammad al-Masri, and Abu al-Khayr al-Masri. Furthermore, two Jordanians, Abu al-Qassam and Sari Shihab were all freed in return for Iranian diplomat Noor Ahmad Nikbakht, who had been abducted by AQAP in Sana'a, Yemen, in 2013. Sirajuddin Haqqani, in conjunction with al-Zawahiri, acted as mediator between Iran and al-Qaeda to secure their release.[96] Al-Zawahiri did not waste time with al-Adel's newfound ability to travel. He sent him to Syria to supervise al-Qaeda's interests there and exploit ISIS's diminishing military status and territorial contraction to ensure the Egyptian jihadists were once more at the vanguard of the global jihad movement.[97]

Subsequently, Abu al-Khayr al-Masri served as al-Zawahiri's deputy and formed a leadership council with the Abu Muhammad al-Masri and Saif al-Adel, who chose to remain Iran for strategic purposes.[98] Abu al-Khayr was one of the planners of the 1998 bombings of two US embassies in East Africa. He eventually went to Syria to assist al-Qaeda affiliates engaged in the civil war that paralysed the country. In February 2017, he was killed in a US air strike in Idlib governate. Significantly, al-Zawahiri's son-in-law Muhammad Abbatay was also discovered to be in Iran. He had not been killed in the 2006 drone strike in South Waziristan, Pakistan, as was thought at the time.[99] Abbatay was yet another example of how key al-Qaeda members have been able to survive for much longer by situating themselves in Iran. Abbatay ran al-Qaeda's External Communications Office in Iran, where he coordinated activities with al-Qaeda's affiliates.[100]

An important aspect of al-Zawahiri was that what he would say publicly did not entirely correspond with what he would instruct his followers privately. In his statements, al-Zawahiri requested that fighters in Iraq regroup and launch an insurgency against the 'Safavid-Crusader occupation' that supported Shiite militias.[101] The Safavid dynasty was a Shiite Persian empire during the sixteenth and seventeenth centuries, insinuating that Iran had aspirations to suppress Sunni Muslims in Iraq. Al-Zawahiri would also state that Iran and the United States had a 'scheme' to eradicate Sunni Muslims in Iraq.[102] Yet, in personal communiques, al-Zawahiri ordered al-Qaeda to 'avoid fighting the deviant sects', a reference to Shiite Muslim civilians.[103] On 3 January 2020, IRGC commander General Soleimani, who had played a role in enabling al-Qaeda to use Iran as a facilitation hub in exchange for not plotting against them, was killed in a targeted US drone strike at

Baghdad International Airport in Iraq.[104] His death raised questions over whether the IRGC would seek to continue a clandestine relationship with al-Qaeda.[105]

Dystopia Redux

On 4 September 2018, the Taliban announced the death of the Haqqani Network leader Jalaluddin Haqqani. Al-Qaeda swiftly issued a glowing eulogy. In a two-page statement, al-Zawahiri also specifically addressed 'our emirs in the Islamic Emirate', meaning the Taliban's top leaders, Haibatullah Akhundzada and Sirajuddin Haqqani, stating that he took 'solace' that Sirajuddin was the 'deputy of the Islamic Emirate of Afghanistan's Commander of the Faithful [*Amir al-Muminin*]' and is following in his father's 'footsteps'.[106]

The Haqqani Network consistently maintained a symbiotic relationship with regional terrorist groups from Pakistan such as the LeT and Jaish-e-Mohammed (JeM). Both are also affiliated with al-Qaeda and gave sanctuary to the al-Qaeda leadership and their families after 9/11. These entities brought vital skill sets and resources. Complicating matters was that all these groups retain a close nexus with the Pakistani military establishment, officially and unofficially.

On 22 September 2018, based on intelligence provided by the United States, several heavily armed al-Qaeda fighters accompanied by family members were tracked to the remote and isolated hamlet of Gharlamai in North Waziristan. A shoot-out with local security forces ensued, resulting in the capture of several al-Qaeda members. Unbeknown at the time, one of the people captured was al-Zawahiri's third wife, Sayyida Halawa, who also went by the name Umm Tasneem.[107] Almost a year later, al-Zawahiri acknowledged the capture of his wife and praised the al-Qaeda fighters who died trying to prevent her capture as 'martyrs' and in a rare rebuke to the Pakistani military, he referred to them as 'treacherous' and called 'their American masters responsible for their criminal acts.'[108] However, the Pakistani military, which has had to long live with loyalties that have been divided at best, duplicitous at worst, were not given much option, as the United States practically pinpointed the location of the al-Qaeda contingent.[109]

Matters were made more complicated when on 29 February 2020, the US special representative for Afghanistan Zalmay Khalilzad and Taliban co-founder Mullah Abdul Ghani Baradar signed a peace deal in Doha, Qatar, the Agreement for Bringing Peace to Afghanistan between the Islamic Emirate of Afghanistan Which Is Not Recognized by the United States as a State and Is Known as the Taliban and the United States of America.[110] The paradoxical and elongated title of the agreement reflected its inherent flaws which directly led to the disastrous events that would eventually unfold in Afghanistan.

Mullah Baradar had spent eight years languishing in a Pakistani prison for being seen as too independent by the Pakistani military. Having fallen out of favour with both the Pakistani military and Taliban, Baradar was released so he could sign the Doha withdrawal deal with the United States on the Taliban's behalf. The problem was that Mullah Baradar exercised no influence or authority. Yet, the Doha agreement was heavily skewed in the Taliban's favour, with the United States making several concessions in return for an entirely dubious counter-terrorism pledge against al-Qaeda and other jihadist groups.

US and Taliban negotiators spent months working out the name of the bizarre, flawed, and sadly ironic title. The Taliban were refusing to remove the term 'Islamic Emirate', and the United States was unwilling to acknowledge it. The agreement provided for a gradual drawdown of American and NATO troops. In return, the Taliban pledged to not allow Afghanistan to be used as a hub for terrorism, cut ties with al-Qaeda, neither hosting them nor allowing fundraising, training, or recruitment.[111] There remained deep concerns that women's rights and civil liberties would plunge back into the dark ages, narcotics would flow in even greater quantities, and al-Qaeda would be allowed safe passage back into Afghanistan. Because it was bilateral, the Doha agreement also excluded the Ashraf Ghani government, which was pressured to release 5,000 Taliban prisoners, setting in motion a process that would see some of Afghanistan's most violent criminals and terrorists walk free.[112]

On 20 February 2020, the *New York Times* published an op-ed attributed to al-Zawahiri ally Sirajuddin Haqqani who used the opportunity to speak on behalf of the entire Taliban and blame the United States for the situation in Afghanistan: 'We did not choose our war with the foreign coalition led by the United States.' However, what was most significant about the unctuous article was what Haqqani didn't talk about. He ignored the Taliban's role in harbouring and assisting al-Qaeda in the years leading up to 9/11 and thereafter giving them safe passage and sanctuary into Pakistan. In fact, al-Qaeda was not mentioned at all. Haqqani did say that 'all Afghans have equal rights, rights of women granted by Islam'. What may have been over-looked was that Haqqani was separating men and women as if women are not part of the first phrase. This language echoed what the Taliban had said back in the 1990s that women will have no role in politics and civil society.[113] Empowering women in Afghanistan post-9/11 had been one of the most powerful success stories as it was a bulwark against misogyny, which in turn leads to radicalisation and terrorism.

As expected, the Taliban who flagrantly disregarded its agreement to end ties with al-Qaeda, and the groups continued to cooperate. In fact, during the deliberations over the Doha Agreement of February 2020, the Taliban quietly assured al-Qaeda that they would remain allies. According to a UN report of May 2020, 'The Taliban regularly consulted with al-Qaeda during negotiations with the United States and offered guarantees that it would honour their historical ties.'[114] They did so in the face of an explicit stipulation in the Doha accord that they would sever ties with terrorist groups including al-Qaeda, which was a key element in justifying the Trump administration's willingness to negotiate with the Taliban in the first place. The UN report further stated, 'The senior leadership of Al-Qaeda remains present in Pakistan, as well as hundreds of armed operatives, Al-Qaeda in the Indian Subcontinent, and groups of foreign terrorist fighters aligned with the Taliban.'[115]

Upon becoming the 46th president of the United States, Joe Biden undertook a policy review on the US presence in Afghanistan. On 14 April 2021 Biden announced, 'I have concluded that it's time to end America's longest war. It's time for American troops to come home.'[116] Biden announced a complete withdrawal of American troops from Afghanistan by 11 September 2021, coinciding with the 20th anniversary of the 9/11 terrorist attacks. Biden's decision went again the advice from his military and the intelligence community, which thought that a US withdrawal would be catastrophic for Afghanistan.[117]

Biden's decision to withdraw all US troops from Afghanistan represented a major shift in US counter-terrorism strategy as it was calendar based rather than being determined by conditions on the ground, irrespective of insecurity and conflicts. In revealing his plans to leave Afghanistan, Biden claimed that 'our reasons for remaining in Afghanistan are becoming increasingly unclear' and al-Qaeda was 'degraded'.[118] However, al-Qaeda may have been degraded but it was not defeated, and the loss of bin Laden did not destroy the group. Under al-Zawahiri, al-Qaeda proved extraordinarily resilient and adaptive, a reminder that the Egyptian terrorist always sought to play the long game.

In commenting on the 10-year anniversary of the bin Laden Abbottabad operation, Biden said, 'We'd follow Osama bin Laden to the gates of hell if need be. That's exactly what we did, and we got him.'[119] What was most telling about Biden's speech was what he didn't say, namely the relevance of Pakistan. Officially the West's counter-terrorism partner, Pakistan had received officially more than $35 billion dollars in the 20 years since 9/11.[120] However, the Pakistani military was the adversary, playing a murderous double game by supporting terrorist groups including al-Qaeda through its intelligence service, the ISI. In fact, the ISI has been energising and maintaining the terrorist conflict in Afghanistan as a facilitator, supporter, and director of terrorist actions against the West. Its two biggest beneficiaries were Sirajuddin Haqqani and al-Zawahiri. The al-Qaeda leader successfully established a reciprocal arrangement of support not only with the Haqqani Network and the Taliban, but also with the Pakistani jihadist groups such as the LeT and the JeM as well as Pakistan's military establishment, most notably the ISI.

Biden also failed to mention that the bin Laden raid was only possible because of the US bases in Afghanistan. The other problem was that bin Laden was not found at 'the gates of hell' but rather in the garrison town of Abbottabad, whose academy's graduates feed into the Pakistani military establishment. As President Obama's vice-president, Joe Biden advised against the Abbottabad operation. Obama revealed in his memoirs that Biden was 'arguing that given the enormous consequences of failure, I should defer any decision until the intelligence community was more certain that bin Laden was in the compound.'[121]

On explaining his decision-making process for the withdrawal from Afghanistan, Biden commented, 'To me, it was absolutely clear. We went for two reasons: get rid of bin Laden and to end the safe haven. I never thought we were there to somehow unify Afghanistan. It's never been done.'[122] The dilemma was that the terrorist safe haven still undoubtedly existed in Pakistan which enabled it to remerge in Afghanistan. Peace eluded Afghanistan because Pakistan's military worked to keep the country weak and divided. Most importantly, the way several US administrations saw Afghanistan differed substantially from how it was seen by Pakistan's military, particularly the ISI. Without a fundamental change in the Pakistan mindset, traditional 'victory' in Afghanistan was never possible or even partially attainable.

Biden's decision to also use 11 September 2021 as a withdrawal date was a propaganda gift to al-Qaeda and its allies, as well as its rivals like the Islamic State Khorasan Province (IS-KP). Bizarrely, the Biden administration chose a date that strengthened the jihadist narrative of resistance and perseverance in the face of the so-called crusader occupation. After belatedly releasing the symbolic error of the departure date, Biden subsequently brought forward the US-led exodus to 31 August 2021 claiming, 'The terrorist threat has metastasized beyond Afghanistan.' Biden was adamant that al-Qaeda's capacity to plot more attacks on the United States from Afghanistan had been permanently extinguished.[123]

However, for the Taliban and al-Qaeda, the twentieth anniversary of 9/11 remained a target to symbolise their renewal and victory of the so-called Islamic Emirate of Afghanistan. Two decades after having to flee Afghanistan and losing several members of his family, al-Zawahiri had survived, with this jihadist vision intact for others to develop. Furthermore, the Biden withdrawal from Afghanistan made a Taliban takeover inevitable and gave al-Qaeda the opportunity to rebuild its network and spawn new aligned movements, to the point it could once again plot and plan attacks around the world.

Without a presence on the ground in Afghanistan, the United States created challenges in monitoring and disrupting emerging terrorist threats. An offshore strategy was never going to be sufficient or a viable alternative. It is often overlooked that Afghanistan experienced a period of relative peace and stability after the Taliban's defeat post-9/11 and that a Taliban-led insurgency did not materialise until 2005. In between, the Bush administration was fixated on Saddam Hussein's Iraq. With Afghanistan less of a priority, as the United States was preoccupied by the ill-fated Iraq War, the Taliban regrouped with the Pakistani military's support.

Therefore, 'winning' in Afghanistan could never have happened when the Bush, Obama, and Trump administrations' most important 'partner', Pakistan, was singularly dedicated to US failure in Afghanistan, despite the lucrative remuneration it received. Principally, the Taliban have been the Pakistani military's strategic asset, and their presence in Afghanistan provided 'strategic depth'. One of the other biggest beneficiaries of that nexus has been al-Qaeda. The Pakistani military was never going to give up the Taliban project just because they were told after 9/11 'you are either with us or against us'.

As the Ashraf Ghani government collapsed, and the Taliban surged across Afghanistan during the summer of 2021, they initially stated that their rule would be more tolerant, broadminded, and inclusive than compared to their previous incarnation in the 1990s. They promised amnesty for adversaries and claimed the rights of women would be protected. To try to win over the international community, the Taliban also asserted that Afghanistan would not be a sanctuary for terrorist groups to operate and plot global attacks. However, over time, the reality looked very different.

The Taliban ruling council was composed entirely of veteran hardliners, and women were entirely absent. The independent media was muzzled, and civil disobedience was outlawed unless sanctioned by the Ministry of Interior run by Sirajuddin Haqqani, the internationally proscribed terrorist who was on the FBI's Most Wanted List. Haqqani took charge of all internal security within Afghanistan and became the most powerful Taliban leader. His uncle, Khalil-ur-Rahman Haqqani, who rescued al-Zawahiri's family during the US Operation Enduring Freedom bombing campaign, was made minister of refugees. Khalil-ur-Rahman Haqqani is also an internationally proscribed terrorist. Amir Khan Muttaqi, who had warned the United States not to conduct operations against bin Laden pre-9/11 and promised al-Qaeda would not attack the United States, was made foreign minister and led the Taliban's diplomatic engagement with the outside world. Taliban 2.0 is Taliban 1.0, and the Haqqanis became the most powerful Taliban faction in Afghanistan.

Tensions over the balance of power in Afghanistan between the Haqqani Network and Mullah Baradar manifested on the evening of 3 September 2021, when a violent altercation broke out in Kabul's presidential palace between Khalil-ur-Rahman Haqqani and Mullah Baradar. A shootout then ensued between their respective security details with Haqqani eventually triumphant. Baradar, was given the symbolic role of first deputy prime minister under the Taliban, but ultimately did not wield any power. He was subsequently jettisoned to Kandahar, and the West's only potential ally in the dystopian Taliban Afghanistan was no longer relevant to matters in that country.[124] The Haqqanis being in charge in Afghanistan meant the country could become a safe haven for terrorism again. According to Secretary

Panetta, 'Al-Qaeda will use the opportunity in Afghanistan as a base from which to conduct attacks.'[125] The situation was compounded with concerns that al-Zawahiri was being protected by the Haqqanis.[126]

The Taliban's pretence of amnesty was in reality a pretext for the execution of former security personnel and government workers during the Ashraf Ghani administration, as well as the torrture of journalists and civil liberty activists. The Taliban also systematically expunged women from public life by enforcing dress restrictions, effectively banned access to secondary and university education and ordered women in the workplaces across Afghanistan to stay home. Compounding the situation, the Taliban terminated the Ministry of Women's Affairs, which was tasked with protecting women's rights. Perversely, they repurposed it into the Ministry for the Promotion of Virtue and the Prevention of Vice, a recreation of the feared 'moral police' that mercilessly terrorized women during the Taliban's previous rule. This entity once again ordered beauty parlours and barber shops to shut down and enforced men to grow beards, ostensibly to demonstrate their 'religious piety'.

Predictably, the Taliban's long-standing ties with al-Qaeda endured and have been reinforced through ideology and family marriages. Furthermore, al-Qaeda and its affiliates praised the Taliban takeover and cited it as the exemplar for spreading their brand of jihad across the world. At the same time, the Taliban not only failed to condemn al-Qaeda but also enabled their quiet return to Afghanistan, and they even flatly denied that al-Qaeda plotted the September 11 attacks. The Taliban's tolerance and patronage of safe havens for terrorism helped create the conditions for terrorist groups to reconstitute inside Afghanistan, where they could eventually launch attacks in the United States and Europe.

Al-Qaeda's senior leadership inevitably praised the Taliban's 'historic victory' in Afghanistan, demonstrating that the decades-long brotherhood between the Taliban and al-Qaeda remained unbroken. Al-Qaeda's affiliates, such as AQAP, AQIM, al-Shabaab in Somalia, and groups in Syria, lauded the Taliban success, with AQAP issuing a *nasheed*, which is vocal music that carries with it Islamic belief and practice, in honour of the Taliban victory. Ultimately, they all saw the Taliban's Islamic Emirate of Afghanistan as a model for their own nascent jihadist states. In fact, key al-Qaeda leaders around the globe began their careers during the reign of the Taliban's first emirate.

Another beneficiary of the Taliban takeover has been the ISIS affiliate in Afghanistan, IS-KP, who have carried out multiple attacks across the country. Civilians, especially women and the Hazara Shiite community, have been the primary targets. The perception has been that the Taliban are enemies of IS-KP, but in reality, the Taliban made little effort to clamp down on the group, with some factions, such as the Haqqani Network, even co-operating for strategic purposes, sometimes to undermine rival Taliban factions. Moreover, the Taliban share IS-KP's misogyny and sectarianism and have forcibly evicted thousands of Hazara families from their homes.

The Taliban offered the promise of security but made the Afghan population insecure and will continue to rule in the only way they know how, through repression via their totalitarian playbook. Following the West's departure from Afghanistan, several terrorist groups have extended their presence from Pakistan into Afghanistan.

Proof of Life

Following the Taliban takeover of Afghanistan, al-Qaeda began releasing a number of al-Zawahiri messages from the as-Sahab backlog. On 10 September 2021, as-Sahab issued a book authored by al-Zawahiri with the date penned as April 2021. The tome was a staggering 852 pages in length. Entitled *Reflections on Political Corruption and Its Effects on the History of Muslims*, al-Zawahiri took shots at rivals and issued an apology of sorts for his long absences, which had led to speculation that the al-Qaeda leader was seriously ill or even dead. Al-Zawahiri thanked his followers for their 'patience over long periods . . . it took me to write this book'.[127]

Al-Zawahiri used the book's introduction to castigate unnamed jihadists and ideologues, accusing them of 'demagoguery' and 'bad morals'. Although the text was written in al-Zawahiri's characteristic finnicky long-winded style, it nevertheless demonstrated the al-Qaeda leader wanted to be able to oversee the transition to the next generation of jihadists by laying out his doctrines and concerns and to avoid complacency, especially as the West had departed Afghanistan.[128]

The following day, on 11 September 2021, the 20th anniversary of the 9/11 attacks, as-Sahab released a video message from al-Zawahiri entitled 'Jerusalem Will Not Be Judaized'. The video was the first of a series, subtitled 'Arab Zionists from Faysal to Bin Zaid'.[129] Al-Zawahiri spent much of the video expressing his anger at Arab leaders for cooperating with Israel, especially in the context of the Abraham Accords. In addition, the video included al-Zawahiri's praise of the 2019 Pensacola attack carried out by Saudi national Mohammed Saeed Alshamrani who murdered three American sailors. He also paid honour to other operatives killed in counter-terrorism operations in Yemen, Mali, Egypt, and Syria, including the former *amirs* of AQAP and AQIM who were killed in the previous year.[130] It was notable that al-Zawahiri's deputy emir, Abu Muhammad al-Masri, who was assassinated in Tehran in 2020, was not mentioned, in large part because of the reluctance to acknowledge that al-Qaeda members have been operating in Iran.

There were also three noteworthy elements in the video that provided proof that al-Zawahiri was still alive. First, it introduced al-Zawahiri with the phrase 'May Allah protect him', which is used in jihadist language to refer to figures who are still alive. Second, al-Zawahiri mentioned the American withdrawal from Afghanistan in the video. He spoke of how the United States was 'making its exit from Afghanistan, broken, defeated, after twenty years of war'. However, he did not explicitly comment upon the Taliban's victory and subsequent takeover of the Afghan government. Nevertheless, images of the Taliban's political delegation inside Kabul's presidential palace were included alongside audio content from AQIM's *amir* which praised the Taliban, especially how they managed to embarrass Trump and Biden. Al-Zawahiri was referencing the US exit from Afghanistan following the highly flawed Doha negotiations in Qatar that occurred in February 2020, and the subsequent gradual pull-out of Western forces from Afghanistan.

Third, and perhaps most concrete, was al-Zawahiri's remark on al-Qaeda affiliate Hurras al-Din's attack on a Russian base in Raqqa, Syria, which took place in January 2021. This demonstrated that al-Zawahiri was alive around this time period and cast doubt on the speculation that he had died in late 2020. Also significant in his praise of Hurras al-Din's attack was al-Zawahiri's emphasis of the unity that allowed it to be executed: 'By ignoring minor issues and differences and focussing on the priorities, this operation turned the compass in the right direction.'[131] Here, the Egyptian ideologue was referring to the cooperation that took place with other jihadist groups in Syria. This call for unity may also be intended as a message to followers of ISIS, al-Qaeda's primary rival in the jihadist landscape.

Another way the theme of unity was conveyed in this video was through the inclusion of speeches given by other *amirs* of al-Qaeda's regional branches. For example, clips of AQAP leader Khalid Batarfi as well as AQIM leader Abu Ubaydah Yusuf al-Anabi are spliced together with al-Zawahiri's speech.

Al-Zawahiri talked about the need to wage jihad in various theatres around the globe as one unified *ummah*: 'Palestine is thus Kashmir, Kashmir is Grozny, Grozny is Idlib, Idlib is Kashgar, and Kashgar is Waziristan.'[132] The mention of Xinjiang's Kashgar is particularly interesting in the context of budding relations between the Taliban government and China, as the former promised Beijing to refrain from offering sanctuary to Uyghurs, and the latter offered substantial aid to the Taliban regime.

Al-Zawahiri concluded his video by citing Abdullah Azzam, despite their personal animosity. Clips of Azzam discussing how jihad must first be undertaken in Afghanistan and then ultimately in Palestine are included: 'We are busy in Afghanistan, it is our duty to help the Muslim *mujahid* people of Afghanistan. We must purify the land of Afghanistan.'[133]

Al-Zawahiri cautioned that the battle against the West was not over and that there remained a need to prepare for a long jihad: 'We must get used to exercising patience. . . . We must understand that repelling this Crusader campaign entails the efforts of successive generations.'[134] Al-Zawahiri then spoke about al-Qaeda's tried and tested strategy of a war of attrition:

> The current stage demands that we exhaust the enemy until it whines and moans due to economic and military bleeding. . . . It is in this context that the importance of operations outside the theatre in which the enemy expects us to strike, operations on enemy soil and beyond enemy lines becomes evident.'[135]

For al-Zawahiri, the success of al-Qaeda's next stage centred on 'a united Ummah' and once again, Afghanistan was the base and sanctuary.

On 23 November 2021, as-Sahab released another video from al-Zawahiri entitled 'Advice for the United Ummah Concerning the Reality of the United Nations'. Much of the video criticizes the UN as an institution, specifically for its role in the creation of the state of Israel, both because of various UN Resolutions and the Oslo Accords. Al-Zawahiri referred to the five permanent Security Council members—the United States, UK, China, France, and Russia—as 'the biggest criminals on the face of the earth'.[136]

Al-Zawahiri stated that since its inception, the value system propagated by the UN has been incompatible with Islam itself, and he provided examples to illustrate this clash. He argued that states who sign the UN

Charter agree to collaborate with 'infidels' to pursue objectives that contradict Shariah. This can take many forms, according to al-Zawahiri. First, he explained how the UN Charter prevents Islamic governments from helping *mujahideen* around the world who are fighting against any member state, such as Palestinians against Israel, Chechens against Russia, or Syrians against the Assad government.

He then highlighted how the UN Charter violates Shariah by pointing to its promotion of gender equality and its prohibition of discrimination upon the basis of things like sex or religion. Al-Zawahiri explained, 'It grants equal rights to men and women, Muslims and unbelievers. . . . And this opposes the Islamic *Shariah* which distinguishes between the rights of men and women, for each sex is entitled to different rights and bears different duties.'[137]

He also commented upon conferences the UN has hosted: 'The UN promoted the spread of indecency such as fornication and homosexuality, late marriage, respect for prostitutes, encouragement of youth to engage in immorality before marriage and equal rights for men and women.'[138] Al-Zawahiri may have included this concentration on gender and homophobia to please the Taliban, as it is not a subject on which he has particularly focused on in the past.

Al-Zawahiri also referenced UNESCO's role when Mullah Omar's Taliban regime destroyed the Bamiyan Buddhas: 'When the Islamic Emirate, during the era of Mullah Muhammad Omar (may Allah have mercy on him), decided to demolish the statues of the Buddha, UNESCO led a vicious smear campaign against the Emirate.'[139] He goes on to recount that 'UNESCO's director at the time, Shiro Motora, a Japanese Buddhist, demanded intervention from different states to stop the destruction of the statues. His delegation stayed in Afghanistan for over ten days to dissuade the Taliban government from destroying the Buddhas. UNESCO gathered 45 ministers of culture from different countries to highlight the "plight" of these statues to generate pressure on the Taliban and save these statues from destruction.'[140] Again, this choice to share an anecdote from the previous Taliban regime may have been a nod to the new Taliban government in Afghanistan that had just come to power.

Finally, al-Zawahiri asked, "So how can a Muslim who holds his *Shariah* in high esteem . . . strives to forbid indecency and heresy . . . is sensitive about his religion and his Prophet and helps his Muslim brethren . . . how can he ever accept to become a part of such an organization [the United Nations]?'[141] This was yet another suggestion of an intended Taliban audience. The Taliban had long courted international recognition and to be allowed to join the United Nations, especially with Sirajuddin Haqqani at the helm in Afghanistan. With all these aspects in mind, the video message and its focus on the Taliban and Afghanistan were directed at the Haqqani regime as well as the UN, who backed Mullah Baradar's Doha-based Taliban as a more 'moderate' faction within the Taliban.

Al-Zawahiri chose to double down on his dislike of Mullah Baradar by criticising the Doha agreement Mullah Baradar brokered with the United States. This was reflected in the second part of al-Zawahiri's series 'Deal of the Century.' The previous edition was issued some 16 months previously, on the 19th anniversary of 9/11.[142] Released on 26 January 2022, al-Zawahiri openly undermined Mullah Baradar by lamenting the Doha Agreement and by extension was creating an opportunity for jihadists loyal to al-Qaeda to support Sirajuddin Haqqani in his play for complete control of the Taliban. Despite the fatal flaws of the Doha Agreement, al-Zawahiri may not have felt entirely safe openly operating within Afghanistan, especially if Mullah Baradar had some authority, for fears that he would work with the United States. This fear was exacerbated by the fact that many in the West identified Baradar as a potential conduit to forming a trustworthy relationship with the Taliban. Therefore, to al-Qaeda, the Haqqani Network represented their best opportunity to return to operational capacity from inside Afghanistan as the group itself was led by a UN designated terrorist, who was thus less likely to work against the group's best interests.

The al-Qaeda leader also made clear his feelings of dissatisfaction towards Qatar and al-Jazeera. Throughout the formative years of al-Qaeda's propaganda campaigns, al-Jazeera would publish much of its material. Al-Zawahiri's discontent with the Qatari newscaster stemmed from claims al-Jazeera made that al-Qaeda's leadership had been in contact with some governmental officials of Arab countries discussing the Abraham Accords. Such an accusation was particularly damning to its jihadist reputation and credentials as it suggested that al-Qaeda may well be compromising on its opposition to the 'internal enemy'. Al-Zawahiri accused Qatar of 'playing a cunning and dangerous role in the Zionist project in the heart of the Islamic world'.[143]

In part 3 of 'Deal of the Century', which was released on 3 February 2022, al-Zawahiri brought out an implied criticism of ISIS and breakaway al-Qaeda factions: 'Al-Qaeda ... has always been based upon ... abstaining from shedding the blood of Muslims in general ... Issuing precise, clear-cut statements. . . . So everyone who abides by his pledge of allegiance to the Organization ... must work in accordance with our guidelines.'[144] He added, 'We do not possess a sharp knife or a piercing bullet to threaten or compel anyone; rather, matters between us are based on oaths, agreements, and the fear of the Hereafter. . . . [Public] awareness ... supersedes that of several groups linked with the Islamic cause.'[145]

Al-Zawahiri also made the clearest statement yet about the US-led withdrawal from Afghanistan: 'We hope that today, with the blessings of Allah, the defeat of the Americans in Afghanistan shall be the beginning of their end too.'[146] Tied to this, the Egyptian doctor also sensed that al-Qaeda's best opportunity was to continue down the path of establishing 'safe bases' across the Islamic world and that its Arab fighters needed to be more patient with and understanding of local sensitivities. To demonstrate his point, al-Zawahiri referred to a well-known Hadith by the Prophet Muhammad in which a Bedouin urinated in a mosque in front of him. The Prophet's companions were outraged at what they considered a serious mark of disrespect in one of the holiest sites of Islam. The Prophet, however, stopped his companions from reacting in fury and rather allowed the Bedouin to finish before instructing someone to pour water over the area.[147]

Through this Hadith, it is understood that the Bedouin was not indigenous to the city and therefore, did not have the same etiquette as his companions, who were from Medina. His action was not a display of disrespectful demeanour to the Prophet's mosque but rather because of his village upbringing instilled differing understandings of acceptable social behaviour. Al-Zawahiri's mention of this Hadith could have several explanations. The most likely was al-Zawahiri's inference that cultural inclusion and sensitivity is key when attempting to bring together individuals from different origins, particularly relevant when jihadists from many cultures and socioeconomic backgrounds come together in one group. He may also have been referring to the pragmatism, patience, and forbearance required in the early stages of the formulation of terrorist groups. Al-Qaeda's message must penetrate people's hearts and minds and cannot solely be enforced with an iron fist.

Some analysts mocked al-Zawahiri for using the Hadith, which they considered too obscure for anyone to understand the connotations. Yet the *hadith* is actually very well-known for showing the Prophet Muhammad rationalising matters and also demonstrating an understanding of different cultural dynamics whilst also seeking to calm potential tensions. The lack of understanding of the relevance of the *hadith* by some exhibited a very narrow prism with which they view things. Al-Zawahiri demonstrated his shrewdness in reinterpreting and misconstruing the Hadith for the purpose of encouraging al-Qaeda's cadres and affiliates to continue to show strategic patience and create 'safe bases' across the Islamic world whilst working to win hearts and minds in the communities where they reside by respecting their traditions. Effectively, there has often been an underestimation of al-Zawahiri's agenda.

In part four of the Deal of the Century, released on 15 February 2022, al-Zawahiri doubled down on his previous sharp criticism of ISIS, highlighting their perceived faults. 'We are in need of a leadership that strives to unite, not a leadership driven by arrogance, obstinance and vilification that divides, excommunicates and spills blood at the altar of an imaginary delusional Caliphate, destroying thereby itself and its deluded followers.'[148] Al-Zawahiri also continued to discuss why the Arab Spring failed to bring the desired change and advised Muslims to take jihadi ideologues as leaders for future revolutions. He also called on Muslims to sacrifice their lives and wealth for that pursuit: 'The media shall try to project and promote "leaders" who will only bring upon us the same tragedies again and again, we must turn away from them. Our real leaders will never be highlighted or mentioned by a media controlled by arrogant powers of the world.'[149]

The two points here are that al-Zawahiri felt triumphant that the ISIS project had ultimately dwindled and that the Arab Spring also failed to deliver for the people in the Middle East and Africa. Al-Zawahiri was blunt in his criticisms that the alternatives to al-Qaeda could not overcome both the 'apostates' and 'infidels' and that the 'internal enemy' and 'external enemy' remain as consequence. Al-Zawahiri reminded his audience that al-Qaeda remained the only viable option for the global jihadist movement. There was some debate that these messages did not establish proof of life, as they covered past events or ideological issues and may have even been recorded when Donald Trump was president or soon after Joe Biden succeeded him. However, al-Zawahiri was about to once again confound the sceptics.

On 5 April 2022, as-Sahab produced a video showing al-Zawahiri speaking about an incident in the southern Indian town of Mandya, Karnataka, where the local academic institution banned women wearing hijabs on campus and in classes, saying it created a lack of cohesion in teaching. The issue attracted some attention beyond India, yet it was most noteworthy that al-Zawahiri chose this incident to prove he was alive and actually seemed to be in good health. The issue subsequently became a cause célèbre for many jihadist groups especially al-Qaeda affiliate, AQIS. Al-Zawahiri sought to criticise countries that banned the hijab and described those in India that chose to wear it as 'the noble Woman of India' who represented a 'battle of consciousness', whereas India represented 'depraved polytheist and atheist enemies'.[150] Al-Zawahiri was so motivated by the issue that he even penned a poem in reference to what had transpired in India entitled 'I Shall Not Surrender, Gallantly Declared the Hijab'.[151]

Al-Zawahiri concluded his proof of life message that al-Qaeda remained committed to its goals across the Islamic world: 'We must understand that the way out is by holding on to our *Shariah*, uniting as a single Ummah, from China to the Islamic Maghreb, and from the Caucasus to Somalia ... a united Ummah waging a concerted war across several fronts.'[152]

The flurry of al-Zawahiri's messages coincided with the Taliban takeover of Afghanistan and the likelihood was that al-Zawahiri's couriers felt more confident to broadcast his messages more frequently than before because there was no longer the threat of a US drone hanging in the air. It also signified that al-Zawahiri was prioritising the regional agenda of AQIS, which has been a strong ally of the Taliban and the Haqqani Network in particular.

The Last Sunrise over the Horizon

As had become abundantly clear, al-Zawahiri had eluded counter-terrorism agencies for more than two decades and endured. Since 9/11 he was in Afghanistan and then Pakistan but was now assessing his options on potentially returning to Afghanistan once more. He had moved around the Pakistani tribal areas and may have moved into urban centres temporarily. With the Haqqani Network taking control of Afghanistan in 2021, al-Zawahiri pondered whether he would be safer there. It raised the questions once more of where al-Zawahiri was and where he could he end up. As Secretary Panetta concluded, 'I've often had the same thoughts of where al-Zawahiri is located because we were ultimately successful with bin Laden. At some point, we'll get a break. Whether it's through his couriers or whether it's through the sounds in whatever tapes he's doing, we'll figure it out one way or the other.'[153] That break would unfold in the unlikeliest of circumstances.

Following the fall of Kabul amidst a messy and consequential Western withdrawal, members of the Haqqani clan had their status enhanced amongst the other Taliban militias with Sirajuddin Haqqani coming out on top.[154] This was in large part through the interference of Pakistan's ISI director general Faiz Hamid. Hamid had flown to Kabul to help the Haqqani Network cement their control in Afghanistan.[155] This also bene-fited Khalil-ur-Rahman Haqqani who attained what initially appeared to be the nondescript position of minister for refugees in the Taliban's new cabinet.

Khalil-ur-Rahman Haqqani had played the pivotal role as the main fun-draiser for the Haqqani Network, enabling them to sponsor the horrific attacks that claimed the lives of thousands of Afghans over the previous two decades and displaced countless more. The subsequent refugee crisis was supposed to be his responsibility to resolve, but instead of helping to ease the plight of ordinary Afghans, Khalil-ur-Rahman surreptitiously used his position as refugees minister to enable entry of terrorists into Afghanistan under the pretence that they were 'returning refugees'. In particular, he acted on behalf of al-Qaeda, encouraging and facilitating the return to Afghanistan of Ayman al-Zawahiri and his family. For Khalil-ur-Rahman, there was an immense personal motivation coupled with his enduring friendship with al-Zawahiri. It was Khalil-ur-Rahman who travelled with al-Zawahiri's family back in 2001 to try to get them across the border into Pakistan during Operation Enduring Freedom. In the process of the US bombing campaign, al-Zawahiri lost some of his family members, which Khalil-ur-Rahman had also felt responsible for, even though he helped save several others of al-Zawahiri's flock.

The Haqqanis felt emboldened and finally considered Afghanistan safe and secure to host al-Qaeda once more, much as they had done pre-9/11. Al-Zawahiri had also waited patiently for two decades for the Taliban's return to power once the US withdrawal was complete. With no apparent sign of the West returning, he chose to avail himself of the Taliban's protection in Afghanistan. Initially, al-Zawahiri's wife, daughter, and grandchildren made the passage from Pakistan's tribal areas to Afghanistan, with al-Zawahiri eventually making the monumental decision to return in April 2022. He was smuggled back into Afghanistan under the guise of a returning refugee, with Khalil-ur-Rahman personally overseeing his safe entry and with the full sanction of Sirajuddin Haqqani, the leader of the Haqqani Network.[156] What was particularly audacious was the location that the Haqqanis chose for al-Zawahiri to stay in: Afghanistan's capital, Kabul. More curious was that the al-Qaeda leader settled in the Kabul hilltop district of Sherpur, which during the years of the Karzai and Ghani administrations was populated by an odd mix of cabinet ministers, warlords, drug traffickers, entrepreneurs, and the emerging class of wealthy Afghan suburbanites who worked in the state bureaucracy.[157]

Before al-Zawahiri dramatically fled Kabul after 9/11 and Operation Enduring Freedom, Sherpur was a largely vacant patch of hillside that had been the site of a dilapidated fort surrounded by modest homes that overlooked the stately area of Wazir Akbar Khan. The land was commandeered by then Afghan president Hamid Karzai after the 2001 overthrow of the Taliban. Locals were evicted in order for the Afghan elite to occupy a gated community styled with ostentatious indulgences. The area reflected the spoils of a gushing drug trade and donor money that divided the haves and have-nots and enabled corruption to permeate throughout Afghan society.[158] Upon al-Zawahiri's low-key return to Afghanistan, Sherpur had transformed itself into the wealthiest enclave in the country but had also contributed to Kabul's cultural erosion.

The Sherpur skyline had swelled through the years and became an eyesore within Kabul, with influences imported from Pakistani's underworld and the haciendas of narcotraffickers in Latin America. Sherpur is a jumble of large mansions, gaudy in design, with sweeping balustrades, multi-tiered wedding-cake plasterwork, pink granite, and lime marble as well as coloured mirrored windows and giant metallic eagles adorning the rooftops. It was arguably the last place al-Zawahiri would want to reside whilst planning al-Qaeda's future, given how it might draw attention to him. Afghans refer to the residences in the area as 'poppy houses' or 'narco-villas'. Sherpur itself is often despairingly referred to as 'Char-pur' in Pashto, which translates into 'City of Loot', a far cry from traditional humble Afghan homes. With many of the previous occupants fleeing following the Taliban's return to Kabul, these homes were now reserved for the senior figures of the regimes as part of the spoils of war.

The Sherpur villa that al-Zawahiri occupied had an imposing entrance, with byzantine floor tiles trailing though the cavernous hallways and Greek columns. Everything inside was concrete and marble. The chandeliers, fixtures, and fittings evoked the stylings of Tony Montana's residence in the film *Scarface*. The balcony had a spacious seating area with a boundary of teal glass panels.[159] The blatantly ostentatious reputation of Sherpur was something which al-Zawahiri had sought to distance himself from for decades, partly to ensure he remained safe from counter-terrorism operations. Aside from the obvious, it also seemed inexplicable that the al-Qaeda leader chose to reside in such opulence—a proverbial den of iniquity that reflected the worst vestiges of Afghan moral decay and corruption and Western apathy. It was also the opposite of the spartan conditions of living in hiding in Pakistan. However, he was a guest of the Haqqanis and most likely could not choose where he stayed, especially as he was dependent on them for security and protection. Curiously, the building is close to several embassies, including those of the United States, United Kingdom, Canada, and Germany, as well as the Iranian and Turkish Missions, who unlike the Western nations, chose to maintain their presence in Afghanistan after the Taliban seized power.[160] Perhaps more concerning was that al-Zawahiri's residence was a stone's throw away from both the Taliban's Ministry for the Promotion of Virtue and the Prevention of Vice and the General Directorate of Intelligence, which were fully staffed and two of the most active ministries in monitoring people, especially in Kabul. They are also led by members of the Haqqani Network. Ultimately, it was incredulous but not surprising that the Taliban were so brazen in hosting al-Zawahiri and especially in Sherpur. They have consistently deceived the international community for generations about their ties with al-Qaeda.

Every day, following sunrise in Kabul and after finishing his prayers, al-Zawahiri would sit down with a book to read and have a cup of tea in the balcony area of his new home.[161] It overlooked the historically famous cemetery in Kabul known locally as Kabre Gora, or 'Graveyard of

Foreigners', which is also located in Sherpur. The cemetery is oddly situated as it juts out from Sherpur's Martyrs Road, forcing the traffic to slow down to navigate around the tree-lined graveyard, with little space to manoeuvre. There is a sign outside that has rusted away by the elements, but it can just about be made out. It says, 'British Cemetery'. The cemetery was built in the nineteenth century, during the Anglo-Afghan Wars. Hundreds of British soldiers are buried there. They represent one of the earliest foreign missions in Afghanistan.[162]

At the end of the cemetery's southern wall, there are dozens of newer plaques that commemorate the names of British, American, Italian, and German soldiers who died in Afghanistan between 2001 to 2014 during the last Afghan mission. For al-Zawahiri, the Graveyard of Foreigners was a reminder that he had endured and survived the 'war on terror'. He could stare down directly at his adversaries, the ones who tried and failed to kill him and permanently dislodge the Taliban and al-Qaeda. However, little did the Egyptian teacher know that he too was in fact being closely monitored.

Despite the US withdrawal from Afghanistan, which reduced the resources available for the American intelligence community and made it more logistically challenging, the CIA took the risky decision to retain some of their intelligence assets in Afghanistan. Information has been collected from closed borders before, and it's part of the spy agency's business to operate in similar conditions since its inception. The Biden administration referred to its 'Over the Horizon' strategy as a key tool for counterterrorism. More important, though, was the decision to keep 'stay-behind agents'. For all the years the West was in Afghanistan, the CIA and other intelligence services chose to keep agents in the country who were willing to stay behind and who retained access to intelligence and a means to communicate, whether through human or electronic channels. These 'principal agents' are locals who have been recruited. Their job isn't necessarily to always provide intelligence themselves but to collect intelligence from others who have access. In particular, these principal agents were tasked with finding out information on al-Zawahiri.[163]

This assignment produced a lot of complications and dangers. Tracking al-Zawahiri in Afghanistan under the protection of the Haqqanis was much more challenging from a counterintelligence perspective. In particular, the difficulty for the CIA was running a network securely, because if agents know one another and if one is compromised, the whole network can be uncovered. The other hurdle was that when dealing indirectly with intelligence, the information would not be in real time but instead staggered and ad hoc. In al-Zawahiri's case, the information was often indirect, second-hand. As a result, the chains of information and acquisition were more extended. Therefore, it became more difficult to vouch for and validate the access of the ultimate source of the intelligence who was in proximity to al-Zawahiri himself, who was not even aware they were providing intelligence that was being used by the CIA. However, what helped the process was that the CIA was able to strengthen its networks over a matter of months, as the number of Afghan dissident groups grew in reaction to the violent and repressive policies of the Taliban.[164]

The odd irony that came from the West's disastrous withdrawal from Afghanistan was that al-Zawahiri concluded it would be safer for him to return to the country because the United States would unlikely choose to return there. Adding to his confidence was the nature of the US-led withdrawal of Afghanistan, which had damaged American credibility in the eyes of its fiercest adversaries, and may have influenced Russian president Vladimir Putin as he calculated his invasion in Ukraine. US interventionism appeared to be slowing down, presenting Russia and China with a window of opportunity to increase their global footprint and antagonise their neighbours. This notion would not have been lost on al-Zawahiri, who also likely believed the West was now distracted with its own internal issues and great power competition squabbles. However, soon after the United States left Kabul, the CIA amplified its efforts to find al-Zawahiri, adamant that the Egyptian ideologue would try to return to Afghanistan. They wanted to be ready and not lose another opportunity.[165] Their instincts proved right.

It is a challenge, turning a man's life inside out without meeting him. Lessons from the triple agent al-Balawi had also been painfully learnt. Testing the validity of the information necessitated finding their sources' character quirks, flaws, or agendas which may signal unreliability. Eventually, after painstakingly creating a viable remote network in Afghanistan, the CIA was able to formulate a pattern-of-life picture of al-Zawahiri residing at the Sherpur villa. A model was subsequently built, drawing parallels with the bin Laden Abbottabad operation. Once again, the National Geospatial-Intelligence Agency was tasked with verifying the information that had been provided by sources on the ground. Everything tallied. Al-Zawahiri's frequent periods sitting in the long balcony and never leaving the villa provided an opportunity for a potential drone operation.[166]

As options for a drone strike were developed, a key dynamic was utilising a missile which could be fired without causing collateral damage to the safe house or the Sherpur neighbourhood around it. Memories were still fresh about the drone strike in Kabul on 29 August 2021, which was purported to target an ISIS terrorist but ended up killing 10 civilians, including seven children, in a catastrophic error that coincided with the end of the 20-year US presence in Afghanistan.[167] The scars of that incident directly impacted on how the al-Zawahiri operation would be conducted and helped amplify targeting rules and protections for civilians in conflict zones where airstrikes from remote-operated drones are conducted.

The decision was made to use a specially modified Hellfire R9X missile, which has six long blades embedded inside the casing. They deploy through the covering of the missile and then rotate moments before impact to ensure that it shreds through its target. Crucially, the missile's payload does not create an explosion, debris, scorch marks, or even powder burns so as to reduce damage and the chances of civilian casualties. Yet it contains a hundred pounds of dense metal, uniquely designed to punch through a building like a wrecking ball. The Hellfire R9X missile was used in other operations against al-Qaeda, including the killings of Jamal al-Badawi in January 2019 and Ahmad Hasan Abu Khayr al-Masri in February 2017. Al-Badawi was part of the cell overseen by al-Zawahiri which was behind the bombing of the USS *Cole*. He was in Yemen when he was targeted. Al-Masri was a trusted Egyptian deputy to al-Zawahiri.[168] The same weapon was also used to kill Qasem Soleimani, the head of Iran's Islamic Revolutionary Guard Corps in 2020. Soleimani had played a key role in harbouring many al-Qaeda fighters, including several of al-Zawahiri's Egyptian cadres.[169]

Flying the drone to Afghanistan was one obstacle, but not the most challenging. More important for the CIA was to be certain that they had al-Zawahiri's location locked in. In addition, the information provided by agents on the ground had to bear out what the electronic intelligence was able to provide. Importantly, members of the Haqqani Network were becoming increasingly complacent about their operational security and equally, security for those around them. To ascertain the veracity of al-Zawahiri's location and activities in Sherpur, agents provided phone numbers, locations of safe houses, orders from Haqqani commanders, times of routines that Haqqani Network guards would take when out and about, and their physical descriptions. A vast array of technical information was being collected and collated.[170]

The input on al-Zawahiri had to be as scrupulous, as possible and the CIA had to be vigilant about the quality of the intelligence. They concluded that it was sound, and the al-Qaeda leader's identity was verified on multiple occasions across several months. Eventually, a decision had to be made on what to do with the information. Ultimately, it required a political decision, and on 25 July 2022, the Biden administration sanctioned a drone strike to eliminate al-Zawahiri once and for all, and at the earliest opportunity, to prevent the re-emergence of al-Qaeda.[171]

The United States decided to carry out the operation with MQ-9 Reaper drones stationed at al-Dhafra Air Base in the United Arab Emirates. The United States has a significant array of defence equipment at al-Dhafra, which provided the most viable and safest unmanned strike basing capability for intelligence, surveillance, and reconnaissance operations in Afghanistan. The drone would have to fly across Pakistan from the Arabian Sea. The United States had given advance notice to Pakistan for airspace permission for several drone missions, but crucially, Pakistan was not made aware of the specific location or the target for the al-Zawahiri strike. Lessons had been painfully learnt over the past two decades about Pakistan's murky ties with al-Qaeda and the Taliban. Far too often, al-Zawahiri was able to escape US counter-terrorism operations because he was tipped off by Pakistani and Afghan jihadists who retained close ties to the Pakistani military. In particular, as al-Zawahiri was residing in a Haqqani safe house, there was serious concern in Washington that even the slightest hint to the Pakistani military over the operation would result in a leak. After all, the Haqqanis retained very close ties with the ISI. Complicating matters was that the al-Zawahiri operation coincided with the Pakistani politician Imran Khan whipping up anti-American sentiment within Pakistan by peddling unfounded allegations about his removal from power as Pakistan's prime minister in a no-confidence vote in April 2022. Despite failing to provide any proof, Khan's conspiracies were resonating with a large segment of Pakistan's population, including the Islamist groups whom Khan was courting to help him return him to power one day.[172]

Just over an hour after sunrise on 31 July 2022, al-Zawahiri walked out onto the balcony of his Sherpur compound. At the same time, an American weapons operator, who had not been born when al-Zawahiri took part in his first act of terrorism at the Egyptian Military Technical College in 1974, sat in an air-conditioned control room in the United States whilst monitoring a live video stream from the drone's camera as it flew inbound to Sherpur. Using the targeting brackets, the weapons operator calibrated the precision-guided laser at the al-Qaeda leader and at 06:18 local time, two Hellfire R9X missiles smashed into the balcony, killing the 71-year-old al-Zawahiri but leaving his family unscathed.[173]

After decades of plotting and planning terrorism, hiding from the authorities, and escaping attempts to capture or eliminate him, al-Zawahiri finally met his end. The Egyptian doctor was not killed in a Navy SEALs operation or a fiery explosion but instead hacked to death in milliseconds by an RX9 missile. His body was not recoverable, as its parts were strewn across the villa. It is doubtful al-Zawahiri even knew what hit him: death by a speeding drone missile is almost certainly instantaneous. For al-Zawahiri, the expression 'what goes around comes around' held true. He was a man who lived by the sword and, ultimately, died by it. However, he perhaps never anticipated it would be a six-bladed one. The smoke that was seen rising from the Sherpur villa by Kabul residents was not from explosives but the result of the motor aboard the R9X missiles colliding with the concrete that once formed part of the Haqqani safe house.

Al-Zawahiri, who meticulously planned his safety for two decades had either become complacent and too trusting of others to guarantee his safety, or, arguably, he knew he would eventually have to face death because of his multiple health issues and was confident that he could leave al-Qaeda intact for others to build on. Although al-Zawahiri opted to return to Afghanistan, he was only able to savour a brief victory over the West, perhaps realising all too late that he never stopped being the primary target for US counter-terrorism agencies. Soon after the operation, the US was able to confirm the death of al-Zawahiri. President Biden then addressed the American people on the monumental development and summarised the Egyptian doctor's role in terrorism across the decades:

> My fellow Americans, on Saturday, at my direction, the United States successfully concluded an airstrike in Kabul, Afghanistan, that killed the emir of al Qaeda, Ayman al-Zawahiri.... He carved a trail of murder and violence against American citizens, American service members, American diplomats, and American interests. And since the United States delivered justice to bin

Laden 11 years ago, al-Zawahiri has been a leader of al Qaeda—the leader.
From hiding, he coordinated al Qaeda's branches and all around the world—
including setting priorities, for providing operational guidance that called for
and inspired attacks against U.S. targets. He made videos, including in recent
weeks, calling for his followers to attack the United States and our allies.[174]

Al-Zawahiri's death signified an important inflection point for not just
al-Qaeda but the global jihadist movement too. Al-Zawahiri was one of
the few remaining veterans who fought against the Soviets in Afghanistan
and helped develop al-Qaeda pre-9/11, a legacy figure who represented al-
Qaeda's first generation and oversaw the emergence of the terror group's
second generation. It took the United States almost 21 years since the
September 11 attacks to find and kill him. The other key dynamic was
that al-Zawahiri represented the thread and continuity of Egyptian jihadists
from al-Banna, Qutb, and Faraj, who shaped the wider jihadist movement
and formed an inseparable bond with the Taliban. There is no clear long-
term successor of al-Qaeda or any terrorist group who can take up the
mantle in the same way. The dark web and encrypted messaging forums
were abuzz with the news of al-Zawahiri's demise. Al-Qaeda sympathisers
showered praise and poetry on al-Zawahiri, referring to him as a 'martyr'
and paying tribute to his long jihadist history. Some cast doubt about his
passing and urged caution about Western conspiracies. Supporters of ISIS
chose to gloat about al-Zawahiri's death, referring to him disparagingly. As
ever, al-Zawahiri was a divisive figure.

In the end it was the Taliban's hubris that led to Ayman al-Zawahiri's
demise. Desperate to be treated as a legitimate government, the Taliban
repeatedly called for the international community to recognise its return
to power. Yet sheltering al-Zawahiri exposed what had been an open secret for decades. The Taliban retained close personal and ideological ties
to al-Qaeda, and they would maintain that relationship at the expense of
everything else. It was deeply naive for politicians and policymakers in the
West to assume the Taliban had evolved or could be reasoned with. This
dangerous delusion could undermine future counter-terrorism efforts.

The Biden administration can take some reassurance that it has a tested
Over the Horizon drone strategy for Afghanistan, coupled with covert intelligence networks to locate and disrupt potential terrorist threats without
having a military presence on the ground in Afghanistan. However, the
discovery of al-Zawahiri in a Taliban safe house in Kabul puts the death
knell on the ill-fated Doha Agreement, which was predicated on the belief

that the Taliban would change their ways, moderate, engage with world, and prevent Afghanistan from becoming a terrorist cesspool again. Al-Zawahiri's presence in the heart of Kabul demonstrated that the Taliban cannot be trusted.

After all, al-Zawahiri was not in Kabul by accident but was consciously hosted by the Haqqani Network. Moreover, soon after the drone strike that killed the al-Qaeda leader, members of al-Zawahiri's family were promptly moved to other safe houses. Antony Blinken, the US secretary of state, called sheltering al-Zawahiri a 'gross' violation of the Doha Agreement.[175] Bizarrely, the Taliban spokesperson Zabiullah Mujahid also claimed that it was the Americans who violated the agreement: 'IEA [the Islamic Emirate of Afghanistan] strongly condemns this attack on any [*sic*] cause and calls it a clear violation of international principles and the Doha Agreement.' Furthermore, a high-level Taliban gathering held in Kandahar, attended by its supreme leader Haibatullah Akhundzada, strongly condemned the US drone strike 'that targeted a residential house in Kabul'. Remarkably, the Taliban also claimed that it 'has no information about Ayman al-Zawahiri's arrival and stay in Kabul'. Reflecting the inevitable tension with the West, the Taliban warned of 'consequences' should future drone operations occur.[176] Subsequently, the Taliban claimed that al-Zawahiri's body could not be found in the Sherpur villa and when speaking about the Egyptian ideologue, deliberately avoided phrases like 'May Allah have mercy on him', which is specifically said for the dead, or 'May Allah protect him', which is meant for the living, as it would indicate they knew whether al-Zawahiri was dead or alive.[177] As for the Haqqani Network's Sirajuddin Haqqani and Khalil-ur-Rahman Haqqani, both chose to reduce their public appearances especially after getting a very humble chill that they remain on the US Rewards for Justice Program and could well be targeted in US drone operations down the road. Rumours and conspiracies also persisted across jihadist web forums and the dark web about al-Zawahiri's fate. Many jihadists refused to believe al-Zawahiri had died or believe that if he passed away, it was because of ill health and not because the United States was able to vanquish him.

Conclusion: 55 Years of Terror

Al-Zawahiri's life in terrorism, which spanned more than half a century, can be framed in three periods. Each phase is defined by al-Zawahiri's personal encounters, reflections of history, and key political events which were intertwined with his own actions of sowing insurrection. To fully understand al-Zawahiri's legacy, it is important to retrace the steps that led him to become the world's most wanted terrorist. The first period is when al-Zawahiri was growing up in Egypt, where he encountered what he viewed as un-Islamic rule from both the Nasser and Sadat regimes which spurred his desire to defy the status quo. Al-Zawahiri appreciated that he hailed from no ordinary family, with relatives who became leaders at al-Azhar and the Arab League, whilst others were also regarded as pre-eminent experts in the field of medicine. This undoubtedly contributed to his strong sense of destiny, even though his heritage was also part of the social establishment in Egypt. Despite having all the trappings of wealth, power, and privilege from both sides of his family, he wanted political change and wasn't shy about expressing his opinions. Throughout all the Egyptian ideologue's experiences and influences, al-Zawahiri conveyed a sense of burden and responsibility in his writings and pursued the concepts of religion and resistance against outside cultural impositions and colonial hegemony. At the same time, he understood there would be trials and tribulations that could hinder the goals he set out to achieve. Therefore, compromise or dialogue was futile. The only solution was direct confrontation and insurrection.

The initial spark can be pinpointed in the mid-1960s in his youth following Sayyid Qutb's execution, when al-Zawahiri turned his back to Hussein al-Shafei, the vice-president of Egypt who had originally sentenced Qutb to prison. Over time, al-Zawahiri increasingly saw himself as a natural successor to Qutb's mission in exposing and removing 'apostate rulers' and their *jahili* practises in the quest to bring about an Islamic state grounded in the Shariah. Much of this was also aided by the fact that al-Zawahiri's own uncle served as Qutb's lawyer. This rebelliousness in al-Zawahiri intensified as he engaged in numerous insurrections against the Egyptian state, including the attempt to take over the Military Technical College. Although he did not succeed, al-Zawahiri managed to escape punishment, and it created a unique trend in his life where he would repeatedly avoid the hangman's noose. Upon being arrested in a massive sweep of jihadists following the assassination of Anwar Sadat, al-Zawahiri not only struck a police officer in retaliation but then under the gaze of the international media, transformed his trial into his own personal show where he warned of future sacrifices. Although al-Zawahiri did not kill Sadat, his poise, passion, and eloquence in defence of the al-Jihad terrorist group made him the voice and face of the Egyptian jihadist movement and served as a defining period in Egypt. It also helped provide the platform for the next stage of his life in Afghanistan and Pakistan as the *mujahideen* war against the Soviets raged on.

By this point, al-Zawahiri was a young jihadist emerging on the scene, and because of his skill at public speaking, he was able to attract both attention and notoriety. This served al-Zawahiri well in Afghanistan. Although he wasn't a front-line *mujahideen* commander against the Soviets, al-Zawahiri benefited the most from the experience of being with fighters from around the Islamic world. For al-Zawahiri, the battle against the Soviets was a means to an end. The real war lay ahead against the Mubarak regime and the other so-called apostate 'internal enemies', which he deemed was a far greater priority than going after Israel and other 'external enemies', as Abdullah Azzam strongly advocated. Al-Zawahiri's aspirations were persuasive enough that they had a profound impact on Osama bin Laden, convincing the Saudi of the merit of the 'internal enemy' strategy with the important caveat that the 'external enemy' was a legitimate target if they sought a presence within the Islamic world.

The rapport and camaraderie al-Zawahiri established with bin Laden cannot be understated as it led to a symbiotic partnership in terrorism that would stand the test of time. Eventually, al-Zawahiri's status, influence, and consolidation within the jihadist movement would be defined by his experiences in Afghanistan across generations, whereas for Azzam, the Soviet withdrawal from Afghanistan would be the last chapter of his life. It was here that al-Zawahiri also demonstrated his cold, calculating, and clinical side. Al-Zawahiri knew that Azzam was an influential ideologue, and as long as he lived, he could divide the global jihadist movement. Al-Zawahiri saw to it that Abdullah Azzam perished in a car explosion in Pakistan. Aside from apostate rulers, al-Zawahiri had become all too aware that his enemies could also be within the ranks of the *mujahideen*. Although al-Zawahiri was unable to unseat Mubarak directly, his EIJ managed to orchestrate numerous acts of terrorism inside Egypt that created significant economic turmoil and had a knock-on effect of eroding investor and tourist confidence. Along with assassinating Egyptian politicians and targeting the embassy in Pakistan, al-Zawahiri demonstrated a frightening aptitude in plotting and directing attacks.

As the mutually beneficial relationship with bin Laden grew, so did their evolving shared goals in carrying out attacks against Western interests in Africa and Asia. Al-Zawahiri concluded that a barrage of attacks against Americans interests would force them to withdraw their diplomatic and armed presence across the Islamic world and in turn, reduce its financial and military support for countries like Egypt. This was a major inflection point for al-Zawahiri as his previous strategy of entirely focussing on Egypt was not working, which in his mind was because the United States provided substantial support for the Mubarak regime. Plots against the American military in Yemen and Somalia convinced both bin Laden and al-Zawahiri that the United States would not responded aggressively, which only further emboldened their targeting. Attacks on the US embassies in Kenya and Tanzania as well as the USS *Cole* demonstrated a clear goal to violently alter the geopolitical balance in the Middle East and East Africa.

For al-Zawahiri, the evolution in expanding the theatre of conflict by targeting the 'external enemy' within the territory of the 'internal enemy' was sufficient. He had successfully relocated from Sudan to Afghanistan and established a safe base of operations for the Egyptian Islamic Jihad (EIJ). There wasn't a need to elevate the strategic agenda beyond what it had attained at that stage, and he had also concluded that it was prudent to keep the EIJ separate from al-Qaeda, despite bin Laden's preference to merge the two groups. Al-Zawahiri also had the foresight to utilise a slew of double and triple agents who were sent to live and work abroad including in the United States to provide intelligence and assist in terrorist attacks. The 'insider threat' was a component of the *Military Studies* manual that al-Zawahiri was developing which would serve as a primary and compulsory text for jihadists in honing their skills in clandestine activities. In fact, virtually all of the EIJ and al-Qaeda plots that emerged from the 1990s can

trace their tactics and strategies to the *Military Studies*. It was so significant, in some circles it was known as the 'Al-Qaeda Handbook', utilised
by operatives across North America, Africa, Europe, and Asia. At the same
time, al-Zawahiri took the lead in al-Qaeda's pursuit of chemical and biological materials. Although not successful in some respects, it demonstrated
a chilling innovation in how he envisaged terrorism and the potential destruction it could inflict.

Yet, bin Laden became more ambitious and wanted to target the US
mainland, which eventually culminated with the 9/11 attacks. Al-Zawahiri
was hesitant to support bin Laden in large part because it was against the
wishes of his EIJ cadres, who believed it would provoke a response. They
feared the United States would go after all the jihadists in Afghanistan and
they would lose their safe bases that had been provided to them by the
Taliban. The EIJ rank and file could plot and plan safely in Afghanistan
without any fear of threat from any entity and didn't want that disrupted.
Al-Zawahiri was torn. He understood the consequences of supporting bin
Laden, but he also was loyal to the person who backed him over Abdullah
Azzam. Not only did al-Zawahiri choose to assist in the September 11 terrorist attacks to demonstrate his commitment to bin Laden; he also formally
merged the EIJ with al-Qaeda. He did this without consulting many of
his EIJ leaders, which caused significant consternation within ranks, but it
reflected his own acerbic, direct approach which was never based on consensus within the EIJ. Al-Zawahiri was also assigned the critical task of ensuring the assassination of Northern Alliance leader Ahmad Shah Massoud,
which was the precursor to 9/11 and if it had not been successful, it could
well have hindered the attacks on the United States. Its purpose was to
weaken and fracture the Northern Alliance to deprive the United States
an ally on the ground when they retaliated for 9/11. The September 11
plot was devastating, killing thousands, and under the George W. Bush administration, the United States commenced the 'war on terrorism' with
the assistance of the intact Northern Alliance and routed the Taliban. Both
al-Qaeda and Taliban leadership lost their strategic foothold in Afghanistan
but were able to escape to Pakistan, where they were given sanctuary by
Pakistani terrorist groups whose murky ties with the Pakistani military establishment hindered counter-terrorism operations for a generation.

One continuous source of support for al-Zawahiri was his close bond
with the Haqqani Network, a relationship al-Zawahiri had finessed over the

years. The leadership of the Haqqani Network personally sought to protect al-Zawahiri and his family and provide them safe passage into Pakistan. However, this came at a great personal cost for al-Zawahiri, who lost one of his wives and two of his children. Al-Zawahiri considered it collateral damage, which he would absorb and accept for the cause he had spent most of his life fighting and killing for. It was this single-minded approach that kept al-Zawahiri fixated on the future for the jihadist movement. During this stage, al-Zawahiri wrote his most important treatise, *Knights under the Prophet's Banner*, which in many ways was meant as his last will and testament, as he feared that the US bombs raining down on the mountains of Tora Bora would lead to his end. Al-Zawahiri envisaged a future jihadist movement that would endure without him, and bin Laden and would take the battle to the West. He warned it would not be without challenges and it would be a multigenerational struggle. It was clear he had to convince himself that all his personal sacrifices had to amount for something in death. However, al-Zawahiri survived, which marked the third period of his life, in Pakistan. For the next two decades, he sought to execute the goals he expressed in *Knights under the Prophet's Banner*, in particular, launching terrorist attacks upon the West.

An important dynamic that intersected with al-Zawahiri's second and third periods was the use of technology for terrorist propaganda. He oversaw a sophisticated public relations and media campaign as it evolved from faxed statements to VHS recordings to audio messages to online appearances and internet postings, and then to the dark web and encrypted messaging. The utilization of modern communications gave him a direct, constant, and permanent tool running parallel with al-Qaeda's ideological and military doctrine. Other terrorist groups and individuals may have eventually harnessed the technology better than al-Zawahiri, but he initiated the communications approach which was instrumental in bringing the jihadist vision to a worldwide audience in real time. Those who doubt the relevance of al-Zawahiri's legacy fail to reckon with the significance of his innovations on a technical level as well as an ideological one.

Indeed, it was al-Zawahiri who originally understood the potential of utilising the media for propaganda, its technological dexterity as well as its efficacy in recruitment and radicalisation. He set the trend for others to follow and develop. He believed that without communication, terrorism would not exist. Using the imagery of a humble and spartan lifestyle, having abandoned a life of wealth and privilege, al-Zawahiri was also aware that presentation and communication mattered as he sought to convince people around the world of his direct knowledge of God's will, even if it came at the cost of losing his own family members and others around him. Curiously, despite being fluent in English and using it in private on occasions and during the Sadat trial, al-Zawahiri never again spoke it publicly, preferring to talk in Arabic. Arguably, al-Zawahiri wanted to show consistency by using the language from the Qur'an, but at the same time he was missing out on the ability to connect online with potential adherents in the West.

Communication became more of a necessity as the terror network had become disjointed as many of al-Qaeda's leadership were strewn across Pakistan and others fled to Iran. The years in Pakistan created significant operational difficulties. One by one, al-Qaeda's leadership were captured or killed by US operations. Al-Zawahiri concluded early on that for al-Qaeda to survive and operate, personal safety and control of the environment were paramount. His inner circle was fiercely loyal and willing to lay down their lives for him. Al-Zawahiri also surrounded himself with fellow jihadists, such as the Haqqani Network, who had the infrastructure in Pakistan to protect him. Sirajuddin Haqqani had continued and strengthened the relationship with the al-Qaeda leader which had begun under his father. This was one of the most important relationships al-Zawahiri established and comparable to the one he had with bin Laden. Crucially, the evolution from Jalaluddin Haqqani to Sirajuddin Haqqani did not the relationship with al-Qaeda but made it closer, suggesting that these relationships are not just strategic but ideological and multigenerational.

For these reasons, al-Zawahiri had escaped the fate of most of his counterparts by observing vigorous security protocols, blending in, and going to ground in Pakistan with the local population. He accepted his operational space was confined from which he could not get out without dying. He had clearly seen the fate of others, including the US Navy Seals operation that eliminated bin Laden. Unlike the other al-Qaeda leaders, al-Zawahiri also ensured that he created a strong counter-intelligence apparatus, with support from the Haqqanis, that could inform him of any impeding American counter-terrorism strikes. Compared to bin Laden, al-Zawahiri also focused more on building a political foundation and made key moves to distribute al-Qaeda's leadership across several countries to prevent a single decapitation. His strategy was to strengthen the periphery to preserve the centre.[1]

It was remarkable that despite being hunted by the Clinton, Bush, Obama, and Trump administrations since the 1990s, al-Zawahiri remained at large throughout the 'war on terrorism'. One of his legacies had been his endurance and longevity. He had been involved in global jihad for decades, placed at the top of the most wanted lists, and eluded law enforcement and intelligence agencies for generations whilst still maintaining a robust propaganda campaign.[2] Al-Zawahiri also survived far longer than his Egyptian predecessors or any of his ideological contemporaries and rivals. It is a complicated business staying one step ahead of the watchful eye of the world's counter-terrorism community. It is even more confounding when comparing the Egyptian ideologue with others who evaded capture for staggeringly long periods and in some cases, spent almost entire lifetimes in hiding—Unabomber Ted Kaczynski; Marxist terrorist Carlos the Jackal; Medellín Cartel drug lord Pablo Escobar; the gangster James 'Whitey' Bulger, who at one time was the Federal Bureau of Investigation's second–most wanted after bin Laden—al-Zawahiri remained at large for far longer.

Aside from al-Zawahiri's own self-preservation efforts, what was significant is that when his fate was in the hands of those in power, serendipity repeatedly favoured him. He was fortunate to escape from the Military Technical College revolt, to avoid a death sentence for the assassination of Sadat, to survive the Afghan-Arab campaign against the Soviets, to be freed from detention by the Russians in Dagestan, to flee Afghanistan following 9/11, and to escape the subsequent American drone operations in Pakistan time and again. This was a long list of 'close calls' which al-Zawahiri managed to thwart.

Whilst in isolation in Pakistan, al-Zawahiri appeared to actively chart the group's broader vision, as well as manage and dictate its direction. In bin Laden's absence, al-Zawahiri served as the glue-man of global jihadism whilst being very careful of his digital footprint and working off the same long-term operational plan.'[3] Al-Zawahiri began the process of making al-Qaeda viable whilst operating in the shadows. In collaborating with Pakistani terrorist groups, camps were created where would-be jihadists who initially intended to engage in terrorism against India in Jammu and Kashmir would be redirected by al-Qaeda's local affiliates such as the Jaish-e-Mohammed (JeM) and Lashkar-e-Taiba (LeT) to serve al-Zawahiri. Their skill sets and Western social skills made them very effective, and they would represent al-Qaeda's second generation tasked with fomenting terrorism around the world.

This coincided with the Iraq War in 2003 driven by George W. Bush and Tony Blair. Although it ousted Saddam Hussein's regime, it also created a security vacuum and gave further impetus and momentum to the jihadist movement. However, al-Zawahiri faced his first direct challenge to his authority from the upstart Abu Musab al-Zarqawi, who had a personal grievance with the Egyptian as he, like many jihadists, believed al-Zawahiri had murdered Abdullah Azzam. Al-Zarqawi's indiscriminate killing of Muslims and filming gory videos of beheadings threatened to cause ruptures within al-Qaeda. Al-Zawahiri demanded al-Zarqawi desist from his graphically violent tactics; al-Zarqawi not only refused but then intensified his attacks. The US ended up killing al-Zarqawi in a drone strike, thus inadvertently taking another rival of al-Zawahiri's off the chess board.

Despite many setbacks against the Mubarak regime and not playing a direct role in the Arab Spring, al-Zawahiri took huge satisfaction when Mubarak was finally pushed out of office and humiliatingly forced to attend court hearings in a cage similar to the one that he put al-Zawahiri in after Sadat's assassination. Many of the nations of the Middle East and North Africa that experienced demonstrations for dignity, employment, freedom, democracy, and justice during the Arab Spring spiralled into war and exacerbated repression of civil rights. The revolution that toppled Mubarak and the subsequent democratic experiment was short lived. A military coup replaced the Muslim Brotherhood government with the army general Abdel Fattah el-Sisi, under whom the memories of Tahrir Square were erased, and the draconian familiarity of the Mubarak regime restored.

Countries across the Middle East and North Africa were either engulfed in conflict or reverted back to autocratic regimes where political elites once again thrived at the expense of ordinary citizens. All of this contributed to creating new enemies, of the old variety, for al-Zawahiri to identify and blame. Throughout the Middle East hope was replaced by resentment, which once again became a tool for al-Zawahiri to exploit. As was demonstrated throughout his life, jihadists flourish anywhere there has been wreckage and disillusionment. The jihadist movement began regenerating, seeking to win hearts and minds and preying on the vulnerable whilst cultivating those motivated by ideology and a propensity for violence.

The Assad regime's violent crackdown on demonstrations in Syria along with the torture and disappearances of civilians turned into a civil war that killed and displaced millions and converged with the sectarianism engulfing Iraq, which in turn led to the emergence and growth of ISIS. Along with having to deal with the US hunting for him, al-Zawahiri faced an equally difficult challenge in countering a growing behemoth that was usurping his and al-Qaeda's position at the helm of the global jihadist movement. ISIS, like al-Zarqawi, had sheer contempt for al-Zawahiri and, embarrassingly for the Egyptian, chose to publicly admonish him and question his credibility and legitimacy. Although initially struggling to counter ISIS, al-Zawahiri adopted strategic patience, which had served him well in the past, and focused on al-Qaeda quietly regenerating in the shadows whilst letting ISIS take the brunt of US counter-terrorism operations. Like with many of the adversaries al-Zawahiri faced, ISIS burnt bright too quickly, and eventually its strength dissipated. Unlike ISIS, al-Zawahiri also understood that if al-Qaeda was to ever succeed in the Islamic world, it should not alienate the local population, and through a series of doctrinal messages, he ordered his fighters and affiliates to avoid Muslim civilian casualties.[4] Under al-Zawahiri, al-Qaeda's affiliates were also accorded more respect and equal status, which bin Laden had been reluctant to do. As a result, al-Zawahiri was able to expanded al-Qaeda's affiliates and presence in sub-Saharan Africa and the Sahel, from Mali to Burkina Faso to Niger.

Throughout his life, al-Zawahiri embedded his writings and commentary in Islamic jurisprudence (*fiqh*). The central thesis of al-Zawahiri's religious and political commentary has been that Muslims must identify themselves as part of a single nation and unite to resist the subjugation of Islam. Therefore, offensive jihad against 'apostate regimes' and their 'Zionist-Crusader' sponsors was both necessary and justified. Al-Zawahiri portrayed himself as an educator of Muslim youth and joining either the EIJ or al-Qaeda as a commitment to both resisting and directly confronting those advocating and maintaining secularism, apostate man-made rule, and democratic governments. This shaped al-Zawahiri's local and global priorities and explains why he came into conflict with a variety of figures within the jihadist movement.

Al-Zawahiri also managed to create an evolving framework through which a wide variety of terrorist groups separated by nationality, class, language, and culture could connect, relate, and empathise. His messages were designed to provoke psychological reactions and communicate ideological guidance to a global audience. Al-Zawahiri united a fragmented jihadist community through rhetoric that insisted on the West as a common enemy of Islam and on the duty of all Muslims to accept the fight against it. He saw the obligation to jihad led by an Islamic vanguard as the stalwart opposition of Western culture and hegemony and attempt to usher in an Islamic governance built on Shariah which would in turn preserve the unity of the *umma*.

In *Knights under the Prophet's Banner*, al-Zawahiri specified that his first goal was ideological clarity and rationality. Even though he was not a trained Islamic scholar, ideology was very important to al-Zawahiri, especially with the shadow of Qutb looming large. Al-Zawahiri's doctrine was shaped as much by the regimes of Nasser, Sadat, and Mubarak as it was by the ideologues Qutb and Faraj. They both used the Pharaoh motif to condemn the respective Egyptian governments of their eras as 'apostate regimes'. They also hated any kind of secularism and Egyptian nationalism that was not connected to Islam and the *ummah*. Importantly, Qutb and al-Banna paved the way for al-Zawahiri's goal of rebuilding an Islamic vanguard, starting with the EIJ and culminating with al-Qaeda. Although al-Zawahiri profoundly valued the Egyptian contribution to jihadism, he drew a line with al-Banna and the Muslim Brotherhood for their involvement in participatory politics. In al-Zawahiri's mind, they legitimised unjust regimes that had pervaded Egypt, whom they were supposed to be fighting against in the first place. As a result, al-Zawahiri sought to continue the doctrines and strategies of Qutb and Faraj and build upon their Egyptian brand of jihadism to make it first grow in Egypt, and then across North Africa, the Middle East, and Afghanistan and Pakistan.

Through his doctrine and use of the media, al-Zawahiri defined himself both as the leader of an ideological movement and a military tactician willing to direct violence to specific political circumstances and to influence events near and far. He also sought to create a lasting leadership role for al-Qaeda as the vanguard of global jihadist movement layered through the Egyptian framework. Al-Zawahiri's world view has oscillated depending on the context and environment he found himself in. There have been several core elements:

1. Muslims are under attack from apostates and infidels based on injustices, both historical and current.

2. Only al-Qaeda as the vanguard are fighting the oppressors of Islam and forces of *jahilliyyah*.
3. There needs to be an *ummah* committed to the cause, willing to migrate (*hijrah*) and sacrifice (*shaheed*).
4. If you are not supporting al-Qaeda, then you are supporting the oppressors both near and far.

As part of this, al-Zawahiri went to great lengths to provide doctrinal sanction for al-Qaeda's actions, to kill with moral authority. He was also able to convince his disciples that their victims constituted reasonable and necessary sacrifices to rid the world of apostasy and heretics and usher in a system of governance bound by a rigid religious interpretation. Time and again, al-Zawahiri manipulated situations for his ideological expediency. He demanded a bitter toll from al-Qaeda's enemies whether it was in hotels, vessels, planes, trains, embassies, or military bases. The men he had been preparing to kill and to die would come into close contact with their targets without ever raising a sense of trepidation. Whether it was politicians or judges, civilians or peace keeping-troops, even rivals of al-Zawahiri, the unsuspecting victims all succumbed to the engulfing roar of terrorist attacks which left misery and destruction in their wake. Contrary to accusations that al-Zawahiri was a micromanager, the Egyptian ideologue was an expert at delegating and choosing the right operatives for specific plots and tasks. Post-9/11, he cultivated and shaped a series of terrorist plots to hit Europe and North America, the most infamous being the 7/7 London bombings in the United Kingdom. However, al-Zawahiri also understood that the effects of terrorism are not only measured by the immediate number of fatalities. The full misery lies in the malign trauma hanging in its aftermath and the consequences of changing how one thinks and feels about one's safety and security.

An example of this was the 2006 transatlantic airline liquid bomb plot that al-Zawahiri oversaw. Although British and American authorities disrupted al-Qaeda's plans to use hydrogen peroxide–based IEDs onboard several transatlantic flights, the plot created massive ramifications for the aviation industry. Security procedures and screening processes became even more stringent, and passengers were only allowed to carry a limited number of 100 ml liquid containers in a resealable plastic bag. Al-Zawahiri's terrorist plot is one of the most consequential in terms of global disruption. Although it was foiled, it had a significant effect on the vulnerable aviation industry, and caused frustrations to the billions of passengers flying every year. Yet it's unlikely many even know the exact reason why those restrictions were imposed in the first place, and the Egyptian doctor who was ultimately behind it.

Al-Zawahiri was not a communicator in quite the same way as bin Laden. Over time, with age, he came across as awkward, long winded, and turgid, and his lengthy statements on theology would be overshadowed by comparisons with bin Laden's charisma. This was a flawed comparison, as bin Laden's gravitas is drawn from the period before 2001. His speeches and commentaries after 9/11 did not carry the same rousing effect. Although at times laboured, al-Zawahiri's messages were a carefully constructed macro of the poetry of religion and violence woven together. He would tell stories from the Qur'an in the same paragraph as calling on people to rise and kill. It was a political sermon interwoven with a call to arms. The interesting dynamic between bin Laden and al-Zawahiri was their comparative messaging. Bin Laden was a passive player in al-Qaeda's ideological development but led through personality, whereas al-Zawahiri directed through doctrine. Al-Qaeda's challenges under al-Zawahiri would have still emerged had bin Laden survived. Jihadists who got involved in the 1970s and 1980s, and even into the 1990s, the Boomer and Gen X generation, were a different breed to the Millennial and Gen Z Jihadis who came of age in the Arab Spring era and gave rise to ISIS.[5]

Demonstrating strategic patience, al-Zawahiri was content to bide his time for the long-term survival of al-Qaeda and future jihadists. Al-Qaeda had entrenched itself in localised conflicts where it operates to advance its transnational aims, which primarily lie in the Islamic world: Afghanistan-Pakistan, the Indian subcontinent, Syria, Yemen, the Horn of Africa, East Africa, the Maghreb, and the Sahel. Each region represents an al-Qaeda affiliate, some of which are stronger than the ISIS factions.

Under al-Zawahiri, mostly out of necessity, al-Qaeda eventually shifted its focus from terrorist attacks in the West to supporting Pakistan-based jihadist groups that operate throughout South Asia. Under al-Zawahiri's guidance, al-Qaeda's members intermarried into Afghan and Pakistani societies, making them inseparable through the bonds of tribe, family, and culture. Their destinies are interwoven. A key component has been al-Zawahiri's support and development of AQIS, whose fighters became an integral component of the Taliban conquest to retake control of Afghanistan in 2021.[6]

Through AQIS, al-Zawahiri had begun a process of localising al-Qaeda to South Asia, with Pakistani cadres that helped the al-Qaeda leadership ingratiate themselves within both Pakistan and Afghanistan. The Taliban has also been inseparable from al-Qaeda, with cultural, familial, and political obligations which it will remain unable to fully abandon, even if its leadership is sincere in seeking to do so. And like many places, politics in Afghanistan is particularly local.[7]

Al-Zawahiri had seen with the experiences of al-Zarqawi and ISIS that cultivating and preserving relationships with local communities was essential as opposed to alienating them through forced, flawed, and rapid state-building projects erected over dead civilians. Al-Zawahiri had always been very concerned that isolation from Sunni Muslim communities increased al-Qaeda's unpopularity and exposure to counter-terrorism strategies and impeded the entire al-Qaeda agenda. Al-Zawahiri forced al-Qaeda and its affiliates to moderate their activities and rhetoric. In fact, despite the logistical challenges, his relationship with the affiliates was essential to the global jihadist movement.

Under al-Zawahiri, al-Qaeda and its affiliates also became more sophisticated by diversifying in social services and proto-governance designed to establish deeper roots within societies, which is a major reason why al-Qaeda's branches have grown in strength across AfPak, the Middle East, North Africa, and sub-Saharan Africa. Although these affiliates seem more localised, the ideology remains global, and part of that strategy entails being embedded within these populations to garner support and operate safely without the concern of betrayal or expulsion.

Aided by warzones, emerging ungoverned spaces, and state complicity coupled with the absence of counter-terrorism monitoring in Afghanistan, Pakistan, and Iraq, al-Zawahiri's envisaged formalisation of his 'safe bases' doctrine has come to fruition. Based on al-Zawahiri's 2013 'General Guidelines for Jihad', al-Qaeda could develop a land corridor that spans all the way from Pakistan to Syria through Afghanistan, Iran, and Iraq. This necessitated cooperation far and wide amongst al-Qaeda, the Taliban, and the Haqqani Network as well as affiliates in Iraq and Syria. It also mandated state elements from Iran's Quds Force and Pakistan's ISI including their proxies. The systematic effort to consolidate these multilayered relationships and alliances demonstrated al-Zawahiri's long-term ambitions, which would persist in some form even if future disputes emerge within the different jihadist factions.

Through his time as head of al-Qaeda, al-Zawahiri was often judged by how many attacks he orchestrated after bin Laden was killed. Although he could not emulate al-Qaeda's previous successes in terrorism, arguably, that is the wrong metric by which to judge him. Al-Qaeda had been withering under bin Laden as its senior leadership was captured or killed. For al-Zawahiri, the goal had to be for al-Qaeda create and maintain 'safe bases' around the Islamic world and if left unchecked, then expand their operations again. To misconstrue the absence of terrorist attacks for fragility or vulnerability is to misinterpret al-Zawahiri's ultimate goals. As the Egyptian teacher once commented about himself and al-Qaeda, 'We adapt to the practical reality wherever it is.'[8] From that vantage point, al-Zawahiri left the terrorist network in a much stronger position than it was in when he inherited when bin Laden died. Al-Qaeda affiliates, AQAP, AQIM, AQIS, and al-Shabaab, have grown and developed the means to operate independently from al-Qaeda core, a key objective of al-Zawahiri's to be self-sufficient.

Throughout al-Zawahiri's time with al-Qaeda, he had to navigate four tiers of jihadists who were ostensibly loyal to him. The first tier comprised the core leadership, led by al-Zawahiri, which still wielded some coordination, if not command capability. The second tier was al-Qaeda affiliates and associates that were bonded to al-Qaeda's ideology, operated independently, yet expressed adherence to al-Zawahiri because of his seniority and therefore retained a *ba'yah* to him. The third tier were locals in territory where al-Qaeda and affiliates operate. This tier consisted of those sympathetic to al-Qaeda's ideology who are not beholden to al-Qaeda; they have their own separate immediate priorities but are willing to respond when called upon for sanctuary, logistics, and resources. The final tier was that of lone actors, individuals who had no direct contact with al-Qaeda but were prepared to carry out attacks in the name of al-Qaeda to support al-Zawahiri's agenda.

For al-Qaeda, the hasty and disastrous withdrawal by the West from Afghanistan, and the Taliban's immediate takeover, enabled the group to meet two other key goals set by al-Zawahiri. Namely, that al-Qaeda and its affiliates can survive 'long wars' with the United States and bleed the West of resources, undermining its influence globally and damaging political will domestically. In Afghanistan, al-Qaeda also once again extended its reach beyond its historical sanctuaries in southern Afghanistan where the

Taliban dominated. Both entities continued to work closely. Al-Qaeda and a plethora of jihadist groups have been indirectly afforded the opportunity to grow and expand by benefiting from their 'safe bases'. More than two decades after 9/11, this 'back to the future' scenario left open the perception many jihadists had, and will continue to have, in pursuing a violent strategy for achieving the eventual goal of defeating both the 'internal enemy' and 'external enemy'. Indeed, in the decades since Sadat's assassination and the 9/11 terrorist attacks, there remains fertile ground for new avatars of jihadism across the Middle East, North Africa, Afghanistan, and Pakistan. They have an opportunity to build on the platform al-Zawahiri helped create with bin Laden.

After having evaded numerous operations that were tasked with eliminating him, al-Zawahiri returned to Afghanistan in 2022, 21 years after he fled under a storm of air strikes. The level of trust he had placed with the Haqqanis once more demonstrated al-Zawahiri's confidence that he would be safe. The Haqqani Network had become the most powerful Taliban faction in Afghanistan and took over several important regime portfolios, including the Interior Ministry that controlled all the security organs. The perception was that this would provide a safe environment for the al-Qaeda leader, assuming that with the United States leaving Afghanistan, they would also forget about him too, especially as they could not launch a the type of ground operation used against bin Laden at Abbottabad. Although al-Zawahiri trusted the Haqqani Network implicitly, he ultimately betrayed his own instincts because despite having an effective security apparatus across the entirety of Afghanistan, they had no control over the skies above.

It is possible that al-Zawahiri's endless health issues and the fatigue of living in the shadows away from all forms of normal life had taken its toll. He may have resigned himself to knowing that he was still monitored. Either way, al-Zawahiri did survive the 'war on terrorism', and he had already begun ceding his role to his confidantes and affiliates. Furthermore, his death is unlikely to be the end of al-Qaeda, although it may generate a new series of problems of fragmentation, internal competition, and dissipation of affiliates. The fact that none of this happened when al-Zawahiri took over from bin Laden demonstrated his own ability to keep the commitment and loyalty of different factions. It is also pertinent to remember the huge $25 million bounty offered for al-Zawahiri by the Rewards for

Justice Program was never claimed or officially paid out. One of the big assumptions was that everybody is for sale. If money was a motivation, al-Zawahiri would have been turned in many times over.

Biden's 'Over the Horizon' counter-terrorism strategy demonstrated that the United States has sophisticated targeting capabilities and human intelligence assets in Afghanistan and Pakistan. However, that is usually in conjunction in working directly with partners on the ground to sustain pressure on al-Qaeda, ISIS, and their respective affiliates. In and around Taliban-controlled Afghanistan, the United States has lacked official local support and infrastructure. The operation that eliminated al-Zawahiri might be the exception rather than the rule as the US utilised its clandestine network of informants in Afghanistan and risks exposing them for future operations as the Taliban closed ranks after al-Zawahiri's death. Whatever technology achieves, it will never be so absolute as to account for every action by a terrorist, let alone measure their thoughts and intent. Human sources have always been the highest objective for the intelligence community as they can provide coveted nuggets of information. Since al-Zawahiri was killed, the Haqqani Network closed ranks and enhanced their operational security to weed out any spies.

Undoubtedly, al-Zawahiri was an opportunist who made a career off the backs of more reckless, wealthy, and violent men. He was stubborn, single minded, and self-serving. However, as a terrorist leader, al-Zawahiri embraced these traits deemed necessary to lead and execute operations. Paradoxically, he was also pioneering, an effective recruiter and delegator, patient and resilient. He retained the boundless capacity of imagination and reinvention of terrorism across his five decades in plotting, instigating, and killing. He may have lacked the magnetism and allure of other jihadists, but he opted for endurance and fortitude. He also was a master in skulduggery.

Following al-Zawahiri's death, some Western policymakers were writing the obituary for al-Qaeda and transnational terrorism, claiming that the bigger concern was from great power competition with Russia and China. In a curious moment of geopolitical symmetry, the drone strike that eliminated al-Zawahiri coincided with the contentious visit to Taiwan by then US House Speaker Nancy Pelosi, which incited China to intensify live-fire military exercises in the Taiwan straits. Along with Russia's invasion of Ukraine in 2022, a multitude of international security challenges with terrorism were eclipsed by the actions of hostile state actors. As history has all too painfully demonstrated, a shift in security priorities could once again enable the global jihadist movement to grow, replenish, and reconstitute, as part of al-Zawahiri's 'safe bases' doctrine. In Afghanistan, combatting terrorism should be seen as a type of 'great power competition'.[9]

The concern for the future is that young, impressionable people from the West may travel back to Pakistan and Afghanistan for terrorist training, as they did from the 1990s to 2007 or like the foreign terrorist fighters (FTF) who travelled to Iraq and Syria between 2012 and 2016 to join ISIS. Afghanistan should be seen through those lenses. Afghanistan, Iraq, and Syria became fertile ground for extremism because of internal wars and ungoverned spaces as well as interference from neighbouring countries. In addition, where women's rights are curtailed and suppressed, radicalisation proliferates and further motivates extremist narratives inspired by misogynistic polices. As feared, after taking power in Afghanistan in 2021, the Taliban began an incremental process of curtailing the rights of women, including to education and to work. This could contribute to a new wave of FTFs, and the West may be unable to deal with it because Afghanistan has been abandoned, and there is no footprint or allies with the ability to openly operate.[10] Both al-Qaeda and ISIS would want to tap into the new generation of jihadists coming of age in the post-COVID-19 era. New entities may be emerging, jockeying for influence, whilst some may prefer to be affiliates of al-Qaeda as they eventually succeed al-Zawahiri. Nevertheless, al-Qaeda has demonstrated the ability to evolve and adapt to surrounding conditions, stepping away temporarily from mass casualty attacks to broaden its reach before it returns stronger to inflict more atrocities.

Looking back, as the bombs were dropping around him during the Tora Bora operation in 2001, al-Zawahiri reflected on one of the most important goals and hopes for the jihadist movement:

> Liberating the Muslim nation, confronting the enemies of Islam, and launching jihad against them require a Muslim authority, established on a Muslim land, that raises the banner of jihad and rallies the Muslims around it. Without achieving this goal our actions will mean nothing more than mere and repeated disturbances that will not lead to the aspired goal, which is the restoration of the caliphate and the dismissal of the invaders from the land of Islam. ... This goal must remain the basic objective of the Islamic jihad movement, regardless of the sacrifices and the time involved.[11]

There would not have been a successful al-Qaeda without al-Zawahiri. Bin Laden started with no top aides; he was an affiliate of Azzam and didn't have the wherewithal to think beyond Afghanistan. Al-Zawahiri had very valuable operatives with intelligence and military training. Al-Zawahiri and bin Laden had a symbiotic relationship, and neither of them could have created al-Qaeda independently. However, al-Zawahiri managed to keep al-Qaeda alive and enabled the growth of the affiliates in bin Laden's absence.[12]

Although the caliphate that al-Zawahiri envisaged was not attained and al-Qaeda was arguably usurped by ISIS for a brief period, the Egyptian ideologue's hope of reaching his long-term goal of a caliphate and winning a war of attrition against the 'apostates' has been preserved as a legacy for others to follow. Al-Zawahiri showed himself to be fatalistic about success, believing that to eventually achieve the goals of the jihadist movement, death in battle was inevitable for its cadres. This enabled al-Zawahiri to demand sacrifices of not just himself but his family, followers, and affiliates too.

From the reign of Gamal Nasser to the era of COVID-19, and everything in between, al-Zawahiri plotted and planned. He created a template for others to develop and follow. His failings and limitations often garner more attention than the atrocities he inflicted as well as the way he kept al-Qaeda afloat. Furthermore, his ability to endure for over five decades and remain relevant to the jihadist agenda across continents demonstrated his importance. Al-Qaeda and the wider jihadist movement did not fear the day al-Zawahiri was no more. Just as was seen with bin Laden's death, al-Qaeda is not dependent on a single individual. Al-Zawahiri ensured that there would be a plethora of experienced leaders based in Pakistan, Afghanistan, and Iran, who may believe that the changed ground conditions would enable them to return to Afghanistan and operate openly. Despite the challenges in communications and logistics, al-Zawahiri groomed his subordinates and heads of affiliates to assume a shared future leadership. Some have been killed, but not all. This generation has evolved and become more resilient during a particularly challenging period and gained experience on the battlefield.

Whilst some other ideologues attracted greater short-term attention, their infamy was eventually their undoing. Al-Zawahiri's approach served to protect him and his plans for the al-Qaeda movement in the long term, as he outlived and out-thought his contemporaries and rivals. His life was based on a myriad of lessons, encounters, plots, strategies, and messages for future generations of jihadists to rise up when the conditions next prove conducive to do so.

Al-Zawahiri never wanted the future of the group to depend on a single individual, and with an overabundance of experienced deputies around and equally dangerous leaders of the affiliates, al-Zawahiri demonstrated confidence that the war against the West and the regimes in the Islamic world would continue. In the meantime, the doctor, teacher, and terrorist has ensured his place as the ideologue who lived, fought, and spoke the longest, whilst ensuring the Egyptian doctrine of jihadism endures at the forefront of people's minds.

Notes

INTRODUCTION

1. Lawrence Wright, *The Looming Tower: Al Qaeda and the Road to 9/11* (London: Allen Lane, 2006).
2. John Calvert, author interview, 20 May 2021.
3. Ali Soufan, *Anatomy of Terror: From the Death of bin Laden to the Rise of the Islamic State* (New York: W. W. Norton, 2017).
4. Cathy Scott-Clark and Adrian Levy, *The Exile: The Stunning Inside Story of Osama bin Laden and Al Qaeda in Flight* (London: Bloomsbury Press, 2017).
5. Fawaz A. Gerges, *The Far Enemy: Why Jihad Went Global* (Cambridge: Cambridge University Press, 2005).
6. Seth G. Jones, *Hunting in the Shadows: The Pursuit of al Qa'ida Since 9/11* (New York: W. W. Norton, 2012).
7. Jerrold Post, 'Military Studies in the Jihad against the Tyrants: The al-Qaeda Training Manual', *U.S. Air Force Counterproliferation Center*, 2004.
8. Montasser al-Zayyat, *The Road to al-Qaeda: The Story of bin Laden's Right Hand Man* (London: Pluto Press, 2004).
9. Ayman al-Zawahiri, *Knights under the Prophet's Banner*, Asharq al-Awsat, December 2001.
10. Thomas Hegghammer, *The Caravan: Abdallah Azzam and the Rise of Global Jihad* (Cambridge: Cambridge University Press, 2020).
11. Peter Bergen, *The Rise and Fall of Osama bin Laden* (New York: Simon & Schuster, 2021).
12. Mitch D. Silber, *The al-Qaeda Factor: Plots against the West* (Philadelphia: University of Pennsylvania Press, 2012).
13. John Miller, Michael Stone, and Chris Mitchell, *The Cell: The Story of the FBI, the CIA, and the Terrorists Next Door* (New York: Hyperion, 2002).
14. Bruce Riedel, *The Hunt for al-Qaeda* (Washington, DC: Brookings Institution Press, 2008); Bruce Riedel, *Deadly Embrace: Pakistan, America, and the Future of the Global Jihad* (Washington, DC: Brookings Institution Press, 2011).
15. Joby Warrick, *The Triple Agent: The al-Qaeda Mole Who Infiltrated the CIA* (New York: Doubleday, 2011).
16. Farhad Khosrokhavar, *Inside Jihadism* (New York: Routledge, 2009).
17. Bruce Hoffman, *Inside Terrorism* (New York: Columbia University Press, 2017).

18. Sajjan Gohel, 'Deciphering Ayman al-Zawahiri and al-Qaeda's Strategic and Ideological Imperatives', *Perspectives on Terrorism* 11, no. 1 (2017).

19. Nimrod Raphaeli, 'Ayman Muḥammad Rabi' al-Zawahiri: The Making of an Arch Terrorist', *Terrorism and Political Violence* 14, no. 4 (2002): 1–22.

20. James D. Jacquier, 'An Operational Code of Terrorism: The Political Psychology of Ayman al-Zawahiri', *Behavioural Sciences of Terrorism and Political Aggression* 6, no. 1 (2014): 19–40.

21. Tim Huffman, 'You Have Atomic Bombs, We Have the Martyrdom-Seekers: Ayman al-Zawahiri's Narrative Arc of the Martyr', *Peace & Conflict Studies* 23, no. 1 (2016): 102–28.

22. Olivier Roy and Tore Hamming, 'Al-Zawahiri's *Bay'a* to Mullah Mansoor: A Bitter Pill but a Bountiful Harvest', *CTC Sentinel* 9, no. 5 (2016).

23. Barak Mendelsohn, 'Ayman al-Zawahiri and the Challenges of Succession in Terrorist Organizations', *Terrorism and Political Violence* 34, no. 8 (2020).

24. Rita Katz, Director of SITE Intelligence Group, https://ent.siteintelgroup.com; Aaron Zelin, Founder, https://jihadology.net/.

CHAPTER 1

1. US intelligence officials, author interview, 27 October 2017.

2. Joseph Votel, author interview, 17 May 2021.

3. Ibid.

4. Umayma Hassan, 'Pure Blood on the Soil of Afghanistan, Part One', *One Ummah*, 15 April 2019.

5. Peter Bergen, 'The Account of How We Nearly Caught Osama bin Laden in 2001', *New Republic*, 30 December 2009.

6. 'Tora Bora Revisited: How We Failed to Get bin Laden and Why It Matters Today', *Report to Members of the Committee on Foreign Relations, United States Senate*, 30 November 2009.

7. Bergen, 'The Account of How We Nearly Caught Osama bin Laden in 2001'.

8. U.S. security official, author interview, 24 April 2011.

9. Gary Berntsen and Ralph Pezzullo, *Jawbreaker* (New York: Crown, 2005), ch. 16.

10. 'Tora Bora Revisited'.

11. Nick Pratt, author interview, 23 August 2011.

12. US security officials, author interview, 27 October 2017.

13. Terry H. Anderson, *Bush's Wars* (New York: Oxford University Press, 2011), 87.

14. US security officials, author interview, 6 February 2013.

15. Ayman al-Zawahiri, *Knights under the Prophet's Banner*, December 2001.

16. Mike Boettcher and David Ensor, 'Reports Suggest al-Qaeda Military Chief Killed', *CNN*, 16 November 2001, http://edition.cnn.com/2001/WORLD/asiapcf/central/11/16/ret.atef/.

17. Al-Zawahiri, *Knights under the Prophet's Banner*.

18. Ibid.
19. Ibid.
20. Ibid.
21. Ibid.
22. Ibid.
23. For the US and Pakistani involvement in Afghanistan during the Cold War, see Peter Bergen, *Holy War, Inc: Inside the Secret World of Osama bin Laden* (New York: Simon and Schuster, 2001); Mohammed Yousaf and Mark Adkin, *Afghanistan the Bear Trap: The Defeat of a Superpower* (Havertown, PA: Casemate, 2001).
24. Al-Zawahiri, *Knights under the Prophet's Banner*.
25. 'Rewards for Justice Program', US Department of State Archive, https://2001-2009..state.gov/m/ds/terrorism/c8651.htm.
26. Lawrence Wright, author interview, 16 January 2022.
27. Samir W. Raafat, *Maadi 1904–1962: Society and History in a Cairo Suburb* (Cairo: Palm Press, 1994).
28. Nimrod Raphaeli, 'Ayman Muḥammad Rabi' al-Zawahiri: The Making of an Arch Terrorist', *Terrorism and Political Violence*, 14 no. 4 (2002): 2.
29. Family member of Ayman al-Zawahiri, author interview, 24 August 2015.
30. Mahfouz Azzam, interview with Rory Carroll, 'Mahfouz Azzam, Egyptian Great-Uncle and Lawyer of Ayman al-Zawahiri', *Guardian,* 11 September 2002, https://www.theguardian.com/world/2002/sep/11/september112002.september1154.
31. Soufan, *Anatomy of Terror*.
32. Family member of Ayman al-Zawahiri, author interview, 24 August 2015.
33. Ibid.
34. Ibid.
35. Said. F. Hassan, 'Al-Azhar', in *Education and the Arab Spring*, ed. Mohamed E. Aboulkacem (Leiden: Brill), 131.
36. Caroline Williams, *Islamic Monuments in Cairo: The Practical Guide* (Cairo: American University in Cairo Press, 2004), 152.
37. Afaf Lutfi al-Sayyid Marsot, *A Short History of Modern Egypt* (Cambridge: Cambridge University Press, 1985), vii.
38. Jackson Sigler, 'Engaging the Middle East: Napoleon's Invasion of Egypt', *History: Reviews of New Books* 38, no. 2 (2010): 40–44.
39. Nathan Schur, *Napoleon in the Holy Land* (London: Greenhill Books, 1999).
40. Juan Cole, *Napoleon's Egypt: Invading the Middle East* (New York: St. Martin's Press, 2007), 157.
41. Al-Zawahiri, *Knights under the Prophet's Banner*.
42. Ibid.
43. J. C. B. Richmond, *Egypt 1798–1952: Her Advance toward a Modern Identity* (London: Routledge, 2013).
44. Fawaz A. Gerges, *Making the Arab World: Nasser, Qutb, and the Clash that Shaped the Middle East* (Princeton, NJ: Princeton University Press, 2018), 41.

45. Al-Zawahiri, *Knights under the Prophet's Banner*.
46. 'The Egyptian Crisis and Arabi Pasha', *The Empire Series*, episode 63, BBC Radio Four, May 10, 2006.
47. Robert L. Tignor, *Modernization and British Colonial Rule in Egypt, 1882–1914* (Princeton, NJ: Princeton University Press, 1995), 15–22.
48. Ibrahim Abu-Lughod, 'The Transformation of the Egyptian Élite: Prelude to the 'Urābī Revolt', *Middle East Journal* 31, no. 1 (1967): 325–44.
49. Tignor, *Modernization and British Colonial Rule in Egypt*, 15–22.
50. Robert T. Harrison, *Gladstone's Imperialism in Egypt* (Westport: Greenwood Press, 1995).
51. Al-Zawahiri, *Knights under the Prophet's Banner*.
52. Milne Cheetham, 'To His Highness Prince Hussein Kamil Pasha', Sir Milne Cheetham Collection, Middle East Centre Archive, St Antony's College, University of Oxford, GB 165 0055, 19 December 1914.
53. George Antonius, *The Arab Awakening* (Philadelphia: J. B. Lippincott, 1939), 243–48, 428–30.
54. Al-Zawahiri, *Knights under the Prophet's Banner*.
55. Ibid.
56. Ibid.
57. Ayman al-Zawahiri, 'The Emancipation of Mankind and Nations under the Banner of the Qur'an', *as-Sahab Media*, 30 January 2005.
58. Ayman al-Zawahiri, 'The Advice of One Concerned', *as-Sahab Media*, 5 July 2007.
59. Ibid.
60. John D. Grainger, *The Battle for Palestine 1917* (Woodbridge: Boydell Press, 2006).
61. Al-Zawahiri, *Knights under the Prophet's Banner*.
62. Ben Halpern, *The Idea of the Jewish State* (Boston: Harvard University Press, 1969), 293.
63. P. J. Vatikiotis, *The History of Modern Egypt* (London: Weidenfield & Nicolson, 1969), 262–67.
64. Arthur Link, ed., *The Papers of Woodrow Wilson, April 5–April 22, 1919*, vol. 57 (Princeton, NJ: Princeton University Press, 1988).
65. Vatikiotis, *The History of Modern Egypt*, 270–94.
66. Al-Zawahiri, *Knights under the Prophet's Banner*.
67. Al-Zawahiri, 'The Emancipation of Mankind and Nations under the Banner of the Qur'an'.
68. Ibid.
69. Ayman al-Zawahiri, 'Realities of the Conflict between Islam and Unbelief', *as-Sahab Media*, 21 December 2006.
70. Ibid.
71. For more on ethnic minorities in the Ottoman Empire, see Molly Greene, *Minorities in the Ottoman Empire* (Princeton, NJ: Markus Wiener, 2005); Salahi Ramadan Sonyel, *Minorities and the Destruction of the Ottoman Empire,*

Publications of Turkish Historical Society, serial 7 (Ankara: Turkish Historical Society Printing House, 1993).

72. Wright, *The Looming Tower*, ch. 2.
73. Family member of Ayman al-Zawahiri, author interview, 24 August 2015.
74. Ibid.
75. Correspondence and Papers relating to the Special Commission in Egypt 1920–1924, Archive of Alfred Milner, Viscount Milner, 1824–1955, Oxford University Bodleian Library, 29 August 1920.
76. Family member of Ayman al-Zawahiri, author interview, 24 August 2015.
77. Maurice Ingram, 'Broad Outlines of the Growth of Nationalism in Egypt', Archive of Alfred Milner, Viscount Milner, 1824–1955, Oxford University Bodleian Library, 4 February 1920.
78. Al-Zawahiri, *Knights under the Prophet's Banner*.
79. Ibid.
80. Correspondence and Papers relating to the Special Commission in Egypt 1920–1924.
81. Daniel Neil Crecelius, 'The Ulama and the State in Modern Egypt' (PhD thesis, Princeton University, 1967), 299.
82. Ibid., 306.
83. Rainer Brunner, 'Education, Politics, and the Struggle for Intellectual Leadership: Al-Azhar Between 1927 and 1945', in *Guardians of Faith in Modern Times: 'Ulama' in the Middle East*, ed. Meir Hatina (Leiden: Brill, 2009), 116–17.
84. Crecelius, 'The Ulama and the State in Modern Egypt', 304.
85. Brunner, 'Education, Politics, and the Struggle for Intellectual Leadership', 117–18.
86. Crecelius, 'The Ulama and the State in Modern Egypt', 309.
87. Brunner, 'Education, Politics, and the Struggle for Intellectual Leadership', 118.
88. Crecelius, 'The Ulama and the State in Modern Egypt', 309.
89. Ibid., 312.
90. Family member of Ayman al-Zawahiri, author interview, 24 August 2015.
91. Crecelius, 'The Ulama and the State in Modern Egypt', 313.
92. Jamal al-Banna quoted in Ana Belén Soage, 'Rashid Rida's Legacy', *Muslim World* 98, no. 1 (2008): 2.
93. Ibid., 3.
94. John Willis, 'Debating the Caliphate: Islam and Nation in the Work of Rashid Rida and Abul Kalam Azad', *International History Review* 32, no. 4 (2010): 711–32.
95. Beth Baron, *The Orphan Scandal: Christian Missionaries and the Rise of the Muslim Brotherhood* (Stanford, CA: Stanford University Press, 2014).
96. British Foreign Office—FO 141/714/3, 3 February 1935.
97. Crecelius, 'The Ulama and the State in Modern Egypt', 318.
98. Family member of Ayman al-Zawahiri, author interview, 24 August 2015.
99. Amir Raafat, 'The World's Second Most Wanted Man', *Star (Amman)*, 22 November 2001.

100. Raphaeli, 'Ayman Muḥammad Rabi' al-Zawahiri', 2.
101. Raafat, 'The World's Second Most Wanted Man'.
102. Family member of Ayman al-Zawahiri, author interview, 24 August 2015.
103. Ralph M. Coury, 'Abd al-Rahman Azzam and the Development of Egyptian Arab Nationalism' (PhD thesis, Princeton University, 1984), 92–137.
104. Saima Raza, 'Italian Colonisation & Libyan Resistance to the al-Sanusi of Cyrenaica (1911–1922)', *Journal of Middle Eastern and Islamic Studies (in Asia)* 6, no. 1 (2012): 87–120.
105. James Heyworth-Dunne in Ralph Coury, 'Arabian Ethnicity and Arab Nationalism: The Case of Abd al-Rahman Azzam', *Journal of the American Research Center in Egypt* 25 (1988): 62.
106. British Foreign Office—FO 371/8988 E5538/3338/16, 17 May 1923.
107. Saad Zaghlul quoted in Anwar G. Chejne, 'Egyptian Attitudes towards Pan-Arabism', *Middle East Journal* 11, no. 3 (1957): 253.
108. Coury 'Arabian Ethnicity and Arab Nationalism', 69.
109. I. H. Baqai, 'The Pan-Arab League', *India Quarterly* 2, no. 2 (1946): 144.
110. Chejne, 'Egyptian Attitudes towards Pan-Arabism', 258.
111. Baqai, 'The Pan-Arab League', 144.
112. Raafat, 'The World's Second Most Wanted Man'.
113. Ralph M. Coury, *The Making of an Egyptian Arab Nationalist: The Early Years of Azzam Pasha, 1893–1936* (Reading: Ithaca Press, 1998), 420.
114. T. R. Little, 'The Arab League: A Reassessment', *Middle East Journal* 10, no. 2 (1956): 145.
115. Abdul Rahman Azzam quoted in David Barnett and Efraim Karsh, 'Azzam's Genocidal Threat', *Middle East Quarterly* 18, no. 4 (2011): 85.
116. Ibid., 436–51.
117. Abdul Rahman Azzam quoted in Chejne, 'Egyptian Attitudes towards Pan-Arabism', 260.
118. Alex Haley, *The Autobiography of Malcolm X* (New York: One World Books, 1992), eBook.
119. Bruce Perry, *The Last Speeches* (New York: Pathfinder Press, 1989), 263–65.
120. Manning Marable, *Malcolm X: A Life of Reinvention* (New York: Viking, 2011), 307–10.
121. Family member of Ayman al-Zawahiri, author interview, 24 August 2015.
122. Ibid.
123. Bruce Rutherford, author interview, 20 May 2021.
124. Hasan al-Banna, *Five tracts of Hasan al-Banna (1906–1949): A Selection from the Majmu'at Rasa'il al-Imām al-Shahid Hasan al-Banna*, trans. Charles Wendell (Berkley: University of California Publications, 1978).
125. Ibid., 60.
126. Abu al-Hasan al-Nadawi, *Mudhakkarat Sa'ih fi al-Sharq al-Arabi* [The diaries of observers in the Arabian Gulf] (Cairo, n.p., n.d.), 26.
127. Hasan al-Banna, 'Mushkilatuna fi Daw' an-Nizam al-lslam' [Our problems in the light of the Islamic Order], in *Majmu'at Rasa'il al-Imam al-Shahid Hasan*

al-Banna (Cairo: Dar al-Shabab, n.d.), 389–93; Hasan al-Banna, *Mabadi'wa Usul fi Mu'tamarat Khassah* [Principles and origins in the private conferences] (Cairo: Mu'ssaasah al-Islamiyah li al-Tiba'ah wa al-Nashr, 1979), 90; Hasan al-Banna, *Majmu'at Rasa'il al-Imam al-Shahid Hasan al-Banna* [The diaries of the martyred Imam Hasan al-Banna] (Cairo: Darul Hadarah al-Islamiyyah, n.d.), 225.

128. Hasan al-Banna, *Selected Writings of Hasan al-Banna Shaheed*, trans. S. A. Qureshi (New Delhi: Millat Book Centre, 1999), 2

129. Ibid., 18.

130. Hasan al-Banna, 'Da'watuna' [Our call], *Jaridat al-Ikhwan al-Muslimin*, 1937, 11–23.

131. Baron, *The Orphan Scandal*, 136.

132. Family member of Ayman al-Zawahiri, author interview, 24 August 2015.

133. Hasan al-Banna, *Nahwa al-Nur* [*The Complete Works*] (Beirut: Al-Risalah, n.d.), 265.

134. Ayman al-Zawahiri, 'The Bitter Harvest: The [Muslim] Brotherhood in Sixty Years', trans. Nadia Masid (Egypt: unpublished, 1991).

135. Ibid., 133.

136. Hasan al-Banna, 'Iftitah' [The beginning], *Al-Nadhir*, 1, 30 May 1937, 146.

137. Al-Zawahiri, *Knights under the Prophet's Banner*.

138. Abdel-Azim Ramadan, *Al-Ikhwan al-Muslimun wal-Tanzim al-Sirri* [The secret organization of the Muslim Brotherhood] (Cairo: Dar al-Shahab, 1977), 13–15.

139. Fred Halliday, author interview, 4 September 2009.

140. Liwaa Hasan Sadiq, *Judhur al-Fitna al-Taifiyya fi al-Firaq al-Islamiyya* [The roots of strife in the Islamic sects] (Cairo: n.p., 1977), 278.

141. Richard Mitchell, *The Society of the Muslim Brothers* (London: Oxford University Press, 1993), 67

142. Ramadan, *Al-Ikhwan al-Muslimun wal-Tanzim al-Sirri*, 85; Hasan al-Banna quoted in Tariq Ismael and Jacqualine Ismael, *Government and Politics in Islam* (London: Frances Pinter, 1985), 70–76.

143. Al-Zawahiri, *Knights under the Prophet's Banner*.

144. William Shepard, *Sayyid Qutb and Islamic Activism: A Translation and Critical Analysis of Social Justice in Islam* (Leiden: E. J. Brill, 1996), xiv; Abdal Fattah al-Khalidi, *Sayyid Qutb: Min al-milad ila al-istishhad* [Sayyid Qutb: The birth of sacrifice] (Damascus: Dar al-Qalam, 1991), 25–72.

145. Paul Berman, 'The Philosopher of Islamic Terror', *New York Times*, 23 March 2003.

146. Adnan A. Musallam, *From Secularism to Jihad: Sayyid Qutb and the Foundations of Radical Islamism* (Westport, CT: Praeger, 2005), 29–32.

147. Abdal Fattah al-Khalidi, *Amrika min al-Dakhil bi-Minzar Sayyid Qutb* [America from the inside through the eyes of Sayyid Qutb] (Cairo: Dar al-Wafa, 1987), 19–20.

148. Adnan A. Musallam, 'The Formative Stages of Sayyid Qutb's Intellectual Career and His Emergence as an Islamic Da' iyah' (PhD thesis, University of

Michigan, 1983); Emmanuel Sivan, *Radical Islam: Medieval Theology and Modern Politics* (New Haven, CT: Yale University Press, 1985); Shepard, *Sayyid Qutb and Islamic Activism.*

149. Shepard, *Sayyid Qutb and Islamic Activism,* 320.

150. Ibid.

151. Ana Belén Soage, 'Islam and Modernity: The Political Thought of Sayyid Qutb', *Totalitarian Movements and Political Religions* 10, no. 2 (2009): 189.

152. Lawrence Wright, author interview, 16 January 2021.

153. John Calvert, *Sayyid Qutb and the Origins of Radical Islamism* (London: Hurst, 2009).

154. Abdal Fattah al-Khalidi, *Amrika min al-Dakhil bi-Minzar Sayyid Qutb,* 38.

155. Shepard, *Sayyid Qutb and Islamic Activism,* 78–80, 182–83.

156. Sayyid Qutb, *Fi Zilal al-Qur'an* [*In the Shade of the Qur'an*], trans. Adil Shamis (New Delhi: Kitab Bhavan, 2007), 19.

157. Danny Orbach, 'Tyrannicide in Radical Islam: The Case of Sayyid Qutb and Abd al-Salam Faraj', *Middle Eastern Studies* 48, no. 6 (2012): 965.

158. Detailed biographies of Maududi and analyses of his political doctrine can be found in Khurshid Ahmad and Zafar Ishaq Ansari, *Mawlana Maududi: An Introduction to His Life and Thought* (Aligarh: Crescent, 1979); Maryam Jameelah, *Who Is Maudoodi?* (Delhi: Taj, 1982); Syed Asad Gilani, *Maududi: Thought & Movement* (Lahore: Islamic, 1984); Seyyed Vali Reza Nasr, *The Vanguard of the Islamic Revolution: The Jama'at-i Islami of Pakistan* (Berkeley: University of California Press, 1994); Seyyed Vali Reza Nasr, *Maududi and the Making of Islamic Revivalism* (New York: Oxford University Press, 1996).

159. Sayyid Abul A'la Maududi quoted in Khurshid Ahmad, *The Islamic Law and Constitution* (Lahore: Islamic, 1960), 43.

160. Robert L. Tignor, author interview, 18 May 2021.

161. Anthony McDermott, *Egypt from Nasser to Mubarak: A Flawed Revolution* (New York: Routledge, 1988), eBook.

162. Anthony McDermott, author interview, 1 August 2009.

163. Peter Mansfield, 'Nasser and Nasserism', *International Journal* 28, no. 4 (Autumn, 1973), 673

164. Mohamed Heikal, author interview, 27 September 2013.

165. Sayyid Qutb and A. Hammuda, *Min al-Qarya ila al-Mishnaqa* [From the village to the hanging rope] (Cairo: Sina li-al-Nashr, 1990), 110.

166. Lawrence Wright, author interview, 16 January 2022.

167. Joel Gordon, *Nasser's Blessed Movement: Egypt's Free Officers and the July Revolution* (Oxford: Oxford University Press, 1992), 58.

168. Musallam, 'The Formative Stages of Sayyid Qutb's Intellectual Career and His Emergence as an Islamic Da' iyah', 157, 158, 263, 264.

169. Abdullah Imam, *Abd-al-Nasir wa al-Ikhwan al-Muslimoon: Al-Unf al-Deene fee Misr* [Nasir and the Muslim Brotherhood: Islamic violence in Egypt] (Cairo: Dar Daral-Khiyal, 1997), 102–108.

170. Lawrence Wright, author interview, 16 January 2022.

171. Daniel Crecelius, 'Al-Azhar in Revolution', *Middle East Journal* 20, no. 1 (1966): 34.

172. P. J. Vatikiotis, 'Islam and the Foreign Policy of Egypt', in *Islam and International Relations*, ed. J. Harris Proctor (New York: Praeger, 1965), 138–45.

173. George Gardner and Sami Hanna, 'Islamic Socialism', *Muslim World* 56, no. 2 (1966): 75.

174. Sayyid Qutb, 'Limadha a damuni' [Why did they hang me?], *Al-Sharika al-Saudiyya li-al-Abhath waal Tawzi*, n.d. 13–14

175. Qutb, *Fi Zilal al-Qur'an* [*In the Shade of the Qur'an*], 252.

176. Robert L. Tignor, *Egypt: A Short History*, Princeton, NJ: Princeton University Press, 2010), 261.

177. Gamal Nasser, *Egypt's Liberation: The Philosophy of the Revolution* (Buffalo, NY: Smith, Keynes and Marshall, 1959), 124.

178. Christina Phelps Harris, *Nationalism and Revolution in Egypt: The Role of the Muslim Brotherhood* (The Hague: Mouton, 1964), 222–23.

179. Lawrence Wright, author interview, 16 January 2022.

180. S. C. Burchell, *The Suez Canal* (Boston, MA: New Word City, 2016), eBook, 148.

181. McDermott, *Egypt from Nasser to Mubarak*.

182. Lawrence Wright, author interview, 16 January 2022.

183. Sayyid Qutb, *Al-'Adala al-ijtima'iyya fi al-Islam* [*Social Justice in Islam*] (Cairo: Dar al-Shuruq, 1983), 76, 80.

184. Sayyid Qutb, *Ma'àlim fi-l-Tarìq* [*Milestones*] (Beirut: Dar al-Shuruq, 1991), 17.

185. Sayyid Qutb, *Milestones* (Indianapolis: American Trust, 1990), 21.

186. Ibid., 98–105.

187. Al-Zawahiri, 'The Bitter Harvest'.

188. Ibid., 63.

189. Ibid., 48, 61.

190. Al-Zawahiri, 'The Bitter Harvest'.

191. Allison Bailey, *The Brothers' Older Sister: Zaynab al-Ghazali and the International Splinters of the Muslim Brotherhood* (Columbia University–London School of Economics & Political Science (LSE), master's dissertation, 2018).

192. Al-Zawahiri, 'The Bitter Harvest'.

193. Jabir Rizq, *Madhabih al-Ikhwan fi Sujoun Nasir* [Slaughterhouses for the brothers in the prisons of Nasir] (Cairo: Dar al-Itisam, 1977), 145.

194. Al-Zawahiri, *Knights under the Prophet's Banner*.

195. Ibid.

196. H. Hanafi, *Al-Haraka al-islamiyya fi misr* [Truth and illusion in Islam] (Cairo: Al-Huda, 1986), 47.

197. Rifat Sayyid Ahmad, *Religion, the State and the Revolution* (Cairo: Al-Dinwal-Dawla wal-Thawra, 1965), 164.

198. Al-Ahram, 7 September 1966.

199. Ibid., 165–66.

200. Lawrence Wright, author interview, 16 January 2022.

201. Al-Zawahiri, *Knights under the Prophet's Banner*.

202. Wright, *The Looming Tower*, 36.

203. Family member of Ayman al-Zawahiri, author interview, 27 August 2015.

204. Ibid.

205. Al-Zawahiri, *Knights under the Prophet's Banner*.

206. Ibid.

207. Family member of Ayman al-Zawahiri, author interview, 27 August 2015.

208. Al-Zawahiri, *Knights under the Prophet's Banner*.

209. Egyptian security official, author interview, March 7, 2010.

210. Ibid.

211. Al-Zayyat, *The Road to al-Qaeda*, 75–77.

212. Al-Zawahiri, *Knights under the Prophet's Banner*.

213. Ibid.

214. Ibid.

215. Ibid.

216. Ibid.

217. Ibid.

218. Ibid.

219. Ibid.

220. Ibid.

221. Raphaeli, 'Ayman Muḥammad Rabi' al-Zawahiri'.

222. Soufan, *Anatomy of Terror*.

223. Tom Pfeiffer and Marwa Awad, 'Zawahri: From Suburban Doctor to Chief of al Qaeda?', Reuters, 3 May 2011, https://www.reuters.com/article/us-binla den-zawahri-idUKTRE7424ZK20110503.

224. Raphaeli, 'Ayman Muḥammad Rabi' al-Zawahiri'.

225. Egyptian security official, author interview, 7 March 2010.

226. Wright, *The Looming Tower*, 40

227. The al-Jihad Case, Case No. 462, Higher State Security Court, Ayman al-Zawahiri statement, 1981.

228. Egyptian security official, author interview, 15 February 2010.

229. 'People in the News, Ayman al-Zawahiri: Bin Laden's Right-Hand Man', CNN, 3 November 2001.

230. The al-Jihad Case, Ayman al-Zawahiri statement.

231. Ayman al-Zawahiri, 'The Open Meeting with Shaykh Ayman al-Zawahiri', *as-Sahab Media*, April 2008.

232. Lawrence Wright, author interview, 16 January 2022.

233. Youseef Aboul-Enein, 'Ayman al-Zawahiri: The Ideologue of Modern Islamic Militancy', *The Counterproliferation Papers, Future Warfare Series, no. 21.*, USAF Counterproliferation Center, 3

234. John R. Harvey, 'Regional Ballistic Missiles and Advanced Strike Aircraft: Comparing Military Effectiveness', *International Security* 17, no. 2 (1992): 48.

235. Ahmed Abdalla, *The Student Movement and National Politics in Egypt 1923–1973* (Cairo: American University in Cairo Press, 2008), 152, 158–59.

236. Al-Zawahiri, *Knights under the Prophet's Banner*.

237. 'President Nasser Dies of Heart Attack', *Guardian*, 29 September 1970, https://www.theguardian.com/theguardian/2014/sep/29/egypt-president-nasser-dies-archive-1970.

238. Al-Zawahiri, *Knights under the Prophet's Banner*.

239. Ibid.

CHAPTER 2

1. Lawrence Wright, 'The Man behind bin Laden', *New Yorker*, 16 September 2002, https://www.newyorker.com/magazine/2002/09/16/the-man-behind-bin-laden.

2. Lawrence Wright, author interview, 16 January 2022.

3. Former EIJ jihadist, author interview, 2 April 2010.

4. Lawrence Wright, 'The Rebellion Within', *New Yorker*, 2 June 2008, http://www.newyorker.com/reporting/2008/06/02/080602fa_fact_wright?currentPage=all.

5. Muhammad Abu Shamaa, 'Former al-Qaeda Ideologue Exposes al-Zawahiri', *Asharq al-Awsat*, 19 November 2008, http://www.aawsat.com/english/news.asp?section=3&id=14775 (accessed 9 March 2016).

6. Ibid.

7. Muhammad Salah, 'Sayyid Imam al-Sharif Interview', part 2, *Al-Hayat*, 9 December 2007.

8. 'Al-Jihad Leader's Son on Father's Links to al-Qa'ida', *Al-Hayat*, 4 April 2004.

9. Lawrence Wright, author interview, 16 January 2022.

10. McDermott, *Egypt from Nasser to Mubarak*.

11. Robert L. Tignor, author interview, 18 May 2021.

12. McDermott, *Egypt from Nasser to Mubarak*.

13. Al-Zawahiri, *Knights under the Prophet's Banner*.

14. Anthony McDermott, author interview, 1 August 2009.

15. Al-Zawahiri, *Knights under the Prophet's Banner*.

16. Robert L. Tignor, author interview, 18 May 2021.

17. Gerasimos Tsourapas, *The Politics of Migration in Modern Egypt: Strategies for Regime Survival in Autocracies* (Cambridge: Cambridge University Press, 2018), 110.

18. R. H. Dekmejian, *Islam in Revolution: Fundamentalism in the Arab World* (Syracuse, NY: Syracuse University Press, 1985), 80.

19. Anthony McDermott, author interview, 1 August 2009.

20. Al-Zawahiri, *Knights under the Prophet's Banner*.

21. Christopher S. Raj, 'US Military Aid to Egypt', *Strategic Analysis* 4, no. 3 (1980): 116–21.

22. Saad Eddin Ibrahim, 'Anatomy of Egypt's Militant Islamic Groups: Methodological Note and Preliminary Findings', *International Journal of Middle East Studies* 12, no. 4 (1980): 435–36.

23. *Al-Ahram*, 13 August 1977.

24. Salih Siriyya, *Risalat al-lman* [The message of faith] (Cairo: n.p., 1973), 21–34.
25. Ibid.
26. Adil Hamuda, *Al-Hijra ila al-Unf* [The migration to violence] (Cairo: n.p., 1987), 171–72.
27. Al-Zawahiri, *Knights under the Prophet's Banner*.
28. Ibid.
29. Rifat Sayyid Ahmad, *Al-Islambuli: Ruya Jadida Fi-Tanzim* [Islambouli: A new view of the Jihad organization] (Cairo: n.p., 1987), 67.
30. Family member of Ayman al-Zawahiri, author interview, 27 August 2015.
31. Nemat Guenena, 'The "Jihad": An "Islamic Alternative" in Egypt', *Cairo Papers in Social Science* 9, no. 2 (1986): 56.
32. John Miller, author interview, 29 April 2021.
33. Marvin G. Weinbaum, 'Egypt's "Infitah" and the Politics of US Economic Assistance', *Middle Eastern Studies* 21, no. 2 (1985): 206–22.
34. Michael Burrell and Abbas Kelidar, *Egypt, the Dilemma of a Nation: 1970–1977* (London: Sage, 1977), 43.
35. Abd al-Halim Mahmud, Radio Cairo, 21 January 1977.
36. Al-Ahram, 5 November 1979.
37. Al-Zawahiri, *Knights under the Prophet's Banner*.
38. Anwar Sadat, 'Peace with Justice' (speech to the Israeli Knesset, delivered 20 November 1977), https://web.archive.org/web/20220609224039/https://www.mtholyoke.edu/acad/intrel/speech/sadat.htm.
39. *Foreign Relations of the United States, 1977–1980*, vol. 1, *Foundations of Foreign Policy*, Office of the Historian, US Department of State, 2014, https://history.state.gov/historicaldocuments/frus1977-80vo1/d114.
40. Ibid.
41. Raafat, 'The World's Second Most Wanted Man'.
42. Family member of Ayman al-Zawahiri, author interview, 27 August 2015.
43. Clayland Waite, 'Peter Jennings', *Museum of Broadcast Communications*, 9 August 2005; '1974 Peabody Award–*Sadat: Action Biography*, ABC Television', https://peabodyawards.com/award-profile/sadat-action-biography/.
44. Family member of Ayman al-Zawahiri, author interview, 27 August 2015.
45. Edwin Diamond, 'Anchor Wars: Dan Rather, Peter Jennings and Tom Brokaw', *Rolling Stone*, 9 October 1986.
46. Family member of Ayman al-Zawahiri, author interview, 27 August 2015.
47. Sam Donaldson, 'Begin, Sadat Sign the Egypt-Israel Peace Treaty at the White House', *ABC News*, 26 March 1979, https://abcnews.go.com/Politics/video/march-26-1979-begin-sadat-sign-egypt-israel-46803366.
48. Former EIJ jihadist, author interview, 17 June 2011.
49. Gabriel R. Warburg, 'The Search for the Sources of the White Nile and Egyptian-Sudanese Relations', *Middle Eastern Studies* 43, no. 3 (2007): 475–86.
50. Mohamed Heikal, *Autumn of Fury: The Assassination of Sadat* (London: Andre Deutsch, 1983), 216.
51. Al-Zawahiri, *Knights under the Prophet's Banner*.

52. Yitzhak Shamir, 'Israel: Statement by the Foreign Minister on the US Policy for Peace in the Middle East' (speech to the Israeli Knesset, delivered September 8, 1982), *International Legal Materials* 21, no. 5 (1982).

53. Duncan L. Clarke, 'US Security Assistance to Egypt and Israel: Politically Untouchable?', *Middle East Journal* 51, no. 2 (1997): 200–214.

54. Anthony McDermott, author interview, 1 August 2009.

55. William Quandt, 'Camp David a Blow to Arab Unity', al-Jazeera, 30 March 2008, https://www.aljazeera.com/news/2008/3/30/camp-david-a-blow-to-arab-unity-2.

56. Robert L. Tignor, author interview, 18 May 2021.

57. Kirk Beattie, *Egypt during the Sadat Years* (New York: Palgrave, 2000), 240–41.

58. Gabriel R. Warburg, *Egypt and the Sudan: Studies in History and Politics* (London: Routledge, 2019).

59. Gabriel R. Warburg, 'Islam and Politics in Egypt: 1952–80', *Middle Eastern Studies* 18, no. 2 (1982): 150–51.

60. Heikal, *Autumn of Fury*, 216.

61. Al-Zawahiri, *Knights under the Prophet's Banner*.

62. Anwar Sadat, *October Magazine*, 30 September 1979, 3–5

63. Robert L. Tignor, author interview, 18 May 2021.

64. Michael Wood, 'The Use of the Pharaonic Past in Modern Egyptian Nationalism', *Journal of the American Research Center in Egypt* 35 (1998): 186.

65. Wright, 'The Man behind bin Laden'.

66. Michelle Shephard, *Guantanamo's Child: The Untold Story of Omar Khadr* (Mississauga: John Wiley & Sons Canada, 2008), 75–76.

67. Ibid.

68. Lawrence Wright, author interview, 16 January 2022.

69. Family member of Ayman al-Zawahiri, author interview, 27 August 2015.

70. Ibid.

71. Israel Altman, 'Islamic Movements in Egypt', *Jerusalem Quarterly*, 10 (1979): 94–95.

72. Al-Zawahiri, *Knights under the Prophet's Banner*.

73. Ibid.

74. Ibid.

75. Azzam, interview with Rory Carroll.

76. Al-Zawahiri, *Knights under the Prophet's Banner*.

77. Bruce Riedel, author interview, 25 November 2019.

78. Family member of Ayman al-Zawahiri, author interview, 27 August 2015.

79. Al-Zawahiri, *Knights under the Prophet's Banner*.

80. Ibid.

81. Heikal, *Autumn of Fury*, 216, 173–74.

82. McDermott, *Egypt from Nasser to Mubarak*.

83. Jaqueline Trescott and Donnie Radcliffe, 'Peace Meal: Carter Serves Sadat Dinner and Hope', *Washington Post*, 9 April 1980.

84. Gilles Kepel, *The Prophet and the Pharaoh: Muslim Extremism in Egypt* (London: Saqi Books, 1985), 71; Heikal, *Autumn of Fury*, 271.

85. McDermott, *Egypt from Nasser to Mubarak*.

86. Ibid.

87. Guenena, 'The "Jihad"', 105–8.

88. Christopher Dickey, author interview, 12 April 2016.

89. Egyptian security officials, author interview, 19 February 2007.

90. Al-Zawahiri, *Knights under the Prophet's Banner*.

91. Egyptian security officials, author interview, 19 February 2007.

92. Ibid.

93. Reuven Paz, author interview, 9 October 2013.

94. David Zeidan, 'Radical Islam in Egypt: A Comparison of Two Groups', *Middle East Review of International Affairs* 3, no. 3 (September 1999): 5.

95. Egyptian security official, author interview, 7 March 2010.

96. Ibid.

97. Muhammad abd-al-Salam Faraj, 'The Neglected Duty', *Al-Ahrar*, 8 December 1981.

98. Ibid.

99. Ibid.

100. Guenena, 'The "Jihad"'.

101. Ahmad, *Al-Islambuli*, 73.

102. Hamied Ansari, 'The Islamic Militants in Egyptian Politics', *International Journal of Middle Eastern Studies* 16, no. 1 (1984): 134–35

103. Guenena, 'The "Jihad"', 60–62.

104. Ibid.

105. Kepel, *The Prophet and the Pharaoh*, 194.

106. Barry Rubin, *Islamic Fundamentalism in Egyptian Politics* (New York: St. Martin's Press, 1990), 58

107. Ayman al-Zawahiri, 'Allegiance and Disavowal', *as-Sahab Media*, 28 December 2002.

108. Al-Zawahiri, 'The Bitter Harvest'.

109. McDermott, *Egypt from Nasser to Mubarak*.

110. Al-Zawahiri, *Knights under the Prophet's Banner*.

111. Ibid.

112. Ibid.

113. Ibid.

114. Mohamed Heikal, author interview, 27 September 2013.

115. Al-Zawahiri, *Knights under the Prophet's Banner*.

116. Egyptian security official, author interview, 7 March 2010.

117. Michael Youssef, *Revolt against Modernity: Muslim Zealots and the West* (Leiden: E. J. Brill, 1985), 176.

118. Ibid.

119. Al-Zawahiri, *Knights under the Prophet's Banner*.

120. Lawrence Wright, author interview, 16 January 2022.

121. Alexander S. Cudsi and Ali E. Hillal Dessouki, eds., *Islam and Power* (London: Croom Helm, 1981).

122. Egyptian security official, author interview, 15 February 2010.

123. Ibid.

124. Ibid.

125. Ibid.

126. McDermott, *Egypt from Nasser to Mubarak*.

127. Orbach, 'Tyrannicide in Radical Islam', 969.

128. Khalid al-Islambouli quoted in Derek Hopwood, *Egypt 1945–1990: Politics and Society* (London: Routledge, 1991), 183.

129. Al-Zawahiri, *Knights under the Prophet's Banner*.

130. Ibid.

131. Egyptian security official, author interview, 3 January 2012.

132. Anthony McDermott, author interview, 1 August 2009.

133. Al-Zawahiri, *Knights under the Prophet's Banner*.

134. Ibid.

135. Ibid.

136. Lawrence Wright, author interview, 16 January 2022.

137. Ibid.

138. Ayman al-Zawahiri, *The Black Book: Torturing Muslims Under President Hosni Mubarak* (n.d.)<<<REFC, www.tawhed.ws (accessed 20 July 2019).

139. Ayman al-Zawahiri, interview with Egyptian security official, 7 March 2010.

140. 'Looking For Answers', PBS, *Frontline*, 14 April 2008.

141. Ibid.

142. Anthony McDermott, author interview, 1 August 2009.

143. 'Muslim Extremist Trial', Associated Press, 15 December 1982.

144. Ibid.

145. Ibid.

146. Ibid.

147. Ibid.

148. 'Cuts 12/12/82 Muslim Extremists Trial', Associated Press Archive, 30 July 2015, https://youtu.be/AY3nM9I19c4.

149. Anthony McDermott, author interview, 1 August 2009.

150. Ibid.

151. Former EIJ jihadist, author interview, 2 April 2010.

152. Ibid.

153. The al-Jihad Case, al-Zawahiri interrogation, 1981.

154. Ibid.

155. The al-Jihad Case, Case No. 462, Higher State Security Court, Ayman al-Zawahiri statement, 1981.

156. Ibid.

157. Al-Zawahiri, *Knights under the Prophet's Banner*.

158. Ibid.

159. Richard Lacayo, 'Public Enemy No. 2', *Time Magazine*, 5 November 2001.

160. Hisham Mubarak, Souhail Shadoud, and Steve Tamari, 'What Does the Gama'a Islamiyya Want? An Interview with Tal'at Fu'ad Qasim', *Middle East Report* (1996): 42.

161. Caryle Murphy, *Passion for Islam* (New York: Scribner, 2002), 67.

162. Wright, 'The Man behind bin Laden'; see also Nabil Abu Stayt, 'Egypt's Islamic Jihad Rises', *Asharq al-Awsat*, 6 February 2000.

163. Sami Moubayed, *Under the Black Flag: At the Frontier of the New Jihad* (London: I. B. Tauris, 2015), 203–4.

164. Musallam, *From Secularism to Jihad*, 14.

165. Charles Robert Davidson, 'Political Violence in Egypt: A Case Study of the Islamist Insurgency 1992–1997' (PhD Thesis, Tufts University, 2005), 251–53.

166. John Calvert, author interview, 20 May 2021.

167. Robert L. Tignor, author interview, 18 May 2021.

168. Michael Petrou, 'The Fall of Hosni Mubarak: After 30 Years of Tyranny in Egypt, the West's Favourite Dictator Admits Defeat', *Maclean's*, 19 February 2011.

169. Hosni Mubarak quoted in John Solecki, *Hosni Mubarak: President of Egypt* (New York: Chelsea House, 1991), 70.

170. Yussef Auf, 'The state of emergency in Egypt: An exception or rule?', *Atlantic Council*, 2 February 2018, https://www.atlanticcouncil.org/blogs/menasou rce/the-state-of-emergency-in-egypt-an-exception-or-rule/

CHAPTER 3

1. Family member of Ayman al-Zawahiri, author interview, 27 August 2015.

2. Ibid.

3. Nick Pratt, author interview, 23 August 2011.

4. Ibid.

5. Ibid.

6. 'GTMO Detainee Report: Abdallah Muhummad Khan', 27 March 2008, *Wikileaks,* http://wikileaks.org/gitmo/pdf/af/us9af-000556dp.pdf.

7. Edger O'Ballance, 'Soviet Tactics in Afghanistan', *Military Review*, 60, no. 8 (1980): 49.

8. Nick Pratt, author interview, 23 August 2011.

9. Ibid.

10. Al-Zawahiri, *Knights under the Prophet's Banner*.

11. Former EIJ jihadist, author interview, 17 June 2011.

12. Masood Farivar, *Confessions of a Mullah Warrior* (New York: Grove Press, 2010), 177.

13. Mary-Anne Weaver, *A Portrait of Egypt: A Journey through the World of Militant Islam* (New York: Farrar, Straus and Giroux, 1998), 477–78.

14. Syed Saleem Shahzad, *Inside al-Qaeda and the Taliban: Beyond bin Laden and 9/11* (London: Palgrave MacMillan, 2011).

NOTES 373

15. Al-Zawahiri, *Knights under the Prophet's Banner*.
16. Thomas Hegghammer, author interview, 12 February 2021.
17. Riedel, *The Hunt for al-Qa'ida*, 38.
18. Muhammad Salah, 'Sayyid Imam al-Sharif Interview', part 2, *Al-Hayat*, December 9, 2007.
19. Muhammad Salah, 'Sayyid Imam al-Sharif Interview', part 1, *Al-Hayat*, December 8, 2007.
20. Wright, 'The Rebellion Within'.
21. Egyptian security officials, author interview, 19 February 2007.
22. Abd al-Qadir bin Abd al-Aziz [Sayyid Imam al-Sharif], *Risalat Al-'Umda Fi I'Dad Al-'Uddah Lil-jihad Fi Sabil Allah* [Treatise on the Pillar of Preparing Oneself for Jihad in the Way of Allah the Almighty] (Peshawar: n.p., 1987).
23. Bruce Riedel, author interview, 25 November 2019.
24. Al-Zawahiri, *Knights under the Prophet's Banner*.
25. Ibid.
26. Andrew McGregor, '"Jihad and the Rifle Alone": Abdullah Azzam and the Islamist Revolution', *Journal of Conflict Studies* 23, no. 2 (2003).
27. Ibid.
28. 'Jordan's 9/11: Dealing With Jihadi Islamism', *International Crisis Group, Middle East Report* 47, no. 3 (2005), https://www.crisisgroup.org/middle-east-north-africa/eastern-mediterranean/jordan/jordans-911-dealing-jihadi-islamism.
29. John Calvert, 'The Striving Shaykh: Abdullah Azzam and the Revival of Jihad', *Journal of Religion and Society, suppl. ser.* 2 (2007): 5.
30. Thomas Hegghammer, 'Abdullah Azzam', in *Al-Qaida dans le texte: Écrits d'Oussama ben Laden, Abdulla Azzam, Ayman al-Zawahiri et Abou Moussab al-Zarqawi* [Al-Qa'ida in the text: The writings of Osama bin Laden, Abdullah Azzam, Ayman al-Zawahiri and Abu Mussab al-Zarqawi], ed. Gilles Kepel (Paris: Presses Universitaires de France, 2005), 120–22.
31. Calvert, 'The Striving Shaykh', 7.
32. Gilles Kepel, *The War for Muslim Minds: Islam and the West* (Cambridge, MA: Belknap, 2004), 172–78.
33. Thomas Hegghammer, *The Caravan: Abdallah Azzam and the Rise of Global Jihad* (Cambridge: Cambridge University Press, 2020), eBook.
34. Al-Zawahiri, *Knights under the Prophet's Banner*.
35. Hegghammer, *The Caravan*.
36. Ibid.
37. Abdullah Azzam, *Join the Caravan* (n.p., 1987).
38. Calvert, 'The Striving Shaykh', 11.
39. Abu Jandal, 'Al Qaeda from Within: As Narrated by Abu Jandal, bin Ladin's Personal Guard', *Al-Quds al-Arabi*, 22 March 2005.
40. Kenneth Katzman, *Al-Qa'ida: Profile and Threat Assessment*, Congressional Research Service Report for Congress, the Library of Congress, 17 August 2005.

41. Ibid.

42. Peter Bergen, *The Osama bin Laden I Know* (New York: Free Press, 2006), 29.

43. Wright, *Looming Tower*, 179.

44. Ahmed Rashid, *Taliban* (London: I. B. Taurus, 2001), 130.

45. Hegghammer, *The Caravan*.

46. Abdullah Anas, *The Birth of the Afghani Arabs: A Biography of Abdullah Anas with Mas'oud and Abdullah Azzam*, trans. Nadia Masid (London: n.p., 2002).

47. Abdullah Azzam, *The Defence of the Muslim Lands: The First Obligation after Iman* (n.p., 1979).

48. Azzam, *Join the Caravan*.

49. Ibid.

50. Wright, 'The Man behind bin Laden'.

51. Al-Zawahiri, *Knights under the Prophet's Banner*.

52. Abdullah Anas and Tam Hussein, *To the Mountains: My Life in Jihad, from Algeria to Afghanistan* (London: Hurst, 2019), 150.

53. Ibid., 197; Bergen, The Osama bin Laden I Know, 68; UAE security official, author interview, 12 December 2020.

54. Bergen, *The Osama bin Laden I Know*, 69.

55. Ibid., 62.

56. Egyptian security official, author interview, 22 March 2009.

57. UAE security official, author interview, 12 December 2020.

58. Lawrence Wright, author interview, 16 January 2022.

59. Sally Neighbour, *The Mother of Mohammed: An Australian Woman's Extraordinary Journey into Jihad* (Melbourne: Melbourne University Press, 2009), 60.

60. Ibid.

61. Ezra Levant, *The Enemy Within: Terror, Lies, and the Whitewashing of Omar Khadr* (Plattsburgh, NY: McClelland & Stewart, 2011), 10.

62. Shephard, *Guantanamo's Child*, 25.

63. Ibid., 29.

64. Leah Farrall, 'Revisiting al-Qaida's Foundation and Early History', *Perspectives in Terrorism* 11, no. 6 (2017).

65. Peter Bergen and Paul Cruickshank, 'Revisiting the Early al Qaeda: An Updated Account of Its Formative Years', *Studies in Conflict & Terrorism* 35, no. 1 (2012): 1–36

66. Mustafa Hamid and Leah Farrall, *The Arabs at War in Afghanistan* (London: Hurst, 2015), eBook, 95.

67. Farrall, 'Revisiting al-Qaida's Foundation and Early History'.

68. Tayseer Allouni, 'Interview with Sheik Osama bin Laden', *al-Jazeera*, October 2001, https://edition.cnn.com/2002/WORLD/asiapcf/south/02/05/binla den.transcript/.

69. Bergen, *The Osama bin Laden I Know*, 50

70. Bergen and Cruickshank, 'Revisiting the Early al Qaeda'.

71. Soufan, *Anatomy of Terror*; Lawrence Wright, author interview, 16 January 2022.

72. Hamid and Farrall, *The Arabs at War in Afghanistan*, 99.

73. Lawrence Wright, author interview, 16 January 2022.
74. Thomas Hegghammer, author interview, 12 February 2021.
75. Bergen and Cruickshank, 'Revisiting the Early al Qaeda'.
76. Egyptian security official, author interview, 3 January 2012.
77. Steve Coll, *Ghost Wars: The Secret History of the CIA, Afghanistan, and bin Laden* (Penguin: New York, 2005).
78. Abdel Bari Atwan, *The Secret History of al Qaeda* (London: Saqi Books, 2006), 76.
79. Abu Walid al-Misri, 'The Story of the Arab Afghans from the Time of Arrival in Afghanistan until Their Departure with the Taliban', *Asharq al-Awsat*, 14 December 2004.
80. Bergen, *The Osama bin Laden I Know*, 108–9.
81. Al-Zawahiri, *Knights under the Prophet's Banner*.
82. Ayman al-Zawahiri, *Kalimat haq* [The word of truth] (n.p.: Dar al-I'tisam, n.d.).
83. Reuven Paz, author interview, 9 October 2013.
84. Stayt, 'Egypt's Islamic Jihad Rises'.
85. Hamdi Rizq, 'Egyptian Jihad Case Highlights Afghan Links', *Al-Wasat*, 22–28 June 1998.
86. Fred Halliday, author interview, 4 September 2009.
87. Mohammad Taqi, 'Jalaluddin Haqqani: Life and Times of a Jihadist Lynchpin', *Wire*, 7 September 2018, https://thewire.in/south-asia/jalaluddin-haqqani-hqn-pakistan-afghanistan-taliban-mujahideen.
88. Nick Pratt, author interview, 23 August 2011.
89. Don Rassler and Vahid Brown, 'The Haqqani Nexus and the Evolution of al-Qa'ida', *Combating Terrorism Center at West Point*, 14 July 2011, 9.
90. 'The Manba-al Uloom Madrasa as a Major Educational Center', *Manba' al-Jihad* (Pashto) 1, no. 1 (July 1989).
91. Nick Pratt, author interview, 23 August 2011.
92. Jeffrey Dressler, 'The Haqqani Network: A Foreign Terrorist Organization', *Institute for the Study of War*, 2.
93. Chris Alexander, author interview, 6 May 2021.
94. Bruce Riedel, *What We Won, America's Secret War in Afghanistan, 1979–89* (Washington, DC: Brookings Institution Press, 2014), 55
95. Charlie Wilson quoted in Anna Mulrine, 'Afghan Warlords, Formerly Backed by the CIA, Now Turn Their Guns on U.S. Troops', *US News & World Report*, 11 July 2008.
96. Mohammed Yousaf and Mark Adkin, *Afghanistan the Bear Trap: The Defeat of a Superpower* (Havertown, PA: Casemate, 2001), 65–66.
97. Ibid.
98. Mitchell, Miller, and Stone, *The Cell*.
99. Benjamin Weiser and James Risen, 'The Masking of a Militant: A Special Report; A Soldier's Shadowy Trail In U.S. and in the Mideast', *New York Times*, 1 December 1998, https://www.nytimes.com/1998/12/01/world/masking-militant-special-report-soldier-s-shadowy-trail-us-mideast.html.

100. Sebastian Rotella, author interview, 25 January 2021.

101. Ibid.

102. Peter Lance, *Triple Cross: How bin Laden's Master Spy Penetrated the CIA, the Green Berets, and the FBI* (New York: Harper Collins, 2010), 11.

103. John Calvert, author interview, 20 May 2021.

104. Benjamin Weiser, 'October 25–31: U.S. Ex-Sergeant Charged in bin Laden Conspiracy', *New York Times*, 1 November 1998.

105. Sebastian Rotella, author interview, 25 January 2021.

106. Joseph Neff and John Sullivan, 'Al-Qaeda Terrorist Duped FBI, Army', *Raleigh News and Observer*, 24 October 2001; Weiser and Risen, 'The Masking of a Militant'.

107. U.S. federal law enforcement official, author interview, 12 December 2018.

108. Weiser and Risen, 'The Masking of a Militant'; Lance Williams and Erin McCormick, 'Bin Laden's Man in Silicon Valley', *San Francisco Chronicle*, 21 September 2001.

109. Sebastian Rotella, author interview, 25 January 2021.

110. Ibid.

111. Mitchell, Miller, and Stone, *The Cell*, 34–35.

112. Nick Pratt, author interview, August 23, 2011.

113. Mitchell, Miller, and Stone, *The Cell*, 34–35.

114. John Miller, author interview, 29 April 2021.

115. Weiser and Risen, 'The Masking of a Militant'.

116. John Miller, author interview, 29 April 2021.

117. Ibid.

118. Mitchell, Miller, and Stone, *The Cell*, 143.

119. *United States of America v. Omar Abdel Rahman et al.*, S(5) 93 Cr. 181, MBM, testimony of Khaled Ibrahim, July 13, 1995, 14241f; Lance, Triple Cross, 48.

120. Mitchell, Miller, and Stone, *The Cell*, 143.

121. *U.S. v. Rahman*, testimony of Colonel Norvell Bonds DeAtkine, 13 July 1995.

122. Ayman al-Zawahiri, *Military Studies in the Jihad against the Tyrants: The al-Qaeda Training Manual* (n.p., n.d.), https://www.justice.gov/sites/default/files/ag/legacy/2002/10/08/manualpart1_1.pdf (accessed 8 May 2021).

123. Service records of Ali Mohamed, as cited in *U.S. v. Rahman*, closing remarks of defence attorney Roger Stavis, 11 September 1995.

124. Neff and Sullivan, 'Al-Qaeda Terrorist Duped FBI'.

125. Lance, *Triple Cross*, 54.

126. Al-Zawahiri, *Knights under the Prophet's Banner*.

127. Al-Zayyat, *The Road to al-Qa'ida*, 107.

128. Ibid.

129. Brynjar Lia, *Architect of Global Jihad: The Life of al-Qaida Strategist Abu Mus'ab al-Suri.* (London: Hurst, 2009), 88–108.

130. Al-Zawahiri, *Knights under the Prophet's Banner*.

131. Rosanne Klass, 'Afghanistan: The Accords', *Foreign Affairs* 66, no. 5 (1998): 922–45.

132. Katya Drozdova and Joseph H. Felter, 'Leaving Afghanistan: Enduring Lessons from the Soviet Politburo', *Journal of Cold War Studies* 21, no. 4 (2019): 31–70.

133. Ibid.

134. U.S. v. Enaam Arnaout, No. 02 CR892, N.D. Ill., government's evidentiary proffer supporting the admissibility of co-conspirator statements, 6 January 2003.

135. Hegghammer, *The Caravan*, 135–136.

136. Abdullah Azzam, 'Open Letter to Every Muslim on Earth', *Al-Jihad*, no. 4 (1985): 22–26.

137. Azzam, *The Defence of the Muslim Lands*.

138. Abdullah Azzam, 'From Kabul to Jerusalem', *Al-Jihad*, no. 52 (1989): 45–49.

139. Abd al-Aziz, *Risalat al-'Umda Fi I'Dad al-'Uddah Lil-jihad Fi Sabil Allah* [Treatise on the Pillar of Preparing Oneself for Jihad in the Way of Allah the Almighty].

140. Ibid., 442.

141. Wright, 'The Rebellion Within'.

142. *U.S. v. Enaam Arnaout*, government's evidentiary proffer supporting the admissibility of co-conspirator statements.

143. Anas and Hussein, *To the Mountains*, 203.

144. Ibid.

145. *U.S. v. Enaam Arnaout*, government's evidentiary proffer supporting the admissibility of co-conspirator statements.

146. Mohamed Heikal, author interview, 27 September 2013.

147. Lawrence Wright, *The Terror Years: From al-Qaeda to the Islamic State* (London: Constable, 2016), eBook.

148. Ibid.

149. Bergen, *The Rise and Fall of Osama bin Laden*.

150. *The 9/11 Commission Report* (New York: W. W. Norton, 2004), 56.

151. Mary Anne Weaver, 'The Short, Violent Life of Abu Musab al-Zarqawi', *Atlantic*, July/August 2006, https://www.theatlantic.com/magazine/archive/2006/07/the-short-violent-life-of-abu-musab-al-zarqawi/304983/.

152. Jordanian security official, author interview, 20 June 2019.

153. Ibid.

154. Michael Weiss and Hassan Hassan, *ISIS: Inside the Army of Terror* (New York: Regan Arts, 2016), 8.

155. US intelligence official, author interview, 29 May 2014.

156. Al-Zawahiri, *Knights under the Prophet's Banner*.

157. Ibid.

CHAPTER 4

1. l-Zawahiri, 'The Bitter Harvest'.

2. Ibid.

3. Ibid.

4. Ibid.

5. Ibid.

6. Abul A'la Maududi quoted in al-Zawahiri, 'The Bitter Harvest'.

7. Al-Zawahiri, 'The Bitter Harvest'.

8. Ibid.

9. Al-Zawahiri, *Knights under the Prophet's Banner*.

10. Ibid.

11. Ibid.

12. Lance Williams, 'Bin Laden's Bay Area Recruiter: Khalid Abu-al-Dahab Signed Up American Muslims to Be Terrorists', *San Francisco Chronicle*, 21 November 2001.

13. David Kaplan, 'Hundreds of Americans Have Followed the Path to Jihad', *US News & World Report*, 2 June 2002.

14. Thomas Hegghammer, 'Why Jihadists Loved America in the 1980s', *Atlantic*, 6 March 2020, https://www.theatlantic.com/politics/archive/2020/03/jihad-abdallah-azzam-america-osama-bin-laden/607498/.

15. John Miller, author interview, 29 April 2021.

16. Nick Pratt, author interview, 23 August 2011.

17. Mary B. W. Tabor, 'Slaying in Brooklyn Linked to Militants', *New York Times*, 11 April 1993, https://www.nytimes.com/1993/04/11/nyregion/slaying-in-brooklyn-linked-to-militants.html.

18. Weiser and Risen, 'The Masking of a Militant'.

19. Tabor, 'Slaying in Brooklyn'.

20. Tabor, 'Slaying in Brooklyn'.

21. US federal law enforcement official, author interview, 12 December 2018.

22. Christopher Dickey, author interview, 12 April 2016.

23. Ibid.

24. John Miller, author interview, 29 April 2021.

25. Tabor, 'Slaying in Brooklyn'.

26. US federal law enforcement official, author interview, 12 December 2018.

27. Former EIJ jihadist, author interview, 17 June 2011.

28. Hegghammer, 'Why Jihadists Loved America in the 1980s'.

29. Susan Sachs and John Kifner, 'A Nation Challenged: Bin Laden's Lieutenant; Egyptian Raised Terror Funds in U.S. in 1990's', *New York Times*, 23 October 2001, 4.

30. Williams, 'Bin Laden's Bay Area Recruiter'; Andrew Martin and Michael J. Berens, 'Terrorists Evolved in U.S.', *Chicago Tribune*, 11 December 2001, https://www.chicagotribune.com/news/ct-xpm-2001-12-11-0112110186-story.html; Lance Williams and Erin McCormick, 'Al Qaeda Terrorist Worked with FBI / Ex–Silicon Valley Resident Plotted Embassy Attacks', *San Francisco Chronicle*, 4 November 2001, https://www.sfgate.com/news/article/Al-Qaeda-terrorist-worked-with-FBI-Ex-Silicon-2861719.php.

31. Stewart Bell, *Cold Terror* (Canada: John Wiley & Sons, 2008), 192.

32. 'Justice Department Secures the Denaturalization of a Senior Jihadist Operative Who Was Convicted of Terrorism in Egypt', US Department of Justice: Office of Public Affairs, 20 April 2017, https://www.justice.gov/opa/pr/justice-department-secures-denaturalization-senior-jihadist-operative-who-was-convicted.

33. Williams, 'Bin Laden's Bay Area Recruiter'.

34. Nick Pratt, author interview, 23 August 2011.

35. Lacayo, 'Public Enemy no. 2'; Wright, 'The Man behind bin Ladin'.

36. Wright, 'The Man behind bin Ladin'.

37. Williams and McCormick, 'Bin Laden's Man in Silicon Valley'.

38. Lance Williams and Erin McCormick, 'Top bin Laden Aide Toured State / Special Report: Al-Zawahiri Solicited Funds under the Guise of Refugee Relief', *San Francisco Chronicle*, 11 October 2001, https://www.sfgate.com/news/article/Top-bin-Laden-aide-toured-state-SPECIAL-REPORT-2871023.php.

39. Nick Pratt, author interview, 23 August 2011.

40. Williams and McCormick, 'Bin Laden's Man in Silicon Valley'; Sachs and Kifner, 'A Nation Challenged'; Williams and McCormick, 'Top bin Laden Aide Toured State'.

41. Bell, *Cold Terror*, 192–95.

42. Tu Thanh Ha and Colin Freeze, 'Canadian Soil a Long-Time Staging Ground for al-Qaeda', *Globe and Mail*, 7 September 2002, https://www.theglobeandmail.com/news/national/canadian-soil-a-long-time-staging-ground-for-al-qaeda/article1026134/.

43. Stewart Bell, 'A Model Life, a Model Operative', *National Post*, 14 October 2005.

44. Shaun Gregory, 'The ISI and the War on Terrorism', *Studies in Conflict & Terrorism* 30, no. 12 (2007): 1013–31.

45. Syed Saleem Shahzad, 'Pakistan Rethink over Support of Militants', *Asia Times*, 20 December 2001.

46. Mohammed Hanif, *A Case of Exploding Mangoes* (New York: Vintage, 2009).

47. Zahid Hussain, *Frontline Pakistan: The Struggle with Militant Islam* (New York: Columbia University Press, 2007), 21–22.

48. Daniel Harrich, 'The Business with Terror', *Deutsche Welle*, 17 June 2021, https://www.dw.com/en/the-business-with-terror/av-57927603.

49. Benazir Bhutto, *Daughter of Destiny* (New York: HarperCollins, 2009), 404.

50. J. Millard Burr and Robert O. Collins, *Sudan in Turmoil: Hasan al-Turabi and the Islamist State* (Princeton, NJ: Markus Wiener, 2010), 70.

51. Ibid.

52. W. J. Berridge, *Hasan al-Turabi: Islamist Politics and Democracy in Sudan* (Cambridge: Cambridge University Press, 2017).

53. Berridge, *Hasan al-Turabi*.

54. *Al-Hayat*, 12 March 2002.

55. Stephen Engelberg, 'One Man and a Global Web of Violence', *New York Times*, 14 January 2001, https://www.nytimes.com/2001/01/14/world/one-man-and-a-global-web-of-violence.html.

56. Jerome Drevon, *Institutionalizing Violence: Strategies of Jihad in Egypt* (New York: Oxford University Press 2022), 94.

57. Ulf Laessing and Khalid Abdelaziz, 'Bin Laden's Sudan Home Left Empty over Attack Fears', *Reuters*, 2 May 2011, https://www.reuters.com/article/us-binla den-sudan-idUSTRE74140Y20110502.

58. U.S. v. Osama bin Laden. No. S(7) 98 Cr. 1023 (S.D. N.Y.), testimony of Jamal al-Fadl, Feb. 6, 2001 (transcript, 218–219, 233); Feb. 13, 2001 (transcript, 514–516); Feb. 20, 2001 (transcript, 890).

59. Ibid.

60. Bergen and Cruickshank, 'Revisiting the Early Al Qaeda'.

61. Anneli Botha, 'The 2010 Suicide Attacks in Kampala', in *The Evolution Of The Global Terrorist Threat*, ed. Bruce Hoffman and Fernando Reinares (New York: Columbia University Press, 2014).

62. Nick Pratt, author interview, 23 August 2011.

63. Egyptian security official, author interview, 22 March 2009.

64. Bergen and Paul Cruickshank, 'Revisiting the Early Al Qaeda'.

65. Ibid.

66. Ayman al-Zawahiri, 'America Is the First Enemy of the Muslims', *as-Sahab Media*, 20 March 2018.

67. Elena Pokalova, *Foreign Fighters after the Conflict Ends. In: Returning Islamist Foreign Fighters* (New York: Palgrave Macmillan, 2020), 72.

68. Osama bin Laden quoted in Michael Scheuer, *Through Our Enemies' Eyes: Osama bin Laden, Radical Islam, and the Future of America* (Washington, DC: Potomac Books, 2006), 147.

69. Alain Bauer, author interview, 5 October 2011.

70. Matthew A. Baum, 'How Public Opinion Constrains the Use of Force: The Case of Operation Restore Hope', *Presidential Studies Quarterly* 34, no. 2 (2004): 218.

71. Nick Pratt, author interview, 23 August 2011.

72. US law enforcement official, author interview, 25 March 2021.

73. Nick Pratt, author interview, 23 August 2011.

74. Al-Zawahiri, *Knights under the Prophet's Banner,* 'Surprises of the Vanguards of Conquest: The First Appearance of al-Jihad since the Assassination of al-Sadat,' *Al-Musawwar*, 27 August 1993, 21–22.

75. Egyptian security official, author interview, 14 July 2015.

76. Al-Zawahiri, *Knights under the Prophet's Banner*.

77. Ibid.

78. Bruce Rutherford, author interview, 20 May 2021.

79. Al-Zawahiri, *Knights under the Prophet's Banner*.

80. Muhammad Salah, 'Sayyid Imam al-Sharif Interview', part 1, *Al-Hayat*, 8 December 2007.

81. Ibid.

82. Ibid.

83. Egyptian security official, author interview, 22 March 2009.

84. Ayman al-Zawahiri, *The Compendium of the Pursuit of Divine Knowledge* (n.p., 1994).

85. Salah, 'Sayyid Imam al-Sharif Interview', part 1.

86. Egyptian security official, author interview, 22 March 2009.

87. Former EIJ jihadist, author interview, 23 November 2013.

88. Tore Hamming, *Jihadi Politics: The Global Jihadi Civil War, 2014–2019* (London: Hurst, 2022), eBook, '2, Explaining Jihadi Fratricide'.

89. Cole Bunzel, 'The Islamic State's Mufti on Trial: The Saga of the Silsila 'Ilmiyya', *CTC Sentinel* 11, no. 9 (October 2018), https://ctc.westpoint.edu/islamic-states-mufti-trial-saga-silsila-ilmiyya/.

90. 'The Trial of the Returnees from Albania', Egyptian Attorney General's Office, Case No. 8/98 Felonies in the Military Prosecutor's Department, March 1999.

91. Al-Zawahiri, *Knights under the Prophet's Banner*.

92. Egyptian security official, author interview, 9 November 2012.

93. Ibid.

94. Azzam, interview with Rory Carroll.

95. Family member of Ayman al-Zawahiri, author interview, 27 August 2015.

96. Jarret Brachman, 'Al-Qa'ida's Changing Outlook on Pakistan', *CTC Sentinel* 1, no. 12 (2008), https://ctc.westpoint.edu/al-qaidas-changing-outlook-on-pakistan//.

97. Bahaa Elkoussy, 'Pakistani Minister in Cairo to Sign Pact Affecting Militants', *United Press International (UPI)*, 25 March 1994.

98. Al-Zawahiri, *Knights under the Prophet's Banner*.

99. 'Bomb Rips Egyptian Embassy', CNN, 19 November 1995, www.cnn.com/WORLD/9511/pakistan_bomb/index.html.

100. Ziad Zafar, 'Who Killed Benazir Bhutto?', *Dawn, EOS*, 24 December 2017.

101. Al-Zawahiri, *Knights under the Prophet's Banner*.

102. Egyptian security official, author interview, 15 February 2010.

103. Williams and McCormick, 'Bin Laden's Man in Silicon Valley'.

104. Ibid.

105. Sebastian Rotella, 'Alleged Al Qaeda Chief Dead, Officials Say', *Los Angeles Times*, 10 April 2008, https://www.latimes.com/world/la-fg-masri10apr10-story.html.

106. Al-Zawahiri, *Knights under the Prophet's Banner*.

107. Egyptian security official, author interview, 9 November 2012.

108. Bhutto, *Daughter of Destiny*, 412.

109. Alan Riding, 'Carlos the Terrorist Arrested and Taken to France', *New York Times*, 16 August 1994, https://www.nytimes.com/1994/08/16/world/carlos-the-terrorist-arrested-and-taken-to-france.html.

110. U.S. v. Ali Mohamed, S(7) 98 Cr. 1023, S.D.N.Y., plea hearing, 20 October 2000, 27; Wright, *The Looming Tower*, 192.

111. 'Al Qaeda No. 2: Sudan's President Pandered to West', CNN, 24 March 2009, http://edition.cnn.com/2009/WORLD/africa/03/24/al-zawahiri.message/.

112. Stuart Elden, *Terror and Territory: The Spatial Extent of Sovereignty* (Minneapolis: University of Minnesota, 2009), 33.

113. Murad Batal al-Shishani, 'Understanding Strategic Change in al-Qaeda's Central Leadership after bin Laden', *Terrorism Monitor, The Jamestown Foundation* 9, no. 23 (June, 2011), https://jamestown.org/program/understanding-strate gic-change-in-al-qaedas-central-leadership-after-bin-laden.

114. Murad Batal al-Shishani, 'Al Qaeda Grows as Its Leaders Focus on the Near Enemy', *National*, 30 August 2013, https://bit.ly/3Orgilu.

115. Paul A. Gigot, 'A Great American Screw Up: The US and Iraq, 1980-1990', *National Interest*, no. 22 (1990): 3–10.

116. Sitara Achakzai, author interview, 13 January 2009.

117. Arshi Saleem Hashmi, 'Historical Roots of the Deobandi Version of Jihadism and Its Implications for Violence in Today's Pakistan', in *Faith-Based Violence and Deobandi Militancy in Pakistan*, ed. Jawad Syed, Edwina Pio, Tahir Kamran, and Abbas Zaidi (London: Palgrave Macmillan, 2016), 144.

118. Mariam Abou Zahab and Olivier Roy, *Islamist Networks: The Afghan-Pakistan Connection* (New York: Columbia University Press, 2002), 22.

119. Christophe Jaffrelot, *Pakistan: Nationalism without a Nation* (New Delhi: Manohar, 2002), 168.

120. Ibid.

121. Egyptian security official, author interview, 9 November 2012.

122. *The 9/11 Commission Report*, 62.

123. Rasul Bakhsh Rais, 'Afghanistan and Pakistan: Difficult Neighbours', *NBR Analysis* 19, no. 5 (2008): 18; Dietrich Reetz, 'Pakistan and the Central Asia Hinterland Option: The Race for Regional Security and Development', *Journal of South Asian and Middle Eastern Studies* 17, no. 1 (1993): 30; C. Christine Fair, *Fighting to the End: The Pakistan Army's Way of War* (New York: Oxford University Press, 2014), 104–5.

124. Peter Tomsen, 'Pakistan: With Friends like These ...', *World Policy Journal* 28, no. 3 (2011); Matt Waldman, 'The Sun in the Sky: The Relationship be-tween Pakistan's ISI and Afghan Insurgents', *London School of Economics: Crisis States Research Centre*, working papers series no. 2 (no. 18), 2010; Olivier Roy, 'The Taliban: A Strategic Tool for Pakistan', in *Pakistan: Nationalism without a Nation?*, ed. Christophe Jaffrelot (London: Zed Books, 2002).

125. Shirin Tahir-Kheli. 'The Military in Contemporary Pakistan', *Armed Forces and Society* 6, no. 4 (1980): 640.

126. Sean P. Winchell, 'Pakistan's ISI: The Invisible Government', *International Journal of Intelligence and Counterintelligence* 16, no. 3 (2003): 374; Anatol Lieven, 'Military Exceptionalism in Pakistan', *Survival* 53, no. 4 (2001): 53.

127. Ahmed Rashid, 'The Taliban: Exporting Extremism', *Foreign Affairs* 78, no. 6 (1999): 31.

128. Ashok K. Behuria, 'Fighting the Taliban: Pakistan at War with Itself', *Australian Journal of International Affairs* 61, no. 4 (2007): 529–43.

129. Winchell, 'Pakistan's ISI', 382.

130. Douglas A. Livermore, 'Pakistani Unconventional Warfare against Afghanistan: A Case Study of the Taliban as an Unconventional Warfare Proxy Force', *Small Wars Journal*, 4 February 2014, https://smallwarsjournal.com/jrnl/art/pakist ani-unconventional-warfare-against-afghanistan.

131. Ijaz Ahmad Khan, 'Understanding Pakistan's Pro-Taliban Afghan Policy', *Pakistan Horizon* 60, no. 2 (2007): 141.

132. Gilles Dorronsoro, 'Pakistan and the Taliban: State Policy, Religious Networks, and Political Connections', in *Pakistan: Nationalism without a Nation?*, ed. Christophe Jaffrelot (London: Zed Books, 2002), 166.

133. Henry Crumpton, author interview, 18 December 2020.

134. Sebastian Rotella, author interview, 25 January 2021.

135. Syed Saleem Shahzad, 'Al-Qaeda's Guerrilla Chief Lays Out Strategy', *Asia Times,* 15 October 2009, http://www.worldsecuritynetwork.com/Terrorism-Broader-Middle-East-United-States-Afghanistan-Pakistan/Shahzad-Syed-Sal eem/Al-Qaedas-guerrilla-chief-lays-out-strategy.

136. Qaiser Butt, 'Strike Two: Ilyas Kashmiri Dead—Again', *Express Tribune,* 5 June 2011, http://tribune.com.pk/story/182727/strike-two-ilyas-kashmiri-dead--again/.

137. 'Ilyas Kashmiri and Retired Pakistan Major Charged in Denmark Plot', FBI: Chicago Division and US Attorney's Office: Northern District of Illinois, 14 January 2010, https://archives.fbi.gov/archives/chicago/press-releases/2010/cg011410.htm.

138. 'Flashback: When The Taleban Took Kabul', BBC News, 15 October 2001, http://news.bbc.co.uk/1/hi/world/south_asia/1600136.stm.

139. Osama bin Laden, 'Declaration of Jihad against the Americans Occupying the Land of the Two Holiest Sites', 1996, republished by *Combatting Terrorism Center at West Point*, https://ctc.westpoint.edu/harmony-program/declarat ion-of-jihad-against-the-americans-occupying-the-land-of-the-two-holiest-sites-original-language-2/.

140. Stefan Goertz and Alexander E. Streitparth, *The New Terrorism: Actors, Strategies and Tactics* (Cham: Springer, 2019), 62.

141. David Winston, author interview, 20 December 2019.

142. Chris Alexander, author interview, 6 May 2021.

143. Nick Pratt, author interview, 23 August 2011.

144. Nick Pratt, author interview, 23 August 2011.

145. US Special Forces official, author interview, 4 February 2015.

146. Sean M. Maloney, author interview, 7 April 2021.

147. Asfandyar Mir and Colin P. Clarke, 'Making Sense of Iran and al-Qaeda's Relationship', *Lawfare*, 21 March 2021, https://www.lawfareblog.com/mak ing-sense-iran-and-al-qaedas-relationship.

148. Ibid.

149. Mohammad Abu Rumman Hassan and Abu Hanieh, 'Infatuated with Martyrdom: Female Jihadism from Al-Qaeda to the "Islamic State"', *Friedrich-Ebert-Stiftung Jordan & Iraq* (2017), 87.

150. Lawrence Wright, author interview, 16 January 2022.

151. Sean M. Maloney, author interview, 7 April 2021.

152. Sean M. Maloney, 'Army of Darkness: The Jihadist Training System in Pakistan and Afghanistan, 1996–2001', *Small Wars & Insurgencies* 26, no. 3 (2015): 518–41.

153. Nick Pratt, author interview, 23 August 2011.

154. Sean M. Maloney, author interview, 7 April 2021.

155. US Special Forces official, author interview, 4 February 2015.

156. Ibid.

157. US intelligence official, author interview, 1 December 2016.

158. Alan Cullison and Andrew Higgins, 'Forgotten Computer Reveals Thinking behind Four Years of al Qaeda Doings', *Wall Street Journal*, 31 December 2001, https://www.wsj.com/articles/SB1009751714799902000.

159. Neighbour, *The Mother of Mohammed*, 60.

160. Shephard, *Guantanamo's Child*, 25.

161. Neighbour, *The Mother of Mohammed*, 60.

162. Ibid.

163. John Miller, author interview, 29 April 2021.

164. Neighbour, *The Mother of Mohammed*, 61.

165. Ibid.

166. Neighbour, *The Mother of Mohammed*, 319–20.

167. Official from the Bosnia-Herzegovina Security Ministry, author interview, 21 March 2010.

168. Aimen Dean, Paul Cruickshank, and Tim Lister, *Nine Lives: My Time as MI6's Top Spy Inside al-Qaeda* (London: Oneworld, 2018), 16.

169. Al-Zawahiri, *Knights under the Prophet's Banner*.

170. Ibid.

171. Ibid.

172. Al-Zawahiri, *Knights under the Prophet's Banner*.

173. 'The Language of Bombs', *Economist*, 9 July 2005.

174. 'Regions and Territories: Dagestan', BBC News, 7 November 2012, http://news.bbc.co.uk/1/hi/world/europe/country_profiles/3659904.stm.

175. Edward W. Walker, 'Russia's Soft Underbelly: The Stability of Instability in Dagestan', *Berkeley Program in Soviet and Post-Soviet Studies Working Paper Series* (Winter 1999–2000).

176. US intelligence official, author interview, 2 June 2019.

177. Al-Zawahiri, *Knights under the Prophet's Banner*.

178. Cerwyn Moore and Paul Tumelty, 'Foreign Fighters and the Case of Chechnya: A Critical Assessment', *Studies in Conflict & Terrorism* 31, no. 5 (2008): 412–33, https://doi.org/10.1080/10576100801993347.

179. US official, author interview, 2 May 2018.

180. CIS official, author interview, 25 October 2016.

181. Ibid.

182. Al-Zawahiri, *Knights under the Prophet's Banner*.

183. Canadian Intelligence Official, author interview, 29 January 2013.

184. Egyptian security official, author interview, 3 January 2012.

185. Cullison and Higgins, 'Forgotten Computer Reveals Thinking behind Four Years of al Qaeda Doings'.

186. Ayman al-Zawahiri, *Al-Mujahideen* (n.p., 1998).

187. Osama bin Laden, 'Declaration of the World Islamic Front for Jihad against the Jews and the Crusaders', *World Islamic Front Statement*, 23 February 1998, republished by Federation of American Scientists, https://fas.org/irp/world/para/docs/980223-fatwa.htm.

188. *The 9/11 Commission Report*, 69.

189. Wright, *The Looming Tower*, 259.

190. Bin Laden, 'Declaration of the World Islamic Front for Jihad against the Jews and the Crusaders'.

191. Ibid.

192. Bin Laden, 'Declaration of the World Islamic Front for Jihad against the Jews and the Crusaders'.

193. Ibid.

194. 'Egypt's Jihad Says Asked by bin Laden to Turn Guns on U.S.', *Agence France Presse*, 24 February 1999.

195. Al-Misri, 'The Story of the Arab Afghans from the Time of Arrival in Afghanistan until their Departure with the Taliban'.

196. Chris Alexander, author interview, 6 May 2021.

197. 'Afghanistan: Taliban Said to Loosen Grip on bin Ladin as They Increasingly Turn to Him for Financial Support and Advice', US Embassy (Islamabad) cable, 12 June 1998, National Security Archive, George Washington University, https://nsarchive2.gwu.edu/NSAEBB/NSAEBB389/docs/1998-06-12%20-%20Haqqani%20as%20UBL%20Advocate.pdf.

198. Ayesha Siddiqa, author interview, 28 April 2021.

199. 'Afghanistan: Jalaluddin Haqqani's Emergence as a Key Taliban Commander', US Embassy (Islamabad) cable, 7 January 1997, National Security Archive, George Washington University, https://nsarchive2.gwu.edu/NSAEBB/NSAEBB295/doc05.pdf.

200. Chris Alexander, author interview, 6 May 2021.

201. Maloney, 'Army of Darkness'.

202. US Department of Defense. 'GTMO Detainee Report: Bendar A al-Ataybi', 25 February 2007. *Wikileaks*, http://wikileaks.org/gitmo/pdf/sa/us9sa-00033 2dp.pdf.

203. US official, author interview, 11 February 2013.

204. Richard Miniter, *Mastermind: The Many Faces of the 9/11 Architect, Khalid Shaikh Mohammed* (New York: Sentinel, 2011).

205. Al-Zawahiri, *Knights under the Prophet's Banner*.

206. Bernard Lewis, 'License to Kill: Usama bin Ladin's Declaration of Jihad', *Foreign Affairs*, November/December 1998.

207. John Miller, author interview, 29 April 2021.

208. Ibid.

209. Ibid.

210. Ibid.

211. Ibid.

212. Ibid.

213. Ibid.,

214. Ibid.

215. John Miller, 'Osama bin Laden Interview', ABC News, *20/20*, 28 May 1998.

216. John Miller, author interview, 29 April 2021.

217. Cullison and Higgins, 'Forgotten Computer Reveals Thinking behind Four Years of al Qaeda Doings'.

218. US official, author interview, 27 August 2017.

219. Cullison and Higgins, 'Forgotten Computer Reveals Thinking behind Four Years of al Qaeda Doings'.

220. *9/11 Commission Report*, ch. 2, n82.

221. Ibid.

222. Muhammad al-Shafi'i, 'Fundamentalist Sources: Al Al-Zawahiri Ousted Following Many Complaints in the Jihad Organization's Shura Council', *Asharq al-Awsat*, 27 January 2000.

223. Ibid.

224. Ronen Shayovitz, 'The Evolution of the Islamist Ideology' (PhD thesis, Cardiff University, 2010), 200–201.

225. Alison Pargeter, *The New Frontiers of Jihad: Radical Islam in Europe* (Philadelphia, PA: University of Pennsylvania Press, 2008), 56.

226. Katherine Zimmerman, 'The al Qaeda Network: A New Framework for Defining the Enemy, Critical Threats Project', *American Enterprise Institute*, 10 September 2013, https://www.criticalthreats.org/analysis/the-al-qaeda-netw ork-a-new-framework-for-defining-the-enemy.

227. Nick Pratt, author interview, 23 August 2011.

228. 'The Trial of the Returnees from Albania'.

229. Muhammad Salah, 'Bin Ladin Front Reportedly Brought CBW from E. Europe', *Al-Hayah*, 20 April 1999.

230. Ayman al-Zawahiri quoted in *Al-Hayat*, 7 August 1998.

231. John Kifner, 'U.S. Agents Said to Thwart Bomb Plot Against US Embassy in Albania', *New York Times*, 21 August 1998, https://archive.nytimes.com/www. nytimes.com/library/world/europe/082198attack-albania.html.

232. Albania State Intelligence Service official, author interview, 6 March 2008; Mohamed Fadel Fahmy, 'Brother of Al Qaeda Leader Offers Peace Plan', *Foreign Policy*, 14 September 2012; https://foreignpolicy.com/2012/09/14/ brother-of-al-qaeda-leader-offers-peace-plan/.

233. 'The Trial of the Returnees from Albania'.
234. UAE security official, author interview, 12 December 2020.
235. 'The Trial of the Returnees from Albania'.
236. Ibid.
237. Ibid.
238. Ibid.
239. Ibid.
240. Ibid.
241. 'Justice Department Secures the Denaturalization of a Senior Jihadist Operative'.
242. 'The Trial of the Returnees from Albania'.
243. Ibid.
244. Ibid.
245. Former EIJ Jihadist, author interview, 4 June.
246. Henry Crumpton, author interview, 18 December 2020.
247. Ayman al-Zawahiri quoted in *Al-Hayat*, 7 August 1998.
248. Nick Pratt, author interview, 23 August 2011.
249. Bell, *Cold Terror*, 192–95, 202–3.
250. *The 9/11 Commission Report*, 68–70.
251. Ibid.
252. Prudence Bushnell, *Terrorism, Betrayal & Resilience: My Story of the 1998 U.S. Embassy Bombings* (Washington, DC: Potomac Books, 2018).
253. *The 9/11 Commission Report*, 68–70.
254. Ibid.
255. 'Islamic Militants Reign of Terror Warning to US', Associated Press, 19 August 1998.
256. Al-Zawahiri, *Knights under the Prophet's Banner*.
257. *The 9/11 Commission Report*, 68–70.
258. Al-Zawahiri, *Knights under the Prophet's Banner*.
259. 'The Open Meeting with Shaykh Ayman al-Zawahiri'.
260. Ibid.
261. Cullison and Higgins, 'Forgotten Computer Reveals Thinking behind Four Years of al Qaeda Doings'.
262. *U.S. v. Ali Mohamed*, plea hearing, 29.
263. Benjamin Weiser, 'U.S. Ex-Sergeant Linked to bin Laden Conspiracy', *New York Times*, 30 October 1998, https://www.nytimes.com/1998/10/30/world/us-ex-sergeant-linked-to-bin-laden-conspiracy.html.
264. Ibid.
265. *U.S. v. Ali Mohamed*, plea hearing.
266. US official, author interview, 27 August 2017.
267. Ibid.
268. US official, author interview, 27 August 2017.
269. Todd R. Phinney, 'Operation Infinite Reach: The 1998 US Embassy Bombing Response', in *Airpower versus Terrorism: Three Case Studies* (Montgomery, AL:

Air University Press, 2007), 25–42, https://www.jstor.org/stable/resrep13
776.9.

270. *The 9/11 Commission Report*, 117.

271. Ibid.

272. Henry Crumpton, author interview, 18 December 2020.

273. 'Pakistan: Reaction to Afghanistan Strikes', US Department of State Cable,
21 August 1998, National Security Archive, George Washington University,
https://nsarchive2.gwu.edu/NSAEBB/NSAEBB344/osama_bin_laden_f
ile_pakistan_01.pdf.

274. 'Usama bin Ladin: Pakistan Seems to Be Leaning against Being Helpful', US
Embassy (Islamabad) cable, 18 December 1998, National Security Archive,
George Washington University, https://nsarchive2.gwu.edu/NSAEBB/
NSAEBB344/osama_bin_laden_file_pakistan_03.pdf.

275. 'Afghanistan: Reaction to U.S. Strikes Follows Predicable Lines: Taliban Angry,
Their Opponents Support U.S.', US Embassy (Islamabad) cable, 21 August
1998, National Security Archive, George Washington University, https://nsa
rchive2.gwu.edu/NSAEBB/NSAEBB253/19980821.pdf.

276. Former EIJ Jihadist, author interview, 13 May 2012.

277. John Miller, author interview, 29 April 2021.

278. Egyptian security official, author interview, 13 November 2012.

279. 'Usama bin Ladin: Pressing High-Level Taliban Official Jalaluddin Haqqani
on bin Ladin', US Department of State cable, 24 May 1999, National Security
Archive, George Washington University, https://nsarchive2.gwu.edu/NSA
EBB/NSAEBB389/docs/1999-05-24%20-%20Haqqani%20Meeting%20
on%20UBL.pdf.

280. US official, author interview, 22 October 2014.

281. P. Scott Thorlin, author interview, 12 December 2017.

282. Maloney, 'Army of Darkness'.

283. Amir Khan Muttaqi, Radio Shariat, 21 January 2000.

284. 'Staff Statement No. 8', National Policy Coordination, National Commission
on Terrorist Attacks, 24 March 2004. http://www.9-11commission.gov/
staff_statements/staff_statement_8.pdf; Craig Whitlock, 'Probe of USS Cole
Bombing Unravels', *Washington Post*, 4 May 2008, 1.

285. Bruce Riedel, author interview, 25 November 2019.

286. Neighbour, *The Mother of Mohammed*.

287. *The 9/11 Commission Report,* 191.

288. Lawrence Wright, author interview, 16 January 2022.

289. Hassan and Hanieh, 'Infatuated with Martyrdom'.

290. US official, author interview, 27 August 2017; US intelligence official, author
interview, 2 June 2019; National Directorate of Security official, author interview, 6 May 2020.

291. Egyptian security official, author interview, 3 January 2012.

292. Ibid.

293. Khalid Sharif al-Din, 'Egypt's Islamic Group Moves toward Establishing a Political Party', *Asharq al-Awsat*, 3 March 1999.

294. Muhammad al-Shafi'i, '*Al Qaeda's Secret Emails*', *Asharq al-Awsat*, 15 December 2002.

295. Former EIJ Jihadist, author interview, 13 May 2012.

296. Al-Zawahiri, *Knights under the Prophet's Banner*.

297. Christopher Dickey, author interview, 12 April 2016.

298. Alan Cullison, 'Inside al-Qaeda's Hard Drive', *Atlantic*, September 2004, https://www.theatlantic.com/magazine/archive/2004/09/inside-al-qaeda-s-hard-drive/303428/.

299. Bruce Hoffman, 'The Evolving Terrorist Threat and CT Options for the Trump Administration', in *How al-Qaeda Survived Drones, Uprisings and the Islamic State* ed. Aaron Zelin (Washington, DC: Washington Institute for Near East Policy, 2017), 14–15

300. US Special Forces official, author interview, 4 February 2015.

301. Ibid.

302. Ibid.

303. Al-Zawahiri, *Knights under the Prophet's Banner*.

304. Egyptian security official, author interview, 13 November 2012.

305. US intelligence official, author interview, 2 June 2019.

306. Stewart Bell, 'Ahmed Khadr provided references for would-be terrorists', *National Post*, 31 December 2005.

307. Canadian official, author interview, 12 February 2020.

308. Saleem Shahzad, author interview, 13 June 2010.

309. D. A. Henderson, author interview, 7 March 2012.

310. Ibid.

311. 'Indonesia Backgrounder: How the Jemaah Islamiyah Terrorist Network Operates', *International Crisis Group*, no. 43, 11 December 2002, 40.

312. Milton Leitenberg, *Assessing the Biological Weapons and Bioterrorism Threat* (Carlisle, PA: US Army War College Press, 2005), 34.

313. D. A. Henderson, author interview, 7 March 2012.

314. Saleem Shahzad, author interview, 13 June 2010; Christopher Dickey, author interview, 12 April 2016.

315. Sajjan M. Gohel, 'The Global-Local Nexus in the Kashmir Insurgency: The Jaish-e-Mohammed, the Pakistani Military and al-Qaeda', in *Exporting the Global Jihad: Critical Perspectives from the Periphery* ed. Tom Smith and Kirsten E. Schulze (London: Bloomsbury, 2020): 99–122.

316. David Albright and Holly Higgins, 'A Bomb for the Ummah', *Bulletin of the Atomic Scientists*, 59, no. 2 (2003): 53.

317. Hoffman, 'The Evolving Terrorist Threat and CT Options for the Trump Administration', 14.

318. Albright and Higgins, 'A Bomb for the Ummah', 49–55; Matthew Bunn, 'Guardians at the Gates of Hell: Estimating the Risk of Nuclear Theft and

Terrorism and Identifying the Highest-Priority Risks of Nuclear Theft' (PhD thesis, Massachusetts Institute of Technology, 2007).

319. Albright and Higgins, 'A Bomb for the Ummah'.

320. US intelligence official, author interview, 2 June 2019.

321. Albright and Higgins, 'A Bomb for the Ummah'.

322. Al-Zawahiri, *Knights under the Prophet's Banner*.

323. Ibid.

324. D. A. Henderson, author interview, 7 March 2012.

325. Joseph Votel, author interview, 17 May, 2021.

326. Christopher M. Davidson, 'Why Was Muammar Qaddafi Really Removed?', *Middle East Policy* 24, no. 4 (2017): 95–96

327. British intelligence official, author interview, 7 August 2019.

328. Eran Berendek and Neil Simon, 'The 2017 Manchester Bombing and the British-Libyan Jihadi Nexus', *CTC Sentinel* 13, no. 5 (May 2020), https://ctc.usma.edu/the-2017-manchester-bombing-and-the-british-libyan-jihadi-nexus/.

329. Daniel Byman, 'Libya's al Qaeda Problem', *Brookings Institution*, 25 February 2011.

330. Phil Hirschkorn, 'Who Is Anas al-Libi?', *CBS News*, 6 October 2013, https://www.cbsnews.com/news/who-is-anas-al-libi/.

331. Berendek and Simon, 'The 2017 Manchester Bombing and the British-Libyan Jihadi Nexus'.

332. British intelligence official, author interview, 7 August 2019.

333. Martin Rudner, author interview, 18 July 2014.

334. Jerrold Post, author interview, 10 December 2016.

335. Cullison and Higgins, 'Forgotten Computer Reveals Thinking behind Four Years of al Qaeda Doings'.

336. al-Zawahiri, *Military Studies in the Jihad against the Tyrants*.

337. Matthew Levitt, 'Zarqawi's Jordanian Agenda', *Washington Institute for Near East Policy*, 16 December 2004, https://www.washingtoninstitute.org/policy-analysis/zarqawis-jordanian-agenda

338. Former EIJ Jihadist, author interview, 23 November 2013.

339. US Department of Defense, 'GTMO Detainee Report: Khair Ulla Said Wali Khairkhwa', 6 March 2008, *Wikileaks*, http://wikileaks.org/gitmo/pdf/af/us9af-000579dp.pdf.

340. Sebastian Rotella, author interview, 25 January 2021.

341. Weaver, 'The Short, Violent Life of Abu Musab al-Zarqawi'.

342. Ibid.

343. Ibid.

344. Ibid.

345. Ibid.

346. Ibid.

347. Ibid.

348. Ibid.

349. Ibid.

350. Ibid.

351. Chidanand Rajghatta, 'Al-Qaeda Tants against India-Israel Ties', *Times of India*, 29 September 2003.

352. Al-Zawahiri, *Knights under the Prophet's Banner*.

353. Ibid.

354. Ibid.

355. Al-Zawahiri, 'The Bitter Harvest'.

356. Al-Zawahiri, *Knights under the Prophet's Banner*.

357. Wright, 'The Man behind bin Laden'.

358. John Miller, author interview, 29 April 2021.

359. Scott-Clark and Levy, *The Exile*, 45–47.

360. Hamid and Farrall, *The Arabs at War in Afghanistan,* 13; Moore and Tumelty, 'Foreign Fighters and the Case of Chechnya'.

361. al-Zawahiri, 'Why This Letter?'.

362. John Calvert, author interview, 20 May 2021.

363. Leah Farrall, 'Interview with a Taliban Insider: Iran's Game in Afghanistan', *Atlantic*, 14 November 2011, https://www.theatlantic.com/international/arch ive/2011/11/interview-with-a-taliban-insider-irans-game-in-afghanistan/ 248294/?single_page=true.

364. Leah Farrall, 'Hotline to the Jihad', *Australian*, 7 December 2009, https:// www.theaustralian.com.au/news/inquirer/hotline-to-the-jihad/news-story/ fa0037fc0776226b0a16021ba64aa23e.

365. Hoda al-Saleh, 'Al-Qaeda's Historian Mustafa Hamed Resumes Digital Activity in Tehran', *al-Arabiya*, 21 January 2018, https://english.alarabiya.net/ News/middle-east/2018/01/21/Al-Qaeda-s-historian-Mustafa-Hamed-resu mes-digital-activity-in-Tehran.

366. Ibid.

367. Farrall, 'Interview with a Taliban Insider'.

368. al-Saleh, 'Al-Qaeda's Historian Mustafa Hamed Resumes Digital Activity in Tehran'.

369. Farrall, 'Interview with a Taliban Insider'.

370. Neighbour, *The Mother of Mohammed*, 65–66.

371. Ibid.

372. Ibid.

373. Paul Cruickshank, 'Bin Laden Documents: Competing Vision of al Qaeda's Top Two', *CNN*, 7 May 2012, https://bit.ly/45hQGNF/.

374. Nick Pratt, author interview, 23 August 2011.

375. US official, author interview, 13 October 2016.

376. Fawaz A. Gerges, *The Rise and Fall of al-Qaeda* (New York: Oxford University Press, 2011), 91; Bergen, *The Rise and Fall of Osama bin Laden*.

377. *9/11 Commission Report*, 252

378. Nick Pratt, author interview, 23 August 2011; Jerrold Post, author interview, 10 December 2016; Bruce Riedel, author interview, 25 November 2019; Douglas London, author interview, 18 December 2020; Henry Crumpton, author interview, 18 December 2020.

379. Henry Crumpton, author interview, 18 December 2020.

380. Lawrence Wright, author interview, 16 January 2022.

381. Aaron Zelin, author interview, 21 January 2022.

382. Christopher Dickey, author interview, 12 April 2016; Aaron Zelin, author interview, 21 January 2022.

383. Cullison and Higgins, 'Forgotten Computer Reveals Thinking behind Four Years of al Qaeda Doings'.

384. Ibid.

385. Ibid.

386. Aaron Zelin, author interview, 21 January 2022.

387. Jean-Pierre Stroobants, 'Vie et mort des assassins de Massoud', *Le Monde*, 11 December 2008, https://www.lemonde.fr/a-la-une/article/2005/04/19/vie-et-mort-des-assassins-de-massoud_640563_3208.html.

388. Amrullah Saleh, author interview, 5 October 2011.

389. Tony Wesolowsky, 'Afghanistan: Masood's Fate Unclear after Apparent Assassination Attempt', *Radio Free Europe*, 10 September 2001, https://www.rferl.org/a/1097356.html.

390. *The 9/11 Commission Report*, 215–323.

391. Mary Fetchet, author interview, 11 January 2022.

392. Faraj, 'The Neglected Duty'.

393. Lawrence Wright, author interview, 16 January 2022.

394. US official, author interview, 2 May 2018.

395. 'Deputy Secretary Armitage's Meeting with Pakistan Intel Chief Mahmud: You're Either With Us or You're Not', US Department of State cable, 13 September 2001, National Security Archive, George Washington University, https://nsarchive2.gwu.edu/NSAEBB/NSAEBB358a/doc03-1.pdf.

396. 'Deputy Secretary Armitage's Meeting with General Mahmud: Actions and Support Expected of Pakistan in Fight Against Terrorism', US Department of State cable, 14 September 2001, National Security Archive, George Washington University, https://nsarchive2.gwu.edu/NSAEBB/NSAEBB358a/doc05.pdf.

397. 'Secretary's 13 September 2001 Conversation with Pakistani President Musharraf', US Department of State, Cable, 19 September 2001, National Security Archive, George Washington University, https://nsarchive2.gwu.edu/NSAEBB/NSAEBB358a/doc10.pdf.

398. Harrich, 'The Business with Terror'.

399. 'Musharraf Accepts the Seven Points', US Embassy (Islamabad), Cable, 14 September 2001, National Security Archive, George Washington University, https://nsarchive2.gwu.edu/NSAEBB/NSAEBB358a/doc09.pdf.

400. Ayesha Siddiqa, author interview, 28 April 2021.

401. 'Michael Morell on 9/11, the CIA and Afghanistan, Part 2', *Intelligence Matters*, CBS News, 22 September 2021, https://www.cbsnews.com/news/intellige nce-matters-michael-morell-on-911-the-cia-and-afghanistan-part-2/.

402. 'Deputy Secretary Armitage-Mamoud Phone Call', US Department of State cable, 18 September 2001, National Security Archive, George Washington University, https://nsarchive2.gwu.edu/NSAEBB/NSAEBB358a/doc09.pdf.

403. 'Mahmud on Failed Kandahar Trip', 29 September 2001, US Embassy (Islamabad), cable, National Security Archive, George Washington University, https://nsarchive2.gwu.edu/NSAEBB/NSAEBB358a/doc12.pdf.

404. Yosri Fouda and Nick Fielding, *Masterminds of Terror* (Edinburgh: London, 2003), 66.

405. US security officials, author interview, 16 September 2019.

406. Ayesha Siddiqa, author interview, 28 April 2021.

407. US security officials, author interview, 27 October 2017.

408. Bruce Riedel, 'Al Qaeda Strikes Back', *Foreign Affairs Magazine*, May/June 2007, http://www.foreignaffairs.org/20070501faessay86304/bruce-riedel/al-qaeda-strikes-back.html.

409. Lawrence Wright, author interview, 16 January 2022.

410. Al-Zawahiri, *Knights under the Prophet's Banner*.

CHAPTER 5

1. US official, author interview, 10 December 2019.
2. 'Tora Bora Revisited'.
3. Ibid.
4. US security officials, author interview, 6 February 2013.
5. Bergen, 'The Account of How We Nearly Caught Osama bin Laden in 2001'.
6. Bergen, *The Osama bin Laden I Know*, 395.
7. Bergen, *The Rise and Fall of Osama bin Laden*.
8. Umayma Hassan, 'Pure Blood on the Soil of Afghanistan, Part One'.
9. US security officials, author interview, 16 September 2019.
10. Bergen, *The Osama bin Laden I Know*, 395.
11. 'Tora Bora Revisited'.
12. Bergen, 'The Account of How We Nearly Caught Osama bin Laden in 2001'.
13. Sumit Ganguly and Michael R. Kraig, 'The 2001–2002 Indo-Pakistani Crisis: Exposing the Limits of Coercive Diplomacy', *Security Studies* 14, no. 2 (2005): 290–324.
14. 'Terror in India', *Economist*, 19 December 2001, https://www.economist.com/unknown/2001/12/19/terror-in-india.
15. Harrich, 'The Business with Terror'.
16. Scott-Clark and Levy, *The Exile*.
17. US security officials, author interview, 16 September 2019.
18. Ayesha Siddiqa, author interview, 28 April 2021.

19. Scott-Clark and Levy, *The Exile*, 32.

20. Bergen, 'The Account of How We Nearly Caught Osama bin Laden in 2001'.

21. Amrullah Saleh, author interview, 5 October 2011.

22. Henry Crumpton, author interview, 18 December 2020.

23. Al-Zawahiri, *Knights under the Prophet's Banner*.

24. Neighbour, *The Mother of Mohammed*, 72.

25. Ibid., 68.

26. Ibid., 70.

27. Ibid., 71.

28. Nelly Lahoud, *The bin Laden Papers* (London: Yale University Press, 2022), eBook, '3, Global Jihad on Autopilot'.

29. Thomas Ruttig, 'Another Bonn-style Conference: A New Plan to "Fix" the War and Enable US Troops to Leave', *Afghan Analysts Network*, 7 March 2021, https://www.afghanistan-analysts.org/en/reports/war-and-peace/another-bonn-style-conference-a-new-plan-to-fix-the-war-and-enable-us-troops-to-leave/.

30. Arif Sahar, 'Ethnicizing Masses in Post-Bonn Afghanistan: The Case of the 2004 and 2009 Presidential Elections', *Asian Journal of Political Science* 22, no. 3 (2014): 289–314.

31. Ivan Watson, 'Ambassador Khalilzad, the "Viceroy of Afghanistan"', *NPR*, 22 October 2014, https://www.npr.org/templates/story/story.php?storyId=4122620.

32. Hans Josef-Beth, author interview, 3 November 2012.

33. Ayman al-Zawahiri, 'Loyalty and Enmity: An Inherited Doctrine and a Lost Reality', *as-Sahab Media*, December 2002.

34. Ibid.

35. al-Zawahiri, 'Why This Letter?'.

36. Ibid.

37. US intelligence official, author interview, 1 December 2016.

38. Bell, *Cold Terror*, 223.

39. Owen L. Sirrs, *Pakistan's Inter-Services Intelligence Directorate: Covert Action and Internal Operations* (London: Routledge, 2017), 351.

40. 'Assault on al Qaeda; Terror in Iraq; Hate Crime Whodunit?', *Anderson Cooper 360 Degrees*, CNN, 18 March 2004, http://edition.cnn.com/TRANSCRIPTS/0403/18/acd.00.html.

41. Sebastian Rotella, author interview, 25 January 2021.

42. Sirrs, *Pakistan's Inter-Services Intelligence Directorate*, 351.

43. Amrullah Saleh, author interview, 25 July 2018.

44. Joseph Votel, author interview, 17 May 2021.

45. Joseph Cirincione, 'Origins of Regime Change in Iraq', *Carnegie Endowment for International Peace*, 19 March 2003, https://carnegieendowment.org/2003/03/19/origins-of-regime-change-in-iraq-pub-1214.

46. US intelligence official, author interview, 9 June 2018.

47. Ibid.
48. Mitchell Silber, author interview, 17 December 2020.
49. US intelligence official, author interview, 9 June 2018.
50. Ibid.
51. Ibid.
52. Sebastian Rotella, author interview, 25 January 2021.
53. US intelligence official, author interview, 23 June 2018.
54. US intelligence official, author interview, 11 June 2018.
55. Al-Zawahiri, *Knights under the Prophet's Banner*.
56. Mitchell Silber, author interview, 17 December 2020.
57. US intelligence official, author interview, 9 June 2018.
58. John Miller, author interview, 29 April 2021.
59. US intelligence official, author interview, 23 June 2018.
60. US official, author interview, 6 March 2017.
61. Jason M. Breslow, 'Colin Powell: U.N. Speech Was a Great Intelligence Failure', *PBS*, 17 May 2016, https://www.pbs.org/wgbh/frontline/article/colin-pow ell-u-n-speech-was-a-great-intelligence-failure/.
62. Lawrence Joffe, 'Abu Musab al-Zarqawi Obituary', *Guardian*, 8 June 2006, https://www.theguardian.com/news/2006/jun/09/guardianobituaries. alqaida.
63. Weaver, 'The Short, Violent Life of Abu Musab al-Zarqawi'.
64. Ayman al-Zawahiri, 'The Defeat of America Is a Matter of Time', *as-Sahab Media*, 9 September 2004.
65. 'Statement from Jama'at al-Tawhid wal-Jihad's Abu Musab al-Zarqawi: Bay'a to Osama bin Laden', *Jihadology*, 18 October 2004, https://jihadology.net/ 2004/10/18/statement-from-jamaat-al-taw%E1%B8%A5id-wa-l-jihads-abu-mu%E1%B9%A3ab-al-zarqawi-bayah-to-usamah-bin-laden/.
66. 'Letter from Wakil Khan October 18, 2004', release of Abbottabad compound material, CIA, November 2017, https://www.cia.gov/library/ abbottabad-compound/51/51A61D0D0F9BFEF9E0524F8F2000C0 35_%D9%85%D9%86_%D8%AA%D9%88%D9%81%D9%8A%D9%82.pdf.
67. Ibid.
68. 'Letter to My Beloved Brother', *Bin Laden's Bookshelf*, Office of the Director of National Intelligence, 20 May 2015, https://www.dni.gov/files/docume nts/ubl/english2/Letter%20to%20my%20beloved%20Brother.pdf.
69. Ibid.
70. 'Appropriate Means', release of Abbottabad compound, November 2017, https://www.cia.gov/library/abbottabad-compound/D5/D5243CC1973928 244D1DDDE221D538A0_%D8%B1%D8%B3%D8%A7%D9%84%D8%A9_ %D8%B1%D9%82%D9%85_1.pdf.
71. 'Ayman al-Zawahiri, letter to Abu Musab al-Zarqawi', Harmony Document, *Combating Terrorism Center at West Point*, 11 October 2005, https://ctc.usma. edu/harmony-program/zawahiris-letter-to-zarqawi-original-language-2/.

72. Ibid.
73. Ibid.
74. Ibid.
75. Ibid.
76. Ibid.
77. Ibid.
78. Shephard, *Guantanamo's Child*.
79. 'Ayman al-Zawahiri, letter to Abu Musab al-Zarqawi'.
80. Ibid.
81. Ibid.
82. Ayman al-Zawahiri, 'The Correct Equation', *as-Sahab Media*, 22 January 2007.
83. Ayman al-Zawahiri, 'Lessons, Examples and Great Events in the year 1427', *as-Sahab Media*, 13 February 2007.
84. Joseph Votel, author interview, 28 April 2021.
85. US intelligence official, author interview, 18 May 2021.
86. Rassler and Brown, 'The Haqqani Nexus and the Evolution of al-Qa'ida'.
87. US intelligence official, author interview, 18 May 2021.
88. Chris Alexander, author interview, 6 May 2021.
89. Carlotta Gall, 'Red Cross Worker Is Killed by Gunmen in Afghanistan', *New York Times*, 28 March 2003, https://www.nytimes.com/2003/03/28/intern ational/worldspecial/red-cross-worker-is-killed-by-gunmen-in.html.
90. Fiona Terry, 'The International Committee of the Red Cross in Afghanistan: Reasserting the Neutrality of Humanitarian Action', *International Review of the Red Cross (Conflict in Afghanistan II)* 93, no. 881 (2011): 173–88.
91. Chris Alexander, author interview, 6 May 2021.
92. 'Taliban commander speaks out', al-Jazeera, 27 June 2010.
93. Chris Alexander, author interview, 6 May 2021.
94. Amrullah Saleh, author interview, 5 October 2011.
95. Al-Zawahiri, *Knights under the Prophet's Banner*.
96. Ibid.
97. US intelligence official, author interview, 18 May 2021.
98. Ayman al-Zawahiri, 'Al-Zawahiri Denounces US, Argues for Reign of Islamic Law and Caliphate, Jihad against Crusaders and Jews', *as-Sahab Media*, 31 January 2005.
99. Ibid.
100. Ibid.
101. British counter-terrorism official, author interview, 12 March 2015.
102. Ayman al-Zawahiri, 'Long-Term Plan', *as-Sahab Media*, 9 July 2005.
103. Mitchell Silber, author interview, 17 December 2020.
104. 'R. v. Khawaja,' The Superior Court of Ontario, Case Number (04 G30282) Exhibit 63. Email of Momin Khawaja to Zeba Khan, 8 August 2003.
105. Canadian official, author interview, 12 February 2020.
106. Sarah Knapton, 'Dateline London: Operation Crevice', *Ottawa Citizen*, 1 May 2007.
107. Peter Clarke, author interview, 29 April 2021.

108. 'Momin Khawaja: Canada Raises Terrorism Sentence', BBC News, 17 December 2010, https://www.bbc.co.uk/news/world-us-canada-12024534.
109. Peter Clarke, author interview, 29 April 2021.
110. Sebastian Rotella and Janet Stobart, 'Terrorism Defendant Cites Fears of Pakistan', *Los Angeles Times*, 20 September 2006.
111. Peter Clarke, author interview, 29 April 2021.
112. British counter-terrorism official, author interview, 12 March 2015.
113. Ibid.
114. Ibid.
115. British counter-terrorism official, author interview, 4 November 2013.
116. Ibid.
117. Peter Clarke, author interview, 29 April 2021.
118. Alan Cowell, 'British Muslim Sentenced in Terror Attacks', *New York Times*, 8 November 2006; 'Dhiren Barot', BBC News, 6 November 2006, http://news.bbc.co.uk/1/hi/uk/6122270.stm.
119. Ayman al-Zawahiri, 'Wills of the Knights of London Raid', *as-Sahab Media*, 16 November 2005.
120. Ayman al-Zawahiri, 'A Message to the British', *as-Sahab Media*, 4 *August* 2005.
121. 'Ayman al-Zawahiri, Interview', al-Jazeera, 1 September 2005.
122. Muhammad Sidique Khan, 'London Bomber: Text in Full', *BBC News*, 1 September 2005, http://news.bbc.co.uk/1/hi/uk/4206800.stm.
123. 'Ayman al-Zawahiri, Interview'.
124. Ayman al-Zawahiri, 'Al Qa'ida's al-Zawahiri Predicts Failure of US Crusade against Muslim States', *as-Sahab Media*, 7 December 2005.
125. David Rohde and Carlotta Gall, 'In a Corner of Pakistan a Debate Rages: Are Terrorist Camps Still functioning?', *New York Times*, 28 August 2005, https://www.nytimes.com/2005/08/28/world/asia/in-a-corner-of-pakistan-a-debate-rages-are-terrorist-camps-still.html.
126. Chris Alexander, author interview, 6 May 2021.
127. Gohel, 'The Global-Local Nexus in the Kashmir Insurgency'.
128. Sebastian Rotella, author interview, 25 January 2021.
129. British counter-terrorism official, author interview, 12 March 2015.
130. Gohel, 'The Global-Local Nexus in the Kashmir Insurgency'.
131. British intelligence official, author interview, 7 August 2019.
132. Sam Kiley, '21/7: The Story of the Bungled UK Terror Attack', *Sky News*, 6 July 2015, https://news.sky.com/story/21-7-the-story-of-the-bungled-uk-terror-attack-10353533.
133. British intelligence official, author interview, 7 August 2019.
134. Cahal Milmo, Ian Herbert, Jason Bennetto, and Justin Huggler, 'From Birmingham Bakery to Pakistani Prison, the Mystery of Rashid Rauf', *Independent*, 19 August 2006.
135. Nic Robertson, Paul Cruickshank, and Tim Lister, 'Document Shows Origins of 2006 Plot for Liquid Bombs on Planes', *CNN*, 30 April 2012, https://edition.cnn.com/2012/04/30/world/al-qaeda-documents/index.html.

136. Mitch D. Silber, *The al-Qaeda Factor: Plots against the West* (Philadelphia: University of Pennsylvania Press, 2012), 117.

137. US security official, author interview, 31 December 2021.

138. Abubakar Siddique, *The Pashtun Question: The Unresolved Key to the Future of Pakistan and Afghanistan* (London: Hurst, 2014), 39.

139. Jeff Stein, 'Ayman al-Zawahiri: How a CIA Drone Strike Nearly Killed the Head of al-Qaeda', *Newsweek*, 21 April 2017, https://www.newsweek.com/2017/05/05/ayman-al-zawahiri-cia-donald-trump-drone-strike-osama-bin-laden-pakistan-587732.html.

140. US security official, author interview, 30 December 2020.

141. Joseph Votel, author interview, 28 April 2021.

142. 'Author of al-Qaeda Chemical and Biological Weapons Manuals Believed Killed in Pakistan', *Nuclear Threat Initiative (NTI)*, 19 January 2006, http://nti.org/7568GSN.

143. Ibid.

144. Ayman al-Zawahiri, 'The Butcher of Washington', *as-Sahab Media*, 30 January 2006.

145. Ibid.

146. Ibid.

147. 'Ayman al-Zawahiri Videotape', al-Jazeera, 4 March 2006.

148. Dominic Casciani, 'Liquid Bomb Plot: What Happened', *BBC News*, 7 September 2009, http://news.bbc.co.uk/1/hi/uk/8242479.stm.

149. John Miller, author interview, April 29, 2021.

150. Ibid.

151. Mir and Clarke, 'Making Sense of Iran and al-Qaeda's Relationship'.

152. Raffaello Pantucci, 'Maulana Masood Azhar in the British Jihad', *Hurst*, 24 January 2013, https://www.hurstpublishers.com/maulana-masood-azhar-in-the-british-jihad.

153. Peter Clarke, author interview, 29 April 2021.

154. Gary Cleland, 'Bomb Plot Suspect Escaped While Praying', *Daily Telegraph*, 17 December 2017, https://www.telegraph.co.uk/news/worldnews/1572870/Bomb-plot-suspect-escaped-while-praying.html.

155. Bill Roggio, 'Al Qaeda Leader Rashid Rauf Killed in Drone Strike, Family Says', *Long War Journal*, 29 October 2012, https://www.longwarjournal.org/archives/2012/10/al_qaeda_leader_rash.php.

156. Alain Bauer, author interview, 5 October 2011.

157. Aaron Zelin, *Your Sons Are at Your Service: Tunisia's Missionaries of Jihad* (New York: Columbia University Press, 2020), 92.

158. Alain Bauer, author interview, 5 October 2011.

159. Al-Zawahiri, 'The Advice of One Concerned'.

160. 'Al-Zawahiri: Egyptian Militant Group Joins al Qaeda', CNN, 5 August 2006, https://edition.cnn.com/2006/WORLD/meast/08/05/zawahiri.tape/index.html.

161. Egyptian security official, author interview, 13 November 2012.

162. 'Al-Qaeda to Give "Open Interview"', BBC News, 19 December 2007, http://news.bbc.co.uk/1/hi/world/middle_east/7153099.stm.

163. Al-Zawahiri, 'The Open Meeting with Shaykh Ayman al-Zawahiri'.

164. Ibid.

165. 'Al-Qaeda Claims Tunisia Attack', BBC News, 23 June 2002, http://news.bbc.co.uk/1/hi/world/middle_east/2061071.stm; David Ignatius, 'The Mombasa Attacks: Al Qaeda's New Weapon', *International Herald Tribune*, 30 November 2002.

166. Al-Zawahiri, 'The Open Meeting with Shaykh Ayman al-Zawahiri'.

167. Ibid.

168. Ibid.

169. Ibid.

170. Albania State Intelligence Service official, author interview, 6 March 2008.

171. 'Trade-Off: The Rendition to Egypt of Sayyid Imam al-Sharif', *Human Rights Watch*, May 2005, http://www.hrw.org/reports/2005/egypt0505/10.htm.

172. Sayyid Imam al-Sharif, 'Wathiqat Tarshid al-'Aml al-Jihad i fi Misr w'al-'alam' [The document for rationalization of jihad in Egypt and the world], *Al-Masri al-Yawm and al-Jarida*, 19 November 2007–3 December 2007.

173. Ibid.

174. Ibid.

175. Salah, 'Sayyid Imam al-Sharif Interview', part 2.

176. Ibid.

177. Ibid.

178. Ibid.

179. Ayman al-Zawahiri, 'The Power of Truth', *as-Sahab Media,* 4 July 2007.

180. Ibid.

181. Ayman al-Zawahiri, *The Exoneration: A Treatise Exonerating the Community of the Pen and the Sword from the Debilitating Accusation of Fatigue and Weakness* (published online, 2008), https://fas.org/irp/dni/osc/exoneration.pdf.

182. Ibid.

183. Ibid.

184. Ibid.

185. Ibid.

186. Ibid.

187. Ibid.

188. Soufan, *Anatomy of Terror.*

189. Cullison, 'Inside al-Qaeda's Hard Drive'.

190. Al-Zawahiri, *The Exoneration.*

191. US federal law enforcement official, author interview, 12 December 2018.

192. 'Ilyas Kashmiri and Retired Pakistan Major Charged in Denmark Plot'.

193. Carlotta Gall, 'Pakistani Militant Chief Is Reported Dead', *New York Times*, 4 June 2011, http://www.nytimes.com/2011/06/05/world/asia/05kashmiri.html?_r=2&ref=world.

194. Sebastian Rotella, author interview, 25 January 2021.

195. 'Ilyas Kashmiri and Retired Pakistan Major Charged in Denmark Plot'.

196. Ibid.

197. Harrich, 'The Business with Terror'.

198. Sebastian Rotella, author interview, 25 January 2021.

199. Declan Walsh and Salman Masood, 'In Pakistan, a Muted Reaction to Kasab's Execution', *New York Times*, 21 November 2012, https://archive.nytimes.com/india.blogs.nytimes.com/2012/11/21/in-pakistan-a-muted-reaction-to-kasabs-killing/.

200. Harrich, 'The Business with Terror'.

201. 'Ilyas Kashmiri and Retired Pakistan Major Charged in Denmark Plot'.

202. 'Tahawwur Rana Guilty of Providing Material Support to Terror Group and Playing Supporting Role in Denmark Terror Conspiracy', U.S. Department of Justice: Office of Public Affairs, 9 June 2011, https://www.justice.gov/opa/pr/tahawwur-rana-guilty-providing-material-support-terror-group-and-playing-supporting-role.

203. 'David Coleman Headley Sentenced to 35 Years in Prison for Role in India and Denmark Terror Plots', US Department of Justice, Office of Public Affairs, 24 January 2013, https://www.justice.gov/opa/pr/david-coleman-headley-sentenced-35-years-prison-role-india-and-denmark-terror-plots.

204. US law enforcement official, author interview, 30 August 2018.

205. Ayman al-Zawahiri, 'Interview with Shaykh Ayman al-Zawahiri', *as-Sahab Media*, 5 May 2007.

206. Ibid.

207. Ibid.

208. Ibid.

209. Ibid.

210. Ayman al-Zawahiri, 'Exit of Bush and Arrival of Obama', *as-Sahab Media*, 19 November 2008.

211. Ibid.

212. Family member of Ayman al-Zawahiri, author interview, 27 August 2015.

213. Sayyid Qutb, *The America I Have Seen: In the Scale of Human Values* (Kashf ul Shubuhat, 1951).

214. Steve Coll, 'Time Bomb: The Death of Benazir Bhutto and the Unravelling of Pakistan', *New Yorker*, 21 January 2008.

215. Heraldo Muñoz, *Getting Away with Murder: Benazir Bhutto's Assassination and the Politics of Pakistan* (New York: W. W. Norton, 2013), eBook.

216. Ibid.

217. Sabrina Tavernise, 'U.N. Report Finds Faults in Pakistani Bhutto Inquiry', *New York Times*, 15 April 2021, 10.

218. Peter Bergen, 'The Killer Question: Who Murdered Benazir Bhutto?', *New Republic*, 30 January 2008, https://newrepublic.com/article/65707/the-killer-question.

219. 'Pakistan: Al-Qaeda Claims Bhutto's Death', *Adnkronos International (AKI)*, 27 December 2007.

220. Syed Saleem Shahzad, 'Al-Qaeda Claims Bhutto Killing', *Asia Times,* 29 December 2007.

221. Zafar, 'Who Killed Benazir Bhutto?'.

222. Eric Schmitt, 'Attack Planner for al Qaeda Reported Dead', *New York Times,* 10 April 2008, https://www.nytimes.com/2008/04/10/washington/10ter ror.html.

223. Saad Sayeed, 'Khan's Interior Minister Pick Raises Questions about "New" Pakistan', *Reuters,* 27 April 2019, https://www.reuters.com/article/us-pakis tan-politics-shah-idUSKCN1S3065.

224. Bruce Riedel, 'Three Ways to Help Pakistan', *Brookings Institution,* 23 June 2011, https://www.brookings.edu/opinions/three-ways-to-help-pakistan/.

225. Daniel Pearl and Steve LeVine, 'Pakistan Has Ties to Nuclear Group Military State Had Vowed to Curb', *Wall Street Journal,* 24 December 2001, https://www.wsj.com/articles/SB1009146749779899360.

226. Karl Vick and Kamran Khan, 'Al Qaeda Tied to Attacks in Pakistan Cities, Militants Joining Forces against Western Targets', *Washington Post,* 30 May 2002.

227. Nick Fielding, 'Omar Saeed Sheikh: The British Jackal', *Sunday Times,* 21 April 2002.

228. Ayman al-Zawahiri, 'Open Discussion with Sheikh Ayman al-Zawahiri', *as-Sahab Media, Minbar al-Tawhid wa al-Jihad,* 15 February 2009.

229. Ibid.

230. Umayma Hassan, 'A Message to the Muslim Sisters', *as-Sahab Media,* December 2009.

231. Ibid.

232. Ibid.

233. Ibid.

234. Umaima Hassan, 'Islamic Spring', *Al-Fajr,* 7 June 2012.

235. Ibid.

236. Ibid.

237. Saleem Shahzad, 13 June 2010.

238. U.S. v. Aafia Siddiqui, 08 Cr. 826 (RMB), S.D.N.Y., government's sentencing submission, 7 July 2010.

239. Ibid.

240. Dan Murphy, 'Aafia Siddiqui, Alleged al Qaeda Associate, Gets 86-Year Sentence', *Christian Science Monitor,* 23 September 2010, https://www.csmoni tor.com/World/Asia-South-Central/2010/0923/Aafia-Siddiqui-alleged-Al-Qaeda-associate-gets-86-year-sentence.

241. Ayman al-Zawahiri, 'Who Will Support Scientist Aafia Siddiqui?', *as-Sahab Media,* 4 November 2010.

242. Ibid.

243. Declan Walsh, 'Pakistan Erupts after US Jailing of "Daughter of the Nation" Aafia Siddiqui', *Guardian,* 24 September 2010, https://www.theguardian.com/world/2010/sep/24/pakistan-aafia-siddiqui-jailed-protests.

244. Hollie McKay and Mohsin Saleem Ullah, 'Pakistani PM Opens Door to Prisoner Swap with US to Free "Hero" Doctor Who Helped Track bin Laden', *Fox News,* 23 July 2019, https://www.foxnews.com/politics/pakistan-pm-prisoner-doctor-laden.

245. Lahoud, *The bin Laden Papers,* '6, The Americans'.

246. Bruce Riedel, 'The Remarkable Case of the Triple Agent and the Bombing in Khost, Afghanistan', *Brookings Institution,* 6 December 2019, https://www.brookings.edu/blog/order-from-chaos/2019/12/06/the-remarkable-case-of-the-triple-agent-and-the-bombing-in-khost-afghanistan/.

247. Ibid.

248. Warrick, *The Triple Agent,* 19–21.

249. Ibid.

250. ' Former Senior CIA Officer Recalls Killing of Service Members by Suicide Bomber', *Intelligence Matters,* CBS News, 30 December 2020, https://www.cbsnews.com/news/former-senior-cia-officer-recalls-killing-of-service-members-by-suicide-bomber-humam-al-balawi/.

251. Ibid.

252. Ibid.

253. Ibid.

254. US security official, author interview 5 October 2016.

255. Warrick, *The Triple Agent,* 43–45.

256. Edmund Fitton-Brown, author interview, 28 January 2022.

257. US security official, 31 December 2021.

258. Ibid.

259. Warrick, *The Triple Agent,* 43–45.

260. Bruce Riedel, author interview, 25 November 2019.

261. Leon Panetta, author interview, 8 April 2022.

262. US security official, author interview, 30 December 2020.

263. Al-Zawahiri, *Knights under the Prophet's Banner.*

264. 'Al-Qaida's Third in Command Killed', NBC News, 1 June 2010.

265. 'Statement on the Abu-Dujanah al-Khurasani Raid (May Allah Accept Him) to Infiltrate the Fortresses of the Americans', as-Sahab Media, 6 January 2010.

266. 'CIA Base Bomber's Message', al-Jazeera, 9 January 2010.

267. Thomas Ruttig, 'The Haqqani Network as an Autonomous Entity', in *Decoding the New Taliban: Insights from the Afghan Field,* ed. Antonio Giustozzi (New York: Columbia University Press, 2009), 53; Alex Spillius, 'CIA Suicide Bomber Worked with bin Laden Allies', *Daily Telegraph,* 7 January 2010.

268. Jalaluddin Haqqani, *Manba al-Jihad,* 2, no. 12 (June 1991).

269. 'Last Will and Testament of Martyr Humam Khalil Abu Mulal al-Balawi', as-Sahab Media, 28 February 2010.

270. 'Late December 2009 al-Qaeda and Haqqani Network Senior Leadership Activities in Miram Shah, Pakistan and Khowst Province, Afghanistan', US Department of State Cable, 11 January 2010. National Security Archive, George Washington University, https://nsarchive.files.wordpress.com/

2016/04/hqn10.pdf; Foreign Intelligence Service and Haqqani Network Involvement in the 30 of December 2009 Suicide Attack on FOB Chapman', US Department of State Cable, 6 February 2010. National Security Archive, George Washington University, Washington, DC, https://nsarchive.files. wordpress.com/2016/04/hqn9.pdf.

271. Mike Mullen, 'Testimony to the Senate Armed Services Committee', 22 September 2011.

272. US intelligence official, author interview, 18 May 2021.

273. Sirajuddin Haqqani, *Military Lessons: For the Legions of Jihadists* (n.p. 2011).

274. 'Sirajuddin Haqqani', Rewards for Justice, 19 September 2012, https://reward sforjustice.net/english/sirajuddin_haqqani.html.

CHAPTER 6

1. Michaelle Browers, 'Egyptian Movement for Change: Intellectual Antecedents and Generational Conflicts', in *Political Ideology in the Arab World: Accommodation and Transformation* (Cambridge: Cambridge University Press, 2009), 109–37.

2. Sherif Mansour, 'Enough Is Not Enough: Achievements and Shortcomings of Kefaya, the Egyptian Movement for Change', in *Civilian Jihad*, ed. Maria J. Stephan (New York: Palgrave Macmillan, 2009), 205–18.

3. Mansour, 'Enough Is Not Enough'.

4. Joseph S. Mayton, 'Kefaya Opposition Movement Is Dead', *All Headline News (AHN)*, 22 May 2007.

5. Ayman al-Zawahiri quoted in Nadia Oweidat et al., *The Kefaya Movement: A Case Study of a Grassroots*, RAND Corporation, 2008, 20.

6. Yasmine Ryan, 'The Tragic Life of a Street Vendor', *al-Jazeera*, 20 January 2011, https://www.aljazeera.com/features/2011/1/20/the-tragic-life-of-a-street-vendor.

7. Ibid.

8. Bob Simon, 'How a Slap Sparked Tunisia's Revolution', *CBS News, 60 Minutes*, 22 February 2011, https://www.cbsnews.com/news/how-a-slap-sparked-tunisias-revolution-22-02-2011/.

9. Ibid.

10. Kara Alaimo, 'How the Facebook Arabic Page "We Are All Khaled Said" Helped Promote the Egyptian Revolution', *Social Media + Society* 1, no. 2 (2015), https://doi.org/10.1177%2F2056305115604854.

11. Thanassis Cambanis, *Once upon a Revolution: An Egyptian Story* (New York: Simon & Schuster, 2015).

12. Charles Levinson, Margaret Coker, and Jay Solomon, 'How Cairo, U.S. Were Blindsided by Revolution', *Wall Street Journal*, 2 February 2011, https://www.wsj.com/articles/SB10001424052748703445904576118502819408990.

13. Jeremy M. Sharp, *Egypt: The January 25 Revolution and Implications for U.S. Foreign Policy*, CRS Report for Congress, Congressional Research Service, 11 February 2011, https://www.refworld.org/pdfid/4d6f4dc5c.pdf.

14. 'Egypt Army: Will Not Use Violence against Citizens', Reuters, 31 January 2011,   https://www.reuters.com/article/egypt-army-idAFLDE70U2JC2 0110131.

15. 'Egypt: President Mubarak Addresses Nation on Transfer of Power', Nile News TV, 1 February 2011.

16. Asef Bayat, 'Plebeians of the Arab Spring', *Current Anthropology* 56, no. 11 (2015): s33–s43.

17. Masooda Bano and Hanane Benadi, 'Official al-Azhar versus al-Azhar Imagined: The Arab Spring and the Revival of Religious Imagination', *Die Welt des Islams* 59, no. 1 (2019), 7–32.

18. US intelligence official, author interview, 12 September 2011.

19. Abdel Latif el-Menawy, *18 Days in Tahrir: An Insider's Account of the Uprising in Egypt* (London: Gilgamesh, 2013).

20. Donald Holbrook, 'Al-Qaeda's Response to the Arab Spring', *Perspectives on Terrorism* 6, no. 6 (December 2012), https://www.jstor.org/stable/26296891.

21. Mohamed Heikal, author interview, 27 September 2013.

22. Bruce Rutherford, author interview, 20 May 2021.

23. Ayman al-Zawahiri, 'Missive of Hope and Joy to Our People in Egypt', parts 1–5, as-Sahab Media, 2011.

24. Al-Zawahiri, Ayman, 'Missive of Hope and Joy to Our People in Egypt, Part 1', as-Sahab Media, 18 February 2011.

25. Al-Zawahiri, Ayman, 'Missive of Hope and Joy to our People in Egypt, Part 3', as-Sahab Media, 28 February 2011.

26. Ibid.

27. Ibid.

28. Ayman al-Zawahiri, 'Missives of Hope and Joy to our People in Egypt', part 5, as-Sahab Media, 14 April 2011.

29. Ayman al-Zawahiri, 'Glad Tidings of Victory to Our People in Egypt'; 'Brief Messages to Our Victorious Ummah', *The Eighth Episode, as-Sahab Media,* 15 February 2018.

30. Atiyah Abdul Rahman, 'Letter from Atiyah to Abu Basir', *Bin Laden's Bookshelf*, Office of the Director of National Intelligence, 27 March 2011, https://www.dni.gov/files/documents/ubl2017/english/Letter%20from%20Atiyah%20to%20Abu%20Basir.pdf.

31. 'Mubarak and Sons Detained in Egypt', al-Jazeera, 13 April 2011, https://www.aljazeera.com/news/2011/4/13/mubarak-and-sons-detained-in-egypt.

32. Paul Owen and Jack Shenker, 'Mubarak Trial—the Defendants and the Charges', *Guardian*, 3 August 2011, https://www.theguardian.com/world/2011/aug/03/mubarak-trial-defendants-charges.; Adrian Blomfield, 'Hosni Mubarak in Court to Answer to the People He Subjugated', *Telegraph*, 4 August 2011, https://www.telegraph.co.uk/news/worldnews/africaandindianocean/egypt/8679930/Hosni-Mubarak-in-court-to-answer-to-the-people-he-subjugated.html.

33. Christopher Dickey, author interview, 12 April 2016.
34. Family member of Ayman al-Zawahiri, author interview, 27 August 2015.
35. Thomas Joscelyn, 'Ayman al-Zawahiri's Brother Released from Egyptian Prison', *Long War Journal*, 19 March 2016, https://www.longwarjournal.org/archives/2016/03/ayman-al-zawahiris-brother-released-from-an-egyptian-prison.php.
36. Lucia Ardovini, 'The Failure of Political Islam? The Muslim Brotherhood's Experience in Government' (PhD thesis, Lancaster University, 2017), 195–208.
37. Ardovini, 'The Failure of Political Islam?', 203–13.
38. Ayman al-Zawahiri, 'Zawahiri Speaks on 12th Anniversary of 9/11, Calls for Attack on U.S.', *Global Terrorism Research Project,* 12 September 2013.
39. Christopher Dickey, author interview, 12 April 2016; Tarek Amara, 'Two Dead as Protesters Attack U.S. Embassy in Tunisia', *Reuters*, 14 September 2012, https://www.reuters.com/article/us-protests-tunisia-school-idUSBRE88D18020120914.
40. Jerrold Post, author interview, 10 December 2016.
41. US security official, author interview, 31 December 2021.
42. Thomas Joscelyn, 'Al Qaeda-Linked Jihadists Helped Incite 9/11 Cairo Protest', *Long War Journal,* 26 October 2012, https://www.longwarjournal.org/archives/2012/10/al_qaeda-linked_jiha.php.
43. 'Protesters Attack U.S. Diplomatic Compounds in Egypt, Libya', CNN, 12 September 2012, https://edition.cnn.com/2012/09/11/world/meast/egpyt-us-embassy-protests/index.html.
44. Bruce Riedel, 'Al Qaeda's Libya Vengeance Plot', *Brookings Institution*, 12 September 2012, https://www.brookings.edu/opinions/al-qaedas-libya-vengeance-plot/.
45. US security official, author interview, 31 December 2021.
46. Ibid.
47. Ayman al-Zawahiri, 'Oh People of Tunisia Support Your Shari'ah', *as-Sahab Media*, 11 June 2012.
48. Aaron Zelin, author interview, 21 January 2022.
49. Thomas Joscelyn, 'Al Qaeda Ally Orchestrated Assault on US Embassy in Tunisia', *Long War Journal,* 2 October 2012; http://www.longwarjournal.org/archives/2012/10/al_qaeda_ally_orches.php.
50. Aaron Zelin, author interview, 21 January 2022.
51. Ibid.; US security official, author interview, 31 December 2021.
52. Benjamin Weiser, 'U.S. Seeks to Use Letters Found in bin Laden Raid in Terrorism Trial', *New York Times*, 15 December 2014.
53. British counter-terrorism official, author interview, 19 December 2014.
54. 'Profile: Anas al-Liby', BBC News, 3 January 2015, https://www.bbc.co.uk/news/world-africa-24418327.
55. British counter-terrorism official, author interview, 19 December 2014.

56. Ayman al-Zawahiri, 'Missive of Hope and Joy to Our People in Egypt', part 7, *as-Sahab Media*, 5 October 2011.

57. Abdel-Fattah el-Sissi, 'Address to the Nation', *ERTU*, 23 June 2013.

58. Sophia Jones, 'No Turning Back: Inside Egypt's Coup', *Atlantic*, 4 July 2013, https://www.theatlantic.com/international/archive/2013/07/no-turning-back-inside-egypts-coup/277535/.

59. Khalil al-Anani, 'Upended Path: The Rise and Fall of Egypt's Muslim Brotherhood', *Middle East Journal* 69, no. 4 (Autumn 2015).

60. Robert L. Tignor, author interview, 18 May 2021.

61. Al-Zawahiri, 'Glad Tidings of Victory to our People in Egypt'; 'Brief Messages to our Victorious Ummah'.

62. Atiyah Abd al-Rahman, 'The People's Revolt … the Fall of Corrupt Arab Regimes … the Demolition of the Idol of Stability … and the New Beginning', *Global Islamic Media Front*, 16 February 2011.

63. 'How al-Qaeda and Islamic State Differ in Pursuit of Common Goal: Strengths and Weaknesses', *IHS Economics and Country Risk,* 16 March 2015.

64. Ayman al-Zawahiri, 'We Shall Fight until There Is No More Persecution', *as-Sahab Media*, 4 October 2017.

65. Ayman al-Zawahiri, 'After Seven Years Where Is the Deliverance?', *as-Sahab Media*, 26 January 2016.

66. Jared Malsin and Owen Bowcott, 'Egypt's Former President Mohamed Morsi Sentenced to 20 Years in Prison', *Guardian*, 21 April 2015.

67. Lizzie Dearden, 'Egypt Sentences al Jazeera Journalists to Death as Mohamed Morsi Given New Life Term in Qatar Espionage Case', *Independent,* 18 June 2016.

68. 'Egypt's Ousted President Mohammed Morsi Dies during Trial', *BBC News*, 4 June 2019, https://www.bbc.co.uk/news/world-middle-east-48668941.

69. Jared Malsin, 'Hosni Mubarak Sentenced to Three Years in Prison', *Guardian*, 9 May 2015, https://www.theguardian.com/world/2015/may/09/egypt-hosni-mubarak-sentenced-to-three-years-in-prison.

70. Sudarsan Raghavan and Heba Mahfouz, 'Egypt's Mubarak Freed from Detention Six Years after His Overthrow', *Washington Post*, 24 March 2017, https://www.washingtonpost.com/world/six-year-after-his-overthrow-egypts-mubarak-is-freed-from-detention/2017/03/24/f5c311e4-f1e8-4894-99c2-ca7fdaa87972_story.html.

71. Auf, 'The State of Emergency in Egypt'.

72. Nathan J. Brown, 'Post-revolutionary al-Azhar', *The Carnegie Papers: Carnegie Endowment for International Peace*, September 2011, https://carnegieendowment.org/files/al_azhar.pdf.

73. Ahmed al-Tayeb, 'Al-Azhar Document', 20 June 2011.

74. 'Rewards for Justice', Bureau of Diplomatic Security, US Department of State, https://www.state.gov/rewards-for-justice/.

75. 'United States: 1984 Act to Combat International Terrorism', *International Legal Materials* 24, no. 4 (1985), 1015–18.

76. 'Rewards for Justice Program', US Department of State Archive, https:// 2001-2009.state.gov/m/ds/terrorism/c8651.htm.

77. Miniter, *Mastermind*, 5.

78. Patricia Davis and Maria Glod, 'CIA Shooter Kasi, Harbinger of Terror, Set to Die Tonight', *Washington Post*, 14 November 2002.

79. Vanessa Barford and Virginia Brown, 'Do Rewards Help Capture the World's Most Wanted Men?', *BBC News*, 25 August 2011, https://www.bbc.co.uk/news/magazine-14666182.

80. John Roth, Douglas Greenburg and Serena Wille, 'National Commission on Terrorist Attacks upon the United States: Monograph on Terrorist Financing', *Staff Report to the 9/11 Commission*, 2004, 7, https://www.hsdl.org/?abstract&did=449287.

81. Nicholas Schmidle, 'Getting bin Laden', *New Yorker*, 1 August 2011, https://www.newyorker.com/magazine/2011/08/08/getting-bin-laden.

82. Leon Panetta, author interview, 8 April 2022.

83. Ibid.

84. US official, author interview, 27 September 2016.

85. Leon Panetta, author interview, 8 April 2022.

86. Elisabeth Bumiller, Carlotta Gall, and Salman Masood, 'Bin Laden's Secret Life in a Diminished World', *New York Times*, 7 May 2011, https://www.nytimes.com/2011/05/08/world/asia/08binladen.html

87. Leon Panetta, author interview, 8 April 2022.

88. US intelligence official, author interview, 6 September 2014.

89. Bob Woodward, 'Death of Osama bin Laden: Phone Call Pointed U.S. to Compound—and to the Pacer', *Washington Post*, 6 May 2011.

90. Garrett Graff, 'I'd Never Been Involved in Anything as Secret as This', *Politico*, 30 April 2021, https://www.politico.com/news/magazine/2021/04/30/osama-bin-laden-death-white-house-oral-history-484793.

91. Leon Panetta, author interview, 8 April 2022.

92. US Special Forces official, author interview, 11 February 2015.

93. Robert O'Neill, *The Operator* (London: Simon & Schuster, 2017), eBook.

94. Ibid.

95. Ibid.

96. Robert Windrem, 'Potential al Qaeda Leaders Eliminated since bin Laden Raid', *NBC News*, 26 February 2014, https://www.nbcnews.com/news/investigations/six-potential-al-qaeda-leaders-eliminated-bin-laden-raid-n38171.

97. Martin Fletcher and Ruth Gledhill, 'We Followed Islamic Rules and Eased Him into the Sea, Says US', *Times*, 3 May 2011.

98. Marc Ambinder, 'The Little-Known Agency That Helped Kill bin Laden', *Atlantic*, 5 May 2011.

99. US Defense official, author interview, 10 May 2015.

100. Douglas London, author interview, 18 December 2020.

101. Sajjan Gohel, *Paula Zahn Now*, CNN, 29 September 2003; Sajjan Gohel, *Newsnight with Aaron Brown. CNN*, 18 July 2005; Sajjan Gohel, 'Creating a

Haven for al Qaeda', *ABC News,* 14 April 2009, https://abcnews.go.com/International/story?id=4067247.

102. Henry Crumpton, author interview, 18 December 2020.

103. S. Khan, 'The Forgotten Case of the bin Laden Doctor', *Deutsche Welle,* 16 November 2017, https://p.dw.com/p/2njWf.

104. Catriona Luke, 'What Did Musharraf Know?', *New Statesman,* 10 May 2011, https://www.newstatesman.com/blogs/the-staggers/2011/05/pakistan-musharraf-military.

105. James Brandon, 'Al-Qa'ida's Involvement in Britain's Homegrown Terrorist Plots', *CTC Sentinel,* 2, no. 3 (March 2009), https://ctc.usma.edu/al-qaidas-involvement-in-britains-homegrown-terrorist-plots/.

106. US intelligence official, author interview, 6 September 2014.

107. US intelligence official, author interview, 27 September 2016; Bruce Riedel, author interview, 25 November 2019.

108. Amrullah Saleh, author interview, 5 October 2011.

109. Pervez Musharraf, *In the Line of Fire* (London: Simon & Schuster, 2006), 258.

110. 'Ayman al-Zawahiri, letter to Abu Musab al-Zarqawi'.

111. Leon Panetta, author interview, 8 April 2022.

112. Ahmed Rashid, *Pakistan on the Brink: The Future of America, Pakistan, and Afghanistan* (New York: Penguin, 2012), 1–22.

113. P. Scott Thorlin, author interview, 12 December 2017.

114. US security official, author interview, 20 April 2019.

115. Amir Mir, 'New al-Qaeda Chief in North Waziristan', *News,* 20 May 2011.

116. Gall, 'Pakistani Militant Chief Is Reported Dead'; Mark Magnier, 'Top al Qaeda–Linked Militant Reportedly Killed by Drone Attack in Pakistan', *Los Angeles Times,* 5 June 2011, https://www.latimes.com/world/la-xpm-2011-jun-05-la-fg-pakistan-qaeda-leader-20110605-story.html.

117. Ayman al-Zawhiri, 'The Noble Knight Dismounted', *as-Sahab Media,* 8 June 2011.

118. Ibid.

119. Ibid.

120. Ibid.

121. Ibid.

122. Jytte Klausen, *Western Jihadism: A Thirty-Year History* (London: Oxford University Press, 2021), 29.

123. 'Ayman al-Zawahiri Appointed as al-Qaeda Leader', *BBC News,* 16 June 2011, https://www.bbc.co.uk/news/av/world-middle-east-13789617.

124. 'AQIM Swears Allegiance to New al-Qaeda Leader Ayman al-Zawahiri', *Middle East Media Research Institute (MEMRI),* 8 July 2011.

125. Matthew Cole and Rym Momtaz, 'Al Qaeda Leader in Yemen Pledges Allegiance to Zawahiri', *ABC News,* 26 July 2011.

126. 'Sadness, Containment and Aspiration', *AQAP Inspire Magazine,* no. 6 (2011).

127. Lahoud, *The bin Laden Papers,* '1, The Birth of the Idea'.

128. Al-Zawahiri, 'Why This Letter?'.

129. 'Letter to Azmarai', Harmony Document—SOCOM-2012-0000006, *Combating Terrorism Center at West Point*, December 2010, https://ctc.usma. edu/harmony-program/letter-to-azmarai-original-language-2/.

130. 'Letter from Usama bin Laden to Mukhtar Abu al-Zubayr', Harmony Document—SOCOM-2012-0000005, *Combating Terrorism Center at West Point*, 7 August 2010, https://ctc.usma.edu/harmony-program/letter-from-usama-bin-laden-to-mukhtar-abu-al-zubayr-original-language-2/.

131. 'A Glad Tiding from Sheikhs Abu al Zubayr and Ayman al-Zawahiri', as-Sahab Media, 9 February 2012.

132. Carlos Igualada and Javier Yagüe, 'The Use of *Bay'ah* by the Main Salafi-Jihadist Groups', *Perspectives on Terrorism* 15, no. 1 (2021).

133. Ibid.

134. Author's assessment of various *ba'yahs* made by jihadists to al-Zawahiri.

135. Cruickshank, 'Bin Laden Documents'.

136. 'Letter to Azmarai', 1.

137. Ibid., 2.

138. Ibid.

139. Elena Mastors, *Breaking al-Qaeda: Psychological and Operational Techniques* (Boca Raton, FL: CRC Press, 2014), 187–88.

140. Soufan, *Anatomy of Terror*.

141. Cruickshank, 'Bin Laden Documents'.

142. 'Letter to Azmarai', 1.

143. Ibid, 2.

144. Ibid, 3.

145. 'Addendum to the Report of the Islamic Maghreb', *Bin Laden's Bookshelf*, Office of the Director of National Intelligence, 19 January 2017, 5, https://www.dni.gov/files/documents/ubl2017/english/Addendum%20to%20 the%20report%20of%20the%20Islamic%20Maghreb.pdf.

146. Ibid, 4.

147. Ibid, 8.

148. Ibid.

149. Letter to 'Atiyatullah al-Libi about Saudi Arabia Scholars', Harmony Document—SOCOM-2012-0000014, *Combating Terrorism Center at West Point*, January 2007, https://ctc.usma.edu/harmony-program/letter-to-atiy atullah-al-libi-about-saudi-arabia-scholars-original-language-2/.

150. Ibid.

151. Ibid.

152. 'Treasury Targets Key al-Qa'ida Funding and Support Network Using Iran as a Critical Transit Point', press release, US Department of the Treasury, 28 July 2011, https://www.treasury.gov/press-center/press-releases/pages/tg1261.aspx.

153. 'Atiyah's Letter to Zarqawi', *Combating Terrorism Center at West Point*, October 2013, https://ctc.usma.edu/harmony-program/atiyahs-letter-to-zarqawi-original-language-2/.

154. 'Abid Naseer Trial Abbottabad Documents', US Department of Justice. 15 February 2015.

155. Ibid.

156. Nick Schifrin, Pierre Thomas, and Jake Tapper, 'Al Qaeda No. 2 Atiyah Abd al-Rahman Killed in Pakistan', *ABC News*, 27 August 2011.

157. 'Letter from Adam Gadahn', Harmony Document—SOCOM-2012-00000004, *Combating Terrorism Center at West Point*, January 2011, 1, https://ctc.usma.edu/harmony-program/letter-from-adam-gadahn-original-language-2/.

158. 'A Draft of Zawahiri's Message to the Egyptians', *Combating Terrorism Center at West Point*, October 2013, https://ctc.usma.edu/harmony-program/a-draft-of-zawahiris-message-to-the-egyptians-original-language-2/.

159. 'Letter Providing Direction', 1.

160. Ibid., 2.

161. 'Letter to Abu-Musa'b 'Abd-al-Wadud', *Bin Laden's Bookshelf*, Office of the Director of National Intelligence, 19 January 2017, 4, https://www.dni.gov/files/documents/ubl2017/english/Letter%20to%20Abu-Musa%20b%20Abd-al-Wadud.pdf.

162. 'Our Honorable Shaykh', *Bin Laden's Bookshelf*, Office of the Director of National Intelligence, 1 March 2016, 12.

163. 'Terror Franchise', 12.

164. Al-Zawahiri, 'Why This Letter?', 3.

165. Ibid., 4.

166. 'Letter to Azmarai', 3.

167. 'Letter Regarding al-Qa'ida Strategy', Harmony Document—SOCOM-2012-00000017, *Combating Terrorism Center at West Point*, Date Unknown, 2.

168. Ibid.

169. Ibid., 3.

170. Ibid., 5.

171. 'Letter from Adam Gadahn', 2.

172. William McCants, 'The Believer: How an Introvert with a Passion for Religion and Soccer became Abu Bakr al-Baghdadi, Leader of the Islamic State', Brookings Institution, 1 September 2015, http://csweb.brookings.edu/content/research/essays/2015/thebeliever.html.

173. Fawaz A. Gerges, *ISIS: A History* (Princeton, NJ: Princeton University Press, 2016), 129–43.

174. Martin Chulov, 'ISIS: The Inside Story', *Guardian*, 11 December 2014, https://www.theguardian.com/world/2014/dec/11/-sp-isis-the-inside-story.

175. McCants, 'The Believer'.

176. Ibid.

177. Benson Bobrick, *The Caliph's Splendor: Islam and the West in the Golden Age of Baghdad* (London: Simon & Schuster, 2012), 165.

178. Cole Bunzel, 'Al-Qaeda's Quasi-Caliph: The Recasting of Mullah 'Umar', *Jihadica*, 23 July 2014, http://www.jihadica.com/al-qaeda%E2%80%99s-quasi-caliph-the-recasting-of-mullah-%E2%80%98umar/.

179. 'The Jihadi Threat: ISIS, al-Qaeda and Beyond', *U.S. Institute of Peace &Wilson Center*, December 2016 / January 2017.
180. William McCants, 'How Zawahiri Lost al Qaeda: Global Jihad Turns on Itself', *Foreign Affairs*, 19 November 2013, https://www.foreignaffairs.com/articles/north-africa/2013-11-19/how-zawahiri-lost-al-qaeda.
181. Soufan, *Anatomy of Terror*.
182. Ayman al-Zawahiri, 'General Guidelines for Jihad', *as-Sahab Media*, 14 September 2013.
183. Ibid.
184. Pieter Van Ostaeyen, author interview, 29 April 2021.
185. Gohel, 'Deciphering Ayman al-Zawahiri and al-Qaeda's Strategic and Ideological Imperatives'.
186. Ibid.
187. Hamming, *Jihadi Politics*, '7, Expanding the Caliphate and al-Qaida's Response'.
188. Scott-Clark and Levy, *The Exile*, 477.
189. Pieter Van Ostaeyen, author interview, 29 April 2021.
190. Alkhshali Hamdi, Barbara Starr and Greg Botelho, 'Al Qaeda Leader, Somali-Based Terror Group Present New Messages', *CNN*, 22 April 2014, https://edition.cnn.com/2014/04/18/world/terrorist-messages-surface/index.html.
191. Pieter Van Ostaeyen, author interview, 29 April 2021.
192. Iraqi security official, author interview, 15 July 2019.
193. 'Syria Suicide Bombers Kill al-Qaeda Rebel Leader in Aleppo', *Associated Press*, 23 February 2014.
194. Soufan, *Anatomy of Terror*.
195. Spanish security officials, author interview, 15 August 2014.
196. 'Syria Suicide Bombers Kill al-Qaeda Rebel Leader in Aleppo'.
197. US security official, author interview, 20 April 2019.
198. Pieter Van Ostaeyen, author interview, 29 April 2021.
199. Ibid.
200. Ibid.
201. US official, author interview, 14 February 2017.
202. Ibid.
203. Ayman al-Zawahiri, 'Exit from the Circle of Inefficiency and Failure', *as-Sahab Media*, February 2014.
204. Ayman al-Zawahiri quoted in Kyle Orton, 'Al-Qaeda Provides Evidence ISIS Was Its Iraqi Branch, Calls for It to Return', *Kyle Orton's Blog*, 3 May 2014, https://kyleorton.co.uk/2014/05/03/al-qaeda-provides-evidence-isis-was-its-iraqi-branch-calls-for-it-to-return/#more-3785.
205. Abu Ayyad al-Tunisi, 'Inspired by the Conquests of Iraq', *al-Bayyariq Media*, 13 June 2014.
206. Ibid.
207. Ayman al-Zawahiri, 'ISIS Is No Longer Part of al Qaeda', *as-Sahab Media*, 3 February 2014.
208. Igualada and Yagüe, 'The Use of *Bay'ah* by the Main Salafi-Jihadist Groups'.
209. Zelin, *Your Sons Are at Your Service*, 193–94.

210. Ibid.

211. Abu Ayyad al-Tunisi, 'Answer to the Essay of Abu Maysarah al-Shami: Letters to Dr. Ayman al- Zawahiri', *Hidayah Media*, 6 January 2016.

212. 'Letter from UBL to 'Atiyatullah al-Libi 4', Harmony Document—SOCOM-2012-0000019, *Combating Terrorism Center at West Point*, May 2010, 2, https://ctc.usma.edu/harmony-program/letter-from-ubl-to-atiyatullah-al-libi-4-original-language-2/.

213. Sami Yousafzai and Sam Seibert, 'ISIS vs. the Taliban: The Battle for Hearts and Minds', *Vocativ*, 5 November 2014, https://www.vocativ.com/world/afghanistan-world/isis-vs-taliban/.

214. Ayman al-Zawahiri, 'The Islamic Spring, Part 1', *as-Sahab Media*, 9 September 2015; Ayman al-Zawahiri, 'The Islamic Spring, Part 2', *as-Sahab Media*, 12 September 2015; Ayman al-Zawahiri, 'The Islamic Spring, Part 3', *as-Sahab Media*, 21 September 2015; Ayman al-Zawahiri, 'The Islamic Spring, Part 4', *as-Sahab Media*, 5 October 2015; Ayman al-Zawahiri, 'The Islamic Spring, Part 5', *as-Sahab Media*, 6 October 2015; Ayman al-Zawahiri, 'The Islamic Spring, Part 6', *as-Sahab Media*, 9 October 2015.

215. Al-Zawahiri, 'The Islamic Spring, Part 1'.

216. Ibid.

217. Bruce Hoffman, author interview, 11 December 2019.

218. Pieter Van Ostaeyen, author interview, 29 April 2021.

219. Scott-Clark and Levy, *The Exile*, 136.

CHAPTER 7

1. Vahid Brown, 'The Façade of Allegiance: Bin Ladin's Dubious Pledge to Mullah Omar', *CTC Sentinel* 3, no. 1 (2010), https://ctc.usma.edu/the-facade-of-allegiance-bin-ladins-dubious-pledge-to-mullah-omar/.

2. Vahid Brown, 'Cracks in the Foundation: Leadership Schisms in al-Qa'ida 1989–2006', *Combating Terrorism Center at West Point* (September 2007), https://www.ctc.usma.edu/posts/cracks-in-the-foundation-leadership-schisms-in-al-qaida-from-1989-2006.

3. 'O Victorious Ummah, Carry Your Arms, Wage Jihad, and Rejoice', *an-Nafir*, 20 July 2014, Jihadology, https://jihadology.net/wp-content/uploads/_pda/2014/07/al-qc481_idah-22al-nafc4abr-122-en.pdf.

4. Ayman al-Zawahiri, 'Al Qaeda Leader Announces Formation of Indian Branch', As-Sahab Media, 3 September 2014.

5. Abdul Basit, 'Asim Umar—New Kid on the Block? *Counter Terrorist Trends and Analysis*', *RSIS* 6, no. 10 (November 2014), 11.

6. Ibid.

7. C. Christine Fair, 'The Foreign Policy Essay: Al Qaeda's Re-launch in South Asia', *Lawfare*, 21 September 2014.

8. Fair, 'The Foreign Policy Essay'.

9. Basit, 'Asim Umar'.

10. Mujib Mashal, Taimoor Shah, and Zahra Nader, 'Taliban Name Lesser-Known Cleric as Their New Leader', *New York Times*, 25 May 2016.

11. Farhan Zahid, 'Death of AQIS Emir Asim Umar Has Serious Implications for al-Qaeda', *Jamestown Terrorism Monitor* 17, no. 20 (2014): 6.

12. Ibid.

13. Usama Mahmoud, 'Targeting of American and Indian Navies', *as-Sahab Media*, 27 September 2014.

14. Bruce Riedel, author interview, 25 November 2019.

15. Mahmoud, 'Targeting of American and Indian Navies'.

16. Zahid, 'Death of AQIS Emir Asim Umar Has Serious Implications for al-Qaeda'.

17. Hannah Byrne, John Krzyzaniak and Qasim Khan, 'The Death of Mullah Omar and the Rise of ISIS in Afghanistan', *Institute for the Study of War*, 17 August 2015, http://www.understandingwar.org/backgrounder/death-mullah-omar-and-rise-isis-afghanistan.

18. Nick Paton Walsh, Peter Bergen, and Jason Hanna, 'Taliban's Mullah Omar Died in 2013, Afghan Government Says', *CNN*, 30 July 2015, http://edition.cnn.com/2015/07/29/asia/afghanistan-mullah-omar; Bruce Riedel, 'Where in the World Is al-Qaida's Leader?', *Markaz Blog, Brookings Institution*, 10 August 2015, https://www.brookings.edu/blog/markaz/2015/08/10/where-in-the-world-is-al-qaidas-leader.

19. J.J. Green, 'Al Qaida's Ayman al Zawahiri: Dead, Duplicitous or Oblivious?', *WTOP*, 10 August 2015.

20. Riedel, 'Where in the World Is al-Qaida's Leader?'.

21. Ayman al-Zawahiri, 'Zawahiri Pledges Allegiance to New Afghan Taliban Leader in Audio Speech', *SITE Intelligence Group*, 13 August 2015, https://news.siteintelgroup.com/Jihadist-News/zawahiri-pledges-allegiance-to-new-afghan-taliban-leader-in-audio-speech.html.

22. Bill Roggio and Thomas Joscelyn, 'New Taliban Emir Accepts al Qaeda's Oath of Allegiance', *Long War Journal*, 14 August 2015, http://www.longwarjournal.org/archives/2015/08/new-taliban-emir-accepts-al-qaedas-oath-of-allegiance.php.

23. 'Taliban Admit Covering Up Death of Mullah Omar'. BBC News, 31 August 2015, http://www.bbc.co.uk/news/world-asia-34105565.

24. Roy and Hamming, 'Al-Zawahiri's *Bay'a* to Mullah Mansoor: A Bitter Pill but a Bountiful Harvest'.

25. Merieme Arif, 'Al Qaeda's al-Zawahiri Purportedly Pledges Allegiance to New Taliban Chief', *CNN*, 11 June 2016, http://edition.cnn.com/2016/06/11/middleeast/al-qaeda-taliban-allegiance/.

26. Ayman al-Zawahiri, 'We Shall Fight You until There Is No More Persecution', *as-Sahab Media*, 5 October 2017.

27. Ayman al-Zawahiri, 'Brief Messages to a Victorious Ummah, Part 2—and Be Not Divided Among Yourselves', *as-Sahab Media*, 21 August 2016.

28. Mujib Mashal, 'Haqqanis Steering Deadlier Taliban in Afghanistan, Officials Say', *New York Times,* 7 May 2016.

29. Vahid Brown and Don Rassler, *Fountainhead of Jihad: The Haqqani Nexus, 1973–2012* (Oxford: Oxford University Press, 2013), 197

30. Al-Zawahiri, 'Brief Messages to a Victorious Ummah, Part 4'.

31. Ibid.

32. Ibid.

33. M. E. McMillan, *Fathers and Sons: The Rise and Fall of Political Dynasty in the Middle East* (New York: Palgrave Macmillan, 2013) 9–17.

34. Sam Heller, 'Al-Qa'ida's Ayman al-Zawahiri Plays Politics', *Gandhara RFE/RL,* 20 May 2016, http://www.rferl.org/a/al-qaeda-al-zawahri-plays-polit ics/27746829.html.

35. Cameron Glenn, 'Al Qaeda v ISIS: Ideology & Strategy', *Woodrow Wilson International Center for Scholars,* 28 September 2015. https://www.wilsoncen ter.org/article/al-qaeda-v-isis-ideology-strategy.

36. Ayman al-Zawahiri, 'Brief Messages to a Victorious Ummah, Part 5—to Other Than Allah We Will Not Bow', *as-Sahab Media,* 5 January 2017.

37. Ibid.

38. Ayman al-Zawahiri, 'Hasten to Syria', *as-Sahab Media* 8 May 2016.

39. Al-Zawahiri, 'Brief Messages to a Victorious Ummah, Part 5'.

40. Ayman al-Zawahiri, 'Brief Messages to a Victorious Ummah, Part 3—Allah, Allah in Iraq', *as-Sahab Media,* 25 July 2016.

41. Ayman al-Zawahiri, 'The Defiers of Injustice', *as-Sahab Media,* 9 September 2016.

42. Benjamin Haas and Daniel McGrory, 'Al-Qa'ida Seeking to Recruit African American Muslims', *CTC Sentinel* 1, no. 8 (2008).

43. 'Nusra Leader: Our Mission Is to Defeat Syrian Regime', al-Jazeera, 28 May 2015, http://www.aljazeera.com/news/2015/05/nusra-front-golani-assad-syria-hezbollah-isil-150528044857528.html.

44. Gohel, 'Deciphering Ayman al-Zawahiri and al-Qaeda's Strategic and Ideological Imperatives'.

45. Ayman al-Zawahiri, 'March Forth to Syria', *as-Sahab,* 8 May 2016.

46. Douglas London, author interview, 18 December 2020; Daveed Gartenstein-Ross and Thomas Joscelyn, 'Rebranding Terror', *Foreign Affairs,* 28 August 2016, https://www.foreignaffairs.com/articles/middle-east/2016-08-28/reb randing-terror.

47. 'Statement by Pentagon Press Secretary Peter Cook on Strike against al-Qaeda Leader', US Department of Defense, 3 October 2016, https://www.defense.gov/News/Releases/Release/Article/962767/statement-by-penta gon-press-secretary-peter-cook-on-strike-against-al-qaeda-lea/.

48. Mattisan Rowan, 'Al Qaeda's Latest Rebranding: Hay'at Tahrir al Sham', *Wilson Center,* 24 April 2017, https://www.wilsoncenter.org/article/al-qae das-latest-rebranding-hayat-tahrir-al-sham.

49. Katherine Zimmerman, 'Al-Qaeda's Strengthening in the Shadows', testimony to the Subcommittee on Counterterrorism and Intelligence, Committee on Homeland Security, US House of Representatives, 13 July 2017, https://www.aei.org/research-products/speech/testimony-al-qaedas-strengthening-in-the-shadows/.

50. Hoffman Bruce, 'Al-Qaeda's Resurrection', *Council on Foreign Relations,* 6 March 2018, https://www.cfr.org/expert-brief/al-qaedas-resurrection.

51. Huda al-Saleh, 'From Iran to al-Qaeda: How Hamza bin Laden's future was secured', *al-Arabiya,* 4 October 2016, https://english.alarabiya.net/en/perspect ive/analysis/2016/10/04/From-Iran-to-al-Qaeda-How-Osama-bin-Laden-secured-son-s-future.html.

52. Al-Saleh, 'From Iran to al-Qaeda'.

53. Martin Chulov, 'Hamza bin Laden Has Married Daughter of Lead 9/11 Hijacker, Say Family', *Guardian,* 5 August 2018, https://www.theguardian. com/world/2018/aug/05/hamza-bin-laden-marries-daughter-of-911-hijac ker-mohammed-atta.

54. 'Bin Laden's Son, Ayman al-Zawahiri Make Joint Threats', *Asharq al-Awsat,* 16 May 2016, http://english.aawsat.com/2016/05/article55350894/bin-ladens-son-ayman-al-zawahiri-make-threats-together.

55. al-Saleh, 'From Iran to al-Qaeda'.

56. Chulov, 'Hamza bin Laden Has Married Daughter of Lead 9/11 Hijacker, Say Family.'

57. Bruce Riedel, 'The Son Speaks: Al-Qaida's New Face', *Markaz Blog, Brookings Institution,* 19 August 2015, https://www.brookings.edu/blog/markaz/2015/ 08/19/the-son-speaks-al-qaidas-new-face.

58. Patrick Wintour, 'Osama bin Laden's Son Vows to Avenge al-Qaida Leader's Death', *Guardian,* 11 July 2016, https://www.theguardian.com/world/2016/ jul/11/osama-bin-ladens-son-vows-to-avenge-al-qaida-leaders-death-video.

59. Russell Goldman, 'U.S. Lists bin Laden's Son as a Global Terrorist', *New York Times,* 5 January 2017, https://www.nytimes.com/2017/01/05/world/mid dleeast/bin-laden-son-terrorist-list.html?_r=0.

60. Thomas Joscelyn, 'Analysis: Osama bin Laden's Son Praises al Qaeda's Branches in New Message', *Long War Journal,* 17 August 2015, https://www. longwarjournal.org/archives/2015/08/osama-bin-ladens-son-praises-alqa eda-branches-in-new-message.php; 'Osama bin Laden's Son Urges Attacks on the West', CNN, 14 August 2015, https://edition.cnn.com/videos/us/2015/ 08/14/osama-bin-laden-son-hamza-bin-laden-todd-dnt-tsr.cnn.

61. 'Hamza bin Laden Highlights Historical Saudi Collusion with British in Speech Inciting Regime Overthrow', *SITE Intelligence Group,* 20 May 2017.

62. US security officials, author interview, 16 September 2019.

63. US security official, author interview, 20 November 2019.

64. Max Burman, 'Trump Confirms Osama bin Laden's Son Hamza Killed in U.S. Operation', *NBC News,* 14 September 2019.

65. US security officials, author interview, 16 September 2019.

66. *One Ummah* magazine, 11 September 2019.

67. Eyal Tsir Cohen and Eliora Katz, 'What We Can Learn about US Intelligence from the Baghdadi Raid', *Brookings Institution*, 6 November 2019, https://www.brookings.edu/blog/order-from-chaos/2019/11/06/what-we-can-learn-about-us-intelligence-from-the-baghdadi-raid/.

68. Bruce Riedel, author interview, 25 November 25, 2019.

69. Bruce Hoffman, author interview, 11 December 2019.

70. Al-Zawahiri, 'America Is the First Enemy of Muslims '.

71. Ibid.

72. Al-Zawahiri, 'How to Confront America?'.

73. Ayman al-Zawahiri, 'Tel Aviv Is Also a Land of Muslims', *as-Sahab Media,* 13 May 2018.

74. Ayman al-Zawahiri, 'The Deal of the Century or the Crusade of the Century, Part 1', *as-Sahab Media*, 11 September 2020.

75. Ibid.

76. Ibid.

77. Ibid.

78. Ibid.

79. Ibid.

80. Dan Ephron, 'How Arab Ties with Israel Became the Middle East's New Normal', *Foreign Policy*, 21 December 2020, https://foreignpolicy.com/2020/12/21/arab-ties-israel-diplomacy-normalization-middle-east/.

81. 'Covert Israeli-Saudi Meeting Sends Biden a Strong Message on Iran', Reuters, 27 November 2020, https://www.reuters.com/article/uk-israel-saudi-analysis/analysis-covert-israeli-saudi-meeting-sends-biden-a-strong-message-on-iran-idUKKBN28714Q.

82. Ellen Nakashima, 'Israel, at Behest of U.S., Killed al-Qaeda's Deputy in a Drive-By Attack in Iran', *Washington Post,* 14 November 2020.

83. Mir and Clarke, 'Making Sense of Iran and al-Qaeda's Relationship'.

84. Cole Bunzel, 'Why Are al Qaeda Leaders in Iran?', *Foreign Affairs,* 11 February 2021, https://www.foreignaffairs.com/articles/afghanistan/2021-02-11/why-are-al-qaeda-leaders-iran.

85. Osama bin Laden, 'Letter to Karim, October 18, 2007', *Bin Laden's Bookshelf*, Office of the Director of National Intelligence, 1 March 2016, https://www.dni.gov/files/documents/ubl2016/english/Letter%20to%20Karim.pdf.

86. Jerrold Post, author interview, 10 December 2016.

87. Mir and Clarke, 'Making Sense of Iran and al-Qaeda's Relationship'.

88. Oubai Shahbandar, 'How Iran Serves as "a Key Geographic Hub for al-Qaeda"', *Arab News*, 9 February 2021, https://arab.news/5y8ns.

89. 'Letter regarding Working in Islamic Countries', 4.

90. Diplomatic Security Service official, author interview, 1 May 2020.

91. Reuven Paz, author interview, 9 October 2013.

92. Diplomatic Security Service official, author interview, 1 May 2020.

93. Tore Hamming, 'Al-Qaeda after Ayman al-Zawahiri', *Lawfare*, 11 April 2021, https://www.lawfareblog.com/al-qaeda-after-ayman-al-zawahiri.

94. 'Bin Laden's Men in Tehran . . . Iran Heavily Indebted to al-Qaeda', *Asharq al-Awsat*, 4 January 2016, http://english.aawsat.com/2016/01/article55346170/bin-ladens-men-in-tehran-iran-heavily-indebted-to-al-qaeda.

95. Abu Muhammad al-Adnani, 'ISI Spokesman Stresses Continuity of Group's Mission', *SITE Intelligence Group*, 8 August 2011, https://ent.siteintelgroup.com/Latest-Multimedia-from-Islamic-State-of-Iraq-ISI/isi-spokesman-stresses-continuity-of-groups-mission.html; Robin Wright, 'Abu Muhammad al-Adnani, the Voice of ISIS, Is Dead', *New Yorker*, 30 August 2016, http://www.newyorker.com/news/news-desk/abu-muhammad-al-adnani-the-voice-of-isis-is-dead.

96. US security official, author interview, 20 April 2019.

97. Hoffman, 'The Evolving Terrorist Threat and CT Options for the Trump Administration', 13.

98. Bunzel, 'Why Are al Qaeda Leaders in Iran?'.

99. 'Muhammad Abbatay ('Abd al-Rahman al-Maghrebi)', *Rewards for Justice*, 24 March 2021, https://rewardsforjustice.net/english/muhammad_abbatay.html.

100. Ibid.

101. Al-Zawahiri, 'Brief Messages to a Victorious Ummah, Part 3'.

102. Ibid.

103. Al-Zawahiri, 'General Guidelines for Jihad'.

104. Borzou Daragahi, Andrew Buncombe, Bel Trew, and Richard Hall, 'Qassem Soleimani: Iran Vows "Harsh Vengeance" after Top General Killed in US Airstrike', *Independent, 3* January 2020, https://www.independent.co.uk/news/world/middle-east/trump-airstrike-iran-general-qassem-soleimani-war-bagdad-airport-a9268511.html.

105. Maysam Behravesh, 'Iran's Unconventional Alliance Network in the Middle East and Beyond', *Middle East Institute*, 7 April 2020.

106. 'Jalaluddin Haqqani, Founder of Afghan Militant Network, Dies', BBC News, 4 September 2018, https://www.bbc.co.uk/news/world-asia-45404817

107. US intelligence official, 18 May 2021.

108. Ayman al-Zawahiri, 'Regarding the Capture by the Traitorous Pakistani Army of Families of the Emigrant Mujahidin', *as-Sahab Media,* 22 August 2019.

109. US intelligence official, 18 May 2021.

110. Agreement for Bringing Peace to Afghanistan between the Islamic Emirate of Afghanistan Which Is Not Recognized by the United States as a State and Is Known as the Taliban and the United States of America, Doha, Qatar, 29 February 2020. https://www.state.gov/wp-content/uploads/2020/02/Agreement-For-Bringing-Peace-to-Afghanistan-02.29.20.pdf.

111. 'Zalmay Khalilzad on *Face the Nation*', CBS News, 24 October 2021, https://www.cbsnews.com/news/transcript-zalmay-khalilzad-on-face-the-nation-october-24-2021.

112. Joe Walsh, 'Trump Denies Releasing 5,000 Taliban Prisoners—but His Administration Negotiated for Their Release', *Forbes*, 13 September 2021, https://www.forbes.com/sites/joewalsh/2021/09/13/trump-denies-releas ing-5000-taliban-prisoners---but-his-administration-negotiated-for-their-release/?sh=109d807c419b.

113. Sirajuddin Haqqani, 'What We, the Taliban, Want', op-ed, *New York Times*, 20 February 2020, https://www.nytimes.com/2020/02/20/opinion/taliban-afghanistan-war-haqqani.html.

114. UN Analytical Support and Sanctions Monitoring Team. 11th Report of the UN Analytical Support and Sanctions Monitoring Team. S/2020/415, UN Security Council, 27 May 2020.

115. Ibid.

116. Joseph Biden, 'Remarks by President Biden on the Way Forward in Afghanistan', *White House*, 14 April 2021, https://www.whitehouse.gov/brief ing-room/speeches-remarks/2021/04/14/remarks-by-president-biden-on-the-way-forward-in-afghanistan/.

117. Statement by General Mark A. Milley, 20th Chairman of the Joint Chiefs of Staff, *Senate Armed Services Committee Hearing on Afghanistan Withdrawal*, 28 September 2021, https://www.armed-services.senate.gov/download/mille y092821.

118. Biden, 'Remarks by President Biden on the Way Forward in Afghanistan'.

119. Ibid.

120. Harrich, 'The Business with Terror'.

121. Barack Obama, *A Promised Land* (New York, Penguin, 2020), eBook.

122. Biden, 'Remarks by President Biden on the Way Forward in Afghanistan'.

123. Joseph Biden, 'Remarks by President Biden on the Drawdown of U.S. Forces in Afghanistan', *White House*, 8 July 2021, https://www.whitehouse.gov/brief ing-room/speeches-remarks/2021/07/08/remarks-by-president-biden-on-the-drawdown-of-u-s-forces-in-afghanistan/.

124. Eltaf Najafizada, 'Taliban Shootout in Palace Sidelines Leader Who Dealt with US', *Bloomberg*, 17 September 2021, https://www.bloomberg. com/news/articles/2021-09-17/taliban-shootout-in-palace-sidelines-lea der-who-dealt-with-u-s.

125. Leon Panetta, author interview, 8 April 2022.

126. Ibid.

127. Ayman al-Zawahiri, 'Reflections on Political Corruption and its Effects on the History of Muslims', *as-Sahab Media*, 10 September 2021.

128. Ibid.

129. Ayman al-Zawahiri, 'Jerusalem Will Not Be Judaized', *as-Sahab Media*, 11 September 2021.

130. Ibid.

131. Ibid.

132. Ibid.

133. Ibid.

134. Ibid.

135. Ibid.

136. Al-Zawahiri, 'Advice for the United Ummah concerning the Reality of the United Nations'.

137. Ibid.

138. Ibid.

139. Ibid.

140. Ibid.

141. Ibid.

142. Al-Zawahiri, 'The Deal of the Century or the Crusade of the Century, Part 2'.

143. Ibid.

144. Al-Zawahiri, 'The Deal of the Century of the Crusade or the Century, Part 3'.

145. Ibid.

146. Ibid.

147. 2 Sahih Muslim 285.

148. Al-Zawahiri, 'The Deal of the Century or the Crusade of the Century, Part 4'.

149. Ibid.

150. Ayman al-Zawahiri, 'The Noble Woman of India', *as-Sahab Media*, 5 April 2022.

151. Ibid.

152. Ibid.

153. Leon Panetta, author interview, 8 April 2022.

154. Najafizada, 'Taliban Shootout in Palace Sidelines Leader Who Dealt with U.S'.

155. David Loyn, 'Punch-Up at the Palace: Why the Taliban Is Tearing Itself Apart', *Spectator*, 20 September 2021, https://www.spectator.co.uk/article/punch-up-at-the-palace-the-bust-up-tearing-the-taliban-apart.

156. US intelligence official, author interview, 26 August 2022.

157. Dexter Filkins, 'For Afghans, a Price for Everything, and Anything for a Price', *New York Times*, 1 January 2009, https://www.nytimes.com/2009/01/01/world/asia/01iht-01kabul.19041046.html.

158. 'Kabul's Poppy Palaces', *GQ Magazine*, 28 July 2014, https://www.gqindia.com/content/kabuls-poppy-palaces.

159. US official, author interview, 16 August 2022.

160. Ibid.

161. Ibid.

162. Andrew North, 'Afghanistan's Graveyard of Foreigners', *BBC News*, 9 June 2012, https://www.bbc.co.uk/news/magazine-18369101.

163. US intelligence official, author interview, 4 August 2022.

164. Ibid.

165. Ibid.

166. US Defense official, author interview, 20 August 2022.

167. Charlie Savage, Eric Schmitt, Azmat Khan, Evan Hill and Christoph Koettl, 'Newly Declassified Video Shows U.S. Killing of 10 Civilians in Drone Strike', *New York Times*, 19 January 2022, https://www.nytimes.com/2022/01/19/us/politics/afghanistan-drone-strike-video.html.

168. Gordon Lubold and Warren P. Strobel, 'Secret U.S. Missile Aims to Kill Only Terrorists, Not Nearby Civilians', *Wall Street Journal, 9 May* 2019, https://www.wsj.com/articles/secret-u-s-missile-aims-to-kill-only-terrorists-not-nearby-civilians-11557403411.

169. James Zumwalt, 'The Unique Weapon That Took Out Soleimani', *Hill*, 20 February 2020, https://thehill.com/opinion/national-security/483393-the-unique-weapon-that-took-out-soleimani/.

170. US intelligence official, author interview, 15 August 2022.

171. 'Al Qaeda Leader Ayman al-Zawahiri Killed in Drone Strike, Biden Says', CBS News, 2 August 2022, https://www.cbsnews.com/live-updates/ayman-al-zawahiri-al-qaeda-terrorist-leader-killed-drone-biden/.

172. US intelligence official, author interview, 28 August 2022; British counter-terrorism official, author interview, 31 August 2022.

173. Debusmann and Partridge, 'Ayman al-Zawahiri'.

174. Joseph Biden, 'Remarks by President Biden on a Successful Counterterrorism Operation in Afghanistan', *White House*, 1 August 2022, https://www.whiteho use.gov/briefing-room/speeches-remarks/2022/08/01/remarks-by-presid ent-biden-on-a-successful-counterterrorism-operation-in-afghanistan/.

175. Antony J. Blinken, 'The Death of Ayman al-Zawahiri', *State Department*, 1 August 2022, https://www.state.gov/the-death-of-ayman-al-zawahiri.

176. 'Declaration of the Islamic Emirate on the Claim of US President Joe Biden', Islamic Emirate of Afghanistan Statement, 4 August 2022.

177. 'Taliban Say They've Not Found Body of al Qaeda Leader', Reuters, 25 August 2022, https://www.reuters.com/world/asia-pacific/taliban-say-the yve-not-found-body-al-qaeda-leader-2022-08-25/.

CONCLUSION: 55 YEARS OF TERROR

1. Bruce Hoffman, author interview, 11 December 2019.

2. Bruce Riedel, author interview, 25 November 2019; Bruce Hoffman, author interview, 11 December 2019.

3. Bruce Hoffman, author interview, 11 December 2019; Mitchell Silber, author interview, 17 December 2020.

4. Zimmerman, 'Al-Qaeda's Strengthening in the Shadows'.

5. Aaron Zelin, author interview, January 21, 2022.

6. 12th Report of the UN Analytical Support and Sanctions Monitoring Team, S/2021/486, *UN Security Council*, 28 April 2021.

7. Douglas London, author interview, 18 December 2020.

8. Al-Zawahiri, 'Brief Messages to a Victorious Ummah, Part 5'.

9. Joseph Votel, author interview, 28 April 2021.

10. Chris Alexander, author interview, 6 May 2021.

11. Al-Zawahiri, *Knights under the Prophet's Banner*.

12. Wright, author interview, 16 January 2022.

Bibliography

PRIMARY SOURCES

'Abid Naseer Trial Abbottabad Documents'. US Department of Justice, 15 February 2015.

'Addendum to the Report of the Islamic Maghreb'. *Bin Laden's Bookshelf.* Office of the Director of National Intelligence, 19 January 2017.

al-Adnani, Abu Muhammad. 'ISI Spokesman Stresses Continuity of Group's Mission'. *SITE Intelligence Group,* 8 August 2011.

'Afghanistan: Jalaluddin Haqqani's Emergence as a Key Taliban Commander'. US Embassy (Islamabad) cable, 7 January 1997. National Security Archive, George Washington University, Washington, DC.

'Afghanistan: Reaction to U.S. Strikes Follows Predicable Lines: Taliban Angry, Their Opponents Support U.S'. US Embassy (Islamabad) cable, 21 August 1998. National Security Archive, George Washington University.

'Afghanistan: Taliban Said to Loosen Grip on Bin Ladin as They Increasingly Turn to Him for Financial Support and Advice'. US Embassy (Islamabad) cable, 12 June 1998. National Security Archive, George Washington University.

'Appropriate Means'. Release of Abbottabad compound material. CIA, November 2017.

'Atiyah's Letter to Zarqawi'. *Combating Terrorism Center at West Point,* October 2013.

'Ayman al-Zawahiri, letter to Abu Musab al-Zarqawi'. Harmony Document. *Combating Terrorism Center at West Point,* 11 October 2005.

Azzam, Abdullah. *The Defence of the Muslim Lands: The First Obligation after Iman.* N.p., 1979.

Azzam, Abdullah. 'From Kabul to Jerusalem'. *Al-Jihad,* no. 52 (1989): 45–49.

Azzam, Abdullah. *Join the Caravan.* N.p., 1987.

Azzam, Abdullah. 'Open Letter to Every Muslim on Earth'. *Al-Jihad,* no. 4 (1985): 22–26.

Azzam, Mahfouz. Interview with Rory Carroll. 'Mahfouz Azzam, Egyptian Great-Uncle and Lawyer of Ayman al-Zawahiri'. *Guardian,* 11 September 2002.

al-Banna, Hasan. 'Da'watuna' [Our call]. *Jaridat al-Ikhwan al-Muslimin,* 1937.

al-Banna, Hasan. *Five Tracts of Hasan al-Banna (1906–1949): A Selection from the Majmu'at Rasa'il al-Imām al-Shahid Hasan al-Banna.* Translated by Charles Wendell. Berkley: University of California Press, 1978.

al-Banna, Hasan. 'Iftitah' [The beginning]. *Al-Nadhir* 1 (30 May 1937): 146.

al-Banna, Hasan. *Majmu'at Rasa'il al-Imam al-Shahid Hasan al-Banna* [The diaries of the martyred Imam Hasan al-Banna]. Cairo: Darul Hadarah al-Islamiyyah, n.d.

al-Banna, Hasan. 'Mushkilatuna fi Daw' an-Nizam al-Islam' [Our problems in the light of the Islamic Order]. In *Majmu'at Rasa'il al-Imam al-Shahid Hasan al-Banna*. Cairo: Dar al-Shabab, n.d.

al-Banna, Hasan. *Nahwa al-Nur* [*The Complete Works*]. Beirut: Al-Risalah, n.d.

al-Banna, Hasan. *Mabadi'wa Usul fi Mu'tamarat Khassah* [Principles and origins in the private conferences]. Cairo: Mu'ssaasah al-Islamiyah li al-Tiba'ah wa al-Nashr, 1979.

al-Banna, Hasan. *Selected Writings of Hasan al-Banna Shaheed*. Translated by S. A. Qureshi. New Delhi: Millat Book Centre, 1999.

Biden, Joseph. 'Remarks by President Biden on a Successful Counterterrorism Operation in Afghanistan'. *White House*, 1 August 2022.

bin Laden, Osama. 'Declaration of Jihad against the Americans Occupying the Land of the Two Holiest Sites'. 1996. Republished by *Combating Terrorism Center at West Point*.

bin Laden, Osama. 'Declaration of the World Islamic Front for Jihad against the Jews and the Crusaders'. *World Islamic Front Statement*, 23 February 1998. Republished by Federation of American Scientists.

bin Laden, Osama. 'Letter to Karim, October 18, 2007'. *Bin Laden's Bookshelf*. Office of the Director of National Intelligence, 1 March 2016.

Blinken, Antony J. 'The Death of Ayman al-Zawahiri'. *State Department*, 1 August 2022.

British Foreign Office—FO 371/8988 E5538/3338/16, 17 May 1923.

British Foreign Office—FO 141/714/3, 3 February 1935.

Cheetham, Milne. 'To His Highness Prince Hussein Kamil Pasha'. Sir Milne Cheetham Collection, Middle East Centre Archive. St Antony's College, University of Oxford, GB 165 0055, 19 December 1914.

Correspondence and Papers relating to the Special Commission in Egypt 1920–1924. Archive of Alfred Milner, Viscount Milner, 1824–1955. Oxford University, Bodleian Library, 29 August 1920.

'Declaration of the Islamic Emirate on the Claim of US President Joe Biden'. Islamic Emirate of Afghanistan Statement, 4 August 2022.

'Deputy Secretary Armitage-Mamoud Phone Call'. US Department of State cable, 18 September 2001. National Security Archive, George Washington University, Washington, DC.

'Deputy Secretary Armitage's Meeting with Pakistan Intel Chief Mahmud: You're Either with Us or You're Not'. US Department of State cable, 13 September 2001. National Security Archive, George Washington University, Washington, DC.

'Deputy Secretary Armitage's Meeting with General Mahmud: Actions and Support Expected of Pakistan in Fight against Terrorism'. US Department of State cable, 14 September 2001. National Security Archive, George Washington University, Washington, DC.

'A Draft of Zawahiri's Message to the Egyptians'. *Combating Terrorism Center at West Point*, October 2013.

Faraj, Muhammad abd-al-Salam. 'The Neglected Duty'. *Al-Ahrar*, 8 December 1981.

'Foreign Intelligence Service and Haqqani Network Involvement in the 30 of December 2009 Suicide Attack on FOB Chapman'. US Department of State Cable, 6 February 2010. National Security Archive, George Washington University, Washington, DC.

'A Glad Tiding from Sheikhs Abu al Zubayr and Ayman al-Zawahiri'. As-Sahab Media, 9 February 2012.

'Hamza bin Laden Highlights Historical Saudi Collusion with British in Speech Inciting Regime Overthrow'. SITE Intelligence Group, 20 May 2017.

Haqqani, Jalaluddin. *Manba al-Jihad* 2, no. 12 (June 1991).

Haqqani, Sirajuddin. *Military Lessons: For the Legions of Jihadists* (n.p., 2011).

Haqqani, Sirajuddin. 'What We, the Taliban, Want'. Op-ed. *New York Times*, 20 February 2020.

Hassan, Umayma. 'Islamic Spring'. *Al-Fajr*, 7 June 2012.

Hassan, Umayma. 'A Message to the Muslim Sisters'. As-Sahab Media, December 2009.

Hassan, Umayma. 'Pure Blood on the Soil of Afghanistan, Part One'. *One Ummah*, 15 April 2019.

Ingram, Maurice. 'Broad Outlines of the Growth of Nationalism in Egypt'. Archive of Alfred Milner, Viscount Milner, 1824–1955. Oxford University Bodleian Library, 4 February 1920.

The al-Jihad Case. Case no. 462. Higher State Security Court, Cairo. Ayman al-Zawahiri interrogation. 1981.

The al-Jihad Case. Case no. 462. Higher State Security Court. Ayman al-Zawahiri statement. 1981.

Khan, Muhammad Sidique, 'London Bomber: Text in Full'. *BBC News*, 1 September 2005.

'Last Will and Testament of Martyr Humam Khalil Abu Mulal al-Balawi'. As-Sahab Media, 28 February 2010.

'Late December 2009 al-Qaeda and Haqqani Network Senior Leadership Activities in Miram Shah, Pakistan and Khowst Province, Afghanistan'. US Department of State Cable, 11 January 2010. National Security Archive, George Washington University.

'Letter from Adam Gadahn'. Harmony Document—SOCOM-2012-00000004. *Combating Terrorism Center at West Point*, January 2011, 1–28.

'Letter from UBL to 'Atiyatullah al-Libi 4'. Harmony Document—SOCOM-2012-0000019, *Combating Terrorism Center at West Point*, May 2010, 1–37.

'Letter from Usama bin Laden to Mukhtar Abu al-Zubayr'. Harmony Document—SOCOM-2012-0000005. *Combating Terrorism Center at West Point*, 7 August 2010, 1–3.

'Letter from Wakil Khan October 18, 2004'. Release of Abbottabad compound material. CIA, November 2017, 1–4.

'Letter Providing Direction'. *Bin Laden's Bookshelf*. Office of the Director of National Intelligence, 19 January 2017, 1–4.

'Letter Regarding al-Qa'ida Strategy'. Harmony Document—SOCOM-2012-00000017. *Combating Terrorism Center at West Point*, n.d, 1–27.

'Letter regarding Working in Islamic Countries'. *Bin Laden's Bookshelf*. Office of the Director of National Intelligence, 1 March 2016, 1–4.

'Letter to Abu-Musa'b 'Abd-al-Wadud'. *Bin Laden's Bookshelf*. Office of the Director of National Intelligence, 19 January 2017, 1–4.

'Letter to 'Atiyatullah al-Libi about Saudi Arabia Scholars'. Harmony Document—SOCOM-2012-0000014. *Combating Terrorism Center at West Point*, January 2007, 1–11.

'Letter to Azmarai'. Harmony Document—SOCOM-2012-0000006. *Combating Terrorism Center at West Point*, December 2010, 1–3.

'Letter to My Beloved Brother'. *Bin Laden's Bookshelf*. Office of the Director of National Intelligence, 20 May 2015, 1–2.

Mahmoud, Usama. 'Targeting of American and Indian Navies'. *As-Sahab Media*, 27 September 2014.

'Mahmud on Failed Kandahar Trip'. US Embassy (Islamabad) cable, 29 September 2001. National Security Archive, George Washington University.

'The Manba-al Uloom Madrasa as a Major Educational Centre'. *Manba' al-Jihad (Pashto)* 1, no. 1 (July 1989), 1–8.

'Musharraf Accepts the Seven Points'. US Embassy (Islamabad) cable, 14 September 2001. National Security Archive, George Washington University.

Muttaqi, Amir Khan. Radio Shariat, 21 January 2000.

Nasser, Gamal. *Egypt's Liberation: The Philosophy of the Revolution*. Buffalo, NY: Smith, Keynes and Marshall, 1959.

One Ummah magazine, 11 September 2019.

'The Open Meeting with Shaykh Ayman al-Zawahiri'. As-Sahab *Media*, April 2008.

'Our Honorable Shaykh'. *Bin Laden's Bookshelf*. Office of the Director of National Intelligence, 1 March 2016, 1–20.

'O Victorious Ummah, Carry Your Arms, Wage Jihad, and Rejoice'. *An-Nafir*, 20 July 2014. *Jihadology*.

'Pakistan: Reaction to Afghanistan Strikes'. US Department of State cable, 21 August 1998, National Security Archive, George Washington University, Washington, DC.

Qutb, Sayyid. *The America I Have Seen: In the Scale of Human Values*. Kashf ul Shubuhat, 1951.

Qutb, Sayyid. *Al-'Adala al-ijtima'iyya fi al-Islam* [*Social Justice in Islam*]. Al-Adalaijtima'iyya fi al-Islam. Cairo: Dar al-Shuruq, 1983.

Qutb, Sayyid. *Fi Zilal al-Qur'an* [*In the Shade of the Qur'an*]. Cairo: Dar al-Shuruq, 1996.

Qutb, Sayyid. *In the Shade of the Qur'an*. Translated by Adil Shamis. New Delhi: Kitab Bhavan, 2007.

Qutb, Sayyid. 'Limadha a damuni' [Why did they hang me?]. *Al-Sharika al-Saudiyya li-al-Abhath waal Tawzi*, n.d.

Qutb, Sayyid. *Ma'àlim fì-l-Tarìq* [*Milestones*]. Beirut: Dar al-Shuruq, 1991.

Qutb, Sayyid. *Milestones*. Indianapolis: American Trust, 1990.

Qutb, Sayyid, and A. Hammuda. *Min al-Qarya ila al-Mishnaqa* [From the village to the hanging rope]. Cairo: Sina li-al-Nashr, 1990.

Rahman, Atiyah Abdul. 'Letter from Atiyah to Abu Basir'. *Bin Laden's Bookshelf*. Office of the Director of National Intelligence, 27 March 2011, 1–20.

Rahman, Atiyah Abdul. 'The People's Revolt . . . the Fall of Corrupt Arab Regimes . . . the Demolition of the Idol of Stability . . . and the New Beginning'. *Global Islamic Media Front,* 16 February 2011.

Sadat, Anwar. 'Peace with Justice'. Speech to the Israeli Knesset, delivered 20 November 1977.

Sadat, Anwar. *October Magazine*, 30 September 1979, 3–5.

'Sadness, Containment and Aspiration'. *AQAP Inspire Magazine*, no. 6 (2011) , 47–54.

Salah, Muhammad. 'Sayyid Imam al-Sharif Interview'. Part 1. *Al-Hayat*, 8 December 2007.

Salah, Muhammad. 'Sayyid Imam al-Sharif Interview'. Part 2. *Al-Hayat*, 9 December 2007.

'Secretary's 13 September 2001 Conversation with Pakistani President Musharraf'. US Department of State cable, 19 September 2001. National Security Archive, George Washington University, Washington, DC.

al-Sharif, Sayyid Imam. 'Wathiqat Tarshid al-'Aml al-Jihad i fi Misr w'al-'alam' [The document for rationalization of jihad in Egypt and the world]. *Al-Masri al-Yawm and al-Jarida*, 19 November 2007–3 December 2007.

el-Sissi, Abdel-Fattah. 'Address to the Nation'. *ERTU*, 23 June 2013.

"Statement by General Mark A. Milley, 20th Chairman of the Joint Chiefs of Staff," *Senate Armed Services Committee Hearing on Afghanistan Withdrawal*, 28 September 2021.

'Statement by Pentagon Press Secretary Peter Cook on Strike against al-Qaeda Leader'. US Department of Defense. 3 October 2016.

'Statement from Jama'at al-Tawhid wal-Jihad's Abu Musab al-Zarqawi: Bay'a to Osama bin Laden'. *Jihadology*, 18 October 2004.

'Statement on the Abu-Dujanah Al-Khurasani Raid (May Allah Accept Him) to Infiltrate the Fortresses of the Americans'. As-Sahab Media, 6 January 2010.

'R. v. Khawaja,'The Superior Court of Ontario, Case Number (04 G30282) Exhibit 63. Email of Momin Khawaja to Zeba Khan, 8 August 2003.

'Terror Franchise: The Unstoppable Assassin, Tech's Vital Role for Its Success'. *Bin Laden's Bookshelf*. Office of the Director of National Intelligence' 20 May 2015.

'The Trial of the Returnees from Albania'. Egyptian Attorney General's Office. Case no. 8/98. Felonies in the Military Prosecutor's Department', March 1999.

al-Tunisi, Abu Ayyad. 'Answer to the Essay of Abu Maysarah al-Shami: Letters to Dr. Ayman al-Zawahiri'. *Hidayah Media*, 6 January 2016.

al-Tunisi, Abu Ayyad. 'Inspired by the Conquests of Iraq'. *Al-Bayyariq Media,* 13 June 2014.

'Usama bin Ladin: Pakistan Seems to Be Leaning against Being Helpful'. US Embassy (Islamabad) cable, 18 December 1998. National Security Archive, George Washington University, Washington, DC.

'Usama bin Ladin: Pressing High-Level Taliban Official Jalaluddin Haqqani on Bin Ladin'. US Department of State cable, 24 May 1999. National Security Archive, George Washington University, Washington, DC.

US Department of Defense. 'GTMO Detainee Report: Bendar A al-Ataybi'. *Wikileaks,* 25 February 2007.

US Department of Defense. 'GTMO Detainee Report: Khair Ulla Said Wali Khairkhwa'. *Wikileaks,* 6 March 2008.

US Department of Defense. 'GTMO Detainee Report: Abdallah Muhummad Khan'. *Wikileaks,* 27 March 2008.

U.S. v. Aafia Siddiqui. 08 Cr. 826 (RMB). S.D.N.Y. Government's sentencing submission. July 7, 2010.

U.S. v. Ali Mohamed. S(7) 98 Cr. 1023. S.D.N.Y. Plea hearing, 20 October 2000.

U.S. v. Enaam Arnaout. No. 02 CR892, N.D. Ill. Government's evidentiary proffer supporting the admissibility of co-conspirator statements, 6 January 2003.

U.S. v. Omar Abdel Rahman. S(5) 93 Cr. 181. MBM. Testimony of Khaled Ibrahim, July 13, 1995, 14241f.

U.S. v. Omar Abdel Rahman. S(5) 93 Cr. 181 MBM. Testimony of Colonel Norvell Bonds DeAtkine, 13 July 1995.

U.S. v. Omar Abdel Rahman. S(5) 93 Cr. 181 MBM. Closing remarks of defence attorney Roger Stavis, 11 September 1995.

U.S. v. Osama bin Laden. No. S(7) 98 Cr. 1023 (S.D. N.Y.). Testimony of Jamal al-Fadl, 6 February 2001 (transcript pp. 218–19, 233); 13 February 2001 (transcript pp. 514–16); 20 February 2001 (transcript p. 890).

al-Zawahiri, Ayman. 'Advice for the United Ummah concerning the Reality of the United Nations'. *As-Sahab Media,* 23 November 2021.

al-Zawahiri, Ayman. 'The Advice of One Concerned'. *As-Sahab Media,* 5 July 2007.

al-Zawahiri, Ayman. 'After Seven Years Where Is the Deliverance?'. *As-Sahab Media,* 26 January 2016.

al-Zawahiri, Ayman. 'Allegiance and Disavowal'. *As-Sahab Media,* 28 December 2002.

al-Zawahiri, Ayman. 'America Is the First Enemy of the Muslims'. *As-Sahab Media,* 20 March 2018.

al-Zawahiri, Ayman. 'MurrAl-Hisad al-Murr: al-Ikhwan al-Muslimin Fi Sitin' (The Bitter Harvest: The [Muslim] Brotherhood in Sixty Years)'. Translated by Nadia Masid. Egypt: unpublished, 1991.

al-Zawahiri, Ayman. *The Black Book: Torturing Muslims under President Hosni Mubarak* (n.d.).

al-Zawahiri, Ayman. 'Brief Messages to a Victorious Ummah, Part 2—and Be Not Divided among Yourselves'. *As-Sahab Media,* 21 August 2016.

al-Zawahiri, Ayman. 'Brief Messages to a Victorious Ummah, Part 3—Allah, Allah in Iraq'. *As-Sahab Media*, 25 July 2016.

al-Zawahiri, Ayman. 'Brief Messages to a Victorious Ummah, Part 4—the Solid Structure'. *As-Sahab,* 25 August 2016.

al-Zawahiri, Ayman. 'Brief Messages to a Victorious Ummah, Part 5—to Other Than Allah We Will Not Bow'. *As-Sahab Media*, 5 January 2017.

al-Zawahiri, Ayman. 'The Butcher of Washington'. *As-Sahab Media*, 30 January 2006.

al-Zawahiri, Ayman. *The Compendium of the Pursuit of Divine Knowledge*. n.p., 1993.

al-Zawahiri, Ayman. 'The Correct Equation'. *As-Sahab Media*, 22 January 2007.

al-Zawahiri, Ayman. 'The Deal of the Century or the Crusade of the Century, Part 1'. *As-Sahab Media*, 11 September 2020.

al-Zawahiri, Ayman. 'The Deal of the Century or the Crusade of the Century, Part 2'. *As-Sahab Media*, 26 January 2022.

al-Zawahiri, Ayman. 'The Deal of the Century or the Crusade of the Century, Part 3'. *As-Sahab Media*, 3 February 2022.

al-Zawahiri, Ayman. 'The Deal of the Century or the Crusade of the Century, Part 4'. *As-Sahab Media*, 15 February 2022.

al-Zawahiri, Ayman. 'The Defeat of America Is a Matter of Time'. *As-Sahab Media*, 9 September 2004.

al-Zawahiri, Ayman. 'The Defiers of Injustice'. *As-Sahab Media,* 9 September 2016.

al-Zawahiri, Ayman. 'The Emancipation of Mankind and Nations under the Banner of the Koran'. *As-Sahab Media*, 30 January 2005.

al-Zawahiri, Ayman. 'Exit from the Circle of Inefficiency and Failure'. *As-Sahab Media*, February 2014.

al-Zawahiri, Ayman. 'Exit of Bush and Arrival of Obama'. *As-Sahab Media,* 19 November 2008.

al-Zawahiri, Ayman. *The Exoneration: A Treatise Exonerating the Community of the Pen and the Sword from the Debilitating Accusation of Fatigue and Weakness*. Published online, 2008.

al-Zawahiri, Ayman. 'Glad Tidings of Victory to Our People in Egypt'; 'Brief Messages to Our Victorious Ummah'. *The Eighth Episode, as-Sahab Media,* 15 February 2018.

al-Zawahiri, Ayman. 'For Incitement and Publishing: You Are Held Responsible Only for Yourself'. Parts 1–2. *As-Sahab Media*, 3 June 2011.

al-Zawahiri, Ayman. 'General Guidelines for Jihad'. *As-Sahab Media,* 14 September 2013.

al-Zawahiri, Ayman. 'Hasten to Syria'. *As-Sahab Media,* 8 May 2016.

al-Zawahiri, Ayman. 'How to Confront America?'. *As-Sahab Media,* 12 September 2018.

al-Zawahiri, Ayman. *Knights under the Prophet's Banner*. *Al-Sharq al-Awsat*, December 2001.

al-Zawahiri, Ayman. 'Interview with Shaykh Ayman al-Zawahiri'. *As-Sahab Media,* 5 May 2007.

al-Zawahiri, Ayman. 'ISIS Is No Longer Part of Al Qaeda'. *As-Sahab Media*, 3 February 2014.

al-Zawahiri, Ayman. 'The Islamic Spring, Part 1'. *As-Sahab Media*, 9 September 2015.

al-Zawahiri, Ayman. 'The Islamic Spring, Part 2'. *As-Sahab Media*, 12 September 2015.

al-Zawahiri, Ayman. 'The Islamic Spring, Part 3'. *As-Sahab Media*, 21 September 2015.

al-Zawahiri, Ayman. 'The Islamic Spring, Part 4'. *As-Sahab Media*, 5 October 2015.

al-Zawahiri, Ayman. 'The Islamic Spring, Part 5'. *As-Sahab Media*, 6 October 2015.

al-Zawahiri, Ayman. 'The Islamic Spring, Part 6'. *As-Sahab Media*, 9 October 2015.

al-Zawahiri, Ayman. 'Jerusalem Will Not Be Judaized'. *As-Sahab Media*, 11 September 2021.

al-Zawahiri, Ayman. 'Kalimat haq' [The word of truth]. Dar al-l'tisam: n.p., n.d.

al-Zawahiri, Ayman. 'Lessons, Examples and Great Events in the Year 1427'. *As-Sahab Media*, 13 February 2007.

al-Zawahiri, Ayman. 'Long-Term Plan'. *As-Sahab Media*, 9 July 2005.

al-Zawahiri, Ayman. 'Loyalty and Enmity: An Inherited Doctrine and a Lost Reality'. *As-Sahab Media*, December 2002.

al-Zawahiri, Ayman. 'March Forth to Syria'. *As-Sahab*, 8 May 2016.

al-Zawahiri, Ayman. 'A Message to the British'. *As-Sahab Media,* 4 *August* 2005.

al-Zawahiri, Ayman. *Military Studies in the Jihad against the Tyrants: The al-Qaeda Training Manual.* n.p., n.d.

al-Zawahiri, Ayman. 'Missive of Hope and Joy to Our People in Egypt'. Parts I–V. *As-Sahab Media*, 2011.

al-Zawahiri, Ayman. 'Missive of Hope and Joy to Our People in Egypt, Part 1'. *As-Sahab Media*, 18 February 2011.

al-Zawahiri, Ayman. 'Missive of Hope and Joy to Our People in Egypt, Part 3. *As-Sahab Media*, 28 February 2011.

al-Zawahiri, Ayman. 'Missives of Hope and Joy to Our People in Egypt'. Part 5. *As-Sahab Media* 14 April 2011.

al-Zawahiri, Ayman. 'Missive of Hope and Joy to Our People in Egypt'. Part 7. *As-Sahab Media*, 5 October 2011.

al-Zawahiri, Ayman. 'Al-Mujahideen'. n.p., 1998.

al-Zawahiri, Ayman. 'The Noble Knight Dismounted'. *As-Sahab Media,* 8 June 2011.

al-Zawahiri, Ayman. 'The Noble Woman of India'. *As-Sahab Media,* 5 April 2022.

al-Zawahiri, Ayman. 'Oh People of Tunisia Support Your Shari'ah'. *As-Sahab Media,* 11 June 2012.

al-Zawahiri, Ayman. 'Open Discussion with Sheikh Ayman al-Zawahiri'. *As-Sahab Media, Minbar al-Tawhid wa al-Jihad,* 15 February 2009.

al-Zawahiri, Ayman. 'The Power of Truth'. *As-Sahab Media,* 4 July 2007.

al-Zawahiri, Ayman. 'Al Qaeda Leader Announces Formation of Indian Branch'. *As-Sahab Media*, 3 September 2014.

al-Zawahiri, Ayman. 'Al Qa'ida's al-Zawahiri Predicts Failure of US Crusade against Muslim States'. *As-Sahab Media,* 7 December 2005.

al-Zawahiri, Ayman. 'Realities of the Conflict between Islam and Unbelief'. *As-Sahab Media,* 21 December 2006.

al-Zawahiri, Ayman. 'Reflections on Political Corruption and Its Effects on the History of Muslims'. *As-Sahab Media*, 10 September 2021.

al-Zawahiri, Ayman. 'Regarding the Capture by the Traitorous Pakistani Army of Families of the Emigrant Mujahidin'. *As-Sahab Media*, 22 August 2019.

al-Zawahiri, Ayman. 'Rise to Support Our People in Gaza'. *As-Sahab Media*, 24 March 2008.

al-Zawahiri, Ayman. 'Tel Aviv Is Also a Land of Muslims'. *As-Sahab Media*, 13 May 2018.

al-Zawahiri, Ayman. 'Together towards Allah'. *As-Sahab Media*, December 2019.

al-Zawahiri, Ayman. 'We Shall Fight until There Is No More Persecution'. *As-Sahab Media*, 4 October 2017.

al-Zawahiri, Ayman. 'We Shall Fight You until There Is No More Persecution'. *As-Sahab Media*, 5 October 2017.

al-Zawahiri, Ayman. 'Who Will Support Scientist Aafia Siddiqui?'. *As-Sahab Media*, 4 November 2010.

al-Zawahiri, Ayman. 'Why This Letter?'. Letter from al-Zawahiri, August 2003. *Bin Laden's Bookshelf*. Office of the Director of National Intelligence, 20 May 2015.

al-Zawahiri, Ayman. 'Wills of the Knights of London Raid'. *As-Sahab Media*, 16 November 2005.

al-Zawahiri, Ayman. 'The Wound of the Rohingya Is the Wound of the Ummah by Shaykh'. *As-Sahab Media*, 12 March 2021.

al-Zawahiri, Ayman. 'Al-Zawahiri Denounces US, Argues for Reign of Islamic Law and Caliphate, Jihad against Crusaders and Jews'. *As-Sahab Media*, 31 January 2005.

al-Zawahiri, Ayman. 'Zawahiri Pledges Allegiance to New Afghan Taliban Leader in Audio Speech'. *SITE Intelligence Group*, 13 August 2015.

al-Zawahiri, Ayman. 'Zawahiri Speaks on 12th Anniversary of 9/11, Calls for Attack on U.S.'. *Global Terrorism Research Project*, 12 September 2013.

PRESS CONFERENCES, TESTIMONIES, AND SYMPOSIUMS

Berrier, Scott, director, Defense Intelligence Agency. 'Statement for the Record: Worldwide Threat Assessment'. *Armed Services Committee, US Senate*, 29 April 2021.

Biden, Joseph. 'Remarks by President Biden on the Way Forward in Afghanistan'. *White House*, 14 April 2021.

Biden, Joseph. 'Remarks by President Biden on the Drawdown of U.S. Forces in Afghanistan'. *White House*, 8 July 2021.

Mullen, Mike. 'Testimony to the Senate Armed Services Committee'. 22 September 2011.

Pompeo, Mike. Speech given at National Press Club, Washington DC, 12 January 2021.

'Secretary of Defense Lloyd Austin and Chairman of the Joint Chiefs of Staff Gen. Mark Milley Press Briefing'. *US Department of Defense*, 6 May 2021.

Shamir, Yitzhak. 'Israel: Statement by the Foreign Minister on the U.S. Policy for Peace in the Middle East'. *Speech to the Israeli Knesset, delivered 8 September 1982. International Legal Materials* 21, no. 5 (1982), 1158–1164.

Zimmerman, Katherine. 'Al-Qaeda's Strengthening in the Shadows'. Testimony to the Subcommittee on Counterterrorism and Intelligence, *Committee on Homeland Security, US House of Representatives*, 13 July 2017, 1–11.

BOOKS

Abdalla, Ahmed. *The Student Movement and National Politics in Egypt 1923–1973.* Cairo: American University in Cairo Press, 2008.

· Ahmad, Khurshid. *The Islamic Law and Constitution.* Lahore: Islamic, 1960.

Ahmad, Khurshid, and Zafar Ishaq Ansari. *Mawlana Maududi: An Introduction to His Life and Thought.* Aligarh: Crescent, 1979.

Ahmad, Rifat Sayyid. *Al-Islambuli: Ruya Jadida Fi-Tanzim* [Islambouli: A new view of the Jihad organization]. Cairo: n.p., 1987.

Ahmad, Rifat Sayyid. *Religion, the State and the Revolution.* Cairo: Al-Dinwal-Dawla wal-Thawra, 1965.

Anas, Abdullah. *The Birth of the Afghani Arabs: A Biography of Abdullah Anas with Mas'oud and Abdullah Azzam.* Translated by Nadia Masid. London: n.p., 2002.

Anas, Abdullah, and Tam Hussein. *To the Mountains: My Life in Jihad, from Algeria to Afghanistan.* London: Hurst, 2019.

Anderson, Terry H. *Bush's Wars.* New York: Oxford University Press, 2011.

Antonius, George. *The Arab Awakening.* Philadelphia: J. B. Lippincott, 1939.

Atwan, Abdel Bari. *The Secret History of al Qaeda.* London: Saqi Books, 2006.

al-Aziz, Abd al-Qadir bin Abd [Sayyid Imam al-Sharif]. *Risalat al-'Umda Fi I'Dad al-'Uddah Lil-jihad Fi Sabil Allah* [Treatise on the Pillar of Preparing Oneself for Jihad in the Way of Allah the Almighty]. Peshawar: n.p., 1987.

Baron, Beth. *The Orphan Scandal: Christian Missionaries and the Rise of the Muslim Brotherhood.* Stanford, CA: Stanford University Press, 2014.

Beattie, Kirk. *Egypt during the Sadat Years.* New York: Palgrave, 2000.

Bell, Stewart. *Cold Terror.* Canada: John Wiley & Sons, 2008.

Bergen, Peter. *Holy War, Inc: Inside the Secret World of Osama bin Laden.* New York: Simon and Schuster, 2001.

Bergen, Peter. *The Osama bin Laden I Know: An Oral History of al-Qaeda's Leader.* New York: Free Press, 2006.

Bergen, Peter. *The Rise and Fall of Osama bin Laden.* New York: Simon & Schuster, 2021, eBook.

Berntsen, Gary, and Ralph Pezzullo. *Jawbreaker.* New York: Crown, 2005.

Berridge, W. J. *Hasan al-Turabi: Islamist Politics and Democracy in Sudan.* Cambridge: Cambridge University Press, 2017.

Bhutto, Benazir. *Daughter of Destiny.* New York: HarperCollins, 2009.

Bobrick, Benson. *The Caliph's Splendor: Islam and the West in the Golden Age of Baghdad*. London: Simon & Schuster, 2012.

Botha, Anneli. 'The 2010 Suicide Attacks in Kampala'. In *The Evolution of the Global Terrorist Threat*, edited by Bruce Hoffman and Fernando Reinares. New York: Columbia University Press, 2014, 600–617.

Browers, Michaelle. 'The Egyptian Movement for Change: Intellectual Antecedents and Generational Conflicts'. In *Political Ideology in the Arab World: Accommodation and Transformation*. Cambridge: Cambridge University Press, 2009, 109–137. Brown, Vahid, and Don Rassler. *Fountainhead of Jihad: The Haqqani Nexus, 1973–2012*. Oxford: Oxford University Press, 2013.

Brunner, Rainer. 'Education, Politics, and the Struggle for Intellectual Leadership: Al-Azhar between 1927 and 1945'. In *Guardians of Faith in Modern Times: 'Ulama' in the Middle East*, edited by Meir Hatina. Leiden: Brill, 2009, 109–140.

Burchell, S. C. *The Suez Canal*. Boston, MA: New Word City, 2016, eBook.

Burr, J. Millard, and Robert O. Collins. *Sudan in Turmoil: Hasan al-Turabi and the Islamist State*. Princeton, NJ: Markus Wiener, 2010.

Burrell, Michael, and Abbas Kelidar. *Egypt, the Dilemma of a Nation: 1970–1977*. London: Sage, 1977.

Bushnell, Prudence. *Terrorism, Betrayal & Resilience: My Story of the 1998 U.S. Embassy Bombings*. Washington, DC: Potomac Books, 2018.

Calvert, John. *Sayyid Qutb and the Origins of Radical Islamism*. London: Hurst, 2009.

Cambanis, Thanassis. *Once upon a Revolution: An Egyptian Story*. New York: Simon & Schuster, 2015.

Cole, Juan. *Napoleon's Egypt: Invading the Middle East*. New York: St. Martin's Press, 2007.

Coll, Steve. *Ghost Wars: The Secret History of the CIA, Afghanistan, and bin Laden*. Penguin: New York, 2005.

Coury, Ralph M. *The Making of an Egyptian Arab Nationalist: The Early Years of Azzam Pasha, 1893–1936*. Reading: Ithaca Press, 1998.

Cudsi, Alexander S, and Ali E. Hillal Dessouki, eds. *Islam and Power*. London: Croom Helm, 1981.

Dean, Aimen, Paul Cruickshank, and Tim Lister. *Nine Lives: My Time as MI6's Top Spy Inside al-Qaeda*. London: Oneworld, 2018.

Dekmejian, R. H. *Islam in Revolution: Fundamentalism in the Arab World*. Syracuse, NY: Syracuse University Press, 1985.

Dorronsoro, Gilles. 'Pakistan and the Taliban: State Policy, Religious Networks, and Political Connections'. In *Pakistan: Nationalism without a Nation?*, edited by Christophe Jaffrelot. London: Zed Books, 2002, 161–178.

Drevon, Jerome. *Institutionalizing Violence: Strategies of Jihad in Egypt*. New York: Oxford University Press 2022.

Elden, Stuart. *Terror and Territory: The Spatial Extent of Sovereignty*. Minneapolis: University of Minnesota Press, 2009.

Fair, C. Christine, *Fighting to the End: The Pakistan Army's Way of War*. New York: Oxford University Press, 2014.

Farivar, Masood. *Confessions of a Mullah Warrior*. New York: Grove Press, 2010.

Fouda, Yosri, and Nick Fielding. *Masterminds of Terror*. Edinburgh: London, 2003.

Gerges, Fawaz A. *The Far Enemy: Why Jihad Went Global*. Cambridge: Cambridge University Press, 2005.

Gerges, Fawaz A. *ISIS: A History*. Princeton, NJ: Princeton University Press, 2016.

Gerges, Fawaz A. *Making the Arab World: Nasser, Qutb, and the Clash That Shaped the Middle East*. Princeton, NJ: Princeton University Press, 2018.

Gerges, Fawaz A. *The Rise and Fall of al-Qaeda*. New York: Oxford University Press, 2011.

Gilani, Syed Asad. *Maududi: Thought and Movement*. Lahore: Islamic, 1984.

Goertz, Stefan, and Alexander E. Streitparth. *The New Terrorism: Actors, Strategies and Tactics*. Cham: Springer, 2019.

Gohel, Sajjan M. 'The Global-Local Nexus in the Kashmir Insurgency: The Jaish-e-Mohammed, the Pakistani Military and al-Qaeda'. In *Exporting the Global Jihad: Critical Perspectives from the Periphery*, edited by Tom Smith and Kirsten E. Schulze, 99–122. London: Bloomsbury, 2020.

Gordon, Joel. *Nasser's Blessed Movement: Egypt's Free Officers and the July Revolution*. Oxford: Oxford University Press, 1992.

Grainger, John D. *The Battle for Palestine 1917*. Woodbridge: Boydell Press, 2006.

Greene, Molly. *Minorities in the Ottoman Empire*. Princeton, NJ: Markus Wiener, 2005.

Haley, Alex. *The Autobiography of Malcolm X*. New York: One World Books, 1992, eBook.

Halpern, Ben. *The Idea of the Jewish State*. Boston: Harvard University Press, 1969.

Hamid, Mustafa, and Leah Farrall. *The Arabs at War in Afghanistan*. London: Hurst, 2015, eBook.

Hamming, Tore. *Jihadi Politics: The Global Jihadi Civil War, 2014–2019*. London: Hurst, 2022, eBook.

Hamuda, Adil. *Al-Hijra ila al-Unf* [The migration to violence]. Cairo: n.p., 1987.

Hanafi, H. *Al-Haraka al-Islamiyya fi Misr* [Truth and illusion in Islam]. Cairo: Al-Huda, 1986.

Hanif, Mohammed. *A Case of Exploding Mangoes*. New York: Vintage, 2009.

Harris, Christina Phelps. *Nationalism and Revolution in Egypt: The Role of the Muslim Brotherhood*. The Hague: Mouton, 1964.

Harrison, Robert T. *Gladstone's Imperialism in Egypt*. Westport, CT: Greenwood Press, 1995.

Hashmi, Arshi Saleem. 'Historical Roots of the Deobandi Version of Jihadism and Its Implications for Violence in Today's Pakistan'. In *Faith-Based Violence and Deobandi Militancy in Pakistan*, edited by Jawad Syed, Edwina Pio, Tahir Kamran, and Abbas Zaidi. London: Palgrave Macmillan, 2016, 133–162.

Hassan, Said. F. 'Al-Azhar'. In *Education and the Arab Spring*. Edited by Mohamed E. Aboulkacem. Leiden: Brill, 129–150.

Hegghammer,Thomas.'Abdullah Azzam'. In *Al-Qaida dans le texte: Écrits d'Oussama ben Laden, Abdulla Azzam, Ayman al-Zawahiri et Abou Moussab al-Zarqawi* [Al-Qa'ida in the text: The writings of Osama bin Laden, Abdullah Azzam, Ayman al-Zawahiri and Abu Mussab al-Zarqawi], edited by Gilles Kepel. Paris: Presses Universitaires de France, 2005, 115–138.

Hegghammer, Thomas. *The Caravan: Abdallah Azzam and the Rise of Global Jihad.* Cambridge: Cambridge University Press, 2020, eBook.

Heikal, Mohamed. *Autumn of Fury: The Assassination of Sadat.* London: Andre Deutsch, 1983.

Hoffman, Bruce. 'The Evolving Terrorist Threat and CT Options for the Trump Administration'. In *How al-Qaeda Survived Drones, Uprisings and the Islamic State,* edited by Aaron Zelin. Washington, DC: Washington Institute for Near East Policy, 2017.

Hoffman, Bruce. *Inside Terrorism.* New York: Columbia University Press, 2017.

Hopwood, Derek. *Egypt 1945–1990: Politics and Society .* London: Routledge, 1991.

Hussain, Zahid. *Frontline Pakistan: The Struggle with Militant Islam.* New York: Columbia University Press, 2007.

Imam, Abdullah. *Abd-al-Nasir wa al-Ikhwan al-Muslimoon: Al-Unf al-Deene fee Misr* [Nasir and the Muslim Brotherhood: Islamic violence in Egypt]. Cairo: Dar Daral-Khiyal, 1997.

Ismael, Tariq, and Jacqueline Ismael. *Government and Politics in Islam.* London: Frances Pinter, 1985.

Jaffrelot, Christophe. *Pakistan: Nationalism without a Nation.* New Delhi: Manohar, 2002.

Jameelah, Maryam. *Who Is Maudoodi?* Delhi: Taj, 1982.

Jones, Seth G. *Hunting in the Shadows: The Pursuit of al Qa'ida since 9/11.* New York: W. W. Norton, 2012.

Jordan, Jenna. *Leadership Decapitation: Strategic Targeting of Terrorist Organizations.* Stanford, CA: Stanford University Press, 2019.

Kepel, Gilles. *The Prophet and the Pharaoh: Muslim Extremism in Egypt.* London: Saqi Books, 1985.

Kepel, Gilles. *The War for Muslim Minds: Islam and the West.* Cambridge, MA: Belknap, 2004.

al-Khalidi, Abdal Fattah. *Amrika min al-Dakhil bi-Minzar Sayyid Qutb* [America from the inside through the eyes of Sayyid Qutb]. Cairo: Dar al-Wafa, 1987.

al-Khalidi, Abdal Fattah. *Sayyid Qutb: Min al-milad ila al-istishhad* [Sayyid Qutb: The birth of sacrifice]. Damascus: Dar al-Qalam, 1991.

Khosrokhavar, Farhad. *Inside Jihadism.* New York: Routledge, 2009.

Klausen, Jytte. *Western Jihadism: A Thirty-Year History.* London: Oxford University Press, 2021.

Lahoud, Nelly. *The bin Laden Papers.* London: Yale University Press, 2022, eBook.

Lal, Bhure. *The Lethal Cocktail of ISI, Taliban & al-Qaida.* New Delhi: Siddharth, 2002.

Lance, Peter. *Triple Cross: How bin Laden's Master Spy Penetrated the CIA, the Green Berets, and the FBI.* New York: Harper Collins 2010.

Leitenberg, Milton. *Assessing the Biological Weapons and Bioterrorism Threat.* Carlisle, PA: US Army War College Press, 2005.

Levant, Ezra. *The Enemy Within: Terror, Lies, and the Whitewashing of Omar Khadr.* Plattsburgh, NY: McClelland & Stewart, 2011.

Lia, Brynjar. *Architect of Global Jihad: The Life of al-Qaida Strategist Abu Mus'ab al-Suri.* London: Hurst, 2009.

Link, Arthur. *The Papers of Woodrow Wilson, April 5–April 22, 1919.* Vol. 57. Princeton, NJ: Princeton University Press, 1988.

Mansour, Sherif. 'Enough Is Not Enough: Achievements and Shortcomings of Kefaya, the Egyptian Movement for Change'. In *Civilian Jihad*, edited by Maria J. Stephan, 205–18. New York: Palgrave Macmillan, 2009.

Marable, Manning. *Malcolm X: A Life of Reinvention.* New York: Viking, 2011.

Marsot, Afaf Lutfi al-Sayyid. *A Short History of Modern Egypt.* Cambridge: Cambridge University Press, 1985.

Mastors, Elena. *Breaking al-Qaeda: Psychological and Operational Techniques.* Boca Raton, FL: CRC Press, 2014.

McDermott, Anthony. *Egypt from Nasser to Mubarak: A Flawed Revolution.* New York: Routledge, 1988, eBook.

McMillan, M. E. *Fathers and Sons: The Rise and Fall of Political Dynasty in the Middle East.* New York: Palgrave Macmillan, 2013.

el-Menawy, Abdel Latif. *18 Days in Tahrir: An Insider's Account of the Uprising in Egypt.* London: Gilgamesh, 2013.

Miller, John, Michael Stone, and Chris Mitchell. *The Cell: Inside the 9/11 Plot, and Why the FBI and CIA Failed to Stop It.* New York: Hyperion, 2002.

Miniter, Richard. *Mastermind: The Many Faces of the 9/11 Architect, Khalid Shaikh Mohammed.* New York: Sentinel, 2011.

Mitchell, Chris, John Jackson Miller, and Michael Stone. *The Cell: Inside the 9/11 Plot, and Why the FBI and CIA Failed to Stop It.* New York: Hyperion, 2002, eBook.

Mitchell, Richard. *The Society of the Muslim Brothers.* London: Oxford University Press, 1993.

Moubayed, Sami. *Under the Black Flag: At the Frontier of the New Jihad.* London: I. B. Tauris, 2015.

Muñoz, Heraldo. *Getting Away with Murder: Benazir Bhutto's Assassination and the Politics of Pakistan.* New York: W. W. Norton, 2013, eBook.

Murphy, Caryle. *Passion for Islam.* New York: Scribner, 2002.

Musallam, Adnan A. *From Secularism to Jihad: Sayyid Qutb and the Foundations of Radical Islamism.* Westport, CT: Praeger, 2005.

Musharraf, Pervez. *In the Line of Fire.* London: Simon & Schuster, 2006.

al-Nadawi, Abu al-Hasan. *Mudhakkarat Sa'ih fi al-Sharq al-Arabi* [The diaries of observers in the Arabian Gulf]. Cairo, n.p., n.d..

Nasr, Seyyed Vali Reza. *Maududi and the Making of Islamic Revivalism.* New York: Oxford University Press, 1996.

Nasr, Seyyed Vali Reza. *The Vanguard of the Islamic Revolution: The Jama'at-façade Islami of Pakistan*. Berkeley: University of California Press, 1994.

Neighbour, Sally. *The Mother of Mohammed: An Australian Woman's Extraordinary Journey into Jihad*. Melbourne: Melbourne University Press, 2009.

The 9/11 Commission Report. New York: W. W. Norton, 2004.

Obama, Barack. *A Promised Land*. New York, Penguin, 2020, eBook.

Osman, Tarek. *Egypt on the Brink from Nasser to Mubarak*. Totten: Yale University Press, 2010

O'Neill, Robert. *The Operator*. London: Simon & Schuster, 2017, eBook.

Pargeter, Alison. *The New Frontiers of Jihad: Radical Islam in Europe*. Philadelphia, PA: University of Pennsylvania Press, 2008.

Perry, Bruce. *The Last Speeches*. New York: Pathfinder Press, 1989.

Pokalova, Elena. *Foreign Fighters after the Conflict Ends: Returning Islamist Foreign Fighters*. New York: Palgrave Macmillan, 2020.

Raafat, Samir. *Maadi 1904–1962: Society and History in a Cairo Suburb*. Cairo: Palm Press, 1994.

Ramadan, Abdel-Azim. *Al-Ikhwan al-Muslimun wal-Tanzim al-Sirri* [The secret organization of the Muslim Brotherhood]. Cairo: Dar al-Shahab, 1977.

Rashid, Ahmed. *Pakistan on the Brink: The Future of America, Pakistan, and Afghanistan*. New York: Penguin, 2012.

Rashid, Ahmed. *Taliban*. London: I. B. Taurus, 2001.

Richmond, J. C. B. *Egypt 1798–1952: Her Advance toward a Modern Identity*. London: Routledge, 2013.

Riedel, Bruce. Deadly Embrace: Pakistan, America, and the Future of the Global Jihad. Washington, DC: Brookings Institution Press, 2011.

Riedel, Bruce. *The Hunt for al-Qaeda*. Washington, DC: Brookings Institution Press, 2008.

Riedel, Bruce. *What We Won, America's Secret War in Afghanistan, 1979–89*. Washington, DC: Brookings Institution Press, 2014.

Rizq, Jabir. *Madhabih al-Ikhwan fi Sujoun Nasir* [Slaughterhouses for the brothers in the prisons of Nasir]. Cairo: Dar al-Itisam, 1977.

Roy, Olivier. 'The Taliban: A Strategic Tool for Pakistan'. In *Pakistan: Nationalism without a Nation?*, edited by Christophe Jaffrelot. London: Zed Books, 2002, 149–160. Rubin, Barry. *Islamic Fundamentalism in Egyptian Politics*. New York: St. Martin's Press, 1990.

Ruttig, Thomas. 'The Haqqani Network as an Autonomous Entity'. In *Decoding the New Taliban: Insights from the Afghan Field*, edited by Antonio Giustozzi. New York: Columbia University Press, 2009, 57–88.

Sadiq, Liwaa Hasan. *Judhur al-Fitna al-Taifiyya fi al-Firaq al-Islamiyya* [The roots of strife in the Islamic sects]. Cairo: n.p., 1977.

Scheuer, Michael. *Through Our Enemies' Eyes: Osama bin Laden, Radical Islam, and the Future of America*. Washington, DC: Potomac Books, 2006.

Schur, Nathan. *Napoleon in the Holy Land*. London: Greenhill Books, 1999.

Scott-Clark, Cathy, and Adrian Levy. *The Exile: The Stunning Inside Story of Osama bin Laden and Al Qaeda in Flight*. London: Bloomsbury Press, 2017.

Shahzad, Syed Saleem. *Inside al-Qaeda and the Taliban: Beyond bin Laden and 9/11*. London: Palgrave MacMillan, 2011.

Shepard, William. *Sayyid Qutb and Islamic Activism: A Translation and Critical Analysis of Social Justice in Islam*. Leiden: E. J. Brill, 1996.

Shephard, Michelle. *Guantanamo's Child: The Untold Story of Omar Khadr*. Mississauga: John Wiley & Sons Canada, 2008.

Siddique, Abubakar. *The Pashtun Question: The Unresolved Key to the Future of Pakistan and Afghanistan*. London: Hurst, 2014.

Silber, Mitch D. *The al-Qaeda Factor: Plots against the West*. Philadelphia: University of Pennsylvania Press, 2012.

Siriyya, Salih. *Risalat al-Iman* [The message of faith]. Cairo: n.p., 1973.

Sirrs, Owen L. *Pakistan's Inter-Services Intelligence Directorate: Covert Action and Internal Operations*. London: Routledge, 2017.

Sivan, Emmanuel. *Radical Islam: Medieval Theology and Modern Politics*. New Haven, CT: Yale University Press, 1985.

Solecki, John. *Hosni Mubarak: President of Egypt*. New York: Chelsea House, 1991.

Sonyel, Salahi Ramadan. *Minorities and the Destruction of the Ottoman Empire*. Publications of Turkish Historical Society. Serial 7. Ankara: Turkish Historical Society Printing House, 1993.

Soufan, Ali, *Anatomy of Terror: From the Death of bin Laden to the Rise of the Islamic State*. New York: W. W. Norton, 2017.

Tignor, Robert L. *Egypt: A Short History*. Princeton, NJ: Princeton University Press, 2010.

Tignor, Robert L. *Modernization and British Colonial Rule in Egypt, 1882–1914*. Princeton, NJ: Princeton University Press, 1995.

Tsourapas, Gerasimos. *The Politics of Migration in Modern Egypt: Strategies for Regime Survival in Autocracies*. Cambridge: Cambridge University Press, 2018.

Vatikiotis, P. J. *The History of Modern Egypt*. London: Weidenfield & Nicolson, 1969.

Vatikiotis, P. J. 'Islam and the Foreign Policy of Egypt'. In *Islam and International Relations*, edited by J. Harris Proctor. New York: Praeger, 1965,, 129–143.

Warburg, Gabriel R. *Egypt and the Sudan: Studies in History and Politics*. London: Routledge, 2019.

Warrick, Joby. *The Triple Agent: The al-Qaeda Mole Who Infiltrated the CIA*. New York: Doubleday, 2011.

Weaver, Mary-Anne. *A Portrait of Egypt: A Journey through the World of Militant Islam*. New York: Farrar, Straus and Giroux, 1998.

Weiss, Michael, and Hassan Hassan. *ISIS: Inside the Army of Terror*. New York: Regan Arts, 2016.

Williams, Caroline. *Islamic Monuments in Cairo: The Practical Guide*. Cairo: American University in Cairo Press, 2004.

Wright, Lawrence. *The Looming Tower: Al Qaeda and the Road to 9/11*. London: Allen Lane, 2006.

Wright, Lawrence. *The Terror Years: From al-Qaeda to the Islamic State*. London: Constable, 2016.

Yousaf, Mohammed, and Mark Adkin. *Afghanistan the Bear Trap: The Defeat of a Superpower*. Havertown, PA: Casemate, 2001.

Youssef, Michael. *Revolt against Modernity: Muslim Zealots and the West*. Leiden: E. J. Brill, 1985.

Zahab, Mariam Abou, and Olivier Roy. *Islamist Networks: The Afghan-Pakistan Connection*. New York: Columbia University Press, 2002.

al-Zayyat, Montasser. *The Road to al-Qaeda: The Story of bin Laden's Right Hand Man*. London: Pluto Press, 2004.

Zelin, Aaron. *Your Sons Are at Your Service: Tunisia's Missionaries of Jihad*. New York: Columbia University Press, 2020.

JOURNALS

Abu-Lughod, Ibrahim. 'The Transformation of the Egyptian Élite: Prelude to the 'Urābī Revolt'. *Middle East Journal* 31, no. 1 (1967): 325–344.

Albright, David, and Holly Higgins. 'A Bomb for the Ummah'. *Bulletin of the Atomic Scientists* 59, no. 2 (2003): 49–55.

Alaimo, Kara. 'How the Facebook Arabic Page "We Are All Khaled Said" Helped Promote the Egyptian Revolution'. *Social Media + Society* 1, no. 2 (2015): 1–10.

Altman, Israel. 'Islamic Movements in Egypt'. *Jerusalem Quarterly,* 10 (1979): 87–94.

al-Anani, Khalil. 'Upended Path: The Rise and Fall of Egypt's Muslim Brotherhood'. *Middle East Journal* 69, no. 4 (Autumn 2015): 527–543.

Ansari, Hamied. 'The Islamic Militants in Egyptian Politics'. *International Journal of Middle Eastern Studies* 16, no. 1 (1984): 123–144.

Bano, Masooda, and Hanane Benadi. 'Official al-Azhar versus al-Azhar Imagined: The Arab Spring and the Revival of Religious Imagination'. *Die Welt des Islams* 59, no. 1 (2019): 7–32.

Basit, Abdul. 'Asim Umar—New Kid on the Block? Counter Terrorist Trends and Analysis'. *RSIS* 6, no.10 (November 2014): 8–12.

Baqai, I. H. 'The Pan-Arab League'. *India Quarterly* 2, no. 2 (1946): 144–150.

Barnett, David, and Efraim Karsh. 'Azzam's Genocidal Threat'. *Middle East Quarterly* 18, no. 4 (2011): 85–88.

Baum, Matthew A. 'How Public Opinion Constrains the Use of Force: The Case of Operation Restore Hope'. *Presidential Studies Quarterly* 34, no. 2 (2004): 187–226.

Bayat, Asef. 'Plebeians of the Arab Spring'. *Current Anthropology* 56, no. 11 (2015): 33–43..

Behuria Ashok, K. 'Fighting the Taliban: Pakistan at War with Itself'. *Australian Journal of International Affairs* 61, no. 4 (2007): 529–543.

Berendek, Eran, and Neil Simon. 'The 2017 Manchester Bombing and the British-Libyan Jihadi Nexus'. *CTC Sentinel* 13, no. 5 (May 2020).

Bergen, Peter, and Paul Cruickshank. 'Revisiting the Early Al Qaeda: An Updated Account of its Formative Years'. *Studies in Conflict & Terrorism* 35, no. 1 (2012): 1–36.

Brachman, Jarret. 'Al-Qa'ida's Changing Outlook on Pakistan'. *CTC Sentinel* 1, no. 12 (2008).

Brandon, James. 'Al-Qa'ida's Involvement in Britain's Homegrown Terrorist Plots'. *CTC Sentinel* 2, no. 3 (March 2009).

Brown, Vahid. 'The Façade of Allegiance: Bin Ladin's Dubious Pledge to Mullah Omar'. *CTC Sentinel* 3, no. 1 (2010).

Bunzel, Cole. 'The Islamic State's Mufti on Trial: The Saga of the Silsila 'Ilmiyya'. *CTC Sentinel* 11, no. 9 (October 2018).

Calvert, John. 'The Striving Shaykh: Abdullah Azzam and the Revival of Jihad'. *Journal of Religion and Society,* suppl. ser. 2 (2007): 83–102.

Chejne, Anwar G. 'Egyptian Attitudes towards Pan-Arabism'. *Middle East Journal* 11, no. 3 (1957): 253–268.

Clarke, Duncan L. 'US Security Assistance to Egypt and Israel: Politically Untouchable?'. *Middle East Journal* 51, no. 2 (1997): 200–214.

Coury, Ralph. 'Arabian Ethnicity and Arab Nationalism: The Case of Abd al-Rahman Azzam'. *Journal of the American Research Center in Egypt* 25 (1988): 61–70.

Crecelius, Daniel. 'Al-Azhar in Revolution'. *Middle East Journal* 20, no. 1 (1966): 31–49.

Davidson, Christopher M. 'Why Was Muammar Qaddafi Really Removed?'. *Middle East Policy* 24, no. 4 (2017): 91–116.

Drozdova, Katya, and Joseph H. Felter. 'Leaving Afghanistan: Enduring Lessons from the Soviet Politburo'. *Journal of Cold War Studies* 21, no. 4 (2019): 31–70..

Farrall, Leah. 'Revisiting al-Qaida's Foundation and Early History'. *Perspectives in Terrorism* 11, no. 6 (2017): 17–37.

Ganguly, Sumit, and Michael R. Kraig. 'The 2001–2002 Indo-Pakistani Crisis: Exposing the Limits of Coercive Diplomacy'. *Security Studies* 14, no. 2 (2005): 290–324.

Gardner, George, and Sami Hanna. 'Islamic Socialism'. *Muslim World* 56, no. 2 (1966): 71–86.

Gigot, Paul A. 'A Great American Screw Up: The U.S. and Iraq, 1980–1990'. *National Interest,* no. 22 (1990): 3–10.

Gohel, Sajjan. 'Deciphering Ayman al-Zawahiri and al-Qaeda's Strategic and Ideological Imperatives'. *Perspectives on Terrorism* 11, no. 1 (2017): 54–67.

Gohel, Sajjan M., and David Winston. 'A Complex Tapestry of Collusion and Cooperation: Afghanistan and Pakistan's Terrorism Networks'. *LSE South Asia Blog,* June 5, 2020.

Gregory, Shaun. 'The ISI and the War on Terrorism'. *Studies in Conflict & Terrorism* 30, no. 12 (2007): 1013–1031.

Guenena, Nemat. 'The "Jihad": An "Islamic Alternative" in Egypt'. *Cairo Papers in Social Science* 9, no. 2 (1986): 1–107.

Haas, Benjamin, and Daniel McGrory. 'Al-Qa'ida Seeking to Recruit African American Muslims'. *CTC Sentinel* 1, no. 8 (2008).

Hamming, Tore. 'Al-Qaeda after Ayman al-Zawahiri'. *Lawfare,* 11 April 2021.

Holbrook, Donald. 'Al-Qaeda's Response to the Arab Spring'. *Perspectives on Terrorism* 6, no. 6 (December 2012): 4–21.

Harvey, John R. 'Regional Ballistic Missiles and Advanced Strike Aircraft: Comparing Military Effectiveness'. *International Security* 17, no. 2 (1992): 41–83.

Huffman, Tim. 'You Have Atomic Bombs, We Have the Martyrdom-Seekers: Ayman al-Zawahiri's Narrative Arc of the Martyr'. *Peace & Conflict Studies* 23, no. 1 (2016): 102–q28.

Ibrahim, Saad Eddin. 'Anatomy of Egypt's Militant Islamic Groups: Methodological Note and Preliminary Findings'. *International Journal of Middle East Studies* 12, no. 4 (1980): 423–453.

Igualada, Carlos, and Javier Yagüe. 'The Use of *Bay'ah* by the Main Salafi-Jihadist Groups'. *Perspectives on Terrorism* 15, no. 1 (2021): 39–48.

Jacquier, James D. 'An Operational Code of Terrorism: The Political Psychology of Ayman al-Zawahiri'. *Behavioral Sciences of Terrorism and Political Aggression* 6, no. 1 (2014): 19–40.

'Jordan's 9/11: Dealing With Jihadi Islamism'. *International Crisis Group.* Middle East Report 47, no. 3 (2005): 1–20.

Khan, Ijaz Ahmad. 'Understanding Pakistan's Pro-Taliban Afghan Policy'. *Pakistan Horizon* 60, no. 2 (2007): 141–157.

Klass, Rosanne. 'Afghanistan: The Accords'. *Foreign Affairs* 66, no. 5 (1998).

Lewis, Bernard. 'License to Kill: Usama bin Ladin's Declaration of Jihad'. *Foreign Affairs* 77, no.6 (November/December, 1998): 14–19.

Lieven, Anatol. 'Military Exceptionalism in Pakistan'. *Survival* 53, no. 4 (2001): 53–68.

Little, T. R. 'The Arab League: A Reassessment'. *Middle East Journal* 10, no. 2 (1956): 138–150.

Livermore, Douglas A. 'Pakistani Unconventional Warfare against Afghanistan: A Case Study of the Taliban as an Unconventional Warfare Proxy Force'. *Small Wars Journal*, 4 February 2014.

Maloney, Sean M. 'Army of Darkness: The Jihadist Training System in Pakistan and Afghanistan, 1996–2001'. *Small Wars & Insurgencies* 26, no. 3 (2015): 518–541.

Mansfield, Peter. 'Nasser and Nasserism'. *International Journal* 28, no. 4 (Autumn 1973): 670–688.

McGregor, Andrew. '"Jihad and the Rifle Alone": Abdullah Azzam and the Islamist Revolution'. *Journal of Conflict Studies* 23, no. 2 (2003).

Moore, Cerwyn, and Paul Tumelty. 'Foreign Fighters and the Case of Chechnya: A Critical Assessment'. *Studies in Conflict & Terrorism* 31, no. 5 (2008): 412–433.

Nasr, Hossein. 'Religion in Safavid Persia'. *Iranian Studies* 7, nos. 1/2 (1974): 271–286.

O'Ballance, Edger. 'Soviet Tactics in Afghanistan'. *Military Review* 60, no.8 (1980): 45–52.

Orbach, Danny. 'Tyrannicide in Radical Islam: The Case of Sayyid Qutb and Abd al-Salam Faraj'. *Middle Eastern Studies* 48, no. 6 (2012): 961–972.

Rais, Rasul Bakhsh. 'Afghanistan and Pakistan: Difficult Neighbours'. *NBR Analysis* 19, no. 5 (2008).

Raj, Christopher S. 'US Military Aid to Egypt'. *Strategic Analysis* 4, no. 3 (1980): 116–121.

Raphaeli, Nimrod. 'Ayman Muḥammad Rabi' al-Zawahiri: The Making of an Arch Terrorist'. *Terrorism and Political Violence* 14, no. 4 (2002): 1–22.

Rashid, Ahmed. 'The Taliban: Exporting Extremism'. *Foreign Affairs* 78, no. 6 (1999).

Raza, Saima. 'Italian Colonisation & Libyan Resistance to the al-Sanusi of Cyrenaica (1911–1922)'. *Journal of Middle Eastern and Islamic Studies (in Asia)* 6, no. 1 (2012): 87–120.

Reetz, Dietrich. 'Pakistan and the Central Asia Hinterland Option: The Race for Regional Security and Development'. *Journal of South Asian and Middle Eastern Studies* 17, no. 1 (1993): 28–56.

Roy, Olivier, and Tore Hamming. 'Al-Zawahiri's *Bay'a* to Mullah Mansoor: A Bitter Pill but a Bountiful Harvest'. *CTC Sentinel* 9, no. 5 (2016).

Sahar, Arif. 'Ethnicizing Masses in Post-Bonn Afghanistan: The Case of the 2004 and 2009 Presidential Elections'. *Asian Journal of Political Science* 22, no. 3 (2014): 289–314.

al-Shishani, Murad Batal. 'Understanding Strategic Change in al-Qaeda's Central Leadership after bin Laden'. *Terrorism Monitor, the Jamestown Foundation* 9, no. 23 (June 2011).

Sigler, Jackson. 'Engaging the Middle East: Napoleon's Invasion of Egypt'. *History: Reviews of New Books* 38, no. 2 (2010): 40–44.

Soage, Ana Belén. 'Islam and Modernity: The Political Thought of Sayyid Qutb'. *Totalitarian Movements and Political Religions* 10, no. 2 (2009): 189–203.

Soage, Ana Belén. 'Rashid Rida's Legacy'. *Muslim World* 98, no. 1 (2008): 1–23.

Tahir-Kheli, Shirin. 'The Military in Contemporary Pakistan'. *Armed Forces and Society* 6, no. 4 (1980): 229–244.

Taylor, Max, and Mohamed E. Elbushra. 'Research Note: Hassan al-Turabi, Osama bin Laden, and Al Qaeda in Sudan'. *Terrorism and Political Violence* 18, no. 3 (2006): 449–464.

Terry, Fiona. 'The International Committee of the Red Cross in Afghanistan: Reasserting the Neutrality of Humanitarian Action'. *International Review of the Red Cross (Conflict in Afghanistan II)* 93, no. 881 (2011): 173–188.

Tomsen, Peter. 'Pakistan: With Friends like These . . .'. *World Policy Journal* 28, no. 3 (2011): 82–90.

'United States: 1984 Act to Combat International Terrorism'. *International Legal Materials* 24, no. 4 (1985): 1015–1018.

Waldman, Matt. 'The Sun in the Sky: The Relationship between Pakistan's ISI and Afghan Insurgents'. London School of Economics: Crisis States Research Centre. Working papers series no. 2 (no. 18), 2010: 1–27.

Warburg, Gabriel R. 'Islam and Politics in Egypt: 1952–80'. *Middle Eastern Studies* 18, no. 2 (1982): 131–157.

Warburg, Gabriel R. 'The Search for the Sources of the White Nile and Egyptian-Sudanese Relations'. *Middle Eastern Studies* 43, no. 3 (2007): 475–486.

Weinbaum, Marvin G. 'Egypt's "Infitah" and the Politics of US Economic Assistance'. *Middle Eastern Studies* 21, no. 2 (1985): 206–222.

Winchell, Sean P. 'Pakistan's ISI: The Invisible Government'. *International Journal of Intelligence and Counterintelligence* 16, no. 3 (2003): 374–388.

Willis, John. 'Debating the Caliphate: Islam and Nation in the Work of Rashid Rida and Abul Kalam Azad'. *International History Review* 32, no. 4 (2010): 711–732.

Wood, Michael. 'The Use of the Pharaonic Past in Modern Egyptian Nationalism'. *Journal of the American Research Center in Egypt* 35 (1998): 179–196.

Wright, Robin. 'Abu Muhammad al-Adnani, the Voice of ISIS, Is Dead'. *New Yorker*, 30 August 2016.

Zahid, Farhan. 'Death of AQIS Emir Asim Umar Has Serious Implications for al-Qaeda'. *Jamestown Terrorism Monitor* 17, no. 20 (2014).

Zeidan, David. 'Radical Islam in Egypt: A Comparison of Two Groups'. *Middle East Review of International Affairs* 3, no. 3 (September 1999).

REPORTS AND MANUSCRIPTS

Foreign Relations of the United States, 1977–1980. Vol. 1. *Foundations of Foreign Policy*. Office of the Historian, US Department of State, 2014.

'Indonesia Backgrounder: How the Jemaah Islamiyah Terrorist Network Operates'. *International Crisis Group*, no. 43, 11 December 2002, 1–50.

'Staff Statement no. 8'. National Policy Coordination, *National Commission on Terrorist Attacks*, 24 March 2004, 1–24.

'Trade-Off: The Rendition to Egypt of Sayyid Imam al-Sharif'. *Human Rights Watch*, May 2005.

'Tora Bora Revisited: How We Failed to Get bin Laden and Why It Matters Today'. *Report to Members of the Committee on Foreign Relations, United States Senate*, 30 November 2009.

'Ilyas Kashmiri and Retired Pakistan Major Charged in Denmark Plot'. *FBI: Chicago Division and US Attorney's Office: Northern District of Illinois*, 14 January 2010.

'Tahawwur Rana Guilty of Providing Material Support to Terror Group and Playing Supporting Role in Denmark Terror Conspiracy'. *US Department of Justice, Office of Public Affairs*, 9 June 2011.

'Treasury Targets Key al-Qa'ida Funding and Support Network Using Iran as a Critical Transit Point'. *Press release. US Department of the Treasury*, 28 July 2011.

'David Coleman Headley Sentenced to 35 Years in Prison for Role in India and Denmark Terror Plots'. *US Department of Justice, Office of Public Affairs*, 24 January 2013.

'How al-Qaeda and Islamic State Differ in Pursuit of Common Goal: Strengths and Weaknesses'. *BALAnce Economics and Country Risk*, 16 March 2015.

'Justice Department Secures the Denaturalization of a Senior Jihadist Operative Who Was Convicted of Terrorism in Egypt'. *US Department of Justice: Office of Public Affairs*, 20 April 2017.

Agreement for Bringing Peace to Afghanistan between the Islamic Emirate of Afghanistan Which Is Not Recognized by the United States as a State and Is Known as the Taliban and the United States of America. Doha, Qatar, 29 February 2020, 1–4.

Andreopoulos, Marcus. '"A Point of Vantage from Which to Dominate the Moslem World": The Impact of the 1919 Egyptian Revolution on Britain's Perception of the Role of Islam in Egypt'. London School of Economics & Political Science (LSE), Master's dissertation, 2021.

Ardovini, Lucia. 'The Failure of Political Islam? The Muslim Brotherhood's Experience in Government'. PhD thesis, Lancaster University, 2017.

Bailey, Allison. 'The Brothers' Older Sister: Zaynab al-Ghazali and the International Splinters of the Muslim Brotherhood'. Columbia University–London School of Economics & Political Science (LSE), master's dissertation, 2018.

Behravesh, Maysam. 'Iran's Unconventional Alliance Network in the Middle East and Beyond'. *Middle East Institute*, 7 April 2020.

Brown, Nathan J. 'Post-revolutionary al-Azhar'. *The Carnegie Papers: Carnegie Endowment for International Peace*, September 2011, 1–30.

Bunn, Matthew. 'Guardians at the Gates of Hell: Estimating the Risk of Nuclear Theft and Terrorism and Identifying the Highest-Priority Risks of Nuclear Theft'. PhD thesis, Massachusetts Institute of Technology, 2007.

Byman, Daniel. 'Libya's al Qaeda Problem'. *Brookings Institution,* 25 February 2011.

Cirincione, Joseph. 'Origins of Regime Change in Iraq'. *Carnegie Endowment for International Peace*, 19 March 2003.

Coury, Ralph M. 'Abd al-Rahman Azzam and the Development of Egyptian Arab Nationalism'. PhD thesis, Princeton University, 1984.

Crecelius, Daniel Neil, 'The Ulama and the State in Modern Egypt'. PhD thesis, Princeton University, 1967.

Davidson, Charles Robert. 'Political Violence in Egypt: A Case Study of the Islamist Insurgency 1992–1997'. PhD thesis, Tufts University, 2005.

Dressler, Jeffrey. 'The Haqqani Network: A Foreign Terrorist Organization'. *Institute for the Study of War*, 2.

Hassan, Mohammad Abu Rumman, and Abu Hanieh. 'Infatuated with Martyrdom: Female Jihadism from al-Qaeda to the "Islamic State"'. Friedrich-Ebert-Stiftung Jordan & Iraq, 2017.

Katzman, Kenneth. *Al-Qa'ida: Profile and Threat Assessment*. Congressional Research Service Report for Congress, the Library of Congress, 17 August 2005, 1–14.

Levitt, Matthew. 'Zarqawi's Jordanian Agenda'. *Washington Institute for Near East Policy*, 16 December 2004.

McCants, William. 'The Believer: How an Introvert with a Passion for Religion and Soccer became Abu Bakr al-Baghdadi, Leader of the Islamic State'. Brookings Institution, 1 September 2015.

Musallam, Adnan A. 'The Formative Stages of Sayyid Qutb's Intellectual Career and His Emergence as an Islamic Da'iyah'. PhD thesis, University of Michigan, 1983.

Oweidat, Nadia, et al. *The Kefaya Movement: A Case Study of a Grassroots. RAND Corporation*, 2008, 1–81.

Phinney, Todd R. 'Operation Infinite Reach: The 1998 US Embassy Bombing Response'. In *Airpower versus Terrorism: Three Case Studies*. Montgomery, AL: Air University Press, 2007, 25–42.

Post, Jerrold. 'Military Studies in the Jihad against the Tyrants: The al-Qaeda Training Manual'. *U.S. Air Force Counterproliferation Center*, 2004, 1–190.

Rassler, Don, and Vahid Brown. 'The Haqqani Nexus and the Evolution of al-Qa'ida'. *Combating Terrorism Center at West Point*, 14 July 2011, 1–56.

Roth, John, Douglas Greenburg, and Serena Wille. 'National Commission on Terrorist Attacks upon the United States: Monograph on Terrorist Financing'. In *Staff Report to the 9/11 Commission*, 2004.

Rowan, Mattisan. 'Al Qaeda's Latest Rebranding: Hay'at Tahrir al Sham'. *Wilson Center*, 24 April 2017.

Sharp, Jeremy M. *Egypt: The January 25 Revolution and Implications for U.S. Foreign Policy. CRS Report for Congress, Congressional Research Service*, 11 February 2011.

Shayovitz, Ronen. 'The Evolution of the Islamist Ideology'. PhD Thesis, Cardiff University, 2010.

UN Analytical Support and Sanctions Monitoring Team. *11th Report of the UN Analytical Support and Sanctions Monitoring Team. S/2020/415, UN Security Council*, 27 May 2020, 1–28.

UN Analytical Support and Sanctions Monitoring Team. 12th Report of the UN Analytical Support and Sanctions Monitoring Team. S/2021/486, *UN Security Council*, 28 April 2021, 1–22.

Walker, Edward W. 'Russia's Soft Underbelly: The Stability of Instability in Dagestan'. *Berkeley Program in Soviet and Post-Soviet Studies Working Paper Series* (Winter, 1999–2000), 1–22.

Youseef, Aboul-Enein. 'Ayman al-Zawahiri: The Ideologue of Modern Islamic Militancy'. *The Counterproliferation Papers, Future Warfare Series*, no. 21, USAF Counterproliferation Center, 1–22.

ARTICLES / NEWS REPORTS

Agence France-Presse, 9 December 2008.

Al-Ahram, 7 September 1966.

Al-Ahram, 13 August 1977.

Al-Ahram, 5 November 1979.

Al-Hayat, 7 August 1998.

Al-Hayat, 12 March 2002.

'Al-Jihad Leader's Son on Father's Links to al-Qa'ida'. *Al-Hayat*, 4 April 2004.

Allouni, Tayseer. 'Interview with Sheik Osama bin Laden'. *Al-Jazeera*, October 2001.

'Al-Qaeda Claims Tunisia Attack'. *BBC News*, 23 June 2002.

'Al Qaeda Leader Ayman al-Zawahiri Killed in Drone Strike, Biden Says'. *CBS News*, 2 August 2022.

'Al Qaeda No. 2: Sudan's President Pandered to West'. *CNN*, 24 March 2009.

'Al-Qaida's Third in Command Killed'. *NBC News*, 1 June 2010.

'Al-Qaeda to Give "Open Interview"'. *BBC News*, 19 December 2007.

'Al-Zawahiri: Egyptian Militant Group Joins al Qaeda'. *CNN*, 5 August 2006.

Amara, Tarek. 'Two Dead as Protesters Attack U.S. Embassy in Tunisia'. *Reuters*, 14 September 2012.

Ambinder, Marc. 'The Little-Known Agency That Helped Kill bin Laden'. *Atlantic*, 5 May 2011.

'AQIM Swears Allegiance to New al-Qaeda Leader Ayman al-Zawahiri'. *Middle East Media Research Institute (MEMRI)*, 8 July 2011.

Arif, Merieme. 'Al Qaeda's al-Zawahiri Purportedly Pledges Allegiance to New Taliban Chief'. *CNN*, 11 June 2016.

'Assault on al Qaeda; Terror in Iraq; Hate Crime Whodunit?'. *Anderson Cooper 360 Degrees. CNN*, 18 March 2004.

Auf, Yussef. 'The State of Emergency in Egypt: An Exception or Rule?'. *Atlantic Council*, 2 February 2018.

'Ayman al-Zawahiri Appointed as al-Qaeda Leader'. *BBC News*, 16 June 2011.

'Ayman al-Zawahiri, Interview'. *Al-Jazeera*, 1 September 2005.

'Ayman al-Zawahiri Videotape'. *Al-Jazeera*, 4 March 2006.

Barford, Vanessa, and Virginia Brown. 'Do Rewards Help Capture the World's Most Wanted Men?'. *BBC News*, 25 August 2011.

Bell, Stewart. 'Ahmed Khadr Provided References for Would-Be Terrorists'. *National Post*, 31 December 2005.

Bell, Stewart. 'A Model Life, a Model Operative'. *National Post*, 14 October 2005.

Bergen, Peter. 'The Account of How We Nearly Caught Osama bin Laden in 2001'. *THE New Republic*, 30 December 2009.

Bergen, Peter. 'The Killer Question: Who Murdered Benazir Bhutto?'. *New Republic*, 30 January 2008.

Berman, Paul. 'The Philosopher of Islamic Terror'. *New York Times*, 23 March 2003.

'Bin Laden's Men in Tehran . . . Iran Heavily Indebted to al-Qaeda'. *Asharq al-Awsat*, 4 January 2016.

'Bin Laden's Son, Ayman al-Zawahiri Make Joint Threats'. *Asharq al-Awsat*, 16 May 2016.

Blomfield, Adrian. 'Hosni Mubarak in Court to Answer to the People He Subjugated'. *Telegraph*, 4 August 2011.

Boettcher, Mike, and David Ensor. 'Reports Suggest al-Qaeda Military Chief Killed'. *CNN*, 16 November 2001.

'Bomb Rips Egyptian Embassy'. *CNN*, 19 November 1995.

Breslow, Jason M. 'Colin Powell: U.N. Speech Was a Great Intelligence Failure'. *PBS*, 17 May 2016.

Brown, Vahid. 'Cracks in the Foundation: Leadership Schisms in al-Qa'ida 1989–2006'. *Combating Terrorism Center at West Point* (September 2007).

Bumiller, Elisabeth, Carlotta Gall, and Salman Masood. 'Bin Laden's Secret Life in a Diminished World'. *New York Times*, 7 May 2011.

Bunzel, Cole. 'Al-Qaeda's Quasi-caliph: The Recasting of Mullah 'Umar'. *Jihadica*, 23 July 2014.

Bunzel, Cole. 'Why Are Al Qaeda Leaders in Iran?'. *Foreign Affairs*, 11 February 2021.

Burman, Max. 'Trump Confirms Osama bin Laden's Son Hamza Killed in U.S. Operation'. *NBC News*, 14 September 2019.

Butt, Qaiser. 'Strike Two: Ilyas Kashmiri Dead—Again'. *Express Tribune*, 5 June 2011.

Butt, Tariq. 'Who Is Ijaz Shah?'. *News International*, 30 March 2019.

Byrne, Hannah, John Krzyzaniak, and Qasim Khan. 'The Death of Mullah Omar and the Rise of ISIS in Afghanistan'. *Institute for the Study of War*, 17 August 2015.

Casciani, Dominic. 'Liquid Bomb Plot: What Happened'. *BBC News*, 7 September 2009.

Chulov, Martin. 'Hamza bin Laden Has Married Daughter of Lead 9/11 Hijacker, Say Family'. *Guardian*, 5 August 2018.

Chulov, Martin. 'ISIS: The Inside Story'. *Guardian*, 11 December 2014.

'CIA Base Bomber's Message'. *Al-Jazeera*, 9 January 2010.

Cleland, Gary. 'Bomb Plot Suspect Escaped While Praying'. *Daily Telegraph*, 17 December 2017.

Cohen, Eyal Tsir, and Eliora Katz. 'What We Can Learn about US Intelligence from the Baghdadi Raid'. *Brookings Institution*, 6 November 2019.

Cole, Matthew, and Rym Momtaz. 'Al Qaeda Leader in Yemen Pledges Allegiance to Zawahiri'. *ABC News*, 26 July 2011.

Coll, Steve. 'Time Bomb: The Death of Benazir Bhutto and the Unravelling of Pakistan'. *New Yorker*, 21 January 2008.

'Covert Israeli-Saudi Meeting Sends Biden a Strong Message on Iran'. *Reuters*, 27 November 2020.

Cowell, Alan. 'British Muslim Sentenced in Terror Attacks'. *New York Times*, 8 November 2006.

Cruickshank, Paul. 'Bin Laden Documents: Competing Vision of al Qaeda's Top Two'. *CNN*, 7 May 2012.

Cullison, Alan. 'Inside al-Qaeda's Hard Drive'. *Atlantic*, September 2004.

Cullison, Alan, and Andrew Higgins. 'Forgotten Computer Reveals Thinking behind Four Years of al Qaeda Doings'. *Wall Street Journal*, 31 December 2001.

'Cuts 12/12/82 Muslim Extremists Trial'. *Associated Press Archive*, 30 July 2015.

Daragahi, Borzou, Andrew Buncombe, Bel Trew, and Richard Hall. 'Qassem Soleimani: Iran Vows "Harsh Vengeance" after Top General Killed in US Airstrike'. *Independent*, 3 January 2020.

Davis, Patricia, and Maria Glod. 'CIA Shooter Kasi, Harbinger of Terror, Set to Die Tonight'. *Washington Post*, 14 November 2002.

Dearden, Lizzie. 'Egypt Sentences Al Jazeera Journalists to Death as Mohamed Morsi Given New Life Term in Qatar Espionage Case'. *Independent*, 18 June 2016.

Debusmann, Bernd, and Chris Partridge. 'Ayman al-Zawahiri: How US Strike Could Kill al-Qaeda Leader—but Not His Family'. *BBC News*, 3 August 2022.

'Dhiren Barot'. *BBC News*, 6 November 2006.

Diamond, Edwin. 'Anchor Wars: Dan Rather, Peter Jennings and Tom Brokaw'. *Rolling Stone*, 9 October 1986.

al-Din, Khalid Sharif. 'Egypt's Islamic Group Moves toward Establishing a Political Party'. *Asharq al-Awsat*, 3 March 1999.

Donaldson, Sam. 'Begin, Sadat Sign the Egypt-Israel Peace Treaty at the White House'. *ABC News*, 26 March 1979.

'Egypt: President Mubarak Addresses Nation on Transfer of Power'. *Nile News TV*, 1 February 2011.

'Egypt Army: Will Not Use Violence against Citizens'. *Reuters*, 31 January 2011.

'The Egyptian Crisis and Arabi Pasha'. *The Empire Series, episode 63. BBC Radio Four*, 10 May 2006.

'Egypt's Jihad Says Asked by bin Laden to Turn Guns on U.S'. *Agence France Presse*, 24 February 1999.

'Egypt's Ousted President Mohammed Morsi Dies during Trial'. *BBC News*, 4 June 2019.

Elkoussy, Bahaa. 'Pakistani Minister in Cairo to Sign Pact Affecting Militants'. *United Press International (UPI)*, 25 March 1994.

Engelberg, Stephen. 'One Man and a Global Web of Violence'. *New York Times*, 14 January 2001.

Ephron, Dan. 'How Arab Ties with Israel Became the Middle East's New Normal'. *Foreign Policy*, 21 December 2020.

Fahmy, Mohamed Fadel. 'Brother of al Qaeda Leader Offers Peace Plan'. *Foreign Policy*, 14 September 2012.

Fair, C. Christine. 'The Foreign Policy Essay: Al Qaeda's Re-launch in South Asia'. *Lawfare*, 21 September 2014.

Farrall, Leah. 'Hotline to the Jihad'. *Australian*, 7 December 2009.

Farrall, Leah. 'Interview with a Taliban Insider: Iran's Game in Afghanistan'. *Atlantic*, 14 November 2011.

Fielding, Nick. 'Omar Saeed Sheikh: The British Jackal'. *Sunday Times*, 21 April 2002.

Filkins, Dexter. 'Al Qaeda Paid for Car Bomb at U.S. Office, Pakistani Says'. *New York Times*, 3 July 2002.

Filkins, Dexter. 'For Afghans, a Price for Everything, and Anything for a Price'. *New York Times*, 1 January 2009.

'Flashback: When the Taleban Took Kabul'. *BBC News*, 15 October 2001.

Fletcher, Martin, and Ruth Gledhill. 'We Followed Islamic Rules and Eased Him into the Sea, Says US'. *Times*, 3 May 2011.

'Former Senior CIA Officer Recalls Killing of Service Members by Suicide Bomber'. *Intelligence Matters. CBS News*, 30 December 2020.

Gall, Carlotta. 'Pakistani Militant Chief Is Reported Dead'. *New York Times*, 4 June 2011.

Gall, Carlotta. 'Red Cross Worker Is Killed by Gunmen in Afghanistan'. *New York Times*, 28 March 2003.

Gartenstein-Ross, Daveed, and Thomas Joscelyn. 'Rebranding Terror'. *Foreign Affairs,* 28 August 2016.

Glenn, Cameron. 'Al Qaeda v ISIS: Ideology & Strategy'. *Woodrow Wilson International Center for Scholars*, 28 September 2015.

Gohel, Sajjan. 'Creating a Haven for al Qaeda'. *ABC News,* 14 April 2009.

Gohel, Sajjan. *Newsnight with Aaron Brown. CNN,* 18 July 2005.

Gohel, Sajjan. *Paula Zahn Now. CNN,* 29 September 2003.

Goldman, Russell. 'U.S. Lists bin Laden's Son as a Global Terrorist'. *New York Times,* 5 January 2017.

Graff, Garrett. 'I'd Never Been Involved in Anything as Secret as This'. *Politico,* 30 April 2021.

Green, J. J. 'Al Qaida's Ayman al Zawahiri: Dead, Duplicitous or Oblivious?'. *WTOP,* 10 August 2015.

Ha, Tu Thanh, and Colin Freeze. 'Canadian Soil a Long-Time Staging Ground for al-Qaeda'. *Globe and Mail*, 7 September 2002.

Hamdi, Alkhshali, Barbara Starr, and Greg Botelho. 'Al Qaeda Leader, Somali-Based Terror Group Present New Messages'. *CNN*, 22 April 2014.

'Hamza bin Laden: Trump Confirms al-Qaeda leader's Son Is Dead'. *BBC News*, 14 September 2019.

Harrich, Daniel. 'The Business with Terror'. *Deutsche Welle,* 17 June 2021.

Hegghammer, Thomas. 'Why Jihadists Loved America in the 1980s'. *Atlantic*, 6 March 2020.

Heller, Sam. 'Al-Qa'ida's Ayman al-Zawahiri Plays Politics'. *Gandhara RFE/RL*, 20 May 2016.

Hirschkorn, Phil. 'Who Is Anas al-Libi?'. *CBS News,* 6 October 2013.

Hoffman, Bruce. 'Al-Qaeda's Resurrection'. *Council on Foreign Relations*, 6 March 2018.

Ignatius, David. 'The Mombasa Attacks: Al Qaeda's New Weapon'. *International Herald Tribune*, 30 November 2002.

'Islamic Militants Reign of Terror Warning to US'. *Associated Press,* 19 August 1998.

Jaafari, Shirin. 'Who Was Abu Muhammad al-Adnani and What Does His Death Mean for ISIS?'. *PRI's The World*, 31 August, 2016.

'Jalaluddin Haqqani, Founder of Afghan Militant Network, Dies'. *BBC News*, 4 September 2018.

Jandal, Abu. 'Al Qaeda from Within: As Narrated by Abu Jandal, Bin Ladin's Personal Guard'. *Al-Quds al-Arabi*, 22 March 2005.

'The Jihadi Threat: ISIS, al-Qaeda and Beyond'. *U.S. Institute of Peace & Wilson Center*, December 2016 / January 2017.

Joffe, Lawrence. 'Abu Musab al-Zarqawi Obituary'. *Guardian*, 8 June 2006.

Jones, Sophia. 'No Turning Back: Inside Egypt's Coup'. *Atlantic*, 4 July 2013.

Joscelyn, Thomas. 'Al Qaeda Ally Orchestrated Assault on US Embassy in Tunisia'. *Long War Journal,* 2 October 2012.

Joscelyn, Thomas. 'Al Qaeda-Linked Jihadists Helped Incite 9/11 Cairo Protest'. *Long War Journal,* 26 October 2012.

Joscelyn, Thomas. 'Analysis: Osama bin Laden's Son Praises al Qaeda's Branches in New Message'. *Long War Journal*, 17 August 2015.

Joscelyn, Thomas. 'Ayman al-Zawahiri's Brother Released from Egyptian Prison'. *Long War Journal*, 19 March 2016.

'Kabul's Poppy Palaces'. *GQ Magazine*, 28 July 2014.

Kaplan, David. 'Hundreds of Americans Have Followed the Path to Jihad'. *U.S. News & World Report*, 2 June 2002.

Khan, Kamran. 'Pakistani Court Finds 4 Guilty in Pearl's Death'. *Washington Post*, 15 July 2002.

Khan, S. 'The Forgotten Case of the bin Laden Doctor'. *Deutsche Welle*, 16 November 2017.

Kifner, John. 'U.S. Agents Said to Thwart Bomb Plot against U.S. Embassy in Albania'. *New York Times*, 21 August 1998.

Kiley, Sam. '21/7: The Story of the Bungled UK Terror Attack'. *Sky News*, 6 July 2015.

Knapton, Sarah. 'Dateline London: Operation Crevice'. *Ottawa Citizen*, 1 May 2007.

Lacayo, Richard. 'Public Enemy No. 2'. *Time Magazine*, 5 November 2001.

Laessing, Ulf, and Khalid Abdelaziz. 'Bin Laden's Sudan Home Left Empty over Attack Fears'. *Reuters*, 2 May 2011.

'The Language of Bombs'. *Economist*, 9 July 2005.

Levinson, Charles, Margaret Coker, and Jay Solomon. 'How Cairo, U.S. Were Blindsided by Revolution'. *Wall Street Journal*, 2 February 2011.

'Looking for Answers'. PBS. *Frontline*, 14 April 2008.

Loyn, David. 'Punch-Up at the Palace: Why the Taliban Is Tearing Itself Apart'. *Spectator*, 20 September 2021.

Lubold, Gordon, and Warren P. Strobel. 'Secret U.S. Missile Aims to Kill Only Terrorists, Not Nearby Civilians'. *Wall Street Journal*, 9 May 2019.

Luke, Catriona. 'What Did Musharraf Know?'. *New Statesman*, 10 May 2011.

Magnier, Mark. 'Top al Qaeda–Linked Militant Reportedly Killed by Drone Attack in Pakistan'. *Los Angeles Times*, 5 June 2011.

Mahmud, Abd al-Halim. *Radio Cairo*, 21 January 1977.

Malsin, Jared. 'Hosni Mubarak Sentenced to Three Years in Prison'. *Guardian*, 9 May 2015.

Malsin, Jared, and Owen Bowcott. 'Egypt's Former President Mohamed Morsi Sentenced to 20 Years in Prison'. *Guardian*, 21 April 2015.

Martin, Andrew, and Michael J. Berens. 'Terrorists Evolved in U.S.'. *Chicago Tribune*, 11 December 2001.

Mashal, Mujib. 'Haqqanis Steering Deadlier Taliban in Afghanistan, Officials Say'. *New York Times*, 7 May 2016.

Mashal, Mujib, Taimoor Shah, and Zahra Nader. 'Taliban Name Lesser-Known Cleric as Their New Leader'. *New York Times*, 25 May 2016.

Mayton, Joseph S. 'Kefaya Opposition Movement Is Dead'. *All Headline News (AHN)*, 22 May 2007.

McCants, William. 'How Zawahiri Lost al Qaeda: Global Jihad Turns on Itself'. *Foreign Affairs*, 19 November 2013.

McKay, Hollie, and Mohsin Saleem Ullah. 'Pakistani PM Opens Door to Prisoner Swap with US to Free "Hero" Doctor Who Helped Track bin Laden'. *Fox News*, 23 July 2019.

'Michael Morell on 9/11, the CIA and Afghanistan, Part 2'. *Intelligence Matters, CBS News*, 22 September 2021.

Miller, John. 'Osama bin Laden Interview'. *ABC News, 20/20*, 28 May 1998.

Milmo, Cahal, Ian Herbert, Jason Bennetto, and Justin Huggler. 'From Birmingham Bakery to Pakistani Prison, the Mystery of Rashid Rauf'. *Independent*, 19 August 2006.

Mir, Amir. 'New al-Qaeda Chief in North Waziristan'. *News*, 20 May 2011.

Mir, Asfandyar, and Colin P. Clarke. 'Making Sense of Iran and al-Qaeda's Relationship'. *Lawfare*, 21 March 2021.

al-Misri, Abu Walid. 'The Story of the Arab Afghans from the Time of Arrival in Afghanistan until Their Departure with the Taliban'. *Asharq al-Awsat*, 14 December 2004.

'Momin Khawaja: Canada Raises Terrorism Sentence'. *BBC News*, 17 December 2010.

Mubarak, Hisham, Souhail Shadoud, and Steve Tamari. 'What Does the Gama'a Islamiyya Want? An Interview with Tal'at Fu'ad Qasim'. *Middle East Report* (1996).

'Mubarak and Sons Detained in Egypt'. *Al-Jazeera*, 13 April 2011.

Mulrine, Anna. 'Afghan Warlords, Formerly Backed by the CIA, Now Turn Their Guns on U.S. Troops'. *US News & World Report*, 11 July 2008.

Murphy, Dan. 'Aafia Siddiqui, Alleged Al Qaeda Associate, Gets 86-Year Sentence'. *Christian Science Monitor*, 23 September 2010.

'Muslim Extremist Trial'. *Associated Press*, 15 December 1982.

Najafizada, Eltaf. 'Taliban Shootout in Palace Sidelines Leader Who Dealt with US'. *Bloomberg*, 17 September 2021.

Nakashima, Ellen. 'Israel, at Behest of U.S., Killed al-Qaeda's Deputy in a Drive-By Attack in Iran'. *Washington Post*, 14 November 2020.

Neff, Joseph, and John Sullivan. 'Al-Qaeda Terrorist Duped FBI, Army'. *Raleigh News and Observer*, 24 October 2001.

'1974 Peabody Award—*Sadat: Action Biography*, ABC Television'. Peabody. N.d.

North, Andrew. 'Afghanistan's Graveyard of Foreigners'. *BBC News*, 9 June 2012.

'Nusra Leader: Our Mission Is to Defeat Syrian Regime'. *Al-Jazeera*, 28 May 2015.

Orton, Kyle. 'Al-Qaeda Provides Evidence ISIS Was Its Iraqi Branch, Calls for It to Return'. *Kyle Orton's Blog*, 3 May 2014.

'Osama bin Laden's Son Urges Attacks on the West'. *CNN*, 14 August 2015.

Owen, Paul, and Jack Shenker. 'Mubarak Trial—the Defendants and the Charges'. *Guardian*, 3 August 2011.

'Pakistan: Al-Qaeda Claims Bhutto's Death'. *Adnkronos International (AKI)*. 27 December 2007.

Pantucci, Raffaello. 'Maulana Masood Azhar in the British Jihad'. *Hurst*, 24 January 2013.

Paton Walsh, Nick, Peter Bergen, and Jason Hanna. 'Taliban's Mullah Omar Died in 2013, Afghan Government Says'. *CNN*, 30 July 2015.

'People in the News, Ayman al-Zawahiri: Bin Laden's Right-Hand Man'. *CNN*, 3 November 2001.

Pearl, Daniel, and Steve LeVine. 'Pakistan Has Ties to Nuclear Group Military State Had Vowed to Curb'. *Wall Street Journal*, 24 December 2001.

Petrou, Michael. 'The Fall of Hosni Mubarak: After 30 Years of Tyranny in Egypt, the West's Favourite Dictator Admits Defeat'. *Maclean's*, 19 February 2011.

Pfeiffer, Tom, and Marwa Awad. 'Zawahri: From Suburban Doctor to Chief of al Qaeda?'. *Reuters,* 3 May 2011.

'President Nasser Dies of Heart Attack'. *Guardian*, 29 September 1970.

'Profile: Anas al-Liby'. *BBC News*, 3 January 2015.

'Protesters Attack U.S. Diplomatic Compounds in Egypt, Libya'. *CNN*, 12 September 2012.

Quandt, William. 'Camp David a Blow to Arab Unity'. *Al-Jazeera*, 30 March 2008.

Raafat, Amir. 'The World's Second Most Wanted Man'. *Star (Amman)*, 22 November 2001.

Raghavan, Sudarsan, and Heba Mahfouz. 'Egypt's Mubarak Freed from Detention Six Years after His Overthrow'. *Washington Post*, 24 March 2017.

Rajghatta, Chidanand. 'Al-Qaeda Rants against India-Israel Ties'. *Times of India*, 29 September 2003.

'Regions and Territories: Dagestan'. *BBC News*, 7 November 2012.

Riding, Alan. 'Carlos the Terrorist Arrested and Taken to France'. *New York Times*, 16 August 1994.

Riedel, Bruce. 'Al Qaeda Strikes Back'. *Foreign Affairs Magazine*, May/June 2007.

Riedel, Bruce. 'Al Qaeda's Libya Vengeance Plot'. *Brookings Institution*, 12 September 2012.

Riedel, Bruce. 'The Remarkable Case of the Triple Agent and the Bombing in Khost, Afghanistan'. *Brookings Institution*, 6 December 2019.

Riedel, Bruce. 'The Son Speaks: Al-Qaida's New Face'. *Markaz Blog, Brookings Institution*, 19 August 2015.

Riedel, Bruce. 'Three Ways to Help Pakistan'. *Brookings Institution*, 23 June 2011.

Riedel, Bruce. 'Where in the World Is al-Qaida's Leader?'. *Markaz Blog, Brookings Institution*. 10 August 2015.

Rizq, Hamdi. 'Egyptian Jihad Case Highlights Afghan Links'. *Al-Wasat*, 22–28 June 1998.

Robertson, Nic, Paul Cruickshank, and Tim Lister. 'Document Shows Origins of 2006 Plot for Liquid Bombs on Planes'. *CNN*, 30 April 2012.

Roggio, Bill. 'Al Qaeda Leader Rashid Rauf Killed in Drone Strike, Family Says'. *Long War Journal*, 29 October 2012.

Roggio, Bill, and Thomas Joscelyn. 'New Taliban Emir Accepts al Qaeda's Oath of Allegiance'. *Long War Journal*, 14 August 2015.

Rohde, David, and Carlotta Gall. 'In a Corner of Pakistan a Debate Rages: Are Terrorist Camps Still Functioning?'. *New York Times*, 28 August 2005.

Rotella, Sebastian. 'Alleged Al Qaeda Chief Dead, Officials Say'. *Los Angeles Times*, 10 April 2008.

Rotella, Sebastian, and Janet Stobart. 'Terrorism Defendant Cites Fears of Pakistan'. *Los Angeles Times*, 20 September 2006.

Rubin, Michael. 'Who Is Responsible for the Taliban?'. *Middle East Review*, March 2002.

Ruttig, Thomas. 'Another Bonn-Style Conference: A New Plan to 'Fix' the War and Enable US Troops to Leave'. *Afghan Analysts Network*, 7 March 2021.

Ryan, Yasmine. 'The Tragic Life of a Street Vendor'. *Al-Jazeera*, 20 January 2011.

Sachs, Susan. 'A Nation Challenged: Bin Laden's Allies; An Investigation in Egypt Illustrates al Qaeda's Web'. *New York Times*, 21 November 2001.

Sachs, Susan, and John Kifner. 'A Nation Challenged: Bin Laden's Lieutenant; Egyptian Raised Terror Funds in U.S. in 1990's'. *New York Times*, 23 October 2001.

Salah, Muhammad. 'Bin Ladin Front Reportedly Brought CBW from E. Europe'. *Al-Hayah*, 20 April 1999.

Salah, Muhammad. 'Sayyid Imam al-Sharif Interview'. Part 1. *Al-Hayat*, 8 December 2007.

Salah, Muhammad. 'Sayyid Imam al-Sharif Interview'. Part 2. *Al-Hayat*, 9 December 2007.

al-Saleh, Hoda. 'Al-Qaeda's Historian Mustafa Hamed Resumes Digital Activity in Tehran'. *Al-Arabiya*, 21 January 2018.

al-Saleh, Huda. 'From Iran to al-Qaeda: How Hamza bin Laden's Future Was Secured'. *Al-Arabiya,* 4 October 2016.

Savage, Charlie, and Eric Schmitt, Azmat Khan, Evan Hill, and Christoph Koettl. 'Newly Declassified Video Shows U.S. Killing of 10 Civilians in Drone Strike'. *New York Times*, 19 January 2022.

Sayeed, Saad. 'Khan's Interior Minister Pick Raises Questions about "New" Pakistan'. *Reuters*, 27 April 2019.

Schifrin, Nick, Pierre Thomas, and Jake Tapper. 'Al Qaeda No. 2 Atiyah Abd al-Rahman Killed in Pakistan'. *ABC News*, 27 August 2011.

Schmidle, Nicholas. 'Getting bin Laden'. *New Yorker*, 1 August 2011.

Schmitt, Eric. 'Attack Planner for al Qaeda Reported Dead'. *New York Times*, 10 April 2008.

al-Shafi'i, Muhammad. 'Al Qaeda's Secret Emails'. *Asharq al-Awsat,* 15 December 2002.

al-Shafi'i, Muhammad. 'Fundamentalist Sources: Al-Zawahiri Ousted Following Many Complaints in the Jihad Organization's Shura Council'. *Asharq al-Awsat*, 27 January 2000.

Shahbandar, Oubai. 'How Iran Serves as "a Key Geographic Hub for al-Qaeda"'. *Arab News*, 9 February 2021.

Shahzad, Syed Saleem. 'Al-Qaeda Claims Bhutto Killing'. *Asia Times,* 29 December 2007.

Shahzad, Syed Saleem. 'Al-Qaeda's Guerrilla Chief Lays Out Strategy'. *Asia Times,* 15 October 2009.

Shahzad, Syed Saleem. 'Pakistan Rethink over Support of Militants'. *Asia Times*, 20 December 2001.

Shamaa, Muhammad Abu. 'Former al-Qaeda Ideologue Exposes al-Zawahiri'. *Asharq al-Awsat*, 19 November 2008.

al-Shishani, Murad Batal. 'Al Qaeda Grows as Its Leaders Focus on the Near Enemy'. *National*, 30 August 2013.

Simon, Bob. 'How a Slap Sparked Tunisia's Revolution'. *CBS News, 60 Minutes,* 22 February 2011.

Spillius, Alex, 'CIA Suicide Bomber Worked with bin Laden Allies'. *Daily Telegraph*, 7 January 2010.

Stayt, Nabil Abu. 'Egypt's Islamic Jihad Rises'. *Asharq al-Awsat,* 6 February 2000.

Stein, Jeff. 'Ayman al-Zawahiri: How a CIA Drone Strike Nearly Killed the Head of al-Qaeda'. *Newsweek,* 21 April 2017.

Stroobants, Jean-Pierre. 'Vie et mort des assassins de Massoud'. *Le Monde*, 11 December 2008.

'Surprises of the Vanguards of Conquest: The First Appearance of al-Jihad since the Assassination of al-Sadat'. *Al-Musawwar*, 27 August 1993, 21–22. 'Syria Suicide Bombers Kill al-Qaeda Rebel Leader in Aleppo'. *Associated Press*, 23 February 2014.

Tabor, Mary B. W. 'Slaying in Brooklyn Linked to Militants'. *New York Times*, 11 April 1993.

'Taliban Admit Covering Up Death of Mullah Omar'. *BBC News*, 31 August 2015.

'Taliban Commander Speaks Out'. *al-Jazeera*, 27 June 2010.

'Taliban Say They've Not Found Body of al Qaeda Leader'. *Reuters,* 25 August 2022.

Taqi, Mohammad. 'Jalaluddin Haqqani: Life and Times of a Jihadist Lynchpin'. *Wire,* 7 September 2018.

Tavernise, Sabrina, 'U.N. Report Finds Faults in Pakistani Bhutto Inquiry'. *New York Times*, 15 April 2010.

al-Tayeb, Ahmed. "Al-Azhar Document," *Al-Azhar*, 20 June 2011.

'Terror in India'. *Economist*, 19 December 2001.

Trescott, Jaqueline, and Donnie Radcliffe. 'Peace Meal: Carter Serves Sadat Dinner and Hope'. *Washington Post*, 9 April 1980.

Vick, Karl, and Kamran Khan. 'Al Qaeda Tied to Attacks in Pakistan Cities, Militants Joining Forces against Western Targets'. *Washington Post*, 30 May 2002.

Waite, Clayland. 'Peter Jennings'. *Museum of Broadcast Communications*, 9 August 2005.

Walsh, Declan. 'Pakistan Erupts after US Jailing of "Daughter of the Nation" Aafia Siddiqui'. *Guardian*, 24 September 2010.

Walsh, Declan, and Salman Masood. 'In Pakistan, a Muted Reaction to Kasab's Execution'. *New York Times*, 21 November 2012.

Walsh, Joe. 'Trump Denies Releasing 5,000 Taliban Prisoners—but His Administration Negotiated for Their Release'. *Forbes*, 13 September 2021.

Warrick, Joby. 'Al-Qaida Tries Comeback with bin Laden Son as Mouthpiece'. *Washington Post,* 28 May 2017.

Watson, Ivan. 'Ambassador Khalilzad, the "Viceroy of Afghanistan"'. *NPR*, 22 October 2014.

Weaver, Mary Anne. 'The Short, Violent Life of Abu Musab al-Zarqawi'. *Atlantic*, July/August 2006.

Weiser, Benjamin. 'October 25–31: U.S. Ex-sergeant Charged in bin Laden Conspiracy'. *New York Times*, 1 November 1998.

Weiser, Benjamin. 'U.S. Ex-sergeant Linked to bin Laden Conspiracy'. *New York Times*, 30 October 1998.

Weiser, Benjamin. 'U.S. Seeks to Use Letters Found in bin Laden Raid in Terrorism Trial'. *New York Times*, 15 December 2014.

Weiser, Benjamin, and James Risen. 'The Masking of a Militant: A Special Report; A Soldier's Shadowy Trail in U.S. and in the Mideast'. *New York Times*, 1 December 1998.

Wesolowsky, Tony. 'Afghanistan: Masood's Fate Unclear after Apparent Assassination Attempt'. *Radio Free Europe*, 10 September 2001.

Whitlock, Craig. 'Probe of USS Cole Bombing Unravels'. *Washington Post*, 4 May 2008.

Williams, Lance. 'Bin Laden's Bay Area Recruiter: Khalid Abu-al-Dahab Signed Up American Muslims to Be Terrorists'. *San Francisco Chronicle*, 21 November 2001.

Williams, Lance, and Erin McCormick. 'Al Qaeda Terrorist Worked with FBI / Ex–Silicon Valley Resident Plotted Embassy Attacks'. *San Francisco Chronicle*, 4 November 2001.

Williams, Lance, and Erin McCormick. 'Bin Laden's Man in Silicon Valley'. *San Francisco Chronicle*, 21 September 2001.

Williams, Lance, and Erin McCormick. 'Top bin Laden Aide Toured State / Special Report: Al-Zawahiri Solicited Funds under the Guise of Refugee Relief'. *San Francisco Chronicle*, 11 October 2001.

Windrem, Robert. 'Potential al Qaeda Leaders Eliminated since bin Laden Raid'. *NBC News*, 26 February 2014.

Wintour, Patrick. 'Osama bin Laden's Son Vows to Avenge al-Qaida Leader's Death'. *Guardian,* 11 July 2016.

Woodward, Bob. 'Death of Osama bin Laden: Phone Call Pointed U.S. to Compound—and to the Pacer'. *Washington Post*, 6 May 2011.

Wright, Lawrence. 'The Man behind bin Laden'. *New Yorker*, 16 September 2002.

Wright, Lawrence. 'The Rebellion Within'. *New Yorker*, 2 June 2008.

Yousafzai, Sami, and Sam Seibert. 'ISIS vs. the Taliban: The Battle for Hearts and Minds'. *Vocativ*, 5 November 2014.

Zafar, Ziad. 'Who Killed Benazir Bhutto?'. *Dawn, EOS*, 24 December 2017.

'Zalmay Khalilzad on *Face the Nation*'. *CBS News*, 24 October 2021.

Zimmerman, Katherine. 'The al Qaeda Network: A New Framework for Defining the Enemy, Critical Threats Project'. *American Enterprise Institute,* 10 September 2013.

Zumwalt, James. 'The Unique Weapon That Took Out Soleimani'. *Hill,* 20 February 2020.

INTERVIEWS

Egyptian security officials, 19 February 2007.

Albania State Intelligence Service official, 6 March 2008.

Egyptian security official, 2 June 2008.

Sitara Achakzai, 13 January 2009.

Egyptian security official, 22 March 2009.

Anthony McDermott, 1 August 2009.

Fred Halliday, 4 September 2009.

Egyptian security official, 15 February 2010.

Egyptian security official, 7 March 2010.

Official from the Bosnia–Herzegovina Security Ministry, 21 March 2010.

Former EIJ Jihadist, 2 April 2010.

Saleem Shahzad, 13 June 2010.

US security official, 24 April 2011.

Former EIJ Jihadist, 4 June 2011.

Former EIJ Jihadist, 17 June 2011.

Nick Pratt, 23 August 2011.

US intelligence official, 12 September 2011.

Alain Bauer, 5 October 2011.

Amrullah Saleh, 5 October 2011.

Egyptian security official, 3 January 2012.

D. A. Henderson, 7 March 2012.

Former EIJ Jihadist, 13 May 2012.

Hans Josef-Beth, 3 November 2012.

Egyptian security official, 9 November 2012.

Egyptian security official, 13 November 2012.

Canadian Intelligence Official, 29 January 2013.

US security officials, 6 February 2013.

US official, 11 February 2013.

Mohamed Heikal, 27 September 2013.

Reuven Paz, 9 October 2013.

British counter-terrorism official, 4 November 2013.

Former EIJ Jihadist, 23 November 2013.

US intelligence official, 29 May 2014.

Martin Rudner, 18 July 2014.
Spanish security officials, 15 August 2014.
US intelligence official, 6 September 2014.
US official, 22 October 2014.
British counter-terrorism official, 19 December 2014.
US Special Forces official, 4 February 2015.
US Special Forces official, 11 February 2015.
British counter-terrorism official, 12 March 2015.
US Defense official, 10 May 2015.
Egyptian security official, 14 July 2015.
Family member of Ayman al-Zawahiri, 24 August 2015.
Family member of Ayman al-Zawahiri, 27 August 2015.
Christopher Dickey, 12 April 2016.
US official, 27 September 2016.
US security official, 5 October 2016.
US official, 13 October 2016.
CIS official, 25 October 2016.
US intelligence official, 1 December 2016.
Jerrold Post, 10 December 2016.
British counter-terrorism official, 17 January 2017.
US official, 14 February 2017.
US official, 6 March 2017.
US official, 27 August 2017.
US intelligence officials, 27 October 2017.
P. Scott Thorlin, 12 December 2017.
US official, 2 May 2018.
US official, 9 May 2018.
US intelligence official, 9 June 2018.
US intelligence official, 11 June 2018.
US intelligence official, 23 June 2018.
Amrullah Saleh, 25 July 2018.
US official, 23 August 2018.
US law enforcement official, 30 August 2018.
US federal law enforcement official, 12 December 2018.
US security official, 20 April 2019.
US intelligence official, 2 June 2019.
Jordanian security official, 20 June 2019.
Iraqi security official, 15 July 2019.
British intelligence official, 7 August 2019.
US security officials, 16 September 2019.
US security official, 20 November 2019.
Bruce Riedel, 25 November 2019.
US official, 10 December 2019.

Bruce Hoffman, 11 December 2019.
David Winston, 20 December 2019.
Canadian official, 12 February 2020.
Diplomatic Security Service official, 1 May 2020.
National Directorate of Security official, 6 May 2020.
UAE security official, 12 December 2020.
Mitchell Silber, 17 December 2020.
Henry Crumpton, 18 December 2020.
Douglas London, 18 December 2020.
US security official, 30 December 2020.
Sebastian Rotella, 25 January 2021.
Thomas Hegghammer, 12 February 2021.
US law enforcement official, 25 March 2021.
Sean M. Maloney, 7 April 2021.
Ayesha Siddiqa, 28 April 2021.
Peter Clarke, 29 April 2021.
John Miller, 29 April 2021.
Pieter Van Ostaeyen, 29 April 2021.
Chris Alexander, 6 May 2021.
Joseph Votel, 17 May 2021.
US intelligence official, 18 May 2021.
Robert L. Tignor, 18 May 2021.
John Calvert, 20 May 2021.
Bruce Rutherford, 20 May 2021.
US intelligence official, 28 May 2021.
US security official, 31 December 2021.
Mary Fetchet, 11 January 2022.
Lawrence Wright, 16 January 2022.
Aaron Zelin, 21 January 2022.
Edmund Fitton-Brown, 28 January 2022.
Leon Panetta, 8 April 2022.
US intelligence official, 4 August 2022.
US intelligence official, 15 August 2022.
US official, 16 August 2022.
US Defense official, 20 August 2022.
US intelligence official, 26 August 2022.
US intelligence official, 28 August 2022.
British counter-terrorism official, 31 August 2022.

Index

For the benefit of digital users, indexed terms that span two pages (e.g., 52–53) may, on occasion, appear on only one of those pages.

Figures are indicated by *f* following the page number